The Culture & Civilization of China

中國文化与文明

Key Concepts in

Chinese Philosophy

Zhang Dainian

Translated and edited by Edmund Ryden

Yale University Press
New Haven and London

Foreign Languages Press
Beijing

Calligraphy for series title by Qi Kong, president of the Chinese National
Calligraphers' Association.

This book was originally published in Chinese in 1989 and is translated here with
the permission of the author.

Printed in the United States of America by Edwards Brothers, Inc.

A catalogue record for this book is available from the Library of Congress and the
British Library.

ISBN: 0-300-09210-5

The paper in this book meets the guidelines for permanence and durability of the
Committee on Production Guidelines for Book Longevity of the Council on
Library Resources.

10 9 8 7 6 5 4 3 2 1

Publication of this book was made possible by the generous support of John and Cynthia Reed.

Yale University Press gratefully acknowledges the financial support given to The Culture & Civilization of China series by:
Patricia Mellon
The Starr Foundation

The Culture & Civilization of China

Each book in this series is the fruit of cooperation between Chinese and Western scholars and publishers. Our goals are to illustrate the cultural riches of China, to explain China to both interested general readers and specialists, to present the best recent scholarship, and to make original and previously inaccessible resources available for the first time. The books will all be published in both English and Chinese.

The partners in this unprecedented joint undertaking are the China International Publishing Group (CIPG) and Yale University Press, which together conceived the project under the auspices of the U.S.-China Book Publication Project. James Peck is director of the U.S.-China Book Publication Project and executive director of The Culture & Civilization of China series.

Honorary Chairs, The Culture & Civilization of China
George H. W. Bush, former President of the United States
Rong Yirong, former Vice President of the People's Republic of China

Yale Editorial Advisory Board
James Cahill, University of California, Berkeley
Mayching Kao, Chinese University of Hong Kong
Jonathan Spence, Yale University
James C. Y. Watt, Metropolitan Museum of Art, New York
Anthony C. Yu, University of Chicago

CIPG Editorial Board
Li Xueqin, Director, History Institute, Chinese Academy of Social Sciences, Beijing
Lin Wusun, Chairman, National Committee for the Accreditation of Senior Translators, and Vice Chairman, Translators' Association of China
Yang Xin, Deputy Director, Palace Museum, Beijing
Zhang Dainian, Professor, Beijing University

Contents

Part Two. Anthropology

A. *Moral Philosophy*

I. Moral Ideals

II. Ethical Concepts

B. *Psychology*

I. Human Nature

Part Three. Epistemology

Translator's Preface

As I came to the end of my doctoral studies at the School of Oriental and African Studies in London, Dr. Sarah Allan asked me to consider translating the present work for Yale University Press. I had in fact bought a copy myself the previous year, 1993, while cycling past the Publishing House of the Chinese Academy of Social Sciences in Beijing. I little realized that this slim volume of 248 pages would become my companion for the next few years.

In the early spring of 1995 Yale arranged for me to spend six weeks in Beijing working with Professor Zhang. I met him in his apartment, crowded with books, and discussed with him how I would set about translating the book. Two points in particular deserve mention. The order of the 64 concepts as laid out in the original would not make much sense to a Western reader, so, while retaining the broad categories of the original, I rearranged the concepts so as to give a better idea of how they fitted together. Professor Zhang not only gave his blessing but also expressed his thanks. The second point I noticed was that in places the text betrayed signs of Marxist jargon. This was not consistently employed throughout, and I felt uncomfortable with it. Professor Zhang explained that in the early years he was obliged to put this in, but since the political climate had improved he was no longer under such an obligation. Hence he authorized me to remove it.

My greatest task for the first few months was to check every single quotation in reliable editions. This was necessary for a twofold reason. First, a Western reader would expect to find detailed footnotes and references and, second, the original text was marred by poor proofreading. Indeed, the work of checking was to go on for several years, and some passages still elude me.

The actual work of translating was begun in London and helped along by a winter stay at the Australian National University thanks to the kindness of Professor Bill Jenner and the hospitality of Dr. John Eddy, S. J. It was completed in Taibei and the first draft was sent to Professor Zhang in early 1996. I saw him again, briefly, that year to finalize a few points.

Changes made in the course of translation fall into three categories.

First, as mentioned above, occasionally comments by the author were omitted. Second, passages were rearranged. The Chinese custom is to place quotations first and then provide the analysis, whereas the Western reader may need a little introduction before being faced with the text as such. This meant placing the comments before the quotations. Third, comments were added. These were of three kinds: those necessary to ensure the flow of a paragraph, those which provided information that the Western reader would need, such as dates and basic biographical information, and some essential comments of a text-critical nature.

In 1996 Professor Allan suggested that I add an introductory paragraph to each section. This may have been the place to give a full summary of Western scholarship and a translation of each term. That would have entailed a new book, however, so the introductions have been kept brief. With the introductory paragraphs in place, I revised the text, making a final check for passages as yet unlocated. I hope that the book serves as a useful guide to the Chinese text, which is the norm to which the reader should refer.

In the course of my work I have become acquainted with a broad range of Chinese philosophical texts. Professor Zhang's ability to cite some obscure phrase from the vast corpus of Zhu Xi or to pull out an important but rare piece by Ouyang Jian is something that deserves admiration. Indeed, this is the work's real value. It is a gateway to the whole field of Chinese philosophy. Lately there has been a tendency for historians of Chinese philosophy to establish a neat system of concepts and categories. It may look good on paper, but, as Professor Zhang himself indicated to me, it is too arbitrary. Awareness of the broad spectrum of Chinese philosophy and its lack of "system" is not a defect but a sign that the philosophical culture of a nation cannot be consigned to the pigeon holes of a modern author. It is this sense of history and of the texts that have emerged in history that gives Professor Zhang's work its own special trait.

It would be wrong, then, to expect to find here a complete treatise on Chinese philosophy or a compendium of the essence of Chinese philosophy. Rather, what the reader will find are the salient comments of key thinkers concerning the important concepts of Chinese philosophy. Of course, what counts as an important concept is a matter of personal judgement, as Professor Zhang admits in the conclusion of his preface. In this regard, perhaps the most obvious omission is the concept of *li*, the rites or ritual. "It is not a philosophical term," Professor Zhang assured me, with a wry smile. He is, after all, a man of his time, the brother of Zhang Shenfu, Bertrand Russell's admirer, and of the New China. Confucius is not his idol. Professor Chen Kuying suggested that Zhang Dainian be considered as the founder of New Daoism, but, when I put this to Professor Zhang in 1996, he replied that that title should go to Chen.

In fact, Zhang Dainian has contributed in a seminal way to the school of *qi*, sometimes translated rather awkwardly as "Materialism." He sees himself as standing in line with a tradition found in the *Guanzi* and exemplified in Zhang Zai, Wang Fuzhi, and Dai Zhen, whom he loves to quote. Dai Zhen, in particular, serves as a role model. Dai devoted himself to exegesis and saw his philosophical work as exegetical, bringing out the true meaning of ancient texts. At the same time he had a perspective on the wholeness of the human person, which he held in contrast to what he saw as Zhu Xi's division of man into a rational part devoted to "principle" and an unruly part dominated by passions. Dai Zhen argued that principle lay in the passions, that a human being fully alive need not exclude essential parts of his nature. Principle is in *qi* and *qi* is not without principle. Zhang Dainian's choice of texts, although trying to be a faithful mirror of history, is nonetheless marked by this same orientation. There is no unbiased history, yet the historian's work can be considered valuable inasmuch as it gives a new angle from which to view the past. This is something Zhang Dainian has succeeded in doing and for which he deserves every credit. If I may count myself among his students, it would be a great honor.

Edmund Ryden

Preface

During thirty years spent in the study of the history of Chinese philosophy, I have paid particular attention to analyzing and investigating the significance of the concepts and categories of classical Chinese philosophy. In 1935 I wrote *Zhongguo Zhexue Dagang* and approached the development of Chinese philosophy from the point of view of the philosophical problems raised. In so doing a preliminary sketch of fundamental categories and concepts was undertaken. Yet the emphasis was placed on the system of philosophical questions without concentrating on the concepts and categories as such. My 1955 essay *Zhongguo Gudian Zhexue zhong Ruogan Jiben Gainian Qiyuan yu Yanbian* only touched on some categories. More than twenty years were to pass before, at the Party Congress in 1978, scholars won a second spiritual liberation. It was then that I decided to write a book specifically dealing with the concepts and categories of Chinese philosophy. In 1981 I wrote the articles on Heaven, the Way, *Qi*, and Principle but, owing to other duties, I was unable to devote all my effort to the task. In 1983 I had to spend a lot of time editing the entry on Chinese philosophy for the philosophy section of the Chinese Encyclopaedia (*Zhongguo Da Baike Quanshu*). In 1985, at the instigation of a number of colleagues, I wrote *Zhongguo Lunli Sixiang Yanjiu*, while at the same time I was often asked to write many shorter articles. Thus my work on the concepts and categories was pushed aside. The years slipped by until in the summer of 1987 I decided to complete my draft. In fact, other things intervened, so it was not until the end of November that the book was by and large completed. I had never before been so remiss in my work.

'Concept' (*gainian*) and 'category' (*fanchou*) are both translations of Western terms. In the pre-Qin era thinkers spoke of 'names' (*ming*); after the Song dynasty the term was 'term' (*zi*). Chen Liang of the Southern Song (1127–1279) wrote *The Meaning of Terms* (*Zi Yi*), and Dai Zhen in the Qing dynasty (1644–1911) wrote *An Evidential Study of the Meaning of Terms in the* Book of Mencius (*Mengzi Zi Yi Shuzheng*). In both of these works the word 'term' (*zi*) means 'concept' or 'category.' 'Name' and 'term' are both based on grammatical function, whereas 'concept' and 'category' refer to the content of the terms. The Chinese term for 'category' (*fanchou*) comes from the *Classic of History*, which talks about the "Great Plan (*fan*) and Nine fields (*chou*)," which refers to the nine kinds of basic principles. This use is rather like the Western use of the term 'category.' In the history of Western philosophy since the time of Aristotle, each school of thought has had its own understanding of the categories. Even today scholars continue to give new interpretations. In brief, 'concepts' express the kinds of ideas, and 'categories' are universal concepts, which express the fundamental kinds of ideas.

Classical Chinese philosophical concepts and categories can be divided into three major kinds: the first are those of natural philosophy, the second those of anthropology, and the third those of epistemology. In traditional terms, the first are the names associated with the Way of heaven, the second the Way of man, and the third the method of study. These three kinds are all interconnected. Some of those that are in the Way of man could equally well be put in the method of study, for instance, but in order to make the exposition clearer, distinctions have to be made.

The concepts and categories of classical Chinese philosophy cover a very broad spectrum. Here the emphasis will be placed on those whose meaning is deeper and more difficult to grasp or whose range of different meanings is greater. As for those that are less meaningful or easier to understand, they will not be discussed. There are also a certain number of terms that appear in the Ming-Qing period (1368–1911) and are now in common use but were rare in philosophical works prior to 1368, such as 'relationship' (*guanxi*). Despite its being an important category, it will not be discussed here because it is not a fundamental concept in classical Chinese philosophy.*

Philosophical concepts and categories all go through a process of emergence, development, diversification, and synthesis. Different thinkers

---

*Author's note: The term *guanxi* first appears in works of the Ming era, such as *Jottings from the Pea Garden* (*Shu Yuan Za Ji*) by Lu Rong (1436–1494), *juan* 9: "The Commissioner of the Office of Transmission, in acting as spokesman for the King's command, is like the throat and tongue of the court. He proclaims to the people below and thus makes the court clear and manifest, and so this relationship [*guanxi*] with the body politic is the most important." *Juan* 10 of the *Great and Full Explanation on Reading the Four Books* (*Du Sishu Daquan Shuo*) by Wang Fuzhi (1619–1692) reads, "Except for this it was a matter of great relevance [*guanxi*], as Confucius' not attaining to an official job, one may suppose that the *qi* was not forthcoming and fate had not determined it." There have been those who have claimed that *guanxi* is a foreign term. This is incorrect.

and schools have differing interpretations of the same category. Philosophers of rival schools rarely have an unbiased view of the concepts and categories of their opponents. This raises an important question: Is it possible for human beings to communicate with each other? Can the past and present speak to each other? It is not possible here to give a complete answer to this problem. I now believe that, to a certain extent, people can communicate with each other. To a certain extent the past and future can speak to each other. If communication were impossible, then society itself would not be possible. If the past could not speak to the present, then human history would be incomprehensible. The very existence of society is proof enough that human beings can communicate with each other. The existence of historical research is ample evidence to demonstrate that the past can speak to the present. The historian Sima Qian said, "Delighting in study, entering deeply into thought; this is something of which the mind knows the meaning." I believe that this is a pointer to research in the history of philosophy. Dispassionate seeking for the truth is possible.

This book is devoted to the study of the concepts and categories of Chinese thought. The origins of Chinese culture lie far back. Even before the oracle bones (c. 1350–1100 B.C.) there was a long history. Yet the oracle bones predate the emergence of philosophy. They mark what could be called a philosophical "prehistory." Some words of those early times are related to later terms; others are not. Insofar as this book takes into account the ancient meaning of the terms it refers to the common usage current since the Western Zhou (1121–771 B.C.) and so does not engage in a study of the origin of Chinese characters.

The material for Chinese philosophy covers all four sections of the *Complete Repository of Books in Four Sections (Siku Quanshu).* Here only the key works by representative philosophers will be selected and the main outlines laid clear without going into great detail. The book is limited to expounding the concepts and categories that arose and were in use in classical Chinese philosophy. It thus excludes terms found in Buddhism, Daoist religion (barring those in common with Daoist philosophy), technical terms from fields such as astronomy, divination, and medicine, literary and artistic terms such as those employed in poetry, art, and music, or those that are not part of the mainstream of Chinese philosophy and that I myself have not sufficiently studied. Apart from these I trust the reader to forgive the omission of any others.

From my heart I thank the Publishing House of the Chinese Academy of Social Sciences for undertaking to publish this work.

Zhang Dainian
Beijing University
December 1987

Introduction: On the System of Categories

Recently scholars of the history of Chinese philosophy have turned their attention to the question of the system of categories of ancient Chinese philosophy. This problem is indeed an important one for the history of philosophy. We often say that Chinese philosophy has its own set of categories, in which case there must be a specific system of these categories. The systematization is a very complex problem. In the history of Chinese philosophy each category has its own path of emergence, development, and change such that even philosophical categories of the same period will be different according to different schools of thought. Which categories belong to the system of ancient Chinese philosophy? How do they relate to each other? These questions call for further research.

'Concept' and 'Category' in Ancient Chinese Philosophy

'Concept' and 'category' are foreign terms that have been imported into Chinese. Although the "Great Plan" chapter of the *Book of History* uses the terms *fan* and *chou* ("Great Plan [*fàn*] and Nine Fields [*chóu*]"), in ancient Chinese the two terms were never linked as one word. In ancient Chinese philosophy the terms that came closest to the modern words for 'concept,' *gainian* and *fanchou*, are 'name' (*ming*) and 'appellation,' or 'term' (*zi*). Confucius talks about the rectification of names:

> If names are not rectified then speech does not match. (*Analects* 13, *Zi Lu* #3, p. 263)

In the *Technique of the Mind A* of the *Guanzi* names and forms are spoken of as follows:

> Things have definite forms. Forms have definite names. One who makes names conform [to real objects] is called a sage. (*Guanzi* 48, *Technique of the Mind A*, 2:9)

The *Zhuangzi* reads,

> Names are what correspond to realities. (*Zhuangzi* 1, *Going Rambling Without a Destination*, line 25)

The *Gongsun Long* says,

> Names are the appellations of things. (*Gongsun Long* 6, *Discussion of Names and Real Objects*, p. 40)

In the logic sections of the *Mozi*, it is said,

> One uses names to refer to real objects. (*Later Mohist Logic*, p. 482)

Thus for all these schools of thought 'names' are what things are called. The *Mohist Canons* distinguish three kinds of names:

'*Ming*' (name). Unrestricted: classifying: private.

These terms are explained in the *Explanations*:

[margin note: general / common]

[margin note: proper]

> 'Thing' is 'unrestricted'; any real object necessarily requires this name. Naming something 'horse' is 'classifying'; for 'like the real object' we necessarily use this name. Naming someone 'Jack' is 'private'; this name stays confined in this real object. (*Later Mohist Logic*, p. 325)

[margin note: similarity (nhu)]

Unrestricted names are those that name universals. Generic names are the names of genera. Both unrestricted and generic names are what we now call concepts. Unrestricted names are universal concepts; generic names are concepts of a given kind of thing. Private names are the names of individuals and are not concepts.

[margin note: ý-niệm]

[margin note: tú danh]

The *Xunzi* distinguishes between common names and generic names:

> For although the myriad things are innumerable, sometimes we want to speak of them as a whole and so we call them 'things.' 'Things' is a great common name.... Sometimes we want to speak of one section of things, and so we call them 'birds' and 'beasts.' 'Birds' and 'beasts' are great particular names. (*Xunzi* 22, *On the Rectification of Names*, lines 23–24)

The great common names are what the Mohists called 'unrestricted names,' whereas the great particular names are what the Mohists called 'classifying names.'

Hence unrestricted names and generic names refer to what we now call 'concepts.' The term 'concept' is said from the point of view of thought, whereas 'name' is a linguistic term. Thought and language may be compared as contents to form. Thought is always expressed in language. There can be no thought that is removed from language. Hence 'names' and 'concepts' are the same.

ý niệm

"'Thing' is 'unrestricted'; any real object necessarily requires this name." This refers to what we now call a *fanchou*, category. The term 'category' comes from ancient Greece. Aristotle described the system of categories. He mentions ten: substance, quantity, quality, relation, location, time, aspect, situation, action, and undergoing. In modern times Kant discussed categories from the point of view of a priori aperception. Hegel discussed categories from the point of view of objective idealism. When we now talk about categories we believe that they are the formal patterns of thought that reflect the unity and universality of things. In other words, they are fundamental concepts with a necessary and universal nature. Ancient Chinese philosophy lacks a system of categories such as that of Aristotle.

(loại danh)
phạm trù

The *Zhuangzi* refers to 'quantity' (*liang*) and 'time' (*shi*), as Aristotle does, but there is very little further discussion of the terms:

lượng (: số)
thời

> The quantity of things is endless; time is without end; kinds without fixed norms; ending and beginning never return to the same old place. (*Zhuangzi* 17, *Autumn Floods*, line 15)

In the *Mencius* and in the *Commentaries on the* Book of Changes the term 'time' refers simply to the ordinary sense of the word.

Han Yu, in his *Inquiry on the Way*, makes a distinction between 'empty positions' and 'definite names':

> Benevolence and justice are definite names. The Way and Virtue are empty positions. (SBBY: *Collected Works of Mr. Chang Li* 11.1, *An Inquiry on the Way*, p. 129a)

Definite names are names that have a definitive content; empty positions are empty boxes that can be filled differently by different schools of thought. Confucians and Daoists both speak of the Way, but what they mean by the 'Way' is different. As for benevolence and justice, they have a determined meaning. Confucians promote benevolence and justice; Daoists oppose them, but the terms 'benevolence' and 'justice' cannot be borrowed so as to give them a different meaning. The Daoists are simply critical of the two concepts. What Han Yu calls definite names and empty positions are both what we now call concepts. If we analyze them further, then 'definite names' are real categories and 'empty positions' are formal categories.

From the Song to the Qing philosophical concepts and categories are called 'appellations' or 'terms.' Some scholars sought to explain the meaning of these appellations. Zhu Xi's disciple Chen Liang wrote a work titled *Detailed Discussion of the Meaning of Terms,** in which he explained the categories and concepts of the philosophy of principle of the Chengs *Ts'êng* and of Zhu Xi. The Qing Confucian Dai Zhen criticized the Chengs and *Chu Hi* Zhu Xi and constructed his own system of philosophy. On the basis of Mencius' categorical and conceptual system he composed *An Evidential Study of the Meaning of Terms in the* Book of Mencius. Here 'term' does not refer to just any word but to philosophical terms. The 'meaning of terms' refers to the explanation of philosophical categories and concepts. The expression 'meaning of terms' is too vague. It lacks the precision of the Western term 'category.' Thus, although Chinese philosophy does not have the term 'category,' it nonetheless certainly does have its own categories.

The Levels and Evolution of the System of Categories

In the history of thought the order in which philosophical categories emerge has a sequence; this is the historical sequence of the philosophical categories.

Between each category there is overlap, implicit containing of others, difference and opposition as well as relationships of mutual negation and affirmation. This can be called the logical relationship of the categories. The order obtained by the logical relationships and formation of categories may be called the logical sequence of the philosophical categories.

Many categories are related to one another and so form a definite system. A system will have different levels. There may be the system of categories of a given school, of a given sect, or of a given period as well as the general categorical system that perdures through time.

In the course of history each thinker who constructs a philosophical

---

* Author's note: The book is now known as *Beixi's Meaning of Terms.*

system will always deal with a number of fundamental problems, which will involve some or many concepts and categories. These concepts and categories form a system, and this is that person's system of categories.

Nearly every important philosopher has his own successors, and thus a philosophical school is formed. The philosophical categories used or constructed by a school will form a system, which is the system of categories of that school.

In each important period of history there may well be several different philosophical schools, each with its own system of categories, which will be interrelated to or in opposition to each other. Taken overall, they form the system of categories of that period.

Over a longer period of history some categories will survive without disappearing and thus form a more universal system of categories.

For each thinker, each school, or each period or for categories that perdure with time each category will have a logical relationship to others. This is the order of logical levels of the philosophical categories.

Aristotle's ten categories begin with 'substance.' The first chapter of *Reflections on Things at Hand*, jointly edited by Zhu Xi and Lu Zuqian, is called *The Substance of the Way*. Wang Tingxiang's *Prudent Words* also has an opening chapter with the same title. Chen Liang's *Beixi's Meaning of Terms* sets out 'destiny,' 'human nature,' and 'mind' in the first section and 'the Way,' 'principle,' 'virtue,' and 'the supreme ultimate' in the second. Dai Zhen's *An Evidential Study of the Meaning of Terms in the* Book of Mencius opens with the 'Way of heaven,' then 'human nature,' and follows with 'the Way' and 'benevolence-justice-ritual-wisdom.' Hegel's *Study of Logic* contains the most categories of all his works. It opens with 'being' and 'nothingness' and concludes with 'idea.'

From ancient times until now there has been no fixed sequence or logical order of philosophical categories. Yet the categories of each thinker, school, or period may be laid out according to two different sequences. One is from the general to the particular; the other is from the simple to the more mysterious. In taking substance as the first category or the substance of the way Aristotle, Zhu Xi, and Lu Zuqian are starting from what is most universal. By starting from 'being' Hegel is beginning from what is simplest.

What categories should be included in the complete system of ancient Chinese philosophical categories? This question demands further analysis.

'Term,' 'concept,' and 'category' all have something in common as well as differing one from another. The terms that express what is universally existent or that name categories of things, such as 'thing' and 'horse,' are concepts. What expresses only one individual person or thing cannot be called a concept. Thus the surname, personal name, or *nom de plume* of a particular person or the name of a historical object cannot be a concept. Among concepts there are some that can be called categories and some that are not categories. Put simply, concepts that express the unity of existence, universal relationships, or universal norms may be called categories, whereas a number of commonly used concepts such as 'mountain,' 'water,' 'white,' 'moon,' 'ox,' and 'horse' cannot be called categories.

The difference between concepts and categories is not only as just stated. In the course of history many philosophers have created their own concepts, some of which have been taken and widely used by later thinkers while others have had no effect. Not all the concepts or terms of any school can be considered to have universal significance. Thus for Mohists the 'three tests' (*san biao*) were very important but they were not adopted by other schools, and after the extinction of Mohism 'three tests' was simply a historical term. The term 'designating' (*zhi*) is proper to Gongsun Long and did not become a generally accepted category. Some concepts may be very popular during a particular period but later disappear without a trace. Thus 'abstruse darkness' (*xuan ming*) and 'independent transformation' (*du hua*) were popular in the period of the two Jins and the Northern-Southern dynasties but by the Tang and the Song dynasties nobody used them and hence they cannot be considered as categories of universal significance. Moreover, there are some thinkers who like to make up their own terms, such as Yang Xiong, who, in his *Classic of the Supreme Abstruseness*, created a set of four terms modeled on a four-character phrase in the *Book of Changes*. This can only be considered as the work of one person and cannot be treated as a category.

There are some thinkers, however, who have proposed that particular concepts, though not universally popular, nonetheless correctly reflect some aspect of the objective and real world and hence have a higher theoretical value and so may be called philosophical categories. Examples are Zhang Zai's 'ability' (*neng*) and Wang Tingxiang's 'contrary cause' (*fan yin*), which can be ranked among the categories of ancient Chinese philosophy.

It is often found that different philosophers use the same category but invest it with different meanings. Han Yu says that the 'Way' and 'virtue' are empty positions. Any category that is an empty position may be filled differently by different thinkers. Thus by the 'Way,' Laozi and Zhuangzi mean what is prior to heaven and earth and the myriad things and yet is also the abstract and absolute cause of the existence of heaven, earth, and the myriad things. The *Commentaries on the* Book of Changes speak of the Way as the universal norm governing the changes of heaven, earth, and the myriad things. Zhang Zai and Dai Zhen take the Way as indicating the process of natural changes. As for *qi*, Boyangfu first suggested the concept of the *qi* of heaven and earth. Mencius, although recognizing that *qi* and the will are opposed to each other, mooted the phrase 'surging *qi*,' which has a level of mystery about it. As for 'principle,' Zhang Zai established that principle is not from man but is in things. Zhu Xi, however, held that from the point of view of principle, even if a thing did not exist, yet its principle could still exist. Wang Shouren emphasized even further that principle was in the mind: "outside the mind there is no thing; outside the mind there is no principle." Since these thinkers express the relationship between principle and things differently, it follows that how they understand 'principle' also differs. Although in the different systems of philosophical categories these terms are treated differently, in the history of philosophy they may be considered as the same category.

Some complicated situations arise in the mention and use of philosophical categories. There are some categories that were first brought forward and expounded by one thinker, such as Laozi's 'Way.' There are categories that may not have been created by any particular thinker but have been explained in detail by a given thinker, such as Confucius' exposition of benevolence. Many categories have been popular over a long period of history, so as to which person first expounded them it is hard to say, given the lack of historical evidence. Thus it is not possible to attribute *qi*, 'principle,' or 'human nature' to any one thinker. Recently some historians of philosophy have said that 'principle' was first propounded by Han Fei and that 'substance and use' (*ti-yong*) and 'root and end' (*ben-mo*) were first advocated by Wang Bi. In truth these suggestions are not in accordance with historical facts. Many concepts arose in the pre-Qin period. Many concepts of the school of principle of the Song and the Ming periods have their roots in pre-Qin texts but the philosophers of the Song and the Ming gave these terms a new interpretation, with the result that they were clarified and assumed a deeper significance as categories of philosophy. The contribution of these later thinkers deserves a full affirmation.

In the pre-Qin period the Confucians, Mohists, Daoists, and Logicians each had their own set of categories. In the post-Qin, post-Han period the Mohists and Logicians disappeared and the Confucians and Daoists merged. Most of the categories of the post-Han and post-Wei period came from pre-Qin Confucianism and Daoism. In the Wei-Jin period the school of mystery had its own set of categories that was largely based on those of pre-Qin Confucianism and Daoism. With the infiltration of Buddhism a new set of categories emerged whose roots were in Indian Buddhism and which was largely different from Chinese categories and concepts. In the course of its development Chinese Buddhism advocated or used some concepts that were not translations of foreign terms, such as 'substance and use' and 'phenomena and principle.' It cannot be said that these categories were not influenced by their original Chinese meaning. Philosophers of principle of the Song-Ming period dabbled in Buddhism and Daoism but, although they entered deeply into them, they ended up by leaving them and attaching their roots to the pre-Qin Confucianism of Confucius and Mencius. Most Buddhist terms, such as 'sex,' 'emptiness,' 'dharma,' and 'awareness,' were not finally adopted by Confucians. Although the Ming-Qing–era philosopher Wang Fuzhi employed the Buddhist category of *neng suo*, he gave it a new meaning. The spirits of Confucianism and Buddhism proved in the long run to be incompatible. Hence, although it can be said that post Wei-Jin philosophical categories were a merging of Confucianism and Daoism, those of Tang and Song times up to the Ming-Qing period were only a case of mutual influence between Confucianism and Buddhism.

The principal philosophical categories of works from the pre-Qin period up until Ming-Qing times are listed below.

Confucian Concepts and Categories

1. *Categories and concepts from the Western Zhou until the Spring and Autumn period*: Decree of heaven, virtue, five agents (*Book of History:*

Books of Zhou); *qi, yin-yang,* harmony (*Saying of the States, Sayings of Zhou*); the Way of heaven and the Way of man, benevolence, ritual, unlucky (*bu qiao*) (*Zuo's Commentary to the* Spring and Autumn Annals).

2. *Categories of Confucius' philosophy:* The Way, the Way of heaven, virtue, benevolence, ritual, loyalty, altruism, filial piety, brotherly love, wisdom, courage, beauty, goodness, the mean and harmony, dual ends, human nature, practice, study, thinking, one thread (*Analects*).

3. *Categories of Mencius' philosophy:* Benevolence-respect-ritual-wisdom; filial piety-brotherly love-loyalty-trustworthiness, the will, *qi,* the mind, thing, principle, respect, awareness, sincerity, innate knowing and innate ability, surging *qi,* value (*liang-gui*) (*Mencius*).

4. *Philosophical categories of the* Great Commentary on the Book of Changes: The supreme ultimate, *yin-yang,* firm-yielding, generating, change, transformation, movement and stillness, the Way and vessel, above and below form, numinous, incipience, daily new.

5. *Philosophical categories of Xunzi (those in common with Confucius are not listed)*: Phenomenon and principle, rule and norm, gathering, kind, group, sincerity, numinous, evidence (*Xunzi*).

6. *Principal categories in the* Record of Rites: Central harmony, virtuous nature, sincerity and clarity, caution when alone (*Mean and Harmony*); bright virtue, highest good, root and branches, research things so as to extend knowledge (*Great Learning*); great commonwealth, small sufficiency (*Evolution of Rites*); principle of heaven, human desire (*Record of Music*).

Daoist Categories

7. *Philosophical categories of Laozi:* The Way, One, simple, vessel, being, beingless, perennial, abstruse, spacious stillness, going back and returning, nature, not-acting, influence.

8. *Philosophical categories of Zhuangzi (those identical to Laozi's are not listed)*: Heaven, man, *qi,* principle, duration and extension, the numinous, genuine. There are also many terms in the *Zhuangzi* that have not become universally accepted categories, such as *yi ming* 以名, the post of the Way, transformation of things, *xuan jie* 懸解, fasting of the mind, sitting and forgetting.

Categories of Other Pre-Qin Schools

9. *Philosophical categories in the* Guanzi *and in the Legalist school*: Ritual-justice-probity-shame, constant, rule, the Way, *qi*, technique of the mind, emptiness, essence, that by which one knows, that which one knows, law, technique, power. The thought of the *Guanzi* synthesizes Daoism and Legalism.

10. *Philosophical categories of the Mohists and the Logicians*: The will of heaven, loving without discrimination, fate, effort, kind, cause, three standards, duration, extension, similarity and difference, without limit, supreme unity, little unity, designating, thing, name, reality.

In the later development of the categories of Chinese philosophy the works that had the greatest influence were the *Analects, Laozi*, and the *Commentaries on the* Book of Changes. In second place are the *Mean and Harmony* and the *Mencius*. Few used the categories created by the Mohists and the Logicians. Although Xunzi was a Confucian, there were few people who took up his categories. The categories of the *Analects, Laozi*, and the *Commentaries on the* Book of Changes are the major categories of traditional Chinese philosophy.

11. *Additional concepts frequently used by Han Confucians*: Original *qi* (*Pheasant Cap Master, Luxuriant Gems of the* Spring and Autumn Annals; as to which work first used the term it is not possible to say); supreme emptiness (*Inner Canon of the Yellow Emperor* and *Outer Chapters of the* Zhuangzi); three relationships, five constants (*Luxuriant Gems of the* Spring and Autumn Annals, *The Understandings Reached at the White Tiger Studio*); stuff (*Apocryphal Changes: Qian Zao Du* distinguishes clearly between *qi*, form, and stuff).

12. *Categories of the abstruse learning of the Wei-Jin period*: Being-beingless, root-branches, substance-function, spontaneity-nature, principle, human nature, fate, meaning of words.

13. *Categories of Sui-Tang Buddhism*: The terms found in Buddhist philosophy are very numerous. A generation ago, Xiong Shili, in his *Fojia Mingxiang Tongshi*, discussed the terms of Sui-Tang Buddhism in great detail. Hence below attention is drawn only to the more important categories: Dharma-world, tathagata, sex, nature, symbol, arising of causes, cause-effect (karma), five concealments, eight consciousnesses, stopping to

meditate, nirvana. In Buddhist books there are also a number of terms that have entered into normal discourse, such as 'reality' (*shi ji*), 'world' (*shijie*), and 'consciousness' (*yi shi*).

Confucianism in the Sui-Tang period did not produce any new concepts. The only exception is Cui Jing's important and clear exposition of substance and function in his *Penetrating the Mystery of the* Book of Changes.

The majority of philosophical concepts and categories of the Song, Yuan, Ming, and Qing periods were derived from the past. Nonetheless they are listed here so as to illustrate which categories survived and which died out in the course of history.

14. *Categories of the philosophy of Zhou Dunyi:* Non-ultimate, supreme ultimate, *yin-yang*, five agents, limit of the human, integrity, numinous, incipience, hard good, weak good.

15. *Categories of the philosophy of Zhang Zai:* Supreme harmony, supreme void, *qi*, nature, numinous, the Way, principle, duality, one, being, phenomenon, mind, ability, integrity, brightness.

16. *Categories of the school of Cheng Hao, Cheng Yi, and Zhu Xi:* In his *Detailed Discussion of the Meaning of Terms*, Chen Liang lists the following categories:

Part One: Fate, human nature, mind, nature, talent, will, meaning, benevolence-justice-ritual-wisdom-trustworthiness, loyal trustworthiness, loyal altruism, one thread, integrity, reverence, respect;

Part Two: the Way, principle, virtue, supreme ultimate, imperial ultimate, central harmony, mean and harmony, ritual and music, light and heavy, justice and profit, ghosts and spirits.

In the *Great and Complete Book on Human Nature and Principle* the following categories are given: Principle and *qi* (supreme ultimate, heaven-earth, *yin-yang*, five agents), ghosts and spirits (life-death), human nature and principle (human nature and fate, mind, the Way, principle, virtue, benevolence-justice-ritual-wisdom-trustworthiness, integrity, loyal trustworthiness, loyal altruism, respectful reverence).

Neither of these works lists the categories in any clear, logical order, but virtually all of the categories of the philosophy of the Cheng brothers and Zhu Xi are present.

17. *Categories of the school of Lu Jiuyuan and Wang Shouren:*

Mind, principle, root-mind, conscience, knowledge and action, justice and profit, principle and desire.

18. *Concepts and categories of the philosophy of Fang Yizhi*: *Tongji* 通幾, *zhice* 質測, *qi-xing-guang-sheng* 氣形光聲, principle, numinous, *fan-yin* 反因, *jiao-lun-ji* 交輪幾, rule by consent (*sui-min-tong* 隨民統). Fang Yizhi's thought has its own special characteristics. Even though the concepts he advanced have not become new categories, they have a notable depth of meaning.

19. *Categories of the philosophy of Wang Fuzhi*: *Qi*, principle, the Way, supreme void, supreme harmony, real being, integrity, numinous, vessel, movement and stillness, ability, knowledge and action, researching things so as to attain the perfection of knowledge, justice and profit, principle and desire, principle and circumstances.

20. *Philosophical categories of Dai Zhen*. The categories set out in *An Evidential Study of the Meaning of Terms in the* Book of Mencius are principle, the Way of heaven, human nature, talent, the Way, benevolence-justice-ritual-wisdom, integrity, authority. Dai's work also includes the following categories: *qi* and transformation, mind and knowing, nature, necessity.

The list above is not complete, because it is hard not to overlook some points, but in gross it presents all the categories of ancient Chinese philosophy from the beginning until recent times. As for the terms that can be called categories and those that are only concepts, it is hard to make an absolute rule but an effort has been made to include all the terms that have important theoretical significance.

Overall System of the Categories of Ancient Chinese Philosophy

As noted above, the concepts and categories of ancient Chinese philosophy underwent a process of historical evolution. The categories that have had a greater effect historically are (1) categories of pre-Qin Confucianism, (2) categories of pre-Qin Daoism, (3) categories of Wei-Jin abstruse learning, and (4) categories of the Song-Ming school of principle. Apart from these groups there are those of Buddhism. Buddhist categories, however, are mostly foreign terms translated into Chinese and have not played a leading role and hence cannot be put on a par with Confucian and Daoist terms. The categories of the Song-Ming school of principle can be said to be a bringing together of the concepts and categories of ancient Chinese philosophy. Thinkers who were opposed to the school of principle were not able to propose any new categories. As we study the categories, we must look for their source and trace their development and so cannot remain limited to the categories of the school of principle.

Can it be said that throughout history ancient Chinese philosophical categories have a common theme and common system? We must answer in the affirmative. This overall system of categories must include those of Confucianism, Daoism, abstruse learning, and the school of principle, which have been handed down and are widely used.

This overall system of categories should have a definite logical structure. The problem now is how to determine this logical structure.

Hegel's *Science of Logic* comprises the complete system of Western philosophical categories. Hegel held that logical and historical sequences were the same. The categories appear in history in a logical order. He set this out according to the pattern of affirmation, negation, and negation of the negation. In fact his so-called historical sequence does not conform to reality and his logical sequence betrays the influence of his own subjective opinion and hence is not strictly arranged according to logic. Hegel himself believed that he had attained the fullness of absolute truth. This is to be out of touch with objective reality. But Hegel's belief in the identity of the logical and historical sequences is full of wisdom. In the history of thought there are indeed the relationships of affirmation, negation, and negation of the negation. But if one is using this as a basis for setting out the historical and hence logical sequence of categories, it will be hard not to force the facts somewhat, for reality is always more complex than the simple formula of thesis-antithesis-synthesis.

In brief, there may be two types of logical pattern. The first is from the commonest categories to the more special, or in traditional Chinese terminology, from what is common (*gong*) to what is particular (*bie*), from what is whole (*quan*) to what is partial (*pian*). The second type is from the superficial to the profound, or in traditional Chinese terminology, from the simple (*jian*) to the occult (*ze*).

In his discussion of categories Aristotle starts with substance. This is to go from the whole to the part. Hegel's *Science of Logic* goes from the simple to the occult.

The first section of *Reflections on Things at Hand* is *On the Substance of the Way*. Although Zhu Xi does not actually set out the system of categories, his theoretical system in fact uses the sequence of whole to part. Chen Liang's *Detailed Discussion of the Meaning of Terms* and the Ming-period *Great and Complete Work on Human Nature and Principle* set out the categories with no proper order, thereby demonstrating how the intellectual level of Zhu Xi's successors had regressed.

Thus our task now is to look at the overall system of the categories of ancient Chinese philosophy according to two patterns: first, according to the logical sequence of general to particular and, second, according to the historical order in which thinkers have dealt with the categories. To a certain degree the historical development of philosophical thought is dictated by logical necessity, yet the order in which philosophical categories emerge in history is not strictly logical. If one tries to force the historical emergence of categories into a definite logical sequence, then one will surely fail. Reality is more complex than logic, and it is important to keep objective facts in mind.

In the course of history, philosophical categories may emerge one by one, such as the Way of Laozi. Again, they may appear in pairs as with *yin-yang* or being and beingless. Categories may form a pair but they can also be used independently. Below two lists are given. The content of each is virtually the same but the logical order varies.

Overall Table of Independent Categories

Highest categories: Heaven, the Way, *Qi* (original *qi*), supreme ultimate, supreme One, space (supreme void), abstruse, limitless/non-ultimate, supreme harmony, principle (10);

Categories of empty position: Virtue, goodness, beauty, root (origin, root), substance (original substance, real substance), function, reality, origin, affirmation (affirmation and negation), reality (truth and falsehood) (10);

Categories of definite names: Decree (the decree of heaven), five agents (water-fire-wood-metal-earth), *yin-yang*, thing, harmony, identity, dual ends, beingless, being, nature, simplicity, vessel, shape, return, constant, change (transformation), movement, stillness, life, change, spirit, numinous, impetus, kind, essence (essential *qi*), integrity, universe, rule and norm, affair, influence, form, stuff, material, incipience, ability (ability to contract, expand, move, be still, end, begin), that by which (that by which it is so), real being; benevolence, justice, human nature, mean and harmony, incorruptible, heavy, public, honor (respect), conscience (innate knowledge), principle of heaven, human desire, great harmony; mind, thought, knowledge, action (put into practice), name, one thread, ability (that by which one knows), what (what is known), experience (58).

In all there are 78 concepts and categories.

Overall Table of Paired Categories

Categories of the Way of heaven: Heaven and man (the Way of heaven, the Way of man), root and branches, being and beingless, the Way and vessel, principle and *qi*, substance and function (stuff and function), the supreme ultimate and the non-ultimate, *yin-yang*, form and spirit (form and stuff, essential spirit), fate and effort, constancy and change, movement and stillness, return and restart, duality and unity, numinous transformation, above and below form, duration and extension, affair and principle, empty and real, mind and thing, identity and difference, symbol and number (22 pairs).

Categories of the Way of man: The Way and virtue, benevolence and justice, innate and learnt, beautiful and good, mean and harmony and excess and falling short, central harmony, justice and profit, principle and desires, will and effort, light and heavy, integrity and clarity, public and private, sincere and false, natural and fabricated, natural and named, honor and lowliness (scale of values), principle and influence (17 pairs).

Categories of epistemology: Learning and thinking, names and realities, knowledge and action, affirmation and denial, wisdom and folly, genuine and false, language and meaning, potentiality and actuality, investigating things so as to know them perfectly (9 pairs).

In all there are 48 pairs given.

The first list gives the highest categories, categories of empty position, and categories of definite names. The order in each kind is a reliable historical order. The highest categories are those that a thinker, when establishing his philosophical system, uses to express the origin of the world or the highest substance. Confucius and Mencius make heaven the supreme substance and have not yet left the primitive theory of the decree of heaven. Laozi and Zhuangzi take the Way as the source of heaven and earth and begin to establish an ontology. (People have recently said that Chinese ontology begins with Wang Bi; this is a great mistake. I have written on the subject elsewhere and do not go into the matter further here.) The earliest notion of *qi* dates from the late Western Zhou in a discourse of Boyangfu. The clear use of *qi* as the highest category is from a later date. In the Wei-Jin period, He Yan and Wang Bi "took heaven as the root" but in fact still took the Way as the supreme category, reading the Way as beinglessness. In the Song-Ming period, Zhang Zai believed that the unity of the world was due to *qi*, whereas the Cheng brothers and Zhu Xi considered principle to be the supreme substance. Lu Jiuyuan and Wang Shouren held that "the mind is principle" and yet still considered principle as the supreme category while, nonetheless, emphasizing that principle is in the mind. Hence beinglessness and mind are not listed among the supreme categories.

The categories of empty position are those used by all schools but given a different meaning by each. The categories of definite names are the categories that have a definite content.

The second list gives the categories of the Way of heaven, of the Way of man, and of epistemology. The main content of Chinese philosophy is "the study of heaven and man," and the main topics of discussion are the Way of heaven, the Way of man, and problems of knowing heaven and knowing man; thus the categories of philosophy can be separated into three kinds. This division has its own necessity. The formation of pairs of categories is also subject to complications. Some categories are not only paired with one other but may have another partner, too. Thus 'identity' is paired with 'harmony' and with 'difference.' 'Integrity' is paired with 'false' and also with 'brightness.' In the Wei-Jin period the relation of appellation to nature was a pressing issue. In the philosophy of Laozi and

Zhuangzi nature was original, in contrast with human endeavor. Later Dai Zhen paired 'nature' and 'necesssity.' This sort of situation is far from rare.

In the two lists above the number of items is rather excessive. If the complexities are removed and the issue is reduced to the bare bones, then one can list sixteen categories as the most important and the most Chinese of all:

1. Heaven and man
2. Being and beingless
3. Substance and function
4. The Way and vessel
5. *Yin-yang*
6. Movement and stillness
7. Constancy and change
8. Principle and *qi*
9. Form and spirit
10. Mind and thing
11. Effort and fate
12. Benevolence and justice
13. Innate and learnt
14. Integrity and illumination
15. Ability
16. Knowledge and action

The system of ancient Chinese categories has a definite and an indefinite nature. In truth, ancient Chinese thinkers did produce a set of concepts and categories, which between themselves have definite relationships and so form a system. It is hard to avoid there being different opinions as to which concepts and categories are important and which less so, or how they are related to and dependent on each other. The development and evolution of concepts and categories has never followed an unchanging model, nor indeed should it. Thus, although we can produce an overall table of categories, it is a temporary summary only.

Ancient Exposition and New Perspectives on Philosophical Categories

In recent times Chinese thought has undergone a change in geographical space. New terms and concepts have come in from the West and from Japan, giving rise to many new philosophical categories. With the progress of the times there have been new changes in philosophical categories.

Xunzi says, "If a [genuine] king should arise, he would certainly keep to old names and also create new names" (*Xunzi* 22, *Rectification of Names*, line 12). He stressed the relationship of the king to the rectification of names. This claim is colored by feudal ideas and does not conform to historical reality. The terms of philosophical systems of thought are all determined in the process of scholars' synthesizing knowledge of the natural world and of society. For the most part this has nothing to do with the king. Yet Xunzi's "keeping to old names and also creating new names" is certainly correct. As for the categories of traditional philosophy, one must examine and analyze them. Some should be retained as they are but some should be changed. Furthermore, new concepts and categories should be made.

Of categories that should be retained and used the following may be listed: duration and extension, nature, movement and stillness, change and transformation, law and norm, identity and difference, kind, thing, goodness, beauty, virtue, public, affirmation and denial, true and false, knowledge and action, study and thought, mind, and essential spirit.

Some categories require a new interpretation and estimation. These are listed here:

1. *Heaven and man.* In ancient philosophy 'heaven' was considered as having will and intentions. For some it was the supreme ruler, for others it was the sky, and for others it was a rational heaven. In the course of the development of ancient philosophy the natural sky has become the chief meaning of 'heaven.' Chinese philosophy can be spoken of as the study of heaven and man, the main question being their relation. In his *Inquiry into Goodness*, Dai Zhen speaks of the Way of heaven and man as being the principal subject dealt with in the classics. Traditional philosophy is based on heaven and man as the main problem. If we thus understand the question of heaven and man as the relation of man and nature, then the problem can be taken as the fundamental category of philosophy.

2. *Being-beingless.* Laozi proposed the categories of being and beingless. By 'beingless' Laozi refers to two objects. First, 'beingless' is the opposite of 'being': " 'Being' is to be taken for advantages; 'beingless' is to be taken for use" (*Laozi* 11). Second, 'beingless' is absolute beinglessness: "The myriad things under heaven are generated from being; being is generated from beinglessness" (*Laozi* 40). Wang Bi takes beinglessness as the root and hence refers to the absolute beinglessness. Absolute beinglessness is a product of thought and does not correspond to any objective reality. Only the first kind of beingless is a necessary logical category.

3. *Substance and function.* Substance and function as discussed in ancient Chinese philosophy are full of complex meanings. 'Substance' as presented by any school of idealism is a product of thought and should not be used. Only the explanation of substance and function given by the Tang scholar of the *Book of Changes*, Cui Jing, may still be employed.

> All the myriad things in heaven and earth have form and stuff. Within form and stuff there is substance and function. Substance is form and stuff itself. Function is the mysterious use superimposed on form and stuff.... As for instance heaven and earth, circular and covering, square and carrying are the substance ..., while the myriad things whose stuff begins and generates are the function.... For animals, form and body are their substance ... and soul and consciousness are their function.... For plants, branches and stems are ... their substance and the fact of living is their ... function. (*SKQS* 7, *Collected Exegeses of the* Book of Changes: *Xi Ci Shang* 1.12, pp. 835b–836a)

'Substance' refers to the physical form of a thing; 'function' refers to the function of the physical thing. Although this interpretation is not acceptable to idealists, it does in truth reflect the state of objective reality.

4. *Qi*. It is not easy to understand what ancient Chinese philosophy means by *qi*. Three meanings are implied. The first is the common concept of *qi*, which refers to all gaseous substances, such as steam, clouds, and the air we breathe. The second is the philosophical category that refers to everything that does not depend on human consciousness but is the objective object of all sensation and awareness, rather like the Western notion of 'matter.' The third is the broad sense in which *qi* refers to any phenomenon, including spiritual phenomena. The important sense is the second, the philosophical category. The Chinese notion of *qi* is very close to yet different from the Western notion of matter. The Western concept is modeled on solids, and the existence of matter is like an atom or a seed. The ancient Chinese concept of *qi* is based on moving, gaseous substances and should be understood as the unity of waves and points. The Chinese concept of *qi* lacks the traditional Western mechanistic interpretation of matter. Instead, it has a chaotic nature. In short, *qi* is an important philo-

sophical category with its own notable significance. Of course, the ordinary notion of *qi* must also be retained and used.

5. *Principle.* The notion of principle also has several meanings in Chinese philosophy. The original meaning of the character *li* is "to carve jade" (*Explanation of the Characters*, p. 12), and it was then extended to apply to the veins in the jade and later extended to refer to the inherent form of substances and the norms by which things move. These norms (*guilü*) are also called norms (*fa-ze*). The term *guilü* is based on Mencius' use of *guiju* and six *lü*; the term *fa-ze* is first seen in the *Zhuangzi* and the *Xunzi*. I believe that in the meaning of norm, *guilü*, or *fa-ze*, 'principle' may still be used. Zhu Xi distinguished between 'the principle by which things are as they are' and 'the principle by which things ought to be.' Today we talk about what is 'reasonable' (conforms to principle) and what is 'unreasonable' (does not conform to principle). The conformity to principle implied is either to the natural norm or to the moral norm. The moral norm is also called *fa-ze*. *Fa-ze* is also a commonly used concept in Song-Ming philosophy. The term 'principle' cannot be discarded. As for the school of the Chengs and Zhu Xi talking about principle as prior to things or events, thus making principle the supreme origin of heaven and earth, this is a product of thought and lost its value a long time ago.

6. *The Way and vessel.* The *Great Commentary on the* Book of Changes says, "What is above form is called 'the Way'; what is below form is called 'the vessel.'" The 'Way' stands for all abstract rules; the 'vessel' refers to all concrete things. The binome 'the Way and the vessel' thus expresses the relationship of things to rules, of phenomena to laws; whether taken according to a special or a general sense the expression still has a certain theoretical value. By saying that "all under heaven is but vessel," Wang Fuzhi established the definitive relationship between things and norms and this is indeed very significant.

7. *Mind and thing.* Mencius was the first to contrast the mind and things:

> The senses of the ears and eyes do not think and are obscured
> by things. Things connect with things and then lead them away.
> The organ of the mind is thinking. By thinking it gains [the
> right view of affairs]. If one does not think then one does not
> acquire [the right view]. (*Mencius 6, Gaozi A, #15*)

Mencius advocates taking the mind to the utmost but also recognizes the existence of external things. Buddhism proclaims that "all is mind" and thereby denies the reality of the objective world. Zhang Zai is opposed to the Buddhist theory that perception of mountains, rivers, and the earth is all an illusion. In contrast he points out that "human beings originally had no mind, it is only drawn by things that they have a mind" (*Record of the Conversations of Zhang Zai*). Wang Shouren, on the other hand, states that outside the mind there are no things. The problem of the relationship of matter to spirit is an old one.

8. *Form and spirit.* Xunzi says, "when form is present then spirit arises" (*Xunzi* 17, *Discourse on Heaven*, line 10). In this he clearly contrasts form and spirit. In the Han dynasty Sima Tan, Huan Tan, and Wang Chong all discuss the relation between form and spirit. During the northern and southern dynasties Buddhism advocated that spirit cannot be extinguished. Fan Zhen wrote his *Treatise on the Destruction of Spirit* in opposition to this view. At the time the problem of the relation between form and spirit was the most prominent issue of the day. 'Spirit' is also called 'essential spirit.' The term 'essential spirit' is often seen in the *Outer Chapters* of the *Zhuangzi*. 'Form' is what is now normally called 'body.' The expression 'essential spirit,' by contrast, remains in use today.

9. *Numinous transformation.* The *Great Commentary* to the *Book of Changes* states that "the unfathomable in *yin-yang* is what is called 'numinous'"; "the numinous is said of the mysteriousness of the myriad things." The 'numinous' here refers to the minute and complex and virtually imperceptible change. This is indeed a profound theoretical point of view. The term 'numinous' (*shen*) is easily confused with the identical term 'spirit' (*shen*), however. An important principle in the rectification of names is that one term should not refer to two entities. The 'spirit' of 'form and spirit' must be retained, hence it is difficult to keep the *shen* that means 'numinous' in the expression 'numinous transformation.'

10. *Integrity.* The *Mean and Harmony* and the *Mencius* both treat 'integrity' as the Way of heaven and also as the supreme moral virtue and hence they easily produce confusion. Wang Fuzhi takes integrity as the supreme category. He says,

> Speaking of integrity, it is a key word and no other word can
> replace or explain it. Even more, there is no manner of speech

that can oppose its form. It is said of all that is good in the world … what goes to the utmost of heaven and earth is but 'integrity' and what is at the utmost in sageliness and worthiness is also just thinking of integrity. (*Great and Full Explanation on Reading the Four Books* 9.1 #10, *Mencius* 4, *Li Lou A*, p. 605)

Integrity is that by which heaven and earth are what they are and is also the highest moral virtue. By 'integrity' Wang Fuzhi is referring to two things. First, he means the nature of objective reality, as in the following passage:

Integrity is what really exists. What is at the beginning has that where it begins; what is at the end has that where it ends. What really is is what is held in common by all in the world. It is what those with eyes can all see and those with ears can all hear. (*Elaboration on the Meanings of the* Book of History 3.6, *Speaking of Destiny* 1, p. 70)

Second, he refers to the nature of objective norms, as in his analysis of a line of *Correcting the Unenlightened* that reads,

The way by which heaven is able to perdure without coming to an end is what is meant by 'integrity.' (*Notes on Master Zhang's* Correcting the Unenlightened 3b, *Integrity and Clarity*, p. 81)

Wang comments, "The transformations of '*qi*' are ordered and have gone on from of old without ceasing; this is solely due to its reality that it has this principle." He also says,

Integrity is the real principle of heaven. (Ibid., 9b, *Qian Cheng* 2, p. 333)

Also, 'integrity' includes the sense of what contains all goodness. This notion, while being very profound, betrays in fact a confusion of concepts. The term 'integrity' originally meant 'trustworthiness,' that one's words match reality, that speech and action are one. This is extended to mean that one's behavior in life is never not in accord with moral norms. This is easy to understand. If one uses 'integrity' to express the Way of heaven or real existence, then this easily leads to confusion of thought. When the idea of the unity of heaven and man in ancient Chinese philosophy is interpreted as the union of nature and spirit, then it has profound significance. If one imposes moral norms on the natural world, however, then this is to fall into error. I believe that today 'integrity' may only be used as a moral concept and should not be treated as a category expressing what really exists.

In the works of recent academics and in modern Chinese there are many new concepts, some of which are closely related to ancient concepts. Some are developed from ancient concepts, whereas some are lacking in ancient Chinese. The important ones are listed below.

Comparative Table of Old and New Concepts and Categories
Old Concepts Appear in Parentheses

Existence 存在 (*you* 有), thought 思維 (*si* 思), course 歷程, process 過程 (*xing* 行), matter 物質 (*qi* 氣), spirit 精神 (mind 心, essential spirit 精神), norm 規律 (principle 理, rule 法則), necessity 必然 (no change), relationship 關係 (no change, related to 相與), development 發展 (*jin* 進), nature 本質 (original nature 本性, no change 本質), accidents 屬性 (nature 性), function 機能 (*yong* 用, ability 能), absolute 絕對 (sole 獨, without pair 無待), relative 相對 (*xiang dai* 相待), opposite 對立 (dual 兩, opposed to 對待), unity 統一 (one 一, united 合一), contradictory 矛盾 (no change), limitless 無限 (endless 無窮), system 系統, 體系 (system of principle 理統), universal 普遍 (all over 周遍), special 特殊 (*fen shu* 分殊), subject 主體 (inner 內, subject 主), object 客體 (outer 外, object 濱), form 形式 (pattern 文), contents 內容 (stuff 質), recognize 認識 (know 知), consciousness 意識 (spiritual brightness 靈明, 意識), put into practice 實踐 (act 行, 實踐), experience 經驗 (seeing and hearing 見聞), principled nature 理性 (virtuous nature 德性, nature of principle 義理之性), rights 權利 (portion 分), duties 義務 (responsibilities 責), freedom 自由 (*zi shi* 自適), equality 平等 (level 平), value 價值 (worth 貴, good worth 良貴), cause 因素, original cause 元素, structure 結構.

From the above table it can be seen that some concepts, such as spirit, contradiction, and necessity, are old. For some, such as principled nature–virtuous nature, opposite–*dui dai*, unity-united, the names may *đối đãi* differ but the idea is roughly the same. Some old concepts have fallen out of use to be replaced by new ones, showing thereby the progress of the times, such as course-*xing*, subject-inner, object-outer, form-pattern, contents-stuff, rights-portion, duties-responsibilities. The concepts 'cause' and 'structure' have no counterpart in ancient Chinese works. This is because ancient Chinese scholarship did not emphasize analysis. The term 'relationship' is found in works of the Song-Ming period, and 'consciousness' is a Buddhist term; both are now very popular.

Modern Chinese philosophy lacks a universal and spiritually profound system but in its use of concepts and categories it already goes far beyond earlier philosophy.

"Keeping to old names and also creating new names" remains the glorious duty of philosophical workers of our new China.*

* Author's note: This essay originally appeared in *Social Sciences in China* no. 2 (1985).

Part One
Metaphysics

A. Ontology

I. Principal Concepts

1. Heaven

Tian THIÊN

天

Although at times there is an intentional conflict between proponents of one view or the other, one may see the concept 'heaven' as embracing a spectrum of views of which the religious idea of God and the popular use of the word to refer to the sky are but the extremes. The division of opinion regarding the sky or divine or heaven has continued down to the present day. It should be noted, though, that it is never as stark as the Western opposition between a transcendent God and a purely scientific view of the sky. The character for 'heaven' is probably derived from that for 'big man.' This is one reason why a human element has always been present in the Chinese conception of heaven as God. Likewise, the heavenly bodies have not traditionally been seen as objective lumps of matter and energy.

Chinese philosophers of later periods inherited their terminology from the past and did not feel at liberty to abandon ancient concepts, but from the Song dynasty onward thinkers sought to systematize their inheritance. 'Heaven' as the supreme concept of Confucius would be worked into the system, but it is effectively neutralized by making it the equivalent of some other more readily available concept such as 'principle' (Cheng Hao), qi (Zhang Zai), 'human nature and principle' (Cheng Yi), or 'mind' (Cheng Hao and Wang Shouren).

God/Sky

'Heaven' is an important concept in ancient Chinese philosophy. It comprises two aspects: on one hand it is an objective infinite reality, the 'sky';

on the other it is 'God,' or the supreme concept. The contrast between these two views is manifest. Ancient religious beliefs maintained that heaven had a will and was the master of the universe. Among the philosophers Confucius held to this belief in heaven as the supreme lord:

> If heaven wished to destroy this culture, it would not have given the said culture to a being who will die like me. Since heaven has not destroyed this culture, what can the people of Kuang do to me?* (*Analects* 9, *Zi Han* #5)

The rise and fall of cultures and the peace and peril of human beings are all decided by heaven. Yet in talking about heaven Confucius also talked about the wide open sky, as when he says,

> Oh how great as a sovereign was Yao! How majestic! Heaven alone is great and Yao alone imitated it.† (*Analects* 8, *Tai Bo* #20)

"Heaven alone is great" cannot be understood as saying that only God is the greatest but rather that heaven is what is broadest. 'Heaven' here means the wide open sky. This may be a late saying of Confucius. Maybe Confucius's thought concerning heaven underwent a change.

In ancient philosophy heaven forms a pair with earth. The *Mean and Balance* is one chapter of the *Record of Rites* and was selected to be one of the four texts that formed the basis of China's civil service exams from the twelfth to the twentieth centuries A.D.‡ It says,

> This heaven is now only as much as what shines here, yet taken as without limit, the sun, moon, and constellations are bespangled in it, the myriad things covered by it. Now this earth

---

*Confucius was passing through the city of Kuang, near Kaifeng in Henan, when he was mistaken for Yang Hu, an official who had caused harm to the people. After five days Confucius escaped. See J. Legge, *The Chinese Classics* (Oxford: Clarendon, 1893; reprint, Taipei: Southern Materials Centre, 1985), 1:217–218, no. 5.

†Yao is the fourth of the legendary emperors of China. See R. Mathieu, *Anthologie des mythes et legendes de la Chine ancienne* (Paris: Gallimard, 1989), #35; W. F. Mayers, *The Chinese Reader's Manual* (Shanghai: Presbyterian Mission Press) I #900.

‡The so-called Four Books include the *Mean and Harmony* and *Great Learning* from the *Record of Rites* and the *Analects* of Confucius with the *Mencius*. Phrases from the first two books are used to name the halls of the university in Beijing where the students studied for and took their exams.

is only as much as a handful of soil, yet taken in its breadth and depth, it supports Mounts Hua and Yue without being weighed down, holds rivers and seas without their seeping away. The myriad things are supported by it. (*Mean and Harmony*, 26)

The *Zhuangzi*, a work full of paradox, asks,

> Is the azure of heaven its true color? Or is it so far away that its furthest limits cannot be reached? (*Zhuangzi* 1, *Going Rambling Without a Destination*, line 4)

Here 'heaven' is in contrast with earth and hence is the sky.

The "canonical" sections of *Guanzi* may perhaps contain the actual words of Guan Zhong. In the *Conditions and Circumstances* chapter heaven and earth are paired:

> Heaven does not change in its constancy; earth does not vary in its regularity; spring, autumn, winter, and summer do not alter their seasonal characteristics. From of old until now it is the same. (*Guanzi* 2, *Conditions and Circumstances*, 1:12)

This passage confirms the regularity and order of heaven and earth.

On the other hand, Mozi, a near-contemporary of Confucius, brought out the religious dimension and wrote of the "will of heaven." The *Mozi* says,

> Those who obey the will of heaven, loving without discrimination, aiding others, will surely obtain a reward; those who oppose the will of heaven, by discrimination and unfriendliness and by doing wrong to others, will surely obtain a punishment. (*Mozi* 26, *Will of Heaven A*, lines 22–23)

Heaven has a will and can reward or punish men and women. What the *Mozi* understands by the content of the will of heaven is loving without discrimination. The will of heaven is the will to love. While the *Mozi* harks back to belief in heaven as God, it nonetheless remodels the ancient Chinese picture of heaven.

Mencius continued in the tradition of Confucius and likewise held that heaven was the lord of the world. The *Mencius* records the following:

> Wan Zhang asked, "Is it the case that Yao gave the empire
> to Shun?" Mencius replied, "Indeed no! The Son of Heaven
> cannot give the empire to anyone." Wan said, "Yes, but
> Shun had the empire so who gave it to him?" He replied,
> "Heaven gave it to him." "Heaven gave it to him," Wan said.
> "Was this with any command to him?" He answered, "No.
> Heaven does not speak. It simply showed what it did through
> his [Shun's] conduct and governance."* (*Mencius* 5, *Wan
> Zhang A, #5*)

The ruler, or "Son of Heaven," is the one appointed by heaven. It is
heaven that is the support of the ruler's authority.

The Han dynasty thinker Dong Zhongshu honored Confucianism,
but on the question of heaven he followed the Mohist "will of heaven"
and held heaven to be the greatest of the spirits:

> Heaven is the great prince of the hundred spirits. (*Luxuriant
> Gems of the Spring and Autumn Annals* 65, *Suburban Talks*,
> p. 398)

Opposition to this religious attitude came from Wang Chong, who held
that heaven was simply the "heavenly body" containing sun, moon, and
stars.

In the Tang dynasty Liu Zongyuan wrote of heaven in contrast to
earth, saying,

> That which is above and is dark the world calls 'heaven'; that
> which is below and is yellow, the world calls 'earth.' (*SKQS*
> 1076, *Collected Works of Liu Hedong* 16, *Speaking of Heaven*
> #1, p. 155a–b)

Liu Yuxi wrote in a similar vein:

> Heaven is the greatest of things having form; human beings are
> the most excellent of animals. (*SBCK: Collected Works of Liu
> Mengde* 12.4, *Discourse on Heaven* I, p. 7a)

---

*Shun is the fifth of the legendary emperors. Yao did not give the throne to his son,
whom he deemed unworthy, but to Shun. See Mathieu, *Anthologie*, #36; Mayers, *Chinese
Reader's Manual* I, #617.

This contrasts heaven and human beings. Both Lius are talking of the heaven of astronomers.

Heaven and Humans

As well as trying to pin down the nature of heaven itself, Chinese thinkers were concerned with the relation between heaven and the human being. Mencius believed that heaven was the source of the human mind and of human nature:

> To the mind pertains the role of thinking. By thinking it obtains its object. If it does not think it does not obtain its object. This is what heaven has given to me. (*Mencius* 6, *Gaozi A* #15)

The mind's ability to think is "what heaven has given," and what the mind is principally concerned with is "principle and respect":

> What is it that our minds feel sympathy for? It is principle and it is respect. (*Mencius* 6, *Gaozi A* #7)

Principle and respect are what please the mind, and Mencius considers this feature to be the defining characteristic of what it is to be human. Human nature and heaven communicate with each other.

> Those who exert their minds to the full know their nature, and those who know their nature know heaven. (*Mencius* 7, *Exhausting the Mind A*, #1)

Human nature is in the mind and has its origin in heaven. Human nature can be understood by the mind, and in the same way so too can heaven. Mind, human nature, and heaven are all of a piece. Mencius affirms the commonality of human nature and heaven, and although he states it only in simple and unclear fashion, yet it was to have enormous influence on philosophy in the Song and Ming dynasties, giving rise to the use of 'heaven' as the highest philosophical category.

The *Guanzi*, in a statement about the constancy of heaven and earth, contrasts heaven and earth as a pair. It also contrasts heaven and the human person:

> Upholding plenitude pertains to heaven; providing security in
> the face of danger pertains to human beings. If one exceeds the
> measure set by heaven, though the country be full it will surely
> dry up. If superior and inferior are not in harmony, though one
> be secure, one will surely come to danger. (*Guanzi* 2, *Conditions and Circumstances*, 1:16)

This saying is also found in the *Sayings of the States*, in which Fan Li addresses King Goujian of Yue (496–465 B.C.):*

> Upholding plenitude pertains to heaven; making firm what is
> unstable pertains to human beings; regularizing affairs pertains
> to earth. (*Sayings of the States* 21, *Sayings of Yue B*, p. 641)

Both the *Sayings of the States* and the *Guanzi* put heaven and human beings on a par.† It is not until the *Zhuangzi* that heaven and human beings are put in opposition, with the *Zhuangzi* favoring heaven and the *Xunzi* giving the preference to the human realm.

The opening line of Chapter 6 of the *Zhuangzi* reads,

> The highest knowledge is to know what heaven does and to
> know what human beings do. (*Zhuangzi* 6, *The Teacher Who Is
> the Ultimate Ancestor*, line 1)

Heaven's doing is spontaneous and natural; the doing of human beings is purposeful. The *Zhuangzi* argues for a clear distinction between the two spheres:

> Do not let the human mind harm the Way; do not let human
> beings abet heaven. (Ibid., line 9)

One should trust to nature and not impose on it. The person who lives out this ideal is called an "extraordinary person":

> Extraordinary persons are extraordinary in the sight of human
> beings but normal in the sight of heaven. (Ibid., line 74)

---

*Yue was a small, barbarian kingdom on the southern fringes of the Chinese cultural world, centered near present-day Hangzhou. It was reduced to ruins in 494 B.C. by Wu, a kingdom of like nature with its capital at present-day Suzhou. Yue rose from the ashes thanks to the wise advice of Fan Li and utterly wiped out its rival in 472 B.C.

†Author's note: It is not possible to say which of these two versions is prior to the other.

Unlike the normal run of people, such persons go along with nature. A later chapter from the *Zhuangzi* corpus, *Autumn Floods*, speaks of heaven and human beings as follows:

> What can be said to be of heaven; what can be said to be of human beings?... Oxen and horses having four feet is of heaven; putting a halter on a horse's head and piercing an ox's nose is of human beings. (*Zhuangzi* 17, *Autumn Floods*, lines 51–52)

Heaven is what is naturally so; human beings alter this natural order. Thus for the *Zhuangzi* heaven is the natural order, which also includes the earth. It can be called the natural heaven.

The *Xunzi* also affirms a distinction between heaven and the human sphere. In chapter 17 the following conclusion is drawn:

> Hence the one who understands the distinction between heaven and human beings is the perfect man. (*Xunzi* 17, *Discourse on Heaven*, line 5)

Heaven and human beings are distinct but the *Xunzi* is opposed to following nature; rather, it emphasizes transforming nature. Instead of admiring the greatness of nature, it is better to transform and use it:

> Instead of magnifying heaven and admiring it why not treat it as a thing and manage it? Instead of obeying heaven and praising it, why not control the Decree of Heaven and use it? (Ibid., line 44)

The upshot of this is that human beings must grasp responsibility for their affairs and not indulge in star gazing:

> Therefore to neglect human measures and think of heaven is to lose the nature of the myriad things. (Ibid., line 46)

Thus in the *Xunzi* heaven is always the natural heaven.

A Philosophical Concept

In the Song dynasty the notion of heaven developed to include new aspects. 'Heaven' is the supreme concept, the highest reality. Zhang Zai thinks that heaven is ultimate space and ultimate space is the state of *qi* when it is scattered and not yet bound together:

> From ultimate space there comes the name of heaven. (*SKQS* 697, *Correcting the Unenlightened* 1, *Great Harmony*, p. 99a)

> The congealing and scattering of *qi* is to ultimate space as the freezing and melting of ice is to water. If we know that ultimate space is *qi* then there is no such thing as 'beingless.'* (Ibid., p. 98b)

He also says that heaven is "great without anything outside it" (p. 100b), meaning that 'heaven' is the collective name for *qi*, a limitless material world.†

Zhang Zai's cousin Cheng Hao speaks of heaven as principle and identifies the two:‡

> Heaven is principle. (*SKQS* 698, *Surviving Works of the Two Chengs* 11, p. 105b)

Cheng Hao's younger brother, Cheng Yi, believed that principle, human nature, and heaven are all the same:

> Human nature is principle. (Ibid. 22a, p. 235a)

> The Way and human nature are one ... the natural order of human nature is called heaven; what comes from nature and has form is the heart-mind; what comes from the nature and moves is called feelings. All these different elements are one. (Ibid. 25, p. 255b)

Heaven is simply the principle of the natural order. The Cheng brothers held both 'principle' and 'heaven' as the highest concepts and thus underlined the unity of heaven and principle.

Cheng Hao also says that "only the mind is heaven" (*SKQS* 698,

---

* On *qi* see concept 5; on 'beingless' see concept 20.
† See E. I. Kasoff, *The Thought of Chang Tsai* (Cambridge: Cambridge University Press, 1984), pp. 55–60, for a longer discussion of Zhang Zai's use of *tian* as "a metaphor for the principles according to which the way of heaven operates" (p. 57).
‡ On 'principle' see concept 3.

Surviving Works of the Two Chengs 2a, p. 19a) and thus equates the mind and heaven. This idea was taken up in the Ming dynasty by Wang Shou-ren:

> The mind is heaven. In talking of the mind one refers to heaven and earth and all the myriad things. (*Complete Collected Works of Wang Yangming: Reply to Ji Mingde*, p. 214)

Again,

> The mind is the Way; the Way is heaven. To know the mind is to know the Way and to know heaven. (*Instructions for Practical Living A #1*, p. 23)

Zhang Zai understood heaven as ultimate space. This is a materialist point of view. The Cheng brothers understood heaven as principle. This is the point of view of objective idealism. Wang Shouren understood heaven as mind. This is the point of view of subjective idealism. In ancient Chinese theories of heaven there was opposition between materialist and idealist points of view. Materialism held that heaven was an unlimited objective entity. Idealism held that heaven was either the supreme spirit or supreme concept. Opposition between these two fundamental points of view is very clear.

2. The Way, The Way of Heaven
Dao ĐẠO
道

The concept dao *is perhaps the most important concept in Chinese philosophy.** *Although its later and more philosophical meanings may develop far beyond the original significance of the word, nonetheless the original image is never wholly lost; hence we can justifiably translate it as the "Way." The most important text for understanding the Way is the* Laozi. *It portrays the Way*

---

* In Wade-Giles transliteration: *Tao.*

as prior—since Chinese grammar is ambiguous here the priority can be logical or temporal—to heaven and earth. In other texts, such as the Four Chapters *of the* Guanzi, *the Way is immanent in heaven and earth rather than prior to them. Of these four chapters the oldest is the one titled* Inner Exercise, *and at least two of the others are commentaries on it. The two in question are* Technique of the Heart *parts A and B. In Song-Qing philosophy the key problems are how the Way relates to other important terms. Thus we may note two stages in the discussion of the Way. In the early period the problem is to situate the Way with respect to the formation of heaven and earth. In the later period the question is one of the relation of the Way to other leading terms, notably 'principle' and* qi.

The original meaning of the character *dao* is a "way," a path along which one can travel. The earliest Chinese dictionary, compiled in A.D. 100, the *Explanation of Words and Characters*, says,

> The *dao* is that way along which one walks; once obtained one calls it the Way. (p. 42a)

What has a definite direction is called the Way.

The Spring and Autumn Period

The original meaning of the term was extended to refer to the norm that people or things must respect. The norm respected by sun, moon, and stars is called the Way of Heaven; the norm governing human life is called the Human Way. An early history of China, *Zuo's Commentary*, records a discussion following the appearance of a comet in 524 B.C. that was a harbinger of fire. Four capital cities did indeed catch fire. Pei Zao of Zheng predicted fire on the appearance of the comet. Confucius' disciple Zi Chan criticized him:

> Heaven's Way is distant; the human way is close. There is no access to the former. How would we know of it? How does

Zao know the Way of Heaven? (*Zuo's Commentary* 10, *Chao* 18 #1, p. 669)

Pei Zao's reliance on astronomical happenings to predict a fire is not to be believed. Zi Chan distinguishes between Heaven's Way, which is distant, and the human way, which is close, and opposes the superstitious practice of determining human affairs by reference to astronomical events. A year earlier, *Zuo's Commentary* recorded another discussion of comets. Shen Xu of Lu said,

> The comet is what sweeps away the old and lays out the new. Heaven's actions always have such omens ... will not the nobles encounter the disaster of fires? (*Zuo's Commentary* 10, *Chao* 17 #4, p. 666)

Shen Xu believed that astronomical happenings portend what will happen in the human world. Indeed, in the Spring and Autumn period astronomy and astrology were inseparable.

Confucius very rarely spoke of Heaven's Way. A disciple, Zi Gong, said,

> The Master's talk of human nature and of the Way of Heaven can not be heard. (*Analects* 5, *Gong Zhi*, pp. 177–178)

Confucius spoke mainly of the human way:

> Who on going out does not go out by the door? Yet how is it that no-one will go out, metaphorically speaking, by this Way? (*Analects* 6, *Yong Ye*, p. 190)

The Way in question is the principle of moral behavior that all should respect. Confucius expands this Way by means of three other key terms:

> Let the will be on the *Way*; rely on *virtue*, trust to *benevolence*, relax in the *arts*. (*Analects* 7, *Shu Er*, p. 196)

Of these four terms, the Way is the founding principle; virtue is the real and visible manifestation of the Way; benevolence is the chief virtue, and the arts, that is, rites and music, are the concrete expressions of benevolence.

Hence in this period the Way may be either the Way of Heaven or the Human Way, but commonly it is the latter that is meant.

The *Laozi* and the *Zhuangzi*

The *Laozi*, or *Canon of the Way and Virtue*, brings a new understanding of the term *dao*. The *Laozi* holds that the Way is the origin of the world, "generated before heaven and earth." In the Spring and Autumn period the Heavenly Way was always the Way of Heaven, with the emphasis placed on 'heaven.' The *Laozi* takes the Way as more fundamental than heaven; heaven comes from the Way:

> There is something formed inchoate;
> Generated before heaven and earth;
> Silent, hush, void, ah!
> Standing alone and not changing,
> Turning round and round and not tiring.
> It may be the mother of all under heaven.
> I do not know its name so I shall call it the 'Way.'
> If pressed I would name it 'great.' (*Laozi* 25/MWD 69)*

By 'great' is to be understood the 'ultimate,' that is, the absolute beginning. In saying that there is "something" *Laozi* indicates that the Way is an objective entity. Quoting the *Laozi* again, we read,

> The way is empty so one who uses it may seem to be not
>   filled;†
> An abyss, ah!, as if it were the ancestor of the myriad
>   things ...
> Murky, yes, as if it only seems to exist.
> I do not know whose child it is;
> It is the image of what is prior to the supreme ancestor.
> (*Laozi* 4/MWD 48)

---

*The *Laozi* has been handed down, copied, and recopied. The chapter numbers used are those of the received text. In 1973 at Mawangdui, Changsha, Hunan Province, two manuscripts were discovered with the first and second parts of the work reversed in order, thus affecting the numbering of the chapters. The first reference is to the received text; the number marked MWD is that of the Mawangdui find.

†This line is difficult. I translate according to Karlgren; see M. Lafargue, *Tao and Method*, p. 525 on 31 (chap. 4). Wing-tsit Chan reads, "It may be used but its capacity is never exhausted." Chan, *A Source Book in Chinese Philosophy* (Princeton: Princeton University Press, 1963), p. 141; D. C. Lau reads, "yet when used there is something that does not make it full." D. C. Lau, *Lao-Tzu: Tao Te Ching* (New York: Knopf, 1994), p. 52.

The Way is the origin of the myriad things; its existence is not like that of the myriad things. If there is a supreme ancestor, then the supreme ancestor has the Way as his origin.

The *Laozi* holds that the Way is neither being nor beinglessness; it has both being and beinglessness. It has a unique form of existence. Chapter 21 reads,

> As 'thing' the Way is vague and unclear;
> Unclear and vague, yet within it is a symbol;
> Vague and unclear, yet within it is a thing;
> Obscure and dark, yet within it is an essence.
> Its essence is truly authentic and within in it is what is reliable.
> (*Laozi* 21/MWD 65)

Again,

> Look at it but you do not see it so you call it 'tiny';
> Listen to it but you do not hear it so you call it 'pianissimo';
> Feel it but you do not touch it so you call it 'minute.'
> These three cannot be ascertained, hence they are muddled
>   into one.
> Up high it does not shine; down below it is not veiled.
> Unending, it cannot be named; it reverts back to what is not
>   a thing.
> This is called the shape without a shape, the image of what is
>   not a thing.
> This is called unclear and vague. (*Laozi* 14/MWD 58)

The Way is on one hand the "symbol" within, the "thing" within and, on the other, what reverts back to nothing, the shape without a shape, the image of what is not a thing. This is to say that the Way is a real, objective presence, yet it is without form or image.

What in fact is this so-called Way? This notion of the Way is derived from the notion of the Way of Heaven. The Way of Heaven is the rule governing all in heaven, but the Way is even more fundamental than heaven. This common rule exists objectively but has no form or image, unlike other things. In fact what the *Laozi* is doing in speaking of the Way is stressing the importance of a universal rule. This rule is seen by the *Laozi* as an objective essence.

The *Laozi* also discusses the formation of the world:

> The Way generates the One: the One generates the Two;
> The Two generate the Three: the Three generate the myriad
>   things.
> The myriad things carry *yin* on their backs and *yang* in their
>   arms
> And take *qi* to be their harmony. (*Laozi* 42/MWD 5)

The "one" is the state before heaven and earth separated, and the Way precedes this; the two are heaven and earth and the three *yin*, *yang*, and *qi*. The Way here is making the abstract absolute. The Way may not be equated, though, with the absolute spirit of modern Western idealism. The *Laozi* says,

> Therefore the Way is great, heaven is great, the earth is great, human beings are also great. Within the universe are these four "greats" and human beings count themselves as one of them. (*Laozi* 25/MWD 69)

The Way is in the universe and hence immanent in space and time.

> The Way is ever not doing and yet nothing is left undone. (*Laozi* 37/MWD 81)

The Way is "not-doing," that is, it has no goal to pursue, nothing that one might associate with the 'spirit' of Hegel.

The *Laozi*'s discourse on the Way may be described as an objective conceptual discourse. It affirms that heaven-earth and the myriad things all have a common rule. This is the *Laozi*'s contribution to philosophy. This rule is also reified. This is to fall into error.

The *Zhuangzi* conceives of the Way in the tradition of the *Laozi* as preceding heaven and earth:

> This Way is really present and can be relied on. It does nothing and has no shape. It may be handed on but not possessed; it may be obtained but not seen. It is itself the root, itself the trunk. Before there was yet heaven and earth from of old it has ever been. It hallows ghosts and hallows the supreme ancestor, generates heaven and generates earth. (*Zhuangzi* 6, *The Teacher Who Is the Ultimate Ancestor*, lines 29–30)

The Way is "really present" but it has no will of its own, no "shape." It is itself the root and trunk and precedes heaven and earth.

In the later corpus the *Zhuangzi* does put the Way below heaven:

> What penetrates heaven is the Way; what accords with earth is virtue; what applies to the myriad things is justice ... the Way belongs to heaven.* (*Zhuangzi* 12, *Heaven and Earth*, lines 4–5)

The Way is subordinate to heaven in this text. Here heaven is more fundamental than the Way. This is a feature proper to the later corpus of the *Zhuangzi*.

The *Great Appendix* to the *Book of Changes*

Written soon after the *Laozi*, the *Great Appendix* to the *Book of Changes* speaks of the Way in a manner that differs from that described in the *Laozi*. The Way does not precede heaven and earth:

> The *Changes* is on a par with with heaven and earth; therefore it can follow through the strands of the Way of heaven and earth. (*Book of Changes: Great Appendix* 1.4, p. 278)
>
> The alternation of *yin* and *yang* is called "the Way." (Ibid. 1.5, p. 280)
>
> What is it that the *Changes* does? The *Changes* opens things up, completes business, and encapsulates the Way of heaven and earth. This it is that the *Changes* does. (Ibid. 1.11, p. 297)

The claim here is that the changing patterns of the hexagrams of the *Book of Changes* encompass all events in the world and can be used to interpret these events. The Way that is referred to is always the Way of heaven and earth and never prior to heaven and earth.

The *Great Appendix* makes a distinction that was to prove highly influential, especially in the Song dynasty, between what is above form, or metaphysical, and what has visible form, the physical:

---

*I quote the text as emended by Wang Shumin, 王叔岷; see Huang Mianhong, *Xinyi Zhuangzi Duben* (Taibei: Sanmin Shuju, 1974), p. 160, n. 3.

> What is above form is called 'the Way'; what is below form is
> called 'vessel.' (Ibid. 1.12, p. 303)

This distinction of "above" and "below" in the original text of the *Changes*
applies to the position of the lines in a hexagram. There are six lines, either
full (—) or broken (- -), in each hexagram, and they are reckoned from the
bottom up.

> As a book the *Changes* should not be kept far away; as a Way it
> is distinguished by frequent changes of the lines. They change
> and move without stopping still, flowing around into the six
> places in the hexagram; above and below have no constancy;
> hard (unbroken) lines and soft (broken) lines alternate. (Ibid.
> 2.8, p. 328)

Each hexagram is a definite pattern of lines, but by changing one line
one changes the whole hexagram into another. Hence by just looking at
the bottom line one does not know which hexagram is being viewed. All
six lines must be considered. The lowest line is the "root," the highest
the "branches." Only when one is at the branches does one know the
whole.

> The six lines intermingle; only according to their proper time
> do they form a figure. The opening line is hard to know, the
> top line easy to know; these are the root and branches. (Ibid.
> 2.9, p. 330)

The root here does not have a logical priority, hence "what is above form"
may not be construed as the root from which what is "below form" might
issue. In fact, what is above form is the formless inasmuch as it appears in
what has form. It is the abstract as opposed to the concrete, or "what has
form." What is above form is the norm of the abstract; what is below form
is concrete things.

The *Changes* are distinguished by a threefold pattern: heaven, earth,
and the human:

> As a book the *Changes* is broad, encompassing everything. In it
> is the way of heaven; in it is the way of humans; in it is the way
> of earth. (Ibid. 2.10, p. 333)

At the level of the way of heaven one speaks of *yin* and *yang*; at the level of the way of earth one speaks of soft (broken) and hard (unbroken) lines; at the level of the way of humans one speaks of benevolence and justice. (*Book of Changes: Treatise of Remarks on the Trigrams* 2, p. 340)

Although there is a difference between these levels, the alternation of *yin* and *yang* is the most abstract and general level of interpretation. In the Song dynasty materialists and idealists gave different interpretations of what is above form and what is below form.

The *Guanzi*, the *Xunzi*, and the *Hanfeizi*

The *Inner Exercise* of the *Guanzi* describes the Way as being formless and soundless, the source of the production of the myriad things:

One does not see its form; one does not hear its voice yet one may trace its accomplishments. . . .

The Way is also that which the mouth cannot speak of; that which the eye cannot see; that which the ear cannot hear. It is the way in which to train one's heart so as to rectify forms. Once lost human beings will die. Once obtained they will come into life. Once lost affairs will fail. Once gained they will be accomplished. (*Guanzi* 49, *Inner Exercise*, 2:123)

The Way is beyond the reach of the senses. It is that by which humans come to life and by which events are brought to fruition. The *Inner Exercise* also speaks of the Way as having no visible form while yet being what causes the myriad things to be:

It is always such that the Way itself lacks a root and a stem. It lacks leaves and fruit. The myriad things depend on it to come to life, they depend on it for their flowering. Its name is said to be the Way. (Ibid.)

The Way in question is the norm governing the coming to life and accomplishment of the myriad things.

The *Inner Exercise* also relates the Way to the heart and *qi*.

> The Way is not in any place, yet it rests in a good heart. When the heart is calm and *qi* is regular then the Way may be made to stop there. (Ibid.)

Although distinct the Way, heart and *qi* are related.

Insofar as the Way may be said to have content it is "harmony":

> As for the coming to life of human beings, heaven produces their essence and earth their form, and when these are united a human being is made. Though in harmony there is life, without harmony there is no life. In examining the way of harmony one discovers that its circumstances cannot be seen, its characteristics cannot be compared with anything else. (Ibid., 2:130)

The "way of harmony" is at the very least the chief content of the Way.

The Han commentary on the *Inner Exercise*, the *Technique of the Heart*, adds more to the notion of the Way. The Way is universal:

> The Way is within heaven and earth: so great it has no outside, so small it has no inside. (*Guanzi* 36, *Technique of the Heart A*, 2:46)

The Way is universal and hence there is nothing outside it. It is present everywhere and thus has no inside. The Way is within heaven and earth and not prior to them as in *Laozi*.

The *Xunzi* emphasized the Way as the path of moral conduct:

> The Way is not the way of heaven nor the way of earth but rather the way that human beings take. (*Xunzi* 8, *The Teachings of the Confucians*, line 24)

Despite this there is some discussion of the universal way of heaven:

> The myriad things only account for one aspect of the Way; one thing only accounts for one aspect of the myriad things. (*Xunzi* 17, *Discourse on Heaven*, line 50)
>
> The Great Way is that by which the myriad things change and are completed. (*Xunzi* 31, *Duke Ai*, line 17)

The Way is that by which the myriad things change, in other words, the norm governing change and development, a Way that is the constant Way of heaven and earth:

Heaven has a constant Way; earth has constant regularity. (*Xunzi* 17, *Discourse on Heaven*, line 23)

The Way is not prior to heaven and earth; hence in speaking of the Way Xunzi supported the materialist point of view.

Xunzi's pupil, Han Fei, explained the Way in terms of principle:

The Way is that by which the myriad things are, the standard which the myriad principles imitate. Principles are the patterns that complete things. The Way is that by which the myriad things come to completion.... The myriad things each have their own principle, and the Way completely gathers the myriad principles. (*Hanfeizi* 20, *Explanations of Laozi* 27:1–7, 15–16)

"Principle" refers to the principles of the myriad things, whereas the Way is their synthesis. The Way comprehends the principles of the myriad things.

In the *Guanzi* the Way is also linked to principle:

The rites come from justice, justice from principle, and principle accommodates to the Way.* (*Guanzi* 36, *Technique of the Heart A*, 2:7)

This passage is a forerunner of Han Fei's explanation of the Way.

In explaining the constant Way of *Laozi*, the *Hanfeizi* points out that the Way is not above heaven and earth:

Indeed any thing that now is and then is not, that now dies and then lives, that flourishes at the beginning and afterwards declines, cannot be said to be for ever. Only that which comes to life with the separation of heaven and earth (out of the amorphous mass) and lasts until the falling apart of heaven and earth and that neither dies nor declines can be said to be for ever. (*Hanfeizi* 20, *Explanations of Laozi* 29:7–12)

What is for ever comes to be with heaven and earth and not before them. The Way is not a metaphysical concept but the norm of the material world. The *Hanfeizi* thus modifies the *Laozi*'s understanding of the Way.

---

* This is the text as emended by Guo Moruo and accepted by Zhang Dainian.

Since the *Laozi* elevated the Way to supremacy it has been a focal point of debate among philosophers. The *Laozi* and the *Zhuangzi* stand on one side in stressing the metaphysical aspects, while from the materialist point of view the *Guanzi, Xunzi*, and *Hanfeizi* all challenge the claim that the Way can be prior to heaven and earth. This was the state of the discussion for the next millennium, until the Song dynasty.

The Song Era

Zhang Zai spoke of the Way in terms of *qi*. He held the way to be the course taken by the changes of *qi*:

> What comes from the transformations of *qi* is called the Way. (*SKQS* 697, *Correcting the Unenlightened* 1, *Ultimate Harmony*, p. 99a)

He further identified the Way with ultimate harmony:

> Ultimate Harmony is what is called the Way. It comprises the nature which contains all the contrasting movements of floating, sinking, rise and fall, movement and rest. It is the beginning which gives rise to fusion and intermingling, of overcoming and being overcome, of expanding and contracting.... Unless it is like wild horses, fusing and intermingling, it does not deserve the name 'ultimate harmony.' (Ibid., p. 97a)

"Wild horses" refers to the fluid, moving *qi*; by "fusion and intermingling" is understood the coming together of *yin* and *yang*. Ultimate harmony includes all moving *qi* and is what binds all *qi* together.

The two Cheng brothers interpreted the Way in terms of principle. Cheng Hao said,

> "The doings of heaven above are without sound or scent" [*Book of Songs* 235 #7, *King Wen*, p. 59]: its substance is called the *Changes* and its principle is called the Way. (*SKQS* 698, *Surviving Works of the Two Chengs* 1, p. 10a)

Here the Way is interpreted in terms of principle. His brother, Cheng Yi, says,

> "The alternation of *yin* and *yang* is what is meant by the Way"
> [*Changes*: *Great Appendix*, 1.5]; the Way is not *yin* and *yang*.
> Rather, that by which *yin* and *yang* alternate is the Way. (*SKQS*
> 698, *Surviving Works of the Two Chengs* 3, p. 61a)

The Way is that by which *yin* and *yang* are what they are. The Way and *qi* are distinguished in terminology that also comes from the *Book of Changes*:

> Apart from *yin* and *yang* there is no Way. That by which *yin*
> and *yang* are is the Way. *Yin* and *yang* are forms of *qi*. *Qi* is
> what is below form; the Way is what is above form. (*SKQS* 698,
> *Surviving Works of the Two Chengs* 15, p. 128b)

Thus, whereas Zhang Zai interprets the Way in terms of *qi*, applying it in a novel way to the whole course of the material world, the Cheng brothers interpret it in terms of principle taken as a universal norm and oppose the equation of the Way and *qi*. In this respect the Cheng brothers are closer to the pre-Qin understanding of the Way. The Cheng brothers, however, go further by reifying this universal norm.

Zhu Xi followed in the Chengs' footsteps and interpreted the Way in terms of principle:

> Insofar as *yin* and *yang* reach to what is far off, they are *qi*. The
> principle, though, by which they do so is what is called the
> Way. (*The Root Meaning of the* Changes: *Great Appendix* I,
> p. 58)
>
> The hexagrams and their lines, *yin* and *yang* are all what
> is below form; the principle by which they are is, however, the
> Way. (Ibid., 1.12, p. 63)

Similar phrases can be found throughout his work; there is no need to quote them all here. Yet at times Zhu Xi writes as if the Way embraces both 'substance' and 'function,' both what is above form and what is below form.* In commenting on a phrase in the *Mean and Harmony* that reads "The way of the gentleman is wide-reaching yet hidden," Zhu Xi says, " 'wide-reaching' applies to the extent of use (of the Way); 'hidden'

---

* The pair 'substance' and 'function' is discussed in concept 32.

applies to minuteness of the body (of the Way)" (*Commentary on the Mean and Harmony* 12).* Zhu Xi goes on to explain,

> Transforming, nourishing, flowing by, going along, above and below shining out, there is nothing which does not have the use of this principle; this is what is called "far-reaching." Yet that by which these things are so cannot be seen or heard; this is what is called 'hidden.' (Ibid.)

"Far-reaching" is said of the "function" and "function" applies to phenomena; "hidden" applies to "substance" and "substance" refers to principle. The Way is what unites the far-reaching and the hidden.

> The Way unites substance and function and is said of the "far-reaching" and the "hidden." (*Conversations of Master Zhu Arranged Topically* 6, p. 99)

This is another of Zhu Xi's theories of the Way.

The Qing Era

Wang Fuzhi fled into early retirement when the Manchus established the authority of their Qing government over his native province of Hunan in 1648.† He continued the tradition of the Chengs and Zhu Xi. In his commentary on one of Zhang Zai's works he wrote,

> The Way is the principle running through heaven, earth, the human sphere, and the world of things. (*Notes to Master Zhang's Correcting the Unenlightened* 1a, p. 15)

The Way is the universal norm of all things. This Way is composed of *qi*:

---

*For this passage the reader should refer to Legge's discussion (*Chinese Classics*, I: 392–393), in which he points out that the meaning of the two terms translated as "wide-reaching" and "hidden" is far from certain.

†Wang Fuzhi (1619–1692) *Zi* (style): Ernong; *Hao* (honorific): Jiang Zhou; known as Chuan Shan, of Hengyang in Hunan Province. He remained loyal to the Ming and served their government in Guilin until it was suppressed. He never shaved his head in the manner prescribed by the Manchu government. He wrote extensively on the classics and the Four Books as well as on Zhang Zai. Partial translations of some of his writings are to be found in Chan, *Source Book*, pp. 692–702.

Outside *qi* there is no principle which can stand up in the void. (*Complete Study After Reading the Four Books* 10, *Mencius* 6A, p. 1241)

Yan Yuan was a pharmacist opposed to excessive book-learning.* He is known for four works called "Preservations," from which the following quotations come. In the first he expresses his belief that the Way is comprised of both *qi* and principle:

> Principle and *qi* are both the Way of Heaven; human nature and form are both decreed by heaven. (*Preservation of Learning* 1, pp. 8b–9a)

Yan held that principle and *qi* cannot be separated:

> This *qi* is indeed the *qi* of principle; principle is the principle of *qi*. (*Preservation of Human Nature* 1, p. 1a)

Principle and *qi* are united to give the way of heaven.

Dai Zhen earned his living by teaching and took part in editing the astrology and geography books included in the Complete Library of the Four Repositories (*Siku Quanshu*).† He understood the Way as said of the path by which *qi* changes:

> In speaking of the Way one refers to the never ending transformation. (*Original Goodness* I, p. 1a)
> *Qi* transforms and flows, generates again and again unceasingly; therefore it is called the Way. (*An Evidential Study of the Meaning of Terms in the* Book of Mencius, p. 287)

---

* Yan Yuan (1635–1704). *Zi:* Yizhi; *Hao:* Xizhai. Of Boye in Hebei Province. He wrote *Preservation of Learning, of Human Nature, of Humankind, of Order* and *Questions on the Notes on a Commentary of the* Analects. A full translation of the *Preservation of Learning* is given by Mansfield Freeman, *Yan Yuan: Preservation of Learning*, Monumenta Serica Monograph 16 (Los Angeles: Monumenta Serica at the University of California, 1972). A partial translation of the *Preservation of Human Nature* is given in Chan, *Source Book*, pp. 704–706.

† Dai Zhen (1723[?]–77). *Zi:* Dong Yuan, of Xiuning, Anhui Province. He was from a merchant family. His philosophy was based on that of the *Mencius*. He was opposed to the idealism of both the Cheng-Zhu school and the Lu-Wang school. His study of the *Mencius* has been translated by Ann-ping Chin and M. Freeman as *Tai Chen on Mencius: Explorations in Words and Meaning* (New Haven: Yale University Press, 1990). His work also includes an essay on *Original Goodness* and letters.

The concrete content of this Way is *yin* and *yang* and the five agents:

> *Yin* and *yang* and the five agents are the real body of the Way.
> (Ibid., B#1, *Heavenly Way*, p. 21)

The Way is the process of change of the material world. In this respect Dai Zhen has clearly developed along the lines set out by Zhang Zai.

Conclusion

In ancient Chinese philosophy the concept of the Way is multifaceted and complex. It covers at least four levels of meaning:

1. The existence of all things is subject to a process of change;
2. Within this process of change there is a contrasting unchanging norm;
3. Each thing has its own particular norm and also a common norm, known as the Way. Some philosophers hold, however, that the entire process of change is itself the Way;
4. Some philosophers, such as Laozi, Zhuangzi, the two Chengs, and Zhu Xi, consider the Way to be above the material world as the highest entity, the origin of the universe and hence a metaphysical construct. *The Great Appendix* to the *Book of Changes* and *Guanzi*, as well as Zhang Zai, Wang Fuzhi, and others, challenge this view of the Way as a metaphysical construct.

At all these four levels the Way always has the sense of a path and of a norm. This is all a reflection of the objective world.

3. Principle
Li   Lí
理

The term "li" originally meant the lines running through a piece of jade. It came to prominence as a philosophical term during the Warring States period. It is then often translated as 'pattern.' By the Song dynasty it rose *to become the most important metaphysical concept and hence is generally translated as 'principle.' For some philosophers it is independent of the material world, whereas for others it is necessarily related to things. As principle it encompasses both the natural and moral orders, both 'is' and 'ought,' there being normally no sense of a clear distinction between the two.**

The Pre-Qin Era

As a philosophical term *li* is first encountered in mid–Warring States works. It is not found in the *Analects* or in the *Laozi*. The *Mencius* talks of principle and respect together:

> With respect to tastes mouths have the same likings; with respect to sounds ears have the same pleasures; with respect to beauty eyes have the same standards; as for minds, why do they alone not have something to agree on? Indeed, they do, namely principle and respect. (*Mencius* 6, *Gaozi A*, #7)

Mencius believes that principle and respect are what minds agree on. Here 'principle' is understood as the standard of moral conduct. The *Mencius* also introduces the term 'blending of principles' in the following comparison of Confucius with an orchestra:

> Confucius is what is meant by a full orchestra. In a full orchestra the bell announces the opening and the stone-chime the ending of the music. The bell indicates the start of the blending of principles; the chime brings the blending of principles to a close. Starting off the blending of principles is the business of wisdom; bringing the blending of principles to a close is the business of sageliness. (*Mencius* 5, *Wan Zhang B* #1)

In commenting on this text the Qing scholar Jiao Xun notes,

---

*For a good definition of the term see Kidder Smith Jr. et al., *Sung Dynasty Uses of the 'I Ching'* (Princeton: Princeton University Press, 1990), p. 257.

'Blending of principles' refers to rhythm and order. (*The Correct Meaning of Mencius* 5b, p. 397)

The bell and the chime stand for the whole course of the concert, in which the sounds of the various instruments are blended together. In modern parlance we might speak of the "system" rather than the "blending" of principles.

The *Great Appendix* to the *Book of Changes* moves the term 'principle' from the moral to the cosmological sphere:

Looking up to contemplate the patterns of heaven; bending down to inspect the principles of earth. (*Great Appendix* 1.4, p. 278)

As symbols are formed in heaven, so shapes are made on earth. (*Great Appendix* 1.1, p. 271)

The heavenly symbols are the patterns of heaven, and the earthly shapes are the principles of earth. Principle and form are related to each other.

Qian knows with ease; *Kun* is able to act with simplicity. . . . Knowing that change is easy and simple, one can obtain the principles of all under heaven.* (Ibid., p. 273)

Here principle is not confined to the earth but applies to heaven, earth, and all that is. Principle is the rule of simplicity underlying the complications of all things.

A story in the *Zhuangzi* has given rise to discussion of the nature of the principles of heaven. Cook Ding carves an ox with perfect skill such that his knife runs so smoothly through the meat that he never hits a bone or ligament and hence in nineteen years has never once needed to sharpen his blade. This is possible because he intuitively follows the patterns of tendons and bones, or 'principles,' that heaven has put in the beast. (*Zhuangzi* 3, *What Matters in the Nuture of Life*, lines 6 ff.). Cheng Xuanying comments,

---

* *Qian* is the first of the hexagrams of the *Book of Changes*. It is composed of six unbroken lines and represents pure *yang*. *Kun* is the second hexagram and is composed of six broken lines and represents pure *yin*. *Qian* is the hexagram of heaven; *Kun* the hexagram of earth.

> This is according to the natural lines (principles) of the meat. (*Zheng Tong Daoist Canon* 27, *Notes to the Southern Flowery True Scripture* 4, p. 21706)

This is not the common meaning of 'principle.' The term is much more frequently encountered in the later parts of the *Zhuangzi* corpus. From the school of *Zhuangzi* comes the following:

> Should we take what is right as our guide and do without what is wrong; should we take what is ordered as our guide and do without what is disordered? To do so would be to misunderstand the principle of heaven and earth and the nature of the myriad things. (*Zhuangzi* 17, *Autumn Floods*, line 38)

Here both right and wrong are parts of the whole; the two are needed to draw the picture.

> "Decreasing and increasing, filling and emptying, what ends then begins": this is said of the scope of the great pattern and refers to the principle of the myriad things. (Ibid., lines 45–46)
> One who knows the Way will surely penetrate principle. (Ibid., line 48)

From the context it is clear that the principle referred to in these quotations is the norm governing heaven, earth, and all that is. From the same school of texts we find the following:

> The myriad things each have their proper principle; the Way does not incline to any one of them. (*Zhuangzi* 25, *Ze Yang*, line 63)

The myriad things have their own principle, whereas the Way is universal in nature.

The *Xunzi* also talks about the principles of things:

> Whatever is able to know is human nature; whatever is able to be known are the principles of things. (*Xunzi* 21, *Removal of Prejudices*, lines 78–79)

This passage affirms that the principles of things are knowable. The *Xunzi* and the *Zhuangzi* both use the expression 'great principle':

> You will be able to speak of the great principle. (*Zhuangzi* 17, *Autumn Floods*, line 7)
>
> All the harms infecting human beings come from being blinkered by one twisted thing and so hidden from the great principle. (*Xunzi* 21, *Removal of Prejudice*, line 1)

The great principle is the fundamental principle.

The *Zhuangzi* and the *Xunzi* claim that heaven and earth and all things have principles but do not explain what principle is. In an explanation of the *Laozi*, the *Hanfeizi* gives a reasonably clear account of principle:

> Principles are the patterns that make things wholly what they are. (*Hanfeizi* 20, *Explanations of Laozi* #27)
>
> Overall, principles are what differentiate square from circular, short from long, coarse from fine, hard from brittle. (Ibid., #29)

Principles are the things that determine the external appearance of a thing. Han Fei's teacher, Xunzi, says,

> The principles of form, shape, and color are distinguished by the eye. (*Xunzi* 22, *Rectification of Names*, line 17)

Han Fei's use of 'principle' is precisely this. In this usage he retains the original meaning of 'principle,' in contrast with the *Zhuangzi*, which makes principle into a cosmic issue.

Six Dynasties, A.D. 222–589

At the time of the Three Kingdoms (A.D. 220–265), Liu Shao wrote about the different qualities of persons in a book titled *Gazette of Human Nature*. In this work he distinguished four kinds of principle:

> The principle of the Way is the changes of the *qi* of heaven and earth, filling and emptying, decreasing and increasing. The principle of affairs is that of the rectification of affairs in the legal system. The principle of justice is what is appropriate to rites and education. The principle of nature is the pivot and

hinge of human feelings. These four principles are not the same. (*SKQS* 848, *Gazette of Human Nature* 4, *Material and Principle*, p. 767b)

The principle of the Way deals with changes in the natural world. The second principle is in the sphere of politics; the third is that of moral conduct and the fourth that of human relations.

Metaphysical explanations of principle were expounded by Wang Bi and Guo Xiang. Wang Bi took 'beinglessness' as the root but affirms that things do have principles:

Things are not disordered; this state must come from their principle. (*Simple Exemplifications of the Principles of the* Book of Changes 1, *Ming Yu*, p. 591)

'Principle' is the principle of a thing. In his commentary on the *Book of Changes*, Wang Bi notes,

Just as one recognizes the movement of things so too the principle by which x is x can also be known. (*Commentary on the* Book of Changes: *Qian: Literary Commentary*, p. 216)

Principle is that by which things move. Wang Bi's interpretation of principle as 'that by which' had a great influence on the Song philosophers.

Guo Xiang denied that being is generated from beingless. Instead he held that

Things each generate themselves and do not come out of anything. (*SKQS* 1056, *Notes on Zhuangzi* 2, *The Sorting Which Evens Things Out*, p. 10b)

Things each create themselves and there is no dependence on another. (Ibid., p. 19a)

He recognized, however, that things do have principles and that the relation between things is governed by principle:

Everything has its principle, every affair has what is appropriate to it. (Ibid., p. 15b)

Ruler and minister, above and below, hand and foot, without and within, these are the natural principles of heaven. Do they not guide the perfect person's conduct? (Ibid., p. 11a)

Things do not have inconstancy. All are combined in heaven and earth, and attain to principle. (*SKQS* 1056, *Notes on Zhuangzi* 5, *The Signs of Fullness of Power*, p. 34a)

According to the principle of nature, a walker is followed by a shadow, a word succeeded by an echo. (Ibid., p. 32a)

According to Guo Xiang, each thing is independent of all others. It is necessarily the case that *x* is *x* and *y* is *y*. It is also necessarily so that there be both *x* and *y*. This type of necessity is what is called principle:

That which cannot be otherwise is the necessity of principle. (*SKQS* 1056, *Notes on Zhuangzi* 4, *Worldly Business Among Human Beings*, p. 24a)

The one who clings to the necessity of principle is wholly in accordance with the 'mean and harmony' and this is to come as close as possible to things. (Ibid., p. 26a)

Guo Xiang's interpretation of 'principle' in terms of necessity had a great influence on the development of thought. It is hard to escape the conclusion, however, that there is a contradiction in his thought between the necessity of each thing creating itself and that existing between form and shadow, between sound and voice.

The Song Dynasty

'Principle' became a key concept in Song-dynasty philosophy. Before the philosophers had discussed the term 'principle,' it was already in use among politicians. As the *Xu Bi Tan* of the *Meng Xi Bi Tan* of Shen Kuo records,

Emperor Tai Zu once asked Zhao Pu, saying, "What thing is the greatest under heaven?" Pu reflected long but before he had yet replied the emperor asked the same question again. Pu replied, "The Way's Principle is the greatest. It rises to the heights and is called the good." (Shen Kuo, *Mengxi Bitan: Xu pian* 2, *Mengxi Bitan Jiaozheng*, p. 1062)

The 'Way's Principle' is simply another way of saying 'principle.' Zhao Pu's use of principle can be said to make him a forerunner of the Chengs and of Zhu Xi.

Zhou Dunyi's *Book of Comprehending* has a line referring to the patterns of *yin* and *yang* that says,

> Now evident, now hidden, if not spiritual one cannot grasp it. (*SKQS* 1101 *Collected Works of Zhou Wengong 2, Book of Comprehending 22, Principle, Human Nature, and Destiny*, p. 430a)

Zhu Xi notes, "this is said of principle" (ibid.). Zhou's meaning is that only the one who has an intelligent mind and the necessary talent can understand. It is Zhou's comment on a line from the *Treatise of Remarks on the Trigrams* of the *Book of Changes*, which reads,

> Exhausting principle, going to the utmost of human nature and stopping at destiny. (*Treatise of Remarks on the Trigrams* 1, p. 338)

Although Zhou mentions principle he does not discuss it in detail.

Zhang Zai interpreted the Way as transformations of *qi* but affirmed that the appearance of these changes is principle:

> Though the *qi* of heaven and earth gathers and scatters, attracts and repels in a hundred ways, yet the principle according to which it acts is ordered and not chaotic. (*SKQS* 697, *Correcting the Unenlightened* 1, *Ultimate Harmony*, p. 97b)

Principle is the underlying order in the transformations of *qi*. Again, Zhang Zai writes,

> Take the *qi* of *yin* and *yang*; they circle round and arrive at their peak, gather and scatter and mutually mingle, ascend and descend mutually demanding each other, entwining and swirling, mutually mingling, now together, now dominating each other. If you want to unite them you will find you cannot do so. This is because their contracting and expanding is endless, their movement without rest; if we do not call this state the principle of human nature and destiny what else can we call it? (*SKQS* 697, *Correcting the Unenlightened* 2, *Trinity and Duality*, p. 105a)

Yin and *yang* are understood on the basis of a circle: ☯. As one increases so the other decreases, and their motion is such that one can never leave the circle or condense it to one. It is this relation between *yin* and *yang* that is called 'principle.' Zhang Zai believed that all things have principles and that principle is the principle of things:

> If principles are not in human beings then they are all in things, the human being is but one thing among others. (*Recorded Sayings* I, p. 313)
>
> The myriad things all have principles. If one does not know how to penetrate to principle it is like living in a dream. (*Recorded Sayings* II, p. 321)

Zhang Zai did not entirely explain how principle and *qi* are related, but he clearly understood *qi* as what is most fundamental, and hence principle is principle in the midst of the transformations of *qi*.

The Cheng brothers made principle the supreme origin of the world. Cheng Hao says,

> Heaven is principle. (*SKQS* 698, *Surviving Works of the Two Chengs* 11, p. 105b)

By saying that heaven is principle, he is saying that principle is what is highest and that on which all things depend. Cheng Yi interpreted principle as 'that by which *x* is *x*':

> It is indeed necessary to penetrate the principles of things, as when one says that by which heaven is high and earth deep, ghosts and spirits are hidden or manifest. (Ibid., 15, p. 125a)

He does not explain any further what this 'that by which' is. He does, however, say that all things have their principle:

> Things under heaven may all be enlightened by principle. For a given thing there is a given standard; each thing has its own principle. (Ibid., 18, p. 155a)
>
> When speaking of the greatness of something one will mention the height of heaven and the thickness of earth; when speaking of the smallness of anything you will mention why it is that a thing is as it is. Scholars all consider matters according

to principle.... When seeking human nature and feeling one will certainly encounter the body; so too each plant and tree has its principle and this is to be examined. (Ibid., 18, pp. 154b–155a)

Whether large like heaven and earth or small like plants and trees, everything has its principle. Cheng Yi also emphasizes the unity of the principles of all things. All things have only one common principle:

There is but one principle in the myriad things, no matter how small a thing or affair all have this one principle. (Ibid., 15, p. 124b)

Things and I have one principle; once *x* is understood then *y* is clear. This is the way to unite without and within. (Ibid., 18, p. 154b)

In saying that things and the self have one principle, Cheng Yi combined the natural and moral orders into one.

Like Cheng Yi, Zhu Xi also interpreted principle as 'that by which *x* is *x*' and also as what *x* ought to be:

Whatever has sound, color, appearance, and shape and flourishes within heaven and earth is a thing. What makes *x* '*x*' is never not the standard by which *x* is necessarily *x* and not self-contained. It is given by heaven and is beyond the capacity of human beings to do. Moreover, if we now speak more precisely, then the mind, for example, is the real master of the body ... next in coming to what the body has, then there is the use of mouth, nose, ears, eyes, and the four limbs; next we come to what the body is related to, that is, the five relationships of ruler-subject, parent-child, husband and wife, older and younger, siblings and friends. These all must have that by which they are necessarily so and this is not self-contained; this is called principle. (*SKQS* 197, *Some Questions of the Great Learning* 2, *Commentary* 10, pp. 232b–233a)

According to this passage, all things have that which makes them what they are. Moreover, all things have the standard that makes them necessarily what they are. Both of these are 'principle.' Zhu Xi explained the method of penetrating to principles as follows:

> Applicable to the virtue of body and mind, human nature and feeling, to the daily constancy of human relations, even to the changes of heaven and earth, ghosts and spirits, to the special characteristics of birds, beasts, plants and trees, indeed to any given thing, none do not have that by which they ought to be and are not self-determined, nor that by which they are and are not able to change. (Ibid., p. 233b)

Principle comprises both that by which x is x and is not able to change into something else and that by which x ought to be x and is not self-determining. The former is the norm of the natural order, the latter the norm of the moral order.

> He was asked, "*Some Questions* said that things have the standard by which they ought to be and also the reason for which they are what they are. What does this mean?" He replied, "In serving one's parents one ought to have filial piety, in serving one's older siblings one ought to have the respect of the younger siblings; this is the standard of what ought to be. Now how does one know that one ought to show filial piety in serving one's parents? How does one know that one ought to show the respect of a younger sibling when dealing with an older sibling? This is the reason for which things are so. As Master Cheng said, "That by which Heaven is high and that by which earth is thick." (*Conversations of Master Zhu Arranged Topically* 18, p. 414)

Although "why things are so" and "that things ought to be so" are different, the two are combined. Zhu's principle includes both the natural and moral norms.

'Principle' is accorded the status of being the origin of the world. Using a term derived from the *Book of Changes*, 'supreme ultimate,' Zhu Xi says,

> The supreme ultimate is but the principle of heaven, earth and the myriad things. . . .
>
> Before there was yet heaven and earth there must have been this principle. Only once there was this principle was

there heaven and earth. If there was not this principle there would be no heaven and earth, no human beings, no things; nothing would be. (Ibid., 1, p. 1)

This means that principle is the supreme origin of heaven, earth, and all that is. Principle is the guiding line of the natural order:

What ensures that *yin*, *yang*, and the five agents, however intricate, do not lose their order is also principle. (Ibid., 1, p. 3)

It is also the norm of moral behavior:

Principle then becomes benevolence, justice, rites, and wisdom. (Ibid.)

Principle is both the origin and universally present:

Above and without limit is the supreme ultimate; below and attaining to the minuteness of each plant, each tree, and each insect is also named principle. One book not read means the loss of one book's principle; one affair not pursued means the loss of one affair's principle; one thing not investigated means the loss of one thing's principle. (Ibid., 15, p. 295)

The principle of the moral order comprises the four Confucian virtues of benevolence, justice, rites, and wisdom. The principle of the natural order comprises four terms from the *Book of Changes*: 'origin,' 'success,' 'advantage,' and 'correct,' or in simpler language, sprouting, growing up, and then coming to completion. The combination of the growth patterns of plants and animals with the four moral virtues is a feature of Zhu Xi's thought.

The Ming-Qing Period

Luo Qinshun was a government official in Nanjing.* Initially interested in Buddhism, he adopted Chang Hao's idea that principle and *qi* were

---

* Luo Qinshun (1465–1547). *Zi:* Yun sheng, *Hao:* Zheng yan, of Taihe, Jiangxi Province.

equivalent. His chief philosophical work, compiled over a period of twenty years toward the close of his life, is titled *Notes on Knowledge Painfully Acquired*. It is composed of 81 short paragraphs of commentary on various works. In discussing the *Book of Changes*, he has this to say about principle:

> What sort of thing is principle? That which penetrates heaven and earth, links past and present is not anything other than *qi* alone. *Qi* is originally one. It circles round without ceasing, now moving, now still, now going, now coming, now opening, now closing, now rising, now falling. Once it has become hidden it then becomes apparent; having become apparent it again becomes hidden. It engenders the warmth and coolness, the cold and heat of the four seasons, the sprouting, growing, harvesting, and storing of the myriad things, the daily social relationships of this people, the success and failure, the gaining and losing of human affairs. Among all these thousand strands and ten thousand threads, there is a complex order and elaborate coherence which cannot ever be undone and which none know why it is that it is so. This is what is called principle. (*Notes on Knowledge Painfully Acquired* 1, #11, pp. 4–5)

Thus principle is the movement of *qi*. It is the strand of stability running through the changes of the world. It does not exist independently: this is a materialist point of view.

> It is not a separate thing, which depends on *qi* to stand up or which "relies on *qi* to operate." (Ibid.)

Although asserting that principle does not exist separately from *qi*, he does not give a more detailed analysis of the relation of principle to the multifarious events and things in the world.

Wang Tingxiang was highly critical of the Chengs' and Zhu Xi's theory that principle precedes heaven and earth. He associated principle and *qi*:

> Principle depends on *qi*; it cannot initiate *qi*. The worldly Confucians say that 'principle can generate *qi*' just as Laozi says that the Way generates heaven and earth. (*Collected Works*

of Wang Tingxiang 3, *Prudent Words* 1, *The Substance of the Way*, p. 753)

Wang held that principle is something *qi* always has:

> *Qi* is the origin of things; principle is what *qi* has; a given object is the fruition of *qi*. (Ibid., p. 751)

Qi is the origin of all things; a given object is what *qi* produces; principle is what *qi* has. Whereas the Chengs and Zhu Xi spoke of one principle in all things, Wang Tingxiang held that each thing has its own principle:

> Within heaven and earth there is one *qi* generating and regenerating. There is what is constant and what varies. The myriad things are not alike; thus if *qi* is one then principle is one, if *qi* is manifold then principle is manifold. The worldly Confucians only talk about principle as one and discard the manifold. This is one-sided. Heaven has the principle of heaven; earth has the principle of earth; human beings have the principle of human beings; things have the principle of things; obscurity has the principle of obscurity; brightness the principle of brightness; each one is different from the other. (*Collected Works of Wang Tingxiang* 3, *Excellent Reviews A*, p. 848)

Different things have different principles.

Wang Tingxiang also discussed the question of the eternity of principle:

> The Confucians say, "In heaven and earth the myriad forms all decline, principle alone does not rot." This is a foolish and stupid statement. Principle has no material form; how then does it rot? Things should be spoken of as they really are. If one is first over generous then, next, one relaxes punishments then, later, one gives license to theft. When the field system went bad then criss-cross paths grew up. When the feudal system failed then the system of commanderies and counties was installed. One who is used to the former cannot act according to the latter. One accustomed to the ancient cannot become accustomed to the modern. Principle suits the time and adapts.

> The past is all straw dogs. Does it not also rot and decline?*
> (Ibid. *B*, p. 887)

Wang's point is that different times have different situations, each expressive of its own principle. Principles are historically bound.

When discussing the *Mencius*, Wang Fuzhi pointed out that principle is within *qi*:

> Principle and *qi* form one body together and outside of *qi* there is no principle, just as outside of principle there can be no *qi* formed. One who talks correctly of principle and *qi* cannot separate one from the other. (*Great and Full Explanation on Reading the Four Books* 10.1, *Mencius: Gaozi A* #2, p. 660)

He explains 'principle' in detail:

> Principle is the order shown up by heaven. Wind, rain, dew, and thunder are not produced at the same time, yet the rise and fall of winter and summer are always reliable. The ruler's conduct keeps both punishments and rewards in store and he employs them according to the changes of the time yet he keeps to the golden mean. Whether to left or right, all things have principle. (*Notes on Master Zhang's* Correcting the Unenlightened 3, p. 136)

The natural world keeps to what is reliable; in the moral world human beings keep to the golden mean between punishments and rewards. Both are principle, but there is a difference between them. Falling short of the golden mean may be said to be lacking the Way but not lacking principle:

> It is evident that what lacks the Way under heaven is not without principle. The Way is a certain principle. Describing

---

*This passage requires some explanation. The field system was an ancient ideal whereby all land was divided into nine squares. The central square was worked in common for the lord. This was then superseded by a system of private ownership, which required paths along the fields. The feudal system was practiced in the Zhou dynasty. Princes were given territory by the king. In time these princes became more powerful than the king, so the Qin-Han emperors introduced greater central control, moving officials from one commandery to another to prevent them from gaining too much local power. A "straw dog" is the *Laozi*'s term for something of no value.

principle as a "certain" principle is the Way. Now if we must say "a certain principle" then it means there is that which makes principle certain and hence that principle itself does not reach certainty. (*Great and Full Explanation on Reading the Four Books* 9.3, *Mencius: Jinxin A* #8, p. 601)

Having the Way is the *qi* which is accomplished by a principle of order; lacking the Way is the *qi* which is accomplished by a principle of disorder. (Ibid. 9, *Mencius 4A*, p. 1127)

Here the Way is the principle of what ought to be, whereas 'principle' includes both the principle of what ought to be and the principle of what actually is.*

Dai Zhen discussed principle and emphasized differences. 'Principle' is the differences between things. His study of the *Mencius* opens with the following:

The term 'principle' is a name given to the distinctive arrangement of a thing that may be observed and analyzed to the smallest detail. Therefore we call it the principle of differentiation. With respect to the stuff of things one talks of principles of the fibers, of principles of skin and flesh, of principles of patterns. When one obtains the differentiation then there is arrangement without a muddle. This is called 'arranged principle.' (*An Evidential Study of the Meaning of Terms in the Book of Mencius* I.1, p. 265)

The principles of things must be obtained by analysis of the thing to its smallest detail.

He insisted on the need for analysis as a necessary prelude to determining the principle of anything. Dai also wrote about principle in terms of what is necessarily so. By 'necessity' he meant 'ideal standard':

As for heaven, earth, human beings, things, and affairs, I have not heard of any principle which cannot be talked about. The *Songs* says, "For any thing there is a rule."† The term 'thing'

---

*Wang Fuzhi also discusses the question of principle and circumstances, for which see concept 29.

† *Book of Odes* 260, *Zheng Min* #1, p. 71.

refers to real objects and real affairs. The term 'rule' refers to their purity and correctness. Real objects and real affairs are nothing if not natural, but by reverting to what is necessary the principles of heaven, earth, human beings, and things are obtained. Despite the greatness of heaven and earth, the proliferation of human beings and things, the complexity and complications of affairs, each has its specific character. Only when in agreement with their principle as straightness matches a plumb-line, levelness matches water, circularity a compass, squareness a square do they become a model for the whole world for ten thousand generations. (Ibid. I. 13, p. 278)

Necessity is the norm of things and affairs. By 'necessity' Dai means what we today call moral obligation.

Conclusion

The term 'principle' emerged in the Warring States period with the original sense of model or form. It was extended to mean the norm of human conduct and of the natural world. By the early centuries of our era it was a fully philosophical concept. Wang Bi spoke of it as 'that by which x is x'; Guo Xiang spoke of it as 'that by which x ought to be x.' In both these ways of speaking there is an implied element of necessity. By the tenth century Cheng Yi understood principle as 'what causes x to be x.' Zhu Xi held principle to be both 'that by which x is x' and 'that which x ought to be.' Both Cheng and Zhu gave principle priority over things. Cheng Yi says, 'there is the principle and then the shape'; Zhu Xi writes, 'before there was any given thing, there was its principle.' Hence principle is not subordinated to things. On this basis both authors constructed an abstract system. Zhang Zai, Luo Qinshun, Wang Tingxiang, Wang Fuzhi, and Dai Zhen, however, criticized the Cheng brothers and Zhu Xi and took 'principle' as the principle of things. It should be noted that there is no attempt to distinguish clearly between that by which x is x and that which x ought to be, that is, between natural and moral norms.

4. Rule
Ze
則

In certain contexts the term ze *has been read as 'law of nature.' In a chapter on military matters in the* Guanzi, *Rickett translates the term thus.* Yet, as noted above, Chinese thinkers do not distinguish the moral and natural spheres very rigidly; hence we should never imagine this 'law of nature' in the sense of the abstract science of eighteenth-century Europe. For this reason it is good to keep to the less specific 'rule.'†*

Closely related to 'principle' is the term 'rule.'‡ As we saw in Dai Zhen's work, this term appears in the *Book of Odes*:

Heaven engenders the mass of peoples;
For any given thing there is a rule;
The people have this normal nature;
They tend to this admirable virtue. (*Odes* 260 #1, *Zheng Min*,
  p. 71)

The standard commentary by Mao glosses the title, *Zheng Min*, as 'the mass of peoples.' 'Thing' is glossed as 'affair' and 'rule' as 'law.' 'Thing' refers in general to all things and affairs. 'Rule' is placed in parallel with 'normal nature' and 'admirable virtue' and hence understood as the standard.

In the *Guanzi* the term 'rule' is mentioned along with what is constant. Among the sayings we find the following:

---

*W. A. Rickett, *Guanzi: Political, Economic, and Philosophical Essays from Early China* (Princeton: Princeton University Press, 1985), 1:126.

†When first published this appeared as a separate section. Zhang later joined it to 'principle' so as to make the total number of concepts discussed add up to sixty. He did not alter the content at all.

‡As John Knoblock notes, *ze* is "law codified by inscription on ritual vessels." *Xunzi: A Translation and Study* (Stanford: Stanford University Press, 1988, 1990).

> Heaven does not change its constancy; earth does not alter its
> rule; sping, summer, autumn, and winter do not vary in their
> succession; from of old until now it has been the same. (*Guanzi*
> 2, *Conditions and Circumstances*, 1:12)

It is in the context of a chapter on military matters that the *Guanzi*
gives its most detailed exposition of 'rule.'

> Taking root in the *qi* of heaven and earth, in the harmony of
> cold and heat, in the nature of water and soil, in the life of
> humankind, birds, beasts, plants and trees, no matter how many
> they be, present in all of them and never changing, this is what
> is called 'rules.' (*Guanzi* 6, *Seven Laws*, 1:71)

This is to say that 'rule' is what people, birds, beasts, plants, and trees all
have in common. This common feature is distinguished by immutability.
This rule is also that in which *qi* and the cosmic world are rooted. The
term *fa*, commonly translated 'law,' is used by the *Guanzi* to apply to
standards of measurement:

> A foot-long ruler, a plumb-line, compass and square, beam and
> weight, decaliter and centiliter and grain-leveler are called
> 'laws.' (Ibid.)

'Law' applies to the standards erected by human beings, 'rule' to what is
naturally so.

The *Zhuangzi* and the *Xunzi* both combine the terms 'law' and
'rule' to form one binome. The following passage comes from a story
about Zhuangzi:

> Now up, now down, taking harmony as the measure, floating
> and roaming over the ancestor of the myriad things, one treats
> things as things and does not let things make one into a thing;
> thus how can you end up being constrained? This was the law-
> rule of the Divine Farmer and the Yellow Emperor. (*Zhuangzi*
> 20, *The Mountain Tree*, lines 6–8)

In the *Xunzi* 'law-rule' is even more clearly the standard to be used in
social life. In talking of the duties of the prime minister, the *Xunzi* notes,

> Establishing the basis of administration and education; correcting the law-codes; gathering reports and reviewing them at fixed times … these are the duties of the high intendent. (*Xunzi* 9, *On the Regulations of a King*, lines 92–93)

Of the feudal lords it is said that they should aim at being

> Sincere about justice in their intentions, encapsulating justice in their laws, rules, standards and measures, and practicing it in their administration of affairs. (*Xunzi* 11, *Of Kings and Lords Protector*, lines 9–10)

The 'laws and rules' show that the *Xunzi* understands the terms as standards.

Thus in ancient Chinese philosophy the term *ze*, 'rule,' applies both to the moral and the natural spheres.

5. Qi
Qi 氣

Perhaps the best translation of the Chinese word qi *is provided by Einstein's equation,* $e = mc^2$. *According to this equation matter and energy are convertible. In places the material element may be to the fore, in others, what we term energy.* Qi *embraces both. The philosophical use of the term derives from its popular use but is nonetheless distinct. In popular parlance* qi *is applied to the air we breathe, steam, smoke, and all gaseous substances. The philosophical use of the term underlines the movement of* qi. Qi *is both what really exists and what has the ability to become. To stress one at the expense of the other would be to misunderstand* qi. Qi *is the life principle but is also the stuff of inanimate objects. As a philosophical category* qi *originally referred to the existence of whatever is of a nature to change. This meaning is then expanded to encompass all phenomena, both physical and spiritual. It is energy that has the capacity to become material objects while remaining what it is. It thus combines 'potentiality' with 'matter.' To understand it solely as 'potentiality' would be wrong, just as it cannot be translated simply as 'matter.'*

In the editing of the quotations that follow the translator has been obliged to fill in details of critical scholarship concerning the dating of certain texts.

Since the air we breathe is essential to life, *qi* was viewed as the principle of life. But the term was applied to all that existed outside of man and woman. In early philosophy it is thus used for "matter," although later philosophy developed another term for this.*

From the Pre-Qin to the Han

Qi is understood as intimately associated with *yin* and *yang*:

> This *qi* of heaven and earth does not lose its order. If it goes beyond the order, the people are in confusion. *Yang* bends over and cannot go out; *yin* rushes and cannot distill away, so there is an earthquake. (*Sayings of the States* 1, *Sayings of Zhou* I, pp. 26–27)

This extract comes from a speech by the Grand Historiographer of Zhou, Boyangfu. *Yin* and *yang* are the two aspects of *qi*. Boyangfu held that the *qi* of heaven and earth has a given order and sequence with a balance between *yin* and *yang*. Although purported to be the earliest exposition of *qi*, the text is dated by Wei Quxian (1898–) to 431 B.C.†

In the Spring and Autumn era there was discussion of six *qi*. The doctor named He advised the marquis of Jin on the need to regulate his passion for women:

---

* For further discussion of this point see concepts 6 and 7, Stuff and Thing.

† M. Loewe, ed., *Early Chinese Texts* (Berkeley: Society for the Study of Early China, 1993), p. 264.

Heaven has six *qi*, which go down and produce the five flavors, develop into the five colors, are verified in the five notes but when overflowing produce the six diseases. The six *qi* are *yin*, *yang*, wind, rain, darkness and brightness. They separate into the four seasons and fall into sequence as the five nodes. If overstepped then they cause disasters. (*Zuo's Commentary* 10, *Zhao* 1 add. #8, p. 573)

The five flavors, five colors, and five notes are the basic or primary flavors, colors, and notes. These are all said to come from the six *qi*. These are all called *qi*, and from this comes the modern Chinese word for the weather: the appearances of *qi*.

The *Mencius* discusses the relation between *qi* and the human will:

The will is the general of the *qi* and the *qi* is the fullness of the body. . . .

When the will is concentrated then it moves the *qi*; when the *qi* is concentrated then it moves the will. Now if some one should fall or run this is due to *qi* and it will come back and affect his mind. (*Mencius* 2, *Gongsun Chou A* #2)

Qi is what fills up the body and what is directed by the will, but the movements of *qi* can have an effect on the will. The *Mencius* claims that *qi* belongs to the body whereas the will belongs to the mind. The body and mind are related just as the will and *qi* are.

The same passage of the *Mencius* contains a famous text on the mysterious "surging *qi*":

I carefully tend my surging *qi*. . . . Like all *qi* it is the greatest and the firmest. It is tended by rectitude and experiences no harm yet it fills up all within heaven and earth. Like all *qi* it accompanies justice and the Way; without it one starves. It is engendered by accumulating justice; it is not acquired by the odd act of justice. If in acting one is not at ease in one's mind then you will starve. (Ibid.)

It is difficult to put into words what the *Mencius* means by this surging *qi*. It is a sort of mystical experience in which the *qi* of heaven and earth invades the self, directing the person in moral conduct. It requires time to accumulate the relevant force to act morally. In the *Mencius*, however, the term *qi* never loses its physical connotation as the fundamental stuff of which the body is composed.

The physical implications of *qi* are found also in the *Guanzi*. In a chapter that Rickett dates to the early Han we find an association of *qi* and what gives life:

> Where there is *qi* there is coming to life; where there is no *qi* there is dying away. [What lives does so by its *qi*].* (*Guanzi* 12, *Cardinal Sayings* 1:160)

The Mencian *qi* filling the body is encountered in *Technique of the Heart*:

> *Qi* is what fills up the body. (*Guanzi* 37, *Technique of the Heart A*, 2:15)

In a description of "fasting of the mind" the *Zhuangzi* distinguishes *qi* from the mind:

> Do not listen with your ears but listen with your heart; do not listen with your heart but listen with *qi*. Listening stops with the ears, the mind stops with the tally [of thought]. As for *qi*, it is space and waits for things [to move it]. Only the Way accumulates space. Space is fasting of the heart. (*Zhuangzi* 4, *Worldly Business Among Human Beings*, lines 26–28)

This *qi* is also a *qi* contained within the body. *Qi* outside the body is mentioned in the following phrase:

> Roaming in the one *qi* of heaven and earth. (*Zhuangzi* 6, *The Teacher Who Is the Ultimate Ancestor*, line 68)

There is no clarification of the relation between heaven and earth and *qi*.

The term *qi* is encountered more frequently in the later corpus of the *Zhuangzi*. A story in which Zhuangzi talks about the death of his wife runs as follows:

---

* Rickett, *Guanzi* (1:216) suggests that the sentence I have bracketed here may be a later marginal note.

I inspected her beginnings and found once there was a time when she was not yet alive. Not only was there a time when she was not yet alive, there was a time before there was any form. Not only was there a time when there was no form, there was a time when there was no *qi*. Muddled up in the midst of chaos, there was a change and so there was *qi*. *Qi* changed and there was a form. The form changed and there was life. Now there is again a change and there is death. It is like the sequence of the four seasons: spring, summer, autumn and winter. (*Zhuangzi* 18, *Perfect Happiness*, lines 17–18)

Here *qi* and form are distinguished. *Qi* is the presence of the formless, and form comes from it. *Qi* is also distinguished from life, in contrast to the quotation from the *Guanzi* above.

In a text ascribed to the Yellow Emperor, the *Zhuangzi* says,

Life is the follower of death; death is the beginning of life; who knows their course [from end to end]? The coming to life of human beings is but the gathering of *qi*. It gathers and so they come to life; it scatters and so they die. Since life and death succeed each other what disaster could I fear? Thus the myriad things are the One.... Thus it is said, "There is but one *qi* running through heaven and earth." (*Zhuangzi* 22, *Knowledge Roams North*, lines 10–12, 13)

Here human life is described as the gathering of *qi*. The myriad things are produced by the changes of *qi*. This is the earliest expression of *qi* as the sole metaphysical origin.

The *Xunzi* shows quite a different approach, distinguishing four levels of being:

Water and fire have *qi* but not life; plants and trees have life but not knowledge; birds and beasts have knowledge but not a sense of justice; human beings have *qi*, life, knowledge and also a sense of justice; thus they are the most valuable thing under heaven. (*Xunzi* 9, *On the Regulations of a King*, lines 69–70)

Human beings possess the distinguishing features of all four levels of being. *Qi* is proper to the lowest level of being, though possessed by all other levels. It is the basis for life, knowledge, and a sense of justice. It refers then to inert matter in a very general sense.

The *Huainanzi* is an early Han compendium of early learning on many topics. Chapter 3 describes the origin of the cosmos and has this to say about *qi*:*

> The Way began in empty space. Empty space produced dimension and duration. Dimension and duration produced *qi*. *Qi* has a shoreline. The light and expanding spread and became heaven; the heavy and stagnant congealed and became earth. The convergence of the pure and mysterious is easy; the congealing of the heavy and stagnant is difficult; thus heaven was formed first and earth established later. (*Huainanzi* 3, *The Pattern of Heaven*, pp. 79–80)

Empty space is the existence of the formless and shapeless. 'Dimension' and 'duration' refer to space and time. By saying "*qi* has a shoreline" the text means that *qi* is a physical entity. It occupies a given space. The text distinguishes two kinds of *qi* with respect to weight, light as opposed to heavy, and with respect to movement, expanding as opposed to stagnant. From this text we may retain three points:

1. *Qi* comes from empty space; empty space is not *qi*;
2. *Qi* occupies physical space and is of two kinds: heavy and light;
3. Heaven and earth are formed from changes of *qi*.

This is the most comprehensive account of *qi* from the Qin-Han period (221 B.C.–220 A.D.).

Original *Qi*

The *Imperial Reader from the Taiping* [A.D. 983] *Period* is a late tenth-century compendium of quotations on selected topics. In its first article, under the rubric of "heaven," it quotes the *Huainanzi*'s "Dimension and duration produced *qi*. *Qi* has a shoreline" but adds the adjective "original" to the noun *qi*:

---

*For a full translation of this chapter, see J. Major, *Heaven and Earth in Early Han Thought* (New York: State University of New York, 1993).

Dimension and duration produced original *qi*, which has a shoreline. (*Imperial Reader from the Taiping Period* 1, *Original Qi*, p. 1a)

The phrase "original *qi*" is frequent in Han-dynasty works, but it is hard to say with any degree of precision in which text it first appeared. It is not found in the *Zhuangzi* or the *Xunzi*. *Mr. Lu's Spring and Autumn Annals* has a phrase that comes close to it but is not yet it:

With the origin the same *qi*. (*Mr. Lu's Spring and Autumn Annals* 13.2, *Responding to the Same*, p. 678)

The phrase does appear in the *Pheasant Cap Master*, a work that may come from the late Warring States era or the early Han:*

Thus heaven and earth were formed from the original *qi*; the myriad things derive from heaven and earth. (*Pheasant Cap Master* 11, *Tailu*, p. 2, p. 27b)

Also controversial in its dating is the work of Dong Zhongshu titled *Luxuriant Gems of the Spring and Autumn Annals*. In a discussion of its authenticity, Loewe notes that it is in the main authentic but that there are grounds for questioning the authenticity of the whole.† The chapter titled *Kingly Way* has the following:

In the *Spring and Autumn Annals* what is more valuable than the origin and than in speaking of it? The origin is the beginning; speaking of the root is correct. The Way is the kingly Way. The king is the beginning of human beings. When the king is correct then the original *qi* is harmonious. (*Luxuriant Gems of the Spring and Autumn Annals* 6, *Kingly Way*, p. 100)

---

*The authenticity of the *Pheasant Cap Master* (*Heguanzi*) was questioned by the Tang scholar Liu Zongyuan. Professor Zhang says that the received text is probably not a Warring States work. Knechtges provides a brief discussion of the problem in M. Loewe, *Early Chinese Texts*, pp. 137–140. This account does not mention the study of Dr. Carine Defoort, *Ho-Kuan-Tzu: a Focal Point of Sinological and Philosophical Unity*, Ph.D. thesis, University of Leuven, 1993. On p. 139 Knechtges refers to an unpublished Dunhuang manuscript of the text. This is known to be a twentieth-century forgery. Knechtges further fails to mention Wu Shigong's edition of the text, which has the best commentary to date.

†Loewe, *Early Chinese Texts*, pp. 77–87.

Here the use of the term "original *qi*" clearly proves that it existed in the early Han. Dong often spoke about the origin as the root of the myriad things and the beginning of heaven and earth:

> Only the sage can bring the myriad things back to one and tie them to the origin.... The origin is like the source and its *raison d'être* is to follow the ending and beginning of heaven and earth.... Therefore the origin is the root of the myriad things and the origin of human beings lies within it. Whence did it come? It came from before heaven and earth. (Ibid. 13, *Emphasising Administration*, p. 147)

Dong also spoke of *qi*:

> Within heaven and earth there is the *qi* of *yin* and *yang*, which constantly bathes human beings just as water constantly bathes fish. Its difference with water is that between the visible and invisible. Its soaking is a soaking.... Within this heaven and earth, it is as if empty and full, human beings are constantly bathed in its soaking. (Ibid. 81, *Heaven, Earth,* Yin *and* Yang, p. 467)

The *qi* referred to here is air. Although Dong Zhongshu talks about *qi* here, it should be borne in mind that he held heaven to be the highest of spirits.

There are a number of Han texts that are modeled on earlier classics and hence are described as apocryphal. These mention original *qi*. The *Apocryphal Spring and Autumn Annals* says:

> When original *qi* is correct then heaven, earth and the eight trigrams are birthed. (*Selected Literature* 1b, *Poem on the Eastern Capital*, p. 14, quoting *Apocryphal Spring and Autumn Annals: Preface to Destiny and the Calendar*)

The Imperial Reader has two quotations from the *River Chart* in which original *qi* is described as the origin of heaven and earth:

> Original *qi* opens for *yang* to be heaven....
>
> Original *qi* is without form, swirling, obscure; going down it becomes the earth; bending over it becomes the

heaven. (*Imperial Reader from the Taiping [983* A.D.*] Period* 1.1, *Original Qi*, p. 1a, *River Chart*)

Following these passages, the *Imperial Reader* quotes a further work called the *System of Rites*, saying,

> Heaven and earth are that which sprout from original *qi* and that which the myriad things come from. (Ibid., p. 1a, *System of Rites*)

Yang Xiong's *Ultimate Abstruseness* does not use the term 'original *qi*,' but his *Dispelling Ridicule* speaks of ultimate abstruseness and refers to original *qi*:*

> The *Ultimate Abstruseness* is a book of five thousand characters. Its branches and leaves spread widely; alone it says over 100,000 words. It plunges deep into the yellow springs; rises high above the vault of heaven; so great as to encompass original *qi*; so constrained as to enter where there is no gap. (Ibid., p. 1b)†

A poem by Yang Xiong contains the following line:

> From the present reflecting back to the past up to when original *qi* begins to transform. (Ibid., p. 1b, *Call to the Soul*)

In the *Han History* there are also references to original *qi*:

> The supreme ultimate, the origin and *qi* though three names are all one. (*Han History* 21, *Gazette of the Calendar A*, p. 964)

The term 'original *qi*' was clearly popular in the later Han dynasty. It refers to the one mass before heaven and earth were separated out.

The *Liezi* descibes the origin of heaven and earth:

> What has form sprouts into life from what does not have form, so where do heaven and earth come from? Thus it is said,

---

*Yang Xiong (53 B.C.–18 A.D.). *Zi:* Ziyun, of Shuqun near Chengdu, Sichuan Province. His principal works, both written late in life, are *Ultimate Abstruseness*, based on the *Book of Changes*, and *Legal Words*, based on the *Analects*. The former is translated by M. Nylan as *Yang Hsiung: The Canon of Supreme Mystery*, (Albany: SUNY Press 1993.)
† See concept 9.

"There is the ultimate 'change'; there is the ultimate start; there is the ultimate beginning, there is the ultimate element."*
At the ultimate "change" *qi* is not yet apparent; the ultimate start marks the beginning of *qi*; the ultimate beginning marks the beginning of form; the ultimate element marks the beginning of stuff. *Qi*, form and stuff were all together and not yet separate; thus it is called 'primeval porridge.' This refers to the mixture of the myriad things before they were distinguished from one another. (*Liezi* 1, *Heaven's Gifts*, p. 2)

Here *qi*, form, and stuff are distinguished: *qi* is visible but without definite form; form is of definite shape but not solid; stuff is solid.

The Han writer Wang Chong says that the myriad things of heaven and earth are all produced by interaction within the *qi* of heaven and earth:

Heaven and earth unite their *qi*; the myriad things sprout from this....

This heaven covers over above; the earth lies down below. The lower *qi* rises, the upper *qi* falls; the myriad things sprout themselves from the midst. (*Balanced Inquiries* 54, *Spontaneity*, pp. 177, 180)

Wang Chong also mentions original *qi*:

Human beings receive original *qi* from above. (*Balanced Inquires* 7, *Unfounded Assertions*, p. 13)

Before human beings are born they are within original *qi*; when they die they return to original *qi*. Original *qi* is vague and diffuse; human *qi* is within it. (*Balanced Inquiries* 62, *Death*, p. 203)

From these passages it is clear that Wang Chong believed human *qi* to be part of original *qi*.

---

*In modern Chinese as in modern English, the words translated here as "start" and "beginning" are similar in meaning. In this text the first of the two is more of a beginning than the second. The English use of "start" is not then inappropriate. The start of a race is a definite point: the "beginning" could refer more generally to the first part of the course run. Graham translated 'beginning' and 'commencement,' but the contrast between these two terms is not as appropriate here.

Wang Chong also discussed whether Heaven was *qi* or a body. He asks,

> "Now is heaven *qi*?" He replies, "No, it is a body." (*Balanced Inquiries* 31, *Talking of Heaven*, p. 105)
>
> This heaven is far away. If taken as *qi* then it is like the sun and the moon; if taken as a body then it is like metal and stone. (*Balanced Inquiries* 19, *Experiencing Space*, p. 48)

He concludes that

> When one speaks of it truly, the heavenly body is not *qi*. (*Balanced Inquiries* 31, *Talking of Heaven*, p. 105)

He held that

> Heaven is removed from what is under heaven by over 60,000 *li*. . . . A single circuit has 365 degrees. . . . What is under heaven is counted in degrees of a circle. What is high is measured in *li*. Were one to compare heaven with *qi*, well, *qi* is like clouds or smoke. How could it be measured in *li* and degrees? (Ibid., p. 107)

Heaven is measurable and hence quite unlike *qi*; thus he concludes,

> Heaven has form and body; what it depends on is not space. (Ibid.)

Heaven is a solid like the earth.

As for the relation between heaven and original *qi*, Wang Chong quotes "Confucian books" thus:

> Those who talk about the *Changes* say that before original *qi* separated all swirled together in one porridge. Further the Confucian books say that all that was dark and swirling belongs to the state of undifferentiated *qi*. Once it had separated then the clear became heaven and the muddy earth. (Ibid., p. 105)

He neither agrees with nor denies this opinion, but in another chapter we read,

> Heaven bestows original *qi*: human beings receive original essence. (*Balanced Inquiries* 39, *Beyond Marvels*, p. 137)

It would seem that Wang Chong did believe that heaven is made of original *qi*. His main interest, however, did not lie in the origin of heaven but rather in advocating the spontaneity of heaven's action, in contrast to those who would stress heaven's action as motivated by moral considerations. By 'spontaneity' he meant 'amorality.'

The later Han commentators on the classics also have something to say about *qi*. Zheng Xuan notes that *qi* is air:

> *Qi* is said of what is breathed in and out.* (*SKQS* 116 *Zheng Xuan's Notes on the* Record of Rites 47, *Meaning of Sacrifices*, p. 274b)

He Xiu agrees with the opinion that original *qi* is the state of unity before heaven and earth separated:

> The origin is *qi*. It arises from the formless and when formed splits, making heaven and earth. It is the beginning of heaven and earth. (*SBBY, Notes on the Gongyang Commentary* 1, *Duke Yin* 1, p. 1a)

The compiler of the first dictionary, Xu Shen, writes,

> *Qi* is the *qi* of clouds.... Clouds are the *qi* of mountains and rivers.... The earth: original *qi* began to separate, the light, clear and *yang* became heaven; the heavy, muddy and *yin* became earth.... Celestial: spring is the celestial heaven; original *qi* is celestial. (*Explanation of Words and Characters*, pp. 148a, 242b, 286a, 215b)

The dictionary explains *qi* as original *qi*. *Qi* flows and is without fixed shape. Original *qi* is the one mass before heaven and earth separated out. This shows that by the later Han the term 'original *qi*' was fairly common.

By the Tang period, Liu Zongyuan held that before heaven and earth separated there was only original *qi*:

> When all was vast, dark, revolving and transforming only original *qi* was present. (*SKQS* 1076, *Collected Works of Liu Hedong* 14, *Replies on Heaven*, p. 260)

---

*This note is to be found in a note on the line "*Qi* is the fullness of the divine" (*Record of Rites* 25, *Meaning of Sacrifices*, p. 260).

After heaven and earth had separated, original *qi* was present within heaven and earth:

> That which is above and is somber the world calls 'heaven'; that which is below and is yellow the world calls 'earth'; that which is muddled and in the middle reaches the world calls 'original *qi*.' (Ibid., 16, *Speaking of Heaven* #1, p. 155a–b)

Liu does not discuss the relation between original *qi* and all that exists.

Thus from the late Zhou to the Tang there are four points made regarding *qi*:

1. *Qi* is formless yet visible; *qi* gathers to make what has form;
2. *Qi* belongs to the body and is in contrast with the mind;
3. *Qi* is the source of life, yet *qi* is not life;
4. *Qi* is rooted in empty space, yet empty space is not *qi*.

In short, *qi* is the original matter of which the myriad things are composed and comes out of empty space.

The Song Dynasty

The notion of *qi* saw new developments in the Song dynasty beginning with the work of Zhang Zai. He believed that *qi* was universally present in all that existed. The opening line of the last chapter of his *Correcting the Unenlightened* reads as follows:

> Everything with shape exists; everything which exists has a visible form; everything with visible form has *qi*. (*SKQS* 697, *Correcting the Unenlightened* 17, *Qian Cheng* 143a)

Zhang Zai held not only that all visible things were composed of *qi* but also that the void was *qi* and the empty space was *qi*:

> When one realizes that space and emptiness are *qi* then being and beinglessness, the hidden and manifest, the wondrous*

---

* On the translation of *shen* in Zhang Zai, see Kasoff, *Thought of Chang Tsai*, p. 61 and note. She reads "marvellous—exciting, marvel, wondrous."

and transformation, human nature and destiny are seen as one and not as separate things. (Ibid. 1, *Great Harmony*, p. 97b)

Again,

The condensation and dispersal of *qi* in ultimate space is like the freezing and melting of ice in water. When one knows that ultimate space is *qi* then there is no beinglessness. (Ibid., p. 98b)

Formless ultimate space is but *qi* when it is dispersed and thus it is never purely nothing. A few lines prior to this statement Zhang explains how visible objects arise from ultimate space:

Qi gathers, then its brightness is effective and there are physical forms; if *qi* does not gather then its brightness is not effective and there are no physical forms. (Ibid.)

Ultimate space is simply what is invisible and not nonbeing.

Zhang Zai's identification of *qi* and space has its forerunners in the *Huainanzi* and the *Liezi*. The *Huainanzi* takes 'space' as the furthest origin of *qi*, whereas the *Liezi* places the appearance of *qi* at the second of its four stages of the origins. It is only Zhang Zai, though, who actually identified *qi* and space as the one source of all. Thus Zhang Zai gave new status to *qi*. It was not only the visible forms. Rather, it is whatever moves or is still, broad or deep, and whatever exists:

The so-called *qi* is not only what appears as steam or gathers together and strikes the eye and so can be known; it is also said of all that swirls and sinks. All this can be said to have form. (Ibid. 4, *The Wondrous and Transformation*, p. 109a)

Zhang Zai emphasizes the movements and changes of *qi*:

Insofar as it is ultimate space, *qi* rises and falls, flies up and never experiences ceasing or stopping; as the *Changes* says, "fusion and intermingling" (2.5) and Zhuangzi says, "the breath blown out by living creatures is like wild horses" (1, #1). (Ibid. 1, *Great Harmony*, p. 98a)

Again, here drawing on the contrast and complementarity of *yin qi* and *yang qi*:

As for the *qi* of *yin* and *yang*, it circles round or reaches its
goal, gathers or scatters, rises or falls, each *qi* depending on the
other, fusing and mingling, now together, now one part dominant. It is impossible to unify them even if one wanted to. This
is why their contracting and expanding are without limit, their
movement without rest even though none set them in motion.
(Ibid. 2, *Trinity and Duality*, p. 105a)

The nature of *qi* is ceaseless movement.

Zhang Zai believed that all that exists has *qi*, including therein the
"thingless" ultimate space as well as measureable objects. Its nature is
movement and change.

The Cheng brothers believed that the myriad things were produced
by transformation of *qi*.

The beginnings of the myriad things all lie in transformations
of *qi*. (*SKQS* 698, *Surviving Works of the Two Chengs* 5, p. 69b)

They denied the existence of formless *qi*:

Whatever has form is always *qi*; whatever is formless is the Way.
(Ibid. 6, p. 71b)

They held that the formless is the Way or principle, which is more fundamental than *qi*.

Zhang Zai held that *qi* coagulated to form things and that when
things were destroyed their *qi* dispersed and returned to ultimate space. *Qi*
itself exists forever. The Cheng brothers held that on the destruction of a
thing its *qi* was also destroyed. Cheng Yi says.

Regarding the dispersal of any thing, its *qi* is used up and does
not return to the original source principle. What is within
heaven and earth is like floods and lamps; even living things
dissolve away. How much more then shall dispersed *qi* not return to existence? Heaven and earth make and transform; do
they do this with dispersed *qi*? Their making and transforming
spontaneously produces *qi*. (Ibid. 15, p. 129b)

The Cheng brothers believed principle to be everlasting, whereas *qi* is
produced and then destroyed, destroyed and then produced. How it is

produced they do not say. Whereas Zhang Zai held that matter always exists, the Chengs believed that this is not the case.

Zhu Xi continued in the tradition of the Chengs but also adopted Zhang Zai's point of view with regard to *qi*. He believed there to be first principle, then *qi*, then things.

> Within heaven and earth there is principle and *qi*. Principle is the Way above form and the root that produces things. *Qi* is the vessel that is below form, that produces the frame of things. (*SBCK: Collected Writings of the Literatus, the Honourable Zhu* 58.4 #1, *Reply to Huang Daofu*, vol. 2, p. 1039b)

Thus principle makes it such that *x* is *x*; *qi* makes it such that *x* is an entity in time and space. Logical priority is given to principle, but *qi* is just as necessary for *x*'s existence.

> Suppose that some given *qi* relies on some given principle, then in the coagulation of this *qi* the principle in question will be present.... If only principle is present then there is but a pure empty world, without form or trace. Principle alone cannot make anything. *Qi*, however, can collect, coagulate and produce things. (*Conversations of Master Zhu Arranged Topically* 1, p. 3)

Thus Zhu Xi believed that *qi* is the stuff out of which the myriad things are composed but not that it is the highest origin.

The Ming-Qing Era

The Ming writer Wang Tingxiang developed Zhang Zai's theory of *qi* as the only substance in the world.

> Both within and without heaven all is *qi*. In the earth it is also *qi*. The emptiness and fullness of things is all *qi*. It communicates with extremes of above and below and is the substance of making and transforming. (*Prudent Words*, p. 753)

The state before heaven and earth were separated is called 'original *qi*':

Before heaven and earth had yet separated, original *qi* was all chaotic, clear, empty and without any fissures. It is the original stuff for making and transforming. (Ibid., p. 751)

Before there were heaven and earth there was only original *qi*. Preceding original *qi* there was no thing; thus original *qi* is the root of the Way. (*Elegant Description A*, p. 835)

Original *qi* had no form; all that has form is also *qi*:

What has form is also *qi*; what is formless is likewise *qi*. The Way lodges within it. What has form is what produces things; what is formless is original *qi*. (*Prudent Words*, p. 751)

Again, just before the text quoted above, we read,

The two *qi* touch and transform; the mass of shapes appears and is constituted; this is what heaven, earth and the myriad things are produced from. Is it not a real body? (Ibid.)

The two *qi* of *yin* and *yang* are those from which the myriad things are produced; thus they are called the *qi* that give life. *Qi* exists both as something with form and something formless, but in fact these two are both the same substance.

Fang Yizhi was a loyal servant of the Ming dynasty who on the arrival of the Qing in southern China retreated into a Buddhist monastery. His early work, *A Little Understanding of the Principles of Things*, is a compendium of notes on the natural sciences. He discusses and develops the theory of *qi* as the sole origin of things. Quoting his father, Fang Kongchi, he says,

The world has only to grasp a form and it is apparent, yet *qi* is subtle. As in winter when breath comes out of the mouth one's *qi* is like smoke. If a person stands in direct sunlight, a haze rises above his head and its shadow is seen on the earth. When you strike a bell or hit a drum the paper in the windows* all moves, yet insofar as it is matter *qi* can certainly be seen. It fills

---

* Paper rather than glass was common in Chinese windows until the twentieth century.

up all spaces, threads through all substances. (*SKQS* 867, *A Little Understanding of the Principles of Things* 1a, *Heaven #2, Qi*, p. 753a–b)

Compared with form, *qi* is tiny, but under certain conditions it can be experienced. The void is full of *qi*, as are all things. Fang Yizhi declares,

> All things are composed of *qi*; all empty spaces are full of *qi*. (Ibid., 753b)
>
> *Qi* coagulates into form, develops into light and sound, like air which has not yet formed into anything and the breath which can be felt. Thus the nature of a form rests in what it is apportioned to do and light and sound are ever an added bonus. *Qi* does not have empty gaps; rather, it turns round, with each part responding to another. (Ibid., p. 755a)

Here he distinguishes between *qi*, which is continuous, and forms, which are "apportioned" to given entities.

Wang Fuzhi also developed Zhang Zai's theory of *qi*:

> The fusion of heaven and human beings is but one *qi*. (*Readings in the Four Books* 10.1, *Mencius: Gaozi A #2*, p. 660)
>
> Principle and *qi* form one entity and without *qi* there is no principle, just as without principle there can be no *qi*. One who speaks well of principle and *qi* does not separate or cut them apart. (Ibid., 10.3, *Mencius: Exhausting the Mind A #7*, p. 724)

The world is a world of *qi* and the union of the world is given by *qi*.

Dai Zhen also developed the thought of Zhang Zai and claimed that the transformations of *qi* constitute the Way while *yin-yang* and the five agents are the embodiment of the Way:

> *Qi* transforms, flows and goes, "producing and reproducing without ceasing"; hence it is called the Way.... *Yin-yang* and the five agents are the embodiment of the Way. (*An Evidential Study of the Meaning of Terms in the* Book of Mencius, p. 287)

Summary

The traditional Chinese understanding of *qi* has several important features:

1. *Qi* is the original material out of which all things are formed by coagulation;
2. *Qi* has breadth and depth and can be spoken of;
3. *Qi* is contrasted with the mind. It exists independent of the mind;
4. *Qi* can move. Indeed, it is normally in a state of flux and transformation.

Hence what Chinese philosophy says about *qi* is basically the same as what Western philosophy says about matter. The Chinese theory, however, is distinctive on two counts:

1. *Qi* is not impenetrable; rather, it penetrates all things;
2. *Qi* is intrinsically in a state of motion and is normally in flux.

As the original matter *qi* itself is without form or any stuff. The Western idea of the atom is best translated as "minute stuff" in Chinese rather than as *qi*. *Qi* is also the condition for life, but at the same time it is present in inanimate objects. It is not impenetrable but rather is in motion.

6. Stuff

Zhi CHẤT

質

'Stuff' is said of that which has fixed form and substance. In ancient Chinese philosophy the term applies to three fields: (1) that which has real content; (2) things with determinate and form; (3) substance or accidents of things.

'Stuff' is used in Chinese philosophy along with *qi*. In the quotation from the *Liezi* above *qi* appears at the second stage whereas 'stuff' is at the fourth stage:

> The ultimate start marks the beginning of *qi* ... the ultimate element marks the beginning of stuff. (*Liezi* 1, *Heaven's Gifts*, p. 2)

The *Apocryphal Classic of Piety* describes the same four stages as follows:

> Before shapes and forms had yet separated out it is called ulti-
> mate 'change.' When original *qi* first begins to appear, it is
> called the ultimate start. The emergence of *qi* and form is
> called the ultimate beginning. When *qi* changes there is stuff;
> this is called the ultimate element. (*Apocryphal Classic of Piety*)

'Stuff' is a more definitive stage of existence than 'form.'
Zhu Xi also distinguishes *qi* from stuff:

> First there was the principle of heaven; thus there was *qi. Qi*
> consolidated into stuff and nature was then present. . . .
>
> *Yin* and *yang* are *qi*; the five agents are stuff. For any
> given stuff, a particular thing is made. Even though the five
> agents are stuff, yet for it to be they have the *qi* of the five
> agents to make a given thing. (*Conversations of Master Zhu
> Arranged Topically* 1, pp. 2, 9)

Yin and *yang* are the two *qi*. The five agents are gathered into stuff by *qi*.
Qi and stuff are linked but are different.

The terms 'form' (*xing*) and 'stuff' (*zhi*) are often linked to form
one binome, literally 'form-stuff.' The Tang scholar Cui Jing wrote a
commentary on the *Book of Changes* that was highly critical of Kong Yingda.
The book is now lost, but quotations from it are preserved in the *Collected
Commentaries on the* Book of Changes by Li Dingzuo. Cui Jing uses the
expression 'form-stuff' to mean the real existence of all things:

> Heaven, earth and the myriad things all have form-stuff. (*SKQS*
> 7, *Penetrating the Mystery of the* Book of Changes, in *Collected
> Commentaries on the* Book of Changes: *Great Appendix* 1.12,
> pp. 835b–836a)

Sometimes 'form-stuff' is a pair of contrasting elements. Wang Fuzhi
comments on Zhang Zai as follows:

> Master Zhang says, "The form of the sun and moon has not
> varied from remote antiquity." 'Form' is said of the ideal model;
> it does not refer to the stuff. The stuff goes through a cycle day

by day but the form is always the same. There is no eternal vessel but there is an eternal Way. The water of the Yangtze and the Yellow Rivers is today as it was in the past but it is not today's water that is the water of the past. The light of a candle yesterday is as it is today but it is not yesterday's flame which is today's flame. Water and fire are close to us and easily known; sun and moon are far and cannot be inspected. (*Complete Works of Chuanshan: Record of Thoughts and Questions* 2, pp. 453–454)

Here 'form' is said of the external appearance and 'stuff' of the internal material of which something is composed.

Another meaning of 'stuff' is original nature or accidents. The *Zhuangzi* says,

Nature is the stuff of life. (*Zhuangzi* 23, *Gengsang Chu*, line 70)

Dong Zhongshu says that nature is stuff and stuff is nature:

If the term 'nature' means what is innate, then the stuff naturally innate is called human nature. Nature is stuff. If one examines the stuff of nature by applying the term 'good' will this be right? If not, why still say that stuff is good? (*Luxuriant Gems of the Spring and Autumn Annals* 35, *Profound Examination of Names and Appellations*, pp. 291–292)

Nature is stuff; stuff is nature.

7. Thing

Wu VẬT

物

In ancient Chinese philosophy the term 'thing' is used mainly of concrete objects or groups of objects. This usage is illustrated clearly in the *Zhuangzi*:

Whatever has traits, appearance, sound, and color are all things. (*Zhuangzi* 19, *Comprehending Life*, line 9)

Because things have appearance they cannot be the origin of the universe. Although this quotation does not state that all things have traits, appearance, sound, and color, the context of the quotation suggests that this is the case. The point is made clearer in a dialogue ascribed to Confucius, who says,

> Is what sprouts before heaven and earth a thing? What makes things things is not a thing; the emergence of a thing cannot have come before things. (*Zhuangzi* 22, *Knowledge Roams North*, line 75)

Here the term 'thing' is applied to concrete things.

> An expression for the number of things is called 'myriad' and human beings are one of them. In the nine inhabited regions, where grain grows, ships and carriages travel, human beings are but one item there. If one compares human beings to the myriad things then are they not like the end of a hair on a horse's body? (*Zhuangzi* 17, *Autumn Floods*, line 11)

The term 'thing' is used of concrete objects considered individually or of the group of myriad things.

The logician Gongsun Long says,

> Heaven and earth and what they produce is a thing. That by which a thing is the thing it is and only that is 'reality.' (*Gongsun Long* 6, *Names and Reality*, p. 39)

The *Orderly Sequence of the Hexagrams* in the *Book of Changes* says,

> There are heaven and earth and then afterwards the myriad things sprout from them. What fills up heaven and earth is but the myriad things. (*Book of Changes*, p. 355)

The nature of a thing is discussed from a logical point of view in the *Mohist Canons* and in the *Xunzi*:

> Name. Unrestricted: classifying; private.
>   [The commentary says,] 'Thing' is 'unrestricted'; any object necessarily requires this name. Naming something 'horse' is 'classifying'; for 'like the object' we necessarily use

this name. Naming someone 'Jack' is 'private'; this name stays confined in this object.* (*Mohist Canons and Explanations*, A78)

An unrestricted name is one that applies to a class of things. 'Thing' is just such a name.

The *Xunzi* says that 'thing' is a broad, general name:

> Thus though the myriad things are innumerable, sometimes one wants to speak of them in general and so one calls them 'things.' 'Thing' is a broad, general name. We infer further and generalize and continue in this way until there is nothing more universal. Sometimes one wants to speak of them in particular and so one calls them 'bird' or 'beast.' 'Bird' and 'beast' are broad particular names. (*Xunzi* 22, *Rectification of Names*, lines 23–25)

Although the basic meaning of 'thing' is a concrete object, the term may be applied to whatever is the object of thought. The *Laozi* speaks of the Way as a 'thing':

> As a 'thing' the Way is obscure and indistinct, indistinct and shadowy. (*Laozi* 21/MWD 65)

This means "taking the Way as an objective existing entity."

> There is something formed inchoate;
> Generated before heaven and earth;
> Silent, hush, void, ah!
> Standing alone and not changing,
> Turning round and round and not tiring.
> It may be the mother of all under heaven.
> I do not know its name so I shall call it the 'Way,'
> If pressed I would name it 'great.' (*Laozi* 25/MWD 69)

Here 'thing' is not said of a visible object but of all that objectively is.

The *Harmony and Balance* makes a contrast between 'thing' and the self:

---

*This is A. C. Graham's own translation. The reading of the *Mohist Canons* is one of Graham's greatest works, unequaled in China or abroad.

The person of integrity does not just complete himself. He also completes things. Completing oneself is benevolence; completing things is knowledge. These are virtues of human nature and they are the way to unite internal and external. Hence whenever one uses them it is appropriate.* (*Harmony and Balance* 25)

In the *Mencius* the contrast between the human agent and the external world is expressed in the terminology of 'mind' and 'things.' Mencius is reported as telling King Xuan of Qi (320–301 B.C.),

If you weigh then you know what is light and what is heavy; if you measure then you know what is long and what is short. Things are all like that and the mind even more so. Let the king please measure it [the mind]. (*Mencius* 1, *King Hui of Liang A*, #7)

The sense organs of ears and eyes do not think, moreover, they can be obscured by things. When one thing meets another, the first leads the second astray. The sense of the mind is to think. If one thinks then one obtains [a correct view]. If one does not think then one does not obtain [a correct view]. (*Mencius* 6, *Gaozi A*, #15)

On one hand are things, on the other the mind. The senses mediate between things and the mind.

The Mencian distinction became an important philosophical issue in the Song-Ming period. Zhang Zai believed that things were of one nature and the mind of another:

Human beings originally did not have a mind, but through things there is mind. (*Collected Works of Zhang Zai: Recorded Conversations* 3, p. 333 [1978 ed.])

Principle is not in human beings but wholly in things. Human beings are but one thing among other things. (Ibid. 1, p. 313)

---

*Note that the words for 'integrity' and 'complete' in this passage have the same sound and similar graphs. The two are considered related. 'Integrity' is the completion of the human person.

A human being is but one thing and the mind is the human capacity to recognize things.

Wang Shouren advocated no principle outside the mind and no thing outside the mind. According to this theory, things do not exist independently. In a letter to Gu Lin* written some time before 1524, he explains.

> With knowing there is the will. Without knowing there is no will. Is knowing not the substance of the will? If the will is to work there must be a thing in which it is to work and the thing is an event. When the will works in serving one's parents, then service of one's parents is a 'thing.' When the will works in administering a people, then administration of a people is a 'thing.' When the will works in studying, then studying is a 'thing.' When the will works in hearing a legal case, then hearing a legal case in a 'thing.' Wheresoever the will is employed there cannot not be a 'thing.' Where there is a will directed to *x*, then there is *x*. Where the will is not directed to *x*, then there is no *x*. Is a 'thing' not then the function of the will? (*SKQS* 1265, *Collected Books of Wang Wencheng 2, Recorded Conversations: Instructions for Practical Living: Letter to Gu Dongqiao*, pp. 44b–45a; WTC #137)

From this passage it is clear that knowing is the substance of the will and that things are its function. Just as substance and function form one, so too things cannot be separated from knowing. This is a clear case of subjective idealism. Things are what the person knows and cannot be separated from the knowing subject.

Wang Fuzhi opposed Wang Shouren's idealism of the mind but followed him in accepting that all events are things. In a discourse attached to Chapter 1 of the *Book of History*, he writes,

> The wind, lightning, rain and dew of heaven are things; so too are the mountains, hills, deeps, plains and crevices of the earth. Moreover, their being *yin* or *yang*, soft or hard is also a thing.

---

*Gu Lin (1476–1545). *Zi*: Huayu; *Hao*: Dongqiao. Poet and painter who lived in Nanjing. Author of *New Edition of National Treasures (Guobao Xinbian)*.

> The flying, diving, moving and staying still of things are also things. The people's generous giving, living and use is also a thing, as also is their gaining or losing, goodness or badness. Fathers, children, older and younger siblings among the people are likewise things as are their good conduct and reputation for tending to sageliness and also their benevolence, justice, ritual and music. (*Elaboration on the Meaning of the* Book of History 1.1 *The Canon of Yao*, p. 6)

All natural and social phenomena are things. 'Thing' refers to objective reality. The origin of the use of 'thing' to apply to events is found among Han-dynasty Confucian scholars, but it is only with Wang Fuzhi that it really enters the philosophical arena.*

'Thing' in ancient Chinese philosophy refers to individual entities. In modern Chinese the terms 'thing' and 'stuff' are combined into 'thing-stuff,' and this new binome is used to translate the Western term 'matter.' In fact, though, it is clear that in Chinese philosophy the concept corresponding to the Western philosophical use of 'matter' is *qi*.

With this we end the first section, in which we have looked at heaven, the Way, principle, qi, *and related concepts. No philosopher can avoid these terms, but different philosophers stress one or the other and establish varying relationships between them.*

II. Apophatic Terms

There are three ontological terms that may be described as apophatic since they point more to what cannot be said than to what can be said. Although

---

*Author's note: In the *Mencius* there is a passage that says, "The myriad things are all complete in me" (*Mencius* 7a, *Exhausting the Mind*, #4). The Han scholar Zhao Ji notes, " 'Things' means 'events'; 'me' means the self." In the *Rites of Zhou* it is said, "The duty of the Grand Director of the multitudes ... is to teach the myriad people the three things of the countryside" (*Rites of Zhou* 2.1, *Officials of Earth*, 21/3. Zheng Xuan (A.D. 127–200) notes, " 'Thing' is like 'event' " (*SKQS* 90 *Zheng's Notes on the Rites of Zhou* 10, p. 192b).

found throughout the philosophical spectrum, they are particularly beloved of Daoist thinkers. The three terms are 'limitless' (or 'endless'), 'abstruse,' and 'space.' hư

vô cực   huyền

8. Limitless, Ultimate of Nonbeing
Wu Ji, Wu Qiong VÔ CƯC, VÔ CÙNG
無極, 無窮

The expression 'limitless' and its relatives are found in the Laozi *and the* Zhuangzi *and also in writings of the logicians. It has no special philosophical meaning. In Song-dynasty philosophy, however, the same expression 'limitless' should be translated as 'ultimate of beinglessness,' for the negative element is no longer qualifying the word 'limit' but is rather qualified by the word 'limit,' here to be translated into Song philosophical jargon as 'ultimate.'*

The term 'limitless' is first encountered in the received text of the *Laozi:**

Know the cock but keep to the hen's role; then you will be a ravine for under-heaven. For one who is a ravine for under-heaven, constant virtue does not leave and one will go back to the state of a baby. Know the white but keep to the black; then

---

* Author's note: Whether the phrase "go back to the limitless" is authentic *Laozi* is a matter of discussion. The Republican scholar Yi Shunding says that 23 characters, from "keep to the black" to "know honour," are a later addition. *Zhuangzi* 33, *Under Heaven*, line 58 quotes the passage without these characters. In the *Zhuangzi* version cock and hen are contrasted and so too are 'white' and 'despised.' Later people did not understand the contrast of 'white' and 'despised' and so, according to Yi, the phrase was changed to contrast black and white, being despised with being honored. Gao Heng (*Laozi Zhenggu* 28, pp. 65–66) says that in chapter 41 it is said, "great white is like being despised," in which 'white' and 'being despised' are contrasted; hence it is clear, he concludes, that the contrast of black and white is not the original text. The conclusions of Yi and Gao seem to be correct, but the "addition" had already occurred by the time of the Mawangdui manuscript, i.e., at least before 168 B.C.

Translator's note: See also Sha Shaohai and Xu Zihong, *Laozi Quanyi* (Guiyang: Guizhou Renmin, 1989), p. 55.

you will be a model for under-heaven. For one who is a model for under-heaven, constant virtue does not turn away and one will go back to the limitless. Know honor but keep to what is despised; then you will be a valley for under-heaven. For one who is a valley for under-heaven, constant virtue is enough, and one will go back to the uncarved block. (*Laozi* 28/MWD 72)

Apart from the *Laozi* we find the term 'limitless' four times in the *Zhuangzi*.

> I was astounded and scared by his words, which went into the limitless like the Milky Way. (*Zhuangzi* 1, *Going Rambling Without a Destination*, line 27)
> Who can climb the sky, wander the mists and go whirling into the limitless, living by forgetting each other without any end or term. (*Zhuangzi* 6, *The Teacher Who Is the Ultimate Ancestor*, line 62)

From the later part of the *Zhuangzi* corpus come the following:

> I enter by the gate of the infinte so as to wander in the wilds of the limitless. (*Zhuangzi* 11, *Preserve and Accept*, line 43)
> There is nothing one does not not forget, nothing one does not not have, serene and limitless and all good things come to one. (*Zhuangzi* 15, *Finicky Notions*, line 7)

Here 'limitless' always refers to the infinite and the boundless.

The term 'infinite' is found twenty-two times in the *Zhuangzi*, and it also appears three times as a sort of proper name.

> so as to wander in the infinite (*Zhuangzi* 1, *Going Rambling Without a Destination*, line 21)
> so as to reply to the infinite (*Zhuangzi* 2, *The Sorting Which Evens Things Out*, line 31)
> going along with the infinite beginning (*Zhuangzi* 4, *Worldly Business Among Humans*, line 11)

The term 'infinite' in all these cases means 'what is without restrictions.' The logician Hui Shi is recorded as saying,

> The south is infinite and finite. (*Zhuangzi* 33, *Under Heaven,*
> line 72)

This paradox is meant to say that the finite and infinite are united.

The *Xunzi* uses 'limitless' and 'infinite' together, both as meaning
"without restrictions":

> Ji, the horse, could run 1,000 *li* in a day; an old nag could do it
> in ten days, but would still get there. Yet what if you try to go
> the end of the infinite and the limit of the limitless? Even if you
> break your bones and wear out your sinews you will never be
> able to get there. (*Xunzi* 2, *Self-Cultivation,* lines 27–28)

These examples suffice to show that pre-Qin philosophy did have the
notion of the limitless and of the infinite.

In the opening of his *Explanation of the Diagram of the Supreme
Ultimate,** Zhou Dunyi used the phrase "the ultimate of beinglessness
and the supreme ultimate (*An Explanation of the Diagram of the Supreme
Ultimate,* p. 187a). Zhu Xi explains as follows:

> The bearing-up of heaven is soundless and tasteless and yet it is
> the hinge of all making-transforming and the root of all kinds
> of things. Thus it is said that there is the ultimate of nonbeing
> and the supreme ultimate. It is not that outside the supreme
> ultimate there is the ultimate of nonbeing. (*SKQS* 1101, *Col-*

---

*Author's note: The early Qing scholar Huang Zongyan wrote a study of the origin
of the *Diagram* and had this to say: "Master Zhou's *Diagram of the Supreme Ultimate,* was
created by Heshang Gong and is the spiritual practice of the diviners.... The name of Heshang Gong's original diagram was the *Diagram of the ultimate of non-being.* Wei Boyang
acquired it and wrote *Cantongqi;* Zhong Liquan acquired it and gave it to Lu Dongbin.
Dongbin later with Chen Tunan became a hermit on Mount Hua and gave it to Chen. Chen
engraved it on a grotto on Mount Hua. Chen also acquired the *Before heaven Diagram* from
a hempen clad Daoist and gave both to Zhong Fang. Fang gave it to Mu Xiu with the bhiksu
Shouya.... Xiu gave the *Diagram of ultimate non-being* to Master Zhou. This diagram was
to be read from the bottom up so as to make clear the way of internal alchemy.... Master
Zhou acquired this diagram but turned its sequence upside down and changed its name,
adding it to the *Book of Changes* and treating it as a secret Confucian work" (Huang
Zongyan, *Tuxue Bianhuo,* quoted in Huang Zongxi, *SBBY: Song-Yuan Schools of Learning* 12, *School of Learning of Jianxi* [Zhou Dunyi] 2, pp. 12b–13a). This lineage is highly
questionable. There was a famous Daoist in the early Song called Chen Tuan and, according
to Song legends, which are probably trustworthy, he possessed a diagram of ultimate non-
being.

lected Works of Zhou Yuangong 1, An Explanantion of the Diagram of the Supreme Ultimate, p. 416b)

Zhou Dunyi's *Diagram of the Supreme Ultimate* and his notion of ultimate beinglessness certainly had Daoist origins, and in this Huang Zongyan's testimony, quoted in the footnote, is valid. Zhu Xi gave his own interpretation of Zhou's phrase. The Confucian philosophy of the Song and Ming dynasties, however, does not often discuss the ultimate of beinglessness. It is not an important Confucian concept.

9. Abstruse
Xuan HUYỀN
玄

The term 'xuan' is originally the description of a color normally translated 'black' but sometimes described as 'red.' It is frequently applied to the sky to indicate the seeming endlessness of the heavens. Close observation suggests that it refers not so much to a given color as to the gloss-matt distinction of a color. Since it is the color of heaven, it might better be translated as 'ultra-x,' as in 'ultramarine' or 'ultraviolet,' as opposed to the burnished yellow-gold of earth. It is this characteristic of 'ultra' that gives rise to its philosophical use to refer to the profound reaches of the Way.

'Abstruse' is another ontological term with Daoist roots.* It is first encountered in a philosophical sense in the *Laozi* but came to the fore in the Han and Jin periods, the first centuries of our era. After that time it was no longer an important philosophical category. Chapter 1 of the *Laozi* reads,

---

*Author's note: Note that the character *xuan* was part of the name of the Kangxi emperor and so was tabooed after his accession and replaced by *yuan*, 'the origin.' Hence Qing editions of the *Laozi* and the *Tai Xuan* write *yuan*, not *xuan*.

The Way that can be taken is not the constant Way; the name that can be named is not the constant name. The nameless is the beginning of heaven and earth; the named is the mother of the myriad things. Thus for constant beinglessness, try to peer at its secrets; for constant being, try to peer at its outcome.* These two come from the same source yet have different names. Both alike are called 'abstruse'; 'abstruse' on 'abstruse,' the gate of all secrets.

The two are constant beinglessness and constant being. Both come from the Way but differ from each other. Together they are called 'abstruse,' which means 'profound, far, and mysterious.' 'Abstruse on abstruse' refers to the Way.

In the *Great Appendix to the* Book of Changes 'abstruse' is used to describe heaven. It is the color of heaven, in contrast to yellow, the color of earth:

> Abstruse and yellow are the mixture of heaven and earth. Heaven is abstruse and earth yellow. (*Book of Changes: Literary Commentary* 2, *Kun*)

Yang Xiong's *Tai Xuan* or *Ultimate Abstruseness* was a late work based on the *Book of Changes*. In it 'abstruse' is a term descriptive of the substance of heaven and earth. Its precise meaning is very hard to pin down, but it at least seems to refer to a state of going beyond all duality.

> The abstruse, while hidden, displays the myriad categories yet does not reveal any form of its own. It supplies the matter of space and of nonbeing yet produces the regulations. It is bound to the numinous and luminous yet fixes the models. It pervades heaven (or assimilates) past and present so as to inaugurate the categories. It unfolds and mingles *yin* and *yang* and emits *qi*. (Zheng Wangeng, *Tai Xuan Xiaoshi: Appendix* 3, *Tai xuan li*, p. 260)

---

*Zhang punctuates this phrase according to the punctuation of Wang Anshi. Heshang Gong and Wang Bi punctuated so as to read, "Thus constantly do away with desires in order to peer at its secrets; constantly have desires so as to peer at its outcome." For a discussion of the translation of this line see Chan, *Source Book*, p. 139. For a discussion of the translation of the whole passage see Sarah Allan's introduction to D. C. Lau, trans., *Lao-Tzu: Tao Te Ching*. (New York: Knopf, 1994), pp. xxi–xxix.

As for this 'abstruseness,' it is the way of heaven, the way of earth and the way of humans. Taken together, the three ways are called heavenly. (Ibid., *Appendix* 8, *Tai xuan tu*, p. 358)

Xuan is the color of heaven; hence the abstruse uses heaven's name. In his later years Yang wrote the *Dispelling Ridicule*, in which he spoke about his earlier work:

I considered silence and wrote the *Tai Xuan*, a book of 5,000 characters ... it plunged deep into the yellow springs, rose high above the vault of heaven; so great as to encompass original *qi*: so constrained as to enter where there is no gap. (*Complete Han Literature* 53, Yang Xiong: *Dispelling Ridicule*, p. 412)*

In fact the *Tai Xuan* itself does not use the expression 'original *qi*.' It is not obvious how the abstruse is related to original *qi*. It would seem, though, that the abstruse transcends all things, forms, and shapes and is the highest origin of the world.

A younger contemporary, Huan Tan (c. 20 B.C.–56 A.D.), refers to Yang Xiong's theories (and equates the abstruse with the origin):

Yang Xiong wrote the Abstruse book, in which he argued that the abstruse was heaven and the Way. He spoke of the sages and worthies establishing laws and doing things, all taking the heavenly way as the uniting element and then applying it to the myriad kinds, kingly administration, human affairs and the legal system. Thus Fu Xi called it the Change; Laozi called it the Way; Confucius called it the Origin; Yang Xiong called it the Abstruse. (*SBBY: New Discourses*, p. 12a)

The Jin-dynasty Daoist Ge Hong also took the abstruse as the origin of the world. In the opening line of his book *The Master Who Grasps the*

---

*This text is also found in the *Imperial Reader from the Taiping [983 A.D.] Period* 1/2b but with "at the bottom of the earth" instead of "yellow springs" and with "*lun*" instead of "gap."

Simple he wrote,*

> The abstruse is the first progenitor of spontaneous nature and
> the great ancestor of the myriad particular things. Its depth is
> subtle and dark; thus it is called 'tiny'; its farthest point is dis-
> tant and obscure; thus it is called 'subtle.' Its height, though,
> goes beyond the nine heavens and its expanse circumvents the
> eight corners.... It embodies itself in the things of nature and
> becomes a being; it incorporates itself in obscurity and solitude
> and thus appears as beingless. It merges into the great darkness
> and dwells in its depths; it rises up to the highest stars (or the
> North Star) and floats on above.... It comprises the Original
> One; it molds and forms the two principles (*yin-yang*); it in-
> hales and exhales the primordial beginning; it stirs up and
> forms all things.... Therefore, where the abstruse is present,
> the pleasure is inexhaustible; where the abstruse has departed,
> the body [outward frame] becomes languid, the spirit passes
> away.... It is only with the said Abstruse Way that one can live
> forever. (*SBBY: The Master Who Grasps the Simple* 1, *Expound-
> ing the Abstruse*, p. 2a)

Ge Hong uses the abstruse in much the same way as Yang Xiong but
writes more clearly. Again, the abstruse is the only absolute transcendent.

10. Empty Space
Xu, Tai Xu THÁI HƯ
虛, 太虛

The character xu *is the drawing of the gap between two mountains. In
English it is often rendered as 'the void,' but the term 'space' retains the original sense of 'gap' as well as the philosophical meaning of the void.*

---

* The best translation of the first three chapters of this work is to be found in E. Feifel,
Pao-P'u Tzu: Nei Pien, chs. 1–3 in *Monumenta Serica* 6 (1941), pp. 113–211. The complete
text is translated in J. R. Ware, *Alchemy, Medicine, and Religion in the China of* A.D. *320: The
Nei P'ien of Ko Hong* (Cambridge: MIT Press, 1966). A review of the latter can be found in
Journal of Asian Studies 27.1: 144–145.

The Wei dynasty (A.D. 220–265) glossary the *Guang Ya* is a compendium of glosses gleaned from ancient texts. For *xu* it reads: "'*xu*' means 'empty'" (*Congshu Jicheng* 1160, *Guang Ya* 3, *Shi Gu* 3, p. 36). The *Laozi* and the *Zhuangzi* both understand *xu* as referring to an inner world, freed from the things of everyday business:

> Attain to the limit of space; keep to extreme stillness. (*Laozi* 16/MWD 60)
>
> Only the Way accumulates space. Space is the fasting of the heart. (*Zhuangzi* 4, *Worldly Business Among Humans*, line 28)

The fasting of the heart is a state of doing away with all the attractions of the sensual world.

In late Warring States and early Han writings *xu* is applied to heaven.

> Heaven is called 'space'; earth is called 'tranquil'; and neither varies. . . .
>
> Space is the beginning of the myriad things. (*Guanzi* 36, *Technique of the Heart A*, 1:4, 9)

Thus space is a cosmological principle. The earth is full of things, whereas heaven is empty and thus described as 'space.' The term 'space' is frequently prefixed by an indicator of the superlative 'ultimate':

> Such a person outwardly never fully contemplates the dimensions of space and time and inwardly does not know the ultimate start. This is why such a one cannot cross Mount Kunlun nor roam in ultimate space. (*Zhuangzi* 22, *Knowledge Roams North*, lines 64–65)

The Han medical text the *Inner Canon of the Yellow Emperor* speaks of ultimate space in words that imply that it is treated as heaven.*

> Great space is broad and vast. It is the foundation of all and the origin of transformations. The myriad things draw their substance and their beginnings from it. The five periods go round

---

*Author's note: Song scholars believed this *juan* to be part of the *Great Treatise on Yin-yang*, an Eastern Han (A.D. 25–220) work.

in sequence in heaven sending out *qi* and true soul, controlling the origins of things on earth. (*Inner Canon of the Yellow Emperor* 66, *Great Treatise on Heaven, the Origin and the Thread*, p. 947c)

The Han work the *Huainanzi* includes 'space' as one of the steps in a cosmogony:

The Way begins in empty space; space gives rise to space-time; space-time gives rise to *qi. Qi* has limits: what is light and *yang* is rarefied and becomes heaven; what is heavy and muddy congeals and becomes earth. (*Huainanzi* 3, *Heaven's Patterns*, 18–19)

The term 'empty space,' *xugou*, is the ultimate beginning. From it come the dimensions of space-time. From these come *qi*, which is thus not the origin itself. *Qi* separates and produces heaven and earth. A similar cosmogony is found in the opening lines of the *Book of Transformations*, a Five Dynasties work by Tan Qiao that understands all things to be in a state of transformation.

The sequence of the Way in space changes into the numinous; the numinous changes into *qi; qi* changes into form; once form is produced then the myriad things are able to fill it up. (*SKQS* 849, *Book of Transformations* 1.1, *Discourse on the Way*, p. 227)

Whereas these two works give priority to *xu* rather than *qi*; Zhang Zai, in the Song dynasty, equates them, thus giving each equal position in the hierarchy:

Ultimate space is *qi*.... Space and emptiness are *qi*.... The condensation and dispersal of *qi* in ultimate space is like the freezing and melting of ice in water. When one knows that ultimate space is *qi* then there is no beinglessness. (*SKQS* 697, *Correcting the Unenlightened* 1, *Ultimate Harmony*, p. 98b)

When one realizes that space and emptiness are *qi*, then 'being' and 'beingless,' the hidden and manifest, the wondrous and transformation, human nature and destiny are seen as one and not as separate things. (Ibid., p. 97b)

Zhang Zai was particularly opposed to the idea that space produces *qi*:

> If one says that space can generate *qi*, then space would be limitless, *qi* limited; space would be substance; *qi* its function; each radically different from the other. This would be to fall into Laozi's theory of natural spontaneity by which being is generated from beingless. (Ibid., pp. 97b–98a)

This criticism of *Laozi* is obviously directed also against the *Huainanzi* and the *Book of Transformations*. Zhang Zai believed that space is the state of *qi* when it is diffuse and not yet congealed. It is not a pure vacuum.*

Wang Tingxiang continued on the lines laid down by Zhang Zai:

> Before heaven and earth were yet split apart, original *qi* was all in a cosmic soup, clear, spacious, with no gaps. It was the original impetus for making and transforming. There was space and hence there was *qi*; space was not independent of *qi*; *qi* was not independent of space. There was the mystery of no beginning and no ending. It is not possible to attain its limits, thus it is called ultimate pole; it is not possible to picture it, thus it is called ultimate space. It is not that outside of *yin* and *yang* there is the pole or space....
>
> Within and without heaven all is *qi*; in the midst of earth is also *qi*; things being abstract or concrete are all *qi*. Penetrating to the peak of up and down is the reality of making and transforming. Therefore space is dependent on *qi* and cannot produce *qi*. (*Collected Works of Wang Tingxiang* 3, *Prudent Words* 1, *The Body of the Way*, pp. 751, 753)

Here again *qi* unites both space and real objects.

The relation of *qi* and space was taken up again by Wang Fuzhi:

> Spacious emptiness is the container of *qi*. *Qi* is fine without boundaries, minute and formless; thus people see spacious

---

* Kasoff, *Thought of Chang Tsai* (p. 37) says about ultimate space in the work of Zhang Zai: "Great Void [ultimate space] ... refers to the same intangible, 'above-form' state as the Great Harmony. But, in contrast to the term Great Harmony, which emphasizes the coexistence of the two polar forces in a harmonious unity, Great Void emphasizes the invisibility of this state."

emptiness but do not see *qi*. Whatever is spacious emptiness is all *qi*. When gathered it is apparent; when it is apparent then people say that it exists. When scattered then it is hidden; when it is hidden then people say it does not exist. . . . As for its reality, then principle is within *qi*; *qi* does not not have principle. *Qi* is within emptiness; emptiness does not not have *qi*. Both are united such that there are not two things. (*Notes on Master Zhang's* Correcting the Unenlightened 1a, p. 23)

Thus, overall, Zhang Zai, Wang Tingxiang, and Wang Fuzhi affirmed that *qi* is without beginning or end, without limit or boundary, and existing forever.

B. Cosmology

Under the heading of cosmology we shall discuss concepts that try to explain the emergence of the cosmos from the principle or principles that are fundamental. Special place is given to yin-yang *and the five agents since these concepts have played a defining role in all fields of Chinese philosophy. These concepts stand close to the ontological principles yet govern the interaction of the principles with the myriad things. In second place attention will be given to concepts that trace the cosmos from its emergence as one via its growth and fruition to a return to the one. The plant metaphor that is illustrated here is a key image of much Chinese philosophy. Third, attention will be given to concepts that have an explicit origin in the* Book of Changes *or its related commentaries. Although later philosophers may give their own interpretation to the concepts in question, there is no doubt that they were conscious of the textual origin of the terms employed. The fourth source of cosmological concepts is Daoism. Finally, we shall consider relational concepts. These five groups may overlap and interact. Daoism, for instance, is certainly fond of the metaphor of growth and return to the one;* yin-yang *are constitutive of the* Book of Changes, *but separate treatment is also justified since the metaphor of growth is as much Confucian as Daoist, and* yin-yang *are not always understood as directly related to the hexagrams of the* Book of Changes.

I. Yin-yang

11. **Yin-yang**

Yin-yang ÂM · DƯỜNG

陰陽

Early Texts

The terms *yin* and *yang* represent what is turned toward the sun, *yang*, and away from the sun, *yin*. This usage is found in the *Book of Songs*:

> He determined the points of the heavens by means of the
>   shadows;
> And then ascending the ridges, he surveyed the *yin* and *yang*.
> (*Book of Songs* 3, *Da Ya* 2.6, *Duke Liu* [Ode 250])

This is the original meaning of the terms.

A classic early text on *yin-yang*, establishing the cosmological use of the pair, is the speech attributed to the Venerable Bo Yang, grand historiographer of Zhou, who uses the concepts to explain earthquakes:

> The *qi* of heaven and earth does not lose its order. If it exceeds its order then it is because people have disturbed it. *Yang* bends down and cannot go out; *yin* is forced and cannot breathe out; thus there are earthquakes. Now the Three Rivers* experience quakes; this is because *yang* has lost its place and is oppressed by *yin*. *Yang* falters and is in *yin*, hence the river's source is blocked. When the source of the river is blocked then the state will certainly perish. The water flows over the soil and the people use it. When the water does not flow over the soil then the people lack the use of wealth. How can it be that they do not perish? (*Sayings of the States* 1, *Sayings of Zhou* 1, pp. 26–27)†

This passage first mentions the *qi* of heaven and earth and then goes on to mention *yin* and *yang*, which are aspects of *qi*: *yang qi* and *yin qi*.

Yin-yang are used to explain the changes in the natural world in *Zuo's Commentary*:

> In Spring, five stones fell in Song; they were falling stars. Six ospreys flew backwards over the Song capital; this was due to the wind. Shu Xing, historiographer of the interior, was in Song, on a visit of friendly inquiries from Zhou, and Duke Xiang asked him about these strange appearances, saying, "What are they portents of? What fortune, good or bad, do they pre-

---

*The Wei, Jing, and Luo Rivers. The Wei and Jing meet just north of the modern city of Xi'an. The Luo joins them 100 kilometers downstream.

†For a full commentary and translation of the whole passage see A. d'Hormon and R. Mathieu, *Guoyu: Propos sur les principautes: Zhouyu* (Paris: Collège de France Institut des Hautes Etudes Chinoises, 1985), pp. 151–155.

dict?" The historiographer replied, "This year there will be the deaths of many great persons of Lu. Next year Qi will all be in disorder. Your lordship will get the presidency of the states, but will not continue to hold it." When he retired, he said to someone, "The king asked me the wrong question. It is not from these developments of the *yin* and *yang* that good fortune and evil are produced. They are produced by human beings themselves. I answered as I did because I did not venture to go against the duke's idea." (*Zuo's Commentary* 5, *Xi* 16, p. 170)

The pair are included among six *qi*, metereological phenomena, in a speech attributed to Doctor He:

Heaven has six *qi* ... the six *qi* are called *yin* and *yang*, wind and rain, darkness and brightness. (*Zuo's Commentary* 10, *Zhao* 1, p. 573)

The *Laozi* uses *yin* and *yang* to speak of the structure of the myriad things:

The Way generates the One; the One generates the Two; the Two generate the Three; the Three generate the myriad things. The myriad things rely on *yin* and embrace *yang* and through the blending of *qi* they come to harmony. (*Laozi* 42/MWD 25)

It is clear that *yin*, *yang* and their blending are all forms of *qi*.

The *Zhuangzi* refers to *qi* many times. *Yin* and *yang* are contrasted with human affairs, *yin-yang* being the factors of change in the natural world.

In all affairs, whether small or great, there are few who reach a successful result except through the Way. If you do not succeed you are sure to encounter disaster sent by human agency; if you do succeed you are sure to encounter the disaster of *yin* and *yang*. (*Zhuangzi* 4, *Worldly Business Among Humans*, line 36)

The context shows that the "disaster of *yin* and *yang*" is an internal fever such that the speaker, Zi Gao, duke of She, is forced to drink cold water.

Yin-yang are clearly related to the natural order in the following quotations. In the first Master Yu is ecstatic about the deformation of old age:

> "It must be some dislocation of *yin* and *yang*." Yet he seemed calm at heart and unconcerned. (*Zhuangzi* 6, *The Teacher Who Is the Ultimate Ancestor*, line 49)

Master Lai is equally happy about the changes involved in dying:

> A child obeys father and mother and goes east or west, south or north. To a human being how much more worthy of obedience are *yin* and *yang*. (Ibid., line 56)

From the later corpus of Zhuangzi we find *yin* and *yang* contrasted, as are movement and stillness:

> Stillness and *yin* have a common virtue; movement and *yang* have a common stream. (*Zhuangzi* 13, *The Way of Heaven*, line 14)

Or again, clear and muddy are allied with *yin* and *yang*:

> One clear, one muddy: *yin* and *yang* blend into harmony. (*Zhuangzi* 14, *Heaven's Movement*, line 17)

The *Autumn Floods* chapter sees the self as constituted by *yin* and *yang*:

> The self receives its form from heaven and earth and receives *qi* from *yin* and *yang*. I am within heaven and earth like a pebble or a bush on a great mountain. (*Zhuangzi* 17, *Autumn Floods*, line 9)

Yin-yang are two fundamental forms of *qi* that together constitute things:

> Heaven and earth are the greatest of forms; *yin* and *yang* are the greatest of *qi*. . . .
> *Yin* and *yang* mutually shine on each other, mutually cover each other, mutually melt into each other. The four seasons mutually succeed each other, mutually give life and deal death. (*Zhuangzi* 25, *Ze Yang*, lines 67, 69)

Thus from Bo Yang to *Zhuangzi*, *yin* and *yang* are forms of *qi*. They are the two *qi* that produce the myriad things of heaven and earth.

The *Book of Changes*

The concepts of *yin* and *yang* are essential to the commentaries of the *Book of Changes*. In a summary of the *Changes* contained in the last chapter of the *Zhuangzi*, it is said,

> The *Changes* discuss *yin* and *yang*. (*Zhuangzi* 33, *Under Heaven*, line 10)*

The *Commentaries* sometimes use the phrase *yang qi*:

> The dragon is hidden; do not act, *yang qi* is hidden away. . . .
> If *yin* puts itself on a par with *yang* there must be conflict.
> (*Literary Commentary*, pp. 10, 20)

The conflict in question is that between *yin* and *yang*. In the *Great Commentary*, *yin-yang* do not refer to two forms of *qi* but to two kinds of stuff.

> In the significance of *yin* and *yang* it matches the sun and moon. (*Great Commentary* 1.6, p. 282)
> The *yang* hexagrams have more *yin*; the *yin* hexagrams have more *yang*. Why is this so? (*Great Commentary* 2.4, p. 315)
> Are *qian* [hexagram of heaven] and *kun* [hexagram of earth] the door to the *Changes*? *Qian* is a *yang* thing, *kun* a *yin* thing. *Yang* and *yin* unite their properties and hard [unbroken] and soft [broken] lines are realized. (*Great Commentary* 2.6, p. 324)

---

*Author's note: Some scholars believe that this chapter of the *Zhuangzi* is an early Han text. It is also argued that the phrase quoted is a later interpolation. There is insufficient evidence to support these arguments. Translator's note: As Roth notes (H. Roth, "Who Compiled the Chuang Tzu?" in Rosemont, H. Jr., *Chinese Texts and Philosophical Contexts* [La Salle: Open Court, 1990], pp. 79–128), doubts about the authenticity of the chapter date from the eleventh-century poet Su Dongbo (1036–1101). See also A. C. Graham, *Disputers of the Tao* (La Salle: Open Court, 1989), pp. 374–376. Both Roth and Graham argue in support of a Han dating.

Here it is not *yang qi* and *yin qi* but *yang* nature and *yin* nature. This marks a further stage in raising *yin* and *yang* to abstract status. *Yin-yang* also embrace the opposition of correct and incorrect and their synthesis:

> The alternation of *yin* and *yang* is called the Way....
>
> What *yin-yang* do not fathom is called the numinous. (*Great Commentary* 1.5, pp. 280, 281)
>
> Establishing the way of heaven is called *yin* and *yang*; establishing the way of earth is called soft and hard; establishing the way of humans is called benevolence and justice. (*Treatise of Remarks on the Trigrams* 2, p. 340)

The fourth-century commentator Han Kangbo (A.D. 317–420) annotated the preceding passage as follows:

> In heaven it forms symbols; on earth it becomes forms. *Yin* and *yang* are said of its *qi*; soft and hard are said of its form. Change and transformation begin with the phenomena of *qi* and then perfect forms. The stuff of the myriad things begins with heaven, becomes form on earth; thus of heaven *yin-yang* is said and of earth soft-hard is said. (*Collected Editions of the Book of Changes*, 3:346)

Yin and *yang* originally refer to *qi*. The rule of change of the two forms of *qi* is called the Way. Thus taken together *yin* and *yang* refer to two natures.

From the Late Warring States Era to the Early Han

The *Guanzi* portrays *yin-yang* as two forms of *qi* but also as principle, that is, as the fundamental division of the universe.

> *Yin-yang* are the great principle of heaven and earth. The four seasons are the great thread of *yin-yang*....
>
> The east is called 'star'; its season is called 'spring'; its *qi* is called 'wind'; ... the south is called 'sun'; its season is called 'summer'; its *qi* is called *yang*; ... the west is called 'planet'; its season is called 'autumn'; its *qi* is called *yin*; ... the north is called 'moon'; its season is called 'winter'; its *qi* is called 'cold.' (*Guanzi* 40, *The Four Seasons*, 2:48, 49, 50, 52, 53)

The great principle of heaven and earth can be understood as the fundamental division of all reality. Another chapter of the *Guanzi* describes principle as making clear distinctions:

> Principle is what clarifies and distinguishes by showing the meaning of what is right. (*Guanzi* 36, *Technique of the Heart A*, 2:7)

Hence, in the *Guanzi, yin* and *yang* are the fundamental division in the world.

The most famous early exponent of *yin-yang* was Zou Yan. Unfortunately, his works are lost, but we know that he made the two principles the basis of his whole system. This was to have a profound influence on Dong Zhongshu in the Han dynasty. Zou Yan's system is described in the *Records of the Historian*:

> He entered deeply into the expansion and contraction of *yin* and *yang* and with strange and torturous meanderings wrote *Ending and Beginning, Great Sageliness*, works of over 100,000 characters. (*Records of the Historian* 74, *Biographies of Mencius and Xun Qing*, p. 2344)

Dong Zhongshu took up Zou Yan's work in a Confucian context. Six chapters of his magnum opus mention *yin-yang* in their titles. By *yin-yang*, Dong refers to *yin qi* and *yang qi*.

> *Yang qi* begins to come out of the earth in the first month. It generates, nutures, causes to grow and fosters all that is above until its task is accomplished and then it collects in the tenth month.... Thus *yang qi* emerges in the northeast and reenters in the northwest. It emerges in the beginning of spring and ends in the beginning of winter and of things none does not respond to it. (*Luxuriant Gems of the Spring and Autumn Annals* 43, *Yang Is Noble; Yin Is Humble*, p. 324)
>
> *Yang qi* begins to come out in the northeast and travels southwards until it reaches its place. It turns west and reenters in the north and is stored in its resting-place. *Yin qi* begins to come out in the southeast and travels northwards also until it reaches its place. It turns west and reenters in the south, con-

cealing its excellence. (Ibid. 47, *The Place of Yin and Yang*, pp. 337–338)

The Way of Heaven comes to its end and begins again at the beginning; thus the north is where heaven both ends and begins, where *yin* and *yang* are united and also differentiated. (Ibid. 48, *The Ending and Beginning of Yin-Yang*, p. 339)

The constancy of heaven and earth is the alternation of *yin* and *yang*. *Yang* is the virtue of heaven; *yin* is the punishment of heaven. (Ibid. 49, *The Significance of Yin-Yang*, p. 341)

The great rule of the Way of Heaven is the mutual opposition of things. Not obtaining both at once, this is *yin-yang*. In spring *yang* emerges and *yin* goes in; in autumn *yin* emerges and *yang* enters. (Ibid. 50, *Yin-Yang Emerging and Entering Above and Below*, p. 342)

Dong Zhongshu understood *yin* and *yang* very specifically as forms of *qi*, one cold, the other warm. Their movement constitutes the four seasons.

The Song Era

In writing the *Explanation of the Diagram of the Supreme Ultimate*, Zhou Dunyi took the supreme ultimate together with *yin* and *yang* as the constitutive factors of the generation and growth of the myriad things:

The limitless and the supreme ultimate. The supreme ultimate moves and generates *yang*. When its movement comes to a peak then it becomes tranquil. It becomes tranquil and generates *yin*. When its tranquility comes to a peak it returns to movement. Movement and tranquility alternate and become the root of the each other, separating into *yin* and *yang* and so establishing the two modes.... The interaction of the two forms of *qi* transform and generate the myriad things. The myriad things sprout up again and again and change without end. (*SKQS* 1101, *Explanation of the Diagram of the Supreme Ultimate*, pp. 416b–418a)

Yin and *yang* are the two *qi* generated by the supreme ultimate. They are two forms of *qi*:

> Heaven by *yang* generates the myriad things, by *yin* brings them to completion. (*SKQS* 1101, *Book of Comprehending* 11, *Harmony and Transformation*, p. 426a)

Sometimes Zhou Dunyi uses the terms to refer to substances that are *yin* or *yang*:

> Water is *yin* and rooted in *yang*; fire is *yang* and rooted in *yin*. The five agents are but *yin* and *yang* and these are the supreme ultimate. (Ibid. 16, *Activity and Tranquility*, p. 428a)

Water and fire are two of the five elements. One is *yin*, the other *yang*. *Yin* and *yang* depend on each other so that the *yin* element, water, is rooted in *yang*, and the converse is true for fire.

Zhang Zai sometimes refers to *yin-yang* as two forms of *qi*, sometimes as two forms of nature. He calls them 'two ends,' that is, two aspects:

> Flowing *qi* moves in all directions, unites and forms concrete objects, generates the myriad variety of humans and things. Its two 'ends' of *yin-yang* in their unending succession establish the great meaning of heaven and earth. . . .
>
> In what making and transforming produces no one thing is like another. From this one knows that although the number of things is infinite, in truth there is one thing which is without *yin* or *yang*.* By this one knows that the transformations and changes in the universe are due to these two 'ends.' (*SKQS* 697, *Correcting the Unenlightened* 1, *Ultimate Harmony*, pp. 10a, 100b)

The 'two ends' stand for two aspects or two kinds of nature. In the next quotation *yin* and *yang* are two kinds of *qi*:

> The earth is pure *yin*; it congeals in the center. Heaven floats in *yang*; it turns and eddies outside. This is the constant nature of heaven and earth. (Ibid. 2, *Trinity and Duality*, p. 101b)

---

* Author's note: The standard text reads: "there is nothing without *yin* or *yang*."

Zhang Zai also talks of the essence of *yin* and *yang*, the two aspects in their pure form, that is, the sun and moon, and contrasts this with their *qi*.

> The essence of *yin* and *yang* conceals the dwelling-place of the other, yet each has its resting place; thus the form of sun and moon has not changed from of old. As for the *qi* of *yin* and *yang*, it turns around, decreases and reaches a peak, gathering and scattering, mingling together, rising and falling, depending one on the other, weaving in and out, mixing together, now side by side, now one dominant over the other. If one wanted to unite them one could not do so. This is why its *qi* contracts and expands without limit, revolves round and moves without ceasing with nothing impelling it to be so. If this is not the principle of life and nature, what is it? (Ibid., p. 105a)

Thus the *qi* of the two aspects is what enables them to interact. The characteristic of each form of *qi* is stated thus:

> The nature of *yin* is to crystallize and condense; the nature of *yang* is to spread out and scatter. (Ibid., p. 106a)

Moreover, he states explicitly that *yin* and *yang* are aspects of *qi*:

> *Qi* has *yin-yang*, its pushing movement brings about a decrease, which leads to transformation. (*SKQS* 697, *Correcting the Unenlightened 4, Wondrous and Transformation*, p. 108b)

In short, Zhang Zai talks of *yin-yang* sometimes as two forms of *qi*, sometimes as two forms of nature.*

Cheng Yi emphasizes that *yin-yang* are *qi*:

> Apart from *yin-yang* there is definitely no Way, so *yin* and *yang* are the Way. *Yin* and *yang* are *qi*. *Qi* is what is below form; the Way is what is above form. (*SKQS* 698, *Surviving Works of the Two Chengs* 15, p. 128b)

In this he was followed by Zhu Xi.

---

*Kasoff (*Thought of Chang Tsai*, pp. 49–53) shows that Zhang Zai understood the relationship of *yin* and *yang* both as cyclical (night and day) and as interactive (union of male and female).

The Ming-Qing Era

In the Ming dynasty He Tang used *yin-yang* to stand for the spiritual and the material, respectively.

> The way of making and transforming is only the alternation of *yin* and *yang*. *Yang* moves and *yin* is still; *yang* is bright and *yin* is dark; *yang* is knowing and *yin* lacks knowing; *yang* has form and *yin* is formless; *yang* lacks substance and takes *yin* as its substance; *yin* has no use and depends on *yang* to obtain use. When the two unite together then things are produced, when they separate then things die. . . .
>
> *Yang* is spirit; *yin* is material form. Form gathers and so is visible, scatters and is then invisible. Spirit does not have the features of gathering and scattering, thus it is never visible. (*Bai Ling Xue Shan*, fascicule 3.8, *Yin-Yang Guan Jian*, pp. 1a, 4b)

Although on the surface this text seems to be about *yin* and *yang*, it is in fact concerned with the relation between spirit and matter. He Tang believed in a creator spirit:

> The human being has a body of blood and flesh; what then allows one to know, judge, feel and respond? It is from the spirit of the human heart/mind. From whence comes this spirit of the heart/mind? It is from the spirit of the creator. (*Scholarly Records of Ming Scholars* 49, *Yin Yang Guan Jian Hou Yu*)

This manifestly dualist theory received criticism from Wang Tingxiang.

> Taking the spirit as *yang* and the form as *yin*, this theory comes from the Buddha's fairy tales. It is erroneous. The spirit must depend on the form and *qi* in order to exist. If there is no form or *qi* then the spirit is destroyed. Inasmuch as it does exist, it must depend on *qi* that has not yet been scattered in order to appear, as the light of a fire must rely on some object before it can be seen. If there is no object how can there be fire? (*Col-*

lected Works of Wang Tingxiang 3, *Collected Inner Terrace* 4, *Reply to He Bozhai's Theory of Creation*, 963–964)

Wang claimed that spirit cannot be independent of form. He also held that *yin* and *yang* were both forms of *qi* and that *qi* was essentially something that was able to change:

> *Yin* and *yang* are *qi*. Change and transformation are the impetus and so the impetus is the numinous. (Ibid., *Prudent Words* 1, *The Substance of the Way*, p. 754)

Further on in the same text, he writes,

> *Yin* and *yang* are the substance of *qi*. Opening, closing, moving, staying still are the potentialities of nature. Contracting, expanding, mutually influencing each other are the products of the impetus. Mingling and interacting and then transforming are the subtlety of the numinous. (Ibid.)

The impetus to change and transform is inherent in *qi*. In a preceding text, Wang posited four levels at which *yin* and *yang* are to be distinguished:

> Within form and *qi*, *yin-yang* have four stages of signification. From the point of view of form there are things such as heaven and earth, man and woman, male and female. From the point of view of *qi* there are things such as cold and heat, day and night, breathing in and out. Taken overall, whatever pertains to *qi* is *yang*; whatever pertains to form is *yin*. Taken precisely, whatever has form and substance even up to the *qi* which is clouds and vapor with a shape is *yin*; any change, transformation, movement, rising and falling, flying around that is invisible is *yang* (Ibid., p. 752)

Notice that the invisible is not independent of the visible, as it was in He Tang. In conclusion, *yin* and *yang* were two forms of *qi*, cold and hot, but in later philosophy they were used as the master concepts for expressing the paired nature of reality. This development began in the *Commentaries to the* Book of Changes and continued especially in the works of Zhang Zai.

12. Five Agents

Wu Xing NGŨ HÀNH

五行

The five agents, or elements, become intimately associated with yin-yang *theory in the Han dynasty. They have an independent origin, however, and mid–Warring States works do not use them along with* yin-yang *theory. The locus classicus for a mention of the five agents is the* Great Plan *chapter of the* Book of History. *The dating of this chapter has long been a subject of dispute, and the question remains a live one even today. As will be seen, Professor Zhang upholds the antiquity of the chapter.*

The Spring and Autumn Period

The earliest reference to the five agents is in the *Book of History*. The emperor of the Xia dynasty (2183–1751 B.C.) said,

> Ah! all you who are in my six armies, I have a solemn announcement to make to you. The prince of Hu wildly wastes and despises the five agents and has idly abandoned the three acknowledged beginnings of the year.* On this account heaven is about to destroy him and bring an end to the favor it has shown him. (*Book of History* 3.2, *The Speech at Gan*, pp. 152–53)

The context of the passage does not permit one to understand what is intended by the phrase "the five agents."

The new text version of the book includes the *Great Plan* chapter among the books of Zhou, but *Zuo's Commentary* quotes it as a book of Shang, the dynasty that preceded the Zhou.† In the *Great Plan* the vis-

---

*Legge (*Chinese Classics*, III: 154 n) explains the three beginnings as the first months of the Xia, Shang, and Zhou dynasties but assumes that these calendars had all been used by the time of the Xia. It is much more credible to suppose the speech to be anachronistic.

†The first emperor of Qin burnt many books in 212. Later scholars reconstructed them from memory or from remaining passages; hence they were called "new texts." Later some copies of the same texts were unearthed from hiding places, and these were called "old texts." Han scholars had bitter disputes as to which texts were superior in quality.

count of Ji talks of the "great plan with nine divisions" granted to Yu. The first of the nine divisions is called the 'five agents':

> First, the five agents: the first is called 'water'; the second is called 'fire'; the third is called 'wood'; the fourth is called 'metal'; the fifth is called 'earth'. Water is called 'what flows down'; fire is called 'what blazes up'; wood is called 'what is bent or straight'; metal is called 'what is malleable and changeable'; earth is what is sowed and from which the harvest is gathered. What flows down becomes salty; what blazes up becomes bitter; what is bent or straight becomes sour; what is malleable and changeable becomes acrid; what is sown and the source of the harvest produces what is sweet. (*Book of History* 5.4, *The Great Plan*, pp. 325–326)

Here the characteristics of each of the agents is set out. The fact that the five agents are expounded as the first of the nine divisions is proof of their fundamental status.

In the 1920s various scholars claimed that the *Great Plan* was not an early text but a work of the Warring States period. There is insufficient evidence for this suspicion, however. The *Great Plan* is quoted in *Zuo's Commentary* by several of the nobles. In 621 B.C. Ying of Ning said,

> In the *Books of Shang* it is said, "For the reserved and retiring there is the rigorous rule; for the lofty and intelligent there is the mild rule.' (*Zuo's Commentary* 6, *Wen* 5, p. 240)

In 584 B.C. Luan Shu, also known as Wu Zi, of Jin quoted the *Books of Shang*, saying,

> When three men divine, the two (with the same result) should be followed. (*Zuo's Commentary* 8, *Cheng* 6, p. 359)

Zuo himself, writing in the early Warring States period, quoted the book in his assessment of Qi Xi:

> The *Books of Shang* say, "Without partiality and without deflection, broad and long is the royal path." (Ibid. 9, Xiang 3)

These quotations do prove that the *Great Plan* is not a Warring States work but is from early Zhou times.

Zuo's Commentary also makes other references to the five agents. In 516 B.C. Zi Taishu quoted Zichan, saying,

> Imitate the brightness of heaven; go along with the nature of earth. [Heaven and earth] will produce their six *qi* and [you] may use their five agents. (Ibid. 10, *Zhao* 25, p. 704)

The historiographer Mo of Jin explained that things occur in twos, threes, fives, or pairs:

> Thus heaven has the three celestial bodies [sun, moon, stars]; earth has the five agents; the body has left and right; each person has a partner. (Ibid., *Zhao* 32, p. 739)

It is worth underlining that the five agents in these texts are attributed to the earth, whereas to heaven belong the six *qi* and the three celestial bodies. The five agents are fundamental to the earth but are not yet seen as the building blocks of the whole universe.

Zuo's Commentary also mentions five materials. Zi Han of Song argued that it is not possible to unilaterally abolish weapons:

> Heaven produces the five materials; the people use them all. It is not possible to exclude any one of them. Who can abolish weapons? (Ibid. 9, *Xiang* 27, p. 531)

The five materials are the five necessary things, that is, the five agents.

The *Xunzi*

The *Xunzi* is critical of Zi Si's and Mencius' theory of the five agents.

> Some roughly imitate the early kings while not knowing their basic principles. Still their abilities are evident, their memory excellent and their experience and learning very varied and broad. They have concocted a theory which they claim to be ancient and call it the Five Agents theory. It is very misguided and without reason, secretive and unjustifiable, esoteric and incomprehensible. To make their theory sound respectable and to win respect for it they claim, "These are the authentic words of the Gentleman [Confucius] of former times. Zi Si provided

the music for [elaborated on] them and Mencius harmonized [systematized] them. The foolish, vacillating and deluded modern Confucians, not realizing that these ideas are false, welcome them warmly. They hand on what they have received believing that, by virtue of these theories, Confucius and Zi You [Zi Gong]* would be highly honored by later generations. It is precisely on this point that they offend against Zi Si and Mencius." (*Xunzi* 6, *Contra 12 Philosophers*, lines 10–14)

Yang Jing notes in his commentary,

The five agents are the five constant things, that is, benevolence, justice, rites, wisdom and trust. (*Zhuzi Jicheng: Xunzi*, p. 59)

Zi Si is traditionally credited with the authorship of the *Mean and Harmony*. This text talks of wisdom, benevolence, and courage as the three virtues. The *Mencius* talks of four virtues: benevolence, justice, rites, and wisdom. It does not describe them as five virtues. The *Mean and Harmony* and the *Mencius* most certainly do not mention water, fire, wood, metal, and earth. It is thus hard to see why the *Xunzi* should criticize Zi Si and the *Mencius*. The five virtues or the five agents are also easily understood, so it is not clear why the *Xunzi* should refer to them as obscure. It would seem that we have insufficient information to fully understand the *Xunzi*'s argument.

The Sequence of the Five

Zou Yan used the succession of the five agents as a historical hermeneutical tool:

Zou Yan ... set out what had happened from the time heaven and earth were split apart, the five virtues moved around, each ruling what was appropriate to it and according to what responded to it. (*Records of the Historian* 74, *Biographies of Mencius and Xun Qing*, p. 2344)

---

* "Zi You" should read "Zi Gong." See Yang Liu Qiao, *Xunzi Guyi* (Jinan: Qi-Lu, 1985), pirated in Taiwan and published at Xinzhu by Yangzhe in 1987, p. 119 n. 31.

In a note to the *Selections of Refined Literature* by Xiao Tong (A.D. 501–531), Li Shan (d. 689)* comments on Zou Yan:

> The *Seven Categories* says, "Master Zou traced the five virtues from beginning to end, following that which was not overcome [earth]. The virtue of wood succeeded it, the virtue of metal came next, the virtue of fire next, the virtue of water next." (*Selections of Refined Literature* 6, *Wei Capital Rhapsody*, p. 166)

Li Shan also quotes Zou Yan's own writings on the succession of the early dynasties:

> The "Master Zou" writes, "The five virtues follow what is not overcome: Yu was earth; Xia was wood; Yin was metal; Zhou was fire. (Ibid. 59, *Memorial Engraving for King Zhao of Qi at An Lu*, p. 1457)

Thus for Zou Yan history proceeds by mutual suppression of the five elements in turn.

The *Sunzi* may represent an earlier understanding of the five agents according to which there was no necessary sequence:

> Thus the five agents do not have constant ascendencies. (*Sunzi* 6, *Emptiness and Fullness*, p. 153)

The *Mohist Canons* echo the same theme:

> The five agents do not have constant ascendencies. Explained by: what it is said of. (*Mohist Canons* B43 [C], p. 411)

The explanation of this canon states:

> That fire melts wood is because there is much fire; that metal uses up charcoal is because there is much metal.† (*Mohist Canons* B43 [E], p. 411)

Văn Tuyền

* D. R. Knechtges, *Wen Xuan or Selections of Refined Literature* (Princeton: Princeton University Press, 1982), p. 53. Li Shan was from Yangzhou and was on the staff of the crown prince, probably Li Hong. He was posted to the College for Honouring Worthies. His commentary was presented to Emperor Gaozong (650–683) in 658.

† This reading is based on that of A. C. Graham.

Whereas Zou Yan held that the five agents succeeded each other according to a necessary sequence, the Mohist logicians believed that the reason for succession was the greater quantity of one of the five.

Dong Zhongshu wrote about the generative sequence of the five and about their sequence of ascendency. He established their order as wood, fire, earth, metal, and water:

> Heaven has five agents: the first is called 'wood'; the second is called 'fire'; the third is called 'earth'; the fourth is called 'metal'; the fifth is called 'water.' Wood is the beginning of the five agents; water is the ending of the five agents; earth is the center of the five agents. This is their heaven-sent order. Wood generates fire; fire generates earth; earth generates metal; metal generates water; water generates wood. (*Luxuriant Gems of the Spring and Autumn Annals* 42, *The Meaning of the Five Agents*, p. 321)

The sequence of ascendencies was as follows:

> Metal overcomes wood.... Water overcomes fire.... Wood overcomes earth.... Fire overcomes metal.... Earth overcomes water. (Ibid. 58, *The Mutual Generation of the Five Agents*, p. 362)

Thus those next to each other in the sequence produce each other but those separated by one element in the sequence overcome each other:

> The *qi* of heaven and earth unites and becomes one, separates into *yin* and *yang*, divides into the four seasons, spreads out into the five agents. The agents are what act but their actions are different; thus there are said to be five agents.... Adjoining ones generate each other and alternate ones overcome each other. (Ibid.)

Dong also matched the five agents with the four seasons:

> Water is winter; metal is autumn; earth is the last month of summer; fire is summer; wood is spring. Spring oversees sprouting; summer oversees growing; the last month of summer oversees fostering; autumn oversees gathering; winter

oversees storing. (Ibid. 38, *The Response to the Five Agents*, p. 315)

Here earth has been forced into the middle position among the four seasons.*

The Song Period

Song-dynasty thinkers did not adopt Dong's sequence but retained the sequence of the *Great Plan*.† Zhou Dunyi gave the cosmological order as the supreme ultimate, *yin-yang*, the five agents, and the myriad things. *Yin-yang* were two kinds of *qi* and the five agents five kinds of *qi*:

> *Yang* changes and *yin* unites and this produces water, fire, wood, metal and earth. The five *qi* flow out in sequence; the four seasons run their course thereby.... The interaction of the two forms of *qi* transform and generate the myriad things. The myriad things sprout up again and again and change without ceasing. (*SKQS* 1101, *Explanation of the Diagram of the Supreme Ultimate*, pp. 417a, 417b–418a)

Wang Anshi‡ wrote a commentary to the *Great Plan* in which he gives a detailed analysis of the five agents:

> The five agents are that by which heaven decrees the myriad things, thus first of all they are called the five agents ... the first

---

* On attempts to reconcile items four and five see Kanaya Osamu, *The Establishment of the Yin-yang, Five Agents' Theory, Zhongguo zhexueshi yanjiu* (1988.3, 22–7).

† In the Qing dynasty Adam Schall (1591–1666) was denounced for following the *Great Plan* sequence rather than the "correct" order of Dong Zhongshu. See the *Veritable Records of Kangxi* year 4 (1665) reference to Yang Guangxian's *Discourse on Fallacies* in the Imperial Archives, Beijing.

‡ Wang Anshi (1021–1086). *Zi:* Jie Fu, from Fuzhou, later in Linchuan, Jiangxi Province. Known as Mr. Linchuan, he was one of the few statesmen of his time to make economic and fiscal issues matters of prime importance. His attitude toward the classics was to capture the intention of the sages and apply their principles to modern situations. He rose to highest office in the 1070s but aroused the opposition of Zhang Zai and Cheng Hao, among others, for his policies, which demanded greater state intervention in the economic life of the country. See H. R. Williamson, *Wang An Shih: A Chinese Statesman and Educationalist of the Sung Dynasty* (London: Probsthain, 1935).

is called 'water'; the second is called 'fire'; the third is called 'wood'; the fourth is called 'metal'; the fifth is called 'earth.' What are they? The five agents accomplish change and transformation and cause ghosts and spirits to act, they come and go within heaven and earth without ceasing and thus are called 'agents.' ... As things the five agents each have their corresponding season, place, material, *qi*, nature, form, affair, features, color, note, smell and taste. This forms a network of correspondences and the changes of the myriad things proceed without ceasing. Their mutually producing each other is that by which they succeed each other. Their mutually taking precedence over each other is that by which they regulate each other. (*SKQS* 1105, *Collected Writings of Lin Chuan* 65, *Commentary on the* Great Plan, pp. 526b, 527a, 527b, 528a)

Wang differentiated the characteristics of the five agents as set forth in the *Great Plan* as corresponding to nature, form, *qi*, and so on:

Flowing down [water] is nature; blazing up [fire] is *qi*; above and below is place; bent and straight [wood] is form; changeable and malleable [metal] is material; sowing and harvesting [earth] is human affairs. (Ibid., p. 528a)

Whereas Zhou Dunyi believed that the five agents were five kinds of *qi*, Zhu Xi tended to say:

Yin-yang are *qi*; the five agents are stuff....
  "*Yang* changes and *yin* unites": first are generated water and fire. Water and fire are *qi*. It flows, moves, glistens and shines, its substance is yet diffuse, its taking form is not yet determined. Next are produced wood and metal and these, on the other hand, have determinate form. Water and fire are at first self-generated. Wood and metal, by contrast, receive their stuff from earth. All the five metals and their like are produced out of the earth. (*Conversations of Master Zhu Arranged Topically* 94, p. 2377)

Overall, it would seem that Zhu Xi believed water and fire to be somehow intermediate between *qi* and form, whereas wood and metal were clearly stuff. By 'stuff' is understood that which has determinate form.

Thus in the early period of Chinese philosophy it was reckoned that the five agents were five fundamental elements in human life. After Dong Zhongshu thinkers took them as constitutive of the myriad things but not the most elementary constituents. The five agents were subordinate to heaven-earth, *yin-yang*.

II. Concepts of Growth

13. One, the Ultimate One

Yi, Tai Yi   NHẤT , THÁI NHẤT

一, 太一

'One' is an important category of Chinese philosophy. Confucius stressed this thread of his teaching:

> The Master said, "Ah, Shan!* It is 'one' that threads through my way." Master Zeng said, "Yes." The Master went out. The disciples asked, saying, "What did he mean?" Master Zeng said, "The Master's Way is but loyalty and compassion." (*Analects* 4, *Li Ren* #15, p. 169)
>
> The Master said, "Si!† Do you think that in studying with me you will learn a lot?" He replied, "Yes, is it not so?" Confucius replied, "Not so. Take 'one' to thread through it all." (*Analects* 15, *Duke Ling of Wei* #2, p. 295)

Confucius is saying that there is only one thing to be grasped and that learning is knowing this one and not accumulating lots of knowledge about things. The one is spoken of from an epistemological point of view.

The *Laozi* uses 'one' as a cosmological principle. The most fundamental principle is the Way, but this generates the 'one,' which in turn gives rise to heaven and earth (the two) and thence to *yin-yang* and *qi* (the three) and so to the myriad things:‡

---

* Zeng Shan, one of the most respected of Confucius' disciples. See Legge, *Chinese Classics* I:117–118.
† Duanmu Si, known as Zi Gong, a disciple of Confucius who occupied government posts in two states. See Legge, *Chinese Classics* I:115–116.
‡ See concept 2, the Way.

> The Way generates the One; the One generates the Two.
> (*Laozi* 42/MWD 5)

The one is the unity that existed before heaven and earth split apart. The term 'generate' is to be taken as a metaphor indicating a temporal relation and not in the sense of a mother giving birth to a child. Before the *Laozi* people all thought that heaven and earth were what was most fundamental. The *Laozi* suggests that there was a time before heaven and earth had established their distinct identities and this is what he calls the one. The one is not, though, the most fundamental. It is the Way that is the foundation of all. This is the meaning of "the Way generates the One; the One generates the Two."

Alongside this cosmological use is a use wherein 'one' refers to the integral unity of any given thing:

> When bearing on your head your troubled sprite can you embrace the One and not let go? (*Laozi* 10/MWD 54)
>
> > Thus the sage embraces the One and is the model for under-heaven. (*Laozi* 22/MWD 67)

The one is a substitute for the Way in chapter 39:

> Formerly of things that obtained the One:
> Heaven obtained the One and became clear;
> Earth obtained the One and became tranquil;
> Spirits obtained the One and became numinous;
> Valleys obtained the One and became full;
> The myriad things obtained the One and sprouted into life;
> Princes and kings obtained the One and became the standard
> > for under-heaven. (*Laozi* 39/MWD 2)

The final chapter of the *Zhuangzi* summarizes the teaching of Guan Zhong and Laozi in these words:

> They established it [their doctrine] on constancy, beingless and being and oversaw it by the Ultimate and the One. (*Zhuangzi* 33, *Under Heaven*, line 55)

According to this statement constancy, beingless, and being are fundamental concepts, whereas the ultimate and the One are important but not fundamental concepts. Notice that the ultimate and the One are to be read as two things. The ultimate is the Way and the one is what is generated by the Way.

> I do not know its name. Its appelation is 'the Way.' If pressed I shall call it 'the Ultimate.'* (*Laozi* 25/MWD 69)

The two terms 'ultimate' and 'one' are combined into one expression in *Mr. Lu's Spring and Autumn Annals*, dating from the late Warring States period:

> The Way is what is quintessential. It is not possible to shape it or name it. If pressed it may be called the 'Ultimate One.' (*Mr. Lu's Spring and Autumn Annals* 5.2, *Ultimate Joy*, p. 256)

The same terminology is found in the early Han work the *Huainanzi*:

> Penetrating to the common identity of heaven-earth, the cosmic soup as the uncarved block, not yet made and forming a thing, it is called the 'Ultimate One.' (*Huainanzi* 14, *Shuan Yan*, p. 132, line 10)

From a similar period comes the *Record of Rites*:

> Therefore these rites must be rooted in the ultimate One. They separate into heaven and earth, circle to become *yin-yang*, change into the four seasons, spread out as ghosts and spirits. (*Record of Rites* 9, *Evolution of Rites*, p. 128)

The Tang commentator Kong Yingda notes,

> It is said of heaven and earth having not yet separated and is the cosmic soup of the original *qi*. It is the greatest and thus it is called 'ultimate'; it has not yet separated and so it is called 'one.' Its *qi* is the greatest and is not yet separated and so it is called the 'ultimate one.' (*SKQS* 115, *The Correct Meaning of the* Book of Rites 22, *Evolution of Rites*, p. 473b)

---

*The character for 'great' (*da*) and that for 'the ultimate' (*tai*) are normally written the same way. Here it should be read *tai*.

In other words, the 'ultimate one' is the state of heaven and earth before they were separated.*

There is a process of evolution from the Way of Laozi to the ultimate one of *Mr. Lu's Spring and Autumn Annals*, the *Huainanzi*, and *Record of Rites*.

> Sometimes the term 'ultimate one' is simply described as 'one.'

> The Way begins with the One. The One does not generate; thus it separates into *yin* and *yang*. *Yin* and *yang* harmonize and join and the myriad things sprout into life. Thus it is said, "The One generates the Two; the Two generate the Three; the Three generate the myriad things." (*Huainanzi* 3, *Heavenly Patterns*, p. 25, lines 17–18)

This text quotes the *Laozi* but omits the phrase "the Way generates the One" and thus considers the Way and the one identical. The point is made even more explicit in another text:

> This non-acting, however, is obtained by the One. The One is the root of the myriad things and the Way without compare. (*Huainanzi* 14, *Shuan Yan*, p. 137, line 8)

The *Explanation of the Characters* is indebted to the *Laozi* for its definition of the one. It does not say, though, that the Way generated the one. Rather, the one and the Way coexist without temporal or logical priority being granted to either.

> At the very start of the ultimate beginning the Way stood by the One. It made and separated into heaven and earth, transformed and formed the myriad things. (*Explanation of the Characters*, p. 7a)

---

*J. Legge argues that the phrase "the ultimate one," which he translates as "the Supreme One," must refer in some sense to the "Almighty One who rules over all things." Legge, *Li Chi: Book of Rites* (1885; reprint, New York: University Books, 1967), pp. 386–388.

14. Origin

Yuan NGUYEN

元

The term 'origin' is similar to the 'one.' Dong Zhongshu writes,

> What is called the one origin is the great beginning. (*Luxuriant Gems of the Spring and Autumn Annals* 4, *Jade Courage*, p. 67)
>
> In the *Spring and Autumn Annals* what is more valuable than the origin and what is said of it? The origin is the beginning. (Ibid. 6, *Kingly Way*, p. 100)
>
> Only the sage can relate the myriad things to the One and tie them to the Origin.... Therefore the *Spring and Autumn Annals* change 'one' and call it the origin. The origin is like the source. Its meaning is bound up with following the beginning and ending of heaven and earth.... Thus the origin is the root of the myriad things and the origin of human beings lies within it. In what way is it in it? It is in it before heaven and earth existed. (Ibid. 13, *Emphasising Administration*, p. 147)

The Qing edition of the *Luxuriant Gems of the Spring and Autumn Annals* by Su Yu notes that Dong's analysis of the 'one' and the 'origin' is based on the observation that the *annals* always refer to the first year of a ruler's reign as the "inaugural [original] year" rather than as the "first year." (*Correct Meaning of the* Luxuriant Gems of the Spring and Autumn Annals 4, *Jade Courage*, p. 67)

In later Chinese philosophical discourse there are references to the one origin or two or many origins. This corresponds in some ways to Western monist, dualist, or pluralist theories. The term 'origin' in each case retains its meaning of the root of the myriad things.

15. Life

Sheng SINH

生

The character sheng *represents a shoot sprouting out of the ground. It is used to talk about all forms of life and coming into life. In the West the dominant image of life is not the sprouting of the plant but the birth of the mammal. Thus* sheng *is often translation as "being born." The contrast of metaphors is not trivial. The birth of a mammal is a dramatic change that we humans recall in parties, whereas the sprouting of the plant is a subtle process that does not draw attention to itself in the same way. Chinese cosmology is marked by this latter image, the slow emergence or generation of the myriad things from the primal cosmic soup.*

Generation, Life, Living Beings, Existence

The term 'life' is applied to all stages of growth from its first emergence to its changes and continuing existence.

Early definitions confirm this picture.

i. Generation

> To generate is to advance, like plants and trees sprout up from the ground. (*Explanation of the Characters* 6B, *Sheng*, p. 127b)
>> To generate is to emerge. (*Guang Ya* 3, *Shi Gu*)

ii. Life

> Plants and trees have life but not knowledge. (*Xunzi* 9, *Kingly Rule*, line 69)

Sheng may be combined with *ming*, 'destiny,' to form a compound:

Shang* has heard it said that death and life are determined by fate, riches and honor and come from heaven. (*Analects* 12, *Yan Yuan* #5, p. 253)

In general whatever is said to live within heaven and earth is said to have a destiny. (*Record of Rites* 23, *Code of Sacrifices*, p. 253)

iii. Living Beings

Kong Yingda opens his preface to the *Book of Songs* by saying:

These odes are songs which speak of effort and praise virtue. They are counsels that put a stop to wrongdoing and prevent evils. Even though they do not act yet they have influence of themselves and then spread to all living beings. (*SKQS* 69 *Preface to the Correct Meaning of the* Book of Songs, p. 47a)

iv. Existence

The way of long life and seeing more days. (*Laozi* 59/MWD 22)

The sequence of the four seasons and the generation of the myriad things is the fundamental operation of heaven and earth, according to Confucius:

What does heaven say? The four seasons circulate and the hundred things are generated. (*Analects* 17, *Yang Huo* #19, p. 326)

Confucius' attention was directed toward human affairs rather than to ghosts, toward what is alive rather than to what might happen after death:

Ji Lu† asked about sacrificing to ghosts and spirits. The Master said, "If one cannot yet serve human beings why ask about serving ghosts?" "Dare I ask about death?" He replied, "If one does not yet know about life how can one know about death?" (*Analects* 11, *Xian Jin* #11, p. 240)

---

* Bu Shang, called Zi Xia, known as a man who read much but lacked deep understanding. See Legge, *Chinese Classics* 1:117.

† Zhong You, called Zi Lu or Ji Lu, a disciple of Confucius. See Legge, *Chinese Classics* 1:114–115.

'Generation' became an important philosophical concept in the *Commentaries to the* Book of Changes. The *Great Commentary* says,

> Generation and regeneration are what is meant by the *Changes*. (*Book of Changes: Great Commentary* 1.5, p. 280)

Han Kangbo notes that

> *Yin-yang* change and revolve so as to complete, transform and generate. (*SKQS* 7, *Book of Changes: Great Commentary* 1, p. 530b)

Kong Yingda adds to this note:

> Generation and regeneration do not stop in their course. *Yin-yang* change and turn: the later is generated while the former is generated; thus the myriad things are ever generated. This is what is meant by the *Changes*. (Ibid., p. 531b)

Here generation is a continuous process of sprouting into life. The *Great Commentary* also says,

> The great virtue of heaven and earth is generation. (Ibid., p. 550a)

Kong Yingda comments,

> By its constancy so it [heaven-earth] generates the myriad things; thus it is said to be its great virtue. (Ibid., p. 551a)

The generation of the myriad things depends on the constant and unchanging nature of heaven and earth. This is the fundamental characteristic of heaven and earth.

> Heaven and earth intermingle and mix. The myriad things transform in purity. Man and woman mix their seminal essence. The myriad things transform and generate. (Ibid., p. 559b)

Kong Yingda explains this text as follows:

> "Intermingling and mixing" has the meaning of each depending on the other.... The two *qi* intermingle and mix and together harmonize and unite. The myriad things experience it,

change and transform and the essence is pure. . . . The mixing
of man and woman refers to their union. It says that man and
woman are like *yin-yang* and mutually touch each other, trusting to their spontaneous bent and acquiring one nature; thus
they unite their essence and then the myriad things are transformed and generated. If man and woman did not have this
spontaneous nature but each kept apart from the other then
the myriad things would not transform and generate. (Ibid.,
p. 559b–560a)

The *Commentaries* take 'generation' as the most fundamental characteristic of heaven and earth. In response to Confucius' silence concerning
death, the *Commentaries* say that if there is life then there must be death:

From the original beginning back to the ending will one know
the theories of death and life. (*Book of Changes: Great Commentary* I.4, p. 278)

Daoist Theories

The *Laozi* brings out the contrasting elements of life. If one pursues the
pleasures of life too much then one will end up losing one's life. If one
does not seek the pleasures of life then one can enjoy long life:

Heaven endures; earth perdures. The reason why heaven and
earth endure and perdure is because they do not generate
themselves; thus they are able to have long life.
    The people's scant consideration of death is because they
seek the blessings of life; thus they pay scant attention to death.
It is only because one disregards life that one is more worthy
than one who values life. (*Laozi* 75/MWD 40)

Not looking for the pleasures of life is better than considering life as valuable. In order to seek long life, the *Laozi* advocates not giving oneself life.
The *Laozi* promotes restraint of one's forces in order to live longer:

In governing the people and serving heaven there is nothing
equal to parsimony. Parsimony can be said to be a case of obedience from early on. Obedience from early on is said to be

putting the emphasis on accumulating virtue. If one puts the emphasis on accumulating virtue then there is nothing one cannot overcome. If there is nothing one cannot overcome then no one knows one's limits. If no one knows one's limits one may possess a state. When one has the mother of a state it is possible to endure and perdure. This is called the way of deep roots, rigid stems, long life and seeing many days. (*Laozi* 59/ MWD 22)

Parsimony is having no desires and not wasting one's energies. In this way one can maintain long life.

The *Zhuangzi* pays more attention to the question of life and death. It advocates the union of life and death. In the following story four men look forward to death:

Who can take nothingness as the head, life as the spine, death as the bottom? Who knows that death and life, existing and not-existing are all one body? (*Zhuangzi* 6, *The Teacher Who Is the Ultimate Ancestor*, line 46)

Death and life are both aspects of the one reality. This statement can be analyzed on two levels. First, it is saying that what lives must necessarily die and that this is a natural process. Second, it is saying that life and death are the same and should be treated equally. One should not enjoy life and hate death. The school of Zhuangzi affirms that life and death are natural processes. But it also denies the value of life.

In the words of a seeming fool the *Zhuangzi* asks,

How do I know that to enjoy life is not a delusion? How do I know that those who hate death are not exiles since childhood who have forgotten the way home? (*Zhuangzi* 2, *The Sorting Which Evens Things Out*, lines 78–79)

The "true person" is not concerned with enjoying life or hating death:

The true persons of old did not know how to enjoy life or hate death. They did not rejoice over their coming forth nor put off their going in. They went promptly; they came promptly. That is all. (*Zhuangzi* 6, *The Teacher Who Is the Ultimate Ancestor*, line 8)

The later sections of the *Zhuangzi* often return to these themes.

Life is borrowed. If one borrows to live then life is a speck of dust. Death and life are like day and night. (*Zhuangzi* 18, *Utmost Happiness*, lines 21–22)

Under heaven the myriad things come to be one. If one grasps this and becomes identical with it, then one's four limbs and hundred joints are all a speck of dust, and death and life, ending and beginning will be as day and night. (*Zhuangzi* 21, *Tianzifang*, line 33)

Life is the follower of death. Death is the beginning of life. Who knows their threads? Human life is an accumulation of *qi*. When it accumulates then one is born; when it disperses then one dies. If death and life are followers of each other can I see any disaster therein? (*Zhuangzi* 22, *Knowledge Roams North*, lines 10–11)

These passages show that life and death succeed each other like night and day according to a natural cycle. They follow each other.*

Despite protestations that one should not enjoy life, the *Zhuangzi* does seek a richer life.

The one who does good should stay clear of fame; the one who does evil should stay clear of punishment. Follow the central vein and make it one's standard; then it is possible to uphold the body and maintain life whole, to care for your parents and last to the end of your years. (*Zhuangzi* 3, *What Matters in the Nurture of Life*, line 2)

From this one can see that the *Zhuangzi* looks for a more complete life, free from the pursuit of material pleasure. In the *Inner Chapters* Zhuangzi is talking to his logician friend, Hui Shi:

Master Hui said to Master Zhuang, "Can a person be without the essentials of personhood?" Master Zhuang said, "Yes." Master Hui said, "If a person is without the essentials of personhood, how can one call him a person?" Master Zhuang

---

* Author's note: The *Zhuangzi* treats life as a speck of dust and says that life can come from death. This is close to Buddhist thought.

said, "The Way gives one the appearance; heaven gives one the shape, so how can one say that such a one is not a person?" Master Hui said, "Granted such a one can be a person but how can he lack the essentials of personhood?" Master Zhuang said, "By the essentials of personhood I refer to the distinction of right and wrong, true and false. What I refer to as being without the essentials of personhood is that the person does inflict self-hurt by likes or dislikes and that he constantly goes by what is spontaneous and does not impose on life." (*Zhuangzi* 5, *The Signs of Fullness of Power*, lines 56–58)

Zhuangzi was critical of Hui Shi's logical categories and argued that human beings should live according to the spontaneity of nature. In this his message is similar to that of the *Laozi*.

In the Warring States period there was also a movement of thought that "valued life." It is represented in the chapter of that name in *Mr. Lu's Spring and Autumn Annals*:

> The sage profoundly considers what is under heaven. There is nothing more valuable than life. Ears, eyes, nose and mouth are the servants of life. Though the ears want to hear a sound, the eyes see a color, the nose smell a perfume, the mouth taste a flavor, if it should hurt life then they desist.... This is the technique of valuing life.... Master Huazi said, "The wholeness of life has priority; diminished life is next; death next and harming life is lowest." Thus the one who respects life is said to be one of wholeness of life. For the one of wholeness of life the six desires are all met together. For the one of diminished life the six desires are all met separately.... For the one who harms life none of the six desires are met. All lead such a one astray into the utmost evil. This is subservience and being shamed. Being shamed has nothing greater than lacking in justice; thus lacking in justice is to harm life. However, harming life is not only a matter of lacking justice. Thus it is said, "Harming life is not as good as death." (*Mr. Lu's Spring and Autumn Annals* 2.2, *Valuing Life*, pp. 74, 75–76)

Wholeness of life is the appropriate fulfillment of the six desires. Harming life is leaving the six desires unsatisfied. Subservience and being dishonored are harmful to life, and this is worse than being dead. A further passage on the same lines is the following:

> Now my life works for me and it profits me greatly. Discussing its scale of value, even an honor like that of Son of Heaven is not its equal. Discussing its worth, even one as rich as to have the empire is not worth changing for it. Discussing its security, if one lost it for as much as one summer one could never ever recover it. These three points are prudently kept by those with the Way. Those who respect them and yet go on to act against them do not attain to the essentials of life.... This world's lords value persons. Whether worthy or unworthy none do not want to have long life and see to the end of their years. Yet if one daily goes against one's life how can one fulfill one's desire? Whatever growth there is in life should be followed. What makes life not followed are desires; thus the sage must first control desires. (Ibid. 1.3, *Stressing Self*, pp. 33, 34)

These texts emphasize control of desires as the way to attain long life. They affirm the value of life. Although the tone may be different from that of the *Laozi* and the *Zhuangzi*, the goal is the same. The *Laozi*'s "not acting in order to live" is in fact a means to attain long life, and the *Zhuangzi*'s "not enjoying life" is a means to uphold the wholeness of life.

Confucian Theories

The Confucians basically underlined the value of life. Perhaps the most famous text in this regard is that on Mencius' respect for justice as well as life. He set greater store by justice, but this was not to denigrate the value of life.

> Fish I like; bear's paw I also like. If I cannot have both together I will forgo the fish and choose the bear's paw. Life I like; justice I also like. If I cannot have both together I will forgo life and choose justice. (*Mencius* 6, *Gaozi A*, #10)

Although in exceptional circumstances one might forgo life, in normal circumstances one will hope to keep both life and justice. The *Xunzi* puts consideration of the value of life on a par with rites and justice:

> A person has nothing they value more than life and nothing they delight more in than peace. In fostering life and taking rest in joy there is nothing greater than rites and justice. (*Xunzi* 16, *Strong States*, line 46)

That rites and justice are conducive to a better life is the heart of Confucian thought. Among later Confucians, Cheng Hao and Wang Fuzhi made the greatest contribution to the appreciation of life.

In a text interspersed with quotations from the *Great Commentary to the* Book of Changes Cheng Hao advocated the view that heaven takes life as its way:

> "Generation and regeneration is what is meant by the *Changes*." This is what heaven takes as the Way. Heaven simply takes life [generation] as the Way. Following this life is principle and this is good.... The myriad things all have the will for spring; thus "to follow it is good." (*SKQS* 698, *Surviving Works of the Two Chengs* 2a, p. 30a)

The "will for spring" refers to the will to live and grow. The *Great Commentary to the* Book of Changes says,

> The alternation of *yin-yang* is what is meant by the Way. What follows from this is good. (*Great Commentary* 1.5, p. 280)

The later Confucians each had their own interpretation of this line. Cheng Hao linked life and goodness together. In another text he links life and benevolence:

> The great virtue of heaven and earth is called 'life.' "Heaven and earth intermingle and mix; the myriad things transform in purity." Life is what is meant by nature. The meaning of the life of the myriad things is what can be best observed. The origin is the growth of goodness, this is what is meant by benevolence. (*SKQS* 698, *Surviving Works of the Two Chengs* 11, p. 97a)

The sense of this text is that the myriad things generate and regenerate without ceasing, and all display the meaning of life. To allow this meaning of life to grow and develop is what benevolence is all about. Things with a meaningful life include plants and animals but not inanimate things.

Hence Cheng Hao's reference to life does not mean generation only but also life itself and growth. It can be said that Cheng Hao laid special stress on the meaning of life and spoke highly of the value of life. He seemed to suggest that the moral virtue of benevolence is directed toward praising the development of life, which fills the myriad things.

Wang Fuzhi uses the expression "prizing life." Inasmuch as one is a human being one has a duty to prize one's life:

> The sage is one of the human race. A human being is one of the living beings. Granted that one is oneself this human being then one cannot not prize one's life. (*Outer Commentary on the* Book of Changes 2.7.1, *Lin*, p. 44)

In a commentary on the *wu wang* hexagram (no. 25),* Wang says that life is to be prized because it is real and not an illusion, as the Buddhists claim.

> What can be relied on is existence and what is most constant is life. Both are without illusion and cannot be said to be illusory. (Ibid. 2, *Wu Wang*, p. 62)
>
> What is constant and can be relied on is life and existence; life and existence are not illusory but are really true. (Ibid., p. 63)

The Buddhists held that human life was without constancy and that it was illusory. By saying that life is what is most constant Wang Fuzhi argued that it has fixed patterns, and by saying that it is not illusory he affirmed the objective reality of this life.

Wang Fuzhi supported Mencius' views of life and justice. Morality and life are bound together, with life forming the basis for morality although in the interests of morality one may renounce life:

> Inasmuch as one values life, life is not such that it cannot not be valued. Inasmuch as one forgoes life, life is not such that one cannot forgo it.... Life is to support justice and then life is to be valued. Justice may be used to establish life and then life can be forgone. (*Elaboration on the Meaning of the* Book of History 5.1, *The Great Announcement*, p. 127)

---

* *Book of Changes*, p. 111. *Wu wang* is the symbol of freedom from error.

Wang Fuzhi had even more to say about the question of life and death.

> The life of heaven and earth is what human beings value. Plants and trees rely on life yet do not regret their death. Birds and beasts fear death yet do not know how to mourn death. Human beings know how to mourn death yet do not need to fear death. Mourning is to want to prolong the life given by heaven and earth; fearing is to nullify the transformation brought on by heaven and earth. Thus mourning and fearing are the great distinction between human beings and birds.... Fools do not know that death must occur; thus they fear death. The clever know that life must die yet they fear life.... Therefore the sage goes to the utmost on the human way and unites to the virtue of heaven. The one who unites to the virtue of heaven stands firm with the principle of existence and life. The one who goes to the utmost on the human way moves by following the impetus of life. (*Outer Commentary on the* Book of Changes 2, *Wu Wang*, pp. 64, 65)

The principle of life is the norm of life; the impetus of life is the inner dynamism of life. By 'life' Wang Fuzhi understood both life and existence. It is all right to mourn the fact of death but not necessary to fear it because what has life must inevitably die. In describing death as a speck of dust the *Zhuangzi* betrayed a fear of death. Wang Fuzhi painted the portrait of the ideal person in face of death.

16. Return

Fan PHĀN

反

The term 'fan' may mean 'to return as the seasons return to the beginning of their sequence' or it can mean 'to be opposed to.' In both senses it is an important concept in Chinese philosophy.

The Point of Return

The origins of the term meaning 'to oppose' are ancient. In 593 B.C., to justify an attack on the nomadic peoples to the north, Bo Zong of Jin said,

> When heaven reverses [*fan*] its seasons there are disasters; when earth reverses [*fan*] its productions there are prodigies; when the people go against [*fan*] virtue, there is disorder. (*Zuo's Commentary* 7, *Xuan* 15, p. 326)

Here the term *fan* means 'to go against.'

It is in the *Laozi* that the term became a philosophical concept.

> Reversal is the movement of the Way. (*Laozi* 40/MWD 4)
>
> Abstruse virtue is profound and far-reaching. It reverses with things and only then does it attain to great conformity. (*Laozi* 65/MWD 28)
>
> Plain words seem paradoxical [*fan*]. (*Laozi* 78/MWD 43)

The *Autumn Floods* chapter of the *Zhuangzi* describes east and west as opposites yet says that one cannot be without the other:

> East and west are opposed [*fan*] to each other and yet cannot do without each other. (*Zhuangzi* 17, *Autumn Floods*, line 32)

Sometimes the term '*fan*' means 'to return to the source.'* This usage is found in the earliest strands of the *Book of Changes*:

> Turn back [*fan*] and return to one's Way. In seven days comes the return [*fu*]. (*Book of Changes* 24, *Fu Hexagram*, p. 107)

Here the terms for turning back (*fan*) and returning (*fu*) are used in the same sense. Used as a binome (*fan-fu*), the term means 'going right back to the beginning and recommencing the cycle.' The *Laozi* also uses *fu* to mean 'return' in this sense:

> Attaining to the utmost space; keeping firmly to stillness. The myriad things all emerge together. I watch their return [*fu*].

---

*In modern Chinese the two senses of 'opposition' and 'return' are distinguished in the writing of the character.

> Things teem and each returns [*fu*] back to its root. (*Laozi* 16/
> MWD 60)

For the *Laozi* the pattern of return is inherent in the Way itself and man-
ifested in all things. Adding to and taking away from are opposites just as
fortune and misfortune are, but one cannot exist without the other:

> Thus a thing is sometimes added to by being taken from and
> taken from by being added to. (*Laozi* 42/MWD 5)
>   Misfortune relies on fortune; fortune hides under mis-
> fortune. (*Laozi* 58/MWD 21)

Thus *fan* may mean 'to be opposed to' or 'to return to.' Both meanings
are simultaneously present in the *Laozi*. In talking about the emergence of
the Way from the cosmic soup the *Laozi* has this to say about how to refer
to it:

> If pressed I shall call it the 'ultimate.' What is ultimate is called
> 'receding'; what recedes is called 'distant'; what is distant is
> called 'turning back [*fan*].' (*Laozi* 25/MWD 69)

In the course of their development things turn back. Having turned back,
they then return again to their previous state. In terms of Hegelian logic
these steps may be described as the negation of an affirmation followed by
the negation of the negation. There can be two kinds of negation of a
negation. According to the first, the situation returns to exactly what it
was in the beginning. Movement is circular. According to the second, the
situation is not precisely the same, for it carries the seed of a new development. Movement is spiral. The *Laozi* tends toward the first pattern.

The *Laozi*, and even more clearly *Mr. Lu's Spring and Autumn
Annals*, say that there is a definite point at which the return motion will
begin. The passage quoted above on the dialectic of fortune and misfortune continues as follows:

> Who knows its limit [turning-point]? Does not the correct
> exist? The correct returns again to become the askew. The good
> returns again to become the prodigious. (*Laozi* 58/MWD 21)

It seems from the context that fortune and misfortune have a given turning point, which when reached will automatically entail the change from

one to the other. The point is made explicit in *Mr. Lu's Spring and Autumn Annals*:

> *Yin* and *yang* change and transform, one above, one below. They unite and become manifest, muddled and obscure. They separate and then return to unite. They unite and then return to separate. This is what is meant by the constancy of heaven. The cartwheels of heaven and earth come to an end and then return to the beginning, reach a peak and then return to go back. Nothing is inappropriate. (*Mr. Lu's Spring and Autumn Annals* 5.2, *Great Happiness*, p. 255)

The turning point is the condition for the turning back.

Han Theories

In his commentary on the *sheng* hexagram (fullness, no. 38) Yang Xiong states that the process of return is a natural one:

> "At the peak of fullness it does not save" means 'the way of heaven turns back.' (*Ultimate Abstruse* I.38.9, *Sheng: Fathoming the Abstruse*, p. 118)

The "peak" or "turning-point" is the key to the return:

> If *yang* does not reach a peak then *yin* will not emerge. If *yin* does not reach a peak then *yang* will not sprout. At the peak of cold warmth is generated; at the peak of warmth cold is generated. (Ibid. II.3, *Evolution of the Mystery*, p. 263)

When something develops to a certain stage, then it will start to turn back. If it fails to reach that point, then it will not turn back. The turning of fortune and misfortune has set conditions:

> Unless one does evil fortune cannot generate misfortune. Unless one does good misfortune cannot generate fortune. (Ibid. II.4, *Shining of the Abstruse*, p. 283)

If one enjoys fortune and does no wrong then one will not encounter misfortune. If one encounters misfortune and does not mend one's ways then one will not obtain fortune. Thus reversal of the situation is dependent on human morality.

In assessing the philosophers Ban Gu had recourse to the theme of development through opposition:*

> There are ten schools of philosophers. Of those that may be considered there are only nine.... Although their words are varied, yet they are like water and fire, which put each other out and also give rise to each other. Benevolence and justice, respect and harmony oppose each other but also produce each other. (*Han History* 30, *Gazette of Arts and Literature: Summary of the Philosophers*, p. 1746)

The Song Period

Among the later Confucians it is Cheng Yi who discusses the theme of reversal. He it is who first coined the following expression:

> When things reach a peak they must go back. The principle for this is as follows. If there is life then there is death; if there is a beginning then there is an ending. (*SKQS* 698, *Surviving Works of the Two Chengs* 15, p. 133a)

When things have developed to their peak then they must go back. The phrase is used frequently in Cheng Yi's *Commentary on the* Book of Changes:

> When the principles of things reach a peak they must turn back, thus at the peak of the *tai* hexagram (prosperous, no. 11), there is the *pi* hexagram (to stop, no. 12) and at the peak of the *pi* hexagram there is the *tai* hexagram.... Coming to a peak and then necessarily turning back is the constancy of principle. (*Commentary on the* Book of Changes 12, *Pi Hexagram*, p. 59)
>
> The principles of things come to a peak and then must turn back. To understand this more nearly take a person ap-

---

*Author's note: It may be that Ban Gu copied this idea from Liu Xin, but there is not sufficient proof to affirm or deny this.

proaching the east. Once he has reached the furthest east then
if he moves on it is west. (Ibid. 38, *Kui*, p. 171)

Things come to a peak and then go back; affairs reach
a peak and then change. When *kun* (distress, no. 47) comes to
a peak then the principle will accordingly change. (Ibid. 47,
Kun, p. 215)

Cheng Yi deserves the credit for formulating this phrase and for applying it as a general principle. Its origins, however, lie further back in the
Laozi and in *Mr. Lu's Spring and Autumn Annals*. Actually, the phrase is
encountered in the last line of the fifth chapter of the much-neglected late
Warring States work the *Pheasant Cap Master*:

Things come to a peak and then go back. The name for this
is 'flowing round.' (*Pheasant Cap Master* 5, *Flowing Round*,
1:15a)

The Ming-Qing Period

The *Balance of East and West* is a late work by Fang Yizhi. It advocates
"mutual opposition and mutual causation." This is a theory of contrasts
and mutual change.

I spoke of the utmost principle within heaven and earth: whenever x causes y then when x comes to a peak it returns to y. . . .
Then the so-called mutually contrasting and mutually causing
is a mutual dependence, mutual overcoming and mutual accomplishing. Day and night, water and fire, life and death, man
and woman, generation and overcoming, hard and soft, clear
and muddied, bright and dark, empty and full, being and
beingless, form and *qi*, the Way and the vessel, true and illusory, going along with and going counter to, secure and perilous, hard-working and lazy, paring and returning (*bo* and *fu*
hexagrams), thunder and mountain (*zhen* and *gen* hexagrams),
decrease and increase (*sun* and *yi* hexagrams) and all that is
expansive or restricted: these are not not dualities. . . . This
opposition is mutual reversal. (*Balance of East and West* 4,
Reversal and Causation, p. 38)

These dualities are all in mutual opposition and give rise to each other. He sets this out in detail:

> Hen and cock are of different natures yet female and male are attracted to each other. Is it not possible to say that they cause each other? Water floods and fire explodes and thus end up in opposition to each other.... The people use them a great deal and they cannot be separated from each other. Water and fire come together in the human body and then the person lives. If they do not come together then the person falls ill. Is it not possible to say that they cause each other?... Silence is deep and motion bobs up. Principle is from ice or charcoal and in the midst of stillness there is movement and in the midst of movement there is stillness. When stillness reaches a peak it must move. When movement reaches a peak it must fall still. If there is the one there must be two. Two is rooted in one. Is it not the case that all mutual oppositions in heaven and earth are all rooted in the one common source? (Ibid.)

To say that when things come to a peak they must return implies that at the peak return is inevitable and also that if the peak is not attained then return will not occur. Wang Fuzhi raised doubts concerning this second implication:

> Transformation between two things, the turning-point of human affairs, going and coming, auspicious and inauspicious, coming to life and dying, good and failure all have a peak to which they come and then go back. Is it not that all have a peak to which they come and then go back?... If there is movement then there is stillness; stillness then movement. Stillness contains movement but movement does not contain stillness.... If one waits for the peak of motion then next there is stillness. If one waits for the peak of stillness then next there is motion. If the peak is not fully attained, its going back builds up and responds violently. (*Record of Thoughts and Questionings: Outer Section*, pp. 32–33)

This is to say that sometimes even though the peak is not reached there is a return. In fact, the situation is not straightforward. The peak can vary for any given kind of thing. Wang Fuzhi was rightly opposed to any attempt to oversimplify the process of peaking and returning. He did not succeed, however, in producing a systematic dialectic. That development proceeds by oppositions, and the fact that when things reach a peak they turn back has become part of popular lore.

17. Destiny

Ming MÊNH

命

The term 'ming' may be translated as 'fate,' 'destiny,' 'decree,' 'command,' or 'life.' It does not figure in the oracle bone script although its cognate ling, *meaning 'command,' does. The original meaning is the mission or gift granted by a higher authority to a lower person. The Zhou interpreted their conquest of the Shang in terms of divine approbation for their rule. The exact conditions for retaining or gaining the approval of heaven are not stated. The last kings of the Shang are presented as morally obnoxious and decadent and thus unworthy of ruling. Possibly on the basis of this the same idea is mirrored back into history and applied to the Shang conquest of the earlier Xia dynasty. Thus a theory of* ming *as the decree from on high came to be used to justify the taking or seizure of political power. There is not, however, a clear revolutionary theory. Mencius, for instance, upheld monarchical rule, but he did expect the ruler to live up to certain moral norms. In popular lore it became identified with fate, and the original sense of 'gift' is lost from sight.*

Early Period A

In the early period the term *ming* referred to the command of God. The divine element decreased, and by the time of the *Mencius, ming* referred to all that was outside the power of human influence to alter. The *Zhuangzi* used *ming* to refer to the attitude of not caring about what happened. The Mohists honored heaven but argued against *ming*, thus separating the two notions. By *ming* they understood a fate already determined. Despite the Mohist rejection of fate, Wang Chong reaffirmed its presence. The Mencian view was the one that was picked up in the Song and continued thereafter. According to this view, *ming* consists of the objective limitations faced by the acting subject.

The concept emerged as a key term in legitimizing the overthrow of a bad ruler:

> The ruler of Xia has many crimes; Heaven has decreed to terminate him. (*Book of History* 4.1, *Shang Books: The Oath of Tang*, p. 173)

The ruler of the Shang justified his usurpation of the throne on the grounds that heaven had decreed it on account of the crimes of Xia. The overthrow of the Shang was seen in the same terms:

> The chief of the West having subdued Li, Zu Yi was afraid and made haste to inform the king.... The king said, "Alas! Is my lifespan not decreed by heaven?" Zu Yi said in reply, "Alas! Your many crimes are amassing above." (*Book of History* 4.10, *Shang Books: The Chief of the West Conquers Li*, pp. 268, 271–272)

The Zhou saw heaven as being on their side:

> Alas! Imperial heaven the high God has changed the decree he gave to his eldest son and this great state of Yin [Shang]. You alone, O King, have received that decree. Unlimited is the happiness and unlimited also the anxiety it brings! (*Book of History* 5.12, *Zhou Books: The Announcement of the Duke of Shao*, p. 425)

The Zhou theory of heaven's decree was that it was not constant but could change. Thus when Feng was appointed to Wei he was told to be careful lest the appointment be withdrawn:

> Alas! You, Feng, my little child, the decree is not constant. You reflect on this and do not make me deprive you of your post.

Understand the decree you have received. Hold dearly what you have heard. Keep the people tranquil and regulated accordingly. (*Book of History* 5.9, *Zhou Books: The Announcement to the Prince of Kang*, pp. 397–398)

One of the most famous expositions of the theory of the decree of heaven is found in the poem on King Wen in the *Book of Songs*:

Majestic, majestic King Wen,
Continuous and bright his sense of reverence!
Great indeed is heaven's decree!
There were the grandsons and sons of Shang,
The grandsons and sons of Shang
Numbered more than hundreds of thousands;
The high God sent his decree;
The princes to Zhou obeyed.
The princes obeyed Zhou.
Heaven's decree is not constant.
. . .
Before Yin [Shang] lost its hosts,
It was the equal of the high God.
Look to Yin as a mirror,
The great decree is not easy to gain.*
(*The Book of Odes* 3, *Great Songs* 1.1 (Ode 235), *King Wen*,
    pp. 429–430, 431)

These thoughts on heaven's decree were to carry over into Confucian learning.

Confucius claimed that at fifty he knew heaven's decree.† This decree determined whether the Way was operative or not:

The master said, "Whether the Way is going to be operative is a matter of decree; whether the Way is not going to be operative is a matter of decree." (*Analects* 14.38, *Xian Asked*, p. 289)

A later section of the *Analects* defines a gentleman in terms of knowing heaven's decree:

---

*Legge (*The Chinese Classics* IV: 431) translates "gain" as "keep."
† *Analects* 2, *On Administration* 4, pp. 146–147.

> The master said, "One who does not know the decree cannot be a gentleman." (*Analects* 20.3, *Yao Said*, p. 354)

The Way is an ideal to be sought. Whether it is attained depends on the decree. Although the term 'decree' is thus used in the *Analects*, it is not elaborated on.

The *Mencius* is much bolder in advocating the moral conditions for earning the approval of heaven.

> That which is done without man's doing is from Heaven. That which happens without man's causing is from the decree of Heaven. (*Mencius* 5, *Wan Zhang A*, #6)

The decree of heaven is something outside human ability to command. It is something that is outside of the self:

> When seeking leads to acquiring and loss to losing then seeking is useful to acquiring and what is sought is within the self. When seeking has the Way and acquiring has decree then seeking is not useful for acquiring and what is sought is outside. (*Mencius* 7, *Exerting the Mind A*, #3)

As Legge explains in his note, the agent is able to seek and acquire the inner virtues by his or her own efforts. Riches and wealth are, however, granted by heaven and cannot be sought; they are only decreed. The agent is not totally powerless, though, in controlling his destiny. The *Mencius* advocates "establishing one's decree," that is, acting in such a way as to be ready for what heaven can do:

> Maintaining one's mind and nourishing one's nature is that by which one serves heaven. When neither short nor long life lead one to be two-faced then one cultivates oneself in expectation of anything. This is how one establishes one's decree. (Ibid., #1)
>
> There is nothing that does not have a decree. One should obediently receive what is correct; therefore the one who knows decree will not stand under an overhanging wall. One who dies whilst exerting himself according to his/her Way may be correctly said to be a case of death by decree. Death under handcuffs and fetters cannot be correctly said to be a case of death by decree. (*Mencius* 7, *Exerting the Mind A* 12, pp. 449–450)

Walking under a dangerous wall is a case of deliberately seeking death, and since what is sought by the self is not the decree, death in those circumstances cannot be described as decreed. The person who dies in the course of duty was not looking for death and hence his or her death is a case of death by decree.

Although the *Xunzi* does not discuss heaven's decree as much, it does mention the topic. 'Decree' is conforming to circumstances:

> What one encounters at the moment is what is meant by 'decree.' (*Xunzi* 22, *On Correcting Names*, line 6)

An example is given to illustrate this:

> The King of Chu has a thousand chariots following him: —this is not due to wisdom; the gentleman eats pulses and drinks water: —this is not due to stupidity. It is what is fitting to the circumstances. (*Xunzi* 17, *Discourse on Heaven*, line 25)

In other words, external forces, rather than one's own choices, determine one's behavior. The king of Chu rules a large country and so needs a large army; a gentleman is not necessarily rich and so eats simply.

Whereas the *Mencius* talks about establishing the decree, the *Xunzi* talks about mastering one's fate:

> To go along with heaven and praise it. Who can master heaven's decree and use it? To look for the right time and wait for it. Who can respond to the time and make it come about? (*Xunzi* 17, *Discourse on Heaven*, lines 44–45)

Mastering heaven's decree and using it is a case of mastering the natural world and adapting it to human needs.

In the *Inner Chapters* of the *Zhuangzi* it is decree that governs the changes and transformations of the world. The individual is powerless to do anything and so is advised not to worry.

> Death and life, survival and ruin, success and failure, poverty and riches, competence and incompetence, slander and praise, hunger and thirst, these are the transformations of affairs, the operations of decree. They alternate before us day and night, and knowledge cannot measure back to where they began. Consequently there is no point in letting them disturb one's

peace; they are not to be admitted into the Spiritual Store-house. (*Zhuangzi* 5, *The Signs of the Fullness of Power*, lines 43–45 [Graham tr.])

In the course of life one cannot avoid encountering poverty and riches, but one should not cling to these; rather, one should follow what is natural. One should keep oneself apart from all the changes of life. Just as a minister obeys his master loyally, so too a human being is toward heaven's decree:

> In the service of one's own heart there is no higher degree of virtue than, without joy and sorrow ever alternating before it, to know that these things could not be otherwise, and be content with them as our destiny. (*Zhuangzi* 4, *Worldly Business Among Human Beings*, line 43 [Graham tr.])
>
> As for recognizing the inescapable and being content with it as destined, only the one who does have virtue within is capable of that. (*Zhuangzi* 5, *The Signs of the Fullness of Power*, line 20 [Graham tr.])

Zhuangzi is arguing that the criminal who complains about unjust treatment is simply upsetting himself. Far better not to worry about the treatment and to maintain peace of mind. The *Zhuangzi* imagines a man who has fallen on hard times saying:

> I have been thinking about what could have brought me to this plight but cannot decide what it is. My father and mother would not wish me to be poor, would they? Heaven is not partial in its covering [the earth], nor earth partial in its bearing up [the land]. Heaven and earth would not choose to make me poor, would they? So I cannot decide who has brought this about. It can only be fate that has brought me to this plight. (*Zhuangzi* 6, *The Teacher Who Is the Ultimate Ancestor*, lines 96–97)

In the later additions to the *Zhuangzi* corpus the whole question of whether there is any destiny is mooted.

> Not knowing why things happen so, how can one say there is no destiny? Not knowing why things happen so, how can one say there is destiny? (*Zhuangzi* 27, *Language*, lines 20–21)

This is a very different picture from that drawn in the *Inner Chapters*. Causes of events of the world are hidden and so we cannot tell if they are decreed by fate or not. Nothing can either prove or disprove the existence of fate.

In the *Circling Sky* destiny is seen as inexorable:

> Nature cannot be changed; fate cannot be altered; time cannot be stopped. (*Zhuangzi* 14, *Circling Sky*, line 79)

In discussing the merits of putting a halter on a horse's neck or a ring in an ox's nose, it is pointed out that

> One does not use what is of human making to destroy what is of heaven's doing; one does not let deliberation destroy what is of heaven; one does not let success wipe out a good reputation. One keeps it carefully and does not lose it. This is called "returning to the authentic." (*Zhuangzi* 17, *Autumn Floods*, lines 52–53)

Human activity should not be allowed to interfere in the course of nature. This is a fundamental Daoist principle.

Early Period B: Mozi

The longest discussion of *ming* as fate is found in the *Mozi*. Mozi was virulently opposed to the idea of fate as automatic punishment. In fact, though, his teaching is not in simple opposition to that of Confucius. The Confucian view is that human affairs are determined both by subjective moral criteria and by objective criteria that lie outside human power to control. A thorough examination of the subjective criteria, however, can enable one to see what it is that is outside one's scope to change. The subjective can indeed be changed. Thus a king can improve his conduct, and this act may affect the destiny of his throne. The *Mozi* is more concerned with the ordinary point of view of ordinary people who blame disasters on fate and so do nothing to improve their lot.

> The fatalists say: When fate decrees that the country shall be wealthy, it will be wealthy. When it decrees that it shall be poor, it will be poor. When fate decrees that the population

shall be large, it will be large. When it decrees that it shall be small, it will be small. When it decrees that the country shall be orderly, it will be orderly. When it decrees that it shall be chaotic, it will be chaotic. When fate decrees that one shall enjoy longevity, one will enjoy longevity. And when fate decrees that one will suffer brevity of life, he will suffer brevity of life. (*Mozi* 35, *Against Fate* 1, lines 3–5 [Chan tr.])

As a ruler he who holds this doctrine will not be righteous. As a minister he will not be loyal. As a father he will not be deeply loving. As a son he will not be filial. As an elder brother he will not be brotherly. And as a younger brother he will not be respectful. The unreasoning adherence to this doctrine is the source of evil ideas and the way of the wicked man.

How do we know that fatalism is the way of the wicked man? Poor people of ancient times were greedy in drinking and eating but lazy in their work. Therefore their resources for food and clothing were inadequate, and the troubles of hunger and cold were approaching. They did not know enough to say, "We are weak and unworthy. We did not work hard." But they would say, "It is originally our fate that we are poor." The wicked kings of ancient times did not check the indulgence of their ears and eyes and the depravity of their minds. They did not obey their ancestors and consequently they lost their countries and ruined their states. They did not know to say, "We are weak and unworthy. Our government has not been good." But they would say, "It is originally our fate that we lost them." (Ibid., lines 34–39 [Chan tr.])

In the Compromising version of this chapter, fate is contrasted with 'endeavor':*

Of old what Jie had left in chaos, Tang was able to put in order. What Zhou had left in chaos, King Wu was able to put in order. . . . Living in the time of Jie and Zhou yet underheaven was in chaos; living in the time of Tang and Wu yet

---

*The first two quotations are from the Purist version of the *Mozi*. The third is from the Compromising version. See Graham, *Disputers of the Tao*, p. 36.

under-heaven was ordered. The ordering of under-heaven was due to the endeavor of Tang and Wu. The chaos of under-heaven was due to the crimes of Jie and Zhou. If one looks at it from this point of view, this security or peril, ordering or chaos, is in how the ruler conducts administration; how is it possible to talk about fate? . . . Now people of worth and integrity honor worthiness and like the technique of the Way and hence are rewarded by kings, dukes and great officers above and renowned by the myriad people below. Can this be ascribed to fate? This is also due to their endeavor. (*Mozi* 37, *Against Fate* 3, lines 8–10, 12–23)

One's status and wealth are due to personal effort and not to fate.

Han-Liang

The Han philosopher Wang Chong believed that everything was determined by fate:

Whatever human beings encounter, whether success or failure, is all due to fate. There is the fate of life, death, long life and short life and also the fate of honor and dishonor, poverty and riches. From kings and dukes to the ordinary people, from sages and worthies to the low and boorish, whatever has head and eyes, or contains blood, none does not have fate. When fate determines poverty and dishonor even though one be rich and honored yet one will run into disaster. When fate determines riches and honor, even though one be poor and mean, yet one will encounter blessings and bounty. (*Balanced Inquiries* 3, *On Destiny and Fortune*, p. 5)

His discussion of fate concentrates on the length of life and the degree of wealth that one enjoys.

Though one's talent be lofty and conduct generous one will not necessarily earn the wealth and honors one requires. Though one's wisdom be paltry and one's virtue scanty, one must not think that one will be poor and mean. Sometimes

one of lofty talent and generous conduct has a bad fate so one
falters and does not progress. One of paltry wisdom and scanty
virtue may have a good fate rise up and jump ahead. Hence
under certain conditions wisdom and stupidity, acting purely
or immorally are matters of nature and talent. Officials being
honored or dishonored, managing property in poverty or riches
are matters of fate and times. (Ibid.)

Fate is not dependent on moral conduct:

When fate determines a short life, even though one be fearful
of going wrong yet in the end one will not attain long life.
When fortune determines poverty and dishonor then even
though one be good natured in the end one will not be otherwise.... Nature and fate are different. Maybe one person is
good by nature and has an evil fate, another is evil in nature
and has a lucky fate.... Nature has good and evil of itself; fate
has lucky and unlucky of itself. (*Balanced Inquiries* 6, *On the
Significance of Destiny*, p. 11)

In truth, Wang Chong's theory was developed as an attack on those in
power in his own day, whom he judged to be stupid and of no virtue
though they enjoyed the blessings of fate.

The relation between virtuous conduct and fate was analyzed according to three categories. The work of Ban Gu, composed after discussions ordered by the emperor at the White Tiger studio, reads,

There are three categories of fate, namely, fate of long life, fate
of encountering and fate of following. (*Understandings of the
White Tiger Studio*, p. 391)

The three are more fully explained by Zhao Ji, author of the earliest extant
commentary on the *Mencius*:*

There are three names given to fate: doing good and attaining
good is called 'receiving fate'; doing good and attaining evil is
called 'encountering fate'; doing evil and attaining evil is called

---

*Zhao Ji (c. 108–201). *Zi*: Binqing, from near modern Xianyang, Shaanxi, a government official. See Loewe, *Early Chinese Texts*, p. 332.

'according with fate.' (*Line by Line Commentary on the* Mencius 7, *Exerting the Mind A*, #4, p. 518 [*Zhuzi Jicheng*])

The first and third recognize the harmony of moral conduct and fate. Good conduct earns a good reward and bad conduct a bad reward. The middle one is the only problematic one, and it is only couched in terms of a bad end for a good person and not the other way around, as in Wang Chong's exposition above. Wang has his own observations on the subject:

> The *Commentary* says, "there are three names applied to fate: the first is called correct fate, the second is called following fate, the third is called encountering fate." 'Correct fate' is said of someone whose nature is good and the person achieves good luck.... 'According with fate' is said of someone who restrains force and acts properly and good luck and happiness come to the person, or of one who abandons himself to the emotions, acts out his desires and evil disasters descend; thus it is called 'following fate.' 'Encountering fate' is when one's conduct is good yet one reaps evil; it is not what one hoped for. One runs up against external things and reaps evil disasters, thus it is called 'encountering fate.' ... To talk about 'following fate' is not to talk about 'encountering fate' and to talk about 'encountering fate' is not to talk about 'following fate.' (*Balanced Inquiries* 6, *On the Significance of Destiny*, p. 11)

The Wei-Jin work the *Liezi* constructs a dialogue between endeavor and fate that presents the same kind of absolute fatalism that is found in Wang Chong:

> Endeavor said to Fate: "How can your effect be as great as mine?"
>
> "What effect on things do you have, that you should wish to compare yourself with me?"
>
> "Whether one lives long or dies young, succeeds or fails, has high rank or low, is poor or rich, all this is within the reach of my endeavor."
>
> "Peng Zu was no wiser than Yao and Shun, yet he lived eight hundred years; Yan Yuan was no less talented than ordi-

nary people, yet he died at eighteen. Confucius was no less virtuous than the feudal lords, but they distressed him in Chen and Cai; the Yin Emperor Zhou did not behave better than the three good ministers he executed, but he sat on the throne. Ji Zha had no rank in Wu, yet Tian Heng became sole master of the state of Qi. Bo Yi and Shu Qi starved to death on Mount Shouyang, but the Ji family grew richer than Zhan Qin. If all this is within the reach of your endeavor, why did you give long life to one and early death to the other, why did you permit the sage to fail and villains to succeed, demean an able man and exalt a fool, impoverish good people and enrich bad ones?"

"If it is as you say, certainly I have no effect on things. But is it you who directs that things should be so?"

"When we say that a thing is destined, how can there be anyone who directs it? I push it when it is going straight, let it take charge when it is going crooked. Long life and short, failure and success, high rank and low, wealth and poverty, come about of themselves. What can I know about it? What can I know about it?" (*Liezi* 6, *Endeavour and Fate*, p. 67 [Graham tr.])*

The contrast of endeavor and fate is similar to that in the *Mozi*, but the *Mozi* gives endeavor a role in altering circumstances, whereas the *Liezi* denies it any role.

Liu Jun (462–521) advocated views similar to those of Wang Chong, denying any connection between morality and wealth or status:

As for so-called 'fate': death and life, honor and dishonor, poverty and riches, order and chaos, disaster and blessing, all these ten things are what heaven bestows. Stupidity and wisdom, good and evil, these four are what human beings can do.... Therefore wickedness and correctness are due to human beings; good luck and bad luck are due to fate. (*Complete Liang Literature* 57, *Discourse on Distinguishing Fate*, p. 3288a)

---

* See Angus Graham, *Book of Liezi: A Classic of the* Tao (New York: Columbia University Press, 1990), p. 122 n for the historical allusions.

His conclusion is that good people do what is right for its own sake and not in the hope of gaining a reward:

> The *Songs** say, "The wind and rain seems dark; the cock crows incessantly." Therefore the good man does what is good; how should he cease to do so?... He trains himself in the virtuous Way, practices benevolence and justice, promotes filial piety and fraternal affection, establishes loyalty and correctness, advances in the rich and flowing streams of ritual and music and treads in the way of the flourishing principles of the former kings. This is what the gentleman pursues; it is not a matter of asking for it and then doing it! (Ibid., p. 3288b)

Moral behavior is not designed as a means of seeking wealth and status. This was a fundamental principle in Confucian thought.

The Song-Ming Era

Wang Chong thought that all encounters that brought disaster were the result of fate. Zhang Zai, however, distinguished between 'fate' and 'chance':

> Fate and endowment are identical with nature; chance is accidental.... When the conduct is the same but the reward different it is difficult to speak in terms of fate, but it is possible to describe this as 'chance.' (*SKQS* 697, *Correcting the Unenlightened* 17, *Qian Cheng*, pp. 143–145)

Fate is what cannot be avoided and is necessarily so:

> The reception of fate is due to a reason.... What is found by truly knowing one's nature and by exhaustive inquiry of principle to be unchangeable is the norm of the self. What heaven itself is not able to change is called 'fate.' (Ibid. 6, *Enlightenment Resulting from Integrity*, p. 113a)

'Fate' is only applicable to what cannot ever be otherwise.

---

* *Book of Songs* 1.7.16, *Guo Feng: Zheng: Wind and Rain* (Ode 90), verse 3, p. 143.

Zhang's nephew and pupil, Cheng Yi, did not agree with his master. His views are shown in the following dialogue:

> Question: "What is the difference between fate and chance?"
>
> The teacher said, "Whether people chance on something or not is simply what is fated."
>
> Question: "At the battle of Chang Ping* 400,000 men died. How can the same death have been fated for all of them?"
>
> He said, "This was nonetheless fated. They chanced on Bo Qi because it was fated that it should be so. This is the less difficult to understand since the Zhao soldiers were all from one country; it is common enough for men from all over the 'five lakes and four seas' to die together."
>
> He asked again, "There are criminals who become kings and ministers who starve to death, men who fell from high rank and men who rise from low rank. Are all such things fated?"
>
> He said, "'Everything is fated.' It is because of what is called fate that there are such inequalities of fortune; there is nothing strange about it." (*SKQS* 698, *Surviving Works of the Two Chengs* 18, p. 164a [Graham tr., p. 25])

Whereas Zhang Zai had distinguished fate and chance, Cheng Yi believed that 'chance' is but the appearance of what is in fact already determined. Cheng did not believe, however, that fate should be used to determine what was morally correct. Right behavior depended on moral principles to be followed at all costs:

> The worthy know only of justice and fate is within it. Middling persons and lower use fate to determine justice as when they say that seeking good luck has the Way and obtaining it is fated. This seeking has no effect on what one obtains. When one knows that fate cannot be sought then one accepts what one has and does not seek it. If the worthy, though, seeks good

---

* At this battle in 290 B.C. the army of Zhao was wiped out by Bo Qi.

luck by the Way and obtains it by justice then it is not necessary to speak of fate. (Ibid. 2a, p. 21b)

This is to say that fate is irrelevant to morality.

The Tang politician Li Mi held that gentlemen could make their
fate. In the Ming dynasty Wang Shouren's pupil Wang Gen (1483–1541)*
held a similar position:

> That Shun was the son of Gusou is fate.† Shun exerted himself
> and Gusou failed [to kill him]. Therefore the gentleman does
> not talk about fate. That Confucius did not have the chance to
> be an official is fate, yet his making the Way clear so as to com-
> fort people is not called fate. If the general people hear of fate;
> the great person makes fate. (*SBBY: Philosophical Records of
> Ming Scholars* 32.1, *Taizhou Scholarly Record*, p. 9a)

'Making fate' is overcoming difficult circumstances and still doing well.

Wang Fuzhi developed Li Mi's theory and expanded it to argue that
all people could create their own destiny. 'Destiny' is the face of natural
law; if people respect this in their way of living then they can grasp hold of
their own destiny.

> Gentlemen can make their own destiny. Life has the principle
> of life, death the principle of death. Order has the principle of
> order, disorder the principle of disorder. Maintaining has the
> principle of maintaining, perishing the principle of perishing.
> Heaven is principle; its decree is the unfolding of principle.…
> Only if one follows principle and is in awe of heaven, then
> destiny will be applicable.… If one prepares oneself to wait for
> destiny and prudently moves along with eternal destiny then
> for a determined person there is nothing he cannot create.
> (*SBBY: Discussion After Reading the* Mirror of Universal His-
> tory 24, pp. 351a–b)

---

*Wang Gen was never an official. His teaching stressed personal moral values and care
for the disadvantaged. His devotion to the classics was such that he dressed in ancient cos-
tume and rode to Beijing in a cart that he supposed to be a model of the kind used by Confucius. See L. C. Goodrich, *Dictionary of Ming Biography*, pp. 1382–1385.

† Gusou twice tried to kill his son, Shun, but was outwitted. See Mathieu, *Anthologie
des mythes et legendes*, pp. 85–86.

18. Integrity

Cheng THÀNH

誠

It is strange to find a moral virtue included among cosmological categories. It is the case that moral and cosmological categories do interweave in the Chinese context. The term 'integrity,' however, was developed as a cosmological category and as a moral category. It came to mean 'one and not permitting of change.' In this sense it has the connotation of integration. Just as a person of integrity is someone who holds fast to his or her principles, so too the cosmos is seen as possessing integrity because it keeps to certain principles of action. The term is also often translated as 'sincerity.'

Union of the Natural and Moral Orders

The etymological sense of *cheng* (integrity) is *xin* (trustworthiness) (*Explanation of the Characters* 3A, *Yan*, p. 52b). The character *xin* depicts a person and a word, meaning that the word matches the person and vice versa.* Such a person is trustworthy. As a philosophical category *cheng* first emerged in the moral sphere in the *Mencius* and the *Mean and Harmony*.† The latter says,

> Integrity is the way of heaven; integrity is the way of human beings. The person of integrity does not force himself and yet hits the mark. Such a one does not reflect and yet apprehends. One who naturally follows and accords with the Way is a sage. The person of integrity chooses the good and keeps to it. (*Mean and Harmony*, #20)

---

* See also Knoblock, *Xunzi*, 1:166–177.

† The *Records of the Historian* say that Zi Si wrote the *Mean and Harmony* (47 *Confucius' Family*, p. 1946). Han and Song scholars believed that the *Mencius* quotes the *Mean and Harmony*. The Qing historian Cui Shu doubted the authenticity of the *Mean and Harmony*, so modern historians of philosophy think that the *Mean and Harmony* copied the *Mencius*. In fact it is very hard to prove either way. The *Mean and Harmony* gives a more detailed and more developed view of integrity.

The *Mencius* has a similar statement:

> Therefore integrity is the way of heaven. Reflecting on integrity is the way of human beings. There has never been one of utmost integrity who does not move others. The one who has not integrity has not yet been able to move others. (*Mencius* 4 *Li Lou* A, #13)

The Han commentator on the *Mean and Harmony*, Zheng Xuan (127–200), notes,

> "Integrity is the way of heaven; integrity is the way of humans." This speaks of integrity as the nature of heaven. The person of integrity studies and thereby is a person of integrity. (*SKQS* 116, *Zheng Xuan's Notes on the* Record of Rites 53, *Mean and Harmony*, p. 368a)

By saying that integrity is the nature of heaven Zheng Xuan means both that integrity is a virtue bestowed on humans by heaven and also that heaven itself can be described as possessing integrity. The *Mean and Harmony* gives a further discourse on integrity:

> Thus utmost integrity is unresting. Because it is unresting so it perdures. Because it perdures so it manifests itself. Because it manifests itself so it goes far. Because it goes far so it is all-embracing. Because it is all-embracing so it is lofty and bright. All-embracing is the means by which it supports things; lofty and bright is the means by which it covers things;* going far is the means by which it accomplishes [*cheng*] things.† The way of heaven and earth may be completely summarized in one phrase: Its making things is without duplicity; its generating things is unfathomable. The way of heaven and earth is extensive and generous, lofty and bright, far-reaching and perduring.... The *Songs* say, "The decrees of heaven, how majestic

---

*Supporting is the activity of earth and covering that of heaven. Integrity is invested with the properties of heaven and earth.

†There is a deliberate use of *cheng*, 'to accomplish,' to describe the operation of its homophone, *cheng*, 'integrity.'

and unending!"* This means, "that is what makes heaven heaven." (*Mean and Harmony*, #26, 27)

Hence integrity is that which is without duplicity and that which is unending. 'Without duplicity' means that before and after match; 'unending' means that there is never a break. In other words, heaven displays a fixed order of acting.

In addition to ascribing integrity to the action of heaven, the *Mean and Harmony* also attributes it to the sage. The sage's action does not require effort or reflection because it naturally agrees with the Way and with principle. This is to say that the moral order and the natural order have the same characteristics and are in fact united.

The *Xunzi* also applies 'integrity' to the moral and natural orders:

"In fostering the mind the sage considers nothing as better than integrity." Utmost integrity admits of no other thing. Benevolence can protect it and justice implement it. The integrated mind/heart keeps to benevolence and then realizes it. It is realized and then is numinous. It is numinous and then can cause transformations. The integrated mind/heart implements justice and then is one with principle. It has principle and so is bright. Is bright and so can change. To cause change and transformation to succeed each other in flourishing is what is meant by heaven's virtue. Heaven does not speak yet human beings can infer it is lofty; earth does not speak yet human beings can infer it is thick. The four seasons do not speak yet the hundred clans act in season. This is because having attained utmost integrity they have constancy. (*Xunzi* 3, *Nothing Indecorous*, lines 26–29)

Hence integrity is on one hand a virtue cultivated by the gentleman and on the other the reliability of the natural order.

Li Ao (772–841) was a proponent of the *Mean and Harmony* in opposition to Buddhist and Daoist thinkers and religions.† He was a

---

* *Songs* IV. i, bk. I, Ode II, st. 1 (Ode 267).
† Li Ao sought to revive Confucianism but in doing so he incorporated insights gained from Buddhism. Carsun Chang believes that Li Ao's notion of 'enlightenment' was in fact a translation of the Buddhist *prajnaparamita*. See C. Chang, *The Development of Neo-Confucian Thought* (New York: Bookman Associates, 1957), pp. 103–112.

student of Han Yu, famous for his satirical essay on veneration of the Buddha's bone. He expands on the theme of integrity:

> Integrity is the nature of the sage. It is "docile and unmoving," broad, great, clear and bright, illuminating heaven and earth. "When influenced it reaches out to all phenomena under heaven." In their going and resting, their speaking and silence there is nowhere they do not attain to the peak.*
> (*SKQS* 1078, *Collected Works of Li Xi* 2, *Book of the Recovery of Human Nature* 1, p. 107a)
>
> The Way is utmost integrity. If one is a person of integrity and yet does not rest then one can be empty. If empty and not resting then one is enlightened. If enlightened and not resting then one illumines heaven and earth and omits nothing. (Ibid., p. 107b)

The Song Period

Zhou Dunyi, in the Song dynasty, titled the first two chapters of his *Book of Comprehending* 'integrity':

> Integrity is the root of the sage. "Great is *Qian* (hexagram no. 1, heaven) the origin. All things begin from it." It is the source of integrity. "The way of *Qian* is to change and transform, so that all is perfectly correct and brilliantly penetrating." Integrity is thus established. It is perfectly pure and perfectly good. (*SKQS* 1101, *Book of Comprehending* 1, *Integrity* 1, pp. 420b–421a)
>
> To be a sage is to have integrity, that is all. Integrity is the root of the five constant virtues [benevolence, justice, rites, wisdom, and trustworthiness] and the source of the hundreds of activities. When still it is beingless; when active it is being. It is perfectly correct and brilliantly penetrating. Without integrity the five constant virtues and hundreds of activities would all not be so. They would be evil, dark and obstructing. Hence

---

*The parts of this text within quotation marks are from the *Great Commentary to the Book of Changes* A 10, p. 295.

> when there is integrity then all goes as if nothing mattered.
> (Ibid. 2, pp. 421b–422a)

According to Zhou, integrity is an a priori moral principle. It is rooted in heaven as its origin and is the foundation of goodness, the virtues, and all proper activity.

Chen Yi speaks even more clearly of integrity:

> Integrity is the reality of principle. It is being integrated and not changing. Throughout the millennia in the human mind and in the principles of things it has always been so. There is one and not two. So-called integrity is when sages whether past or to come agree with this moral rule. Integrity is the way of heaven. (*SBBY: Discourse on the Classics* 8, *Explanation of the* Mean and Harmony, pp. 5a–b)
>
> Sincerity is the reality of principle. (*SKQS* 698, *Surviving Works of the Two Chengs* 1, *Discourse on the Way*, p. 357a)

Cheng Yi reckoned that integrity is being integrated and not changing. It is a universal and necessary law. It is the reality, that is, the objective rule, of principle. The moral law and natural law are one.

Zhu Xi also discusses integrity:

> Integrity is said of what is truly the case and shows "no illusion" [hexagram no. 25, *wu wang*]. It is the fundamental nature of heaven. (*Exegesis of the* Mean and Harmony, pp. 19a–b)
>
> Integrity is said of what is most real and has "no illusion." It is the correct principle bestowed by heaven and received by things. (*SKQS* 1101, *Explanation of the* Book of Comprehending, p. 420b)

Zhu Xi interprets the hexagram 'no illusion' in the sense of what must necessarily be the case. Cheng Yi and Zhu Xi both consider the five constant virtues to be self-evident and necessary for all.

Wang Fuzhi

Wang Fuzhi gives the most detailed analysis of integrity. Integrity means that heaven and earth have principle:

Heaven and earth having their principle is integrity. (*Notes on Master Zhang's* Correcting the Unenlightened 3b, *Integrity and Clarity*, p. 98)

Integrity is the reality of the principle of heaven. It does not have any of the artifice of human manufacture. (Ibid., p. 116)

Integrity is the real principle of heaven. (Ibid. 9b, *Qian Cheng* 2, p. 333)

Integrity is that which integrates all the principles:

Integrity binds together the principles under heaven and does not exclude anything. It threads through the centre of the myriad affairs and there is nothing it does not penetrate. (*Great and Full Explanation on Reading the Four Books* 3.20, *Mean and Harmony*, p. 134)

Integrity includes the principles of morality:

Speaking of integrity, it is a key word and no other word can replace or explain it. Even more, there is no manner of speech that can oppose its form. It is said of all that is good in the world. It is said of all that penetrates my body, mind, will and knowledge and is not not one with goodness. (Ibid. 9.1 #10, *Mencius* 4, *Li Lou A*, p. 605)

Integrity unites inside and outside and embraces the five virtues and amalgamates *yin* and *yang*. (Ibid. 10.3, *Mencius* 7, *Exhausting the Mind A*, p. 6984)

Wang Fuzhi thus also combines the natural and moral orders. He also talks about the relation of integrity to things:

Integrity depends on things to make its efforts apparent. Things take integrity as their stem. (Ibid. 3, *Mean and Harmony* 25.1, p. 162)

Integrity cannot be made manifest without a concrete medium. In reverse, things depend on integrity as their principle.

Wang also glosses 'integrity' as really existing:

Integrity is what really exists. What is at the beginning has that where it begins; what is at the end has that where it ends. What really is is what is held in common by all in the world. It is

> what those with eyes can all see and those with ears can all hear. (*Elaboration on the Meanings of the* Book of History 3.6, *Speaking of Destiny* 1, p. 70)
>
> Integrity is reality. What is real is what always exists ... just as water is always flowing and always going down, fire is always blazing and always going up. (Ibid. 4.7, *Great Plan* 3, p. 116)

What really exists in Wang's philosophy is principle. 'Integrity' means, then, that objective reality has set rules. Integrity expresses the fact that reality and its law are one.

Hence from the *Mean and Harmony*'s proclaiming integrity as the Way of heaven to Wang Fuzhi's integrity as the real principle of heaven, the sense of the term has remained largely unchanged.

III. Concepts Derived from Daoism

Whereas the preceding seven concepts were used in various schools of thought, the next four are specifically Daoist in origin, if not in later use. They sketch the contours of the Daoist world. Daoism takes notice of the unsayable mystery at the heart of the world and thus is concerned with pointing to what cannot be said; at the same time Daoists advocate flowing spontaneously with the flow of nature. The sage is to behave like the Way itself and to appropriate its qualities to himself or herself.

It has been a commonplace of Chinese philosophy that Daoism tends to be other-worldly. This view has been challenged through study of the key text, the Dao De Jing, *and its practical, political, and military applications. A more serious challenge has been given, however, by the discovery in Changsha of manuscripts that are Daoist in inspiration but manifestly concerned with* realpolitik. *Reassessment of Daoism in the light of these manuscripts has led scholars to understand three major currents present in its formation: the "metaphysics" of the* Dao De Jing, *political and military reflections on the sage ruler or sage general, and meditation practices.*

19. Dimension: Extension-Duration

Yu-zhou VŬ-TRU

宇宙

The modern Chinese word for 'universe' is a binome (yu-zhou) composed of characters that when read separately mean 'extension' (yu) and 'duration' (zhou). One could also translate it as 'space-time,' but I have used 'space' to mean 'empty space' when translating xu. *'Space' as in 'space-time' suggests what is measurable, whereas the more Bergsonian 'extension-duration' is probably nearer to the original meaning of the term* yu-zhou.

Yu-zhou

The earliest known use of *yu-zhou* is in one of the *Inner Chapters* of the *Zhuangzi*:

> Alongside sun and moon, seizing extension and duration. (*Zhuangzi* 2, *The Sorting Which Evens Things Out*, line 77)

The *Zhuangzi* itself gives no explanantion of the terms. For that one can look at another Warring States work, the *Shizi*, whose claim to fame is its definition of these two concepts:

> The four quarters of Heaven and earth are called 'extension'; going back to the past and coming forward to the present are called 'duration.' (*Shizi*, quoted in commentary of Lu Deming (556–627) in *Explanation of the Writings of Zhuangzi* by Guo Qingfan, p. 48)

The term appears several times in the later corpus of the *Zhuangzi*:

> If it is so, outside one does not look at extension-duration and within one does not know the ultimate start. (*Zhuangzi* 22, *Knowledge Roams North*, lines 64–65)
>
> If it is so, going astray ... one does not know the ultimate start. (*Zhuangzi* 32, *Lie Yu Kou*, lines 20–21)

'Extension-duration' refers to the outside world and is contrasted with the ultimate start. It is the visible universe, in contrast to the 'big bang.'

The terms are defined separately in the *Keng Sang Chu* chapter:

> What is real and yet not confined to a place is 'extension'; what endures and has no trunk nor branches is 'duration.' (*Zhuangzi* 23, *Keng Sang Chu*, lines 55–56)

The *Huainanzi* states:

> Going back to the past and coming to the present is called 'duration'; the four directions, above and below are called 'extension.' (*Huainanzi* 11, *Leveling Customs*, p. 99, line 20)

This definition agrees with that of the *Shizi*. Another Han work is the *Ling Xian* by Zhang Heng:

> The measure of 'extension' is without limit: the ends of 'duration' are infinite. (*Yuhan Shanfang Ji Yishu*, p. 2816a)

Although heaven and earth are limited, the concepts 'extension-duration' are without limit.

In a commentary on the *Zhuangzi*, Guo Xiang notes,

> 'Extension' is the four directions, above and below, and the four directions, above and below, are without limit. 'Duration' is what perdures from the past to the present and neither in past nor present does it have a limit. (*Explanation of the Writings of Zhuangzi*, *Zhuzi Jicheng* 3, *Collected Exegesis of Zhuangzi*, p. 348)

Guo Qingfan's edition includes a further note:

> The *Three Cang* says, "the four directions, above and below are 'extension.' Although extension is real it does not have a fixed place in which it can be found." The *Three Cang* says, "going back to the past and coming up to the present is called 'duration.' ... Although duration increases in time one cannot know its beginning nor yet its ending." (Ibid.)

Thus 'extension' refers to the space of space and time. This is real but not located. 'Duration' refers to the time of space and time. This perdures but has no beginning or ending that may be spoken of. This confirms the reality of space and the continuing nature of time and the limitlessness of both.

Jiu-yu

A more logical analysis of the terms is given in the *Mohist Canons*. The term used for duration in these canons is *jiu* 久 rather than *zhou*, but otherwise the definitions are similar to the above:

> Canon: 'Duration' is pervasion of different times. (A40)
> Explanation: 'Present' and 'past' combine mornings and evenings. (A40)
> Canon: 'Extension' is pervasion of different places. (A41)
> Explanation: 'East and west' covers 'north and south.' (A41)
> (*Later Mohist Logic*, p. 293)

Thus 'duration' is what applies to all dimensions of time and 'extension' is what applies to all dimensions of space. Together they refer to the four-dimensional world: the three dimensions of space with time.

Zhou-he

In the *Guanzi* there is a chapter titled *Zhou-he, the All-Embracing Unity*. *Zhou-he* are what embrace heaven, earth, and the myriad things.

> Heaven, earth encapsulate the myriad things; '*zhou-he*' encapsulates heaven and earth. (*Guanzi* 11 *All-Embracing Unity*, 1:135)
> The meaning of '*zhou-he*' is that above it reaches to above heaven and below it has its source below the earth, outside it goes beyond the four seas. It unites heaven and earth so as to make of them one bundle. (Ibid., 1:152)

The term *zhou-he* refers to the inclusion of all.

Thus, the *Zhuangzi* and *Shizi* used *yu-zhou*, the Mohist logicians used *jiu-yu* and the *Guanzi* used *zhou-he*. Of these three expressions only the former lasted. The combinations with *jiu* and *he* failed because the words have too many different meanings. In Han-dynasty and later works it is the formulation *yu-zhou* that appears.

20. Being and Beingless

You-wu HŨU - VÔ

有無

The Chinese language does not have any word that corresponds to the Greek εἶναι, *which is both a grammatical copula and an affirmation of existence. The closest to the verb 'to be' is* 'you,' *which equally well means 'to have.' This point must be borne in mind. In places* 'you' *may be better translated as 'be' but often 'have' is more congruent. Aquinas explains this in terms of* esse non subsistens. *The Laozi tries to say the same by saying that beinglessness has a symbol though it lacks form. It is unfortunate that in Chinese 'wu' can mean both the contrasting pair of* 'you' *and the metaphysical source of both* 'you' *and 'wu'. It would help if the Cantonese negation of* 'you', *namely* 'mou' 冇, *were to be used in the first case, leaving 'wu' to function in the second.*

There are two forms of the character for 'beingless': 無 *and* 无. *The exact origin of the two characters and why they should come to be synonymous need not detain us here. Within philosophical writings the two are perfectly synonymous.*

The Classical Period

Being and beingless are compared in the *Analects*:

> Master Zeng said, "To be able and yet ask those who are not able; to have much and yet ask those who have little; having [*you*] while appearing to have not [*wu*]; full yet seeming to be empty; when offended not contradicting. Long ago my friend used to do things in this way."* (*Analects* 8, *Tai Bo* #5, p. 210)

The contrast between 'having' and 'not-having' is a reference to personal ability rather than a metaphysical distinction. Yan Yuan was very humble and hence although he had ability he nonetheless asked advice of others who were not as advanced as he was.

---

* He is referring to Yan Yuan, who died young; hence Zeng says, "long ago."

It is in the *Laozi* that 'being' and 'beingless' first emerge as a philosophical pair. By 'being' the *Laozi* refers to the concrete existence of heaven, earth, and the myriad things. 'Beingless' in the *Laozi* has different meanings. It can refer first to the empty part of a given thing; second to the state before or after a particular thing existed; third to the highest origin that transcends all particular things.

The first meaning is found in the reference to the hub of an axle:

> Thirty spokes congregate in one hub. It is by what is not that the cart has its use. Clay is shaped into a vessel. It is by what is not that the vessel has its use. One cuts out doors and windows to make a room. It is by what is not that the room has its use. Hence being is what can be put to advantage and what is not can be put to use. (*Laozi* 11/MWD 55)

A wheel is made of spokes, a pot of clay, a door of a frame. These features are the 'being' of the objects. But the usefulness of a door is that it is empty and can be passed through, of a pot that it is empty and can contain things, of a wheel that it has a hub which is a point around which the wheel turns. Thus there is a contrast between the being and the beinglessness of things.

The second sense is found in the contrast of being and beingless in the following text:

> When all under heaven know beauty as beauty then there is awareness of ugliness; when all know good as good then there is awareness of evil. Thus being and beingless give rise to each other; difficult and easy form each other; long and short compare with each other; high and low correspond to each other; sound and voice harmonize with each other; fore and aft follow each other. (*Laozi* 2/MWD 46)

In any circumstances in which being should cease to exist then beingless arises, just as what is high is always in contrast with what is low.

The third meaning of 'beingless' is found in the metaphysics of the *Laozi*, according to which beingless is more fundamental than being:

> Reversal is the motion of the Way; weakness is the use of the Way. The myriad things under heaven are generated from being. Being is generated from beingless. (*Laozi* 40/MWD 4)

Here 'being' refers to heaven and earth whereas 'beingless' refers to the Way. Heaven and earth have form and name and so are said to be. The Way is formless and nameless and so is said to be beingless. This is absolute beinglessness. It is not just a void but is the source of all that is.

> Look and one does not see it, its name is indistinct; listen and one does not hear it, its name is faint; touch and one does not feel it, its name is subtle. These three may not be further examined and so merge into one. Its upper part is not bright; its depths are not gloomy; reeling on and on it is not possible to name it. It returns back to there not being a thing. This is called the shape without a shape, the symbol of what is not a thing. It is vague and elusive. (*Laozi* 14/MWD 58)

This beinglessness transcends the opposition between being and beingless.

In the *Laozi* being is generated from beingless. There is a beginning of being:

> All under heaven has a beginning. It may be taken as the mother of all under heaven. (*Laozi* 52/MWD 15)

The *Zhuangzi*, by contrast, says that the beginning is not an absolute beginning, nor is beingless absolute beingless. Merely to state that there is beingless is to state that there is something, hence a being.

> There is a beginning. There is not yet beginning to be a beginning. There is not yet beginning to be this not yet beginning to be a beginning. There is being. There is beingless. There is not yet beginning to be beingless. There is not yet beginning to be this not yet beginning to be beingless. However, suddenly there is 'beingless' but one does not know which out of 'being' and 'beingless' there is and which there is not. (*Zhuangzi* 2, *The Sorting Which Evens Things Out*, lines 49–51)

As Graham explains, 'nothing' can only be postulated in contrast with something. The assertion that there is nothing is contradictory because it is asserting of nothing that it is.* Being and beingless are always a pair:

---

*A. C. Graham, *Chuang-Tzu* (London: Allen and Unwin, 1981), pp. 55–56.

Considering it with respect to their being, then none of the myriad things are not. Considering it with respect to their beingless then none of the myriad things are not beingless. When one knows that east and west are opposites and one cannot be without the other, then what belongs to each will be appropriately assigned. (*Zhuangzi* 17, *Autumn Floods*, lines 31–33)

The use of 'being' and 'beingless' in logic is employed by the *Zhuangzi* to say something about the metaphysical status of the two terms. A similarly logical approach is found in the *Mohist Canons*:

Canon: Beingless does not necessarily require being. Explained by: what it is said of. (B49)

Explanation: In the case of the beingless of something, it is beingless only if it is. As for the cases of the sky falling down not being, they are altogether non-existent. (B49)

(*Later Mohist Logic*, p. 418)

Unlike the *Zhuangzi*, the Mohist logicians asserted that there can be cases in which beingless is not dependent on there ever having been that thing.

The Wei-Jin Period

The Wei-Jin period is generally known for its formation of Daoist metaphysics. He Yan and Wang Bi (226–249) both stressed beingless, whereas Pei Gu (267–300) stressed being. Guo Xiang (252–312) also questioned Wang Bi's emphasis on beingless.

The *Jin History** contains an account of Wang Bi and He Yan:

In the time of King Zheng Shi of Wei, He Yan, Wang Bi and others commented on the theories of Laozi and Zhuangzi. They reckoned that "heaven and earth and the myriad things all took beingless as their root. Beingless inaugurates things and completes their task. Beingless tends towards not existing. *Yin* and *yang* go to it to transform and generate. The myriad

---

* References in this section are to the history of the Jin (265–420) and not to the Jin (1115–1234).

things depend on it to produce their forms. The worthy depend on it to produce their virtue. The unworthy depend on it so as to save their person." Thus the use of beingless is that it has no rank and yet is valuable. (*Jin History* 43, *Biography of Wang and Yan*, p. 1236)

He Yan's work *Discourse on the Way* gives priority to beingless:

What makes being to be being is its reliance on being generated by beingless. What makes affairs to be affairs are their reliance on being produced from beingless. Should one talk about it there is nothing to say. Should one name it there is nothing to name. Should one see it it has no form. Should one listen to it it has no sound. Yet it is the completeness of the Way. Thus it is able to illuminate sounds and echoes and make *qi* and things stand out. It can embrace outer form and inner spirit and make light and shadows shine out. By it is the abstruse black. By it is the elemental white. By it is the square square. By it is the compass round. Round and square get their form yet it itself is without form. White and black get their name yet it itself is without name. (*Discourse on the Way*, quoted by Zhang Zhan (fl. 310) in his commentary on the *Liezi* 1, *Heaven's Gifts*, p. 3)*

Here beingless, formless, and nameless are what make things what they are. Although these negative terms have no form or name, they are the completeness of the Way. In other words, beingless transcends all contrasts.

Wang Bi died young and his extant works are all commentaries on the classics, especially on the *Laozi*. His point of view is at one with the point of view of He Yan.

Of the myriad things under heaven all are produced by being. The beginning of being is to have beingless as its root. If one wants to have complete being it is necessary to go back to beingless. (*Laozi–Zhou Yi* [Wang Bi ed.], *Laozi* 40, p. 110)

---

* In Chan, Wing-tsit, *Source Book in Chinese Philosophy*, p. 324.

Wang's exegesis of the *Analects* was lost but not before it was quoted by later authors:

> The Way is what beingless is called. There is nothing that it does not penetrate and nothing that it arises from. How much more then should it be called the Way. Flowing naturally without substance so it is not possible to picture it. (*Analects* 7, *Shu Er*, note preserved by Xing Bing, p. 624)

Pei Gu, by contrast, wrote *Discourse Honouring Being*.

> This extreme beinglessness, nothing can be produced by it. Thus what inaugurates generation is self-generated. What generates itself must have substance yet if it has a lack then it generates a lack. Generation takes being as its own part; thus space and beingless are what is said to be lacking in being. Thus if fostering involves the transformations of being it is not the case that the function of beingless is able to complete this. If principles are many it is not the case that non-action is able to follow them.... If there is even a drop of being, then all must be being. How can space and beingless add anything to the existence of the mass of generated things? (*Jin History* 35.2, *Biography of Pei Xiu*, appendix pp. 1046–1047)

Here being is self-generating and cannot come from beingless. Beingless is a lack of being in some respect.

By 'being' Pei Gu refers to concrete beings. He does also hold that there is absolute being. In the opening line of his essay he says that it is the Way, which gathers together all the self-generating 'roots':

> This collective gathering of all roots is the way of the highest peak. (Ibid., p. 1044)

Pei Gu's interpretation of the Way is peculiar to his own philosophy.

Guo Xiang built up his philosophy by expanding on the *Zhuangzi*. In his writings he opposed the idea that being is generated by beingless.

> Let me ask, "Is the maker of things being or beingless? If it is beingless then how can it make things? If it is being then it

does not suffice to make the many forms of things. Thus it is evident that the many forms make themselves into things. And later the beginning may be said to be the maker of things. (*SKQS* 1056, *Notes on the* Zhuangzi 2, *The Sorting Which Evens Things Out*, p. 19a)

What was before things? ... Suppose I say the utmost Way was before and further that the utmost Way is utmost beingless. How then can it be before? (Ibid. 22, *Knowledge Roams North*, p. 112a)

Thus Guo Xiang believed that beingless could not generate being. Guo Xiang understood beingless as a pure zero. He held all things to be in contrast with one another and denied any transcendence.

The next contribution to the debate came from the bhiksu Zhao (384–414), a pupil of Kumarajiva (344–413), the most famous translator of Buddhist manuscripts into Chinese. Zhao used Buddhist logic to discuss the problem of being and beingless:

The myriad things have that by which they are beingless and that by which they are not beingless. Having had that by which they are beingless, they exist and yet do not exist, and having had that by which they are beingless, they are beingless and yet not beingless. Being beingless yet not beingless, this being-lessness is not an absolute void; being existent yet beingless, this existence is not the real being. (*On the Unreal Void*, p. 31)

The myriad things are not truly existent because their existence is dependent on something else:

If being really is, it must constantly be. Does it depend on causes and relative causes [*hetupratyaya*] to become being? And, likewise, if beingless really is, it must constantly be. Does it depend on causes and relative causes for it to become so? If being cannot be by itself and must depend on causes and relative causes for coming into being then it can be known that it is no real being. As it is no real being it cannot be called being though it is existent. (Ibid., p. 35a)

Yet the myriad things are not nonexistent.

> With regard to not beingless: If all is beingless in which no activity arises in a perfect stillness then it may be called beingless. Then there should be nothing that arises. If things arise then things are not beingless. It is clear that causes and relative causes give rise to everything so the universe is not beingless. (Ibid., p. 35b)

Thus the myriad things are not existent, nor are they nonexistent.

> If one says that all is being, this being is not produced from reality. If one says all is beingless, we see all phenomena are obviously there. The phenomenal appearances are not beingless, yet they are unreal. As they are unreal, they are then not really existent. (Ibid., p. 37c)

The myriad things are not truly real; thus they are not existent. The phenomena have already appeared, however; hence things are not beingless.

The bhiksu Zhao was influenced by Mahayana Buddhism, but his use of the terms 'being' and 'beingless' betrays the influence of "abstruse" neo-Daoism, too. His use of the terms is different from that current in Chinese philosophy, however. He Yan, Wang Bi, Pei Gu, and Guo Xiang used 'being' to refer to given individual 'beings.' He Yan and Wang Bi used 'beingless' to refer to what transcends all duality. Pei Gu and Guo Xiang used 'beingless' to refer to the denial of the existence of a being. Zhao used 'being' to refer to reality and 'beingless' to refer to illusion. Thus, although he may have used the same terms his motive was quite different, and the reference they have is Buddhist rather than Chinese.

Chinese Daoism accepts that beings are dependent but does not go on to say that therefore they are not real. Buddhism argues from the contingency of things to a denial of their real existence.

Liu Yuxi

In an essay probably written sometime between 806 and 814, Liu Yuxi produced a novel interpretation of the formless. He held that it was simply too diffuse to be seen by the human eye but that it was not really nothing or beingless. He identifies 'formless' with the Buddhist notion of 'empti-ness' and from this point begins his argument:

> As for the so-called 'formless,' is it not empty? What is empty is
> form at its most diffuse; in its substance it is not opposed to
> things and in its function it is always dependent on 'being.' It
> must rely on things for it to be able to take a form. Now in
> making buildings the form of their height and breadth is con-
> tained within [their structure]. In making tools the form of the
> square and compass is contained within [their structure]. When
> a sound, whether loud or soft, is produced then the echo can-
> not outdo it. When a sundial is erected, whether straight or
> crooked, the shadow cannot outdo it. Are these not the nu-
> merical dimensions of emptiness? Now when the eye sees, it is
> not that it has its own light. Rather, it is necessary to rely on
> the sun, moon or fire for there to be light. The so-called 'hid-
> den by darkness' is simply that for which the eye cannot find a
> light. Would one say that for the eyes of cats and weasels or
> dogs and rats that which is in darkness is hidden? I therefore
> say that seeing with the eyes is making out the coarsest of
> forms; seeing with wisdom is making out the subtlest of forms.
> How could there be anything formless in heaven and earth?
> What of old was called 'without form' was simply 'without
> constant form' and this must depend on things in order to be
> seen.* (SBCK, *Collected Works of Liu Mengde* 12.5, *Discourse
> on Heaven* 2, pp. 10b–11a)

Zhang Zai and Wang Fuzhi

Zhang Zai based his interpretation of 'being' and 'beingless' on a theory of *qi*. He rejected the Buddhist interpretation of this world as illusory but was also opposed to the Daoist belief that 'being' was generated from 'beingless':

---

* This translation is indebted in part to H. G. Lamont, "An Early Ninth Century Debate on Heaven," *Asia Major* 18.2 (1973): 181–208, 19.1 (1974): 37–85, especially 19.1, p. 78.

When one realizes that space and emptiness are *qi*, then 'being' and 'beingless,' the hidden and manifest, the wondrous and transformation, human nature and destiny are seen as one and not as separate things. One who considers condensation and dispersal, going out and coming in, form and non-form and is able to infer to the root whence they come can fathom the *Changes*. If one says that space can generate *qi*, then space would be limitless, *qi* limited; space would be substance, *qi* its function, each radically different from the other. This would be to fall into Laozi's theory of natural spontaneity by which 'being' is generated from 'beingless' and one does not recognize the constant rule of 'being' and 'beingless' being undifferentiated and united. If one says that the myriad phenomena are the visible things produced within ultimate space, then things and space are taken to be not mutually contingent. Forms would produce themselves; natures would produce themselves. Forms, natures, heaven and human persons would not be mutually dependent for their existence. This would be to fall into the erroneous opinion of the Buddhists, who hold that mountains, rivers and the great earth are illusions.... They speak of the way of heaven, nature and destiny and if they do not fall into theories that all is illusion then they decree that 'being' is generated from 'beingless.' They hold this the path of entering into virtue. They do not know how to choose a technique to inquire. It is abundantly obvious that they are deluded by partial views and lapse into folly. (*SKQS* 697, *Correcting the Unenlightened* 1, *Ultimate Harmony*, pp. 97b–98a)

The distinction between 'being' and 'beingless' is simply that of the degree of gathering or scattering of *qi*. Scattered *qi* is 'beingless'; gathered *qi* is 'being.' Space is scattered *qi*. It cannot produce *qi*.

Zhang Zai goes on to deny the distinction between 'being' and 'beingless':

When *qi* gathers then its brightness becomes effective and it has form. When *qi* does not gather then its brightness does not become effective and it is without form. When *qi* is gathered how can one not say that it has being? When it is scattered how can one rush to say that it is beingless? Hence the sages raise their head to look at and bow their head to examine but say they only know the causes of being hidden or being manifest. They do not say they know the causes of 'being' and 'being-less.' ...

The condensation and dispersal of *qi* in ultimate space is like the freezing and melting of ice in water. When one knows that ultimate space is *qi* then there is no beinglessness. Hence in talking of the ultimate questions of nature and the way of heaven, the sages restrict their research to the numinous sequence of the five agents and the transformations of the changes. All those philosophers of shallow and erroneous thought who distinguish 'being' and 'beingless' do not investigate principles to the fullest. (Ibid., pp. 98b–99a)

What is visible is bright; what is invisible is dark. There is only the distinction between bright and dark and not between 'being' and 'being-less.'

Zhang Zai was opposed to the cosmology that places 'beingless' as the origin of the universe. The Daoist 'being' generated from 'beingless' and the Wei-Jin 'beingless' as the root both take the origin of the universe as an absolute. Zhang Zai believed that the only absolute is the collective name applied to *qi* in its successive states of change. He called this absolute the 'ultimate harmony':

The ultimate harmony is the so-called Way. (Ibid., p. 97a)

It comes from the transformations of *qi* and has the name of the Way. (Ibid., p. 99a)

Only this state of the transformations of *qi* can be considered an absolute.

Wang Fuzhi developed Zhang Zai's theories. He also held that there was no such thing as 'beingless.'

What people see is utter space. It is *qi* and not space. Space contains *qi*; *qi* fills up space. There is no so-called 'beingless-ness.' (*Notes on Master Zhang's* Correcting the Unenlightened 1a, *Ultimate Harmony*, p. 14)

Those who talk about 'beingless' do so because they are egged
on by those who speak of 'being' and want to demolish their
opinion. Thus in response to what the latter call 'being' they
say that there is no such 'being.' In the world is there indeed
anything that can be called 'beingless'? To say that a turtle has
no hair is to talk about a dog and not a turtle. To say that a
rabbit has no antlers is to talk about a deer and not a rabbit.
The one who speaks must have a foundation and only then can
one's theory stand. Suppose a speaker wants to establish 'beingless' as the foundation; even should a search for it high and
low and to the four corners and from past to present, existing
and departed be conducted it would not be possible to find it.
(*Record of Thoughts and Questionings (Inner Chapter)*, p. 411)

Wang Fuzhi's point is that 'beingless' is only suggested by reason of
comparison. Wondering whether a turtle has hair is on the basis of comparison with a dog. Asking if a rabbit has antlers means that one is thinking
of deer. Likewise, talk about 'beingless' is only possible on the basis of talk
about 'being.' 'Beingless' cannot be a state in itself.

Looking over the evolution of the concepts of 'being' and 'beingless,' one can say in general that 'being' is used of individual objects and as
a collective term for all such beings. 'Being' applies to objective beings and
phenomena. Such beings exist independent of the human observer. The
phenomena, however, depend on the observer, and here objectivity and
subjectivity become confused.

The sense of 'beingless' is even more complicated. What given objects lack, for example, a hole, can be termed 'beingless.' The coming into
existence of a being can be said to be a coming of 'beingless' from 'being.'
The destruction of a being can be described as a movement from 'being'
to 'beingless.' 'Beingless' is used to describe a change of state. Early Daoist
philosophy applied 'beingless' to whatever went beyond all oppositions,
was formless, anonymous, and without a rule. This 'beingless' is certainly
not a mere zero. Guo Xiang interpreted it as zero, however. The bhiksu
Zhao understood it as describing the unreal nature of illusion. Zhang Zai
and Wang Fuzhi affirmed that heaven, earth, and all they contain are certainly not an illusion.

21. **Spontaneous**

Ziran TỤ NHIÊN

自然

The term 'zi ran' is composed of two characters, the first meaning 'self' and the second 'what is so.' Together they may be translated as 'what is so of itself.' In simpler English one could say 'spontaneous.' The term is also translated 'nature.' Indeed in modern Chinese the word for the ecologist's 'nature' is literally 'great what is so of itself.' The term 'nature' is to be understood as 'spontaneity' rather than the opposite of the divine or of the artificial. The latter contrasts derive from Western thought and are quite foreign to the Chinese pattern of thought. Angus Graham spent a lot of time reflecting on the theme of spontaneity as it is expounded in the Zhuangzi and in other Daoist writings. He summarized his views as follows:

> *While all other things move spontaneously on the course proper to them, man has stunted and maimed his spontaneous aptitude by the habit of distinguishing alternatives, the right and the wrong, benefit and harm, self and others, and reasoning in order to judge between them. To recover and educate his knack he must learn to reflect his situation with the unclouded clarity of a mirror, and respond to it with the immediacy of an echo to a sound or shadow to a shape.**

Zhang's discussion here is confined to the period from the Laozi *to the deaths of Xi Kang and Ruan Ji in* A.D. *263.*

The *Laozi* and the *Zhuangzi*

The term first appears in the *Laozi* as the model for the sage. Wang Chong took it up in opposition to the Han Confucians' purposive thought. Xi

---

* Graham, *Chuang Tzu*, p. 6.

Kang used it in contrast to the artificial hypocrisy of contemporary ritual education. Ruan Ji first used the term as a general term for heaven, earth and all they contain, our modern idea of 'nature.' From and including the Tang onward there has been no substantially new interpretation of the term.

Chapter 25 of the *Laozi* contains the following line:

> Humans imitate the earth; the earth imitates heaven; heaven imitates the Way; the Way imitates what is so of itself. (*Laozi* 25/MWD 69)

By saying that the Way imitates what is so of itself, the text means that the Way just is as it is and not that there is something else beyond the Way.

> The work is accomplished; affairs performed; the people all say I am so of myself. (*Laozi* 17/MWD 61)
>
> Esteem of the Way; honoring virtue is not the result of anyone's order but arises of itself. (*Laozi* 51/MWD 14)
>
> Therefore the sages desire to not desire, do not esteem objects difficult to obtain. They study how to not study and return to what the mass of persons have passed by. They support the spontaneity of the myriad things and do not dare to act actively. (*Laozi* 64/MWD 27)

The contrast is between the natural occurrence of things and the forced striving of human agents.

In the *Zhuangzi* the spontaneous is what originally was so.

> What I mean by being without the essential nature of a person is to say that a person does not inflict injury on himself by tending to likes or dislikes. Rather, one goes constantly by spontaneity and does not add to life. (*Zhuangzi* 5, *The Signs of the Fullness of Power*, line 58)

An anonymous writer refuses to say how to rule the empire; rather, he advocates spontaneity:

> May your heart roam in the insipid, unite your *qi* to the desert, flow along with things spontaneously and do not give place to

self inclination; then you can order the empire. (*Zhuangzi* 7, *Responding to the Emperors and Kings*, line 11)

Flowing along with things spontaneously implies following both the spontaneity of human beings and that of things. In the later corpus of the *Zhuangzi* the doctrine of spontaneity is carried to the point of anarchy by an advocate of total withdrawal from social life:

> The people of ancient times dwelt in the midst of chaos and desert and found the insipid and the desert along with their contemporaries.... At that time nothing was done yet things went along spontaneously. (*Zhuangzi* 16, *Menders of Nature*, lines 7, 9)

The *Zhuangzi* also contains chapters that Graham associates with the Yangists, advocates of the benefits of a comfortable private life as opposed to the vicissitudes of social engagements. An old fisherman tells Confucius:

> Rites are what the customs of the time prescribe. The authentic is what one receives from heaven; it is spontaneous and cannot be exchanged for something else. (*Zhuangzi* 31, *The Old Fisherman*, line 38)

Wang Chong

Wang Chong included a chapter titled *Spontaneity* in his *Balanced Dialogues* in which he fervently advocates the Daoist ideal. The chapter opens with the following:

> Heaven and earth unite their *qi*; the myriad things are generated of their own accord just as when husband and wife unite their *qi* a child is generated by its own accord. The living things among the myriad things, those that have blood, know hunger and know cold. They see that the five grains can be eaten. They take and eat them. They see silk and hemp can be worn. They take and wear them. Some say that heaven produces the five grains so as to feed human beings and produces silk and hemp so as to clothe them. This is to say that heaven is the

farmer for human beings or the silk-weaver. This does not accord with spontaneity; therefore its import is doubtful and it
cannot be followed. Suppose one turns to the Daoist theory,
then heaven universally sends out *qi* among the myriad things.
Grains satisfy hunger while silk and hemp ward off cold; therefore human beings eat grains and wear silk and hemp. That
heaven does not purposefully produce the five grains, silk and
hemp so as to clothe and feed human beings follows from the
fact that disasters produce changes but not in order to reprove
human beings. Things produce themselves and human beings
wear or eat them; *qi* changes itself and people fear it. For the
usual theory is disheartening.... Consider a person who sends
forth his *qi*. It is not that he wants to produce a child. The *qi*
is sent forth and the child produces itself. Heaven moves
not because it wants to produce things. Rather, things produce
themselves. This is what spontaneity is about then. Sending
forth *qi* and not wanting to make things and things make
themselves, this is what is meant by 'not acting making.' In
talking of the spontaneity of heaven what is its 'not acting'? It
is *qi*. Quite simply it is without desires, without action and
without anything to do. (*Balanced Inquiries* 54 (18.1), *Spontaneity*, p. 177)

Wang Chong exalted the notion of spontaneity as a riposte to the Han
Confucian theory of heaven and earth mutually influencing each other
with its concomitant corollary that heaven sends disaster to reprove
people. He claimed that heaven and earth produce things spontaneously
and naturally and not in order to serve human interests. Heaven is spontaneous and nonacting in its movement. This is so because *qi* is itself not
engaged in purposive activity.

The Wei-Jin Period

Spontaneity became a much-debated topic in the Wei-Jin period. In his
commentary on the text of the *Laozi* that reads, "the Way imitates what is
so of itself," Wang Bi says,

> The Way does not go against spontaneity and hence it attains to its nature. To imitate what is so of itself is for a square to imitate a square, a circle to imitate a circle and not to go against what is so of itself in any way. Spontaneity is a term which cannot be named, a word that reaches to the utmost. (Lou Yulie, *Wang Bi: Laozi* 25, p. 65)

Just as a square is by definition square, so too the Way is so of itself. In commenting on the line of the *Laozi* that runs "heaven and earth are not benevolent; they treat the myriad things like a straw-dog," Wang Bi writes,

> Heaven and earth trust to what is so of itself; they neither act nor make. The myriad things manage themselves by themselves; thus they are not benevolent. The benevolent person must make, establish, promote and change things. Such a one bestows favor and acts positively. In being made, established, promoted and changed things lose their authenticity. When favors are bestowed and positive actions received then things are no longer complete. When things are no longer complete then heaven and earth do not suffice to cover* and support them. Heaven† and earth do not produce straw for animals yet animals eat straw. It does not produce dogs for human beings yet human beings eat dogs.‡ If one does not act on behalf of the myriad things then each will fit its function and then there is nothing that is not sufficient. (Ibid., p. 13)

In this text spontaneity, what is so of itself, is not making and not positively acting. This agrees with the original meaning of the *Laozi*. In saying that spontaneity is a concept that cannot be spoken of Wang Bi means that it is the term of all investigation. When one can no longer uncover any further causes then one says that something is so of itself.

---

* For this reading as 'cover' see A. Rump, *Commentary on the Lao Tzu by Wang Pi* (Honolulu: University Press of Hawai'i, 1979), p. 19 n. 3.

† Text emended following Lou Yulie, *Wang Bi Laozi*, p. 15 n. 5.

‡ Author's note: Wang Bi misunderstands the phrase 'straw dogs.' It should be a dog made of straw and not straw and dogs separately.

Zi ran in the more modern sense of 'nature,' as that which embraces heaven, earth, and all therein, appears in Ruan Ji's *Discourse on Fathoming Zhuangzi*:

> Heaven and earth are produced from Nature. The myriad things are produced from heaven and earth. Nature has nothing outside it; thus it is the name of heaven and earth together. Heaven and earth do have an inside; thus the myriad things are produced from them. Inasmuch as it has no outside what can be said to differ from it? Inasmuch as it has an inside what can be said to be special to it? (*Complete Three Kingdoms Literature* 45, *Discourse on Fathoming Zhuangzi*, p. 9a)

Nature is the great whole that encompasses all, and heaven and earth are within it. By using the term *zi ran* in this sense Ruan Ji invested it with new meaning. The modern use of the term has its origins in Ruan Ji's use here.

Ruan's contemporary, Xi Kang, advocated a rejection of logical name-chopping and a return to spontaneity.

> The one called a gentleman does not apply his mind to distinguishing 'so' and 'not so;'* rather, his conduct does not contravene the Way. How can this be explained? The one whose *qi* is calm and spirit vacant does not apply his mind to acquiring honors. The one who sees his body as a shell and whose mind penetrates does not confine his essential nature to his desires. If honors are not present in the mind then one can go past the logicians and trust to the spontaneous. If one does not confine one's essential nature to one's desires then one can examine noble and base rank and penetrate to the myriad natures. If one can fluidly penetrate to the nature of things then one does not contravene the great Way. If one goes past the logicians and trusts to the spontaneous then one is not restrained by 'so' and 'not so.' (Ibid. 50, *Discourse on Explaining Selfishness*, p. 1a)

---

*This may be read as 'right' and 'wrong,' 'true' and 'false.'

Xi Kang rejected the logicians' distinguishing what is right and wrong, true and false and advocated spontaneity instead.

Ruan Ji's great-nephew, Ruan Zhan, however, combined logic and spontaneity.

> He saw the Minister of Education, Wang Rong. Rong asked him, "The sages value logic, Laozi and Zhuangzi expound spontaneity, is their purpose the same?" Zhan replied, "Much about the same." (*Jin History* 49.3, *Biography of Ruan Zhan*, p. 1363)

Guo Xiang found no opposition between the activity of the human agent and the spontaneous course of nature. Both can be described as spontaneous or 'natural.'

> What came before things? I say *yin* and *yang* came before things and *yin-yang* are themselves but things. What came before *yin* and *yang*? I say Nature came before *yin* and *yang* and Nature is the self-appointed name of things.... To make clear the Nature of things, it is not what is made to be so. (*SKQS* 1056, *Notes on Zhuangzi* 22, *Knowledge Roams North*, p. 112a)
>
> Movement and staying, death and life, prosperity and decline, disintegration and rising, not yet begun and always present all are just naturally so. It is not that they are purposely so; thus one can leave them and they will obtain of their own accord. (Ibid. 12, *Heaven and Earth*, p. 64b)

What is natural or spontaneous is what is such by itself.

Guo Xiang also used the phrase *tian ran*, 'so by heaven' or 'naturally so':

> What is it that generates and regenerates? It is what is freely so and that generates itself. It generates itself which means I do not generate it. Indeed I cannot produce things and nor can things produce me. Rather, I am so spontaneously. Being so of one's own accord is then what is called 'naturally so.' Being naturally so means it is not made to be so and thus it is said of heaven. Since it is said of heaven it makes clear its spontaneity.

Is it not said of its bright vault? ... Thus 'heaven' is the collective term for the myriad things. (Ibid. 2, *The Sorting Which Evens Things Out*, p. 10)

Unlike Xi Kang, Guo Xiang believed that logic and spontaneity are compatible. Distinctions between ruler and minister, and a Confucian moral education are natural.

The one whom the times value is the prince and the one whose talent is not comparable with his contemporaries is the minister. Just as heaven is high of itself and earth is humble of itself, the head is above of itself and the feet of themselves touch the ground, how can one replace the other? (Ibid., p. 11a)

The Confucian moral education can be summed up in the terms benevolence and justice:

Benevolence and justice are the essential nature of human beings and so one should rely on them.... Those who fear that benevolence and justice are not the essential nature of human beings and worry about them can truly be said to worry overmuch. (Ibid. 8, *Webbed Toes*, p. 48b)

The one who is good at charioteering puts all his effort into it.... Suppose he were to rely on the strength of the fastest steeds and press them to their utmost; then even if their footprints reached to the edge of the desert yet the nature of the ordinary mass of horses would be good enough. It is erroneous to say that trusting to the nature of the horse entails letting it go and not driving it. If one hears about 'non-activity' and then says that walking is not as good as lying down, why not let the horse live* and not come back? (Ibid. 9, *Horses' Hooves*, p. 50b)

Human activity is a part of nature and hence using a horse to pull a chariot is as natural as just letting the horse roam wild, if not more so.

---

* The *SKQS* edition reads *sheng*, 'live'; Zhang reads *wang*, 'go.' The two characters are easily confused.

22. Essence and Spirit

Jingshen   TINH-THÂN

精神

The term 'spirit' in English can refer to the deity or to an inner force within a human being or human society. In Chinese philosophy the term shen *carries the same range of connotations. 'Jing' in the Warring States period refers to the purest, the most quintessential. It would seem that the combination* jing-qi *came to the fore in Daoist meditation texts, where it may be translated as 'essence.' In the* Zhuangzi, jing *and* shen *are combined into one notion that is interpreted in a cosmic setting.*

The Religious Sense

The term 'spirit' originally referred to the object of religious adoration.* The following extracts from *Zuo's Commentary* and the *Analects* all illustrate the religious use of the term:

> The state of the people is what the spirits regard. The sage kings, therefore, first secured the welfare of the people, and then put forth their strength in serving the spirits. (*Zuo's Commentary* 2, *Huan* 6, p. 47)
>
> A spirit came down in Xin.... The Duke of Guo caused the prayer-master Ying, the superintendent of the ancestral temple, Qu, and the historiographer, Yin, to sacrifice to it.... The historiographer Yin said, 'Ah! Guo will perish. I have heard that, when a State is about to flourish, its ruler receives his lessons from the people. When it is about to perish, he receives his lessons from the spirits. (Ibid. 3, *Zhuang* 32, p. 119)
>
> The Master did not talk about potents, bravado, disorder or spirits. (*Analects* 7, *Shu Er* #20, p. 201)
>
> Fan Chi asked about wisdom. The Master said, "To undertake the duties assigned to the people, respect ghosts

---

*The term *shen* is used in Chinese religion for the spirits of the spirit world in general. Some Protestants use it to translate the Judeo-Christian YHWH.

and spirits yet keep them at a distance; this may be said to be wisdom." (*Analects* 6, *Yong Ye* #20, p. 191)

Jing-shen

In the Warring States period 'spirit' began to be paired with the term 'form' and thus was divested of its religious connotations. Graham translated it as the demonic. Cook Ding explains to Wen Hui how he cuts up an ox:

> Your servant makes contact by the spirit and does not look with the eye. With the senses I know how to stop but the spirit wants to go on. (*Zhuangzi* 3, *What Matters in the Nurture of Life*, line 6)

Perceiving by the spirit is contrasted with perceiving by the eyes.

> When power is complete then form is complete; when form is complete then spirit is complete. (*Zhuangzi* 12, *Heaven and Earth*, line 64)
>
> Your highness's spirit and form. (*Zhuangzi*, 24 *Xu Wu Gui*, line 16)

Xunzi also uses the distinction of spirit and form:

> The form is present and the spirit lives. (*Xunzi* 17, *Discourse on Heaven*, line 10)

Sometimes both the Zhuangzi and the Xunzi use the term *jing*, 'essence,' rather than *shen*, 'spirit,' to refer to the inner nature of a human being. In a dialogue with Hui Shi, Zhuangzi says,

> Now you expel your spirit outside of yourself, exhaust your essence. You lean on a tree and mumble, repose on a dried-up *wu-tong* tree and snooze.* (*Zhuangzi* 5, *The Signs of the Fullness of Power*, line 59)

---

* Graham, *Chuang Tzu*, pp. 82–83, explains that the reference is probably to a desk of the wood of the *wu-tong* tree (*Sterculia platanifolia*).

Jing and 'form' are contrasted in the following passage, in which *jing* means 'essential spirit':

> Abandon affairs and then one's form [body] will no longer be worn out. Forget about life then one's essence [*jing*] will be unharmed. When the form is whole and essence restored one is at one with Heaven. (*Zhuangzi* 19, *Fathoming Nature*, lines 5–6)

In the *Xunzi*, *jing* also means 'essential spirit,' as in the following story about a man in a cave who loved to think.

> When the desires of ear and eye assailed him, they destroyed his thought. When he heard the sound of mosquitoes or gnats, it disturbed his essential spirit. (*Xunzi* 21, *The Removal of Prejudices*, line 62)

Jing Qi

The *Inward Training* of the *Guanzi* introduces the phrase 'essential *qi*.'

> In general the essence of things when compared is what generates. Below it generates the five grains, above it becomes the constellations. It flows within heaven and earth and is called ghosts and spirits. It is stored in the bosom and is called the sage. (*Guanzi* 49, *Inward Training*, 2:121)

According to this passage there is a lot of essence within heaven and earth. In the sky it gathers into stars; on the earth it becomes the five grains; among human beings it is the wisdom of the sages. The *Inward Training* explains 'essence' as follows:

> Essence is the essence of *qi*. (Ibid., 2:124)

In other words, 'essence' is a diffuse form of *qi*. Its presence in the sages is explained thus:

> It affirms the mind in the center, makes the ears and eyes perceptive and keen, strengthens the four limbs and so it may be the dwelling place of essence. (Ibid.)

The mind and bosom of the person can be the dwelling place of essence, hence essential *qi* can reside there and then the person is wise.

> Respectfully clear out the dwelling then essential *qi* will enter. (Ibid., 2:126)
>
> The life of all human beings is as follows: heaven produces their essence; earth produces their form. The two unite to become a human being. (Ibid., 2:130)

Hence essence is what heaven provides.

The *Inward Training* speaks of essence as the essence of *qi* but further mentions 'essential *qi*':

> Think of it, think of it and think of it again. Thinking of it yet not penetrating; ghosts and spirits will penetrate it. This is not due to the strength of ghosts and spirits but to the nature of essential *qi*. (Ibid., 2:129)

From this it is clear that essence is essential *qi*.

The *Inward Training*'s understanding of essential *qi* is not that it is the fruit of human endeavor but that it is given by heaven. Within heaven and earth there is a lot of essential *qi*, and the human mind is suited to receiving it and so the mind becomes the dwelling place of essence and then one is wise. This is a crude theory of the relation between spirit and form. Moreover, the *Inward Training* holds that essential *qi* is the source of the sage's wisdom as well as being what produces the life of the five grains. Life and wisdom are seen as one. If essence is what gives life to the five grains, why is it not also the cause of the form, the body, of a person rather than just the source of wisdom?

Mr. Lu's Spring and Autumn Annals also mention essential *qi*:

> It is necessary to enter into the collecting of essential *qi*. It collects in feathered birds and enables them to fly high. It collects in running beasts and enables them to move smoothly. It collects in pearls and jade and enables them to be essentially lustrous. It collects in trees and plants and enables them to grow luxuriantly. It collects in sages and enables them to be very perspicacious. (*Mr. Lu's Spring and Autumn Annals* 3.6, *Exhausting Number*, p. 136)

This is to say that the soaring of birds, the running of beasts, the brightness of pearls and jades, the luxuriance of trees, and the wisdom of sages are all signs of the gathering of essential *qi*. Essential *qi* is given by heaven:

> The Way of heaven is circular.... why do we say that the Way of heaven is circular? Essential *qi* goes up and comes down, going round in a circle returning and including all without there being a point of rest; thus it is said that the Way of heaven is circular. (Ibid. 3.5, *The Circular Way*, pp. 171–72)

The later chapters of the *Zhuangzi* also mention the essence of heaven and earth:

> I want to take hold of the essence of heaven and earth so as to assist the five grains so as to foster the people. (*Zhuangzi* 11, *Preserve and Accept*, line 30)

> Now I want to unite the essence of the six *qi* so as to nourish the mass of living *things*. (Ibid., line 47)

It may be that the essence referred to here is the same as that mentioned in the *Inward Training*.

Essential Spirit

The linking of the words 'essence' (*jing*) and 'spirit' (*shen*) is first encountered in the later chapters of the *Zhuangzi*.

> The essence of water is to be bright; how much more so then for essential spirit? The sage's mind is calm, the mirror of heaven and earth, the mirror of the myriad things. (*Zhuangzi* 13, *The Way of Heaven*, line 4)
>
> [They] require the workings of essential spirit and the exercise of the techniques of the mind before they can be put into practice. (Ibid., line 26)
>
> Confucius asked Lao Dan, "Today while you are at rest dare I ask about the utmost Way?" Lao Dan replied, "You should fast and train yourself and clean out the channels of your mind, wash white the essential spirit and bash up your

knowledge. The Way is deep and difficult to speak about."
(*Zhuangzi* 22, *Knowledge Roams North*, line 29)

'Essential spirit' is said of the activity of the human mind. The term remains an important one in modern philosophy.*

In ancient philosophy the same idea could be conveyed by the phrase 'spiritual brightness.'

To exhaust the spiritual brightness in you and treat it as one.
(*Zhuangzi* 2, *The Sorting Which Evens Things Out*, line 37)

Here 'spiritual brightness' refers to the human spirit. The reference is the same in a text from the *Xunzi*:

The mind is the ruler of form and the lord of the spiritual brightness. (*Xunzi* 21, *The Removal of Prejudices*, line 44)

It means 'human thought and consciousness' in the following:

If one gathers soil to form a mountain wind and rain spring from it. If one gathers water to form an ocean, *jiao* dragons and dragons come to life from it. If one gathers goodness to produce virtue then spiritual brightness is autonomously obtained and sagely minds are complete from it. (*Xunzi* 1, *An Exhortation to Learning*, line 18)

In ancient Daoist philosophy the terms 'spirit,' 'essential spirit,' and 'spiritual brightness' had a further layer of meaning. They did not only refer to the human; they also applied to the universe. The Confucian commentaries on the *Changes* have the phrase:

What cannot be fathomed in *yin-yang* is called 'spirit.' (*Great Commentary* I.5, p. 281)

Daoist texts are not so explicit but contain many difficult phrases using 'spirit.' 'Spirit' (numinous) is used as an honorific in talking of heaven:

Nothing is more numinous than heaven, nothing richer than earth. (*Zhuangzi* 13, *The Way of Heaven*, line 22)

---

*The term is used to translate the Absolute Spirit of Hegel. In common parlance it is found in the phrase "essential spirit illness," psychological illness.

The numinosity of heaven and earth has the sequence of respected-despised, in front and behind. (Ibid., line 30)

In the next passage, from the syncretist section of the *Zhuangzi*, 'spirit' applies to the human spirit and 'essential spirit' to the cosmic spirit:

> To be pure and delicate without admixture, to be still and integrated without alteration, to be indifferent and not to purposively act and when moving to go along with heaven, this is the way to nuture the spirit.... Essential spirit flows to the four directions with everything else. There is nothing it does not reach. Above it borders heaven; below it loops round the earth. It transforms and nurtures the myriad things and it may not be pictured. It is to be named 'one with God.' By the way of the pure and the simple, one can keep only to the spirit. Keeping to it, do not lose it. Be one with spirit. (*Zhuangzi* 15, *Finicky Notions*, lines 18 ff.)

The cosmic essential spirit may have existed before heaven and earth:

> Brightness is produced from darkness; what is sorted is produced from what is formless. Essential spirit is produced from the Way. Bodily form is produced from essence and the myriad things produce each other by means of form. (*Zhuangzi* 22, *Knowledge Roams North*, line 30)

The late final chapter of the *Zhuangzi* corpus summarizes the philosophy of Zhuang Zhou:

> Alone he went back and forth with essential spirit but did not look down on the myriad things. (*Zhuangzi* 33, *Under Heaven*, line 66)

The essential spirit of heaven and earth seems to be something that transcends the individual person.

'Spiritual brightness' appears to be an expression of heaven and earth in the following text from the syncretist portion of the *Zhuangzi*:

> Heaven is honorable, earth humble. This is the set position of spiritual brightness.... Heaven and earth are utterly numinous

yet have sequences of the high and the low, first and last. (*Zhuangzi* 13, *The Way of Heaven*, lines 29, 30)

This passage is clearly based on the *Great Commentary to the* Changes, whose opening line reads,

Heaven is honorable, earth is humble. *Qian* (trigram of heaven) and *kun* (trigram of earth) are determined thereby. (*Great Commentary* 1.1, p. 271)

Again:

Now whether in that most quintessential of the daemonic-and-illumined or in those hundredfold transformations, already things live and die. (*Zhuangzi* 22, *Knowledge Roams North*, line 18)
   Where does spirit come down from? Where does bright-ness come out of? Sagehood has that from which it is generated; kingship has that by which it is accomplished. All have their origin in the One. (*Zhuangzi* 33, *Under Heaven*, line 2)

The author of this chapter understood the differing doctrines of philosophy as grasping only part of what had once been a whole and complete system:

Did not the people of old provide for everything! They were peers of the daemonic-and-illumined and equals of heaven and earth, they fostered the myriad things and harmonized the empire, their bounty extended over the hundred clans....
   Now the empire is in utter confusion, sagehood and excellence are not clarified....
   People split the glory of heaven and earth down the middle, chop up the patterns of the myriad things, and scrutinize some point in what for the ancients was a whole. There are few who are able to have the whole glory of heaven and earth at their disposal, and speak of the full scope of the daemonic-and-illumined. (Ibid., lines 7–9)

In the *Great Commentary* the phrase "the virtue of spiritual brightness" may apply to a cosmic power or it may refer to the wisdom of the sages. The *Commentary* describes the creation of the trigrams by Fu Xi (Bao Xi):

> Of old, when Bao Xi reigned over all under heaven, he looked up and saw the symbols in heaven. He looked down and saw the patterns on earth. . . . Nearby he made inferences from his own person. Far away he made inferences from things. Hence he created the eight trigrams to penetrate the virtue of spiritual brightness and to classify the natures of the myriad things. (*Great Commentary* 2.2, p. 309)

In another passage it means 'making manifest the excellence of the sages' wisdom':

> They understood the Way of heaven and examined what makes the people tick. They created these numinous things as a propaedeutic for the people's use. The sages used them by restraining and holding back and so lent spiritual brightness to their virtue. (*Great Commentary* 1.11, p. 298)

The numinous things are the *yin-yang* and the hexagrams. They enable one to make predictions about the unknown and hence are numinous. Use of them requires spiritual discipline. The sage who can use them is not only virtuous but also far-seeing.

IV. Concepts Derived from the *Book of Changes*

Although a number of concepts already discussed were prominent in the Commentaries to the Book of Changes, the six that follow are exclusively derived from those commentaries, and their use in Chinese philosophy has been determined by explicit reference to the same source. The six terms are largely concerned with expressing the nature and stages of change. They apply to the cosmological development from the original chaos to the complexities of the world as it now is. The Book of Changes sought to look for the underlying principles that explain how the multifarious world came out of pure simplicity.

23. Supreme Ultimate

Tai ji THÁI-CỤC

太極

Any philosophy that asserts two elements such as the yin-yang *of Chinese philosophy will also look for a term to reconcile the two, to ensure that both belong to the same sphere of discourse. The term 'supreme ultimate' performs this role in the philosophy of the* Book of Changes. *In the Song dynasty it became a metaphysical term on a par with the Way.*

The Changes

The term 'supreme ultimate' is used to refer to the unseparated state of heaven and earth:

> The *Changes* have the supreme ultimate, which generated the two modes. The two modes generated the four symbols; the four symbols generated the eight trigrams. (*Great Commentary to the* Changes 1.11, p. 299)

The two modes indicate heaven and earth. Zheng Xuan, in his commentary on this text, notes,

> The Way in the midst of the ultimate is undifferentiated and harmonized *qi*. (*SKQS* 7, *Additions to Mr. Zheng's Zhou Yi*, Hui Dong (ed.), p. 176a)

Another Confucian of the Han dynasty, Yu Fan, comments thus:

> The supreme ultimate is the supreme One. It separated into heaven and earth and thus generated the two modes. (*SKQS* 7, Yu Fan quoted by Li Dingzuo, *Collected Exegesis of the Zhou Yi*, p. 832a)

In the later apocrypha the supreme ultimate is also understood as the state of primordial unity. Confucius is quoted as saying,

> The *Changes* began with the supreme ultimate. The supreme
> ultimate separated and became two; thus it generated heaven
> and earth. (*SKQS* 53, *Zhou Yi Qian* Zao Du, ed. Zheng Kang-
> cheng A, p. 867a)*

Zheng Xuan notes on this text:

> This is the time when *qi* and the symbols had not yet sepa-
> rated, when heaven and earth were just beginning.

A similar text is found in another of the apocryphal works:

> The *Changes* have the supreme ultimate, which generated the
> two modes. The two modes had not yet separated, their *qi* was
> all a primordial soup. (*He Tu kua Di Xiang*, Sun Ke, ed., p. 608)

As Original *Qi*

The supreme ultimate is linked to original *qi* in the calendrical portion of
the *Han History*, part of the work inspired by Liu Xin:†

> The supreme ultimate, origin and *qi* are three in one. The
> ultimate is the center; the origin is the beginning. (*Han His-
> tory* 21, *Calendrical Gazette*, p. 964)
>
> The supreme ultimate is the central and original *qi*. (Ibid.,
> p. 981)
>
> The supreme ultimate rotates the three heavenly bodies
> and five planets above and original *qi* turns the three forms of
> rulership and the five agents below. On the human level the
> imperial ultimate rules over the three virtues and five affairs.
> Thus the three heavenly bodies match the three forms of
> rulership: the sun matches the rulership of heaven; the moon
> matches the rulership of earth; the pole star matches the ruler-
> ship of human beings. The five stars match the five agents:
> water matches Mercury; fire matches Mars; metal matches Ve-

---

* Zheng Kangcheng is Zheng Xuan.

† Liu Xin (?–23 A.D.) *Zi*: Zijun, later changed name to Liu Xiu, *Zi*: Yingshu, from
Peixian, Jiangsu Province. He followed his father, Liu Xiang, in editing the classics.

nus; wood matches Jupiter; earth matches Saturn. The three
heavenly bodies and the five planets form one system together.
(Ibid., p. 985)

Here the terms 'supreme ultimate' and 'original *qi*' can be used of one and
the same thing but may also be differentiated.

In literary works of the period the term 'supreme ultimate' was used
with the same sense. The historian Ban Gu wrote a work titled *Quoting the
Classics*:

> At the origin of the supreme ultimate the two modes began
> to separate. Misty and vague, some sank and was mysterious,
> some floated and was light. What sank and what floated inter-
> acted with each other; all kinds of things were muddled
> up. (*Complete Later Han Literature* 26, *Quoting the Classics*,
> p. 614b)

The poet Cao Zhi wrote,

> The start of this supreme ultimate is the primordial soup with-
> out distinctions in which the myriad things are all interwoven
> and have equal majesty with the Way. What has form must
> corrupt; what has a path must come to an end. Mysterious
> original *qi*, who can know its end? (*Selections of Refined Liter-
> ature* 34, *Seven Revelations*, p. 481)

All of the above concur in affirming that the supreme ultimate is the primordial unity.

The *Zhuangzi* also refers to the supreme ultimate:

> This Way has a nature and is reliable. It does not act, nor does
> it have form. It may be passed on but may not be possessed. It
> may be obtained but cannot be seen. It is its own root and
> stem. Before heaven and earth were, from of old it has always
> existed. It hallows ghosts and god. It generated heaven and
> earth. It was before the supreme ultimate and yet is not reck-
> oned high. (*Zhuangzi* 6, *The Teacher Who Is the Ultimate An-
> cestor*, lines 29–30)

This text is proof of an opposition between Daoism and Confucianism.
Daoism posited the Way as primordial to the supreme ultimate.

As 'Beingless'

In the Three Kingdoms period, Han Kangbo wrote a commentary on the *Great Commentary to the* Changes and used the Daoist idea that 'being' is generated from 'beingless' to comment on the line that the "*Changes* have the supreme principle which produces the two modes":

> 'Being' must be produced by 'beingless': therefore the su-preme ultimate produces the two modes. The supreme ulti-mate is the name which cannot be named. It cannot be laid hold of and named. It is only by acquiring 'being' that it can be referred to as the supreme ultimate. (Yan Lingfeng, ed., *Collected Editions of the Yi Jing: Great Commentary*, 3:308)

In other words, the two modes are being, and the supreme ultimate is beingless. It is on the basis of the former that the latter is postulated.

During the fifth and sixth centuries, the question as to whether the supreme ultimate was 'being' or 'beingless' became a hot topic. Su Yan, Emperor Wu of the Liang dynasty (reigned 502–549), discussed the issue with Li Yexing:

> Yan asked once more, "The *changes* talk about the supreme ultimate. Is it being or beingless?" Yexing replied, "The supreme ultimate that is handed on is being." (*Gazette of the Three Kingdoms (Wei)* 28.8, *Biography of Tong Hui*, p. 795 n. 1)

Li Yexing was a classics scholar of the northern dynasties and interpreted the supreme ultimate as being according to the tradition of Zheng Xuan. The southern dynasties' scholars advocated the opinion of Han Kangbo that the supreme ultimate was beingless.

The Tang commentator Kong Yingda used Wang Bi's edition of the *Changes*, which preferred the Daoist 'beingless,' but on the relevant passage of the *Great Commentary* Kong held that the supreme ultimate was original *qi*:

> The supreme ultimate is said of the state before heaven and earth separated, the original *qi* that was all one mass together, that is the ultimate start and the ultimate One. Thus Laozi

said, "The Way generated the One" that is this same supreme ultimate. It is also said that the original mass separated and so there was heaven and earth; thus it is said "the supreme ultimate produced the two modes," that is, what Laozi says, "the One produced the Two." (*The Correct Meaning of the Zhou Yi* 7, p. 17a)

Kong Yingda places the Way above the supreme ultimate, thereby indicating that he accepts the Daoist view of the Way.

Song Metaphysics

In the Song dynasty the notion of the supreme ultimate underwent new developments. Zhou Dunyi wrote his *Explanation of the Diagram of the Supreme Ultimate* and took the supreme ultimate as the origin of *yin-yang* and the five agents:

> The limitless and the supreme ultimate. The supreme ultimate moves and generates *yang*. When its movement comes to a peak then it becomes tranquil. It becomes tranquil and generates *yin*. When its tranquility comes to a peak it returns to movement. Movement and tranquility alternate and become the root of each other, separating into *yin* and *yang* and so establishing the two modes. *Yang* changes and *yin* unites and this produces water, fire, wood, metal and earth. The five *qi* flow out in sequence; the four seasons run their course thereby. The five agents combine in one system of *yin-yang*. *Yin-yang* form one supreme ultimate. The supreme ultimate is rooted in the limitless. The generation of the five agents is such that to each name corresponds one nature. The reality of the limitless and the essence of two [*yin-yang*] and five [agents] marvelously unite and coagulate. The Way of *Qian* [heaven] perfects the male; the Way of *Kun* [earth] perfects the female. The two *qi* intermingle, transform and generate the myriad things. The myriad things generate and regenerate and their changes and alterations are endless. (*SKQS* 1101, *Collected Works of Zhou*

Yuangong 1, Explanation of the Diagram of the Supreme Ultimate, pp. 416b–418a)*

Although Zhu Xi may have read Zhou Dunyi correctly, in his own exegesis he used Zhou's text to draw out his own very different philosophical view.

> The supreme ultimate is the Way which is above form while *yin-yang* are the vessel that is below form. (*SKQS* 1101, *Exegesis of the Explanation of the Diagram of the Supreme Ultimate*, p. 417a)

He claimed that Zhou's philosophy

> Greatly supported the view of the distinctness and unity of one principle, two *qi* and five agents so as to produce a systematic body of thought. (*Appendix to Master Zhou's* Book of Comprehending)

According to this interpretation the supreme ultimate is the one principle. In Zhou's own work 'principle' is not such an important concept.

> Principle is called 'rites.' . . .
>   Rites are principle; music is harmony. When *yin-yang* keep to principle then there is harmony. . . . The myriad things

---

*Author's note: There is a problem with the editing of the first line of this text. Zhu Xi saw a version that had "From the limitless the supreme ultimate comes" (*Complete Works* 71.4, *Records of the Biography of Lianxi*, p. 1260b). This interpretation is correct. The Ming scholar Han Bangqi saw otherwise. He wrote, "Master Zhou's 'limitless' and 'supreme ultimate' is the same as Laozi's 'beingless produces being.' . . . How much better than the original text which read, 'from the limitless the supreme ultimate comes.' Zhu Xi's excising the words 'from' and 'comes' is the result of his own Confucian bias" (*SKQS* 1269, *Collected Works of Yuanluo* 18, *Following Record of Testing, Seeing and Hearing*, p. 638b). Mao Qiling was of the same opinion (*Taijitushuo yi yi*). It seems that the original text of Zhou Dunyi read "the supreme ultimate is rooted in the limitless." This could mean that the root of the supreme ultimate is limitless or that the supreme ultimate has the limitless as its root. Both explanations are possible. The next line discusses the limitless, two, and five but does not mention the supreme ultimate. In another work Zhou talks of the supreme ultimate, two, and five but does not mention the limitless: "The five agents and *yin-yang*, *yin-yang* and the supreme ultimate" (*SKQS* 1101, *Book of Comprehending* 16, *Activity and Tranquility*, p. 428a). In other words, it would seem that Zhou can talk of the five agents and the two *qi* in the context of the limitless or of the supreme ultimate as if both were the same. The title of the diagram is the *Diagram of the Supreme Ultimate*, suggesting that this is the key concept and that it is unlikely that there could be a 'limitless' more primordial. Zhu Xi's exegesis is correct.

each keep to their principle and then there is harmony. (*SKQS* 1101, *Book of Comprehending* 13, *Rites and Music*, p. 427a)

The term 'principle' also appears in the heading of the 22nd chapter of the same book, but it is not used within the body of the chapter.

One who is not wise cannot understand the manifestations and concealment. (Ibid., 22, *Principle, Human Nature and Destiny*, p. 426b)

According to Zhu Xi, this phrase refers to 'principle.' It is not, however, the highest concept. In the *Explanation of the Diagram of the Supreme Ultimate*, Zhou describes the five agents as five *qi* and *yin-yang* as two *qi*. He does not say if the supreme ultimate is to be considered one *qi* or not. In Zhou's philosophy 'principle' and *qi* are not the supreme concepts.

The pupils of Zhou Dunyi, the two Cheng brothers, are the first to exalt 'principle,' but they do not mention the supreme ultimate. The preface in the traditional edition of the *Book of Changes* edited by Cheng Yi mentions the supreme ultimate, but since Cheng Yi wrote another preface the traditional one is unlikely to be his.*

Zhu Xi used the philosophy of principle developed by the Cheng brothers to explain Zhou's *Explanation of the Diagram of the Supreme Ultimate*. He retained the structure of Zhou's book and many of his terms. Hence Zhu Xi took the term the 'supreme ultimate' as the key philosophical term. He interpreted the opening line of Zhou's book to refer to the formless and to principle:

"The limitless and the supreme ultimate." This simply means "the formless and having principle." (*Conversations of Master Zhu Arranged Topically* 94a, *Explanation of the Diagram of the Supreme Ultimate*, p. 2365)

The supreme ultimate is to be understood like the ridgepole of a roof or the pole of heaven. Once one has reached this point one can go no further. One has attained to the utmost principle. (Ibid., p. 2374)

The principle that unites heaven, earth and the myriad things in the supreme ultimate. (Ibid., p. 2375)

* For the traditional preface, see *Yi Cheng Zhuan* (Taibei: Shijie Shuju, 1988), pp. 1–2.

The supreme ultimate is the highest principle, the one that subsumes all other principles. From it all things are produced:

> "The limitless and the supreme ultimate"; this does not mean that there was some object shining brightly up there. Rather it simply says that at the very start this principle was not an object; there was just this principle alone. If there was this principle then there was *qi*; if there was *qi* then it separated into *yin* and *yang* and from this were produced a great variety of things. (Ibid., p. 2387)

In other words, Zhu Xi understood the supreme ultimate as absolute principle.

Zhu Xi also advocated the theory that each person has his or her own supreme ultimate and so too does each thing.

> Speaking from the point of view of their unity the myriad things all together form one supreme ultimate. Speaking from the point of view of their difference each thing has its own supreme ultimate. (*SKQS* 1101, *Collected Works of Zhou Yuangong* 1, *Exegesis of the Explanation of the Diagram of the Supreme Ultimate*, p. 418a)

The supreme ultimate is the highest form of principle, on which all things rely for their existence, and hence all things possess this principle:

> The supreme ultimate is but the most perfect and the best moral principle. Each person has a supreme ultimate and each thing has a supreme ultimate. (*Conversations of Master Zhu Arranged Topically* 94a, *Explanation of the Diagram of the Supreme Ultimate*, p. 2371)

This supreme ultimate is supreme in both cosmic and moral terms.

With regard to the original statement in the *Great Commentary to the* Book of Changes to the effect that the *Changes* has the supreme ultimate, Zhu Xi's exegesis differed widely from that of the Han Confucian scholars. He interpreted the phrase in terms of the drawing of the strokes in the trigrams.

> One producing Two is a spontaneous principle. Change is the alternation of *yin* and *yang*. The supreme ultimate is their

principle. The two modes begin with one stroke and so separate into *yin* and *yang* (- - and —). The four symbols come
next and have two strokes forming major and minor (major
yang = and major *yin* = =; minor *yang* and minor *yin*). The
eight trigrams come next and have three strokes and are the
complete expression of the three materials (heaven, earth and
human beings). (*The Original Meaning of the* Book of
Changes, p. 62)

The strokes are written from the bottom up:

It was asked, "The *Changes* have the supreme ultimate which
produced the two modes. The two modes produced the four
symbols; the four symbols produced the eight trigrams." He
said, "This supreme ultimate is indeed said of the drawing of
the trigrams. Before the trigrams were drawn the supreme ultimate is simply a primordial soup [of] moral principle. Within
it contains *yin-yang*, hard-soft, odd-even, indeed there is
nothing it does not have. At first one odd and one even line
were drawn then the two modes were produced. Above one
odd stoke an even stroke was drawn and this is the *yin* emerging from the *yang*. Also above one odd stroke another odd
stroke was drawn and this is the *yang* within *yang*. Then above
one even stroke an odd stroke was drawn and this is the *yang*
emerging from *yin*. Also an even stroke was drawn above an
even stroke and this is the *yin* within the *yin*. These are called
the four symbols. As for the so-called eight trigrams, above
each of the symbols are two trigrams produced by adding an
even or an odd stroke to each to make the eight trigrams.
(*Conversations of Master Zhu Arranged Topically* 75, *Changes
11: Great Commentary II*, p. 1929)

Zhang Zai does not say much about the supreme ultimate. When he
does mention it, he uses it to talk about the unity of *yin-yang*, hard-soft:

The earth is two because it separates into hard and soft, man
and woman which imitate it. This is the law. Heaven is three,
one supreme ultimate and two modes which model themselves
on it. This is nature. (*SKQS* 697, *Correcting the Unenlightened
2, Trinity and Duality*, p. 101a)

The unity of the complementary pairs is the third, hence heaven has three. The text continues,

> One thing with two bodies, that is *qi*. Because it is one so it is numinous; because it is two so it can change, this is why heaven has three. (Ibid.)

It would seem that Zhang Zai might have understood the supreme ultimate as *qi*:

> One thing; two bodies. Is this what its supreme ultimate is said to be? (Ibid. 14, *Da Yi*, p. 133b)

Ming-Qing Metaphysics

Wang Tingxiang succeeded Zhang Zai and opposed Zhu Xi's interpretation of the supreme ultimate as principle:

> The theory of the supreme ultimate began with the phrase, "the *Changes* have the supreme ultimate." The inferred origin of making-transforming cannot be spoken of; thus it is called the supreme ultimate. If one seeks for it in reality then it is the pure and vacuous *qi* of the primordial soup before heaven and earth had been split apart.... From the Southern Song onwards, the Confucians alone interpret the supreme ultimate as principle and dislike encountering *qi*.... Alas! This is to turn things upside down. How can it be so? The myriad principles all come from *qi*. There is no principle hanging alone in the void.... Principle is vacuous without shape. How then could *yin* and *yang* come out of principle? ... Outside original *qi* there is no supreme ultimate; outside *yin* and *yang* there is no *qi*.... To talk of principle and not to talk of *qi* is to dispose of the form and make do with the shadow. Is it not so? (*Collected Works of Wang Tingxiang* vol. 2, *Collected Works Stored in Mr. Zhang's House* 33.1, *Debate on the Supreme Ultimate*, pp. 596–597)

In saying that the supreme ultimate is original *qi* Wang Tingxiang was reverting to the Han Confucian point of view but arguing his case in a more systematic manner.

The early Qing scholar Li Gong (1659–1733) rejected Zhu Xi's interpretation of the supreme ultimate without, however, reverting to the early Han interpretation:

> Bao Xi inaugurated the eight trigrams such that the *Changes* themselves produced the trigrams. I have never heard that it was said that he first made the supreme ultimate. As for making the even and odd strokes of the trigrams, the Diagram of the Supreme Ultimate does not mention this.... What made the symbols is called *Qian*, so first *Qian* was drawn and what imitates this is called *Kun*, so next *Kun* was drawn. Both have three strokes to symbolize the three materials. I have never heard it said that there was first one stroke, then two strokes so that there was *yin* and *yang*, then major *yang*, minor *yin*, minor *yang* and major *yin*. (*Collected Books of Yan and Li, Commentary and Notes on the* Book of Changes 5, *Great Commentary on the* Book of Changes 1, pp. 38b–39a)

Li Gong's rejection of the early Han interpretation is in fact unjustified. Li argued that it is not the *Changes* that have the supreme ultimate but rather the inverse.

> Change is change so there must be that which changes produced from that which does not change. Cui Jing says, "Out of fifty there is one that is not used, this is the supreme ultimate. It does not change." (Ibid.)

In fact, Cui Jing only said that the one of the fifty that is not used is like the supreme ultimate and not that it is the supreme ultimate.

Thus in the course of history there have been different interpretations of the line "the *Changes* have the supreme ultimate." The Han Confucians thought it was talking about cosmogenesis. Zhu Xi thought that it was about the order in which the trigrams are to be written. Li Gong held that the traditional reading was back to front and that in fact the supreme ultimate was the source of the *Changes*. As to its content, the Han Confucians, Zhang Zai, and Wang Tingxiang all thought it was said of *qi*, whereas Zhu Xi and his disciples held that it was principle. This division reflects a basic division between these two currents of thought.

24. Numinous Transformation

Shenhua THÂN-HÓA

神化

In concept 22 we saw the use of 'shen' in combination with 'jing' to refer to the essence. 'Shen' is also found in combination with 'hua,' 'change,' to refer to the mystery of the process of transformation. As such it may be translated as 'numinous.' In the work of Zhang Zai the mysterious aspect is not to the fore, so 'wondrous' is a more appropriate translation.

The term *shen*, in addition to meaning 'the spirits' or 'the human spirit,' is also used to mean 'a tiny, almost imperceptible change.' In this usage it is always combined with the term *hua*, 'transformation.' This concept figures highly in the works of Zhou Dunyi, Shao Yong, Zhang Zai, and Cheng Hao, that is, in early Song-dynasty philosophy.

The *Changes*

The term first occurs in the *Great Commentary*:

> That which is unfathomable in *yin* and *yang* is called 'numinous.' (*Great Commentary on the* Book of Changes 1.5, p. 281)
> The numinous is without place and change-as-such is without substance. (Ibid. 1.4, p. 279)
> One who knows the way of changing and transforming knows what the numinous does. (Ibid. 1.9, p. 293)

In the *Treatise of Remarks on the Trigrams* 'the numinous' refers to the inexpressible in the alternations of *yin* and *yang*:

> The numinous is what is marvelous in the myriad things and what gives them expression. (*Treatise of Remarks on the Trigrams* 6, p. 345)

The term 'marvelous' could also be translated 'minute.' What this minuteness is is explained in the *Great Commentary*:

As a book the *Changes* is one that should not be put far away.
As a way it is marked by constant shifting. The lines change
and move without stopping and go round in a circle into any
of the six spaces in the hexagrams. Above and below have no
constancy. Hard and soft lines change places with each other
so that one cannot make a hard and fast rule. It is only change
that is appropriate to them. (*Great Commentary* 2.8, p. 328)

The lines in a hexagram can be continually moved so as to produce new
hexagrams. Han Kangbo notes,

The numinous is the peak of change and transformation. It
is what is marvelous in the myriad things and gives them expression. It cannot be tied down to any given form. Thus it is
said that *yin* and *yang* cannot be fathomed. If one tries to discuss this further then one might say that originally as for the
turning of the two modes and the movement of the myriad
things, is it not that they are made to be such? There is nothing which does not by itself transform in ultimate space; suddenly it makes itself. (Yan Lingfeng, ed., *Collected Editions of
the Yi Jing*, vol. 3, *Great Commentary*, notes of Han Kangbo,
pp. 292–293)

Here Han interpreted the numinous as the sudden change in ultimate
space.

The *Book of Changes* calls on its readers to investigate the mysteries
of change:

When one carefully investigates the reasons of things and enters into their minute changes, one comes to know their use.
When one employs this use to give security to one's person,
one comes to highest virtue. If one goes beyond this one ar-
rives at a point which is virtually beyond knowing. To understand the numinous and know transformation is the ultimate
virtue. (*Great Commentary* 2.5, p. 317)

Xunzi also uses the term 'numinous' to refer to spontaneous change:

The constellations follow each other around, the sun and moon
change their stations as lights, the four seasons succeed each

> other, *yin* and *yang* produce great transformations, wind and
> rain go forth everywhere. The myriad things each obtain their
> harmony and are produced thereby. Each acquires its fostering
> and is completed. One cannot see the cause of this, only its
> fruit, and this is what is called the numinous. (*Xunzi* 17, *Discourse on Heaven*, lines 8–9)

Heaven and earth, *yin* and *yang* are in continual flux, generating and perfecting the myriad things. This is what is called the numinous.

The Song Era

Zhou Dunyi revived the term 'numinous':

> Heaven generates the myriad things by *yang* and perfects the
> myriad things by *yin*.... As for great concordance and great
> transformation one does not see their trace. None know how
> they are so. This is called 'numinous.' (*SKQS* 1101, *The Book of
> Comprehending* 11, *Concordance and Transformation*, p. 426a)

Chapter 16 of the same book is here quoted in full:

> When *x* moves then *x* is not still. When *x* is not still then *x* is
> not moving. *X* is a thing. When *y* moves it does not move.
> When *y* is still it is not still. *Y* is numinous. "When *y* moves it
> does not move; when *y* is still it is not still" does not mean that
> *y* is neither moving nor still. Things cannot interpenetrate; the
> numinous makes marvels with the myriad things. Water is *yin*
> and rooted in *yang*; fire is *yang* and rooted in *yin*. The five
> agents are but *yin* and *yang* and these are the supreme ultimate. The four seasons revolve on their course; the myriad
> things end and begin. The primal soup! The undifferentiated! It is infinite! (Ibid. 16, *Activity and Tranquility*, pp.
> 428a–b)

Whereas most things are either at rest or in motion, the numinous transcends the distinction of movement and rest. It is a mysterious kind of change that comprises both stillness and movement.

Shao Yong (1011–1077) was not of a scholarly background and never served in government office.* He became famous for his systematic scholarship, which tried to describe all things according to mathematical patterns. His use of the binary system of numbering inspired Leibniz and from him came the modern computer industry. Although numbers can express relationships between things in a way that is easy to grasp, no mathematical model can completely exhaust the intricacies of the world: the numinous.

> That which makes things is the numinous. The numinous does not die; its changes are the four seasons....
>
> Sunk in heaven and sunk in earth, not going and yet arriving, not under the grasp of yin-yang: this is the numinous.† (*SKQS* 803, *The Book of the Supreme Principles Ordering the World, Outer Chapters: On the Observation of Things*, pp. 1084a–b)

The numinous is the mysterious power by which the myriad things are made.

Wondrous

Zhang Zai discussed the numinous or wondrous in greater detail.

> The wondrous means ultimate space in its marvelous operations and response....
>
> That which cannot be fathomed in heaven is called the wondrous. What is wondrous and also constant is called 'heaven.' (*SKQS* 697, *Correcting the Unenlightened* 1, *Ultimate Harmony*, pp. 99b, 107b)

For Zhang Zai ultimate space was heaven and the mysterious resonances within ultimate space were the wondrous. Zhang Zai believed that the wondrous is the nature of *qi*:

---

* Shao Yong. *Zi*: Yaofu, posthumous title Kang Jie, called Bai Yuan, from Gongcheng, Huixian, Henan Province. K. Smith, Jr., P. K. Bol, J. A. Adler, and D. J. Wyatt, *Sung Dynasty Uses of the I Ching* (Princeton: Princeton University Press, 1990), 47–49; 100–135.
  † See Smith et al., *Sung Dynasty Uses*, p. 128.

> The nature of *qi* is rooted in space and the wondrous. Yet the wondrous and nature are what *qi* has by definition. (Ibid. 17, *Qian Cheng*, p. 143a)

The wondrous is what *qi* has by definition.

> The wondrous is the virtue of heaven; transformation is the Way of heaven. Virtue is its substance and the Way is its use. They are simply one with *qi*. (Ibid. 4, *The Wondrous and Transformation*, p. 108b)

Qi has the wondrous for its essential nature and it is also what transforms. Here the terms 'wondrous' and 'transformation' are two sides of the same coin.

Zhang Zai's special contribution is to have examined the causes of wondrous transformation. *Qi* is able to be wondrous because it is the reconciliation of contraries itself:

> One thing with two substances, that is *qi*. Because it is one it is wondrous; because it is two it is transformed. (Ibid. 2, *Trinity and Duality*, p. 101a)
>
> *Qi* has *yin* and *yang*. These increase and decrease and so produce transformation, unite into one that cannot be fathomed and this is the numinous. (Ibid. 4, *The Wondrous and Transformation*, p. 108b)

Qi comprehends opposites, and their opposition is in fact their unity. Because of their opposition there is change and transformation; because of their unity that same process of change is unfathomable and wondrous.

More accurately put, the wondrous, for Zhang Zai, was the potential for change:

> The potential for contracting, stretching, moving, resting, ending and beginning is one; thus what makes "the myriad things marvelous is called the wondrous," what "penetrates the myriad things is called the Way," what "gives substance to the myriad things is called nature." (Ibid. 17, *Qian Cheng*, p. 143b)

What makes possible the marvelous changes of the myriad things is the wondrous. Zhang Zai believed that all change is a manifestation of the wondrous:

> Movement under heaven is at the inspiration of the wondrous. (Ibid. 4, *The Wondrous and Transformation*, p. 108b)
>
> Only the numinous is able to instigate change and transformation inasmuch as it is the one movement under heaven. (Ibid., p. 110a)

This wondrous power is not an external force but is an inherent property of *qi*.

The Cheng Brothers

His nephew, Cheng Hao, believed that the numinous is what inspires the process of generation in the world:

> "The workings of heaven above are soundless and odorless" (*Odes* 50, p. 431). Its substance is called the *Changes*; its principle is called the Way; its function is called the numinous. (*SKQS* 698, *Surviving Works of the Two Chengs* 1, p. 10a)
>
> "Generation and regeneration are what is meant by the *Changes*"; the function of generation and regeneration is the numinous. (Ibid. 11, p. 102b)
>
> Exhausting the numinous and knowing transformation. The mystery of transformation is the numinous. (Ibid., p. 97b)

Cheng Hao believed that the *Changes* embraced all phenomena as they came into existence. The numinous is the mysterious way by which they come into existence.

Sometimes in talking about the wondrous Zhang Zai differentiated between 'clear' and 'muddy.' He held that the clear is what best represents the wondrous.

> All *qi* if clear can then penetrate, if dark then block. At its clearest it is the wondrous. (*SKQS* 697, *Correcting the Unenlightened* 1, *Ultimate Harmony*, p. 99a)

In a preceding remark he notes,

> Ultimate space is clear. Since it is clear it is without obstacle. Since it is without obstacle therefore it is wondrous. The opposite of clear is muddy. What is muddy is an obstacle. What is an obstacle is form. (Ibid.)

Here form and the wondrous are opposed as if to say that form is not wondrous. This is a contradiction in Zhang Zai's thought. Cheng Hao criticized him on this score:

> Outside *qi* there is no numinosity, outside the wondrous there is no *qi*. Some may say that the clear is wondrous and is it then the case that the muddy is not wondrous? (*SKQS* 698, *Surviving Works of the Two Chengs* 11, p. 97b)

The numinous is the root nature of *qi* and since the muddy is *qi* it cannot be said to be without the numinous. Neither Zhang nor Cheng succeeded in explaining how the numinosity of the clear and that of the muddy were related.

Cheng Yi differed from both his brother and his uncle. He did not make the numinous a key term in his philosophy.

Zhu Xi, on the other hand, interpreted the numinous as principle. Commenting on Zhou Dunyi's observation that things and the numinous differ in their relation to movement and rest, he noted that

> The numinous is this principle. (*Conversations of Master Zhu Arranged Topically* 94, p. 2404)

> " 'When *y* moves it does not move; when *y* is still it is not still' does not mean that *y* is neither moving nor still." This is talking about the principle which is above form. Principle is the numinous which cannot be fathomed. When it is moving it is not not still; thus it is said, "it does not move." When it is still it is not not moving; thus it is said, "it is not still." In the midst of stillness there is movement and in the midst of movement there is stillness. In stillness there is the potential for movement and in movement there is the potential for stillness. In the midst of *yang* there is *yin* and in the midst of *yin* there is *yang*. The two are unceasingly interwoven (Ibid. p. 2403)

Despite this remark the numinous was not an important concept for Zhu Xi.

25. Change, Transformation, Movement-Stillness
Bianhua, Yi, Dong-jing BIẾN HÓA , DỊCH , ĐỘNG-TÌNH
變化, 易, 動靜

Change is spoken of in various types of terminology. The title of the Book of Changes *is yi. This character may have two possible origins. It may be the picture of a chameleon, which can change color, or it may be a picture of the sun and moon, which indicate times and periods of change.* In later literature the use of yi for "change" nearly always implies a conscious allusion to its use in the* Book of Changes. *The character* bian *is the most general word for change of any kind. The term* hua, *with which* bian *is associated in modern Chinese to produce the compound* bianhua, *can be translated as 'transformation.' Further on, our discussion will touch on the pair 'movement' and 'stillness,' which from early times have been used to express the two poles between which change takes place.*

The *Great Commentary*

Change is one of the most important concepts in ancient Chinese philosophy. According to the *Great Commentary*, change is a universal phenomenon:

> In heaven images are perfected; on earth forms are perfected, thus change and transformation [*bianhua*] may be seen. (*Great Commentary* 1.1, p. 271)

**Wu Jingnuan, *Yi Jing* (Washington, D.C.: Taoist Center, 1991), pp. 34–35.

> Of change and its implementation, none is greater than the four seasons.... Heaven and earth change and transform; the sage imitates them. (*Great Commentary* 1.11, p. 300)

Within heaven and earth all is in a state of flux. This is most evident from the changes of the seasons. Change is here defined in terms of advancing and retreating, opening and shutting:

> Change and transformation are the image of advancing and retreating. (*Great Commentary* 1.2, p. 274)
>
> The alternation of shutting and opening is what is meant by 'change.' (*Great Commentary* 1.11, p. 298)

The *Great Commentary* also mentions the root of change:

> Hard and soft impel each other and generate change and transformation. (*Great Commentary* 1.2, p. 274)

The reference here is to the alternation of lines, which are broken (soft) and unbroken (hard) in the hexagrams. As the lines change position a new hexagram is formed. It is the fact that there are two contrasting elements, hard and soft, that makes change possible. 'Change' is defined separately from 'transformation':

> Transformation and shaping is what is meant by 'change.' (*Great Commentary* 1.12, p. 303)

Transformation is the act of moving into another state. When that state is obtained then a change may be confirmed. Zhang Zai elaborated on this point.

The term *yi* is used to refer to the cosmic phenomenon of change as such or to the *Book of Changes* itself.

> Generation and regeneration are what is meant by change as such. (*Great Commentary* 1.5, p. 280)

With respect to this text Han Kangbo notes:

> *Yin-yang* revolve and change such that they perfect, transform and generate. (*Collected Editions of the* Book of Changes vol. 3, p. 292)

The cosmic status of change is indicated in the following passage:

> Heaven and earth establish their position and change-as-such proceeds within them. (*Great Commentary* 1.7, p. 284)

The Tang commentator Kong Yingda notes,

> If one is talking about the realization of the images then heaven is above and earth below, that is, "heaven and earth establishing their position." The myriad things transform and change within heaven and earth, that is, "change-as-such proceeds within them." (*The Correct Meaning of the* Book of Changes 7, p. 9b)
>
> The numinous is without place and change-as-such is without substance. (*Great Commentary* 1.4, p. 279)
>
> *Qian* [trigram of heaven] and *Kun* [trigram of earth] perfect their sequence and change-as-such is established between them. Were *Qian* and *Kun* to be destroyed then change-as-such could not be seen. Were change-as-such to not be seen then *Qian* and *Kun* would be at the point of fading away. (*Great Commentary* 1.12, p. 303)

Kong Yingda notes,

> Here change-as-such is said of the changes and transformations of *yin* and *yang*. (*The Correct Meaning of the* Book of Changes 7, p. 18b)

The whole system of the *Book of Changes* is dependent on the hexagrams *Qian* and *Kun*. Without them there would be no change.

Of all these quotations the most influential in determining the nature of change has been the one that defines change-as-such in terms of generation and regeneration. Kong Yingda remarks on this passage:

> Generation and regeneration is a term that means going on without a break.... The myriad things continually generate and this is what is meant by change-as-such. (Ibid., p. 8a)

In his *Original Meaning of the Book of Changes*, Zhu Xi writes,

> *Yin* generates *yang*; *yang* generates *yin*. Their changes are infinite. (*Original Meaning of the* Book of Changes p. 58)

The image of the sprouting grain is, then, the dominant motive in understanding the phemonenon of change. Change is the whole process of the generation of new life.

The term 'movement,' *dong*, is closely linked to that of change.

> Movement and stillness have a constant norm; hard and soft are determined thereby. (*Great Commentary* 1.1, p. 271)
>
> [The explanations of the lines of a hexagram] speak of the finest movements under heaven yet there is nothing in them that can provoke confusion. (*Great Commentary* 1.8, p. 285)

Thus the *Great Commentary* claims that there is an order in the process of movement and rest that is inherent in the universe.

Zhuangzi to Guo Xiang

In the syncretist chapters of the *Zhuangzi* change and movement are affirmed:

> Spring and summer come first and autumn and winter later; this is the sequence of the four seasons. The myriad things transform and are inaugurated, following the direction they sprout, they take on form: this is passing through stages of growth and decline, going through change and alteration. (*Zhuangzi* 13, *The Way of Heaven*, line 29)

The *Autumn Floods* dialogue mentions the relentless process of change:

> The life of a thing is like a stampede, like a gallop. There is not a movement when it does not change, not a moment when it does not shift. (*Zhuangzi* 17, *Autumn Floods*, line 46)

The question of change is treated in early Chinese logic. Among the 21 paradoxes of Hui Shi recorded in the final chapter of the *Zhuangzi* corpus is one on change:

> The shadow of a flying bird has never yet moved. (*Zhuangzi* 33, *Under Heaven*, lines 76–77)

Sima Biao* explained this by saying that, though the bird moves, the shadow is always a new shadow, rather as the moving image at the cinema is in fact a succession of still shots:

> The bird moves and the shadow is produced. What produces the shadow is an absence of light. An absence is not a going nor is production coming. (*Zhuzi Jicheng* 3, *Collected Editions of the* Zhuangzi: *Exegetical Literature*, p. 479)

The same topic is treated in the Mohist canons:

> B17 (C) A shadow does not shift. Explained by: remaking.
> B17 (E) Where the light arrives, the shadow disappears.
> (*Later Mohist Logic*, pp. 373–374)

Gongsun Long is quoted in the *Liezi* as saying,

> What is a shadow does not shift. (*Zhuzi Jicheng* 3, *Liezi* 4, *Confucius*, p. 48)

And Prince Mou said,

> "What is a shadow does not shift": —the explanation is that it is replaced. (Ibid.)

This is also saying that the "movement" of the shadow is created by a constant series of still shadows. The same logic was not, however, applied to the movement of the bird.

Just as Wang Bi's commentary on the *Laozi* propounded the view that beingless is generated by being, so too in his commentary on the *Book of Changes* he held that movement is rooted in stillness. The *Fu* hexagram (meaning 'to return') says:

> In *Fu* we see the mind of heaven and earth! (*Book of Changes* 24, *Fu: Commentary on the Decision*, p. 107)

In his exegesis of the last line of the *Commentary on the Decision* Wang Bi writes,†

---

*Sima Biao (?–c. 306). *Zi*: Shaotong, from the region west of modern Wenxian, Henan Province. He was a member of the Jin imperial family, a historian, and an exegete.

† For a complete translation of Wang's commentary on *Fu*, see Smith et al., *Sung Dynasty Uses*, pp. 240–242.

Fu means 'returning to the root.' Heaven and earth take the root as their mind. Any movement stops and is then still. However, stillness is not the opposite of movement. Speaking stops and then is silent. However, silence is not the opposite of speaking. Hence it is that even though heaven and earth are great, rich enough to contain the myriad things, such that thunder moves and wind progresses, revolving and transforming in myriad changes, nonetheless tranquility and utter beinglessness are their root. Therefore when movement stops in the earth only then can the mind of heaven and earth be seen. (Lou Yulie, ed., *Wang Bi's Edition of the* Laozi *and* Changes: *Fu*, pp. 336–337)

Guo Xiang, on the other hand, affirmed the all-pervasiveness of change. The self I am today is not the same as the self I was yesterday:

Of the force which is without force there is none greater than change and transformation; thus it opens up heaven and earth so as to press on to what is new, bears up mountains and hills so as to dismiss what is old; thus it does not stop for a moment, rushing on it has already encountered something new, thus the myriad things of heaven and earth are never at any moment not shifting. The world is completely new yet we take it as old. A boat changes daily and we look at it as if it were old. A mountain alters daily and we look at it as if it were in the past.... Therefore, the self I was is not the self I will be or now am. I go forward with the now; how could I then continue to keep hold of the past? Yet none in the world are aware of this and so they say that what I encounter now can be and exist, how foolish! (*SKQS* 1056, *Notes on Zhuangzi* 6, *The Teacher Who Is the Ultimate Ancestor*, p. 38a)

Buddhism

Buddhism brought with it Indian logic and a complete denial of the reality of change. Bhiksu Zhao reckoned that change was simply an illusion:

What others mean by movement is that past things do not attain to the present; therefore they say there is movement and
not stillness. What I mean by stillness is also that past things do
not attain to the present; therefore it is said that there is stillness and not movement.... People indeed know that bygone
things do not come to the present yet they say present things
can go on to the future. Bygone things indeed do not come to
the present. Where do present things go on? Why? If one seeks
past things in the past, one finds that they were never not existent in the past. Nonetheless if one looks for past things in
the present then one finds that they are never existent there.
That the things are never in the present shows clearly that the
things have not come. From the fact that they are never non-
existent in the past one knows that the things never left it. (*The
Immutability of Things*, p. 7)

Zhao denies that there is any connection between past and present. The
past cannot carry through to the present; hence there are no grounds on
which to base a theory of change.

This is to say that past things are only in the past. They do not
go from the present to the past. Present things are only in the
present. They do not go from the past to the present. (Ibid.)

In other words, the time in relation to the speaker is a defining characteristic of the given thing.

As there is not even the slightest link that goes or returns, what
thing can there be that can move? Since this is so the tempest
that overturns mountains is yet always still; rivers in torrents
do not flow; wild forces blowing and pounding do not move;
sun and moon coursing through heaven do not revolve. (Ibid.,
p. 9)

Although there may be the appearance of change, in fact it is only an appearance and everything is tranquil. Hence the past and the present always
exist.

Therefore in speaking of something as having gone does not
necessarily mean it has gone away: the past and present are

always in existence because they do not move. To claim that a thing has gone does not necessarily mean that it has gone away. One says that from the present one cannot attain to the past because the latter does not come to the present. Things do not come; therefore there is no rushing or galloping between past and present. There is no movement; therefore each thing, according to its nature, remains in its own time. (Ibid., p. 15)

The main point of this passage is to deny the flow of time. What is past is past and what is present is present. There is no flow from past to present and hence there is no such thing as movement or change.

The Song Era

The Song philosophers returned to the *Book of Changes* in their discussion of change. Zhang Zai wrote,

Therefore the sage speaks of the ultimate of nature and the way of heaven, examining the wondrous of threes and fives, change that is. (*SKQS* 697, *Correcting the Unenlightened* 1, *Ultimate Harmony*, p. 98b)

What applies to both human nature and the Way of heaven is simply change-as-such. (Ibid., p. 100b)

Qi has *yin* and *yang*. These increase and decrease and so produce transformation; because of their unity that same process of change is unfathomable and wondrous. (Ibid. 4, *The Wondrous and Transformation*, p. 108b)

In other words, the highest things in the world, such as the Way of heaven and human nature, are subject to change.

Zhang Zai differentiated between two aspects of change.

If there is change then there is transformation; this is moving from the coarse to the fine. "Transformation with shaping is what is meant by change-as-such," this making the minute apparent by reference to the obvious. (Ibid., p. 109a)

'Change' is said of what is obvious, 'transformation' of
what is increasing. (*Collected Works of Zhang Zai: Hengqu's
Explanation of the* Book of Changes: *Qian Hexagram*, p. 70)

By 'transformation' Zhang Zai meant the minute stirrings of change,
whereas he applied 'change' (*bian*) to the obvious changes. This distinction is a reflection of Zhang Zai's dialectical approach.

Cheng Hao was an advocate of generation:

"Generation and regeneration is what is meant by change-as-
such," this is what makes heaven to be the Way. Heaven simply takes generation for its Way. (*SKQS* 689, *Surviving Works
of the Two Chengs* 2a, p. 30a)

The great virtue of heaven and earth is called "generation." Heaven and earth interweave and intermingle; the myriad things transform. Generation is what is meant by human
nature. The meaning of the generation of the myriad things is
what can be best observed. (Ibid. 11, p. 97a)

Cheng Yi followed the Song tradition inaugurated by Ouyang Xiu of
questioning the Han and post-Han commentaries on the classics. These
later commentaries were seen as obscuring the original meaning of the
classics. Hence Cheng Yi's commentary on the last line of the *Commentary on the Decision* of the *Fu* hexagram is a rejection of Wang Bi's reading
of the same:*

"Seven days and it comes back again": the revolution and
progress of heaven and earth is like this. Decline and growth
influencing each other is the principle of heaven. . . . One *yang*
comes back below, this is the mind of heaven and earth's generating things. Former scholars [Wang Bi] all took stillness as
what makes apparent the mind of heaven and earth. They did
not know that the first stirrings of movement are in truth the
mind of heaven and earth. How can those who do not know
the Way recognize this? (*Mr. Cheng's Commentary on the* Book
of Changes: *Fu Hexagram*, p. 106)

*For a complete translation of Cheng's commentary on *Fu*, see Smith et al., *Sung
Dynasty Uses*, 245–251.

Here the emphasis is clearly laid on movement rather than stillness, in direct contrast with Wang Bi's reading.

The Qing Era

Wang Fuzhi also gave priority to movement rather than stillness:

> The supreme ultimate moves and generates *yang*; this is the movement of movement. It is still and generates *yin*, which is the stillness of movement. Were one to discard "movement and then stillness" where would *yin* be generated from? The alternation of movement and stillness is said of closing and opening. From closing to opening and from opening to closing are both movements. If one were to discard stillness then this would stop. "The greatest integrity is without stopping." How much more is this so of heaven and earth! "The decree of heaven is what is most awesome." What stillness lies therein!
> (*Record of Thoughts and Questionings* 1, *Inner Chapters*, p. 402)

Both movement and stillness are relative to each other, although if priority is to be assigned then it is given to movement.

Wang Fuzhi talks even more about the transforming process of heaven and earth:

> The virtue of heaven and earth does not change, yet the transformation of heaven and earth is new every day. Today's wind and thunder are not yesterday's wind and thunder so one knows that today's sun and moon are not yesterday's sun and moon. Wind is one with *qi*; thunder is one with sound; the moon is one with the earthly ghost *po*; the sun is one with brightness. These are all one. Or in knowing that today's sense organs and sinews are not yesterday's sense organs and sinews, and seeing and hearing have the same sensation; touching and feeling have the same, knowing each by the fact that its proper nature does not change and hence distinguishes and synthesizes and transforms so that each element received matches what is provided by another sense. (Ibid. 2, *Outer Chapters*, p. 42a)

The water of the rivers today is like it was in the past but it is not today's water that has come through from the past. The light of a candle yesterday is as today but it is not yesterday's flame that is today's. Water and fire are close and we know their changes. The sun and moon are far and cannot be investigated. Nails and hair grow daily and the old drops off. This is something people know about. The daily growth of muscles and flesh and the discarding of the old is something people do not know about. People see that the form has not changed and do not know that the matter has already gone, thus they imagine that the sun and moon of here and now are the sun and moon of the past, the muscles and flesh of the here and now are those of the newborn baby. How is this sufficient to justify talk of the transformation inherent in daily renewal? (Ibid., p. 67)

Hence in the history of Chinese thought there have been two attitudes toward change. On one hand those who follow the *Book of Changes* asserted the universality of change; on the other, Wang Bi and the Buddhists stressed stillness.

26. Incipience

Ji

Although 'transformation' can be distinguished from 'change' by the degree of variation, the Great Commentary *has a further term for speaking of the initial tendency to change that is even more minute than 'transformation.' The term in question is 'incipience,' or 'impetus.'*

The *Changes* are the means by which the sages searched the profound and examined incipience. Only by the profound can one penetrate to the purposes under heaven; only by incipience

can one perfect the tasks under heaven. (*Great Commentary*
1.10, pp. 295–296)

The Master said, "Ah, to know the numinosity of incipience!" The gentleman in dealing with his betters does not
flatter, in dealing with his inferiors is not rude for does he not
know incipience? Incipience is the most minute of aspect of
movement and the first appearances of good fortune. The
gentleman sees incipience and inaugurates; he does not wait
until the ending of the day. (*Great Commentary* 2.5, p. 321)

The gentleman is attuned to the slightest sign of change and thus is able to
see not only the good but the better in other people. Kong Yingda comments on this passage as follows:

Incipience is the minute. It is the minuteness of a movement
that has already begun. Movement is said of movements of the
mind and of events. At the very start of motion its principle is
not yet apparent, it is only extremely minute. When it has already appeared then the mind and affair are clear and evident.
Such does not deserve the name incipience. If it has not yet
moved and is tranquil, not yet present at all, then this also
cannot be called incipience. Incipience is the leaving of beingless to enter being and is on the fringe of beingless and being;
thus it is the tiniest kind of change. (*The Correct Meaning of
the* Book of Changes 8, p. 8a)

Kong Yingda's analysis includes both movements of the mind and physical
movement of objects.

Incipience or impetus was equally important in Zhou Dunyi's
thought:

Integrity does not act but is the impetus to good and evil.
(*Book of Penetration* 3, *Integrity Is the Incipient Virtue*, p. 1a)

The fourth chapter of the same book, quoted here in full, relates incipience to the sage.

"Tranquil and not moving" (*Great Commentary* 1.10) is integrity. "Touched and then penetrating" (*Great Commentary*
1.10) is the numinous. Movement but not yet becoming form,

in the interstice of beingless and being is incipience. Integrity is quintessential therefore bright; the numinous is responsive therefore mysterious; incipience is tiny therefore hidden. Integrity, the numinous and incipience can all be said of the sage. (*Book of Penetration* 4, *Sagehood*, p. 1a)

The sage is one who is attuned to the finest things of the world. Notice how this chapter is looking for a terminology that will go behind the dichotomy of this or that. Incipience is neither in the world of the beingless nor in the world of being. It is an attempt to verbalize the middle term. In Zhou's philosophy 'integrity' is applied to human nature; 'the numinous' points to the responsiveness of the person to stimuli, and 'incipience' is the first stirring of thought. Thus for Zhou incipience is confined to mental activity.

The late Ming scholar Fang Yizhi advocated "penetrating incipience" or "insight" into the changes of things. All things arise from one source, belong to one universe:

> In looking right through heaven and earth we see that heaven and earth are one thing. One extrapolates to the point at which it is not possible to know. One turns back to what it is possible to know and grasps it. From the visible one knows the hidden; the most original is one reality. This is the profound insight which makes things things and the numinous numinous. To profoundly plummet the roots from which the storehouse of silent feeling comes is called penetrating to incipience. Things have a reason for being as they are. One can examine the reality of this thoroughly. At its greatest it meets the origin; at its smallest it emerges in plants and creepy-crawlies. Classify the nature and characteristics of a thing and determine its likes and aversions, extrapolating to predict what in it is unchanging and what changes. This is called fathoming the substance. Fathoming the substance is that in which penetrating to incipience is concealed. (*SKQS* 867, *Author's Preface to the* Little Recognition of the Principles of Things, p. 742b)

Fang's "penetrating to incipience" refers to the process of knowing the intrinsic causes of change in things, whereas "fathoming substance" is an in-depth study of the rules governing the changes in the appearance of things.

The notion of incipience presented by the *Great Commentary* and the derivative terms 'studying' or 'knowing incipience' are important concepts in ancient Chinese dialectics.

27. Image
Xiang TƯỢNG
象

Three distinct uses of the term xiang *are discussed: 'image' (in the* Great Commentary*), 'symbol,' (in the* Great Commentary *and the* Laozi*), and 'phenomenon' (in Song and post-Song works).*

Image

The term *xiang* was originally the picture of an elephant. It was borrowed to mean 'image,' 'figure,' or 'symbol' and became an important concept in philosophy based on the *Book of Changes*. In ancient thought it has two meanings: 'symbol' and its cognates and 'metereological phenomenon.'

These two uses are both found in the *Great Commentary*:

> In heaven perfecting symbols; on earth perfecting forms: change and transformation become apparent. (*Great Commentary* 1.1, p. 271)

Han Kangbo explained the use of *xiang* in this sentence as referring not to symbols but to the heavenly bodies:

> Images are the sun, moon, stars and planets; forms are mountains, rivers, plants and trees. (*Collected Editions of the* Book of Changes 3, p. 283–284)
>
> What perfects images is called *Qian*; what imitates them is called *Kun*. (*Great Commentary* 1.5, p. 281)

> Since they are visible they are called 'images'; since they are forms they are called 'vessels.' (*Great Commentary* 1.11, p. 298)

Both images and vessels can be perceived, but images are the objects of seeing, whereas vessels can be both seen and felt.

> Of the things that model themselves on images nothing is greater than heaven and earth. Of the things that change and course along nothing is greater than the four seasons; of the things that display images and are bright nothing is greater than the sun and moon. . . .
>
> Heaven causes images to descend to reveal good and bad fortune. (*Great Commentary* 1.11, p. 300)
>
> Of old Bao Xi reigned over all under heaven; raising his head he contemplated the images in heaven, bending down he looked at the models on earth. (*Great Commentary* 2.2, p. 309)

Here images and forms are contrasted: images belong to heaven and forms pertain to earth. Images are also contrasted with vessels. Vessels have a determined shape, whereas images do not. Furthermore, images pertain to heaven and models to earth. Compared with forms, models have an even more definite shape.

Symbol

The meaning of 'symbol' is illustrated by the following examples:

> The sages set out the hexagrams and observed the symbols ... therefore good fortune and bad fortune [as expressed in the line-statements of the *Book of Changes*] are the symbols of gain and loss; and the repentance and sorrow are the symbols of concern and anxiety. The changes and transformations are the symbols of advancing and retreating. Hard and soft are the symbols of day and night. (*Great Commentary* 1.2, p. 274)
>
> The sages contemplated and surveyed all under heaven. They mused on all the forms and appearances and pictured

what they represented and their character. Therefore it is said that they are symbols. (*Great Commentary* 1.8, p. 285, 1.12, p. 304)

A book does not adequately express speech; speech does not adequately express thoughts. Is it then that the sage's thoughts cannot be known? The master said, "The sages established symbols to adequately express their thoughts." (*Great Commentary* 1.12, p. 302)

The eight trigrams form a sequence and the symbols are in their midst. (*Great Commentary* 2.1, p. 306)

Symbols are symbols of these things. The lines and symbols move within and good fortune and bad fortune are seen outside. (*Great Commentary* 2.1, pp. 307–308)

Therefore the *Changes* is symbolic; symbols are representations. (*Great Commentary* 2.3, p. 314)

The eight trigrams inform by symbols. (*Great Commentary* 2.12, p. 336)

In the *Symbolic Commentary to the* Book of Changes, the symbols are the images associated with each of the eight trigrams. Thus 'heaven' is associated with *Qian*. In the *Great Commentary* symbols are seen as able to express what cannot be put into words. There are also four symbols singled out to serve as mediating points between the eight trigrams and the two modes of *yin* and *yang* (*Great Commentary* 1.11, p. 301).

The use of *xiang* to mean 'symbol' is found in *Zuo's Commentary*. The following is the discussion of how babies' names are to be chosen:*

---

*This text and the following passage require some explaining. A baby may be born with a mark on it that is in the form of a Chinese character; that is the first kind of naming. A baby may be named after a moral virtue, such as Prudence. Third, and most relevant here, a baby may be named from some particular trait, thus: Longshanks. Fourth, a baby may be named after an object (Daisy), and finally a baby may take the father's name as in Donald MacDonald.

The process of divining that was undertaken at the royal court and elsewhere gave a powerful impetus to the notion of symbolism. The turtle plastron was popular, possibly because its shape suggested the shape of the earth, while the round shell suggested the dome of heaven. The turtle came from water but the necromancy was done in fire. Hence the turtle was singularly apt for discerning the patterns of heaven and earth. The other means of divining was by yarrow stalks. These would be counted and thrown in groups.

There are five ways of naming: by pre-intimation, by the name of a virtue, by striking appearance, by analogy, by similarity. When the child is born with its name this is naming by pre-intimation; naming by virtue is naming by what is auspicious; naming by symbols is naming by striking appearance; naming by borrowing from some other object is naming by analogy; naming by similarity is to name after the father. (*Zuo's Commentary* 2, *Huan* 6, p. 47)

The turtle is symbolic; the milfoil is numerical. Things are generated and then there are symbols. Once there are symbols then they multiply. Once they multiply then there are numbers. (*Zuo's Commentary* 5, *Xi* 15, p. 165)

Symbols are representations of things.

The term 'great symbol' is used in the *Laozi* to refer to the Way. Whereas symbols in the *Great Commentary* are visible objects; in the *Laozi* the symbol stands for the invisible Way in contrast to things that can be seen:

Grasp the great symbol and all under heaven will come to you. (*Laozi* 35/MWD 39)

The great symbol is formless. (*Laozi* 41/MWD 3)

As 'thing' the Way is vague and unclear; unclear and vague, yet within it is a symbol; vague and unclear, yet within it is a thing. (*Laozi* 21/MWD 65)

Unending it cannot be named; it reverts back to what is not a thing. This is called the shape without a shape, the image of what is not a thing. (*Laozi* 14/MWD 58)

The *Hanfeizi* explains the meaning of 'symbol' in the *Laozi* as follows:

People have rarely seen a living elephant but have obtained the bones of dead elephants. From the layout they have imagined the living creature; thus whatsoever people imagine is called an 'elephant.' Now even though the Way cannot be acquired, heard or seen, the sages grasped the effects of its appearance in order to make its form visible; thus it is said, "the shape without a shape; the image of what is not a thing." (*Hanfeizi* 20, *Exegesis of the* Laozi #28)

Despite differences between the *Changes'* use and that of the *Laozi*, both are using the term 'symbol' to express what language is inadequate to express.

Phenomenon

Han and Song *xiang-shu* (symbol and number) philosophers developed the use of the term in the *Great Commentary* to apply it to every symbolic association of the trigrams and to the system of relationships established thereby.* From the Song onward the term *xiang* was used in its modern sense of 'phenomenon.' This usage can be illustrated with passages from Zhang Zai and Wang Fuzhi.

Zhang Zai related phenomena to *qi*:

> The so-called *qi* is not specifically its state as diffuse vapor or congealed mass, what can be seen by the eye and known. It is also said of what is firm or compliant, moving or stopping, flooding or trickling. All these can be called phenomena. Suppose that phenomena were not *qi*, then what would produce phenomena? If seasons were not *qi*, then what would produce seasons? (*SKQS* 697, *Correcting the Unenlightened* 4, *The Wondrous and Transformation*, p. 109a)

Phenomena are contrasted with the mind as its objects:†

> From phenomena one can recognize the mind but if one follows phenomena one can lose one's mind. What knows phenomena is the mind. A mind that merely stores phenomena is itself but a phenomenon; is it possible to call it a mind? (Ibid. 7, *Great Mind*, p. 116b)

The last chapter of Zhang's book opens with this line:

> Whatever is shapable is all 'being'; whatever is 'being' is all phenomena; whatever is a phenomenon is *qi*. (Ibid. 17, *Qian Cheng*, p. 143a)

---

* Smith et al., *Sung Dynasty Uses*, pp. 255–256.

† The chapter from which this passage comes is an attack on Buddhism. The Buddhist mind, if it only acts as a repository for what it sees, is itself only another phenomenon of the same class as the things themselves. Zhang Zai is arguing that the mind is substantially different from phenomena.

Wang Fuzhi's comments on phenomena are found in his commentaries on Zhang Zai. Although phenomena and forms are all composed of *qi*, there is nonetheless a distinction between them:

> The two *qi* of *yin* and *yang* fill up ultimate space. Here there are certainly no other things nor is there any gap to fill. The phenomena of heaven and the forms of earth each have their scope. (*Notes on Master Zhang's* Correcting the Unenlightened 1a, *Ultimate Harmony*, p. 25)

Despite this text Wang did not confine the use of 'phenomena' to what pertains to heaven.

> The movement of the two *qi* is such that they interact and generate, coagulate and drip and produce the myriad phenomena including things and persons. (Ibid., p. 40)

The distinction between the self and things is not that only the latter are phenomena but that the latter are outer and the former inner. Phenomena are real but need not have form. In explaining the phrase that the numinous cannot be fathomed, Wang Fuzhi writes,

> The unfathomable has its phenomenon but not its form. It is not the case that it is possible to compare, classify, broaden or extend and grasp it. (Ibid. 2b, *The Wondrous and Transformation*, p. 80)

Phenomena may not have form but nonetheless they are still realities that can be apprehended.

28. Cosmic Moral Order

Yuan heng li zhen

元亨利貞

It would be strange for the Western reader to find the heading 'origin-sacrificial offering-profit-divination' in a book of philosophy. The four characters—yuan, heng, li, and zhen—are found in a text that is placed at the beginning of the Book of Changes *and occurs in many other places. It is possibly a form of ritual incantation. According to Gao Heng, the original meaning of the four terms is as follows:* yuan, *'great';* heng, *'sacrifice';* li, *'profit'; and* zhen, *'divination'.* Their importance to philosophy, however, lies in their being interpreted in a moral and cosmological sense.*

The Tang Dynasty

The moral interpretation is seen in the Tang dynasty in the work of Kong Yingda:

> These are the four virtues of *Qian*. In his Commentary Zi Xia says, "the origin is the beginning; *heng* is penetration; *li* is harmony and *zhen* is correctness [*zheng*]." They say that the virtue of this trigram is to be pure *yang*. It can spontaneously begin to generate the myriad things by *yang qi* such that *yuan* begins and *heng* penetrates. They are able to make the nature of things harmonious with each obtaining what it requires and they are also able to make things firm, correct and able to achieve their end. This trigram naturally leads things in these four ways so that they obtain their proper place; thus they are called the four virtues. They say that the sages must imitate this trigram and practice the good way so as to enable the myriad things to grow. Things obtain life and existence and are thus able to be the origin. Also they must accord with the myriad things by performing excellent affairs, making it such that they open up and penetrate and are auspicious [*heng*]. Also they must harmonize with the myriad things by justice such that each thing obtains its principle and produces profit. Also they must firmly establish things by *zhen* such that each thing is

* Gao Heng, *Zhouyi Gujing Jinzhu* (Shanghai: Kaiming Shudian, 1947), p. 1; there is a longer discussion in Gao Heng, *Zhouyi Gujing Tongshuo* (Hong Kong: Zhonghua Shuju, 1963), pp. 87–100. See also Loewe, *Early Chinese Texts*, p. 217, where E. L. Shaughnessy cites two translations that both try to convey the original meaning of the phrase: (1) "primary receipt: beneficial to divine" and (2) "perform the great sacrifice: a beneficial divination."

correct and is able to bring about success [*zhen*]. (*The Correct Meaning of the* Book of Changes: *Qian*, p. 1a)

Kong's moralistic interpretation is in fact a development out of the *Literary Commentary*, which reads,

The origin is the growth of goodness; *heng* is the gathering of excellence; profit is the harmony of justice; *zhen* is the root of affairs. The gentleman embodies benevolence sufficiently to give growth to people. He gathers excellent qualities sufficient to unite the proper codes of behavior. He profits things sufficiently to harmonize with all that is just. He is correct and firm sufficiently to be the root of affairs. The gentleman practices these four virtues, thus *Qian* is *yuan, heng, li, zhen*. (*Literary Commentary*, p. 5)

Kong Yingda also quotes one Mr. Zhuang:*

In saying that the origin is the growth of goodness, it is talking about the nature of heaven, which generates and fosters the myriad things. Even the greatest kind of goodness is not able to engender life but the origin is the ancestor that can engender life; thus it is said that the origin is the growth of goodness. *Heng* is the gathering of excellences. What is excellent is beautiful. It is said of heaven being able to penetrate and complete the myriad things such that things are the gathering together of all beauty; thus it is said that they are the gathering of excellences. Profit is the harmony of justice. This is said of heaven being able to benefit and increase everything such that each thing obtains what is fitting to it and all unite together. *Zhen* is the root of affairs. This is said of heaven being able to perfect the myriad things by central and correct *qi*, such that things all are firm and even. (*The Correct Meaning of the* Book of Changes I, *Qian: Literary Commentary*, p. 6b)

Kong Yingda continues with his own remarks:

---

*All I can find about this gentleman is that he was from the Northern and Southern Dynasties period.

The origin is the beginning of things. In accordance with the seasons it accompanies spring. Spring is what stimulates life; thus it is said below that it embodies benevolence. Benevolence is then spring. *Heng* penetrates and completes the myriad things. In accordance with the seasons it accompanies summer; thus it is said below that it accords with proper conduct. Proper conduct is then summer. Profit is the harmony of justice. In accordance with the seasons it accompanies autumn. Autumn is when things are perfected. Each thing obtains what is fitting to it. *Zhen* is the root of affairs. In accordance with the seasons it accompanies winter. Winter is for gathering and storing. Things are all rooted.... The origin is benevolence; *heng* is proper conduct; profit is justice and *zhen* is reliability. (Ibid., p. 7a)

Here the four terms are linked with the four seasons and the four moral virtues.

An even earlier interpretation of the sequence of four is found in *Zuo's Commentary*. Mu Jiang, duchess of Lu, was confined to a particular part of the palace. The diviner told her that according to the hexagram *sui* she would get out because it means 'to follow, to get out.' She argued that this would not happen because divination must take into account the moral qualities of the person concerned. Since she had contributed to disorder in the state, her fate would be death. Her words are as follows:

"The *Sui* hexagram [no. 17] comprises beginning, a sacrificial offering. The divination will be profitable. 'No error' being great, penetrating, beneficial, firmly correct, without blame." Now that greatness is the lofty distinction of the person; that penetration is the assemblage of excellences; that beneficialness is the harmony of all righteousness; that firm correctness is the stem of all affairs. The person who is entirely virtuous is sufficient to take the presidency of others; admirable virtue is sufficient to secure an agreement with all propriety. Beneficialness to things is sufficient to effect a harmony of all righteousness. Firm correctness is sufficient to manage all affairs. But these things must not be in semblance merely. It is only thus that *Sui* could bring the assurance of blamelessness. (*Zuo's Commentary* 9, *Xiang* 9, p. 437)

Both the commentary here and that of the *Literary Commentary* interpret the phrase in a moral sense.*

The Song Dynasty

Song-dynasty philosophers continued with the moral interpretation. Cheng Yi writes,

> *Yuan, heng, li* and *zhen* are the four virtues. *Yuan* is the beginning of the myriad things; *heng* is the growth of the myriad things; *li* is the completing of the myriad things and *zhen* is the perfection of the myriad things. (*Commentary on the* Book of Changes: *Qian*, p. 1)
>
> The 'origin' with respect to the four virtues is like 'benevolence' with regard to the five constant virtues; speaking generally they are the same thing; speaking specifically it includes all four. (Ibid., *Commentary on the Declaration*, p. 4)

Here the four terms are applied to the cosmic order of evolution.

Zhu Xi expanded on Cheng Yi's exegesis as follows:

> *Yuan* is the beginning of life of a thing; *heng* is the luxuriant growth of a thing; *li*, however, is its tendency to bear fruit while *zhen* is the realization of its fruit. Once the fruit is produced then its stalk falls off and it can produce seeds which will grow anew. These four virtues go around in a circle without ceasing. (*Original Meaning of the* Book of Changes: *Qian: Commentary on the Declaration*, p. 2)
>
> *Yuan* is the beginning of living things. Within heaven and earth there is no virtue prior to this; thus in accordance with the seasons it is spring, among human beings it is benevolence and it is the growth of all good. *Heng* is the penetration

---

*There are also some slight changes of terminology that reinforce the moral interpretation. See Yang Bojun, *Notes on Zuo's Commentary on the* Spring and Autumn Annals (Beijing: Zhonghua Shuju, 1981), p. 965.

of living things. When a thing reaches this point there is nothing more excellent; thus in accordance with the seasons it is summer, among human beings it is profit and it is the gathering of all good points. *Li* is the completing of living things. Each thing obtains what is its due and there is not any harm done among things; thus in accordance with the seasons it is autumn, among human beings it is justice and what obtains its share is in harmony. *Zhen* is the perfection of living things. Reality and principle are both present. Following their presence each is sufficient unto itself; thus in accordance with the seasons it is winter, among human beings it is wisdom and it is the stem of all affairs. The stem is the body and branches and leaves depend on it in order to exist. (Ibid., *Literary Commentary*, p. 2)

The virtues that Cheng Yi and Zhu Xi caused to correspond with the four terms are not the same as those chosen by Kong Yingda. But the use of the four terms to speak about the moral and cosmic orders in the one sphere of discourse is the same.

In brief, from the earliest times those who came under the influence of the *Book of Changes* believed that the four characters discussed here applied to both the moral and the cosmological spheres. To link benevolence, justice, ritual, and wisdom to the four seasons is rather artificial. Yet even though it may be mistaken the theory cannot be entirely overlooked, for moral values may not be wholly divorced from principles governing the natural order.

V. Concepts of Relation

The next set of terms is concerned with expressing relationships such as unity of two things, harmony, and causality. A common theme is the use of different terms to express two aspects of the world: the metaphysical and the physical. This division is never as clearly marked in Chinese thought as in some types of Western philosophy. As authors experimented with a vocabulary that distinguishes contrasting pairs they also looked for ways in which to express the complementarity and unity of the poles.

A. Binary Relations

29. The Way and Vessel: Metaphysics and Physics

Dao-qi, Xing shang–Xing xia DAO KHÍ HÌNH THƯỢNG. HÌNH HA

道器, 形上形下

Aristotle's distinction between physics and metaphysics has had a profound influence on Western philosophical terminology. The equivalent Chinese terms are used to express both the relation of the Way to phenomena and that of universals to particulars. The discussion was taken up particularly in the Song and the Qing dynasties.

The *Great Commentary*

The twelfth chapter of part 1 of the *Great Commentary* has the following line:

> What is above form is called the 'Way'; what is below form is called the 'vessel.' (*Great Commentary* 1.12, p. 303)

The Tang commentator Kong Yingda analyzed this distinction in terms of time and of substance. The Way is prior in time and is without substance, whereas 'vessel' is subsequent in time and has substance.

> The Way is the name of what is without body; form is the appellation of what has stuff. Whatever is is produced from beingless. Form is erected from the Way such that there is first the Way and then form so the Way is above form and form is below the Way; therefore what is outside form and above it is called the Way. What is inside form and below it is called 'vessel.' Even though form is at the frontier of the Way and vessel yet it pertains to vessel and not to the Way. Anything with the stuff of form may be used as a vessel; thus it is said that what is below form is called the 'vessel.' (*The Correct Meaning of the* Book of Changes 7, p. 18b)

The *Great Commentary* also says,

What is visible is called 'image'; what is form is called 'vessel.' (*Great Commentary* 1.11, p. 298)

Kong Yingda annotated this passage thus:

Substance and stuff form vessels so they are called vessel things. (*The Correct Meaning of the* Book of Changes 7, p. 17a)

The meaning of both these phrases from the *Commentary* is identical.

The Song Dynasty

In the Song dynasty 'Way and vessel' became an important part of Song philosophy based on 'principle,' although it was expressed in varying ways.

Zhang Zai understood what is above form as formless *qi*, and this was equivalent to the Way:

What comes from the transformation of *qi* has the name of the Way. (*SKQS*, 697 *Correcting the Unenlightened* 1, *Ultimate Harmony*, p. 99a)

What revolves in the formless is called the Way; what is below form does not suffice to talk about it. (Ibid. 3, *The Way of Heaven*, p. 107b)

What is above form, though by name is 'formless' yet has its image. (Ibid. 3, *The Wondrous and Transformation*, p. 108b)

Cheng Hao did not agree with his uncle in supposing the Way to be *qi*:

There are some who suppose that the clear, spacious, one and great are the heavenly Way but these are all attributes of vessel and are not said of the Way. (*SKQS* 698, *Surviving Works of the Two Chengs* 11, p. 95b)

Cheng Hao was referring to his uncle and his theory of ultimate space. The nephew believed that ultimate space is vessel and not the Way. Cheng postulated a sharp distinction between the Way and vessel but without totally separating them:

The *Great Commentary* says, "What is above form is called the Way; what is below form is called the vessel"; and again, "what establishes the Way of heaven is called *yin* and *yang*; what establishes the way of earth is called soft and hard; what establishes the way of human beings is called benevolence and justice"; and again, "the alternation of *yin* and *yang* is what is meant by the Way." *Yin* and *yang* are also what is below form yet they are called the Way, so only the first of these quotations clearly expresses the distinction between above and below. Originally this alone was the Way. It demanded that human beings be silent and thus know it. (Ibid.)

Yet at times Cheng Hao did not retain a clear distinction. Thus he says,

Vessel is also the Way and the Way is also vessel. (Ibid. 1, p. 10a)

His brother made a more rigorous distinction between the two:

The alternation of *yin* and *yang* is what is meant by the Way. The Way is not *yin-yang* but that whereby there is the alternation of *yin* and *yang* is the Way. (Ibid. 3, p. 61a)

Apart from *yin-yang* there is most definitely no Way. That by which *yin-yang* are is the Way. *Yin-yang* are *qi*. *Qi* is below form while the Way is above form. (Ibid. 15, p. 128b)

The Way is the root and origin of all things, that by which they are, and so is not equivalent to any one of them:

The Way, however, spontaneously generates the myriad things. Now spring brings to life and summer causes to grow, this is all due to the life of the Way.... The Way spontaneously produces and reproduces without ceasing. (Ibid. 15, p. 118b)

Hence the alternation of *yin* and *yang* is what produces the myriad things.

Zhu Xi's comment on "the alternation of *yin* and *yang* is what is meant by the Way" (1.5) is as follows:

What causes *yin* and *yang* to exchange positions and revolve is *qi*; their principle is the Way. (*The Original Meaning of the Book of Changes*, p. 58)

In other words, the distinction between what is above and what is below form is made in terms of 'principle' and *qi*. The distinction is also temporal:

> Principle has never yet left *qi*. And so principle is what is above form; *qi* is what is below form. When one speaks of what is above or below form is this not also to speak of before and after? (*Conversations of Master Zhu Arranged Topically* 1, p. 3)

Wang Fuzhi

Wang Fuzhi produced a novel theory of the relationship arguing that vessel was the root:

> "Is called" is said of something to which a name applies and on which the name depends. At first above and below do not have a clearly defined boundary. They are predicated according to what one intends to express. Thus it is evident that above and below have no absolute limits and that the Way and vessel cannot exchange their substances. Under heaven there is only vessel and that is all. The Way is the Way of vessel. The vessel cannot be said to be the vessel of the Way. If there is not a thing's Way there is not its vessel yet people can talk about it. However, supposing one has a thing's vessel, could it not have the Way? ... If there is not the vessel then there would not be the Way. People could scarcely talk about it or affirm its existence. ... If there were not bow and arrow there would not be the way of archery. If there were not carriages and horses there would not be a way of driving. If there were not sacrificial animals, sweet wine, jade disks and money, bells, stone chimes, pipes and strings there would be no way of rites and music. (*Outer Commentary on the* Book of Changes 5.4, *Xi Ci* 1.12.2, pp. 202–203)

Vessel is the concrete, existing object, the Way is the norm that is evidenced by the vessel. All concrete objects are vessels, and the Way belongs to them. Wang Fuzhi held that the metaphysical is not the root; rather, form is the root:

What is above form is not said of the formless. As for what has form, it has form and then comes what is above form. What is above the formless from of old until now, penetrates the myriad changes, goes to the utmost in heaven and in earth, in people and things. All these are what is not yet.... Thus what is understanding are the ears and eyes; what is perceptive is the mind's thinking; what is benevolent is the human being; what is just are affairs; what is harmonious are rites and music; what is for all and is most correct are punishments and rewards; what is useful are water, fire, metal and wood; what favors life are grains, gourds, silk and hemp; what is correct virtue are ruler and minister, father and son. If one should get rid of the concrete objects and try to get hold of what was before the vessel existed, then from of old until now, penetrating the myriad changes, going to the utmost in heaven and in earth, in people and things, yet one would not be able to name them, how much less acquire the real thing. (Ibid., pp. 203–204)

He concludes,

There is the vessel and then there is its form. There is the form and then there is what is above it. If there is not form there is no below, this is something people say. If there is no form then that there is no above is evidently and manifestly the case. (Ibid., p. 204)

Wang Fuzhi did not accept that metaphysical and physical are related as above and below but affirmed that form is the basis of what is above form. The metaphysical is not prior to form but an expression of form.

Dai Zhen

Dai Zhen returned to Zhang Zai's theory of *qi*. He took the *qi* of *yin-yang* to be what is above form:

The Way is like walking. *Qi* transforms and flows along, generating and regenerating without ceasing; therefore it is called the Way.... In the transformations of *qi* with regard to given things there is a distinction between what is above or below form. 'Form' is said of given things and not of the transformations of *qi*. The *Book of Changes* also says, "They established the way of heaven, calling it *yin*, calling it *yang*." This simply refers to *yin-yang*, it does not say that what makes the *yin* and *yang* to begin is called the Way. Could it be that the sages established this saying but that it was inadequate? The alternation of *yin* and *yang* goes on without a halt. This is what is called the Way. That is all.... 'Form' is said of completed forms. 'What is above form' is likewise said as 'what is before form.' 'What is below form' is likewise said as 'what is after form.' *Yin-yang* having not yet taken shape are 'what is above form' and it is clear that it is not the case that they are 'what is below form.' (*An Evidential Study of the Meaning of Terms in the* Book of Mencius 2, #17, 1a, 1b–2a, 2b)

Dai Zhen accepted that there is a distinction between what is above and what is below form. The *qi* of *yin-yang* that has not yet become things is the formless, and this is above form and not below it.

Conclusion

In summary it may be said that in ancient Chinese philosophy the notion of the Way encompassed two meanings. On one hand it is a process, on the other, a norm. In taking the Way as the transformation of *qi* Zhang Zai understood it as a process. In reading it as principle the Cheng brothers and Zhu Xi considered it to be a norm.

When the Way is considered a process then the relation of the Way to vessels is that of the universal to particulars. In the course of Chinese philosophy, however, this is not the principal issue at stake under the heading of the Way and vessel.

Taken as a norm the Way is contrasted with vessel as the universal to the multifarious, the abstract to the concrete. Can the universal be independent of the multifarious, or of individuals, and still exist? Of the universal and the particular, which is to be considered as the root? The dispute behind the terminology here is whether to talk of the universal from the point of view of the particular as Wang Fuzhi did or to talk of the particular from the point of view of the universal as Cheng Yi and Zhu Xi did.

30. Phenomena and Principle
Shi-li   sù lí
事理

Professor Zhang's interest was in autochthonous Chinese philosophical concepts. The pair discussed in this section are best known from their use in Buddhist translations. By showing how the terms were borrowed by the Buddhists from existing terminology and how they remained in use in non-Buddhist contexts, Professor Zhang has filled a lacuna in the writing on Chinese philosophy.

In the Sui and Tang dynasties the Garland School of Buddhist thought arose in China.* It distinguished four dharma worlds: (1) the phenomenal dharma world; (2) the principle dharma world; (3) the principle and phenomena having no obstacle dharma world, and (4) the phenomena and phenomena having no obstacle dharma world.† Fa Zang expounded this doctrine to Empress Wu Zetian (r. 684–704) of the Tang. The terms translated as 'phenomenon' and 'principle' existed in Chinese before the introduction of Buddhism and were used in the course of Chinese philosophy to talk about the relation of the metaphysical to the physical.

---

* It was the most philosophical of the Chinese Buddhist schools and was based on the *Avatamsaka Suutra*. Its first teachers were Da Shun (557–640), Zhi Yan (602–668), and Fa Zang (643–712). See D. Howard Smith, *Chinese Religions* (London: Weidenfeld and Nicolson, 1968), 133–134.

† For a partial exposition of this see "A Hundred Gates to the Sea of Ideas of the Flowery Splendour Scripture," Taishoo Shinshuu Daizookyoo 45. 1875 (1990): 627b.

Pre-Buddhist Use

The two terms were already used together in the earliest period of philosophy. In the Wei-Jin period they were used as a contrasting and complementary pair. Naturally these uses were not the same as the later Buddhist use. In Buddhist use 'principle' is also termed the 'substantial principle,' and it refers to the substance of a phenomenon. 'Phenomenon' refers to all that appears to the eye. In ancient Chinese thought 'principle' is the norm of things and affairs, whereas 'phenomenon' refers to natural changes and human affairs and hence may be better translated as 'affairs.' The 'root of affairs' refers to human activities. According to tradition in ancient China the official on the ruler's left hand took down his words while the one on his right recorded his deeds (affairs). The term 'deeds-affairs' was then extended in usage to changes in the natural world. Thus in *Zuo's Commentary* the appearance of a comet is referred to as the affairs of heaven:

> The affairs of heaven are constantly accompanied by such appearances. (*Zuo's Commentary* 10, *Zhao* 17, p. 666)

'Affair' and 'principle' used as one word are found in the *Xunzi*:

> Those who were anciently called 'scholar-officials' gave of themselves with great generosity, brought harmony to the masses.... They were committed to their affairs and to principle. (*Xunzi* 6, *Contra Twelve Philosophers*, line 34)

The commentator Yang Liang* notes,

> They were committed to carrying out their affairs and did so with principle. (*Zhuzi Jicheng* 2, *Collected Exegesis of the* Xunzi, p. 63)

Although brief, this use is evidence that the two terms were juxtaposed. The *Huainanzi* juxtaposes 'affairs' and the Way.

> Thus why the sages act is called the 'Way'; what they do is called 'affairs.' The way is like a gong or stone-chime. Once hit

---

* See Loewe, *Early Chinese Texts*, p. 179. Yang Liang's preface to the *Xunzi* is dated A.D. 819.

it does not change. Affairs are like '*qin*' and '*se*,' each string
alters its note.* (*Huainanzi* 13, *Fanlun*, 121/24)

The Way endures over time, but affairs change according to the time. The
final chapter of the *Huainanzi* also discusses the same issue:

> Thus in talking of the Way and not talking of affairs then one
> does not float and sink with the world; in talking of affairs and
> not of the Way one does not roam and breathe with transfor-
> mations. (*Huainanzi* 21, *Yao Lue*, 223/4)

The distinction between the Way and affairs here is similar to that between
principle and affairs in the *Xunzi*.

Wang Chong distinguished the Way and affairs even more emphatically.

> What the Confucians study is the Way; what civil historians
> study are affairs.... Affairs have their ending in the Way. The
> Confucians regulate the root; the civil historians manage the
> tip. In comparing the Way as root and affairs as the tip one
> determines honorable and lowly, high and low. (*Balanced In-
> quiries* 34, *Weighing up Talents*, p. 121)

Wang Chong honored the Way as the root and denigrated affairs as the
tip.

The first to clearly and consciously contrast affairs and principle was
Wang Bi. This he did when referring to Confucius' saying that the Way
can be grasped in one thread (*Analects* 4, *Li Ren* #15, p. 169).

> Affairs have a going back; principle gathers together. Therefore
> if one obtains the going back, even though affairs be vast it is
> still possible to talk of them with one name. If one gathers all
> together, even if principle is broad, it is possible to completely
> grasp it. (Lou Yulie, ed., *Wang Bi's Edition of the* Laozi *and*
> Changes: *Exegesis of the* Analects, p. 622)

---

*The *qin* and *se* are boards laid on a table with strings that are hit by hammers or
plucked. On a stringed instrument one string can produce a succession of notes, but this is
not so for the gong or the stone-chime, because one spot on the stone can only produce one
note that cannot then be altered.

Here 'affairs' and 'principle' can both be grasped by one term. Affairs all return to unity; principles can be gathered into one. "What is universal yet gathers to one" is a good definition of 'principle.'

Zhang Zhan (fl. sometime between 317 and 420) also mentions affairs and principle. In a note on the *Liezi* he writes,

> Fate is a period of necessity and the allotting of straight determination. Even if a given thing has not yet been experienced yet a given principle is already fixed. If one supposes long life or early death are a matter of proper health-care or fulfilling and arriving at are dependent on the strength of wisdom, then this is to mistake heaven's principle. (*Liezi* 6, *Li Ming*, p. 67)

This is to say that principle is necessary. Long life, short life, fulfilling, and attaining are all decreed by a necessary principle and human affairs cannot change them.

Wang Bi's and Zhang Zhan's use of the pair shows that they already existed before they were adopted by Buddhism. The Buddhists took the terms to express their own philosophy but tried to use terms that already existed in Chinese. Buddhist use of the term 'principle' differed, however, from its Chinese use in that in the latter it stood for the norm governing change, whereas in Buddhist thought it was the only real world.

Post-Buddhist Use: The Song Dynasty

In Song philosophy it was Cheng Yi who returned to the theme of principle and affairs:

> Of what is most apparent none is more so than affairs. Of what is most hidden none is more so than principle. Yet affairs and principle are one. The hidden and apparent have a single source. Those whom the gentlemen of old pronounced to be good scholars were able to understand this matter alone. (*SKQS* 698, *Surviving Works of the Two Chengs* 25, p. 259b)

In his preface to the *Book of Changes*, Cheng Yi writes,

> The most hidden is principle. The most obvious is image. Substance and use have a common origin; the apparent and

hidden have no division between them. (*Preface to the Commentary on the* Book of Changes, p. 2)

In the first of these quotations the contrast is between principle and affairs; in the second it is between principle and image. Clearly Cheng Yi was not wedded to either reading.

Zhu Xi had more to say about the distinction of principle and affairs. He argued that principle is amid affairs but also that principle is prior to affairs. The following is an exegesis of a line from the Analects:*

> What one studies below are affairs; what one attains to above is principle. Principle is only with affairs. If one can truly completely study affairs below then the principle one attains to above will be found therein. Studying below is simply affairs while attaining above is principle. Studying below and attaining above must only hold to affairs and things and one will see principle. (*Conversations* 44, *Lun Yu* 26, *Xian Wen*, pp. 1139–40)

Zhu Xi here says that principle is immanent in affairs and can be attained by a thorough knowledge of affairs. He continues,

> Studying below is affairs and attaining above is principle. Principle is amidst affairs and affairs are not outside principle. Within one thing there is one principle. In any given thing to perceive the principle within it is indeed a case of attaining to the above. (Ibid. p. 1141)

In other contexts Zhu Xi asserts the priority of principle over affairs:

> Before there is affair *x*, there is first principle *x*. As for instance before there was yet ruler and minister there was already the principle of ruler and minister. Before there was yet father and child, there was already the principle of father and child. Before they existed can one suppose there was originally not this principle, simply waiting for there to be rulers and ministers, fathers and children, and then putting the principle into them? (*Conversations* 95, *Book of Master Cheng* 1, p. 2436)

---

* *Analects* 14.37, Legge, *Chinese Classics* I, 288–289; "My studies lie low and my comprehension rises high."

From the epistemological point of view principle is immanent in affairs, but from the ontological point of view principle precedes affairs. The two points of view remained unreconciled in his work.

Post-Buddhist Use: The Qing Dynasty

The early Qing philosophers Wang Fuzhi, Yan Yuan, and Li Gong all affirmed the immanence of principle and denied its priority.

Wang Fuzhi argued that by studying things thoroughly one could attain their principle. In a work probably written in the winter of 1668, he criticized the reading into natural events of human moral principles:*

> There is examining affairs so as to understand their principles. There is no such thing as establishing principle so as to define affairs. (*Extensive Discourse to Supplement Zuo's Commentary on the* Spring and Autumn Annals pt. 2 (xia), p. 8a, *Shi Wenbo Speaks of a Solar Eclipse*)

In imposing the principle that the fate of a nation can be seen in the advent of an eclipse, one is imposing human principles on natural phenomena. This is to impose subjective criteria. By contrast, in going from phenomena to principle one is conducting an objective investigation.

Yan Yuan held that the way to acquire knowledge was by investigating affairs. Li Gong distinguished between "principle immanent in affairs" and "principle based on affairs":

> Affairs have a condition called 'principle,' that is, it is immanent in affairs. Now it is said that principle is above things; this is to make principle another thing apart from other things. 'Principle' is a mere word. How can it be a thing? Heavenly affairs are called heavenly principle; human affairs are called human principle; affairs of things are called principles of things. The *Odes* (*Book of Songs: Da Ya* 3 *Tang* 7 *Zheng Min* [Ode 260]) says, 'There is a thing and there is its rule. Apart from affairs and things how can there be any principle?' (*SKQS* 47, *Questions on*

---

* This date is given in Wang Fuzhi, *Shi Guang Zhuan* ed. Wang Xiaoyu, p. 2.

an Annotated Commentary on the Analects 2, On Analects 19,
p. 26a)

Li Gong here gives a reply to the contradiction we noted in Zhu Xi. If
'principle' were above things then there would be a thing that had no
principle, and yet it was said that by investigating things one would dis-
cover principle.

In talking of principle, Zhu Xi, Wang Fuzhi, and Li Gong all understood it as a rule, as what is to be contrasted with the variations of
things. The fact that the question as to whether principle is within affairs
can still be discussed today shows that it is a feature of Chinese thought.

'Affair' and 'thing' are often combined into one word. 'Thing' refers
to concrete objects and 'affair' to their changes. Chen Liang* gives a very
neat definition of the two words:

> Whatsoever takes up space in the universe is a 'thing'; whatso-
> ever is used under the sun is an 'affair.' (*SBBY* 80, *Collected
> Works of Longchuan* 10a.1, *Topics on the Classics*: The Book of
> History, p. 61a)

The term 'affair' is at first said of human activity and then extended to refer
to all changes in the natural world, the affairs of heaven. This latter is its
most comprehensive meaning.

31. Influence and Principle
Shi, Li-shi   LÍ THẾ
勢, 理勢

The term *shi* means 'influence, tendency, strategic power, authority.' In
ancient Chinese philosophy it can describe the relation between one thing
and another, their mutual influence. It can also describe the movement of
one thing toward another, its tendency; and finally it can describe the ef-

---

* Chen Liang (1143–1194). *Zi*: Tongfu; *Hao*: Longchuan, from Yong Kang, Zhejiang
Province. He was twice imprisoned for opposing the court eunuchs. Late in life he was given
a government post but died before he could assume it. In contrast to the reigning ideology of
the Southern Song, he advocated military reform with a view to winning back the north of
China from the Jin, ancestors of the Manchu, who established China's last dynasty.

fect of the ruler on the ruled, authority. In all these cases it is expressing a relation between two or more things.

Military and Political Thought

The term occurs in the received text of the *Laozi* but not in the Mawangdui versions, where it is replaced by 'vessel':

> The Way generates it; virtue nourishes it; things form it; influence perfects it. (*Laozi* 51/MWD 14)

In military philosophy *shi* can mean 'strategic power.' If the army makes proper use of the advantages of the terrain then even the cowardly soldiers will prove brave.

> Courage and fear are a matter of strategic power; strength and weakness are an issue of deployment [of forces].... Therefore one who is good at war seeks [victory] through strategic power and not from relying on troop numbers. Thus such a one is able to select troops and employ strategic power. One who uses strategic power commands troops in battle as if rolling logs or stones. Wood and stone are such that they remain still when stable but move when on steep slopes. If square they stop; if round they roll. Thus the strategic power of one who is good at using troops in war is like rolling round stones down a slope of a thousand fathoms.* This is strategic power. (*Master Sun's Military Methods* 5, *Strategic Power* #15, p. 145; #18–20, p. 146)

Courage and fear are a matter of strategic power insofar as when strategic power is on their side fearful troops gain courage. When strategic circumstances are against them then the courageous troops will be afraid. Thus courage and fear depend on the circumstances in which the battle is engaged. "Like rolling logs and stones" refers to using objective circumstances to move the army. Logs and stones are heavy and can be moved when the terrain is favorable but otherwise are very difficult to budge. If

---

*Literally, "a thousand *ren*." One *ren* is eight feet. One fathom is six feet.

one makes use of the objective circumstances then one can lead the army to victory. Thus in the *Sunzi shi* is used principally of 'strategic power.'

In the military philosophy of Sun Bin the same term is used. The manuscript is damaged but seems to say the following:

> There are in all four ways for the army: the first is deployment; the second strategic power; the third change; the fourth authority. If one examines these four then this is the way to destroy powerful enemies and win over fierce generals. (*Sun Bin's Military Methods* 9, *Possession of Strategic Power*, p. 80)

Since the title of this chapter is "Strategic Power" it may be that this was the most important of the four issues. In *Mr. Lu's Spring and Autumn Annals* we learn:

> Sun Bin valued strategic power. (*Mr. Lu's Spring and Autumn Annals* 17.7, *Not Two*, p. 1124)

In the Warring States period, however, it was Shen Dao who made a special place for *shi* in his philosophy.

> Thus the monster roams the mist; the flying dragon rides the clouds. If clouds disappear and mist is no more then they are like earthworms because they have lost what they ride on. (Thompson, *The Shen Tzu Fragments*, Fragment 10)
>
> Therefore if the worthy bow to the unworthy authority is held light; if the unworthy are able to obey the worthy, positions are respected. (Ibid., Fragment 11)
>
> As a commoner Yao was not able to administer his neighborhood. From this it can be seen that the worthy suffice to obey the masses and that authority and position suffice to make the worthy bow. (Ibid., Fragment 12)

A similar passage is quoted by Han Fei and attributed to Shen Dao:

> Master Shen said, "The flying dragon rides the clouds, the monster roams in the mist. If clouds disappear and mist is no more then the dragon and monster are like earthworms because they have lost what they rode on. If the worthy bow to the unworthy authority is held light and positions disregarded;

if the unworthy are able to obey the worthy, then authority is valued and positions are respected. As a commoner Yao was not able to administer even three people yet as emperor Jie could throw all under heaven into disorder. From this I know the need for authority and positions to be upheld and the unattractiveness of worth and wisdom. If a bow is weak yet the arrow goes high it is because it relies on the wind. If a person is unworthy yet his or her commands run it is because he or she is assisted by the masses. Yao taught his serfs and dependents and the people did not listen but once he attained the throne he reigned over all under heaven; his commands ran and his punishments stopped evil. Seen from this perspective to be worthy and wise does not suffice to bring the masses to submission, while authority and position suffice to make the worthy bow down." (*Hanfeizi* 40, *A Critique of the Doctrine of Authority*, #1)

Shen Dao interpreted *shi* as the influence of the ruler, his authority. He paired it with the position of the ruler and contrasted position and authority with wisdom and moral worth.

The *Hanfeizi* does not quote Shen Dao uncritically; rather, it offers its own evaluation:

As for authority ... if the worthy uses it then the empire is ordered; if the unworthy uses it then the empire is disordered. (Ibid., #3)

A comparison is drawn with riding a horse.

Suppose the chair of state [position] is like a chariot, authority like the horses and commands like the bridle, punishments like the whip. Now if Yao and Shun are driving then the empire is ordered. If Jie and Zhou are driving then the empire is in disorder, yet the worthy and unworthy are far apart. (Ibid., #4)

The *Hanfeizi* goes on to say that it is not necessary to wait for the sage ruler, as Shen Dao's statements could be taken to imply. Rather, authority alone suffices.

The first emperor of Qin did indeed rely on legalist arguments such as those advanced by Shen Dao and Han Fei. In his hands authority turned into autocracy and despotism. Although initially successful, his empire failed to last, and two years after his death his son was overthrown. This failure of legalism inspired thinkers to look elsewhere for political ideology.

Han Fei's own teacher, Xun Qing, had already advocated the need to maintain both moral worth and authority.

> Therefore being the ruler of men and women is the position of most profit and authority in the empire but it alone is not able to guarantee one's security. One who wants to make himself secure must pursue the Way. (*Xunzi* 11, *Of Kings and Lords-Protector*, line 3)

Xun Qing contrasts the intelligent ruler, one of moral worth, and the one who resorts to dark schemes:

> Therefore the intelligent ruler soon obtains the right people while the scheming ruler quickly secures his authority. The first finds himself at ease and his state ordered, achievements great and name renowned, at the most he can reign and at the worst he can be a lord-protector. The latter finds himself worn-out and the state in disorder, achievements nullified and name disgraced. His altars of soil and grain will surely be in peril. (*Xunzi* 12, *On the Way of a Lord*, lines 4–6)

Although moral worth and authority are both necessary for the ruler, the former is the more valuable.

> To abide in an authoritative post and practice the way of dominion such that in the empire none are resentful: such were Tang and Wu. To abide in an authoritative post and not practice the way of dominion, even if one's position is surer than that of any other in the empire, yet be unable to find even the contentment of a humble commoner: such were Jie and Zhou. Thus obtaining an authoritative post is not nearly as good as having the way of dominion. (*Xunzi* 16, *On Strengthening the State*, lines 23–25)

This was Xun's comment on the rapaciousness of contemporary rulers, but it was not accepted by his pupil, Han Fei.

The term *shi* appears again in a work of Liu Zongyuan on ancient social order. The circumstances (*shi*) of the times dictated the type of social structures that emerged.

> That kind of feudal system could not be dismantled even by ancient sage kings such as Yao, Shun, Yu, Tang, Wen and Wu. It is not that they did not think of destroying it but rather that circumstances did not permit. The origin of these circumstances, was it not among primitive human society? If not then it would not give rise to feudalism. Feudalism was not intended by the sages.

In primitive human society people fought with one another. This gave rise to the tribal chief who would "certainly look for those able to distinguish crooked and straight and obey orders." A hierarchy of leadership was established:

> There is the head of the *li* and then the official of the country, and then the lords and after the lords the earls of districts and generals and after them the Son of Heaven.

Next the positions attained were passed on by heredity:

> Those who bestow kindness on the people die and one must call on their descendants and honor them. (*SBBY: Collected Works of Liu Hedong* 3.1, *Discourse on Feudalism*, pp. 43b–44a)

Liu Zongyuan contrasted the circumstances that dictate what happened in history with the intention of the sages.

Philosophical Use

The fullest account of *shi* in all Chinese philosophy is that given by Wang Fuzhi.

> All talk about *shi* is to do with what flows smoothly and is not opposed, thus what goes from high to low, from great to include the small, where the former is no longer able to contain it and is not obstructed. (*Readings in the Great and Compre-*

hensive Theories on the Four Books 9.7, *Mencius Li Lou Shang*,
p. 601)

High and low differ in position, great and small in how much they contain.
Water falls from high to low and the sea envelops a puddle. These are
natural tendencies (*shi*).

Wang's commentary on the *Mencius* turns to the relation of tendency to principle. *Shi* is circumstances and tendency, *li* is rule and norm.
The two are complementary.

> The small virtue serves the great virtue, small worth serves
> great worth; this is principle. Principle is what is necessarily so,
> but it is borne out by *shi* [force of circumstances]. The small
> serves the great, the weak serves the strong; this is *shi*. *Shi*
> is what is unavoidably so but it becomes a principle. (Ibid.,
> p. 599)

Principle is what ought to be so, but it can only be translated into reality
by the force of circumstances. The force of circumstances can then be taken
as displaying the principle. In one case it is a question of morality, in the
other of the natural order, which may or may not conform to the moral
order. Thus Wang distinguished principle from the Way.

> The Way is the definite principle. By adding 'the definite' to
> principle we have the Way. (Ibid. 9, *Mencius* 4A, p. 1129)

The Way is the moral norm, whereas principle consists of both the moral
and natural norms.

Wang Fuzhi believed that principle and the force of circumstances
were complementary. One gave rise to the other. In a work dated to
c. 1671–72, he expounded this theory in the context of what the ruler can
expect to get from the people.* If the ruler looks to the surplus produced
by the people then he can use this, but if he considers the needs of the
state first and taxes the people accordingly, whether or not they have the
means, then the people will be resentful. Proper concern for the people is
in accordance with principle, and the same ruler's concern for the state will
be in accord with what circumstances permit.

---

* For date, see Wang Xiaoyu's preface to *Shi Guang Zhuan*, p. 2.

> Going with and against the flow is principle. What principle controls is the Way. Possibility and impossibility apply to affairs. Affairs determine the force of circumstances. By what is compliant in something one can realize its possibility; by what is contrary in something one confirms its impossibility. Principle perfects the force of circumstances. If one follows what is possible then things go smoothly. If one attempts what is not possible then one is obstructed. Force of circumstances perfects principle. (*Extensive Commentary on the Odes* 3, *Xiao Ya* #41, pp. 97–98)*

In this passage Wang mentions the Way, principle, affairs, and force of circumstances. The Way is the universal norm, and one may go with it or against it. If one acts in conformity with the Way then what one wants to do is possible; this is a case of principle perfecting the force of circumstances. If what is possible also conforms to the Way then this is a case of force of circumstances perfecting principle.

Wang Fuzhi's account is not wholly clear, but it does represent a good attempt to deal with a difficult problem. By *shi* he meant the relation between the norm governing change and the tendency of things to develop. The question remains a difficult topic today.

32. Substance and Function

Ti-yong THỂ DỤNG

體用

The relation between an object and its inherent movement or activity, between the fundamental metaphysical nature of a thing and its expression, between moral principles and their being carried out by individuals, is all encompassed in a common pair of terms. Given the variety of uses and contexts, various translations could be employed, but so as to preserve the coher-

---

* This section was not included in the first printed edition.

ence of this section the Chinese terms ti-yong *will be translated consistently as 'substance and function.'*

'Substance and function' is a pair of concepts that proved popular from the Tang period to the Qing. Its origin lies in Warring States philosophy. The pair 'substance and function' is probably modeled on an earlier pair, 'root and function.' By the Tang dynasty both Confucian and Buddhist scholars used 'substance and function,' but with rather different meanings.

Root and Function

The notion of 'root' is found early on. In the *Analects* 'root' means 'the main point':*

> Lin Fang† asked about the root of rituals. The Master said, "What a great question! In festive ceremonies it is better to be sparing than extravagant. In the ceremonials of mourning, it is better that there be deep sorrow than a minute attention to observances." (*Analects* 3, *Ba You* #4, pp. 155–156 [Legge tr.])

The *Analects* does not oppose 'root' and 'function,' for we find the latter also applied to rituals:

> Master You said, "In the function of ritual, harmony is to be valued." (*Analects* 1, *Xue Er* #12 [Legge tr.])

The function is the practice of ritual.

The two do occur as a complementary pair in the *Xunzi*. The opening line of the tenth chapter says,‡

---

* But Legge, *Chinese Classics*, vol. 1, *Confucian Analects*, notes that Zhu Xi believed that 'root' here meant the first thing to be attended to.

† Lin Fang, styled Zi Qiu of Lu, is known only by this question. Legge, p. 155, n. 4.

‡ This follows the punctuation of the Tang commentator of the *Xunzi*, Yang Liang, and rejects an emendation proposed by Wang Niansun.

> The myriad things occupy the same space but have different substances. Even if a thing has no intrinsic appropriateness yet it has a function. (*Xunzi* 10, *On Enriching the State*, line 1)

The ninth-century commentator Yang Liang noted that things are produced together in space but have different substances. Although from the human point of view they lack any permanent intrinsic definition yet they all have a principle by which they can be used for people (*Zhuzi Jicheng* 2, *Collected Exegesis of the* Xunzi 10, p. 113). Here 'substance' means the shape and body of a thing and 'function' means its usefulness. At times he uses 'substance' in a more abstract way to refer to the essential core of a thing:

> This Way has a constant substance yet it goes through the utmost changes and one corner is not enough by which to comprehend it. (*Xunzi* 21, *Removal of Prejudices*, line 24)

Although Xun Qing often speaks of the Way as the way of human beings, here he refers to the Way of heaven.

> Heaven has a constant Way; the earth has a constant number; the gentleman has a constant substance. (*Xunzi* 17, *Discourse on Heaven*, line 24)

The gentleman's constancy reflects that of heaven. From these two quotations we can see that 'constant substance' may be predicated of both heaven and human beings.

In his assessment of Daoism the Han writer Sima Tan, father of the historian Sima Qian, contrasted 'root' and its usage or movement:

> Daoism advocates no positive action and also no not-doing. It is easy to put into practice but its language is difficult to understand. Its technique is to take beingless space as the root and cause and effect as its usage. (*Records of the Historian* 130, *Summarised Discussion of the Six Schools*, p. 3292)

The usage is derived from the root.

The last chapter of the *Zhuangzi* was written at almost the same time and by someone of views similar to those of Sima Tan. In talking of Lao Dan and Guan Yin it contrasts 'root' and 'thing':

> Taking the root as the essence and taking things as crude ob-
> jects. (*Zhuangzi* 33, *Under Heaven*, line 54)

The Daoists are said to be concerned with the Way as what is formless and
not an object. The *Zhuangzi* also combined 'root' and 'stem' to form a
metaphor based on trees:

> Obscurely as if not existing, something exists. Slippery and
> formless and yet numinous. The myriad things flourish and do
> not have consciousness; this is what is meant by the root-stem.
> (*Zhuangzi* 22, *Knowledge Roams North*, lines 20–21)

The myriad things are like the leaves and branches on the tree of the Way.

Pre-Buddhist Use

Wang Bi, in his notes on Chapter 38 of the *Laozi*, contrasted 'substance'
and 'function':

> Even though [virtue] is "involved in great endeavors and has
> much wealth" (*Great Commentary* 1.5) yet with regard to the
> myriad things, each one obtains its own virtue [and they can-
> not be perfect alone. Therefore heaven cannot support; earth
> cannot cover; human beings cannot suffice unto themselves.
> The myriad things,] even though valuable, take 'beingless' as
> their function. They cannot dispense with beingless and make
> themselves to be substances.* (*Commentary on the* Laozi 38,
> p. 94)

Here it is said that the myriad things take beingless both as substance and
as function. Han Kangbo used the pair in a similar way:

> Even though the sages deal with the Way for its function they
> are not able to completely do without it as substance. (Yan
> Lingfeng, 3, p. 292 on the *Great Commentary* 1.5)

---

* For the editing of this passage and the insertion of the words in square brackets, see
Lou Yulie, *Wang Bi's Edition of the Laozi*, p. 94 and nn. 33–36. For the translation of this
passage see A. Rump, trans., with W. T. Chan, *Commentary on the Lao Tzu by Wang Pi*,
Monographs of the Society for Asian and Comparative Philosophy, no. 6, Honolulu: University of Hawai'i Press, 1979, p. 112 and p. 117 nn. 7, 8.

In a brief passage, Yuan Zhun of the Western Jin distinguished 'stuff' and 'function':

> To be bent or straight is the nature of wood. What is bent fits the sickle. What is straight aligns itself with a rope. This is the material of wheels and laths. To be worthy or unworthy is the nature of human beings. The worthy become teachers and the unworthy are the matter. This is the material of teachers and their matter. Hence then it is clear that 'nature' refers to the stuff and 'material' names the function. (*Complete Jin Literature* 54, *Discussion of Material and Nature*, p. 2a, p. 1769b)

'Stuff' refers to the inner substance, wood or worthiness, whereas 'function' refers to the outward function.

Zheng Xianzhi (364–427) used 'root' and 'function' to explain the relation of form and spirit:

> Form rests and revolves with *qi*; spirit is aware and likewise flowing with the mysterious. Even though movement and stillness generate each other yet the pure and the coarse have different sources. Is it not that each has its root and their causing each other to come about is their function? (*SBBY: Hong Ming Ji* 5, *Treatise on the Indestructibility of Spirit*, p. 39b)

Fan Zhen (c. 450–c. 510) was a poor student who wrote a response to Zheng Xianzhi called the *Treatise on the Destruction of the Spirit* in which he equated form with stuff and spirit with function. He used the relation of stuff and function to explain the relation of form and spirit:

> Form is the stuff of spirit; spirit is the function of form. Thus any given form refers to the stuff of that thing and 'spirit' refers to its function.... Spirit is to stuff as sharpness is to a knife. Form is to function as a knife is to sharpness. (*Complete Liang Literature* 45, *Treatise on the Destruction of the Spirit* pp. 6b, 3209b; also *Liang History*, pp. 665, 666)

'Stuff' applies to the material substance and 'function' to its function.

Early Buddhist Use

The Buddhist Hui Yuan (334–416 or 417) came from Shanxi and was a pupil of the great Buddhist Dao-an. He used the philosophy of Zhuangzi to support Buddhism.* Hui Yuan believed that bhiksus need not kneel or bow before kings or lords.

> Form becomes substance by having dimensions. Principle takes heterodox and orthodox as its functions. The origin of both is that each rests on its own root. If one allows the stem to remain and does not render it bright then phenomena are not able to reply to it. Form and principle are mutually shaped, their way is mysterious. (*SBBY: Hong Ming Ji* 5.7, *On the Sramana Baring His Right Shoulder*, p. 44a)†

Su Yan, Emperor Wu (r. 502–549 or 550), founder of the Liang dynasty, promoted Buddhism at the expense of Daoism.‡ He used the pair 'root' and 'function' in his writings and talks on the sutras:

> The mind is the root of function. There is only one root but many functions. The many functions may flourish or fade but the nature of the one root is unchangeable. The one root is indeed the spiritual brightness of non-brightness. Suppose we try to name non-brightness. It is not the eye of ultimate space. Soil and stones have no feeling; are they what is meant by non-brightness? No. Therefore knowing, recognizing and having concern for respond to brightness. The body cannot avoid mistakes. Mistaken concern is not knowing; therefore it is called non-brightness yet non-brightness experiences what is above. Being generates the destruction of being. Generation and destruction are its various functions. The heart of non-brightness

---

* For a biography of Hui Yuan see R. H. Robinson, *Early Maadhyamika in India and China* (Madison: University of Wisconsin Press, 1967), pp. 98–99; Tsukamoto Zenryuu, *A History of Early Chinese Buddhism*, trans. L. Hurvitz (Tokyo: Kodansha International, 1985), pp. 757–898.

† For a complete, annotated translation into Japanese see Kimura Eiichi, ed., *Eon Kenkyuu (Studies on Hui Yuan)* (Kyoto: Soobunsha, 1960) 2:94–95 (text), 412–418 (translation and notes).

‡ For an account of his Buddhist career, see K. K. S. Ch'en, *Buddhism in China: A Historical Survey* (Princeton: Princeton University Press, 1964), pp. 124–128.

does not vary. (*Complete Liang Literature* 6, *Record of Establishing Spiritual Brightness as the Meaning of Buddhism*, p. 2982b)

This passage is not easy to understand. It should be noted that 'non-brightness' can mean 'lack of intelligence'; hence Su Yan says that error in thought is an example of non-brightness. At the same time 'non-brightness' is a transcendent quality that cannot be spoken of in words. It is unchanging and roots both correct and mistaken judgements, which are the functions of the root.

Shen Ji* wrote notes on the emperor's discourse and clearly used the pair 'substance and function.'

> If there is the substance of *x* then there is its function. He says that the function is not the substance and discusses how the substance is not the function. The function flourishes and fades; the substance does not have generation nor destruction.... The substance is to the function as something that neither is apart from nor close to it. If one is apart from the substance there is no function; therefore it is said it does not leave it. The significance of function is not substance and therefore it is said it is not close.

The distinction is that substance is unchanging, whereas function changes.

Hui Yuan, Su Yan, and Shen Ji were all Buddhists They used the terms 'substance' and 'function,' but was it conformity to Buddhism?†

Non-Buddhist Usage in the Tang Dynasty

By the Tang dynasty of all the above formulations it was 'substance and function' that remained current.

Kong Yingda used the pair in his discussion of the *Qian* hexagram:

---

* Shen Ji is mentioned in the *Liang History* as wearing cotton clothes and eating vegetables. (*Liang History* 53, *Good Ministers* 2, *Shen Yu*, p. 769 [Beijing: Zhonghua Shuju]).

† The Sanskrit word translated as 'substance' in the formula 'substance and function' is *dhaatu*. This literally means 'whatever is differentiated, has a boundary or limit or is contained.' It also means 'nature or provenance of a thing.' The term *dhātu* is also translated into Chinese by *jie*, 'limit.'

This is indeed the symbol of heaven. Why then does one not call it heaven but rather *Qian*? 'Heaven' is the name of the definite substance. '*Qian*' is the name of the function of the substance. Thus the *Discussion of the Trigrams* says, "*Qian* is strength" (#7). It talks of the substance of heaven taking strength as its function. The sages wrote the *Changes* originally to teach people. They wanted human beings to imitate the functions of heaven and not to imitate its substance, thus they named it *Qian* and did not call it heaven. Heaven takes strength for its function, revolving without ceasing, responding and transforming without end; this is the natural principle of heaven. (*The Correct Meaning of the* Book of Changes 1, p. 1a)

Here heaven is the material substance and *Qian* is its active functioning.

Cui Jing (Tang, dates uncertain) wrote a commentary, *Penetrating the Mystery of the* Book of Changes, that was deliberately critical of Kong Yingda. The book itself is lost, but it is quoted by Li Dingzuo (eighth century).

All the myriad things in heaven and earth have form and stuff. Within form and stuff there is substance and function. Substance is form and stuff itself. Function is the mysterious use superimposed on form and stuff. To talk of the function of the mysterious principle coming to aid the substance is to refer to the Way. Substance is to function as vessel is to thing. Substance insofar as it is below form is vessel. As for instance heaven and earth, circular and covering, square and carrying are the substance and the vessel, while the myriad things whose stuff begins and generates are the function and the Way. For animals form and body are their substance, their vessel, and soul and consciousness are their functioning, their Way. For plants branches and stems are their vessel, their substance, and the fact of living is their Way, their function. (*SKQS* 7, *Collected Exegesis of the* Book of Changes: *Xi Ci Shang* 1.12, pp. 835b–836a)

'Substance' refers to the physical form of a thing; 'function' refers to the

function of the physical thing. This can be said to be a materialist interpretation of the substance-function terminology.

Tang Buddhism

In Buddhist language, however, the substance is on the ideal level. In the
Tang dynasty the two terms 'substance' and 'function' are very common.
An example is the Platform sutra of Hui Neng (638–713), the sixth patri-
arch of Zen Buddhism.*

> 'To think' means 'to think of the original nature of true such-
> ness [*bhūta tathatā*].' True suchness is the substance of think-
> ing; thinking is the function of true suchness. (*Taishō Shinshū
> Daizōkyō* 48 (no. 2008); *The Sixth Patriarch's Dharma Jewel
> Platform Scripture* 4, *Samādhi and Prajñā*, p. 353b)

True suchness is a rendering of Sanskrit meaning 'what really is.' It is not
material. The same chapter also distinguishes the relative roles of *samādhi*,
'concentration, meditation,' and *prajñā*, 'wisdom, discernment,' in terms
of substance and function:

> Meditation and discernment are one substance, not two. Med-
> itation is the substance of discernment and discernment is the
> function of meditation. (Ibid., p. 352c)

In other words, the purpose of meditation is to discern, and discernment
must be done in the context of meditation. The relationship is explained
by an analogy:

> What are meditation and discernment like? They are like a
> lamp and its light. With the lamp there is light. Without the
> lamp there is darkness. The lamp is the substance of the light
> and the light is the function of the lamp. Even though there
> are two names yet there is only one substance. (Ibid.)

This use of 'substance' to refer to what a thing really is and of 'function' to
refer to its subordinate functioning was to prove popular in later thought.

---

* For a complete translation of this text, see The Buddhist Text Translation Society, *The
Sixth Patriarch's Sutra*, 2d ed. (San Francisco: The Sino-American Buddhist Association, 1977).

Hu Yuan

In the early Song, Hu Yuan (993–1059) applied the distinction between substance and function to refer to the classics and the application of the moral principles contained therein.* His goal was to encourage students to see how the principles of the classics could be applied to concrete issues. He propounded a system of learning known as "clarifying the substance and reaching to its function." His disciple Liu Yi described his master's teaching thus:

> In the way of the sage there is substance, function and literary embellishment. The relationship of ruler and minister, father and child, the virtues of benevolence and justice, rituals and music cannot be changed in the course of history; these are the substance. The *Odes, Book of History,* the historical annals and collections of the Masters give examples to later generations; these are the literary embellishment. Raising up and managing the empire, being able to send compassion down on the people so that they turn to the imperial center, these are the function. (*SBBY: Song and Yuan Scholarly Records* 1, *Secure and Established Record*)

This is to say that the fundamental unchanging principles are the substance and their application in specific circumstances is function. This reading of 'substance' was already noted in the *Xunzi.*

Another of Hu Yuan's pupils was Cheng Yi. He used 'substance and function' to describe the relation between principle and phenomenon:

> The most hidden is principle; the most apparent is phenomenon. Substance and function have one source; there is no gap between the apparent and the hidden. (*Preface to the Commentary on the* Book of Changes, p. 2)

This use of 'substance' to refer to principle as what is most hidden and of 'function' to apply to phenomena is concordant with Hu Yuan's usage.

* See Smith et al., *Sung Dynasty Uses*, pp. 25, 32, 34, 37–39, 227.

Zhang Zai

Hu Yuan's contemporary Zhang Zai frequently used 'substance and function.' The meaning of the term 'substance' differs according to context, however. In *Correcting the Unenlightened* 'substance' has three possible meanings: 'original nature,' 'physical form,' 'part or aspect of a thing or affair.'

The first usage is illustrated by the following phrase:

> What does not yet not exist is what is meant by substance. By substance is to be understood nature. (*SKQS* 697, *Correcting the Unenlightened* 6, *Enlightenment Resulting from Sincerity*, p. 112b)
>
> Spirit is the virtue of heaven; transformation is the Way of heaven. Virtue is its substance; the Way its functioning. Both are simply one with *qi*. (Ibid. 4, *The Wondrous and Transformation*, p. 108b)

Here substance is the fundamental virtue.

> Responsivity is the wondrous nature; nature is the substance of responsivity. (Ibid. 17, *Qiancheng*, p. 143b)

Here substance is again equated with nature.

The following examples illustrate the use of 'substance' as physical form:

> Spirit is without a fixed place; change has no substance. (Ibid. 4, *The Wondrous and Transformation*, p. 108b)

This line is based on the *Great Commentary* (I.4, p. 279). Being without substance is being without physical form. Again,

> Ultimate space is without substance. (Ibid. 2, *Trinity and Duality*, p. 102a)

The third usage is illustrated by the following quotations:

> *Qi* is one thing with two substances. Since it is one therefore it is numinous; since it is two therefore it transforms. (Ibid. 2, *Trinity and Duality*, p. 101a)

The two substances are empty and full, movement and stillness, gathering and dispersal, clear and muddy. (Ibid. 1, *Ultimate Harmony*, pp. 99b–100a)

The same work also uses the term 'original substance,' taken up by
later Chinese philosophy to translate the Greek term ὄν. It is used to describe the relation of ultimate space and *qi*:

Ultimate space has no form. It is the original substance of *qi*,
its gathering and scattering, changes and transformations are
its objective form. (Ibid., p. 97b)

Original substance is contrasted with objective form. Objective form is the
state of flux, whereas original substance is the situation that does not
change.

When one knows that space and emptiness are indeed *qi*, then
being and beingless, the hidden and apparent, the numinous
and transformation, nature and fate are united and are not two
separate things. (Ibid.)
When one knows that ultimate space is indeed *qi* then
there is no beingless. (Ibid., p. 98b)

The use of 'indeed' shows that ultimate space and *qi* are one. It is not the
case that ultimate space is a higher level of reality than *qi*.

Zhu Xi

Zhu Xi followed Cheng Yi in speaking of principle as substance.

Principle is the substance of heaven; fate is the function of principle. (*Conversations 5, Nature and Principle 2, The Meaning
of Feeling, Nature, Mind and Intention and Such Topics*, p. 82)

Zhu did not limit the meaning of substance to principle.

As for saying that this patch of still water is the substance and
the ability of water to flow, stop, spout forth, make waves is
function, well, indeed this patch of water can flow and can
stop, can spout forth and make waves and this is truly sub-

stance. Or as for saying this body is substance: the eyes see, ears hear, hands and feet move, these are indeed function. Or as this hand is substance then the movement of pointing and grasping is its function. (*Conversations* 6, *Nature and Principle* 3, *The Meaning of Benevolence, Justice, Rituals and Wisdom and Such Topics*, p. 101)

This is to say that the terms 'substance and function' refer to a relationship and not to static entities. The moving hand is function with regard to the body as substance, but the hand is equally well substance with regard to the movement of pointing.

What is seen below is substance and what is produced above is the function. This body is the substance and its movements are function. Heaven is substance; 'the beginning of the myriad things' is function. The earth is substance and 'the productivity of the myriad things' is function. If one is speaking of *yang* then *yang* is substance and *yin* is function; if one is speaking of *yin* then *yin* is substance and *yang* is function. (Ibid.)

This passage echoes Cui Jing's words, quoted above. It also illustrates how 'substance and function' describe a relationship as established by the speaker and not an inherent metaphysical relationship.

Zhu Xi often referred to 'original substance.' He referred to principle as the original substance of nature and the original substance of physical form.

Before human beings and things were yet produced one can but speak of principle. Saying that nature was not yet in existence is to refer to fate when spoken of heaven. When one says that talent is nature then it is already not nature. Saying that talent is nature is to speak of something that comes after birth. Here principle has already fallen amidst form and *qi*. It is no longer wholly the original substance of nature; therefore it is said that it is already not nature. This is what is meant by nature among human beings. Human beings have a given form and *qi* and the corresponding principle begins to be amidst form and *qi* and is what is meant by nature. If one says that talent is nature then one has already mentioned what is generated and also *qi* and stuff. It does not merit to be the original substance of nature. So the original substance of nature is free from any impurities. It is necessary that people understand that their original substance is originally not apart from nor yet confused in them. (*Conversations* 95, *Master Cheng's Book A*, p. 2430)

The original substance of human nature is principle. Whereas Cheng Yi held that human nature was principle *tout court*, Zhu Xi argued that there is a distinction: principle exists in heaven before anything else but human nature only emerges when principle begins to descend into the human physical form. In describing principle as the original substance of human nature Zhu Xi was referring to what it essentially is.

Zhu Xi also maintained that principle is the original substance of form and vessel, of physical objects. It is that by which physical things exist.

However, the original nature of form and vessel when apart from form and vessel is what is meant by the Way while form and vessel considered alone are what is meant by vessel. (*Conversations* 75, *Changes* 11: *Xi Ci* 1.12, p. 1936)

He also held that the Way is the original nature of the heavenly principle of spontaneous nature. This is principle itself:

Nature is what human beings receive from the heavenly principle. The Way of heaven is the original nature of the heavenly principle of spontaneity. In truth they are the one principle. (*Collected Annotation on the* Analects 3)

In all these cases Zhu Xi was referring to principle but, as we have noted, in various different ways.

Zhu Xi also wrote about the original substance of the mind:

Someone asked, "Is the mind good or evil or not?" He said, "The mind moves according to things and events, thus quite spontaneously it is good or bad. Now for instance compassion is good. When one sees an infant about to fall into a well and one does not have compassion then this is evil. Apart from good is evil. Yet the original nature of the mind has never yet not been good." (*Conversations* 5, *Nature and Principle* 2, *The Meaning of Feeling, Nature, Mind and Intention and Such Topics*, p. 86)

Mencius' example of the infant on the brink of the well is used to affirm the same Mencian point that human nature is essentially good.

The original substance of the mind is what it has essentially:

Pure consciousness is itself the original substance of the mind. (Ibid., p. 87)

Wang Shouren

The same topic occurs in the writings of Wang Shouren, who says,

Utmost goodness is the original substance of the mind. (*Collected Books of Yangming* 1, *Instructions for Practical Living* 1, p. 2a; WTC #2)

Knowledge is the original substance of the mind: the mind naturally is able to know. On seeing a father it naturally knows to be filial. On seeing an elder sibling it naturally knows to behave like a younger sibling. (Ibid. 1, p. 5a; WTC #8)

The original substance of the mind is indeed nature; nature is in fact principle. (Ibid., p. 18b; WTC #81)

The original substance of the mind is in fact heavenly principle. (Ibid., p. 20a; WTC #96)

Integrity is the original substance of the mind. If one seeks to restore one's original substance then this is the work of thinking and integrity. (Ibid., p. 26b; WTC #121)

This quotation shows that it is not simply a matter of metaphysics. It is a moral quest for rectitude and honesty in thinking that is at stake. The point is made using an analogy:

The human mind is a heavenly abyss; there is nothing that the mind's original substance does not contain. Originally it was one with heaven. It is only that it is blocked by selfish desire and then it loses the original substance of heaven. The principle of the mind is without limit. Originally it was one with the abyss. It is only that it is blocked by selfish desire and then it loses the original substance of the abyss. (*Collected Books of Yangming* 3, *Instructions for Practical Living* 3, p. 5a [Taiwan ed.]; WTC #222)

There is an innate a priori capacity to know in the mind, which is the conscience:

The original substance of this mind is in fact heavenly principle. The conscience is the place of awareness in which the heavenly principle sheds its brightness on the spirit. (*Collected Books of Yangming* 2, *Instructions for Practical Living* 2, *Letter in Reply to Ouyang Chongyi*, p. 24b [Taiwan SBBY ed.])

Original substance is innate and a priori.

Wang Fuzhi

Wang Fuzhi built on Zhang Zai's thought and discussed substance and function in more detail. In his writings 'substance' has three levels of meaning: (1) the concrete existence of things, their physical shape; (2) their essential nature; and (3) the supreme original source of heaven, earth, and the myriad things.

Substance and function contain each other.... Substance is fully present in function and function is present in substance.... If there was no carriage what would one travel in? If there was no vessel what would one store things in? Therefore it is said that substance is fully present in function. What does not store things is not a vessel; what one does not travel by is not a carriage. Therefore it is said that function is present in substance. (*Outer Commentary on the* Book of Changes 5, p. 198)

'Substance' refers to the carriage and vessel, 'material objects' and 'function' to traveling and storing. The sentences are constructed so as to be tautologous, even though this would not be apparent at first reading, perhaps. One would have to understand 'carriage' and 'vessel' as very general terms, including airplanes and barns, for instance.

'Substance' means 'original nature' in the following comment on a remark of Zhang Zai saying that the nature of water is to be still or move and from this it generates its properties of intermingling and spreading out:

> It contains as water contains the form of a shadow: this is its substance. What this generates is its function. (*Notes on Master Zhang's* Correcting the Unenlightened 1a, *Ultimate Harmony*, p. 13)

The third sense of 'substance' is present in the following:

> Therefore one who talks well of the Way is able to reach the substance from the function. The one who does not speak well of the Way rashly establishes one substance and relegates function to following after it. (*Outer Commentary on the* Book of Changes 2, p. 38)

Wang Fuzhi emphasizes the close connection between substance and function:

> *Qian* and *Kun* have substance and hence must generate a function. Function returns back and forms the substance. (*Notes on Master Zhang's* Correcting the Unenlightened 1a, *Ultimate Harmony*, p. 14)
>
> Substance is that by which there is function; function is in truth the function of this substance. (Ibid. 2b, p. 76)

There is a necessary connection between substance and function such that there can be no substance without a function and any function will always be dependent solely on this one substance.

Wang Fuzhi advocated a materialist view of substance and function:

> The functions under heaven all have their being. I infer from their function and know the existence of their substance. How can one doubt this? The being of functions is that they have effects; the being of substances is in their nature and characteristics. Substance and function co-exist and require each other in order to be. (*Outer Commentary on the* Book of Changes 2, p. 37)

The effects produced by something and its nature and characteristics must be the same and so too the function, which produces the former, and the substance, on which the latter depend, must also be equal.* Therefore, since effects and characteristics concur, so too must substance and function.

Wang Fuzhi was critical, then, of Daoist and Buddhist idealism.

33. Dual Ends; Duality

Liang Duan, Liang Yi LƯỠNG ĐOAN

兩端, 兩一

That Chinese philosophers frequently thought in terms of complementarity is well known. Here some of the key terms for complementarity, duality, and opposition are discussed.

Relations between things may be expressed as conflicting or complementary duality. This is the foundation of dialectics.

Ancient Sources

The expression 'dual ends' is first found in the *Analects*:

> The Master said, "Do I indeed have knowledge? I do not know anything. But if a lowly seemingly empty-headed person asks me then I expound both ends and exhaust the topic." (*Analects* 9.7, *Zi Han*, p. 219)

---

* One could illustrate this with an example: water is a liquid substance one of whose functions is washing. If the function is washing, then water has the effect of cleaning away dirt. If the substance is liquid then it has the characteristic of being wet. What cleans away dirt must be wet and what is wet must be able to clean away dirt. This conclusion is impossible in Western logic unless it is restated in tautologous form. Chinese thinkers do not have a rigorous logic and appeal more to commonsense analogies.

Kong Yingda commented on the dual ends here by saying that it means 'from start to finish.'* Zhu Xi notes that

> The dual ends are like as if one said the dual heads. They refer to the ending and beginning, the root and branches, top and bottom, general and detailed. There is nothing they do not encompass. (*Collected Notes on the* Analects 9, p. 37)

The expression is found also in the *Mean and Harmony*:

> The Master said, "How great was the knowledge of Shun! Shun liked to question and liked to study even shallow words. He concealed the bad and exalted the good, grasped the dual ends of a matter and used their central message for the people. It was because of this that he was Shun!" (*Mean and Harmony* 6, p. 388)

Zheng Xuan interpreted the dual ends as excesses with respect to the center.

> The dual ends are exceeding and falling short. He used the central message for the people and worthy and unworthy alike were able to put it into practice. (*SKQS* 116 *Zheng Xuan's Notes on the* Record of Rites 52, *Mean and Harmony*, p. 353a)

Zhu Xi understood them as the widest extremes among the answers received:

> The dual ends refer to the various different extremes among the many opinions advanced. In general all things have dual ends. This applies to anything measurable in length or breadth. From the point of view of the central good one can grasp the dual ends and one can examine a measure so as to grasp its center and then use it. (*Chapter and Verse Exegesis of the* Mean and Harmony 6, p. 3)

Since the phrase 'dual ends' is only found once in the *Analects* and once in the *Mean and Harmony*, it is hard to determine which interpretation is

---

* *Zhuzi Jicheng* 1, *Correct Meaning of the* Analects: *Collected Exegesis of the* Analects 9.7, p. 179.

correct. From the literal meaning of the words one must suppose Confucius to have held that everything had dual aspects.

Zuo's Commentary contains the record of statements made by a certain historiographer named Mo, who explains things in numerology:

> Things are produced in duals, in threes, in fives, in pairs. Thus in heaven there are the three heavenly bodies [sun, moon, planets]; on earth there are the five agents; the body has left and right and everyone has a partner. (*Zuo's Commentary* 10, *Zhao* 32, p. 739)

It may be that this passage enlightens Confucius' use of 'dual ends,' namely, to refer to dual aspects or a pair.

The Song Dynasty

Although the *Book of Changes* used paired terminology, it did not describe pairs such as hard and soft, day and night, *yin* and *yang* as duals. Not until the Song dynasty was the term 'dual' used to speak of these pairs. Thus Zhang Zai writes,

> If the dual are not established then even one cannot be seen. If one cannot be seen then the functioning of the dual is nullified. Take any dual substances, space and fullness, movement and stillness, gathering and scattering, clear and muddy, they are each pairs that prove to be one. (*SKQS* 697, *Correcting the Unenlightened* 1, *Ultimate Harmony*, pp. 99b–100a)
>
> If there are not the dual then there is not the one. Therefore, the sages took hard and soft to establish the root. If *Qian* and *Kun* are destroyed then there is no means by which to see the *Changes*. (Ibid., p. 100a)
>
> Fluid *qi* was all intermingled. It united and formed stuff and produced people and things in their infinite variety. Its *yin-yang*, the dual ends, revolved around without ceasing and constitute the chief principles of heaven and earth. (Ibid.)

Clearly Zhang Zai applied the term 'dual' to the pairs of the *Book of Changes* but also extended them to any such pairs while using 'one' to refer to their unity.* It is not clear whether he thought of the possibility of there being a central term between the two as in the *Mean and Harmony*.

He did, however, emphasize that each thing has two substances. *Qi*, for instance, comprises two constituent parts, which are in contrast and hence a perpetual source of movement. The unity of this duality is called 'trinity.' The following text contains Zhang's own annotations:

> One thing with two substances, that is *qi*. One, therefore it is numinous [since it is a duality it cannot be fathomed]. Dual, therefore it transforms [deduced from the one]. This is the trinity of heaven. (Ibid. 2, *Trinity and Duality*, p. 101a)

Sometimes the duality may be described as an opposition:

> Since there are symbols, there are their opposites. Opposites must oppose each other in what they do. Since there is opposition, there is enmity. Enmity must harmonize and be reconciled. (Ibid. 1, *Ultimate Harmony*, p. 100b)

Opposition must always be conflictual.

In the works of the Cheng brothers there is more detailed discussion of opposition.

> The principle of heaven, earth and the myriad things is not independent but must have opposition within it. Things are just like that; it is not as if they have been deliberately ordered that way. (*SKQS* 698, *Surviving Works of the Two Chengs* 11, p. 97b [Cheng Hao])
>
> Of the myriad things none do not have oppositions. There is one *yin* and one *yang*, one good and one evil. If *yang* grows then *yin* diminishes; if good increases then evil grows less. (Ibid., p. 99a [Cheng Hao])
>
> There must be duality. It is the root of generating and regenerating. (*SKQS* 698, *Mr. Cheng's Pure Words*, p. 358a [Cheng Hao])

---

* Author's note: Zhang Zai sometimes used 'two ends' rather than 'dual ends': "The changes and transformations of heaven and earth are but two ends" (*SKQS* 697, *Correcting the Unenlightened* 1, *Ultimate Harmony*, p. 100b).

His brother wrote:

> Within heaven and earth everything is in opposition. If there is
> *yin* then there is *yang*. If there is good then there is evil....
>
> The Way has nothing that is not in opposition. If there is
> *yin* then there is *yang*. If there is good then there is evil. If
> there is 'is the case,' then there is 'is not the case.' (*SKQS* 698,
> *Surviving Works of the Two Chengs* 15, p. 128b)

Ye Shi* was a contemporary of Zhu Xi who, though opposed to the
philosophy of the Cheng brothers, did not side with attempts at court to
act too rigorously against Zhu Xi. He undertook a study of state institutions from a utilitarian and practical point of view. He discussed duality as the fruit of the unity of the Way. In this passage he expresses regret
that people fail to see that all things are related in patterns of duality:

> The Way has its origin in unity and becomes embodied in du-
> ality. Of old those who talked of the Way had to do so in terms
> of duality. Any forms that there are, whether *yin* or *yang*, hard
> or soft, going contrary to or going along with, going towards
> or away from, odd and even, separating and uniting, latitude
> and longitude, warp and woof are all dual. Not only this but
> whatever can be spoken of under heaven is also dual and not
> one. If even one thing is so, how much more the myriad
> things? The myriad things are all so and how much more is
> their mutual yielding to each other? (*Collected Works of Ye Shi*
> 2, *Other Collected Works of Mr. Shuixin* 7.4, *Centrality and
> Commonality*, p. 732)

Wang Fuzhi

Wang Fuzhi also wrote about the dual ends and the one:

> The dual ends are space and fullness, movement and stillness,
> gathering and scattering, clear and muddy. If pursued to the
> end they will be found to be one. Fullness does not shut out

*Ye Shi (1150–1222). *Zi*: Zhengze; *Hao*: Shuixin, from Yongjia, Zhejiang Province.

space; to know space is to know fullness too. Stillness stills movement. It is not not moving. When one gathers from *x*, then one scatters from *y*; when one scatters from *x*, then one gathers from *y*. Muddiness enters clarity and embodies clarity; clarity enters muddiness and dynamizes muddiness. And then one knows their unity. It is not a case of uniting a duality and making unity their pivot. (*Record of Thoughts and Questionings* 1, *Inner Chapters*, p. 411)

This passage is reasonably clear. One should, however, note that clarity is change and muddiness is the fixed embodiment of one state of change. The two are related rather as the solid and liquid forms of a substance are. The final point is that the unity is the unity of the duality and not a third unity superimposed from without.

Wang also explained duality in terms of opposition, using a term, *dui-li*, that has passed into modern discourse as the standard term for opposition:

The dual ends exchange functions and thus form the image of opposition. Thus it can be known that there movement and stillness, gathering and scattering, space and fullness, muddiness and clarity all are taken from and given by the real substance of intertwining great harmony. (*Notes on Master Zhang's* Correcting the Unenlightened 1a, *Ultimate Harmony*, p. 20)

34. Identity and Difference

Tong-yi ĐÔNG DỊ

同異

Logic is one of the weaker points of Chinese philosophy. Nonetheless the later Mohists developed a highly complex logic with a precise definition of terms. The degrees of sameness and difference are thus best exposed in their writings.

The question of identity and difference was taken up by Warring States logicians. Hui Shi classified things into genera. Within a given genus things would be similar; he called this 'great similarity.' Likewise with a given species things would be similar, thus, 'small similarity.'

> Being similar in great matters but different from similarity in small matters, this is what is meant by 'similarity and difference in small things.' For every single one of the myriad things to be wholly similar or wholly different, this is what is meant by 'similarity and difference in great things.' (*Zhuangzi* 33, *Under Heaven*, line 72)

Oxen and horses are both animals and thus are similar in great things. They belong to the same genus. White horses and bay horses belong to the species 'horse' and thus are similar in small things. Belonging to a genus and belonging to a species are not the same. Yet if one considers that any one thing belongs to some species and genus then there will always be something else similar to it. On the other hand, if one considers that any given thing is never quite the same as another then all things are different from one another. Hui Shi did not resolve the problem; he merely stated its paradoxes.

For all its anti-logic the *Zhuangzi* depends on the work of people such as Hui Shi to proclaim the subversion of logic. The man with the chopped foot is a sage who roams in the oneness of all things and regards the loss of his own foot as highly as wiping off mud. His view of the myriad things is as follows:

> When you look at them from their difference, then from the liver to the gall is as from Chu to Yue.* When you look at them from their similarities, then the myriad things are all one. (*Zhuangzi* 5, *The Signs of the Fullness of Power*, line 7)

The goal of the unity of all things is that espoused by Zhuang Zhou himself:

---

* Chu was a state centered around modern Hubei Province; Yue was a state centered around Hangzhou in Zhejiang. In 333 B.C. Chu conquered Yue. The text cited here is presumably anterior to this date.

Heaven and earth and I were generated together; the myriad things and I are one. (*Zhuangzi* 2, *The Sorting Which Evens Things Out*, line 52)

In a later metaphysical development of Zhuang Zhou's thought it is pointed out that what a word refers to is a whole that is more than the sum of the named parts:*

A 'group' word establishes the custom of taking ten surnames or a hundred given names as a whole. It joins what is different and treats them as the same, distinguishes what is similar and treats them as different. Now when you indicate the hundred parts of a horse you do not have the horse, though the horse is tied up there in front. This is because you must establish the hundred parts on another footing in order to call them 'horse.' (*Zhuangzi* 25, *Ze Yang*, line 60)

The most sophisticated elaboration of classificatory language is found in the Mohist Canons. Here four kinds of similarity are distinguished:†

Same: identical, as units, as together, of a kind. (A86C)
There being two names but one object, is the sameness of 'identity.'
Not being outside the total, is the sameness 'as units.'
Both occupying the room, is the sameness of being 'together.'
Being the same in some respects, is sameness in being 'of a kind.' (A86E) (*Later Mohist Logic*, p. 334)

---

* This is to say that the process of classification overlooks certain differences in order to subsume all species under a common genus, as when a flock of yellow-faced honeyeaters (*Lichenostomus chrysops*) and white-naped honeyeaters (*Melithreptus lunatus*) is described as a flock of honeyeaters. It is also a process of making distinctions that are not obvious to the ordinary eye, as when a flock of honeyeaters is described as a flock of yellow-faced honey-eaters and white-naped honeyeaters. The classification 'honeyeater' or 'horse' works on one level; that of 'yellow-faced honeyeater' or 'hooves and tail' works on another level.

† "Laughing jackass" is another name for the laughing kookaburra (*Dacelo novaegui-neae*) and hence an example of the sameness of identity. Any one of a flock of forty sulphur-crested cockatoos (*Cacatua galerita*) is the same as any other with regard to the number of birds in the flock, one of forty. Two rabbits in one hole are the same; insofar as they are members of the same family in the same warren, they are together. One eastern gray kangaroo and another eastern gray kangaroo are the same in that they both belong to the species 'eastern gray kangaroo.'

Corresponding to the four degrees of similarity are four degrees of difference:

> Different: two, not units, not together, not of a kind. (A87C)
> The objects, if the names are two, necessarily being different, is being 'two.'
> Not connected or attached, is 'not units.'
> Not in the same place, is 'not together.'
> Not the same in a certain respect, is 'not of a kind.' (A87E)
> (Ibid., p. 334)

The first kind of difference is a simple statement of lack of identity. The second is saying that things belong to different sets. The third is a statement of difference due to spatiotemporal factors, and the last is the difference resulting from species or genus classification.

The Mohist logicians give some of the types of difference and identity statements that are applied to given contexts:*

> Sameness and difference. In interplay the following become relative:
> Having and lacking ... (A88C)
> In interplay the following become relative:
> In the case of a rich family of native intelligence: having and lacking;
> In the case of putting side by side and measuring: more and less;
> In the case of a son, son and mother within a family: elder and younger;
> In the case of the body being here and the thoughts on something else:
> Present or absent;
> In the case of a price being right: dear or cheap. (A88E) (Ibid., pp. 338–339)

In other words, the classifications of identity and difference are relative to each other and applicable within a given context only.

---

* Distinctions of identity and difference are made within contexts and are thus dependent on what the speaker determines as necessary to distinguish. Among birds, length of beak, color of feathers, and sound of voice are all noted as indications of difference in species. In modern biology differences in genetic structure are important.

The Confucian View

In the *Great Commentary* sameness and difference receive little attention. A world-weary Confucius is said to have remarked on the theme of death:

> The Master said, "Under heaven what is thinking? What is worrying about? Under heaven all return to sameness, by death to mud. There is one outcome, though there be a hundred worries. For under heaven what is thinking? What is worrying about?" (*Great Commentary* 2.5, p. 316)

In general, the question of identity and difference is not one that exercised Confucians.

B. *Coordinating Concepts*

35. **The Whole**
Yi Ti   NHẤT THỂ
一體

From a logical assertion to the fact that all things belong to the same universe of discourse to a political ideal of coordination between ruler and subjects, the notion of unity and wholeness took on cosmic dimensions.

In Logic

Ancient Chinese philosophy used the expression "one body." All things were seen as composing one whole body. This term originated with the logician Hui Shi:

> May love flood over the myriad things: heaven and earth are one body. (*Zhuangzi* 33, *Under Heaven*, line 74)

This is to say that all things together, despite their multitude, can be considered one unit. The comparison of the world with a body is also found in the thought of Zhuang Zhou, Hui Shi's friend:

Who can take beingless as the head, life as the backbone, death as the rump? Who knows that the quick and the dead, the existing and the perished are all one body? I shall take such a one as my friend. (*Zhuangzi* 6, *The Teacher Who Is the Ultimate Ancestor*, line 46)

In the later parts of the *Zhuangzi* it is by death that one becomes one with the whole of nature:

Heaven and earth are the father and mother of the myriad things. Uniting they form into one body;* separating they return to their beginning. (*Zhuangzi* 19, *Fathoming Nature*, line 7)

The *Zhuangzi* also uses the term 'the great whole' to refer to the totality of things. Confucius speaks in praise of Lao Dan:

Unless the master had turned me upside down I would not have known the great whole of heaven and earth. (*Zhuangzi* 21, *Tianzifang*, lines 37–38)

Family and Politics

In *Mr. Lu's Spring and Autumn Annals* the term 'one body' is used to refer to members of the same family:

Father and mother are to their children and children are to their father and mother as one body but two parts,† with the same *qi* but different breathing. (*Mr. Lu's Spring and Autumn Annals* 9.5, *Essence Penetrating*, p. 508)

There is a physical basis for this assertion of unity.

The term 'one body' is also used in a metaphorical way for the body politic. The *Guanzi* presents ideal government in these terms:

---

* This is the author's reading. Angus Graham (*Chuang-Tzu: The Inner Chapters*, London: George Allen & Unwin, 1981, p. 182) understands the subject of the sentence to be the myriad things and not heaven and earth. The things emerge out of the primordial soup when the energies unite. Thus bodies are formed. The same disperse at death.

† Variant reading: "one body yet separate forms."

> The early kings were one body with the people. Since they were one with the people then they were able to defend the state with the state and keep the people with the people. (*Guanzi* 30, *Rulers and Ministers A*, 1:403–404)

The people were on the side of the ruler and so he was able to depend on them to maintain the autonomy of the state. A commentary attributed to Fang Xuanling (578–648) but probably by Yin Zhizhang (d. 718) notes,*

> By taking the heart of the hundred clans as his own heart, thus it is said, 'one body.' When one state is of one mind the myriad peoples have one heart. (*Ershierzi: Guanzi* 30, *Rulers and Ministers A*, p. 133c)

The picture here is highly idealistic, but even in more practical politics the expression 'one body' is used with the sense that the people will obey all commands of the ruler.

> There is the governing 'of one body.' Therefore one is able to issue commands and orders, enunciate constitutions and laws.... The governing of 'one body' is to eliminate heterodox opinions and forbid changes of custom.... When one decrees regulations and laws, issues commands and orders then no one will not respond. In this way one can govern the people as one group. (*Guanzi* 6, *Seven Laws*, 1:78–79)

The image here is of military obedience in the one *corps*.

The Cosmic Whole

In the Song dynasty the image of one body was elevated to cosmic proportions. Cheng Hao believed that the highest ideal of human life was to realize the unity of heaven, earth, and the myriad things:

> Benevolence is what makes heaven and earth and the myriad things to be one body. (*SKQS* 698, *Surviving Works of the Two Chengs* 2a, p. 19a)

---

*M. A. N. Loewe, ed., *Early Chinese Texts*, p. 249.

The student should first come to know benevolence. Benevolence is like the primordial unity and is one body with things. (Ibid., p. 20a)

This is to consider the whole as a great self and to ask for the breaking down of the limits of the ordinary self. This view was to have a great influence on the Song and Ming periods.

36. Unity

He Yi

合一

'Gathering into one' became an important theme in Chinese philosophy from the Han dynasty onward. The expression may have found its origin in the following passage:

Each affair concords with its name; each name concords with heaven. Between heaven and humans they unite and form one. (*Luxuriant Gems of the Spring and Autumn Annals* 35, *Profound Examination of Names and Appellations*, p. 288)

Zhang Zai wrote about different levels of unity:

Justice and decree unite in principle; benevolence and wisdom unite in sageliness; movement and stillness unite in the numinous; *yin* and *yang* unite in the Way; human nature and the Way of heaven unite in integrity. (*SKQS* 697, *Correcting the Unenlightened* 6, *Enlightenment Resulting from Integrity*, p. 112b)

The great theme of neo-Confucian philosophy was to be the unity of heaven and human beings:

Confucian scholars achieve integrity through enlightenment and enlightenment through integrity; therefore heaven and human beings are united. If one achieves scholarship then one can become a sage; if one acquires heaven then one cannot not even begin to discard human beings. (*SKQS* 697, *Correcting the Unenlightened* 17, *Qiancheng*, p. 144b)

Later Wang Shouren expounded the unity of knowledge and action (WTC #5).

Although they used the term 'to unite,' however, neither Zhang Zai nor Wang Shouren explained it. From their use of the term we can conclude that it involves both the recognition of difference and the assertion of a very close relationship. It would seem to include the second and third kinds of identity outlined in the *Mohist Canons*.

37. Harmony, Ultimate Harmony

He, Tai He HOÀ , THÁI HÒA

和, 太和

The most frequently used conjunction in modern Chinese is perhaps the word *he*, meaning 'and.' The original meaning of the term is 'harmony' as applied to singing. In ancient forms of singing one singer would reply to the other. Indeed, these practices continue among certain tribes in China today. The *Explanation of Words* has the following definition:

> 'Harmony' is one replying to another. (*Explanation of Words and Characters* 2a, *kou bu*, p. 32a)

Incorporating Difference

From the meaning given above, the term *he* was extended to describe the unity of any nonidentical objects. A famous passage in the *Guo Yu* gives the description of harmony presented by the grand historiographer of the late Western Zhou, Shi Bo.

> Harmony fulfills living things; but identity does not lead to growth. Putting *x* on a level with *y* is harmony; therefore it is able to promote abundance and growth and things revert to it. If identity is used to put down identity then in the end one will dismiss the object. Therefore the former kings mixed together earth, metal, wood, water and fire so as to form the hundred things. Therefore they harmonized the five tastes so as to please the palate; fashioned the four limbs so as to maintain the

body; harmonized the six tonic notes so as to attune the ear; rectified the seven internal organs so as to serve the heart; leveled the eight elements to form human beings; affirmed the nine threads so as to establish pure virtue, united the ten numbers so as to instruct the hundred units.... Hence the former kings gave different surnames to the princes, looked for talent wherever it was to be found, chose ministers, took practiced workers and did this so as to increase variety. If voices are the same no one will listen; if things are alike none have decoration; if tastes are the same there is no fruit; if things are the same there is nothing to talk about. (*Sayings of the States* 16, *Sayings of Zheng*, pp. 515–516)

Shi Bo's definition of 'harmony' as putting x on a level with y means to accept diversity and not to reduce all to uniformity. This gives the possibility of new things arising.

Another early definition of 'harmony' is to be found in *Zuo's Commentary*. 'Harmony' is here distinguished from 'assent':

When the marquis of Qi returned from his hunt, Yanzi was with him in the tower of Chuan and Zi You (Liang Qiuju) drove up to it at full speed. The marquis said. "It is only Ju who is in harmony with me." Yanzi replied, "Ju is an assenter merely; how can he be considered in harmony with you?" "Are they different," asked the marquis, "harmony and assent?" Yanzi said, "They are different. Harmony may be illustrated by soup. You have the water and fire, vinegar, pickle, salt and plums with which to cook fish. It is made to boil by the firewood, and then the cook mixes the ingredients, harmoniously equalizing the several flavors, so as to supply whatever is deficient and carry off whatever is in excess. The master eats it, and his mind is made more equable. So it is in the relations of ruler and minister. When there is in what the ruler approves of anything that is not proper, the minister calls attention to that impropriety, so as to make the approval entirely correct. When there is in what the ruler disapproves of anything that is proper, the minister brings forward that propriety, so as to remove occasion for the disapproval. In this way the government is made equal, with no infringement of what is right, and there is no quarrelling with it in the minds of the people.... Now it is not so with Ju. Whatever you say 'yes' to, he also says 'yes.' Whatever you say 'no' to, he also says 'no.' If you would try to give water a flavor with water, who would care to partake of the result? If lutes were to be confined to one note, who would be able to listen to them? Such is the insufficiency of mere assent." (*Zuo's Commentary* 10, *Zhao* 20, p. 679)

Yanzi was arguing that harmony allows for the reconciliation of both assent and rejection. It is not enough to be a yes man.

A similar distinction is to be found in the *Analects*:

The gentleman harmonizes but is not a 'yes' man; the mean man is a 'yes' man but does not harmonize. (*Analects* 13, *Zi Lu* #23, p. 273)

With respect to this passage He Yan (190–249) noted,

The mind of the gentleman is harmonious; thus he notices the difference in things, hence it is said that he is not a 'yes' man. What the mean man likes is all one so each competes for the winning stake, hence it is said he does not harmonize. (*Correct Meaning of the* Analects: *Collected Exegesis of the* Analects 13, *Zi Lu*, pp. 296–297)

The sage is able to accept difference and so produce harmony, whereas the mean man can only choose one thing and hence different things compete for his attention; he is not at harmony. He Yan has moved the focus from the degree of assent with another as in the *Sayings of Zheng* and presumably in the *Analects* and concentrated on the state of mind of the speaker.

In the Cosmos

The value of harmony to the Confucian tradition can be traced to the saying of the *Analects* on the function of ritual:

In the functioning of ritual, harmony is the most important thing. (*Analects* 1, *Xue Er* #12, p. 143)

In the *Laozi* harmony is a feature of the cosmos:

> The myriad things carry *yin* on their backs and *yang* in their arms. Blended *qi* is their harmony. (*Laozi* 42/MWD 5)

Blended *qi* is that which combines *yin* and *yang*.

> To know harmony is called the constant; to know the constant is called enlightenment. (*Laozi* 55)

The Mawangdui version of this line is as follows:

> Harmony is called the constant; to know the constant is called enlightenment. (MWD 18)

Here the Mawangdui version is better. The constant is the norm governing the processes of change. According to the *Laozi*, harmony is the basic principle of the universe and things cannot leave harmony and still exist. Harmony is not, however, contrasted with identity, as it was in the above Confucian texts:

> Blunt its sharpness; unravel its knots; harmonize (*he*) its light; unify (*tong*) its dust*—this is called 'abstruse identity.' (*Laozi* 56/MWD 19)

In this passage *he* and *tong* are considered roughly equivalent. From the time of the *Laozi* the term 'harmony' came to mean 'without conflict,' as it still does today.

Shi Bo's use of the term still had a mitigated influence, as can be seen in late Warring States and early Han writings:

> Utmost *yin* is solemn, somber; utmost *yang* is brilliant, shining. The solemn and somber comes from heaven; the brilliant and shining comes from earth. The two intermingle, interpenetrate, perfect harmony and so things are generated from them. (*Zhuangzi* 21, *Tianzifang*, line 27)

The *Inward Training* chapter of the *Guanzi* says:

---

*Lau (*Tao Te Ching*, p. 21) translates this as "Follow along old wheel tracks."

With regard to all human life, heaven issues its essence; earth issues its form. By joining these it becomes a human being. When there is harmony there is coming to life; when there is not harmony there is no coming to life. (*Guanzi* 49, *Inward Training*, 2:130)

'Harmony' also plays a role in the cosmogenesis of the *Huainanzi*:

The Way begins with One. One is there but does not generate; therefore it separates into *yin-yang*. *Yin-yang* unite and harmonize and the myriad things are generated. (*Huainanzi* 3, *Heavenly Patterns*, 25/17)

Harmonizing is what produces the myriad things, but the emphasis is on the mixing rather than on the variety, as in Shi Bo's remarks.

Also from the Han period was Gongsun Hong (200–121 B.C.). In his use of 'harmony' he combined cosmic and political speculation:

When *qi* unifies then things follow; when voices are in a duet then there is responding. Now the lord of men harmonizes with virtue above and the hundred clans harmonize with unity below; therefore the mind is harmonious and so *qi* is harmonious. When *qi* is harmonious then form is harmonious. When form is harmonious then voices are harmonious. When voices are harmonious then the harmony of heaven and earth responds. Thus when *yin* and *yang* are harmonious, the wind and rain are timely, sweet dew falls, the five grains grow, the six animals flourish, the best wheat rises, oxen and plants are productive. The mountains do not fall; the marshes do not dry up. This is the utmost harmony. Thus when form is harmonious then there is no sickness. When there is no sickness then there is no dying young. Thus fathers do not mourn their children; elder brothers do not weep for younger brothers. Virtue accords with heaven and earth and is as bright as sun and moon. (*Han History* 58, *Biography of Gongsun Hong*, p. 2616)

Whereas Shi Bo and Yanzi used 'harmony' to refer to the unity of variety, Gongsun Hong uses it to refer to coordination between phenomena. The term shifted in meaning.

Ultimate Harmony

The term 'ultimate harmony' comes from the *Commentary on the Decision* in the *Book of Changes*. It was to experience great popularity in the Song dynasty. The original use comes in a paean in praise of the *Qian* hexagram. Supreme harmony is the state in which each thing is in its correct place and no thing interferes with another.

> Great is *Qian* the origin. The stuff of the myriad things begins there, and it still rules over heaven.... The Way of *Qian* is change and transformation. Each thing in its proper nature and destiny, guarded and united in ultimate harmony and so there is profit in the divination. (*Commentary on the Decision* 1, *Qian*, p. 3)

Zhang Zai used the concept to express the complete course of the transformation of *qi*. The opening paragraph of his work states:

> The ultimate harmony is the so-called Way. Within, it contains the nature of mutually interacting, floating and sinking, rising and falling, moving and being still. It generates intermingling and interweaving and is the beginning of mutual overcoming and bearing up, of bending and stretching.... What is not like wild horses in intermingling and interweaving is not worth being called 'ultimate harmony.' (*SKQS* 697, *Correcting the Unenlightened* 1, *Ultimate Harmony*, p. 97a)
>
> What comes from the transformations of *qi* has the name of the Way. (Ibid., p. 99a)

From these two remarks it is clear that both 'the Way' and 'ultimate harmony' refer to the transformations of *qi*.

In his comments on Zhang Zai's writings Wang Fuzhi notes,

> Supreme harmony is utmost harmony.... *Yin* and *yang* have different roles but their intermingling and interweaving in the midst of the supreme ultimate is such that they unite and unify and do not interfere with or harm each other, as in the primordial soup with no gaps. This is utmost harmony. Before there was yet form and vessel there was originally nothing inharmonious. Since there is now form and vessel, their harmony

is not lost; thus it is called ultimate harmony. (*Notes on Master Zhang's* Correcting the Unenlightened 1, *Ultimate Harmony,* p. 1a)

Both Zhang Zai and Wang Fuzhi are saying that in the face of the diversity of things in the world what matters most is their reconciliation and harmony. This is a key theme of Confucian thought.

C. Causal Concepts

38. Causality and Consequence
Suoyi, Gu, Yin
所以, 故, 因

In the previous sections we have looked at relations of coordination between things. In this section we look at the various ways of expressing causality and consequentiality.

Gu

In ancient Chinese philosophy the commonest ways of expressing 'thus' were *gu* and, more emphatically, *shi gu*; for 'hence' there was *suoyi*. *Gu* was used to express a reason in the following passage in the *Laozi*:

> One who is courageous in daring-do will be killed; one who is courageous in not daring will live. Of these two one is profitable and one is harmful. Heaven hates what it hates; who knows the reason for it? (*Laozi* 73/MWD 38)

This passage merely illustrates the use of the word. A full analysis of it is given in the *Mohist Canons*:

> The reason/cause of something is what it must get before it will come about. (A1C)
> 'Minor reason': having this, it will not necessarily be so; lacking this, necessarily it will not be so.

It is the unit [which precedes all others (?)]. (Like having a starting point.)
'Major reason': having this, it will necessarily [be so];
lacking [this, necessarily it will not] be so.
(Like the appearing bringing about the seeing.) (A1E) (*Later Mohist Logic*, p. 263)

The minor reason is a necessary condition, whereas the major reason is a sufficient condition.

Examples may help. In order to travel to Adelaide, I will need to start from somewhere. Unless I start from somewhere I will never get there. Even if I start, however, I still might not reach the destination. Having a starting point is thus a minor reason. Assuming I am not blind or asleep, if an elephant walks in front of me I will see it but if it does not walk in front of me then I will never see it. The appearance of the elephant is a major reason.

Suoyi

The term *suoyi* can also be illustrated with passages from the *Laozi*:

> Heaven is long-lived and earth enduring. That by which [*suoyi*] heaven and earth are long-lived and enduring is that they do not generate themselves; thus [*gu*] they are able to enjoy long life. (*Laozi* 7/MWD 51)
>
> That by which [*suoyi*] rivers and seas are the kings of the hundred valleys is that they are well able to descend; thus [*gu*] they are able to be the kings of the hundred valleys. (*Laozi* 66/ MWD 29)

'That by which' may be also translated as 'the reason why.'

The *Inner Chapters* of the *Zhuangzi* contain a little story about a shadow that recognizes the dependence of one thing on another. The Chinese term is *suo dai*, 'that on which one depends.' Again this may be taken as 'the reason why.'

The penumbra asked the shadow, saying, "A moment ago you were walking; now you have stopped; a moment ago you were sitting; now you are standing. Why don't you decide to do one or the other?" "Is it that there is something on which I depend to be so? And does what I depend on too depend on something else to be so? Would it be that I depend on snake's scales or cicada's wings? How would I recognize why it is so? How would I recognize why it is not so?" (*Zhuangzi* 2, *The Sorting Which Evens Things Out*, line 93)

In later works the terms pile on top of one another for emphasis. Thus Dong Zhongshu used the expression 'the reason whereby *x* is so.'

The *Spring and Autumn Annals* record the losses and gains under heaven and illustrate the reason why they are so (*suo yi ran zhi gu*). (*Luxuriant Gems of the Spring and Autumn Annals* 3, *Bamboo Forest*, p. 56)

The purpose of history writing was to reveal the causes of events and particularly, for a Confucian, the moral causes.

Wang Bi used the expression 'whereby *x* is so' in conjunction with the term 'principle' or 'reason':

Should one recognize the movement of things then the reason why they are so can also be known. (*Notes on the* Book of Changes: *Literary Commentary* 1, *Qian*, p. 216)

The Cheng brothers and Zhu Xi were particularly concerned with investigating why things should be so. Cheng Yi writes,

All things have root and branches. It is not possible to separate root and branches into two separate things. Mopping and brushing are a pair. (*SKQS* 698, *Surviving Works of the Two Chengs* 15, p. 117a)

Heaven has a reason for being high and earth has a reason for being deep, although what those reasons are is not explained.

It is necessary to examine the principles of things, as when one says that by which heaven and earth are high and deep respectively or that by which ghosts and spirits are hidden or manifest. If one is only saying that heaven is high and earth is deep then this is just a matter of language and what more is there? (Ibid. 15, p. 125a)

There must be a reason for every assertion.

Zhu Xi believed that the reason something is as it is is that it ought to be that way. Moral necessity is the grounding of all necessity:

> Investigating principle is simply this: wanting to know that whereby events and things are so and that whereby they ought to be so. If one knows that whereby they are so then one's will does not waver. If one knows that whereby they ought to be so then one's conduct does not go astray. (*Collected Writings* 64 #33.7, *Reply to a Certain Person*, p. 1162b)
>
> In dealing with the things under heaven then there must be for each the reason whereby it is so and the norm whereby it ought to be so; this is what is called 'principle.' (*SKQS* 197, *Some Questions on the Great Learning*, pp. 222a–b)

For Zhu Xi moral virtues are founded on the relationships that are given. 'Ought' is derived from 'is':

> The reason whereby something is so is given by that which is above it. The reason whereby a ruler should be benevolent is that the ruler is the leading brain and the people and land are all entrusted to his care. He must use benevolence and favor. Suppose one considers what will happen if he is not benevolent and loving, then things would certainly not get done! It is not that this is said of the ruler: that he cannot not use benevolence and favour. It is rather that this is to conform to principle. Suppose one discusses one household. The head of the household uses love towards the people of the household and cherishes the things of the household. This is because this is to conform to principle, as if heaven had commissioned it to be so.... As for the reason why a father is compassionate and a son filial, it is because father and son were originally of one *qi* and it is just a case of one person's body becoming a pair. Their bounty and love belong to them together. It is from their being so and not able not to be so. Other important discussions

are all alike. In all cases the heavenly principle has commissioned it to be so. (*Conversations of Master Zhu* 17, *The Great Learning* 4, p. 383)

Yin

The translation of the term yin *is not easy, since English prefers to use prepositional compounds rather than Latin nouns and verbs. Various usages are current: 'in accord with,' 'adapt to,' 'accommodate to,' 'go along with,' 'adjust to,' 'conform to.'*

The term *yin* originally meant 'to depend on.' In the earliest dictionary it is defined as 'thereupon.' A gloss by Gao You in *Mr. Lu's Spring and Autumn Annals* defines it as 'to depend on':

To depend on wisdom and clarify it. (*Mr. Lu's Spring and Autumn Annals* 3.2 *Exhausting Number*, p. 139, n. 13)

Confucius says,

The Yin/Shang dynasty depended on the Xia dynasty rituals and so what has been lost and gained can be known; the Zhou depended on the Yin/Shang rituals and so what is lost and gained can be known. (*Analects* 2, *On Administration* 23, pp. 153–154)

Shen Dao talks about a policy of adjusting to others and not imposing on them:

The Way of heaven adjusts [*yin*] and is great, transforms and is then small; adjustment is adjusting to the people's emotions. (Fragment 28)

There is nothing people do not do themselves. If you transform them and order them to submit to yourself, then nothing can be attained or used. (Fragment 29)

Therefore use what people do themselves and do not use people for oneself and then there is nothing that cannot be done and used. This is what is meant by 'adjusting to.' (Fragment 32)

In *Mr. Lu's Spring and Autumn Annals* there is a whole section on the topic of valuing accommodation or adjustment.

> Of the things the three dynasties valued there was nothing more precious than 'accommodation.' If one accommodates to others then one will have no enemies. Yu pierced the three rivers and five lakes, cut Yi Jue, channeled Hui Lu and poured them into the Eastern Sea following [*yin*] the force of the water. Shun made a village into a town, two villages into a city, three villages into a capital and Yao accepted the abdicated seat. This was accommodating to the mind of the people. Tang and Wu overcame Xia and Shang with a thousand chariots. This was accommodating to the desire of the people. In Qin people stood and traveled, because there were chariots. In Yue people sat and traveled because there were boats. Qin and Yue are geographically far apart but whether standing or sitting one could reach either, by accommodating to their forms of transport.... One who examines heaven will examine the seried stars and know the four seasons; this is accommodation. One who predicts by the almanac sees the moon's course and knows the last days of the old moon and the first days of the new moon; this is accommodation. (*Mr. Lu's Spring and Autumn Annals* 15.7, *Valuing Accommodation*, pp. 925, 927)

A Han-era part of the *Guanzi* discusses a meditation technique known as accommodation:

> 'The Way [affair] of non-acting' is accommodation. Accommodation knows no loss or increase. By its form accommodate to it and give it its name; this is the technique of accommodation....
>
> Accommodation is to dispense with self and take things as one's norm. (*Guanzi* 36, *Technique of the Mind A*, 2:9)

Here 'accommodation' means 'to become as objective as possible in one's regard.'

In Buddhist philosophy the term *yin* was combined with *guo* to translate the law of karma.

Part Two
Anthropology

A. Moral Philosophy

I. Moral Ideals

This part begins with five sections on moral ideals: benevolence and justice, the public interest, human relations, nondiscrimination, and moderation.

39. Benevolence and Justice

Ren-yi

仁義

The character ren *is composed of the graph for human being and that for the number two. It is expressive of the relations that should pertain among human beings. Hence it has been translated as 'humanity,' 'benevolence,' 'love,' and, to bring out the sense of relationship, 'co-humanity.' It is also the supreme virtue that encompasses all others and so is rendered 'goodness,' 'perfect virtue.'* Professor Zhang's own definition of* ren *stresses establishing oneself and establishing others, that is, ensuring the social and cultural standing of each person. It is thus preeminently a virtue of society rather than an internal matter of conscience alone.*

The concept of empathy, shu, *is a further extension of the idea of benevolence. The term* shu *means 'to put oneself in the position of another and to look at the world from that perspective.' It has been translated as 'altruism' by W. T. Chan and is glossed by him as "the extension of one's originally good mind to others." It has been taken up in a long discussion by Fingarette.†The character itself combines the graphs for the mind/heart with that meaning 'to be like,' thus signifying sympathy and empathy.*

---

* See Wing-Tsit Chan, *A Source Book in Chinese Philosophy* (Princeton: Princeton University Press, 1963), pp. 788–789.

† H. Fingarette, *Confucius: The Secular as Sacred* (New York: Harper and Row, 1972).

Yi, *what is right, is applied particularly to a person in authority, the father or the prince. It implies the correct use of authority according to moral norms. In the* Mencius, *yi is a sense of respect for others born of a consciousness of right and wrong; hence I shall translate the term as 'respect' in the* Mencius.

The Pre-Han Period: Ren

Ren is the virtue associated with Confucius.

Mr. Lu's Spring and Autumn Annals note that

Confucius valued benevolence. (*Mr. Lu's Spring and Autumn Annals* 17.7, *Not Two*, p. 1123)

This is correct, but Confucius was not the first to use the term. Several examples from *Zuo's Commentary* may be cited to show that benevolence was already seen as a moral principle. The grand minister of Jin, Jiu Ji, said,

I have heard: to go out of the door as a guest and to undertake affairs as if one were performing a sacrifice is the norm of benevolence. (*Zuo's Commentary* 5, *Xi* 33, p. 223)

Ying Xin of Chu is recorded as saying,

The Odes [Ode 260, *Zheng Min*] say, "He neither devours the mild, nor violently rejects the strong. He does not insult the poor nor the widow; nor does he fear the violent or powerful." Only the person of benevolence is able to do so. (*Zuo's Commentary* 11, *Ding* 4, p. 751)

The *Commentary* also includes a judgment by Confucius of King Ling of Chu:

Zhong Ni [Confucius] said, "It is contained in an ancient book that to subdue self and return to propriety is benevolence. True is the saying and excellent." (*Zuo's Commentary* 10, *Zhao* 12, p. 638)

Thus in glossing 'benevolence' as subduing the self and returning to propriety Confucius was but quoting an ancient source.

The *Great Learning* quotes a close relative of Duke Wen of Jin, Fan, as saying,

> A dead person takes beinglessness as the jewel, takes benevolence and closeness as the jewel. (*Great Learning*, p. 377)

"Benevolence and closeness" here refers to the close family ties that bind the dead to the living. In the *Sayings of Jin* it is noted that

> You Shi taught Li Yi in the middle of the night and wept. He said to the duke [Duke Xian of Jin]: "... I heard a saying of foreigners that ran: Acting for benevolence and acting for the State is not the same. One who acts for benevolence loves his relatives and by this is meant benevolence. One who works for the State profits the State and by this is meant benevolence." (*Sayings of the States* 7, *Sayings of Jin* 1, pp. 274, 275)

Loving one's relatives is loving and respecting one's parents. Profiting the state is working for the good of the state. Benevolence is both a specific family virtue and the term for the universal virtue.

What makes Confucius' treatment of the term stand out is that he made it the highest moral principle. The *Analects* record various definitions of the term that differ according to the person to whom they are given. This illustrates Confucius' method of replying to individuals according to their talent. Previously it was held that the *Analects* do not provide a full definition of 'benevolence,' but this is not the case. Paragraph 6.28 of the *Analects* does indeed give an adequate description.

> Zi Gong said, "If there is someone who extensively spreads his learning to the people and can benefit the masses, what about him or her? Would you say this was benevolence?" The Master said, "Why say only benevolence, such a one must be a sage. Even Yao and Shun fell short of it. A benevolent person while wanting to establish him- or herself also establishes others, while wanting to be outstanding him- or herself also makes others outstanding. To be able to judge others by what is near to

ourselves may be called the full scope of benevolence." (*Ana-lects* 6, *Yong Ye* #28, p. 194)

Here Confucius distinguished between being a sage and being benevolent. Zi Gong failed to make this distinction. Since a distinction has to be made, the two terms must be clearly defined, and hence we can suppose Confucius' definition of benevolence to be a complete definition.

In order to draw out the import of this definition of 'benevolence' it is necessary to examine the terms used in the body of the definition, in particular the terms 'establish' and 'make prominent.' The term 'establish' (*li* 立) appears in a number of passages in the *Analects*. It means 'to attain a certain level of achievement' and 'to attain recognized social position.' Confucius says that

> At thirty I was established. (*Analects* 2, *On Administration* #4, p. 146)

He Yan explains this text as meaning that

> He had some success/achievement. (*Correct Meaning of the* Analects: *Collected Exegesis of the* Analects 2, *Wei Zheng*, p. 23)

Being established involves knowing the rites. The rites form the basis of society and music its crowning achievement:

> To be established by rites and to attain completion in music. (*Analects* 8, *Tai Bo* #8, p. 211)

The same sentiment is taken up in the post-Confucian final chapter of the *Analects*.

> If one does not know the rites one has nothing by which one can be established. (*Analects* 20, *Yao Yue* #3, p. 354)

From these passages it is clear that to be established is to have a certain social standing in the sense that one knows the social customs and is able to act as a social being.

That being established denotes a high degree of cultural status is clear from the following:

> There are those with whom one can study together but cannot yet promulgate the Way. There are those to whom one can

promulgate the Way but with whom one cannot be established together. There are those with whom one can be established but with whom one cannot share authority. (*Analects* 9, *Zi Han* #29, pp. 225–226)

'Being established' is the third in the hierarchy describing teacher-pupil relationships. At the lowest level one can be a fellow pupil of someone. At the second level one can teach the other. At the third one can stand on an equal footing in social circles (be established), and finally one can share one's teaching authority with the other. 'Being established' can also mean having a certain position at court:

Was not Zang Wen* like one who had stolen his situation? He knew the virtue and talents of Hui-under-Willow, and yet did not arrange that he should stand with him in court. (*Analects* 15, *Duke Ling of Wei* #13, pp. 298–299)

The tenth-century scholar Xing Bing noted that

He did not call him and raise him to stand with him in court. (*Correct Meaning of the* Analects: *Expansion of the* Analects 15, *Duke Ling of Wei*, p. 340)

'To be outstanding' means to have real virtue oneself and for this to be recognized by others. Confucius distinguished it from the mere possession of reputation without substance to support it.

Zi Zhang asked, "How can an official be said to be outstanding?" The Master said, "What do you understand by outstanding?" Zi Zhang replied, "He should be renowned in the State and at home." Confucius said, "That is renown. It is not being outstanding. One who is outstanding is straight of character and dedicated to justice. He examines what is said and observes people's faces and is concerned about humbling himself before others. Such a one is outstanding in the State and in the family. The one who is renowned seems to adopt benevolence but acts contrary to it and remains thus with no self-doubt. He will be

---

*Zang Wen knew that Hui-under-Willow was more competent than himself but would not recommend him for a post in court lest he lose his own position.

renowned in the State and at home." (*Analects* 12, *Yan Yuan* #20, pp. 259–260)

Thus Confucius' definition of 'benevolence' involves establishing oneself in society and being outstanding in virtue. Furthermore, it supposes that one wants the same for others. In other words, it recognizes the value of the self and of others. As a fundamental principle of morality this is an essential part of the Confucian worldview.

Benevolence is also discussed in other sections of the *Analects*, the more important passages of which must be quoted here.

> Yan Yuan asked about benevolence. The Master said, "To master oneself and return to the rites is benevolence. If for one day one can master oneself and return to the rites then all under heaven will go back to benevolence. Does practicing benevolence depend on oneself or on others?" Yan Yuan said, "Please tell me what you mean in detail." The Master said, "Do not look at what is without the rites; do not listen to what is without the rites; do not say what is without the rites; do not do what is without the rites." (*Analects* 12, *Yan Yuan* #1, p. 250)
>
> Zhong Gong asked about benevolence. The Master said, "When you go outdoors act as if entertaining a great guest. Treat the people as if you were undertaking a great sacrifice. What you yourself do not want do not impose on others. Then there will be no resentment against you in the State nor at home." Zhong Gong said, "Although I am not clever let me henceforth act according to this word." (Ibid. #2, p. 251)
>
> Fan Chi asked about benevolence. The master said, "To love others." (Ibid. #22, p. 260)

The first and second of these quotations, in which Confucius calls on the hearer to return to the rites and to act hospitably toward others, were already present in the texts cited from *Zuo's Commentary*. Confucius' unique contribution was to define 'benevolence' as 'loving others' and as not doing to others what you do not want done to yourself.

'Returning to the rites' is to be understood as showing respect for the moral and social norms of society. It is not a political program. Kong

Yingda and Liu Baonan* both gave useful interpretations of the phrase. Kong says,

> To return is to go back to. If one can go back to the rites then one can practice benevolence. (*Correct Meaning of the* Analects: *Collected Exegesis of the* Analects, 12 *Yan Yuan*, #1, p. 262)

Liu Baonan says,

> To go back is to revert to. If I first reflect on what I see, hear, say and do in terms of the rites, this is what is meant by returning to the rites. It does not mean that one first has private matters or first is without the rites and that one should return to this state. (Ibid.)

'To return to the rites' is to respect the rites. This is a moral issue and not a political program.

Not doing to others what you would not want done to yourself is also called 'empathy' (*shu* 恕). Confucius singled it out as one word worth practicing:

> Zi Gong asked, "Is there one word which can be practiced throughout one's life?" The Master said, "It is empathy. What you yourself do not want do not impose on others." (*Analects* 15, *Duke Ling of Wei* #23, p. 301)

Benevolence would seem to contain empathy within it. Empathy is the same virtue taken from a narrow perspective; 'benevolence' also expresses the need to establish others and make them outstanding.

The Pre-Han Era: Yi

As Confucius valued benevolence, he also promoted justice. Benevolence is the highest moral norm, whereas *yi* 義, what is right, refers generally to the existence of moral norms.

---

* Liu Baonan (1791–1855). *Zi*: Chuzhen; *Hao*: Nianlou, from Baoying, Jiangsu Province. His most famous work is the *Correct Meaning of the* Analects, a work completed by his son, Liu Gongmian (1824–1883). In this work he gathered and edited editions of the *Analects*. See M. Loewe, *Early Chinese Texts* (Berkeley: Society for the Study of Early China, 1994), pp. 318–319.

The gentleman puts what is right in the highest place. (*Ana-lects* 17, *Yang Huo* #23, p. 329)

The gentleman takes what is right as the substance of his conduct and ritual norms as the way to practice it. (*Analects* 15, *Duke Wei of Ling* #17, p. 299)

To see what is right and not to do it, is not being courageous. (*Analects* 2, *On Administration* #24, p. 154)

Perform your duties so as to do what is right for the living, respect the spirits and ghosts of the departed and keep them at a distance. This can be said to be wisdom. (*Analects* 6, *Yong Ye* #20, p. 191)

The gentleman is regarded as one who

when he sees a chance to make gains thinks of what is right. (*Analects* 16, *Ji Shi* #10, p. 314)

Although Confucius used the terms *ren*, 'benevolence,' and *yi*, 'what is right,' he never, according to the *Analects*, treated them as a binomial pair, *ren-yi*. The same is true of *Zuo's Commentary*. The references to benevolence in the latter work have already been quoted. The following are references to *yi*.

Zhao Shuai said, "The *Odes* and the *Histories* are the storehouse of what is right." (*Zuo's Commentary* 5, *Xi* 27, p. 200)

Ji Wenzi said, "Promulgate the five precepts in the four quarters: the father should do what is right; the mother should be full of tenderness; the elder sibling friendly; the younger sibling respectful and the child show filial piety." (*Zuo's Commentary* 6, *Wen* 18, p. 280)

Xie Yang said, "The prince is able to regulate his destiny as to what is right." (*Zuo's Commentary* 7, *Xuan* 15, p. 326)

The Pre-Han Era: *Ren-yi*

Perhaps the first use of *ren* and *yi* as a pair is to be found among Confucius' disciples. If we accept the traditional ascription of the *Mean and Harmony* to Confucius' grandson, Zi Si (492–431 B.C.), then it may represent one of the earliest uses of the pair.* Each is defined according to a homophone.

> Benevolence [*ren*] is to do with human beings [*ren*] and is most conspicuous in one's love for relatives. What is right [*yi*] is to do with what ought to be done [*yi* 宜] and is most conspicuous in honoring the worthy. The degrees of love for relatives and the grades accorded the worthy are the source from whence ritual springs. (*Mean and Harmony* 20)

This homophonic definition was to prove very popular. Zheng Xuan commented on the term 'human being' as used in the definition of 'benevolence':

> 'Human being' is to be read as meaning taking others to be the same kind of being as oneself. (*SKQS* 116, *Notes on the* Record of Rites, p. 363a)

Kong Yingda explained the need to first love one's relatives:

> Benevolence means benevolent love for one's relatives and those one encounters. It says that the method of practicing benevolence is to be intimate with others. If one wants to love others whom one does not know well, one must first love one's own relatives then starting from them reach out to those one does not know well. (Ibid., p. 363b)

The homophone *yi*, used to define what is right, is to be glossed as meaning what ought to be done.†

---

*Author's note: *Records of the Historian* 47, *Confucius' Family*, p. 1946: "Zi Si made [wrote, compiled, edited] the *Mean and Harmony*."

†Author's Note: Some scholars of ancient Chinese believe that *yi* is the name of an ancient sacrifice. This view is not without foundation. The *Book of Rites* contains the following passage, in which *yi* and *lei* are types of sacrifice: "When the Son of Heaven goes out on a tour of inspection, he is to perform the *lei* sacrifice to the Lord Above and the *yi* to the spirits of earth and the *cao* to the ancestors. The feudal lords will go out and perform the *yi* to the spirits of earth and the *cao* to the ancestors" (*Record of Rites* 5, *On the Regulations of a King*, p. 70). The *lei* and the *yi* are both names of sacrifices. Ancient sacrifices all involved the slaughter of animals as victims or the killing of captives. But the killing was only one part of the sacrifice. The main part was to pray to the spirit. To say that the root meaning of *yi* is to kill is unwarranted. Moreover, when the *Mean and Harmony* uses *yi* to gloss 'what is right' it uses the meaning then current and not the original meaning of the character.

The dating of the different elements of the *Mozi* is also unclear. There are certainly instances in which *ren* and *yi* are paired.

> Master Mozi said, "Now under heaven kings, dukes, great persons, officials and gentlemen sincerely desire to practice benevolence and justice and be superior people. If they want to attain the way of the sage kings and also be of benefit to the hundred clans of the state and then arrive at the theory of conforming to superiors, they cannot not examine conforming to superiors as the root and the key to order." (*Mozi* 13, *On Conforming to Superiors C*, lines 58–59)

A similar phrase occurs in another chapter of the same work:

> Master Mozi said, "Now, however, kings, dukes, great persons, officials and gentlemen sincerely desire to produce benefits which enable all under heaven to flourish and to remove all the evils under heaven—and the spread of wars is indeed the greatest evil under heaven. Now if they want to practice benevolence and justice and to be superior people, and attain to the way of the sage kings and also be of benefit to the hundred clans of the state, then they cannot not examine the theory of non-aggression." (*Mozi* 19, *Against Aggression C*, lines 62–64)

It is clear from these passages that the pairing of *ren* and *yi* was a common practice at the time. The *Mozi* associates the phrase with Gaozi in particular. Gaozi was one of Mencius' adversaries.

> Master Mozi said, "... Now Gaozi speaks with a lot of dialectic. He talks of benevolence and of what is right and does not blame me." (*Mozi* 48, *Gong Meng*, line 83)

According to the *Mencius*, Gaozi believed benevolence to be a matter for the internal forum and what is right to be a matter for external relationships. Mencius may well have picked up the pair *qua* pair from Gaozi.*

---

*Author's note: Here I am rejecting the view of Zhao Ji that Gaozi "formerly studied under Mencius" (*Correct Meaning of the* Mencius: *Notes on the* Mencius, p. 431).

Another possibly pre-Mencian text that uses *ren* and *yi* as a pair is the *Explanation of the Hexagrams Commentary* on the *Book of Changes.**

> Formerly the sages composed the *Changes* in accordance with the principles of human nature and destiny so that they established the way of heaven and called it *yin* and *yang*. They established the way of earth and called it soft and hard. They established the way of human beings and called it benevolence and what is right. (*Explanation of the Hexagrams Commentary*, pp. 338–339)

The use of *ren* and *yi* as a pair is common in the *Mencius*. The *Mencius* retained Confucius' definition of benevolence as a family virtue par excellence but insisted that its scope be extended to include all peoples under heaven.

That the two terms form a pair is clear from the following examples.

> Why should the king† ask about profit? There is only benevolence and respect worth talking about. (*Mencius* 1, *King Hui of Liang A*, #1)
>
> Benevolence is the secure dwelling of human beings. Respect is the correct road of human beings. (*Mencius* 4, *Li Lou A*, #27)
>
> Benevolence is the mind of human beings. Respect is the road of human beings. (*Mencius* 6, *Gaozi A*, #11)

---

*Whether this text is pre-Mencian or not, it should not be quoted without a reference to the recently unearthed *Yao Pian* from the *Silk Commentaries to the* Book of Changes from Mawangdui. The latter text mentions *yin-yang*, hard and soft but instead of *ren-yi* it reads 'superior and inferior.' In other words, what distinguishes the human sphere is not the moral virtues but social hierarchy: "Therefore the *Changes* has the way of heaven and this cannot be fully expressed by the sun and moon, stars and planets; therefore it is said by *yin* and *yang*. There is the way of earth, which cannot be fully expressed by water, fire, metal, earth and wood; therefore it is described by soft and hard. There is also the way of human beings, which cannot be fully expressed by father and child, ruler and minister, husband and wife, previous and next and is therefore described by superior and inferior" (Mawangdui *Silk Commentaries: Yao Pian*, lines 21–22) (Liao Mingchun and Chen Songchang, "Boshu 'Yao' shiwen," in Chen Guying, *Daojia Wenhua Yanjiu* 3 (Shanghai: Shanghai Guji, 1993) 3:434–435).

This latter text should be cited, but the fact that it lists the five agents as proper to the way of earth is a sign that it is perhaps from the late Warring States period.

† Duke Hui (370–319 B.C.) was then at Liang. He had usurped the title of king. Mencius arrived in Liang in 320 B.C., shortly before the ruler's demise.

If one abides in benevolence and proceeds from respect then the great person's affairs will all be included. (*Mencius* 7, *Exhausting the Mind A*, #33)

People all have that which they cannot bear. To apply this feeling to all that one can bear is benevolence. People all have that which they will not do. To apply this feeling to all that one does is respect. (Ibid. *B*, #31)

From these texts it can be seen not only that Mencius used *ren* and *yi* as a pair but that they formed the heart of his moral philosophy.

Mencius discussed benevolence and emphasized its foundation within the human heart. No person likes to see another suffering, and from this feeling benevolence springs. Moral principles are grounded in the movements of the heart:

People all have the heart of one who cannot bear [to see the suffering of] others.... What I mean by saying that people all have the heart of one who cannot bear to see the suffering of others is that if today you happened to see an infant about to fall into a well you would have a heart of alarm and compassion. This would not be motivated by any desire to know the father and mother of the child nor for any hope of reputation in the district or among one's comrades and friends nor because one can't stand the wailing of the child.... The heart of compassion is the starting point of benevolence. (*Mencius* 2, *Gong Sun Chou A*, #6)

The heart that cannot bear the sufferings of others is the heart that shows compassion. Mencius believed this to be the inner basis for benevolence.

Mencius also discussed benevolence with respect to relatives.

To be close to relatives is benevolence and to respect one's elders is respect. There is no other. One should extend it to all under heaven. (*Mencius* 7, *Exhausting the Mind A*, #15)

The gentleman's attitude towards things is to like them but not to show benevolence to them; to the people to show benevolence to them but not to be intimate with them. One is intimate with relatives but benevolent to the people. One is benevolent to the people but loving towards things. (Ibid., #45)

Taken in the broad sense, 'benevolence' may be considered to include intimacy with relatives and one's love for things, but in the narrow sense benevolence is the virtue proper to relations with people in general rather than just one's family members. While recognizing the special relationship a person enjoys with his or her family the *Mencius* called on human beings to extend their concern to all, without the circumscription of family intimacy.

Mencius explained the virtue of respect in a similar way. Respect is born of a heart that can experience shame.

> A heart that can be ashamed and that can have dislikes is the starting point of respect. (*Mencius* 2, *Gongsun Chou A, #6*)
>
> People all have that which they will not do. To apply this feeling to all that one does is respect.... If a person can allow the full growth of his desire to not break in and steal then one's respect will be more than enough for use. If a person can allow the full growth of his desire to not be greeted "Hey, you!" then wheresoever he goes he will act with respect. (*Mencius* 7, *Exhausting the Mind B #31*)

Not wanting to break in and steal and not wanting to be called rudely, "Hey, you!" are both expressions of one's awareness of what is wrong. These are the things that one will not do, that one would be ashamed to do. Mencius was calling for respect for property and persons, and it is this that he summed up in the term *yi*.

In other Confucian works the meaning of *yi* was not 'respect' as in the *Mencius*. The *Great Commentary to the* Book of Changes reads,

> Proper administration of wealth, correct instruction, prohibits the people from doing what is wrong. This is called 'what is right.' (*Great Commentary* 2.1, p. 308)

The *Xunzi* says,

> A sense of what is right is what is to be used to stop people acting in an evil and treacherous way. (*Xunzi* 16, *On Strengthening the State*, line 76)*

---

* Knoblock translates *yi* in this sentence as "moral principles and a sense of what is just."

The *Record of Rites* sought to clarify the relationship of benevolence and *yi*.

> Justice is the apportioning of the arts and the discipline of benevolence.... Benevolence is the root of justice. (*Record of Rites* 9, *Evolution of Rites*, p. 130)

Kong Yingda explained this passage as follows:

> Justice is what governs decisions and accords with what ought to be done. Art is talent. Benevolence is generosity. If people have talents and also have generosity but do not decide according to justice then they will go to excess and fail. Hence by using justice one attains the correct measure. (*SKQS* 115, *Correct Meaning of the* Record of Rites 22, *Evolution of Rites B*, p. 475b)
>
> Benevolence is the ideal of under heaven. Justice is the regulatory rule of under heaven. (*Record of Rites* 32, *Record of the Gnomon Debates*, p. 291)

Benevolence is like the gnomon of the sundial, the ideal to which all should conform, whereas justice is that which determines the application of benevolence.

> To honor the honorable and respect the respectable is the main significance of justice. (*Record of Rites* 49, *Four Regulations on Mourning Dress*, p. 339)

These passages all bring out the regulatory aspect of justice. It moderates, regulates, and determines the way for human conduct. The last quotation shows that this function is directed toward maintaining the established social order.*

Daoist philosophers brought a fierce criticism of benevolence and justice. The Daoists saw the definition of these virtues as a step away from the world of the great Way. The *Laozi* describes the decline of society in these terms:

---

*Author's note: The *Mean and Harmony* talks about respecting the worthy rather than respecting the respectable. It may be that this formulation of the phrase indicates slightly more social mobility. The expression "respecting the respectable" depicts a very conservative society.

When the great Way was discarded then there was benevolence and justice. (*Laozi* 18/MWD 62)

The solution is to do away with the virtues and then one will return to real values:

Stop benevolence and do away with justice; the people will return to filial piety and compassion. (*Laozi* 19/MWD 63)

Zhuang Zhou himself questioned the two virtues:

From the way I see things, the starting points of benevolence and justice, the path of right and wrong is the source of confusion. How should I know how to discriminate? (*Zhuangzi* 2, *The Sorting Which Evens Things Out*, line 70)

In the later *Zhuangzi* material there is even more criticism of the two virtues. The Daoists failed to come up with any viable alternative moral principles, however.

In the late Warring States period *Mr. Lu's Spring and Autumn Annals* provided a summing-up of the Confucian view of benevolence and justice. The opening line of a chapter on loving different kinds of things says:

To be benevolent to other things and not to human beings does not deserve the name 'benevolence.' Not being benevolent to other things and being benevolent to human beings alone is indeed benevolence. Benevolence is a matter of being benevolent to one's own kind. Therefore it is possible to employ the person who is benevolent to the people. There is nothing he cannot do. (*Mr. Lu's Spring and Autumn Annals* 21.5, *Loving Different Kinds*, p. 1462)

Here there is little doubt that benevolence is the virtue proper to human society. The opening line of another chapter defines justice:

Justice is the measuring cord of the myriad affairs, from whence arise the degree of distance and the relations of ruler and minister, superior and inferior. It is that by which one orders confusion, secures against danger, and wins victory and profit. (*Mr. Lu's Spring and Autumn Annals* 8.2, *Discussing Awe*, p. 430)

These texts express the same conservative social structure found in the *Record of Rites*.

Summing Up

According to Confucius, benevolence can be expressed as not wanting to do to others what you would not want done to yourself. Confucius valued filial piety but he did not explain benevolence as loving one's relatives. Mencius sometimes spoke of benevolence with regard to one's relatives, perhaps in response to Mozi, who could be viewed as denigrating one's relatives at the expense of strangers. This development of the idea of benevolence is in fact a narrowing-down of the original concept.

When Confucius used the term *yi* he was referring to what is right in general and did not have any specific virtue in mind. The *Mean and Harmony* first put benevolence and *yi* together, interpreting *yi* in terms of what ought to be done, in particular, confining it to honoring the worthy. Mencius interpreted *yi* as respecting one's superiors. The latter two interpretations reinforced distinctions between people. The *Appendices of the Book of Changes* and the *Xunzi* interpreted *yi* as preventing the people from doing what is wrong. Both brought out the limiting force of *yi*. Thus *yi* came to serve as a means of reinforcing social distinctions. As a moral principle, however, *yi* preserved a distinction between what should be done and what should not be done.

Han and Tang Thought

Dong Zhongshu interpreted *ren* and *yi* in a new way. He held that *ren* must involve love of others. Love of oneself alone could never merit the name *ren*. *Yi* he understood as self-correction. Merely to correct others is not *yi*.

> What the *Spring and Autumn Annals* deal with are the relationships between the self and others. What deals with these relationships is *ren* and *yi*. By *ren* one brings peace and security to others; by *yi* one corrects oneself. The character *ren* refers to

human beings, while the character *yi* refers to the 'self.'* ...
The *Spring and Autumn Annals* give the models of *ren* and *yi*.
The model of *ren* is to love others, not to love oneself. The
model of *yi* is to correct oneself, not to correct others. If I
cannot correct myself, then even if I correct others this cannot
be called *yi*. If others are not loved by one then even if one
loves oneself a lot this cannot be called *ren*.... *Yi* does not
mean correcting others. It means correcting oneself. Even in
an exceptionally disordered era there is no one who does not
want to correct others. How can this be called *yi*? *Yi* is a matter
of doing what ought to be done [*yi* 宜] to oneself and only
then can it be called *yi*.... Loving others is what is meant by
ren. Applying *yi* to oneself is what is meant by *yi*. *Ren* governs
others; *yi* governs the self. (*Luxuriant Gems of the Spring and
Autumn Annals* 29, *Models of* Ren *and* Yi, pp. 249–254)

The interpretation of *ren* in this text comes from Confucius, but the
reading of *yi* is the creation of Dong himself. Hence it is not tautologous
to say "applying *yi* to oneself is what is meant by *yi*," since this can be read
as, "applying what everyone understands as *yi* to oneself is what I [Dong
Zhongshu] mean by *yi*."

Dong Zhongshu further elaborated on the meaning of *ren* in a passage that defines the virtue as loving others and not harming them.

What is meant by *ren*? *Ren* is loving others with compassion,
living in concord and not competing. It has no mind to hurt or
wrong others; it has no will to scheme behind someone else's
back. It has no *qi* to be jealous. It has no desire for making
others sad. It does not engage in backbiting and flattery. It
does not act against others. Therefore its mind is at ease; its
will at peace; its *qi* harmonious; its desires moderated; its affairs
easy; its conduct according to the Way. Therefore it is able to
be at peace and in accord with principle and not to compete.

---

*From the point of view of linguistic history this is not true. Dong bases his remark on
the fact that the character *ren* contains the character for human being as part of its shape,
whereas the character for *yi* contains the character for 'self' as part of its makeup.

Such as this is what is meant by *ren.* (*Luxuriant Gems of the Spring and Autumn Annals* 30, Ren *and Wisdom,* p. 258)

In an introduction to the bibliography of the philosophers in the *Han History,* Ban Gu summed up their views and comments on *ren* and *yi.* Although not stated explicitly, his understanding of the pair seems to be influenced by the interpretation of Dong Zhongshu. *Ren* and *yi* are mutually opposed and mutually related such that one requires the other.

Though their words be varied, as different as water and fire, yet these destroy each other and give rise to each other. *Ren* and *yi,* respect and harmony are opposed to each other and yet come into being together. (*Han History* 30, *Bibliography: Summary of the Philosophers,* p. 1746)

'Respect' and 'harmony' refer to the respective roles of rites and music. It is in this Confucian perspective that *ren* and *yi* are presented. It is a Confucianism that has integrated the language of *yin-yang* in their mutual opposition and generation.

Han Yu of the Tang dynasty lamented the rise of Buddhism and Daoist religion and sought to promote true Confucianism. In the opening paragraph of his *Original Way* he presented the twin virtues of *ren* and *yi* as the kernel of the ancient Confucian moral philosophy:

Extensive love is what is meant by *ren.* To practice this in accordance with what ought to be done is what is meant by *yi.* To act according to these is what is meant by the Way. To have enough in oneself and not to depend on what is without is what is meant by virtue. *Ren* and *yi* are terms with a definite content; the Way and virtue are abstract terms....

Yao transmitted this to Shun. Shun transmitted it to Yu. Yu transmitted it to Tang. Tang transmitted it to Kings Wen and Wu and the Duke of Zhou. These three transmitted it to Confucius. Confucius transmitted it to Meng He [Mencius]. After Mencius died the message was no longer handed on. (*SBBY* 70, *Collected Works of Mr. Chang Li* 11.1, *The Original Way,* pp. 129a, 130b)

Han Yu's interpretation of *ren* as 'extensive love,' although pretending to be a reflection of the original Confucian ideal, in fact took up the definition of *ren* given by Xu Gan in the second century A.D.* In fact, Dong Zhongshu had already used the definition as part of his analysis of the good:

> Trustworthy and charitable [extensive love], generous and consciously practicing the rites is what can be called good. (*Luxuriant Gems of the Spring and Autumn Annals* 35, *The Profound Examination of Names and Appellations*, p. 304)

The Song and Post-Song Periods

Zhou Dunyi and Zhang Zai both interpreted *ren* in terms of loving others. Zhou writes,

> The virtue of loving is called *ren*; that of doing what is right is called *yi*. (*SKQS* 1101, *Book of Comprehending* 3, *Sincerity Is the Impetus of Virtue*, p. 422b)

Zhang Zai interpreted love of others from the point of view of love of self:

> To love others with the same heart with which one loves oneself is to fulfill the demands of *ren*. (*SKQS* 697, *Correcting the Unenlightened* 8, *Central Correctness*, p. 122a)
>
> To show reverence, respect, moderation, giving way to others so as to clarify what is ritual is the utmost *ren* and the peak of the way of love. (Ibid. 9, *The Most Appropriate*, p. 126a)

Ren is the way of love, interpreted in accordance with the proper norms of conduct (ritual). Zhang Zai also discussed the relation of *ren* and *yi*:

> *Yi* is the movement of *ren*. Proceeding only in accordance with *yi* may result in harm to *ren*. *Ren* is the constant force of the body. To be excessive in *ren* may result in harm to *yi*. (Ibid., p. 124b)

If one proceeds only according to justice then Shylock will have his pound of flesh. If one proceeds only according to mercy then indulgence will

---

* Chan, *Source Book*, p. 455. (See *SKQS* 696, *Discourses That Hit the Mark* 9, p. 482a.)

replace justice. There may be conflict between *ren* and *yi*. This is Zhang Zai's theory of the mutual influence of *ren* and *yi*.

The Cheng brothers interpreted *ren* in a new way. Cheng Hao explained it as becoming one with things; his brother said it was concerned with what was in the public interest.

Cheng Hao said,

> The scholar must first recognize *ren*. The person of *ren* is all involved and forms one with things. *Yi*, ritual, wisdom and trust are all aspects of *ren*. . . . This way cannot be compared to things. Even the greatest thing is not big enough to name it. The use that heaven and earth make of it is the use I make of it. Mencius spoke about the myriad things all being present in the self. One must turn back on oneself and be sincere and then one truly attains great joy. (*SKQS* 698, *Surviving Works of the Two Chengs* 2a, p. 20a)
>
> Medical books describe the lack of feeling in hands and feet as 'not-*ren*.' This formulation is indeed excellent. The person of *ren* forms one body with heaven-earth and the myriad things. There is nothing that is not part of oneself. By recognizing all as oneself then one can surely attain to all places, can one not? If there is even anything which does not pertain to the self then the self is not even in touch with itself, just as when the hands and feet lack feeling [are not-*ren*]. *Qi* also does not penetrate and nothing pertains to the self. (Ibid. 2a, p. 19a)
>
> As for what is most *ren*, it involves seeing heaven and earth as one body and the many things within heaven and earth as the four limbs and many parts of the body. Who is it that does not love his or her four limbs and the many parts of his or her body? The sage attains the perfection of *ren* and thus is able to simply embody this heart. (Ibid. 4, pp. 66a–b)

To embody *ren* is to transcend one's own little ego and to treat the whole world as one's body. People naturally love their own bodies. To apply this love to the world is to display *ren*.

The idea that heaven and earth form one body emerges in Warring States philosophy. The logician Hui Shi stated:

Universally loving the myriad things and heaven and earth are
one body. (*Zhuangzi* 33, *Under Heaven*, line 74)

His friend Zhuang Zhou maintained that

the myriad things and I form one. (*Zhuangzi* 2, *The Sorting
Which Evens Things Out*, line 52)

Neither, however, thought of *ren* in these terms. Mencius talked of all
things as being present in the self but again did not mention *ren* in this
context. Cheng Hao's definition thus gathered together the Confucian
idea of *ren* and a view of the world that owes more to Zhuangzi than to
Confucius. On the basis of these strands of thought he built a new philosophy. The kernel of his doctrine of *ren* is the transcendence of one's
own ego.

Cheng Yi interprets *ren* in terms of what is in the public interest.*

Ren is to be in the public interest [disinterested]. (*SKQS* 698,
Surviving Works of the Two Chengs 9, p. 85a)

Confucius said, "A benevolent person while wanting to
establish him- or herself also establishes others, while wanting
to be outstanding him- or herself also makes others outstanding. To be able to judge others by what is near to ourselves
may be called the full scope of benevolence." (*Analects* 6, *Yong
Ye* #28, p. 194)

To say that Confucius spoke of *ren* as educating others,
this is sufficient. To sum up one can say it does not go beyond
what is in the public interest. (*SKQS* 698, *Surviving Works of
the Two Chengs* 9, p. 85a)

The way of benevolence may be summed up adequately
by the one word, 'public interest.' The 'public interest' is only
the principle of benevolence and one may not say that the public
interest is benevolence. When the public interest becomes embodied in a person then it becomes benevolence. It is because
when we consider the public interest then things and the self
are seen in equal light and then benevolence is that by which

---

* Graham translates this idea as 'disinterestedness.' Graham, *Two Chinese Philosophers*,
p. 97.

we are able to show consideration and that by which we are able to love. Consideration is the application while love is the function of benevolence. (Ibid. 15, p. 122a)

Cheng Yi also commented on Mencius' definition of *ren*:

Mencius says, "The heart of compassion is benevolence." Later people interpreted benevolence as love because compassion is indeed love. Love by itself is a feeling while benevolence is nature. How then can one turn it such that love is benevolence? Mencius' reference to compassion as benevolence must be taken as from the preceding phrase, which says that the heart of compassion is the starting point of benevolence. Since it is the starting point only it cannot be interpreted as benevolence itself. (Ibid. 18, p. 146a)

Cheng Yi was opposed to the interpretation of benevolence as love. He preferred to interpret it in the light of the principle of the public interest, by which he meant seeing the self and things in equal light. This is the norm governing the use of the term 'benevolence.' Love is simply the function of benevolence. Zhu Xi explained Cheng Yi's definition as follows:

In the world there are those who have the public interest at heart but who lack any compassion whatsoever. To put the public interest and a compassionate heart together is a task incumbent on a 'human' being. (*Conversations* 95, *Master Cheng's Book* 1, p. 2454)

Cheng Hao interpreted benevolence using the example of hands and feet that could not feel. Based on this interpretation, his pupil, Xie Liang-zuo, explained benevolence in terms of the Buddhist notion of awareness.*

Benevolence is the benevolence present in the definition of the four limbs as not benevolent. To be not benevolent is to not

---

*Xie Liangzuo (1050–1103). *Zi*: Xiandao; called Shang Cai, from Shang Cai (in modern Henan Province). He advocated the heart as the principle of heaven.

feel pain or sensations; to be benevolent is to feel pain and sensations. The benevolence of the Confucians is the awareness of the Buddhists. (*SKQS* 698, *Recorded Conversations of Shang Cai* 2, p. 578a)

Zhong Gong went out as if to meet a great guest and served the people as if undertaking a great sacrifice but the heart which underlay this activity was in fact that of recognizing pain and sensations. (Ibid. 1, p. 575a)

Zhu Xi took Cheng Yi's viewpoint as the basis on which to build his own theory of *ren*. He said,

Ren is the principle of love and the virtue of the heart. (*Collected Notes on the* Analects 1, *Xue Er* #2, p. 1)

By this he meant that *ren* is the principle governing love. "The virtue of the heart" is the original substance of the heart. Zhu Xi distinguished between the principle governing love, which he called *ren*, and the feelings of love. In so doing he opposed Cheng Yi's definition of *ren* as love, but while opposing he also continued and amplified the legacy of Cheng Yi. Zhu Xi placed even more emphasis on *ren* as complete purification of selfish desires and putting into practice the principles of heaven.

Ren is the complete virtue of this heart.... The complete virtue of this heart is nothing if it is not the principle of heaven and then it cannot but not interfere with human desires. Therefore, the one who practices *ren* must have that by which to overcome selfish desires and to return to ritual.... Then if one purifies one's selfish desires and practices the principles of heaven then *ren* cannot be not used enough. (Ibid. 12, *Yan Yuan* #1, p. 49)

Zhu Xi also wrote a treatise on *ren* in which he explained what he meant by the virtue of the heart and the principle of love:

The heart of heaven and earth is to give life to the myriad things and the life of each person and thing is such that they obtain their heart from the heart of heaven and earth. Thus we speak of the virtue of the heart. Even though it encompasses and is present in all things such that there is nothing it does not contain, yet it may be covered by one word, namely *ren*.... What is this heart? In heaven and earth this is the heart that gives life to things. In the human sphere it is the heart which is warm and loving to others and that brings profit to things.... Someone asked, "Is what you say what Master Cheng said when he wrote that love is feeling and *ren* is nature? In which case, can one not then take love as *ren*?" I reply, "No." What Master Cheng said was that one could take the development of love and call it *ren*. What I talk about is to take the principle of love and call it *ren*. (*SBBY: Collected Writings* 67.31, *Treatise on* Ren, pp. 20a, 20b–21a)

In thus explaining *ren* in terms of the virtue of the heart and the principle of love, Zhu Xi made it wholly abstract and in reality lost sight of the intimate and straightforward view of *ren* advocated by Confucius and his disciples.

Zhu Xi also criticized Cheng's disciples for their theories of *ren*.

Someone said, "The disciples of Mr. Cheng who talk about *ren* are many. There are those who deny that love is *ren* and who say that the unity of the self with the myriad things is the body of *ren*. There are also those who deny that love is *ren* and who interpret *ren* as the heart having knowledge and feeling. Now if the master's view is such [as just expounded] can all of these sayings be untrue?" I say, "Those who say that things and the self are one can see that *ren* must involve love for everyone and everything but not how it is that *ren* is the body of truth. Those who say that the heart has knowledge and feeling are able to see that *ren* includes wisdom but not what it is that makes *ren* gain the reality of its name.... As for those who talk about there being all one body, this simply confuses people and lacks all prudence. There are even some who imagine things are their own selves. For those who more specifically talk about knowledge and awareness, this makes people exaggerate and not enter deeply into things or leads to their thinking that desires are principles. (Ibid., pp. 21a–b)

Zhu Xi opposed the view that *ren* was being one with things and the view that *ren* was being aware of pain and sensations.

Zhu Xi's theory of *ren* as the principle of love and the virtue of the heart had a profound impact on post–Southern Song thinkers. Later Wang Fuzhi turned the saying around:

> Master Zhu said, "*Ren* is the principle of love." This saying can be turned upside down and looked at in another way. If one wants to bring out the riches of *ren* then one may say that it is the principle of love. If one wants to express the distinction between the *ren* of nature and feelings and what is not yet *ren* then one should say principled love. (*Complete Commentary on Reading the Four Books* 10, p. 668)

By 'principled love' is to be understood love that is reasonable as contrasted with mere feelings.

Zhu Xi's explication of *ren* stressed the purification of selfish desires and the need to practice the principles of heaven. This distinction between desire and principle was refuted by Dai Zhen, who said,

> '*Ren*' is the virtue of generation and regeneration. "The people are secure. They drink and eat each day."* This is to simply say that the human way is generation and regeneration. People living fulfilling lives and then moving on to enable all others under heaven to live fulfilling lives, this is *ren*. (*An Evidential Study of the Meaning of Terms in the* Book of Mencius B, pp. 316–317)

Dai Zhen also wrote,

> In the life of human beings there is nothing worse than not being able to lead a fulfilling life. To lead a fulfilling life oneself and also to bring others to lead fulfilling lives is *ren*. To want to lead a fulfilling life oneself and not to care about the harm one does to others is a denial of *ren*. In truth, this denial of *ren* has its origin in the desire to lead a fulfilling life oneself.

* *Book of Songs*, Ode 166.

> Suppose someone had no such desire anyway; then of course such a person would not be able to deny *ren*. But if one does not have the desire to lead a fulfilling life then one will not even look at the poorest and most desperate conditions of human life on the earth. On the other hand, there is no such desire as wanting others to lead a fulfilling life and not needing to lead a fulfilling life oneself.... In governing all under heaven, the sages sympathized with the feelings of the people and went along with their desires and so the kingly way was complete. (Ibid. *A*, pp. 273, 275)

Dai Zhen's definition of *ren* as wanting to lead a fulfilling life oneself and also to bring others to lead a fulfilling life is a straightforward and neat way of describing *ren*.

Conclusion

From Confucius to Dai Zhen *ren* has been explained in a series of different interpretations. The fundamental meaning is that given by Confucius, namely, loving others and wanting to establish oneself and others, wanting to be outstanding oneself and also make others outstanding. Dong Zhongshu's description of loving others with *ren* and Han Yu's statement that extensive love is what is meant by *ren* both built on Confucius' formulation. In the Song dynasty Cheng Hao's concept of forming one body with heaven and earth and the myriad things did not avoid the risk of falling into unreal abstraction. Neither Cheng Yi's opposition to interpreting *ren* in terms of love nor Zhu Xi's description of *ren* as the principle of love and the virtue of the heart avoided the danger of being too abstract. Dai Zhen's definition of *ren* as wanting to lead a fulfilling life oneself and also to bring others to lead a fulfilling life was clearer and rather more to the point. To sum up, Confucius' theory of *ren* retains an important place in theoretical thought today as in the past.

The Confucian doctrine of *ren* advocates the love of human beings but also holds that the separation of people according to social class is correct. This produces an internal contradiction in Confucian thought. How to truly implement the great ideal of love of humankind is a matter that still awaits a solution today.

40. Public Interest
Gong
公

We saw in the preceding section that Cheng Yi explained ren *in terms of the public interest. By so doing he made the public interest become the first principle of moral philosophy. The major protagonists of the idea of the public interest, however, were the legalists. There is thus a tension between Confucian philosophy, with its stress on the moral person in a family setting, and the legalist concern for the public forum, in which the person runs the risk of being reduced to a mere cipher.*

The Great Commonwealth

The term 'public interest' (*gong* 公) first emerged as a key term in the *Record of Rites*, which explains the regime of the great commonwealth as one in which "all under heaven is for the general public."

> When the great Way runs, all under heaven is for the general public. One chooses the worthy according to their ability. Their speech is trustworthy and they bring about harmony. Thus people do not only love their relatives, do not only treat their own children as children. Hence the old have a place to end their days, the strong a use and the young a place to grow up. Widows, orphans, the sick are all cared for. Men have their role in society; women have a home to go to [marriage]. Wealth is despised and thrown on the ground. There is no need to store it for oneself. Force is disdained and is not displayed. It is not necessary to act for oneself. Therefore if one plots in secret it will not succeed. Thieves and confusion will not occur, thus doors are open and not closed. This is what is meant by the great commonwealth. (*Record of Rites* 9, *Evolution of Rites*, p. 120)

This passage gives an excellent concrete picture of what is meant by 'public interest.' The most important features are not limiting one's love to one's own relatives and children and not hoarding wealth or relying on one's own strength. In essence the connotation is to transcend the self and not to have a selfish and self-seeking heart.

The public interest is the fundamental principle of morality, and the ideal of all under heaven being for the public is a noble ideal for human society.

It is not easy to determine when this text was written. Han-dynasty Confucian scholars believed it to be an exposition of Confucius' own views. Modern scholars believe it to be by Han Confucians. I believe that the *Evolution of Rites* chapter is a Confucian work of the Warring States period.

Warring States Legalist Texts

In Warring States legalist texts there are many references to the public interest. It is a fundamental principle of administration. The *Guanzi*, the *Book of Lord Shang*, and the writings of Shen Dao and Hanfeizi all advocated such a view.

According to the *Inner Training* chapter of the *Guanzi* the public interest encompasses an ordered mind and well-ordered affairs. Only when these are achieved will the people submit to one's government.

> Since such people obtain the principle of the one, an ordered mind is within them, ordered words issue from their mouth, ordered affairs are done to others, then all under heaven is ordered. When the one word is obtained then all under heaven submits; when the one word is established then all under heaven listens. This is the meaning of "being in the public interest."* (*Guanzi* 49, *Inner Training*, 2:125)

The one word and the principle of the one both refer to the Way. In another chapter the *Guanzi* distinguishes between public and private interests:

---

*Author's note: The Qing-dynasty Confucian scholar Wang Niansun amended "this is the meaning of 'being in the public interest'" to "this is what it means." Wang's reading is without foundation. The character *gong*, 'in the public interest,' is not an error.

What is done in the public interest, even if it is a matter of imposing a heavy punishment, will not arouse resentment among
the people. What is done for private motives, even if it is a
matter of giving substantial rewards, will not be welcomed by
the officials.* (*Guanzi* 53, *Imprinting "Prohibitions" on One's
Heart*, 2:178)

Here it is also a matter of acting in the public interest and winning the
obedience of the people.

Related to this issue is the *Guanzi*'s theory of forming one body with
the people. The ruler is instructed to pay attention to the people:

When one listens to the people as individuals they are foolish; if
one unites the people and then listens to them they are sage-
like. . . . The former kings were good at forming one body with
the people. Since they formed one body with the people they
were able to defend the State with the State and defend the
people with the people. (*Guanzi* 30, *Rulers and Ministers A*,
1:403–404)

"Forming one body with the people" in fact means complying with the
people's wishes:

That which makes for the flourishing of government is to
comply with the mind of the people. That which makes for the
disintegration of government is to go counter to the mind of
the people. (*Guanzi*, 1 *On Shepherding the People*, 1:4)

When one's rule is united as one body then one can issue
commands and orders and clarify decrees and regulations. . . .
The rule is united as one body because one eliminates hetero-
dox views and prohibits extravagant customs. (*Guanzi* 6, *Seven
Laws*, 1:78)

"Forming one body" means that superiors and inferiors see eye to eye and
share a common mind as if they were one body. On one hand the rulers
must find out the wishes of the people; on the other the people must accept the point of view of the rulers.

---

* Another version has "superiors" for "officials."

The distinction between public and private interests is also found in the *Book of Lord Shang*:

> When the distinction between public and private interests is clear, then little people do not hate the worthy and the unworthy do not envy those of merit. Thus when Yao and Shun ruled over all under heaven it was not for the sake of private advantages that they ruled but rather for the sake of all under heaven. They selected the worthy and chose the capable and passed it on to them. It was not that they distanced their fathers and sons and drew close to people from afar but that they were clear about the way of ordering chaos. Therefore the three kings drew close to [all under heaven] by justice while the five hegemons corrected the feudal lords by law. In neither case did they appropriate the profit of all under heaven to themselves. They ruled all under heaven for the sake of all under heaven and therefore those who had positions had the requisite merit. All under heaven rejoiced in their administration and none were able to harm it. The rulers and ministers of today's disturbed generation each seek to work for the benefit of one State only and undertake the weight of one office alone so as to further their own interests. This is what brings about a danger for the State. For the relation of public and private interests is the root of survival or destruction. (*Book of Lord Shang* 14, *The Cultivation of the Right Standard*, p. 18, lines 13–16)

The fate of a state depends, then, on whether a regime favors public or private interests. The public interest is to govern all under heaven for the sake of all under heaven. The private interest is to work for the benefit of only one state. The rule of law is to be upheld in contrast to that of private opinion:

> Those who act as rulers in this world mostly relax laws and rely on private standards of morality. This is why the State is in disorder. (Ibid., p. 18, line 21)

Among the things that are given as harmful to the public interest are "extensive learning and skill in debate" and "scholarly learning":

> The great officials and leading ministers of the State should all not be permitted to have extensive learning, skill in debate and suchlike distracting affairs. (*Book of Lord Shang* 2, *An order to cultivate waste lands*, p. 3, line 26)

To do these things is to fall into biased and erroneous ways. Instead the people "should not value scholarly learning" (Ibid., line 18).

Shen Dao also wrote about the distinction between public and private interests:

> Of old it was considered fortunate to establish the Son of Heaven and honor him. It was not a matter of benefiting one person. (*The Shen Tzu Fragments*, Fragment 21)
>
> Therefore to establish the Son of Heaven is for the sake of all under heaven. It is not a matter of establishing all under heaven for the sake of the Son of Heaven. To establish the ruler of a State is for the sake of the State. It is not a matter of establishing a State for the sake of the ruler. To establish a departmental official is for the sake of the department. It is not a matter of establishing the department for the sake of the official. (Fragment 22)
>
> Therefore consulting the turtle is the way to know what it is that will establish what is public.* One weighs up on a balance so as correct what is established in the public interest. One writes contracts so as to guarantee the reliability of what is established in the public interest. One controls measures so as to determine the exactitude of what is established in the public interest. One has a legal system and codes of rites so as to maintain the justice of what is established in the public interest. Whatsoever is geared to what is established in the public interest is that by which one does away with private interests. (Fragment 73)

The final chapter of the *Zhuangzi* contains an assessment of Shen Dao's philosophy:

---

* "Consulting the turtle" refers to the ancient Chinese practice of divination using heated turtle plastrons and bovine scapulae.

> His thought was in the public interest and not in favor
> of cliques. It was easy and without any self appropriation.
> (*Zhuangzi* 33, *Under Heaven*, line 41)

Today's *Shenzi* is in fragments and incomplete.

Han Fei placed even greater emphasis on the contrast between
public and private interests:

> Of old when Cang Jie composed characters, setting up oneself
> in one's own domain was what was meant by serving one's
> private interests and turning one's back on these was what was
> meant by serving the public interest. Public and private inter-
> ests are mutually opposed to each other. This is something
> Cang Jie certainly knew. (*Hanfeizi* 49, *Five Vermin* #10)

He discusses this mutual opposition in more detail:

> The way of the enlightened lord must include being cognizant
> of the distinction between public and private interests, clarify-
> ing the legal system and removing private emoluments. That
> commands must run and prohibitions must hold is the public
> justice of the lord of men. That one must practice one's private
> concerns, trust one's friends, not encourage by rewards or stop
> by punishments is the private justice of the minister. When
> private justice runs then there is disorder. When public justice
> runs then there is order. Therefore, public and private are dis-
> tinct. The minister of men may have private interests at heart
> or he may act in the interest of public justice. To keep oneself
> shining white and practice what is in the public interest and
> practice what is correct and occupy one's office without in-
> clining to private affairs is, for the minister of men, to act in the
> interests of public justice. To do wrong and follow one's de-
> sires, to make oneself secure and profit one's family is, for the
> minister of men, to have private interests at heart. When an
> enlightened lord is above then the minister of men casts aside
> the private concerns of his heart and practices public justice.
> When a disorderly lord is on top then the minister of men dis-
> cards public justice and acts out of his private concerns. Thus
> the minister and ruler have different ways of looking at things.

The ruler calculates how to use all his ministers. The ministers calculate how to serve their ruler. The relationship of ruler and minister is one of calculation. To injure himself and profit the State is something no minister would do. To injure the State and profit the ministers is something no ruler would do. The feeling of the minister is such that to injure himself would be profitless. The feeling of the ruler is that to harm the State would be lacking in love. Ruler and minister are drawn together by calculation. (*Hanfeizi* 19, *Covering up Wickedness* #6)

This text distinguishes between public justice and private justice. Public justice is in the interests of the state and the ruler. Private justice is in the interests of oneself and one's family. By associating the distinction between public and private with the minds of ruler and minister the text clearly makes the ruler the symbol of what is in the public interest. In fact this so-called public interest is simply the private interest of the ruler. In traditional thought the public interest in fact had two levels of meaning. On one level it referred to the common good of society; on the other it indicated the good of the ruler or of the state. In the course of history rulers often interpreted the good of the ruling group as being the public interest. Han Fei's point of view is precisely that. The early Qing scholar and pro-Ming loyalist Huang Zongxi (1610–1695) had this in mind when he wrote the following critical remarks:

Those who later became rulers of men were not so. They thought that the power of determining what was to the advantage or disadvantage of the empire could be obtained solely from themselves.... They took self-interest on a grand scale as the great public interest. (*SBBY* 362 [Taibei 1965], *Ming Yi Dai Fang Lu* 1, *The Original Rulers*, pp. 1b, 2a)

In short, the good of the people, the good of the state, and the good of the rulers are three things whose relationship is very complicated.

Han Fei included Confucius among those he deemed useless from the point of view of the state:

Nowadays the lords of the world make enquiry into useless disputations. They honor practices which are far from bringing practical benefits and hope to make the State wealthy and strong. This cannot be. They have extensive thought and disputing wit such as that of Confucius and Mozi. Confucius and Mozi did not farm the land and so what does the State get from them? One may practice filial piety and reduce one's desires like Ceng and Shi but Ceng and Shi did not win battles and so what profit accrues to the State? The common man has his own inclinations; the lord of men thinks of the public interest. Not doing anything but making sure one has enough, not being an official yet making a name for oneself, this is one's own inclinations. Cutting down on the study of cultural things and making the legal system clear, putting a hold on private inclinations while working for one common cause, this is the public interest. (*Hanfeizi* 47, *Eight Fallacies*, #3)

By saying that the lord of men thinks of the public interest, Han Fei was establishing a close relation between the lord of men and the public interest, thus showing that by 'the public interest' he understood the ruler's private interest. By including Confucius, Mozi, and other scholars as well as all academic activities among the private inclinations, Han Fei showed that his view of the distinction between the public and the private was very narrow.

By contrast, in *Mr. Lu's Spring and Autumn Annals* there is a chapter dedicated to the subject of the public interest that gives a much fuller analysis of the term according to three levels of meaning. The first is that of the people of one's own state, the second is that of humankind as a whole, and the third transcends humankind:

In the past the former sage kings' way of administering all under heaven was to first consider the public interest. Once the public interest was catered for then all under heaven was calm. Calm was obtained from the public interest being met. There are many who have tried to observe from the highest social vantage point and have obtained all under heaven. They acquired it by thinking in the public interest. That they lost it must be because of selfish bias.... The empire is not one person's empire. The empire belongs to all that is under heaven. If *yin* and *yang* were not to unite then not one species of thing would grow. Sweet dew and timely rain do not selfishly fall on one thing alone. The life of the myriad peoples is not limited to that of one person.... There was a man of Jing who lost his bow and did not bother to look for it. He said, "A man of Jing has lost his bow; a man of Jing will find it, so why go looking for it?" Confucius heard of this and said, "Forget the qualifier 'of Jing' and this saying is good." Lao Dan heard of it and said, "Forget the term 'a man' and this saying is good." Thus Lao Dan was more public minded than Confucius. (*Mr. Lu's Spring and Autumn Annals* 1.4, *In Honour of the Public Interest*, p. 44)

The original saying by the man of Jing was that a man of his own state will find the bow. This is the public interest of one's fellow nationals. Confucius amended the saying such that it reads, "another man will find it," thus including all humankind. Lao Dan amended to "it will be found" and thereby included all beings in the world. In general the term 'the public interest' takes humankind as the measure. The mere pursuit of human good to the exclusion of all other considerations can, however, lead to an imbalance and destruction of the environment and thence to damage to the conditions of human life. From this perspective it is also important to take into consideration a view of the public interest that transcends the human point of view.

The Song Dynasty

In the Song dynasty the two Cheng brothers particularly emphasized the public interest. Cheng Hao took work in the public interest to be an important principle of self-cultivation while Cheng Yi explained *ren* in terms of the public interest.

In a reply to a letter from Zhang Zai on calming one's nature, Cheng Hao expounded his view of the public interest:*

The constancy of heaven and earth is that its heart reaches to the myriad things and yet it is without thought for itself. The constancy of the sage is that his feelings go along with the myriad things and yet he is without his own feelings. Therefore

---

* According to Zhu Xi (*Conversations* 93, p. 2359) this was written when Cheng Hao was 22 or 23, i.e., in 1054 or 1055.

in the learning of the gentleman there is nothing like being open and welcoming to the great public. Things come and one goes along and responds to them.... The feelings of a person each have their clouded aspects; therefore one cannot adapt to the Way. A great proportion of disasters come from selfishness and use of cleverness. If one is selfish then one cannot take active steps to respond to what passes. If one uses cleverness then one cannot take simple awareness as natural. Now if one has a mind that dislikes things outside oneself and yet seeks enlightenment in a mind where there is nothing, this is to turn the mirror around and look for one's reflection.... Instead of considering the external wrong and the internal right it is better to forget both internal and external. If one forgets both then one plainly is without any affairs. If one is without affairs then one is fixed. If fixed, then clear. If clear then how can one's replying to things be a hinderance? The joy of the sage is to rejoice as things dictate; the anger of the sage is to be angry as things dictate. Thus the joy and anger of the sage are not bound to his own heart but to things. If one does thus then what is there that the sage cannot respond to? ... Now if one takes the joy and anger of selfishness and the use of cleverness and looks at the correctness of the joy and anger of the sage how will it appear? (*Mr. Mingdao's Collection of Literary Works 3, Reply to Master Heng Qu's Letter on Calming Human Nature, Juan* 3.1, p. 213a)

Cheng Yi interpreted *ren* in terms of what is in the public interest.

Ren is to be in the public interest [disinterested]. (*SKQS* 698, *Surviving Works of the Two Chengs* 9, p. 85a)
   Confucius said, "A benevolent person while wanting to establish him- or herself also establishes others, while wanting to be outstanding him- or herself also makes others outstanding. To be able to judge others by what is near to ourselves may be called the full scope of benevolence" [*Analects* 6, *Yong Ye* #28, p. 194]. To say that Confucius spoke of *ren* as educating others, this is sufficient. To sum up one can say it does not go beyond what is in the public interest. (Ibid.)
   The way of benevolence may be summed up adequately

by the one word, 'public interest.' ... It is because when we consider the public interest then things and the self are seen in equal light and then benevolence is that by which we are able to show consideration. (Ibid. 15, p. 122b)

The public interest is seeing things and the self in equal light and thus it is benevolence. By explaining *ren* as the public interest Cheng Yi made the public interest the first principle of morality.

41. Five Human Relationships
Wu Lun
五倫

The late Warring States period established five human relationships—ruler-minister, father-son, husband-wife, elder-younger, friend-friend—that were to be determinative for all later Chinese philosophy. The identification of these relationships is prescriptive rather than merely descriptive. To say that some-one is my ruler or father implies a certain attitude I am to have toward him and he toward me. Hence, each of the relationships is characterized by two norms expressing the virtues to be displayed by either member. In later impe-rial times the system could develop into a rigid justification of social hierarchy, neglecting the responsibilities incumbent on the superior in each relationship.

The modern Chinese term for 'ethics' comes from this discussion of hu-man relationships. Hence Professor Zhang provides a note on its origins.*

* Author's note: In modern Chinese the term 'ethics' is translated as 'the principles of relationships' (*lunli*). The term has its origin in the *Record of Rites*: "Music is what inspires the principles of relationships" (*Record of Rites* 19, *Record of Music*, p. 205). Zheng Xuan explains the distinction between 'relationships' and 'principles' as follows: "Relationships are what constitute categories of things; principles are what serve to distinguish things" (*SKQS* 116, *Notes and Comments on the* Record of Rites 37, *Record of Music*, p. 98b). Kong Yingda expands this explanation: "*Yin-yang* and the myriad things each have categories of relationship and distinction of principles (ibid., p. 99b). The expression 'principles of relationships' refers to re-lationships in general and is not yet confined to human relationships alone. In modern Chi-nese the term 'principle of relationships' refers to the relationships between human beings.

Early References

The term 'human relations' first appeared in the *Mencius*:

> Prince Millet taught the people to sow and reap, to cultivate
> the five grains. The five grains ripened and the people were
> nourished. The way of human beings is such that if they are
> well fed and warmly clad, have comfortable housing and no
> education then they will approach the state of birds and beasts.
> The sage [Shun] was concerned about this and deputed Xie to
> be minister of Education so as to teach the people human
> relations. Between father and son there should be affection;
> between ruler and minister justice; between husband and wife
> distinction of roles; between old and young proper order; be-
> tween friends trustworthiness. (*Mencius* 3, *Duke Wen of Teng
> A*, #4)

Human relations, then, are the five listed here as taught by Xie.

In the *Book of History* the Zhou legend surrounding the origin of the
same relationships is given:

> The emperor said, "Jie, the people continue unfriendly with
> one another, and do not observe docilely the five orders of re-
> lationships. It is yours as the minister of Instruction, reverently
> to set forth the lessons of duty belonging to those five orders.
> Do so with gentleness. (*Book of History* 2.1, *The Canon of
> Shun*, p. 44)

Confucius mentioned three of the five relationships. In dialogue
with Duke Jing of Qi (546–489 B.C.) he set out the first two alone, namely,
ruler-minister, father-son:

> Let the ruler be a ruler, the minister a minister, the father a
> father and the son a son. (*Analects* 12, *Yan Yuan* #11, p. 256)

A third relationship was touched on by Confucius' disciple Zi Lu when
talking about a person who refuses to take up office:

> Not to take office is not right. If the relations between young
> and old may not be neglected, how is it that he sets aside the
> duties that should be observed between sovereign and minis-

ter? Wishing to maintain his personal purity, he allows that great relation to come to confusion. A superior man takes office and performs the duties he ought to do and which belong to that office. As to the failure of right principles to make progress he is aware of that. (*Analects* 18, *The Viscount of Wei* #7, pp. 335–336)

Here the just relationship between ruler and minister is described as the great relationship. The passage also mentions the relations of old and young.

The *Commentary on the Decision* of the *Book of Changes* begins with the relationship of husband and wife:

The family: the woman's correct place is within; the man's correct place is outside. For man and woman to be correct is the great measure of heaven and earth. The family has a stern ruler; this means the parents. The father is to be a father, the son a son, the younger brother a younger brother, the husband a husband, the wife a wife and then the way of the household is correct. When there are correct households then all under heaven is fixed. (*Book of Changes* 37, *Jia Ren: Commentary on the Decision*, p. 159)

Here only three of the five relationships dealing with the family are mentioned.

The *Mean and Harmony* says,

There are five ways [of human relationships] under heaven and there are three means of implementing them. The five are ruler and minister, father and son, husband and wife, elder and younger sibling, friend and friend. These are the five relationships under heaven. Wisdom, benevolence, courage, these three, are the three virtues under heaven. (*Mean and Harmony* #20)

The five ways are the same as what the *Mencius* spoke of as the five relationships.

In his discussion of human relationships Xunzi brought out the distinction between noble and mean, older and younger.

Someone who is honored like the son of heaven, is rich enough to have all under heaven. This is something towards which all human beings have a common desire. Were one to follow human desires then authority would not be able to contain them and things would not suffice to satisfy them. Thus the first kings decided to create rites and justice to bring about distinctions among human beings. Hence there is the grading of noble and base, the difference between old and young, the distinction between wise and foolish, capable and incapable. All of these mean that a people undertake their own affairs and each obtains what is appropriate.... The great mass of people thus remain secure on the one way. Therefore the benevolent people are top in the hierarchy while the farmers use their muscle to till the fields, the merchants use their judgement to make money, the hundreds of workers use their skill to make machines. From the scholars and officials up to the dukes and lords there are none who do not undertake the duties of their office without benevolence, generosity, wisdom and ability. This is what is meant by the utmost peace. Therefore some bring blessings to all under heaven yet do not reckon it as much. Some keep the door and receive guests, keeping the gates and closing the bolt and yet do not reckon it as too little. Thus it is said "irregular but uniform, oppressive but favorable, dissimilar and so similar," this is what is meant by human relations. (*Xunzi* 4, *Shame and Dishonor*, lines 72–77)

This text differs from the *Mencius* in advocating the necessity of social and class distinctions. In another passage the *Xunzi* mentions four of the five relations:

Ruler and minister, father and son, elder and younger brothers, husband and wife—these all have a beginning and ending and then from the ending begin again. They have the same principle as heaven and earth and endure from generation to generation for ever. This is what is called the great body.... The ruler being a ruler, the minister a minister, the father a father, the son a son, the elder brother an elder brother, the younger brother a younger brother are all one. For the farmer to be a farmer, the official an official, the merchant a merchant are all one. (*Xunzi* 9, *On the Regulations of a King*, lines 66–67, 68–69)

Of the five relations, this passage makes no mention of that between friends.

The same relationship is also lacking in the list of ten moral norms in the *Record of Rites*:

> The father is to be compassionate, the son filial, the elder brother kind and the younger brother respectful, the husband just and the wife obedient, the old person gracious and the young compliant, the ruler benevolent and the minister loyal. These ten are called the human norms. (*Record of Rites* 9, *Evolution of Rites*, p. 126)

Here the relationship of elder and younger brother is complemented by one between older and younger people in general. Thus although there is no mention of friends there are still five relationships with ten norms in all.

Concomitant Virtues

From the Han dynasty onward, when most philosophical works mention human relations they generally have in mind the Mencian set of five: father-son, ruler-minister, husband-wife, elder brother–younger brother, and friend-friend.

The *Great Learning* lists the virtues associated with three of these relationships:

> To act as the ruler of men one must practice benevolence; to act as the minister of men one must practice respect; to act as the son of a man one must practice filial piety; to act as the father of men one must be compassionate. In dealing with fellow nationals one must be trustworthy. (*Great Learning*, p. 362)

Notice how this passage emphasizes the relationships that should exist between people of the same state rather than just between friends. This addition expands the scope of friendship and represents a new contribution. Both the *Great Learning* and the *Mean and Harmony*, however, keep to the same line of thought as Mencius.

The five relationships as expounded by Mencius all involve mutual respect between two parties. In the ten norms of the *Record of Rites* the mutual obligations of each of the parties are also spelled out. One must bear in mind that all these relationships were seen as mutual exchanges. In pre-Qin Confucianism there was never the demand for absolute obedience of son to father, minister to ruler, or wife to husband.

42. Nondiscrimination
Jian Ai
兼愛

Nineteenth-century translators seized on the Mohist jian ai *as a Chinese equivalent of Christian love for all men. This resulted in a certain bias. The Mohists had a highly developed military-style organization in which complete obedience was demanded. They sought to defend small states and preached against war while also building machines to defend besieged cities. Hence the term* jian ai *is more properly translated as 'loving without discrimination'—the emphasis being on the lack of discrimination rather than on the love.*

Mozi

The expression "loving without discrimination" is associated with Mozi. In detail the expression is as follows:

> To show no discrimination and mutually love; to have dealings with others and mutually benefit. (*Mozi* 15, *Loving Without Discrimination B*, lines 10–11)

Expressed in brief, it is "no discrimination."

The rule of showing no discrimination in one's love for others and of dealing with others so that each party benefits is set out as follows:

To look on the State of others as one's own State; to look on the family of others as one's own family; to look on the person of others as one's own person. (Ibid., lines 11–12)

Mozi advocated allowing no discrimination so as to change distinctions:

> Of those who distinguish names in the world and who hate others and steal from them, are they advocates of no discrimination or of making distinctions? One must say that they advocate 'making distinctions.' The fruit of making distinctions in social intercourse is a great disaster in the world, is it not? Therefore making distinctions is wrong.... Therefore Master Mozi said, "Show no discrimination so as to change distinctions." ... Of those who distinguish names in the world and who love others and benefit others, are they advocates of no discrimination or of making distinctions? One must say that they advocate 'no discrimination.' The fruit of no discrimination in social intercourse is a great benefit for the world, is it not? Therefore Master Mozi said no discrimination is right. (*Mozi* 16, *Loving Without Discrimination C*, lines 6–7, 8–9, 14–15)

The Mohists proclaimed attaining correctness by means of using no discrimination. They believed that nondiscrimination included all the virtues of graciousness, loyalty, compassion, filial piety, friendship, and fraternity:

> Therefore the gentleman considers nothing as on a par with examining no discrimination and implementing it in his business. As a ruler one must be gracious, as minister of men one must be loyal, as father of men one must be compassionate, as son of a man one must be filial, as elder brother of men one must be friendly, as younger brother of others one must be respectful. Thus the gentleman values nothing better than wanting to be a gracious ruler, a loyal minister, a compassionate father, a filial son, a friendly elder brother, a respectful younger brother but if there is any discrimination then none of these virtues may be practiced. (Ibid., lines 84–86)

The principle of nondiscrimination is to love others as oneself. Practicing universal love is not the same as what the Confucians meant when they said that one expands from what is applicable to oneself to extend it to others or from what is close to reach out to what is far away. But the Mohist loving without discrimination did not remove class distinctions. The Mohist ideal is stated thus:

> When all under heaven love one another: the strong do not oppress the weak; the many do not take from the few; the rich do not denigrate the poor; the nobles are not haughty to the base; the schemers do not cheat the foolish. (*Mozi* 15, *Loving Without Discrimination B*, line 14)

Even in this ideal the divisions between rich and poor, noble and base persist. Hence the love between human beings that the Mohists proclaim is still not truly equal love for all.

Xunzi

Xunzi opposed Mozi's loving without discrimination and in reply spoke of weighing without discrimination and the art of nondiscrimination.

> Weighing the relative merits of choosing or refusing desires and aversions: When a person sees something desirable, he must reflect on the fact that with time it could come to involve what is detestable. When he sees something that is beneficial, he should reflect that sooner or later it, too, could come to involve harm. Only after weighing the total of the one against that of the other and maturely calculating should he determine the relative merits of choosing or refusing his desires and aversions. In this fashion, he will regularly avoid failure and being ensnared by what he has chosen. (*Xunzi* 3, *Nothing Indecorous*, lines 45–47 [Knoblock tr.])

He further stated,

> Hence, the gentleman, though worthy, is able to tolerate the unfit. Though wise, he is able to suffer the stupid. Though profound, he is able to endure the superficial. Though pure, he

can tolerate the adulterated. This may be described as the 'art of nondiscrimination.' (*Xunzi* 5, *Contra Physiognomy*, line 49 [Knoblock tr.])

'Weighing without discrimination' means weighing up one's options from all points of view. 'The art of nondiscrimination' means the technique of acceptance and toleration. In talking of learning Xunzi said,

> Be complete and whole in it, and then you will be truly learned.... So the gentleman is to be valued for his complete-ness. (*Xunzi* 1, *An Exhortation to Learning*, lines 45, 51)

The art of nondiscrimination is the path by which one comes to a full picture of the matter.

43. Moderation
Zhong Yong
中庸

The character zhong *literally means 'the center.' It is used in moral philoso-phy to refer to moderation in all things, neither going to excess nor falling short of the mean. Even in popular culture the Chinese see this as one of the greatest ideals of daily life. This ideal was well expressed by Wang Fuzhi. Liu Shao gave an interesting version of the theory based on the five agents, whereas Ye Shi produced a dialectical theory.*

The Pre-Han Era

Zhong is a basic concept of Confucian philosophy. It is also called 'centrality' and 'commonality.'

In the *Analects* the affairs of Yao and Shun are thus described:

> Yao said: "Oh! Shun, the heavenly ordered succession now rests on you. Sincerely hold fast to moderation. If there be distress and want within the four seas, the blessings of heaven

will come to a final end." Shun also used the same words in giving the charge to Yu. (*Analects* 20, *Yao Said* #1, p. 350)

Here 'moderation' is taken to be the fundamental principle of morality. The *Analects* also record Confucius' views on the subject:

> As a virtue moderation goes far indeed! The people seldom keep to it. (*Analects* 6, *Yong Ye* #27, p. 193)

The same work also includes Confucius' comment on his followers:

> Since I cannot acquire people who act according to moderation whom I may instruct, I must first find the zealous and prudent. The zealous will advance and grasp the truth; the prudent will keep from wrong-doing. (*Analects* 13, *Zi Lu* #21, p. 272)

According to tradition Confucius' grandson Zi Si wrote the *Mean and Harmony*.* This work quotes Confucius as saying:

> The gentleman aims at moderation and harmony; the little person is opposed to moderation and harmony. The moderation and harmony of the gentleman lies in his always keeping to the center; the little person's opposition to moderation and harmony lies in having no prudence. (*Mean and Harmony* #2)

It also includes Confucius' praise of Shun:

> How great was the wisdom of Shun! Shun liked to ask and liked to inspect the words of those close to him. He hid evil and displayed good. He grasped both extremes and used the center for the people. This is what made him Shun! (*Mean and Harmony* #6)

These are the principal passages in which Confucius spoke about moderation and harmony. The most important expressions of the idea are grasping both extremes and using the center for the people (*yun zhi qi zhong*), "moderation and harmony," going in moderation, and "always keeping to the center."

---

*Author's note: The *Records of the Historian* say, "Zi Si wrote the *Mean and Harmony*" (*Records of the Historian* 47, *The Family of Confucius*, p. 1946).

It is first of all necessary to examine the meaning of the phrase 'moderation and harmony.' Two explanations of it were given by Han-dynasty Confucian scholars. The first involved a homophonic pun on the second of the two characters, *yong*. The *yong* meaning 'harmony' was read as the *yong* meaning 'use,' hence the whole phrase meant 'gathering all together so as to use the center.' The second reading of *yong* was as 'constancy.' The phrase would then mean 'the constant way without excess or falling short.' Kong Yingda quoted Zheng Xuan's *Index* 目錄 as saying,

> Its name is called the *Mean and Harmony* because it records how to gather all together so as to use the center. '*Yong*' [harmony] is '*yong*' [use]. (*Record of Rites* 31, *Mean and Harmony*)

In his notes on the *Record of Rites* Zheng Xuan explained the phrase "the gentleman aims at moderation and harmony" by saying,

> *Yong* [harmony] is constancy. It is to use the center as the constant way. (*SKQS* 116, *Notes on the* Record of Rites 52, *Mean and Harmony*, p. 352a)

Regarding the line "he grasped both extremes and used the center for the people" Zheng said,

> The two ends are to go to excess and to fall short. If one uses the center for the people then worthy and unworthy can all practice it. (Ibid., p. 353a)

That Zheng used both senses of *yong* suggests that he was not able to fully express his meaning.

Cheng Yi explained the phrase by saying:

> What is not biased is what moderation means; what is unchangeable is what harmony means. Moderation is the correct way of all under heaven; harmony is the fixed principle of all under heaven. (*Mean and Harmony*, p. 1 [Shanghai ed.])

Zhu Xi said,

> Moderation is the name for what does not go to excess nor fall short. Harmony is what is ordinary. (quoted in *Collected Exegesis of the* Analects 6, *Yong Ye*, p. 427)

He also said,

> Moderation and harmony is to be unbiased and impartial, neither going to excess nor falling short, and the principle of what is ordinary, that is the ought of heaven's decree. It reaches to the utmost minute things. (*Mean and Harmony*, p. 2b [Shanghai ed.])

Zhu Xi also noted that 'constancy' has two meanings. The first is what happens with regularity, the second, what is ordinary. The two are slightly different. Zheng Xuan's description of 'harmony' as what is constant used the first meaning, whereas Zhu Xi's definition used the second.

By testing the meaning of the *Mean and Harmony* against that in the *Analects* we find that "moderation and harmony" has the meaning of "using the center." The clearest expression of this is the following line: "He grasped the two extremes and used their center for the people." The phrase means the use of the principle of the center; thus it is also said that "the gentleman always keeps to the center." By "always keeps to the center" is meant that at any time one always chooses the center. Although *yong* (harmony) can mean both constancy and what is ordinary, it clearly ought to mean 'use' in this phrase. One ought not bring these other meanings of *yong* into the picture. From the Song dynasty onward, however, Zhu Xi's exegesis became the leading one. Most people know the definition: "What is not biased is what moderation means; what is unchangeable is what harmony means." The definition is Cheng Yi's but it was Zhu Xi who propagated it.

What the *Analects* describe as going by the center the *Mencius* terms the central way. Moderation and harmony, moderation in doing, and the way of moderation all focus on moderation as the key note.

> Wan Zhang asked, saying, "When Confucius was in Chen he said, 'Let me go back. The scholars of my school are ambitious but hasty. They want to advance and seize their object but cannot forget their early ways.' Why did Confucius, when he was in Chen, think of the ambitious scholars of Lu?" Mencius replied, "Confucius, not getting people to pursue the central way whom he might teach, decided to take the zealous and prudent. The zealous would attain their object; the prudent

would avoid errors. It is not to be thought that Confucius did not wish to get people pursuing the central way but being unable to find such he thought of the next best." (*Mencius* 7, *Exhausting the Mind B*, #37)

Moderation means grasping the center and not falling into any extreme.

The *Commentaries on the* Book of Changes gave various formulations with 'moderation': 'correct moderation,' 'moderation and correctness,' 'the way of moderation,' 'going by moderation.' These are all praised and in general it is held that if one keeps to the path of moderation then one will be lucky. If not then one will be unlucky. This can be seen from a number of texts.*

The influence of the *Mean and Harmony* went far and deep, especially since the Song dynasty, so the ideal of "what is not biased is what moderation means; what is unchangeable is what harmony means" was not only accepted by scholars but also penetrated generally into society.

The Post-Han Era: Liu Shao

After the Han dynasty there were three people who had especially noteworthy interpretations of moderation and harmony: Liu Shao of the Three

---

*Author's note: The following are examples: "'*Meng*': good luck. By acting in good luck one's time will be right on [*zhong*]" (*Commentary on the Decision* 4, *Meng Hexagram*, p. 27). "Its place is in the position of heaven and it takes correctness as its center [*zhong*]" (ibid. 5, *Xu Hexagram*, p. 31). "It is profitable to meet the great person. Such a one values the center [*zhong*] and the correct" (ibid. 6, *Song Hexagram*, p. 35). "The trigram of the arts and enlightenment is on that of strength. The line is in the center and the correct place and corresponds [to the line above]. This is the correct course of the gentleman" (ibid. 13, *Tong Ren Hexagram*, p. 63). "Wining and dining is firm and fortunate as shown by the central and correct position" (*Symbolism Commentary* 5, *Xu Hexagram*, p. 34). "The good fortune of the shining of '*bi*' [union] is placed in the correct and central position" (ibid. 8, *Bi Hexagram*, p. 46). "Not waiting for the end of the day, fortunate; good luck. As shown by its position in the correct and central place" (ibid. 16, *Yu Hexagram*, p. 77). "Placed in yellow: great good fortune. One will obtain the central way" (ibid. 30, *Li Hexagram*, p. 132). "One will receive this great blessing because one is in the central and correct position" (ibid. 35, *Jin Hexagram*, p. 152). "The second nine: fortunate; good luck. One obtains the central way" (ibid. 40, *Jie Hexagram*, p. 173). "Though there be warfare do not fear. One obtains the central way" (ibid. 43, *Guai Hexagram*, p. 185). "The good fortune of the fifth nine is because of its place as correct and central" (ibid. 57, *Sun Hexagram*, p. 241). "The second nine: fortunate; good luck. It is in the central place so it leads to correctness" (ibid. 64, *Wei Ji Hexagram*, p. 268).

Kingdoms period, Ye Shi of the Southern Song, and Wang Fuzhi at the turn of the Ming-Qing period.

In the *Gazette of Human Nature*, Liu Shao expressed the belief that the five agents, wood, metal, fire, earth and water, are made manifest in human beings as five virtues: benevolence, ritual, trust, justice, and wisdom. These five are also called the five constants. Taken by itself each has its own bias. Taking all together in such a way that the whole transcends the sum of the five is what is meant by moderation and harmony.

> If one weighs up their material and stuff then one appeals to the five things. The proof of the five things is that each is in one's own body. In the body wood is bone, metal is tendons, fire is *qi*, earth is flesh, water is blood. These are the symbols of the five things.... Therefore bones flourish and are soft. This is called great resolution. Great resolution is the stuff of benevolence. *Qi* is light and clear. It is called the principle of culture. The principle of culture is the root of ritual. The body is right and fleshed out. It is called authentic and firm. What is authentic and firm is the foundation of trust. Tendons are vigorous yet supple. They are called courage and bravado. Courage and bravado are the determinants of justice. One's outlook is calm and expansive. It is called communicating with the minute. Communicating with the minute is the origin of wisdom. The five substances are of everlasting nature; thus they are called the five constants.... Though the body changes continually it always relies on the five substances.... The five substances are different from this kind. When the five constants are all present, embrace them with simplicity. The five substances fill up the interior; the five spirits are shown outside.... Therefore what inclines to one material takes the name of that material as its name. The person who gathers all the materials takes virtue as his or her goal. The person who gathers together all the virtues has an even better reputation. Therefore to gather together the virtues and arrive at one's goal is called moderation and harmony. Moderation and harmony are the goal of the sage. (*SKQS* 848, *Gazette of Human Nature* A1, *Nine Points of Physiology*, pp. 762–764)

Moderation and harmony form the supreme ideal of gathering together all the virtues and arriving at one's goal. This ideal is Liu Shao's exegesis of the term 'moderation and harmony.'

The Post-Han Era: Ye Shi

Ye Shi interpreted moderation and harmony in terms of uniting opposites and overcoming contradictions between things.

> The Way has its origin in unity and it becomes embodied in duality. Of old those who talked of the Way had to do so in terms of duality. Any forms that there are, whether *yin* or *yang*, hard or soft, going contrary to or going along with, going towards or away from, odd or even, separating or uniting, latitude and longtitude, warp and woof are all dual.... Moderation and harmony is that whereby one smoothes off the duality of things so as to make clear the unity of the Way so as to make clear what the duality rests on and not that the pair are able to be present. Water comes to the level and then stops. The Way comes to moderation and harmony and then stops. (*Collected Works of Ye Shi* 2, *Other Collected Works of Mr. Shuixin* 7.4, *Mean and Harmony*, p. 732)

The harmony is the point at which water no longer falls, the moment of stillness between each conflicting pair.

The Post-Han Era: Wang Fuzhi

Wang Fuzhi, rejecting the interpretation of *yong* as what is ordinary, analyzed the meaning of the phrase as follows:

> As for the meaning of this '*yong*,' in the *Explanation of the Characters* it says that '*yong*' [harmony] is '*yong*' [use]. In the *Book of History* the use of '*yong*' is never inconsistent with its meaning '*yong*' [use]. Before Master Zhu no one had ever read this character as meaning ordinary.... Hence one who knows how to talk about moderation and harmony is speaking about

the use of moderation. (*Great and Comprehensive Readings of the Four Books* 2.1, *Mean and Harmony: Ming Pian Da Zhi*, pp. 62, 63)

This explanation of the phrase is correct. Wang Fuzhi went on to reject the interpretation of moderation and harmony as neither exceeding nor falling short.

> The phrase with the two characters '*zhong*' [moderation] and '*yong*' [harmony] most certainly cannot be compared with exceeding and falling short. Early Confucian scholars seem not to have realized this point. They said that moderation and harmony was like the character 川 '*chuan*' [river]. When one has written the first stroke then it is as if one had fallen short; the last stroke is like going to excess while the middle stroke is moderation and harmony. Is this not a great mistake? (Ibid. 6.1, *Analects: Xianjin Pian*, p. 365)

Wang believed that moderation is the highest standard. There can only be falling short of it; there can be no exceeding it.

> Wickedness will always be a matter of falling short. How can it be to go beyond? The sagely Way is the peak of majesty, the best, what is so lofty it is like heaven. How can one go beyond it? ... One must take moderation as the utmost, be a partner of heaven and earth, praise transformation and generation and there can be nothing that can be exceeded. Do not want to let people say that the Way has limits and boundaries and thus take refuge in the vale of wrong. (Ibid.)
>
> It is not that originally there were three roads: one of excess, one in the center and one of falling short.... The separation into these three roads of excess, the center and falling short does not even hold water when applied to children's games. (*Great and Comprehensive Readings of the Four Books* 7.5, *Analects: Yaoyue Pian*, p. 497)

The reading of moderation and harmony as the utmost peak, the highest ideal that is, means that there can only be a falling short. There can be no going to excess. Commonly excess does in fact mean 'falling short.'

Wang's interpretation, however, establishes a new meaning of the phrase 'moderation and harmony,' a meaning that is a denial of the traditional interpretation.

The ideal of moderation and harmony suggests that all things have a norm, that is, a limit. To exceed this limit and to fall short of it amount to the same thing. This implies a view of contrasting opposites and interrelated poles that is correct. But the concept of moderation and harmony also requires one to uphold this standard and maintain these limits. It prevents movement in any other direction. It stifles any point of view that would encourage progress and development. This is the limitation of moderation as a way of thought. In daily life one needs the principle of neither going to excess nor falling short. It is applicable to food, drink, and clothing, for instance. But scientific development may require breaking through traditional concepts. Social progress depends even more on breaking out of the shackles of tradition. In this respect the concept of moderation and harmony becomes an obstacle to progress.

II. Ethical Concepts

The following section discusses the terms for virtue, obligation, value, authority, and duty.

44. Virtue, Power
De, Dao-de
德, 道德

The term de *has such a broad scope of meaning that any single equivalent will always fall short. In some contexts the term 'power' is an appropriate translation, suggesting the inherent force present, whereas in other contexts 'virtue' is more apt. If the latter is understood as the power within something by which it expresses its true nature then one can see how the moral and nonmoral uses can all come from the same concept. Professor Zhang con-*

centrated on the moral uses of the term de *and noted when it began to be found in the binome* dao-de.

The original meaning of the term *de* is difficult to determine. Some guesses have been made by scholars of early writing but no reliable conclusion has been reached. The modern meaning of the term is 'morally praiseworthy behavior,' 'high moral character.' The *Explanation of the Characters* says,

> '*De*' is what is won from others outside and from the self inside. (*Explanation of the Characters* 10B, p. 217a)

In other words, it refers to the proper means of dealing with social relations between the self and others.

Confucian Use

The modern use is already evidenced in the *Book of Poetry* and the *Book of History*, dating from the western Zhou.

> Heaven engenders the mass of peoples;
> For any given thing there is a rule;
> The people have this normal nature;
> They tend to this admirable virtue.
> (*Book of Poetry* 3, *Da Ya* 6, *Zheng Min*, Ode 260.1, p. 71)

> It was your greatly distinguished father, King Wen, who was able to illustrate his virtue and be careful in the use of punishments. (*Book of History* 5.9, *Announcement to Kang*, p. 383)

This line was quoted in *Zuo's Commentary* by Wu Chen, duke of Shen:

> The *Books of Zhou* say, "Because he was able to illustrate his virtue and be careful in the use of punishments so King Wen was able to establish the Zhou. By illustrating his virtue is meant he did all he could to exalt it, by being careful in his use of punishments is meant he did all he could to abolish them." (*Zuo's Commentary* 8, *Zheng* 2, p. 341)

The *Book of History* further says,

> Let the king sedulously cultivate the virtue of reverence. (*Book of History* 5.12, *Announcement to Shao*, pp. 426–427)

According to the evidence of *Zuo's Commentary*, *de* in the Spring and Autumn period also referred to moral conduct, as the following examples show:

> Zhong Zhong said, "I have heard that one should unite the people by virtue." (*Zuo's Commentary* 1, *Yin* 4, p. 15)
>
> The duke said, "... Keep to one's duty, practice virtue so as to wait for the time." (*Zuo's Commentary* 3, *Zhuang* 8, p. 81)
>
> Zhou Zhiqiao said, "To give a salary to those without virtue is a disaster." (*Zuo's Commentary* 4, *Min* 2, p. 126)
>
> Qu Wan ... said, "If, my Lord, you use virtue to win over the feudal lords, who will dare not to submit?" (*Zuo's Commentary* 5, *Xi* 4, p. 139)
>
> Gong Zhiqi ... said, "... Ghosts and spirits do not respect the status of human beings, they adhere to virtue alone. Thus the *Books of Zhou* say, 'August Heaven is not doting, it only sustains virtue.'" (Ibid., p. 143)
>
> Fu Chen said, "The Highest Above treats the people with virtue." (Ibid. 24, p. 189)
>
> Qi Que said, "Correction of virtue, conveniences of life and serving abundant means of sustenance are known as the three important matters." (*Zuo's Commentary* 6, *Wen* 7, p. 247)
>
> Zi Chan said, "*De*, that is the foundation of the State." (*Zuo's Commentary* 9, *Xiang* 24, p. 505)

In all these cases *de* is to be understood as virtuous conduct.

In the Spring and Autumn period *de* was used apart from *dao*, 'the Way,' although in modern Chinese the two normally form a binome: *dao-de*, 'virtue.' *Dao* as the Way refers to the principle, whereas *de* is respect and application of the principle.

> The will fixed on the Way; relying on virtue, trusting to benevolence, relaxing in the arts. (*Analects* 7, *Shu Er* #6, p. 196)

Unless one attains to perfect virtue, one cannot keep to the perfect Way. (*Mean and Harmony* #27)

The terms *dao* and *de* are not found as a binome in the *Analects* nor in the *Mencius*. It was in the *Explanation of the Trigrams Commentary on the* Book of Changes and in the *Xunzi* that they first appeared as one. In the former, although the two characters were juxtaposed they were not necessarily used as a binome:

> He observed the changes of *yin* and *yang* and established the trigrams, followed the course of hard and soft (unbroken and broken lines) and created the lines of the trigrams; went along with *Dao* and *De* (or *Dao-de*) and followed the principles of what was right, exhausting principle and going to the utmost in nature so as to arrive at what was decreed [for that object]. (*Explanation of the Trigrams Commentary on the* Book of Changes, p. 338)

In the *Xunzi* the two terms began to coalesce:

> Therefore to study up to and including rites and stop there is called the peak of *Dao-de*. (*Xunzi* 1, *An Exhortation to Learning*, line 29)
>
> In talking about what should be looked for in *Dao-de*, he does not have a divided allegiance to the Later Kings. (*Xunzi* 8, *The Teaching of the Ru*, lines 124–125 [Knoblock tr.])
>
> There are three kinds of awe: the awe of *Dao-de*, the awe inspired by cruel judicial investigations, the awe generated by complete madness. (*Xunzi* 16, *On Strengthening the State*, line 5)

Here the *Xunzi* used the same word, 'awe,' for all three kinds, but one would more normally translate these as awe, fear, and terror. The first is a kind of respect; the second is fear of being maltreated; the third is a reign of terror such as that unleashed by the French Revolution. *Dao-de* inspires awe. The two terms were not yet a full binome. It was only from the Han dynasty onward that they definitely formed a binome.

Daoist Use

With the *Laozi* the term *de* took on a new meaning: the internal support by which the myriad things exist. It is the "power" of the Way:

> The Way produces them (the myriad things); *De* nourishes them; matter gives them physical shape; surrounding forces complete them. Hence the myriad things honor the Way and value *De*. The honoring of the Way and the valuing of *De* does not depend on anyone's command but is constantly so of itself. (*Laozi* 51/MWD 14)

This is not to say that the sense of *de* as virtue is absent in the *Laozi*. Indeed in many passages *de* simply refers to virtue and virtuous conduct:

> The quality of great virtue follows simply from the Way. (*Laozi* 21/MWD 65)
>
> The person of high virtue is not aware of his or her virtue, and so really possesses virtue. The person of low virtue looks at his or her virtue, and so does not possess virtue. (*Laozi* 38/MWD 1)
>
> High virtue is like a valley. (*Laozi* 41/MWD 3)
>
> Repay resentment with virtue. (*Laozi* 63/MWD 26)

In referring to the practice of writing a contract on a tally of bamboo or silk, the *Laozi* says,

> Those who have virtue are in charge of the tally; those without virtue take charge of collecting the taxes. (*Laozi* 79/MWD 44)*

The new usage introduced by the *Laozi* was taken up and expounded in the *Zhuangzi*:

> Hence forms without the Way are not produced. What is produced without power (*de*) is not bright. (*Zhuangzi* 12, *Heaven and Earth*, lines 14–15)

---

*On tallies see R. Henricks, *Lao-Tzu: Te-Tao Ching* (New York: Ballantine, 1989), p. 184.

The same idea of inner creative force or power is present in the *Guanzi*:

> What is spacious and formless is called the Way. What transforms and fosters the myriad things is called the Power. (*Guanzi* 36, *Technique of the Heart A*, p. 3)
>
> The Power is the dwelling of the Way. When things acquire it they come to life. (Ibid., p. 7)*

In a well-known pun *De*, virtue or power, is equated with *de*, obtaining:†

> Therefore Power (*De*) is obtaining (*de*). Obtaining means obtaining that by which things are what they are. (Ibid.)‡

The internal force that is obtained, power, is what the Confucians called 'nature.' In these Daoist works the Way stands for the universal nature common to all things whereas power is the specific identity of each object by which it differs from all other things.

In the *Inner Chapters* of the *Zhuangzi*, *de* refers to virtue alone and is never used to form the binome *Dao-de*.

> Whether one succeeds or not and later does not encounter disaster is something only a person of virtue is able to do. (*Zhuangzi* 4, *Worldly Business Among Human Beings*, line 37)
>
> Knowing that one can do nothing about it and yet rest secure as if decreed is the peak of virtue. (Ibid., line 43)
>
> Therefore wherever virtue grows appearances are forgotten. (*Zhuangzi* 5, *The Signs of the Fullness of Power*, line 51)

In these cases virtue is high moral value.

---

* Rickett, *Kuan-Tzu*, p. 174, has "The Power is the release of the Way."

† Author's note: The *Guanzi's* homophonic explanation of virtue as obtaining is also found in Confucian literature. The *Record of Rites* says, "When both rites and music are obtained this is called having virtue. Virtue is acquiring" (*Record of Rites* 19, *Record of Music*, p. 205); "Virtue is that which is obtained by the self" (*Record of Rites* 45, *Xiangyinjiuyi*, p. 328). The *Guang Ya* collection of glosses also repeats the same homophonic definition (*Congshu Jicheng* 1160, *Guang Ya* 3, *Shi Gu* 3, p. 35).

Zhu Xi gives a more detailed exposition of the pun: "As a word 'Virtue' is obtaining. This means to practice the Way and obtain its fruits in one's mind" (*SKQS* 191, *Collected Notes on the* Analects 2, *On Administration*, #1, p. 17a). Zhu Xi means that in any given circumstances one is able to follow a definite norm.

‡ Following amendments by Guo Moruo; see Rickett, *Kuan-Tzu*, p. 175 n. 122.

In the *Outer Chapters, De* was also used in the sense of 'virtue.' In the following passage, it embraces the Confucian virtue of benevolence as well:

> This virtue is harmony; the Way is principle. There being noth-
> ing virtue does not embrace is benevolence. There being noth-
> ing the Way does not have a principle for is justice. (*Zhuangzi*
> 16, *Shan Xing*, line 2)

The *Outer Chapters* used the binome *Dao-de* but with a Daoist rather than a Confucian meaning. This shows that the two terms, *Dao* and *De*, moved together both in the sense of virtue and in the sense inaugurated by the *Laozi*.

> Many trust in benevolence and justice and use them, classifying
> them according to the five internal organs. Yet they are not the
> correct form of the Way and Power. (*Zhuangzi* 8, *Webbed Toes*,
> line 2)
>   If the Way and Power do not disappear, where then would
> one acquire benevolence and justice? (*Zhuangzi* 9, *Horses'
> Hooves*, line 12)
>   To destroy the Way and Power so as to make benevo-
> lence and justice is the fault of the sage. (Ibid., line 14)
>   This spacious calm, restful simplicity, this quiet expan-
> siveness and non-acting is the peace of heaven and earth and
> the utmost in the Way and Power. (*Zhuangzi* 9, *The Heavenly
> Way*, line 14)
>   Riding on the Way and Power and floating and roaming
> . . . (*Zhuangzi* 20, *Mountain Tree*, line 6)

These passages constitute an attack on the Confucian ideals of benevolence and justice. In the last the Way and the Power are the origin of all that is.

The Zhuangzian primitivist considered virtue to be that which is closest to nature:

> Moreover the one who uses the carpenter's curve and measur-
> ing cord, compass and square to correct things is one who cuts
> away from nature. To depend on cords, knots, glue, and lac-

quer to stick things firmly is to violate your powers. (*Zhuangzi* 8, *Webbed Toes*, line 14)

To be at one with not-knowing is to not depart from virtue. To be at one with not-desiring is called essential simple nature. If one has essential simple nature then the life of the people is obtained. (*Zhuangzi* 9, *Horses' Hooves*, line 10)

Thus the movement to use *dao* and *de* together is to be found in Confucian and Daoist writings of the late Warring States period.

45. Moral Obligation
Dangran
當然

We might expect to find terms that express the idea of moral obligation in an ethical theory. In fact, as we have seen, terms descriptive of human relationships are already prescriptive. Moreover, since terms that may apply to natural necessity can equally well apply to moral necessity, the two were not distinguished in early Chinese philosophical terminology. By the Song dynasty, however, Zhu Xi showed a clear difference between what is so by nature and what ought to be so. Dai Zhen acknowledged this type of distinction but argued that moral obligation coalesces with natural necessity.

Dang

The term *dang* literally means 'what is in face of': "*dang* is fields aligned with each other" (*Explanation of the Characters* 13b, p. 291). To be aligned with each other is to face each other. The *Guang Ya* collection of glosses says that *dang* is "to be straight" (*Guang Ya* 3, *Shi Gu* 3, p. 30). The word took on the sense of fittingness or appropriateness. Zang Xuanshu of Lu explained the roles of officials in states of differing sizes:

In the next State [medium-sized State] the Prime Minister is fit to be the middle-ranking minister of a large State and its middle ranking minister is fit to be the lower ranking minister while its lower minister is fit to be its highest civil servant. The Prime Minister of a small State is fit to be the lower-ranking minister of a large State; its middle ranking minister is fit to be the highest civil servant and its lower-ranking minister is fit to be the lower civil servant. High and low being thus is the ancient system of administration. (*Zuo's Commentary* 8, *Cheng* 3, p. 351)

The term was then extended to the moral sphere to refer to conduct that was in accordance with moral norms. It thus came to mean moral obligation.

The *Mencius* says,

For the one who knows, there is nothing that he does not know, accomplishing his duties is a matter of urgency. (*Mencius* 7, *Exhausting the Mind A*, #46)

Here the idea of obligation is contained in the term *dang*, translated as 'accomplishing.' The *Guanzi* defines *dang* as follows:

Responding to changes and not losing them is what is called '*dang*.' (*Guanzi* 11, *Zhou He*, 1:152)

These examples illustrate the early use of the term. It was not until the Song dynasty, however, that it became an important concept. Zhang Zai wrote,

What is most fitting [*zhi dang*] is what is called virtue [*de*]. (*SKQS* 697, *Correcting the Unenlightened* 9, *What Is Most Fitting*, p. 123b)

Dangran

Zhang Zai did not give an explanation of the term *dang* itself. It was Zhu Xi who was to use the expression *dangran*, 'what is necessarily so,' frequently and to give an explanation of it. In a note on the *Analects* Zhu Xi explained the Way in terms of what is necessarily so. The text of Confucius reads,

> In the morning I heard of the Way. (*Analects* 4, *Li Ren* #8, p. 168)

Zhu Xi comments,

> The Way is the principle by which things and affairs are necessarily so. (*Chapter and Verse Commentary on the* Analects 4, *Li Ren* #8, p. 14)

In his late work, *Some Questions on the Great Learning*, Zhu Xi distinguished between that which makes a thing to be that thing (*suo yi ran zhi li*) and that which makes it necessarily that thing (*suo dang ran zhi li*). The latter has the sense of moral obligation.

> As for the things under heaven they must each have a reason that makes them what they are and a norm which obliges them to be what they are. (*SKQS* 197, *Some Questions on the Great Learning*)

He discussed the relation between the two in the following terms:

> Whatever has sound, color, appearance and shape and flourishes within heaven and earth is a thing. If there is this thing then what makes it to be this thing cannot not be a norm of obligation particular to it and yet not contained within it. This norm is obtained from the gift of heaven and is not something human beings can make. Now to come closer to the point, the mind as a thing is the master of the body. Its substance has the nature of benevolence, justice, proper conduct and wisdom while its function has the feelings of compassion, shame, respect and moral discrimination. Though all mixed together yet in responding to circumstances each response has a governing principle and so there can be no confusion. (Ibid.)

What makes a thing what it is is its nature. The norm to which the same thing is bound is the principle by which it responds to circumstances. The mind has the four virtues by nature. Moral obligation only arises when the mind is required to respond to challenges. Thus when one sees an infant about to fall into a well one is obliged to respond with compassion and thus exercise the benevolence of the mind. The same passage is further discussed in the *Conversations*:

> It was asked, "The *Some Questions* says that things must each have a reason that makes them what they are and a norm which obliges them to be what they are. How can this be?" He replied, "In the case of serving one's parents one must be filial or serving one's elder brother one must be fraternal and the like; these are cases of norms of obligation. As for how one must be filial in serving one's parents or fraternal in serving one's elder brother these are the reasons which make something what it is." (*Conversations* 18, p. 414)

The moral norms impose obligations, but the content of those obligations must be spelled out by the nature of the things in question. One's obligations to parents and to elder brothers will differ because the natural relations of the self to parents and to elder brothers are different. Zhu Xi also explains the same point by expounding the first line of *Ode* 260:

> "Heaven engenders the mass of the peoples; for any given thing there is a rule." Seeing has a norm by which one sees; hearing a norm by which one hears. To see as things are and to hear as things are is the correct way. To see not as things are nor hear as things are is not correct. (*Conversations* 59, p. 1382)

To keep to the moral norm is not a matter of simply looking. One is obliged to make an effort to look at things as they really are and not to be led by simple appearances. Morality and reality are thus bound together. To act morally presupposes that one sees how things really are.

This point is made even clearer in Zhu Xi's explanation of the phrase 'thoroughly investigating principle':

> The one who thoroughly investigates principle wants simply to know what it is that makes things so and what it is that they ought to be. If one knows what it is that makes things so then one's intentions do not go astray. If one knows what it is that

they ought to be then one's conduct does not falter. (*Collected Writings* 64, #33.7, *Reply to Someone*, p. 1162b)

It is only by knowing the true reality of what things are that one can make correct decisions about what to do. Once one knows the truth about things then one must know what moral principles to apply so that one acts as one ought.

Bi-ran

Dai Zhen discussed the relation between obligation and nature in terms of a discussion of the terms *bi-ran*, 'what ought to be so,' and *zi-ran*, 'what is so of itself.' His *bi-ran* was the *dangran* of Zhu Xi. The term did, however, put the emphasis on the necessity of obligations:

> Examining from the point of view of the nature [*zi-ran*] of blood and *qi* so as to know why something is necessarily so is what is meant by the significance of principles. Nature and obligation are not two things. If one considers the nature of something then the clearer one makes it without straying from it in the slightest then this is what it necessarily ought to be. If one does so then there is no trepidation. If one does so then one has security. It is simply the utmost principle of what is naturally so. If one goes from what is naturally so and lets things flow away to be lost then one loses what is naturally so and this is not what is naturally so. Thus to return to what necessarily ought to be so is fitted to completing what is naturally so. (*An Evidential Study of the Meaning of Terms in the* Book of Mencius *A*, p. 18)

This is a natural morality. There is no conflict between moral obligation and reality. Moral obligation perfects the real nature of things and cannot go counter to them.

Dai Zhen's term *bi-ran* existed at least from the Wei-Jin period (from the third to the sixth century A.D.). It was employed without any sense of moral obligation. It expressed instead the way things necessarily are. Wang Bi used it in his commentary on the *Book of Changes*:

One makes clear from whence blessing and misfortune arise and so one does not speak wrongly. One discerns the principle of necessity [*bi-ran*] and so one does not vary in one's conduct. (*Notes on the* Book of Changes 16, *Yu hexagram*, p. 299)

Guo Xiang also used the phrase:

Not being able to be otherwise is the necessity of principle. (*SKQS* 1056, *Notes on Zhuangzi* 4, *Worldly Business Among Human Beings*, p. 24a)

46. Value

Gui, Liang-gui
貴, 良貴

The term gui *could be translated by 'noble,' since it refers both to the class of persons we term the nobility and to what is of genuine value, as in 'noble ideals.' Professor Zhang points out how the moral and social senses were both present in ancient texts. There is, though, little discussion of value in itself; rather, we are told what things are valuable. It is humans who emerge as beings of supreme worth and so some time is spent showing on what grounds humans may lay claim to such superiority.*

Gui, what is valuable, is an important concept in ancient Chinese philosophy. In ancient texts the term had two meanings. One was what is of social value; hence aristocratic titles and official posts are valuable. The second was moral value. In the latter sense it corresponded to the modern Chinese term for value, *jia-zhi* 價值. According to the *Explanation of the Characters* the terms referred to things:

'*Gui*' is that things are not cheap. (*Explanation of the Characters* 6b, p. 131a)

Jia is the value (*zhi*) of things. (Ibid. 8a, *New Appendix*, p. 168a)

From this application to things the term *gui* was extended to refer to social worth and then further to include moral worth. In a work by the Han-dynasty scholar Liu Xi the philosophical meaning of the term was further enhanced by a homophonic gloss:

> *Gui* is to turn back to [*gui* 歸]. It is that to which things turn back and look up to. (*SKQS* 221, *Explication of Terms* 4.1, *Explication of Language*, p. 400b)

Social and Moral Value

Many texts could be cited to illustrate the meaning of *gui*. As an initial illustration we shall confine ourselves to the *Mozi* and show the social use of *gui* and its use to refer to moral worth.

> If the people under heaven do not love each other then the strong will necessarily seize the weak, the rich will necessarily shame the poor, the noble [*gui*] will necessarily lord it over the base, the devious will necessarily cheat the simple.... If the people under heaven all love each other then the strong will not seize the weak; the many will not take from the few, the rich will not shame the poor and the noble will not lord it over the base. (*Mozi* 15, *Mutual Love B*, lines 8–9, 14)

Here *gui* refers to the nobles in society.

> Of all things none is more valuable [*gui*] than justice. (*Mozi* 47, *Valuing Justice*, line 1)

Here *gui* is a term of moral approbation.

Both meanings are found in the *Laozi*, sometimes in close proximity to each other. The social sense is evident in the following:

> To be rich and honored [*gui*] and to be proud is to set oneself on the road to disaster. (*Laozi* 9/MWD 53)
>
> The Way produces them (the myriad things); *De* nour-ishes them; matter gives them physical shape; surrounding forces complete them. Hence the myriad things honor the Way and value *De*. The honoring of the Way and the valuing of *De*

do not depend on anyone's command but is constantly so of itself. (*Laozi* 51/MWD 14)

Here *gui* means 'showing respect for.'

Blunt its sharpness; unravel its knots; harmonize its light; unify its dust*—this is called abstruse identity. Therefore one cannot bring it about that one is close. One cannot bring it about that one is distant. One cannot bring it about that one profits. One cannot bring it about that one is harmed. One cannot bring it about that one is honored [*gui*]. One cannot bring it about that one is demoted. Therefore it is what is valuable [*gui*] under heaven. (*Laozi* 56/MWD 19)

The first use of *gui* in this passage refers to social status, the second to moral value. The second use is likewise present in the following line from the *Analects*, attributed to Youzi:

Among the uses of the rites, bringing harmony is the most valuable. (*Analects* 1, *Xue Er* #12)

The value of human beings was brought out by both Xunzi and the *Classic of Piety*:

Among the species in heaven and earth human beings are the most valuable. (*Classic of Piety* 9, *Sheng Zhi*, line 1)

Water and fire have *qi* but not life; plants and trees have life but not knowledge; birds and beasts have knowledge but not a sense of justice; human beings have *qi*, life, knowledge and also a sense of justice; thus they are the most valuable thing under heaven. (*Xunzi* 9, *On the Regulations of a King*, lines 69–70)

Human beings are valuable in that they have a specific moral nature that is not possessed by other things.

Mencius distinguished between the value that a person has, given by heaven, simply by virtue of being that human being and the value that

---

* Lau translates this line as "Let your wheels move only along old ruts."

human society accords to others by granting ranks and honors. The former cannot be taken away but the latter are expendable.

> To want to be honored is common to the heart of all and all persons have within them that which is worthy of honor but they do not think of it. The value given by human beings is not truly honorable. Those whom Zhao the Great honors he can demote.* The Odes say, "He has given us our fill of wine; he has filled us with his virtue."† "Filled us with his virtue," that is "filled us with benevolence and respect." One who is so fed does not yearn for the rich meat and fine millet of human beings. On him rests a good reputation and renown so such a one does not desire the elegant embroidered garments of human beings. (*Mencius* 6, *Gaozi A*, #17)

Mencius discussed the ranks accorded by heaven and those accorded by human society:

> There are ranks accorded by heaven and ranks accorded by human beings. Benevolence, justice, loyalty, trustworthiness and delighting in the good without tiring of it: these are ranks accorded by heaven. Being a duke, prime minister, government official: these are ranks accorded by human beings. (Ibid. #16)

What was important for Mencius were the natural endowments of the human being. Notice, though, that they were moral virtues and a moral disposition to delight in the good. It was this that was of real value.

The *Zhuangzi* questioned commonly accepted social values and the Confucian way of treating human beings as more valuable than other things.

> From the point of view of the Way things do not have honorable and base. From the point of view of things each considers itself honorable and despises others. From the point of view of ordinary people honorable and base are not intrinsic to

---

*J. Legge explains that "Zhao the Great" refers to the name of one of the four great families in Jin who held sway in the country. Legge, *The Chinese Classics* (Oxford: Clarendon, 1863; reprint, Taipei: Southern Materials Centre, 1985), 2:420 n. 2.

† *Book of Songs* 3, *Da Ya* 2.3, *Ji Zui*, Legge, 4:475 (Ode 247).

things.... Formerly Yao and Shun abdicated the throne and yet ruled as emperors. Zhi Kuai abdicated and his realm ended. Tang and Wu fought and reigned. Duke Bai fought and was defeated. From this it can be seen that with regard to the rites of fighting and abdicating or the conduct of Yao and Shun, honorable and base have their proper time. It is not possible to make either into a constant rule. (*Zhuangzi* 17, *Autumn Floods*, line 29, 34–35)

In referring to honorable and base as not being evident from the point of view of ordinary people, the text is referring to social rank accorded by human beings. In referring to honorable and base as having their own time the text implies both social rank and natural rank. Although this passage relativizes all forms of ranking among things, it does so at the expense of the Way, which is to be valued above all else:

What is more honorable than the Way? (Ibid., line 47)

Another chapter expresses this in terms of the One:

Penetrating to the one *Qi* under heaven, the sage therefore honors the one. (*Zhuangzi* 22, *Knowledge Roams North*, line 13)

The highest form of existence is to roam independent of all things:

If one understands that what makes things things is itself not a thing, how would one not then be able to manage the hundred clans under heaven? To go out and enter the six apertures,* to roam amidst the nine continents, to go independently and return independently: this is called being independent. A person who is independent is one who is said to be most valuable. (*Zhuangzi* 11, *Preserve and Accept*, lines 62–63)

In other words, although these parts of the *Zhuangzi* denied the relative worth of different things, they did not rule out the absolute value of the Way. This goes to show that it is not possible to avoid all assessment of values.

---

* Or: go in all directions.

Value of the Human Being

Dong Zhongshu adopted the Confucian line according to which human beings are more valuable than other things. Their value lies in their ability to establish social relationships and to master the other things of the world.

> Human beings receive a decree from heaven; thus they transcend and are different from the mass of living things. At home there are the intimacies of father and child, elder and younger sibling. Outside there are the norms of ruler and minister, superior and inferior. They meet and gather and encounter each other and so there are the distinctions of venerable, aged, mature and young. There is decorum in their coming together and grace in their loving each other. This is what makes human beings valuable. They grow the five grains to feed themselves; use silk and hemp to clothe themselves, the six beasts to nourish themselves. They yoke oxen and harness horses, cage leopards and put tigers behind bars. This is the spirit that they are endowed with from heaven and that makes them more valuable than things. (*Han Shu* 56, *Biography of Dong Zhongshu: On the Policy of Xian Liang*, p. 3516)

While discussing the relative value of human beings, it is not inappropriate to consider another category, ability [*neng*].* The most interesting passage on this topic is one by Liu Yuxi that spells out what human beings are able to do in contrast with what heaven is able to do.

> In general within the realm of forms all have some abilities and some inabilities. Heaven is the greatest of things having form; human beings are the greatest of living beings. What heaven

---

*Zhang Dainian devotes a whole, though brief, section to this term in cosmology. The section quotes the *Analects, Mencius, Xunzi*, and the *Great Commentary of the* Book of Changes from the early period to show that *neng* means 'human ability.' Apart from the passage by Liu Yuxi translated here, the only other post-Han writer mentioned is Zhang Zai. Like Liu Yuxi, Zhang Zai distinguishes between heaven and human beings. "Heaven's ability is nature whilst human beings' planning is their ability" (*SKQS* 697, *Correcting the Unenlightened* 6, *Enlightenment Resulting from Sincerity*, p. 112b)

can do human beings are certainly not able to do. What human beings can do, heaven likewise in part cannot do. . . . With *yang* there is abundant growth; with *yin* there is death. Water and fire harm material things. Wood is solid; metal is sharp. In youthful vigor there is strength and health; in old age there is wasting away and blindness. Powerful energies contend for mastery; mighty forces contend for preeminence: such are the capabilities of heaven. With *yang* human beings do the planting; with *yin* they gather and reap. . . . They cut down timber and hollow out the solid [wood]. They sap and mine; they put the swordpoint to the whetstone. With righteousness they control the powerful and contentious; with the rites they distinguish the senior and junior. They favor the worthy and esteem the meritorious. They establish the highest excellence and prevent vice. Such are the capabilities of human beings. (*SBCK: Collected Works of Liu Mengde* 12.4, *Discourse on Heaven A*, p. 7a)

This list describes dominance over nature, social hierarchy, and moral virtues as all proper to human beings.

The special value of human beings lies in their intellectual grasp and hence practical application of knowledge, according to Shao Yong.

Only human beings can stand side by side with the myriad things and be the soul of the myriad things. Take the calls of birds and beasts. Each makes one sound according to its species. Human beings are those for whom there is nothing that they cannot do. If one extends this to other things there is nothing that is not so. Only human beings can make use of the juxtaposition of heaven and earth, sun and moon. Other species cannot do this. The life of human beings can truly be said to be valuable. If one considers heaven and earth and the value of human beings and does not value oneself this is to go counter to the principles of heaven and earth and there is nothing more unlucky than this. (*SKQS* 803, *Book of the Supreme Principles Governing the World: Outer Chapters on the Observation of Things*, pp. 1082b–1083a)

Shao Yong believed that human beings contained the perfection of all other species and also that they transcended all other species.*

Virtue as True Value

Zhou Dunyi used the example of Confucius' best pupil, Yan Hui, to point out the true values of life.

> Master Yan had a single bamboo dish of food and a single gourd to drink from and lived in an obscure lane. Others could not have coped with this distress but he did not let it change his joy. Riches and honor are what people like but Master Yan neither liked nor sought them and yet was happy in his poverty. What is the reason for this? Within heaven and earth there are the highest honors and greatest loves to be sought but he was different because he saw what was really great and ignored what was of little import. (*SKQS* 1101, *Book of Comprehending* 23, *Master Yan*, p. 430b)

In another chapter of the same work Zhou Dunyi stated that it is virtue that is valuable.

> Within heaven and earth the most respected thing is the Way and the most valuable thing is simply virtue. (Ibid. 24, *Teachers and Friends A*, p. 431a)

The value of moral principles lies not in them as such but in their use by human beings.

> As for the Way and justice [moral principles], it is only when one has them that they are valuable and respectable. When human beings are born they are ignorant. They remain fools if they do not have teachers and friends. This Way and justice are possessed through the help of teachers and friends and are then honored and respected. Is their significance not also important? Is their accumulation not also a joy? (Ibid. 25, *Teachers and Friends B*, p. 431b)

---

*For more on this topic see Chan, *Source Book*, p. 492.

This emphasis on the value of the moral life is a constant thread running throughout Confucian works.

47. Authority

Quan

權

The term *quan* is correctly translated as 'authority or power' when used in Legalist works, but in Confucian works the same term means 'assessment or moral authority.' It originally described a balance used to weigh things. From this meaning come the twin uses of power and assessment.

Assessment, Moral Authority

Confucius said,

> There are some people with whom one may study together but they cannot go on with us to understand principles. Should one indeed be able to go on with them to understand principles yet they maybe cannot be established in them with us nor be able to make assessment with us. (*Analects* 9, *Zi Han* #29, pp. 225–226)

With respect to this text, He Yan stated,

> Even if one studies with them perhaps they will reach unorthodox conclusions and thus not be able to attain to the Way. Even if they attain to the Way yet they will not have anywhere to be established. Even if they have somewhere to be established they will not be able to assess the extent of the weightiness of an issue. (*The Correct Meaning of the* Analects: *Collected Exegesis of the* Analects 9, *Zi Han*, p. 193)

Huang Kan quoted Wang Bi as saying,

> Assessment relates to the changes of the Way. Change does not have a constant substance. The numinous makes it clear. It is

present in a given person. It cannot be predicted. It is especially difficult. (*Wang Bi Jixiaoshi*, p. 627)

Thus in this passage *quan* is the assessment of relative weight that enables one to adapt to changes in circumstances.

A similar definition is found in the *Mencius*:

> By assessing one knows what is light, what heavy; by measuring, one knows what is long, what short. (*Mencius* 1, *King Hui of Liang A*, #7)
>
> Chun-yu Kun said, "Is it the norm that in giving and receiving presents men and women should not touch?" Mencius said, "It is the norm." He asked, "If one's sister-in-law is drowning may one rescue her by hand?" He replied, "To not rescue one's drowning sister-in-law would be to be a ravenous wolf. That in giving presents men and women should not touch is the norm. Saving one's drowning sister-in-law by hand is a matter of assessment." (*Mencius* 4, *Li Lou A*, #17)

Although assessment is here opposed to the norm, it is nonetheless obligatory in the circumstances. Mencius discussed three philosophers whom he believed guilty of doctrinaire adherence to principles irrespective of circumstances:

> Master Yang held "each for oneself." He would not have plucked out even one hair in order to benefit all-under-heaven. Master Mo proclaimed disinterested love. He would have rubbed his body from head to toe if he could thereby benefit all-under-heaven. Zi Mo holds a mid-way position. By holding a mid-way position he is nearer what should be but by holding a mid-way position without assessment he is like those who hold to their one doctrine. The reason I so dislike this holding to one point is that it offends against the Way. It makes one point and misses a hundred. (*Mencius* 7, *Exhausting the Mind A*, #26)

Doctrinaire adherence to maxims is inappropriate in the moral life. The moral person is one who can make the appropriate judgment in the circumstances.

A viewpoint similar to that of Confucius and Mencius was expressed in the *Gong Yang Commentary* to the *Spring and Autumn Annals*:

What is meant by assessment? Assessment is acting against the norm so that good may result. (*Gong Yang Commentary* 2, *Duke Huan* 11 pp. [56–57])

In modern speech 'the norm' is 'a general rule' whereas 'assessment' is 'lively awareness.' While respecting the general principles one should be careful to be alive to circumstances.

The trader holds the balance in his hand. If he holds it correctly the measure weighed out is correct. If he holds it incorrectly or uses false weights then what is weighed out will be incorrectly estimated:

People never obtain what they want in pure form. In dismissing what they dislike they never purely get rid of it. Hence whatever actions people do they should always conform to the balance. When the balance is held incorrectly, a heavy object will make it swing up and people will think it is light; a light object will make it swing down and people will think it is heavy. This makes people confused about what is light and what is heavy. When the balance is held incorrectly then disaster is mingled with desire and people think it is a blessing; blessing is mingled with dislike and people think it is disastrous. This is what makes people confused about what brings blessing and what is disastrous. The Way is the correct balance both in the past and today. If you depart from the Way and choose your own standard then you will not know what disasters and blessings will come to you. (*Xunzi* 22, *On the Rectification of Terms*, lines 71–74)

The correct balance shows what is weighed out correctly, that is, what is light and what is heavy. The opposite is scheming after *quan*, which is here best translated as 'power':

Lords who honor the rites and respect the worthy will reign; those who stress law and love the people will be lords-protector; those who like profit and are much inclined to trickery will be in danger; those who scheme for power, plot revolutions and fall into intrigues will perish. (*Xunzi* 16, *On Strengthening the State*, line 5)

Scheming after power involves not respecting what is right and what is worthy of trust:

> Thus those who use the State to establish what is right will reign; those who establish what is worthy of trust will be lords-protector; those who establish scheming after power will perish.* Among these three the intelligent ruler will make a prudent choice. (*Xunzi* 11, *Of Kings and Lords-Protector*, line 4)

In his discussion of *quan*, Dong Zhongshu distinguished between the normal rites and the varying rites. To fit the sense of the term in his exposition it is best to translate it as 'authority.'

> In the *Spring and Autumn Annals* there are normal rites and varying rites. Thus the method of pacifying one's nature and quietening one's mind is a normal rite. When one's nature is not pacified nor one's mind quiet and yet one still does not deviate from the Way, then this is a varying rite.... When one is clear about what is normal and what is varying then one can distinguish between light and heavy and exercise proper authority. (*Luxuriant Gems of the Spring and Autumn Annals* 4, *Jade Courage*, pp. 74, 75)

Although what is a matter of varying rites is not in accord with the norm, it nonetheless does not depart from the Way. Dong quoted two examples from history† in which a person did something wrong in order to attain a greater good and concluded,

> Thus in all human conduct to put what is crooked first and what is right last is what is meant by attaining authority. (Ibid. 3, *Bamboo Forest*, p. 60)

There is, however, a certain limit on what "wrongs" are permissible:

> Even when authority must be opposed to the norm yet it must still be in the realm of what is permissible. What does not lie

---

*Although in the previous quotation Knoblock translates *quan mou* as 'scheming after power,' here he translates the same phrase as 'a record of expediency and opportunism.'

†Feng Choufu was a spearman caught in battle who pretended to be his master and delivered himself up to death so as to allow his master to escape (Legge, *Chinese Classics*, vol. 5, *Zuo's Commentary* 8, *Cheng* 2, p. 345); Ji Zhong was forced to make an oath to the people of Song so as to save the heir to the throne of Zheng. (Legge, ibid. 2, *Huan* 11, p. 57).

within the realm of the permissible is not to be done even in
the face of death. (Ibid. 4, *Jade Courage*, p. 79)

Thus within the sphere of what is permitted according to fundamental
principles there is a distinction between adherence to the norm and exercise of one's own authority when special circumstances demand it. This
moral authority enables the person to make judgments not foreseen in
normal guidelines.

Authority: Power

The early Confucians did not discuss authority as the exercise of power by
the ruler. This was a topic discussed by the Legalists. It is found in the
Conversations of the Lord Protector, a chapter of the *Guanzi* based in particular on the thought of Shen Buhai:

> Now arms flourish on authority and authority flourishes on
> lands. Thus when the feudal princes acquire the benefits of
> land then authority follows from this. When they lose the
> benefits of land their authority goes away.... Now authority is
> what the divine sage takes as his capital. (*Guanzi* 23, *Con-
> versations of the Lord Protector*, 1:340)

The chapter of the same work titled *Conforming to the Law* was closer
to the Confucianism of Xunzi than to Legalist philosophy. It discussed
power:

> What makes a prince a prince is power [*shi*]. Thus if a prince
> loses power then his ministers will dominate him.... Regal
> sway and power are more valuable than ranks and salaries....
> Do not share your regal sway and power for the sake of rank
> and salary. Thus it is said, "Power is not to be given to others."

Authority and power are closely connected. The ruler must have a firm grip
on his position and authority and not allow the ministers to control him.

The *Book of Lord Shang* discussed authority as one of three methods
of managing a country:

> There are three ways to manage a State: the first is by law, the
> second by confidence and the third by authority. Law is what

the prince and ministers make together; confidence is what the prince and ministers establish together; authority is what the prince alone controls. When the lord loses his grip then he is in peril. When prince and ministers relax the law and give rein to private interests then there will inevitably be disorder. Thus one establishes the law and clarifies roles and does not allow private interests to harm the law, then one can manage. When authoritative control is confined to the prince then he holds sway. When the people have confidence in his rewards then affairs are successful. When the people do not have confidence in his punishments then there is trickery without end. Only the enlightened lord loves authority and stresses confidence and does not allow private interests to harm the law. (*Book of Lord Shang* 14, *Practising Authority*, p. 18, lines 13–16)

Authority is the absolute power of the ruler. In enumerating the three, law, confidence, and authority, the *Book of Lord Shang* was arguing that all are needed to direct a state.

Shen Dao associated authority with position. When one's position is respected then one has authority.

Therefore when the worthy are subject to the unworthy then authority is slighted. When the unworthy are able to be subject to the worthy then position is respected. Yao was a commoner and was not able to regulate even the neighboring families but once installed on the throne as king his commands ran and his prohibitions were effective. From this it can be seen that worthiness does not suffice to command obedience while power and position are enough to cause the unworthy to be subject. (Fragments 11, 12, appendixes 3, 13)

The same passage occurs in a slightly different form quoted in the *Hanfeizi*:

When the worthy are subject to the unworthy then authority is slighted and position low. When the unworthy are able to be subject to the worthy then authority is respected and position honored. (*Hanfeizi* 40, *A Critique of the Doctrine of Position* #1)

Han Fei in particular discussed the problem of the invariability of authority and power. He believed that if the great ministers took authority to themselves then the state would perish. The fifteenth chapter opens thus:

> In general when the State of the lord is small while the fiefs of private families are big then authority is slighted and the ministers respected and there is the possibility of perishing. (*Hanfeizi*, 15 *Portents of Ruin* #1)

He emphasized that the ministers should not be allowed to share in the authority of the ruler:

> Though Wang Liang and Zao Fu were skilled charioteers, if you let them hold the reins together and drive they would not be able to manage the horses. How then can the lord share authority with his ministers and still manage the government? (*Hanfeizi* 35, *Outer Congeries of Sayings: Lower Right Series* #6)

The chapter on the lord opens in a similar vein:

> What puts the person of the lord in peril and his State in danger is that the great minister is overesteemed and the advisors on left and right have too much sway. By 'overesteemed' one means that there is no law; rather, usurpation runs riot. They have hold of the handles of the State and give rein to private interests. By 'sway' one means that which has a grasp of authority and power and weighs up what is light and what is heavy. These two matters cannot but be examined. (*Hanfeizi* 52, *The Lord* #1)

These observations reflect the way in which ministers were exercising power in the states of the Chinese oecumene in the fourth and third centuries B.C. Han Fei advocated concentrating all power in the ruler's hands. He also used the term 'authority' in the Confucian sense discussed above:

> The early sages have a saying which runs, "When compasses have faults or water has waves, should I want to correct them there is nothing that can be done." This saying is applicable to the issues requiring authoritative assessment. (*Hanfeizi* 47, *Eight Fallacies* #5)

48. Rights and Duties

Fen, Ming-fen

分, 名分

The terms for rights and duties in modern Chinese are borrowed translations of Western concepts. Ancient Chinese lacked any terms that corresponded exactly to the modern usage. In ancient Chinese works, however, there was a notion that combined both concepts in one term, namely *fen*, 'portion.'* The fact that there was but one term emphasizes the close relation between rights and duties. It would be wrong to demand that others fulfill their duties without simultaneously recognizing their rights. Likewise, it is wrong to concentrate only on one's rights and refuse to shoulder the burden of one's duties.

The term appears in the *Great Commonwealth* text of the *Record of Rites*:

> Men have their portion; women have a home [to be married into]. (*Record of Rites* 9, *Evolution of Rites*, p. 120)

Zheng Xuan gave it the following annotation:

> 'Portion' is one's job. (*SKQS* 115, *Zheng Xuan's Notes on the Record of Rites* 21, *Evolution of Rites*, p. 444a)

That is, the portion comprises a given set of rights with a corresponding set of duties. In the *Autumn Floods* dialogue in the *Zhuangzi* the term 'portion' occurs in a passage on the relativity of all things:

> Throughout the realm of things, measuring has no limit, times have no stop, portions have no constancy, nothing whether ending or starting stays as it was. Therefore the wisest, because they have a full view of far and near, do not belittle the smaller or make much of the greater, knowing that measuring has no limit; because they have an assured comprehension of past and

---

*The term 'portion' is used here in the sense of 'part' as in the Christmas carol "In the Bleak Mid-Winter," which reads, "If I were a wise man, I would do my part," "part" being the role and contribution expected of me. Since 'part' has many other meanings, too, the term 'portion' is here adopted.

present, they are not disheartened by indefinite delay or on tiptoes for that which is in reach, knowing that times have no stop; because they are discerning about cycles of waxing and waning, they are not pleased when they win or anxious when they lose, knowing that our portions have no constancy. (*Zhuangzi* 17, *Autumn Floods*, lines 15–17 [Graham tr.])

The portions are what one gains or loses, which means in effect what rights accrue to one.

There is a chapter in *Mr. Lu's Spring and Autumn Annals* dedicated to the topic of portions:

> In general the lord should examine portions and only then will his administration attain its objectives and trickery, deceit, treachery and undercover operations be annihilated. . . . For the lord who has the Way what makes it possible for him to employ his ministers is that he has the reins. What are the reins? Rectifying titles and examining portions are the reins. Thus one allots according to what a person really does and then examines the title of his office so as to ask for the required work. One listens to what a person says so as to investigate what kind of person one is dealing with and then one does not employ the corrupt. Should many titles not correspond to reality then many affairs will not correspond to what is employable. Thus the lord cannot not examine titles and portions. (*Mr. Lu's Spring and Autumn Annals* 17.1, *Examining Portions*, pp. 1029, 1030)

"Rectifying titles and examining portions" means to see what the rights and duties of each officeholder are as stated on paper and then to see how far actual performance matches what is written. Gao You commented on this text as follows:

> Portion is said of the portions of benevolence, justice, rites and statutes, killing and giving life, giving and taking. (Ibid., p. 1032 n. 2)

Here benevolence, justice, rites, and statutes can be seen as duties whereas killing, giving life, giving, and taking are rights.

The same work also discussess the right to life and the duty to die for a greater good than life:

> The outstanding person attains to the portions of life and death. When one attains to the portions of life and death then profit and harm, existence and passing away are not able to deflect one. (*Mr. Lu's Spring and Autumn Annals* 20.3, *Knowing Portions*, p. 1345)

'Portion' here means being ready to die when one ought to die. Gao You makes the point more clearly:

> The gentleman dies for justice and does not seek to maintain life at all costs. If a thing be unjust yet he can keep his life he will not do it. . . . He does not keep hold of life in order to gain profit or existence nor does he relinquish death because of the risks of harm or passing away. (Ibid., p. 1348 nn. 2, 3)

Life has the right to life but under certain conditions one prefers to forgo the right to life and exercise one's duty to die.

Gao You also annotated the term 'portion' in the *Huainanzi*:

> In ancient times the Son of Heaven had one imperial domain and the feudal princes each had their own similar domain. Each had his own portion and they could not invade each other. (*Huainanzi* 8, *Ben Jing*, p. 60, line 19)

Gao notes that

> A portion is a boundary. (*Huainanzi [Zhuzi jicheng xinbian]*, p. 267)

The boundary delimits the area in which each has rights.

Thus we must recognize that the term 'portion' comprises both rights and duties. It is only a very general concept, however, and is not as clear as the distinction of rights and duties in modern discourse.*

---

*Note that the United Nations Declaration of Human Rights also entails duties for citizens and governments.

B. Psychology

I. Human Nature

This part considers three terms: xing, *'human nature,'* qing, *'emotions,' and* cai, *'talent.' These are descriptive of what it is that constitutes a human person as such. The following part looks at the terms used for mental activities.*

49. Human Nature
Xing, Qi-zhi
性, 氣質

In Western philosophy the question of what is innate in man arose especially in epistemology. In China the question is one of moral philosophy. In fact, under the rubric of xing *Chinese philosophers discussed various issues: What is it that distinguishes man from other animals? How are body and mind related? Are moral principles naturally inherent in all human beings or are they to be learnt? The debate originated with Mencius and Gaozi but was dominated by Zhu Xi, who argued for a clear separation between moral principles and the animal side of man. In response, the Qing thinkers chosen by Professor Zhang argued for the unity of the human person.*

Theories of human nature in ancient Chinese philosophy abound and are very complicated. In my previous work, *The Scope of Chinese Philosophy*, I have already laid out the essential points and so do not need to go into so much detail now.* Here I set out the special meanings of the concept and analyze its evolution.

By and large two trends of interpretation are to be found. On one

---

* *Collected Works of Zhang Dainian*, vol. 2, *The Scope of Chinese Philosophy* (Beijing: Qing Hua University, 1990). This work was written in 1936 (author's handwritten note in the volume presented to the present translator.) On human nature see pp. 220–292.

hand 'human nature' refers to what is innate; on the other, it refers to what distinguishes human beings from animals and is thus specific to humans.

Pre-Song Theories

Gaozi defined human nature as what is innate:

> What is innate is what is meant by human nature. (*Mencius* 6, *Gaozi A* #3)

What is innate is what is 'natural' in the most immediately obvious sense:

> To enjoy food and admire beauty is human nature. (Ibid. #4)

Gaozi took native ability to be human nature. The *Mencius* records the debate between Mencius and Gaozi whereas the *Mozi* contains an assessment of Gaozi's thought. Mencius did not give his own views of human nature but the nature of his questions carried certain implications. He asked Gaozi,

> Is the nature of a hound like the nature of an ox and the nature of an ox like the nature of human beings? (Ibid. #3)

This would seem to imply that all three have different natures according to Mencius. In another context Mencius discussed grounds for asserting similarity of nature:

> Thus for whatsoever is of the same kind there is always likeness. Why should human beings be an exception? The sage and I are of the same kind. (Ibid. #7)

All human beings have a common likeness. Although there is no definite statement to the effect that humans differ in nature from animals, this is in fact implicit:

> That whereby human beings differ from animals is minute. The common people dismiss it while the gentleman fosters it. (*Mencius* 4, *Li Lou B* #19)

The difference lies in the a priori human moral consciousness.

Xunzi held a view of nature that is similar to Gaozi's definition of human nature as life, but unlike Gaozi, who believed that human nature was amoral, Xunzi held it to be immoral.

> Whatsoever is a matter of nature is the fruit of heaven. It cannot be studied nor effected.... What cannot be studied nor effected and is in the human person is what is meant by human nature. (*Xunzi* 23, *The Nature of Man Is Evil*, lines 11–12)
>
> That whereby life is as it is is called nature. (*Xunzi* 22, *On the Rectification of Terms*, line 2)

Xunzi also discussed the specific characteristics of human beings, but he did not consider these to be part of human nature:

> What is it that defines a human being as a human being? I say it is his ability to distinguish.* (*Xunzi* 5, *Contra Physiognomy*, lines 23–24)

The Han authors Dong Zhongshu and Wang Chong defined human nature in a similar way. Dong said,

> The traits that follow naturally from life are what is meant by human nature. Human nature is the basic stuff. (*Luxuriant Gems of the Spring and Autumn Annals* 35, *The Profound Examination of Names and Appellations*, pp. 291–292)

Wang wrote,

> Human nature is rooted in what is naturally so. Good and evil have stuff. (*Balanced Inquiries* 13, *On Original Nature*, p. 29)

In the Tang dynasty, Han Yu related human nature to the Confucian virtues:

> Human nature is born along with birth.... There are five things which distinguish it as human nature: benevolence, rites, trust, justice and wisdom. (*SBBY: Collected Works of Mr. Chang Li* 11.2, *Original Nature*, pp. 131a–b)

---

*John A. Knoblock (*Xunzi: A Translation and Study of the Complete Works*: I.) explains this as the ability to make distinctions of social class.

These varying views, which span the Warring States and the Tang periods, can be summarized in two points. The first is that what is innate is human nature and the second is that human nature is the distinguishing trait of human beings. Xunzi, Dong Zhongshu, Wang Chong, and Han Yu all expressed the first point. While agreeing on this point they nonetheless held different opinions as to the nature of what is innate. Gaozi believed that it is amoral. Xunzi believed that it is immoral. Dong Zhongshu and Wang Chong both thought that human nature is a mixture of good and bad but were inclined to believe in its innate goodness. Han Yu came down clearly on the side of the moral virtue of human nature.

The Song Dynasty Prior to Zhu Xi

The philosophers of 'principle' of the Song dynasty had new theories about human nature. Zhang Zai distinguished between the nature of heaven and earth, common to all things including persons, and the nature of *qi* and stuff [*zhi*], which is specific to each individual thing:

> First there is the form and then there is the nature of *qi* and stuff. If one reflects well then one will find the nature of heaven and earth. Thus the nature of *qi* and stuff is something the gentleman has and is not part of nature. (*SKQS* 697, *Correcting the Unenlightened* 6, *Enlightenment Resulting from Sincerity*, p. 114a)

The "form" is the human body. One is first aware of one's own special nature, "the nature of *qi* and stuff," but if one reflects then one will realize that one also has a nature in common with all other things in heaven and earth. The nature of *qi* and stuff is particular to the individual and therefore partial, whereas the nature of heaven and earth is common to all and therefore universal and unbiased:

> As regards human strength and weakness, slowness and speed, having talent and lacking talent: this is the bias of *qi*. Heaven is rooted in and shares in harmony without bias. If one nourishes one's *qi* and goes with it back to its root and does so without bias then one will fully understand one's nature and this heaven. (Ibid., p. 114b)

Cheng Hao recognized that what is innate is nature, but believed that this refers to what is given by *qi*. More fundamental is the stillness that underlies human life and that cannot be grasped:

> What is above 'human life being still.' . . .
>
> It is not possible to comprehend and talk about what is above 'human life being still.' (*SKQS* 698, *Surviving Works of the Two Chengs* 1, p. 14b)

The phrase "human life being still" comes from the *Record of Rites*:

> Human life being still is the nature from heaven. Once it encounters things it moves. This is the desires of nature. (*Record of Rites* 19, *Record of Music*, p. 206)

"Nature from heaven" means what is naturally so.

Cheng Yi proposed the theory that nature is principle:

> Nature is principle. It is what is called the principle of nature. All the principles of under heaven originally emerge from it. There are none that are not good. (*SKQS* 698, *Surviving Works of the Two Chengs* 22a, p. 235a)
>
> Mencius says that human nature is good. This is so. Even though Xunzi and Yang Zhu neither understand nature what makes Mencius stand out among the Confucians is that he alone understood nature. Nature has nothing in it which is not good. . . . Nature is principle. Principle from Yao and Shun down to the common person is all one. (Ibid. 18, pp. 164b–165a)

The content of nature is principle, and this is benevolence, justice, rites, wisdom, and trust:

> What is undertaken from nature is all good. The sage goes along with its goodness and this has the names of benevolence, justice, rites, wisdom and confidence. (Ibid. 25, p. 255b)

Cheng Yi also accepted that what is innate is human nature but did not believe that this was the root of nature:

> Anyone who talks about the place of human nature must look at how its meaning is established. Moreover, if one talks about

human nature as good then it is the root of nature. What is
innate is what is meant by nature. It refers to what is given.
(Ibid. 18, p. 167a)

What he here termed "the root of nature" is elsewhere referred to as "the
utmost root and the deepest source of nature":

When Mencius talks about goodness he refers to the utmost
root and deepest source of nature. (Ibid. 3, p. 58a)

In other words, Chen Yi distinguished two levels of human nature. The
deepest source is principle, which can be couched in terms of the Confucian moral virtues. Nature is what is innate and is given by qi. The latter
is illustrated by the following passage:

As in popular speech like saying that one's nature is fast or
slow. How can nature be fast or slow? This way of talking of
nature is the nature that is innate. (Ibid. 18, p. 167a)

Nature in terms of principle cannot be fast or slow. Only nature derived
from qi can have these characteristics.

Zhu Xi

Zhu Xi continued in the line set by Zhang Zai and the Chengs but developed and explained their theories in greater detail. He modified Gaozi's
theory that what is innate is nature to produce a new theory:

What is innate is what is meant by qi; the principle of what
is innate is what is meant by human nature. (*Conversations* 59,
p. 1376)

He explained the principle of what is innate as follows:

Regarding human nature it is not as if there is something
within that is called 'nature'; rather, it is just that things ought
to be so; that is what is called 'nature.' It is just that human
beings ought to do so that is what is 'nature.' (*Conversations*
60, p. 1426)

Hence 'nature' simply consists of the norms human beings ought to observe. He distinguished two kinds:

> There are two kinds of 'nature': there is what is called 'the nature of principle' and there is what is called 'the nature of *qi* and stuff.' (*Conversations* 95, p. 2431)

He explained the lower kind in these terms:

> 'What is innate is nature' refers to what is born as the nature which is composed of the interchange and mingling of what is given by '*qi*.' It is not the nature of principle. (*Conversations* 95, p. 2425)

The nature of principle is what Cheng Yi called 'principled nature.'

Zhu Xi explained the relation of these two kinds of nature in ontological terms:

> *Grosso modo* human beings have a given form and *qi*; thus it is this principle begins from amidst form and *qi* and is called 'nature.' Yet in speaking of it as nature one has already encountered the fact that there is life and at the same time there is *qi* and stuff. It does not merit being termed the original substance of nature. Moreover, the original substance of nature is not muddled up within it. It is required that a person should see beyond this that his original substance is originally not removed from it nor is it muddled up inside it. (*Conversations* 95, p. 2430)

The original substance of nature is principle. What is not amid form and *qi* is what is called 'principle'; the principle that is within form and *qi* is called 'nature.' Principle in its pure form is not embodied; when it is embodied it is called 'human nature.' Principle is the nature of heaven and earth:

> In discussing the nature of heaven and earth then one is speaking solely of principle. In discussing the nature of *qi* and stuff then one is speaking of the mixture of principle and *qi*. (*Conversations* 4, p. 67)

Note that whereas Zhang Zai used the phrase 'the nature of heaven and earth' to refer to what is universal and common to all things, for Zhu Xi it was a matter of principle alone.

Zhu Xi also explained what he meant by *qi* and stuff:

> 'Stuff' when spoken of along with *qi* is the 'stuff' of *qi*-stuff. (*Conversations* 4, p. 76)

'*Qi*-stuff' is *qi* and stuff. *Qi* and stuff are distinguished from one another: *qi* is the *qi* that is given, whereas stuff is the form and body. He explained how *qi* is given:

> When what is given is the *qi* of essence and courage then one is a sage or a worthy. This is indeed to receive *qi* in its entirety and principle in its correctness. If what is received is clear and bright then one is courageous and chirpy. If what is received is generous then one is gentle and peaceable. If what is received is clear and lofty then one is honorable. If what is received is plentiful then one is rich. If what is received is longevity then one has a long life. If what is received is run-down, decrepit, feeble and sullied, then one is stupid and unworthy. One is then poor, mean and short-lived. Heaven has a given *qi* to give birth to a person and then many other things flow from it. (*Conversations* 4, p. 77)

This was to ascribe all differences between peoples to what is received from *qi*. These differences included social distinctions of wealth and status. This was certainly biased and false. Zhang Zai's theory of *qi* and stuff as the particular nature of each individual was more reasonable.

Because Zhu Xi insisted that human nature is principle he made a sharp distinction between human nature and the mind. He opposed any view of knowledge, awareness, or movement as human nature:

> The mind and nature have but one principle. They can be spoken of together or separately. One must know that which unites them and that which separates them. So much is possible. As for saying that nature is the mind that is not possible. Nor can one say that the mind is human nature. (*Conversations* 18, p. 411)
>
> Mind and human nature are distinct. The spiritual part is mind; the substantial part is nature. The spiritual part is knowing and being aware of. (*Conversations* 16, p. 323)

Knowing and being conscious are proper to the mind and not to nature as such. He reckoned that Gaozi's theory that what is innate is human nature was said of knowledge and consciousness and was thus erroneous:

> What is innate refers to human knowing, consciousness and movement. Gaozi's talk about human nature ... is very like modern Buddhist descriptions of nature as being what is used.... Human nature is what human beings obtain from heavenly principle. What is innate is what human beings obtain from the *qi* of heaven. Human nature is what is above form; *qi* is what is below form. In the life of human beings and things, there is nothing that is not nature and also nothing that is not *qi*. Now in talking about it from the point of view of *qi* one is referring to knowing, consciousness and movement and in this human beings and other things do not differ, while in talking about it from the point of view of principle then one refers to the gifts of benevolence, justice, rites and wisdom and on this how can things obtain the wholeness of these qualities? This is what makes it so that human nature is in no respect not good and that humans are the soul of the myriad things. (*SKQS* 197, *Collected Notes on the* Mencius 6, *Gaozi A*, p. 167b)

In his conversations Zhu Xi expanded on this issue:

> Gaozi merely says that what is innate is human nature. He refers to the movement of hands and feet, the hearing and seeing of ears and eyes and the knowing and awareness of the mind. ... He only speaks of what is innate, such as essence and spirit, the spiritual and material souls and whatsoever is used and moves. Just as the Zen masters ask, "What is it to be Buddha?" and reply, "To see human nature is to be Buddha." Or "What is human nature?" "Human nature is what is used and what moves." This is said of the seeing of the eyes, the hearing of the ears, the grasping of the hands, the moving of the feet, which are all nature. They talk all about this but only refer to what is below form. (*Conversations* 59, p. 1376)

Zhu Xi distinguished between nature and mind on the basis of the distinction between what is above form and what is below form. His theory of human nature can be described as a metaphysical theory built on Mencius' suggestion that there is a distinction between the nature of human beings and of animals. For Zhu Xi human beings and animals had a common ability to move and to be conscious, but they differed in that human beings possess the Confucian virtues. Hence *human* nature was but benevolence, justice, rites, and wisdom. In fact, animals and humans differ widely in their movements and abilities to know. Moreover, the principles of morality cannot be divorced from the faculties that enable one to be aware of those principles. Zhu Xi made human nature into something too overtly metaphysical.

The principle of human nature is also referred to as the 'principle of nature and justice.'

> "Is the virtuous nature also spoken of as the nature of principle and justice?" He said, "Yes." (*Conversations* 64, *Mean and Harmony* 27, p. 1585)

Zhu Xi's pupil Chen Zhi said,

> Nature is the heavenly principle which is in the human mind. It is not the equal of what is received; thus the early Confucians made a distinction between what they termed the nature of justice and principle and the nature of blood and *qi*. Benevolence, justice, rites and wisdom are the nature of justice and principle. Knowing, awareness and movement are the nature of *qi* and stuff. (*SBBY: Song and Yuan Confucian Schools of Learning* 65, *Scholarly Record of Muzhong*, p. 10a)*

Although Chen was referring to the distinction made by the early Confucians, in fact it was Zhu Xi whom he had in mind.

Zhu Xi rigorously separated nature and mind. The reason for his so doing was to drive a wedge between reason and emotions. Although it is true that Cheng Yi's principled nature, Zhu Xi's nature of principle, and Chen Zhi's nature of justice and principle are not the same as modern philosophers' rational nature, they are all close to it. 'Knowing,' 'aware-

---

*Chen Zhi (from the late twelfth to the early thirteenth century). *Zi*: Qi Zhi, known as Qian Shi, from Yong Jia (now in Zhejian Province). He was a teacher whose works are published as *Collected Works of Mu Zhong*.

ness,' and 'movement' refer mainly to the emotions. What Zhu Xi referred to as the nature of principle was the inner moral imperative. He believed that this inner moral imperative was given by heaven and was a priori. His theory of human nature may be termed a form of a priori ethics.

The Ming Dynasty

Lu Jiuyuan took a view opposite to that of Zhu Xi.* He believed that the mind and nature are basically without any difference:

> As for 'emotion' [*qing*], 'nature' [*xing*], 'mind' [*xin*] and 'talent' [*cai*], they are in fact all much about the same. The words are different, that is all. (*SKQS* 1156, *Selected Sayings of Mr. Xiang-shan* 3, p. 580b)

Wang Shouren concluded a letter by saying,

> If one tries to see and understand from the point of view of human nature then *qi* is nature and nature is *qi*. Originally there is no possibility of separating nature and *qi*. (*SBBY: Complete Books of Yang Ming* 2, *Instructions for Practical Living* 2, *Letter to Zhou Daotong*, p. 16b, WTC #150)†

By opposing the view that there is any distinction between nature and the mind he was also opposing the view that there are two distinct types of nature. The point was made firmly by the late Ming scholar Liu Zongzhou:‡

> Whoever talks about nature always refers to *qi* and stuff. Some might say that there is the nature of *qi* and stuff and the

---

*Lu Jiuyuan (1139–1193). *Zi*: Zi Jing, called Xiang Shan, from Jinxi, near Fuzhou (now called Linchuan), Jiangxi Province. He was a minor official and teacher who was considered the founder of the school of mind by Wang Shouren. His works were edited by his son. On his philosophy see C. Lyman van Law, *The Philosophy of Lu Hsiang-shan, a Neo-Confucian Monistic Idealist* (Ph.D. thesis, Union Philosophical Seminary, New York, 1939).

† Zhou Heng (fl. 1510–1530), a minor official. This letter dates from 1524.

‡ Liu Zongzhou (1578–1645). *Zi*: Qi Dong; *Hao*: Nian Tai, known as Ji Shan, from Shan Yin, modern Shao Xing, Zhejiang Province. He died on a hunger strike following the collapse of Ming rule in southern China. He was a teacher of Huang Zongxi.

nature of justice and principle but this is not the case. Filling up heaven and earth there is only the nature of *qi* and stuff. There is certainly no nature of justice and principle. If one says there is the principle of *qi* and stuff how can there also be the principle of justice and principle? (*SBBY: Scholarly Records of Ming Confucians* 62, *Scholarly Record of Ji Shan*, pp. 492a–b)

This is to say that human nature should not be split into two parts.

His pupil, Huang Zongxi, discussed the relation between nature and mind:

Humans receive the *qi* of heaven and come into life. There is but one mind alone and movement and stillness, joy and anger, grief and happiness circle around in unending succession. When it [the mind] should be compassionate, it is compassionate; when ashamed, it is ashamed; when respectful it is respectful and when able to distinguish right and wrong, it is able to distinguish right and wrong. With a thousand ends and ten thousand threads, weaving and intermingling, on in sequence such that one cannot fathom it, this is what is called human nature. At the beginning there is no question of a thing established before the mind which is added on to the center of the mind.... Therefore nature is the nature of mind. It houses awareness and naturally has a reasonable mind so there is no need to look for any so-called nature. Also it houses the *qi* of contracting and expanding, going and coming so there is no need to look for any so-called principle. (Ibid. 47, *Scholarly Record of All Confucians* B1, pp. 361a–b)

This is to look at the relation of mind and nature from the point of view of principle and *qi*. As principle is within *qi* so nature is within the mind. One should not oppose the awareness of the mind to nature. Zhu Xi was opposed to the view that the uses of the mind could be deemed 'nature' whereas Huang Zongxi held precisely that nature lies in the awareness of the mind.

The Qing Dynasty

Wang Fuzhi did not support the view that human beings have two natures. He reached his own conclusion as to what the nature of *qi* and stuff is:

> The so-called nature of *qi* and stuff is a reference to the nature within *qi* and stuff. Stuff is the stuff of human form and stuff. It includes the principle of life. What is within *qi* and stuff is full of *qi*.... Thus stuff includes *qi* and *qi* includes principle. Stuff includes *qi*; thus one person has the life of one person. *Qi* includes principle so one person has the nature of one person. (*Collected Complete Surviving Books of Chuanshan* 12, *Great and Full Explanation on Reading the Four Books* 7.2, *Analects* 17, *Yang Huo*, pp. 9a–b)

Here *qi*, stuff, and nature are separated into three levels. It is stressed that nature is the nature that lies with *qi* and stuff. He also says,

> Nature is rooted in the principle of *qi* and so exists in *qi*; thus when speaking of nature one must speak of *qi* and first grasp this *qi* which contains it [principle]. (Ibid., p. 11a)

Nature exists within *qi* and stuff and cannot exist independent of *qi* and stuff.

In his exegesis of Zhang Zai's view that first there is the bodily form and then the nature of *qi* and stuff, Wang Fuzhi writes,

> Regarding *qi* and stuff: *qi* completes stuff and stuff then produces *qi*. *Qi* completes stuff; thus *qi* coagulates and collects into forms, taking its capital from things so as to nourish its stuff. Stuff produces *qi* so alike and unlike, attacking and being defeated each follow their kind. Thus the *qi* of the ears, eyes, mouth and nose encounter sounds, colors, tastes and smells and do so naturally and cannot dismiss them. This begins from forms and is not the intermingling of the *qi* of ultimate harmony. It is rather what healthy and normal things constantly have. The old theory that the nature of *qi* and stuff is of the ilk of unequal things such as darkness and brightness,

> strong and weak accords with the theory of Master Cheng. Now Master Zhang allies the bias of darkness and brightness, strong and weak obtaining *qi* with talent and not with nature.... And this nature of *qi* and stuff is close to what Mencius meant when he spoke of the relationship of mouth, ears, eyes and nose to sounds, colors, tastes and smells. This nature is the principle of life. That one is a human being means that this is no different from the principle that comes with life; thus the principles of benevolence, justice, rites and wisdom are things that even the stupidest person cannot destroy. Nor can the desires of sound, color, taste and smell be abolished by the person of greatest wisdom. This is what can be called human nature. (*Notes on Master Zhang's* Correcting the Unenlightened 3, p. 91)

Although here Wang Fuzhi did not ascribe the old theory to Zhang Zai, in fact it is a reasonably accurate assessment of Zhang's views. Taking Mencius' comments on the relations of the four sense organs to their appropiate senses as the nature of *qi* and stuff was indeed Wang's own interpretation. The original text in the *Mencius* reads,

> For the mouth to be inclined to tastes, the eyes to colors, the ears to sounds, the nose to smells and the four limbs to ease and rest is human nature. However, there is the decree of heaven to consider in their regard and the gentleman does not call [pursuit of] them 'nature.' (*Mencius* 7, *Exhausting the Mind B* #24)

Wang Fuzhi believed that this statement expressed the nature of *qi* and stuff. Wang Fuzhi accepted Zhu Xi's theory that nature is the principle of life but included both the Confucian virtues and the desires of the senses in the definition of 'nature.' On this point he differed from Zhu Xi.

Yan Yuan was a virulent opponent of the Chengs and Zhu Xi. He believed that nature and *qi*-stuff should not be separated:

> This *qi* is the *qi* of principle and principle is the principle of *qi*. How does it come about that one can say that principle is good while *qi*-stuff is bad?.... Even less is it necessary to separate the nature accorded by heaven's decree and the nature

of *qi* and stuff. (*Congshu Jicheng Xin Bian* 23.21, *Preservation of Human Nature A*, [p. 1], p. 450a)

All people can become Yao or Shun. The spirit that makes this possible is the nature of *qi* and stuff. Without *qi* and stuff there is nothing that can be human nature. Without *qi* and stuff human nature cannot be seen. (Ibid., [p. 16], p. 454a)

Here Yan Yuan was simply saying that human nature cannot be separated from *qi* and stuff. As for the relation of *qi* and stuff to the nature of *qi* and stuff, however, it is not at all clear from what Yan Yuan says.

Dai Zhen produced a new theory about human nature. He was opposed to the view that principle was nature and held that human nature is blood, *qi*, the mind, and knowing:

The blood, *qi*, mind and knowledge of human beings which are rooted in *yin-yang* and the five agents are human nature. (*An Evidential Study of the Meaning of Terms in the* Book of Mencius A, p. 272)

Yin-yang and the five agents are the substance of the Way; blood, *qi*, the mind and knowing are the substance of human nature. (Ibid. *B*, p. 287)

Dai Zhen emphasized that each kind of creature has its own nature. Human beings have blood, *qi*, a mind and knowing that are different from those of other animals:

Nature separates from *yin-yang* and the five agents to form blood, *qi*, the mind and knowing and differentiates according to the nature of things. If one considers all that comes after birth, all one's capacities, the whole of one's virtue, now all take this as their root. Thus the *Changes* say that what completes things is nature. *Qi* transforms and produces human beings. Once it has produced things each separates with its own life-span. Moreover, the distinctions of things have been so from of old and always.... The nature of persons and things separates from the Way and each produces its own characteristics. (Ibid., pp. 291–292)

> Nature is that blood, *qi*, the mind and knowing are rooted in *yin-yang* and the five agents and no persons or things do not differ in this respect. (Ibid., p. 295)

'Blood and *qi*' refers to the inner constitution of the body, whereas 'the mind and knowing' refers to the intellectual abilities. By taking these elements as human nature Dai Zhen was flatly contradicting Zhu Xi's theory of human nature.

Zhu Xi believed that as regards knowledge, awareness, and movement, human beings are the same as animals. Dai Zhen, however, believed that human blood and *qi* are not the same as those of the animals, and human awareness is even more different:

> From of old until now, regarding what has been said about the nature of human beings and all the other things, it is the case that each kind has its own *qi*. Speaking specifically about blood and *qi*, it is not only that *qi* is proper to each kind but also that knowledge and awareness are different. Human beings differ from birds and beasts in respect of rites and justice but it is also the case that human knowledge and awareness far surpasses that of things. This is what Mencius meant by saying human nature is good. (Ibid., p. 302)

In basing the theory of the goodness of human nature on the fact that the knowledge and awareness of human beings outstrips that of birds and beasts, Dai Zhen was advocating a position quite different from that of the Chengs and Zhu Xi.

Dai Zhen had more to say about the content of the nature of blood, *qi*, the mind, and knowing:

> Human beings are born and then there are desires, feelings, and knowing. These three are the natural outcomes of blood, *qi*, the mind and knowing. As for desires, they are for sounds, colors, tastes and smells and they lead to loving and standing in awe of. What is produced at the level of feelings are joy, anger, sorrow and happiness and they lead to grief and delight. What is distinguished by knowing is beautiful and ugly, right and wrong and this leads to liking and disliking.... Only when

there are desires, feelings and knowing can desires achieve their end, feelings come to fruition. (Ibid. *C*, pp. 308–309)

The actual content of human nature is desires, feelings, and knowing. There is no reference to the principle of the Chengs and Zhu Xi. Dai Zhen related moral awareness to cognition.

Thus we complete this rough survey of views of human nature. From Gaozi's theory that what is innate is human nature to the more complex theory of Dai Zhen, one is dealing with a natural theory of human nature. Mencius' establishing a distinction between the animals and human beings and the Song philosophers' use of 'principle' to express this difference can be called a priori theories of human nature. These are two different models of thinking about human nature.

50. Emotions
Qing
情

The concepts of 'emotions' (qing) and 'talent' (cai) are both closely related to that of human nature (xing). Debate about the emotions is similar to that about human nature: are they morally neutral or are they pernicious? Tradition provides two lists of the emotions: one with seven members and another, found in the Mencius *and promulgated by Zhu Xi, with four.*

Specific singling out of 'emotions' is first encountered in the *Xunzi*:

The bodily form is present and the spirit is living and liking, disliking, joy, anger, grief and happiness are within it. These are what are called the heaven-sent emotions. (*Xunzi* 17, *Discourse on Heaven*, lines 10–11)

    The liking, disliking, joy, anger, grief and happiness of human nature are what is meant by 'emotions.' (*Xunzi* 22, *On the Rectification of Terms*, line 3)

This states clearly that the six attributes cited are to be understood as 'emotions.' The *Record of Rites* gives a list of seven such attributes:

> "What is meant by human emotions?" "Joy, anger, grief, fear, love, dislike, desire, these seven. They cannot be acquired by study." (*Record of Rites* 9, *Evolution of Rites*, p. 126)

This work substituted fear for the *Xunzi*'s happiness, read "love" rather than "liking," and added desire to the list. It was this list of seven that was taken up by Han Yu in the Tang dynasty:

> The emotions arise from contact with things.... There are seven such emotions: joy, anger, grief, fear, love, dislike and desire. (*SBBY: Collected Works of Mr. Chang Li* 11.2, *An Inquiry on Human Nature*, p. 131b)

Dong Zhongshu discussed the relation of human nature to emotions:

> What heaven and earth give birth to is called nature and emotions.... The emotions are also human nature. If it is said that human nature is good then how must it be for the emotions? (*Luxuriant Gems of the Spring and Autumn Annals* 35, *The Profound Examination of Names and Appellations*, p. 298)

The *Balanced Inquiries* quote Dong Zhongshu answering this question as if human nature were good and emotions inclined to be bad:

> The great thread of heaven is the alternation of *yin* and *yang*; the great thread of human beings is the alternation of emotions and nature. Nature is produced from *yang* and emotions are produced from *yin*. *Yin qi* is mean and *yang qi* is benevolent. (*Balanced Inquiries* 13, *On Original Nature*, p. 120)

The same chapter also quotes Liu Xiang as saying,

> Nature is what one is born with. It is just so. It is in the person and does not develop out. The emotions reach out to things and are so. They go out of the bodily form and encounter the outside. (Ibid.)

The *Extended Reflections* quote Liu Xiang as saying:

Nature and emotions mutually influence each other. Nature is not alone in being good; the emotions are not alone in being bad. (*SBBY: Extended Reflections* 5.7, *Various Sayings B*, pp. 11b–12a)*

In other words, Liu Xiang was critical of a divorce between nature and emotions such that one can be portrayed as wholly good and the latter wholly bad.

In the third century He Yan and Wang Bi discussed the problem of the emotions. Their debate was recorded by He Shao:

He Yan believed that the sage is without joy, anger, grief or happiness. His arguments are very spiritual. Zhong Hui and others put them into practice. [Wang] Bi was different. He thought that what makes the sage flower among people is numinous perspicacity. What he has in common with other people are the five emotions. Numinous perspicacity flowers; thus he can experience the reconciliating harmony so as to communicate with beinglessness. He has the five emotions in common so he cannot but respond to things with grief and happiness. Hence it is that the emotions of the sage respond to things and do not become tied up in things. Now people say that to be not tied up is to not react to things. This is to fall wide of the mark. (*Gazette of the Three Kingdoms* 28, *Books of Wei* 28.8, *Biography of Zhong Hui*, p. 795 n. 1)

Here the main contents of the emotions are joy, anger, grief, and happiness.

The debate as to the relative goodness of human nature and emotions continued throughout the Tang and Song dynasties. Li Ao held that human nature was good and emotions were bad:

---

* On the *Extended Reflections* see Ch'en Ch'i-yun, *Hsun Yueh and the Mind of Late Han China: A Translation of the* Shen-chien *with Introduction and Annotations* (Princeton: Princeton University Press, 1980); Ch'en Ch'i-yun, *Hsun Yueh (A.D. 148–209): The Life and Reflections of an Early Medieval Confucian* (Cambridge: Cambridge University Press, 1975); M. Loewe, *Early Chinese Texts*, pp. 390–393. A summary in French and a partial concordance to the Chinese text are to be found is *Shen Jian Tongjian* (Shanghai: Shanghai Guji, 1987), pp. i–x.

> That which enables a person to be a sage is human nature. That
> which causes a person to make nature go awry is emotions.
> Joy, anger, grief, fear, love, dislike and desire, these seven are
> all produced by emotion.... Human nature is what is decreed
> by heaven. When the sage obtains it then he or she will not go
> astray. Emotions are the motion of human nature. The com-
> mon folk flounder in them and are not able to know their root.
> (*SKQS* 1078, *Collected Works of Li Wengong 2, The Recovery of
> Nature A*, p. 106b)

The contents of the emotions in Li Ao's statement are the same as those
listed by his contemporary, Han Yu.

Writing roughly two hundred years later, Wang Anshi voiced opposition to this division of nature and emotions into good and bad:

> Human nature and the emotions are one. In the world there
> are those who discourse saying, 'human nature is good; emo-
> tions are bad.' This is to merely know the names 'human na-
> ture' and 'emotions' and not to understand their real content.
> Joy, anger, grief, happiness, likes, dislikes and desire, before
> having emerged outside, are present in the heart and are hu-
> man nature. When joy, anger, grief, happiness, likes, dislikes
> and desire emerge outside and are shown in behavior they are
> emotions. Human nature is the root of the emotions; emotions
> are the application of human nature.... Therefore regarding
> these seven, when human beings are born they have them and
> it is in contact with things that they then move from the en-
> counter. When their motion agrees with principle then the
> person is a sage and a worthy. When it does not agree with
> principle then one is a mean person. Now when someone only
> sees how emotions are expressed externally and how they are
> tied up in external things and then lead into evil one will say
> that the emotions are bad. But good human nature is also the
> emotions. Is it that when one has not yet examined how emo-
> tions emerge externally that [one supposes] external things af-
> fect them and so cause them to enter into goodness? The gen-
> tleman nourishes the goodness of nature; thus his emotions are

also good. The mean person nourishes the badness of nature; thus his emotions are also bad. Thus what makes the gentleman a gentleman, is it not not his emotions? And what makes a mean person a mean person, is it not not his emotions? Those who fall short of this reasoning look for human nature among gentlemen and emotions among mean persons. (*SKQS* 1105, *Collected Works of Lin Chuan* 67, *Discussion of Justice* 6 #6, *Human Nature and Emotions*, pp. 555a–b)

Wang Anshi believed that emotions are both good and bad. His list of seven emotions differs slightly from that of Han Yu and Li Ao.

Zhu Xi's comments on the subject arose in the context of a discussion of Mencius. The text in the *Mencius* reads as follows:

The heart of compassion is the starting point of benevolence; the heart of shame is the starting point of respect; the heart of yielding is the starting point of rites; the heart of right and wrong is the starting point of wisdom. (*Mencius* 2, *Gong-sun Chou A*, #6)

Zhu Xi explained these qualities as emotion:

Compassion, shame, yielding and distinguishing right and wrong are emotions. Benevolence, respect, rites and wisdom are nature. The heart/mind controls nature and emotions. (*Collected Notes on the* Mencius 2, *Gong-sun Chou A*, p. 25)

Thus the emotions are not limited to the lists of seven cited in earlier works. When the *Mencius* was discussing the four qualities it was referring to one's general awareness, but by ascribing the four qualities to the emotions Zhu Xi could not avoid, particularly in the fourth case, confusing the rational and the emotional spheres. Zhu Xi also criticized Li Ao explicitly:

Li Ao's *Recovery of Nature* amounts to 'destroying the emotions to return to nature.' This cannot be so. How can the emotions ever be destroyed? (*Conversations* 59, p. 1381)

After the Song the notion of emotions encompassed both Zhu Xi's list of four qualities derived from the *Mencius* and the traditional lists of seven.

51. Talent
Cai
才

The notion of talent is also closely bound to those of human nature and emotions. It is the material nature of a thing. In moral philosophy, however, it is seen as what is intrinsically proper to the human being. For Confucius this was defined as moral worth, whereas Cheng Yi saw it as amoral and Zhu Xi read it as ability.

For Confucius the notion of 'talent' was to be understood as moral worth.

> Zhong Gong, as chief minister to the head of the Ji family, asked about administration. The Master said, "First employ the services of your officers, forgive minor transgressions and raise to office the worthy and talented." (*Analects* 13, *Zi Lu* #2, pp. 262–263)

Confucius judged his best pupil, Yan Yuan, to have been just such a talented person:

> When Yan Yuan died, [his father] Yan Lu asked for the [sale of the] Master's chariot so that he might [buy] an outer coffin. The Master said, "Whether talented or not everyone calls his son his son. When [my son] Li died, there was a coffin but no outer coffin. I would not walk on foot just so that he might have an outer coffin because having followed in the rear of great officers it was not proper that I should walk on foot." (*Analects* 11, *Of Former Times* #7, p. 239)

The details of the case need not concern us here; we simply note the use of the word 'talent.'

Mencius used the terms 'mind,' 'nature,' and 'talent' without making clear what distinctions, if any, he understood there to be. In talking about human nature, he said,

From the emotions that pertain to it, it can be good. This is what I mean by talking of its goodness. If people do what is not good, the fault is not due to their talent. (*Mencius* 6, *Gaozi A, #6*)

Moral wrongdoing is to be blamed on the human heart/mind and not on heaven's endowment of talent:

In years of abundance the children of the people are mostly good. In bad years the children of the people are mostly wicked. This is not because the talents endowed by heaven are any different but rather inasmuch as the people let their hearts fall and flounder. (Ibid. #7)

Mencius drew an analogy with Mount Niu, which should have been covered in trees but was now denuded. Human nature possesses talent in the same way the mountain possesses trees:

And so also of what properly belongs to human beings; shall it be said that the mind of any person was without benevolence and respect? The way in which one loses one's proper goodness of mind is like the way in which the trees are denuded by axes and machetes. Hewn down day after day can it [the mind] retain its beauty? . . . People see that it is like that of birds and beasts and imagine that it never had talents. But does this represent the real aspect of the human person? (Ibid. #8)*

Benevolence and respect, along with the rites and wisdom, are the talents that all people have by virtue of being human beings:

Benevolence, respect, the rites and wisdom are not infused into us from outside. We are certainly provided with them. To hold differently betrays a lack of thought. Thus it is said, "Seek and you will find them; neglect them and you will lose them." People differ from one another in regard to them; some as

---

*Author's note: The term translated as 'aspect' is the same *qing* that was discussed under the heading of 'emotions.' Dai Zhen explains that here *qing* is not to be read as 'emotions' but as meaning the real nature or true integrity of the person. (*An Evidential Study of the Meaning of Terms in the* Book of Mencius C, #1, *Cai*, p. 41).

much as twice, some five times and some to an incalculable amount. It is because they cannot fully employ their talents. (Ibid. #6)

Talents, then, are moral virtues. As a commentary on the Mencian view the following note from Lu Jiuyuan is not out of place:

As for 'emotion,' 'nature,' 'mind' and 'talent,' they are in fact all much about the same. The words are different, that is all. (*SKQS* 1156, *Selected Sayings of Mr. Xiang-shan* 3, p. 580b)

Cheng Yi advocated the view that talent is not good:

Human nature has nothing about it that is not good whereas what is not good is talent. Human nature is principle. Principle is one and the same from Yao and Shun down to the common person. Talent is received from '*qi*.' '*Qi*' is clear and muddy. If one receives its clarity one is a worthy; if one receives its muddiness one is a fool. (*SKQS* 698, *Surviving Works of the Two Chengs* 18, p. 165a)

In distinguishing human nature and talent on the grounds of the distinction between principle and *qi* Cheng's theory was quite different from that of the *Mencius*.

Zhu Xi explained talent as ability:

Talent is the ground of trust for one to undertake something. . . . Talent is the force of the mind. It is to use the force of *qi* to go and do something. . . . Human nature is the principle of mind. Emotions are the motion of the mind. Talent is the ground on which the emotions gather and rest. (*Conversations* 5, p. 97)

In explaining the use of the term 'talent' in Confucius' reply to Zhong Gong, Zhu Xi noted,

The worthies are those who have virtue; the talented are those who have ability. (*Collected Exegesis of the* Analects 7, p. 54)

Again 'talent' is glossed as 'ability.'

Dai Zhen did likewise:

As for talent: persons and things all take their nature as their basic form-stuff and those of ability are able to distinguish them according to their differences. This is what Mencius meant by the talent that comes down from heaven. (*An Evidential Study of the Meaning of Terms in the* Book of Mencius *C*, p. 307)

The debate about talent and nature has been largely inspired by the *Mencius.* In the Wei-Jin period there was also a discussion of the same topic. Zhong Hui and others produced four different theories of the relation of talent and human nature. Liu Xiaoji recorded the debate as follows:

The *Gazette of the Wei* says, "[Zhong] Hui discussed the similarity and difference between talent and human nature and this was spread around in his generation. The four theories are, talent and human nature are the same; talent and human nature are different; talent is united to human nature; talent and human nature are separate." (*Zhuzi Jicheng* 8, *The World Speaks a New Language* 4, *Literary Study*, p. 48n)

The original discussion was lost long ago and the report given here is unreliable. It had no influence on thought in the Tang and Song dynasties.

II. Concepts of Intentionality

52. Mind/Heart

Xin

心

Xin, *the heart or mind, is the center of human thought and feeling. It is not just one organ among others but something that coordinates the work of all organs of thinking. The* Mencius *brought the term to prominence and was to serve as a source for much later reflection. The* Guanzi *also had some early texts that bore evidence of meditative practices. Professor Zhang quotes these but the critical remarks on dating have been supplied by the translator.*

Buddhism introduced a trend toward idealism, and this was to reappear in the work of Wang Shouren. It is in the work of Dai Zhen that the relation between mind, principle and the human emotions and feelings is best expressed.

The *Mencius* and the *Guanzi*

Although the *Analects* and the *Laozi* refer to the mind/heart, neither text discusses its meaning. It is in the *Mencius* that the term is given its first explanation. In the *Mencius* the mind is the faculty that thinks:

> The organs of the ears and the eyes do not think and are glued to things. One thing calls forth the other thing and thus the organ functions. The role of the mind is to think. Only when one thinks can one grasp [what the mind is about] and if one does not think one will never grasp it. (*Mencius* 6, *Gaozi A*, #15)

The mind is contrasted with the ears and eyes and assigned its own specific role. The precise nature of this mind remained to be determined. It would appear that it is not exactly the heart, which is one of the five inner organs:

> Therefore if it [the mind] receives its proper nourishment, there is nothing which will not grow. If it loses its proper nourishment, there is nothing which will not decay. Confucius said, "Hold it fast and it remains with you. Let it go and you lose it. Its outgoing and incoming cannot be defined as to time or place." It is the mind of which this is said. (Ibid. #8)

The movements ascribed to the mind indicate that Mencius was clearly not referring to the physical organ of the heart. Further proof is afforded by the following remark:

> When people's chickens and hounds are lost, they know how to look for them again; but when they lose their mind they do not know how to look for it again. The Way of learning is nothing else other than looking for the lost mind. (Ibid. #11)

The mind that can be lost is not the heart but the capacity to know.

> The mind is also moral awareness. It is the mind of compassion, shame, yielding and discrimination of right and wrong. (*Mencius* 2, *Gong-sun Chou A*, #6)

The *Technique of the Heart* and its related chapters in the *Guanzi* discuss the relation of the mind to other sense organs. The *A* chapter contains the longest exposition of the subject:

> In the body the mind/heart is in the place of the prince. The roles of the nine apertures are the portions of the offices/sense-organs.* If the mind remains in the Way the nine apertures will keep to their principle but if it is filled with desire and lust, the eyes will not see colors and the ears will not hear sounds.... The ears and eyes are the sense-organs for seeing and hearing. If the mind does not interfere in matters of seeing and hearing, the sense organs will be able to maintain their separate roles. Now if the heart has desires, when things go past the eyes will not see them, when sounds come the ears will not hear them. Thus it is said, "When the superior falls from the way, the inferior cannot do its duties." Therefore,† the technique of the mind lies in not acting and thereby controlling the apertures. (*Guanzi* 36, *Technique of the Heart A*, 2:1)

The later explanatory section of the chapter reads as follows:

> The heart is the lodging of wisdom. (Ibid., 2:5)

Although it bears a similar name, *Technique of the Heart B* is quite a different work, being a commentary on the *Inner Training*. It states:

> Do not use things to confuse the organs. Do not use the organs to confuse the mind. This is what is called 'inner virtue.'‡ (Ibid. *B*, 2:15)

---

* The nine apertures are the (1, 2) eyes, (3, 4) ears, (5, 6) nostrils, (7) mouth, (8) anus, and (9) genitals; the term *guan* in Chinese means both 'office' and 'sense organ.' Both senses may be intended here.

† Omitting "it is said"; see Rickett, *Kuan-Tzu*, p. 172 n. 96.

‡ Versions: "inner obtaining"; see *Guanzi* 37, 2:16 n. 6.

Here external things, sense organs, and the mind are distinguished and the role of the mind in relation to the organs is brought out. The oldest text of the three considered here, the *Inner Training*, states:

> The form of the mind is always such that it is naturally full and naturally complete, naturally produced and naturally perfected. It loses these only through sorrow and joy, happiness and anger, desires and profiteering. If one can discard sorrow and joy, happiness and anger, desires and profiteering one's mind will go back to fullness. The emotions of this mind profit from calm and tranquility. If there is neither trouble nor confusion harmony will be produced naturally. (*Guanzi* 49, *Inner Training*, 2:122)
>
> Do not let things confuse the senses. Do not let the senses confuse the heart. This is called 'inner obtaining.' ... When our hearts are ordered then the senses are ordered. When our hearts are calm then the senses are calm. What orders them is the heart. What calms them is the heart. The heart contains another heart [the mind]. Within the heart there is another heart [the mind]. (Ibid., 2:125, 126)

There is a reciprocity between the heart and the senses such that the latter should not upset the former and the former should pacify the latter. In saying that the mind is naturally full and complete, the passage is stressing the subject's mastery of what is happening. By saying that there is a heart within the heart the text refers to self-consciousness.

The *Xunzi*

The most detailed discussion of the mind in pre-Qin philosophy is to be found in the *Xunzi*. On the subject of the relation of the mind to the sense organs, the *Xunzi* has this to say:

> The ears, eyes, nose and mouth each are receptors and cannot exchange their faculties. These are what are meant by the senses given by heaven. The heart/mind is lodged in the central cavity [the thorax] to control the five senses. This is what is

meant by the heavenly prince. (*Xunzi* 17, *Discourse on Heaven*, line 12)

Whenever anything is judged to be the same sort or the same emotion, it is because the perception of the sense given by heaven says that it is the same thing.... The mind gives meaning to impressions.* It gives meaning to impressions, and only then, by means of the ear, sound can be known. But the giving of meaning to impressions must depend on the senses given by heaven, each noting its particular kind of sensations, and only then can there be knowledge. When the five senses note† something but do not understand it, and the mind tries to give it a meaning but has no explanation, nobody would differ; everyone would call this ignorance. (*Xunzi* 22, *On the Rectification of Terms*, lines 16, 19–21)

The five senses encounter external objects and the mind is able to recognize them by the impression left on the senses. The mind leads the whole process:

How can a person know the Way? By the mind.... The mind is the prince of the bodily form and the master of intellect. When it issues a command there is nothing that does not obey it. It itself makes prohibitions; it itself gives commands; it itself makes decisions; it itself makes choices; it itself causes action; it itself stops action. Thus the mouth can exert itself forcibly and make the silent speak; the body can exert itself forcibly and make the bent straight; the mind can exert itself forcibly and change one's perception. If it does this, then it would be in error and must resign its lordship. Hence I say: the mind is as it chooses.‡ It cannot prevent the results of its action appearing

---

* Author's note: "Impressions": the ability to recognize external objects through the senses. In a note on the same character in *Zuo's Commentary* (9 *Xiang* 28, p. 539, "to reveal the fault"), Du Yu (222–284) says, "'to reveal' is to judge," that is, to reveal is to make an assessment. For translation and notes, see H. H. Dubs, *The Works of Hsuntze*, 3d ed. (Taibei: Confucius Publishing House, 1983), p. 490 n. 2.

† To note is to encounter directly.

‡ Translation based on notes of Wang Xianqian, *Collected Exegesis of the* Xunzi (1891), p. 265.

of themselves. (*Xunzi* 21, *On the Removal of Prejudices*, lines 34, 44–47)

Here it is not said that the mind can know independently of the senses but merely that the mind has the ability to make decisions and that it is free in this regard. It is the mind that determines conduct:

> Desire does not worry about the possibility of being fulfilled and yet achieves its goal while lusting goes after what it thinks is possible to attain. The desire that does not worry about the possibility of being fulfilled and yet achieves its goal is received from heaven. The lusting which goes after what it thinks is possible to attain is received from the heart.... Therefore if one's desire outstrips what one's actions can attain then the mind rejects it. If what the mind agrees to does not depart from principle then even though desires be many what harm can they do to one's self-control? If one's desires are few but one's actions outstrip them it is the mind which has caused this situation. When what the mind agrees to departs from principle then even though desires are few, how would that stop disorder? Therefore the control of disorder lies in what the mind agrees to and passing away lies in what the emotions desire. (*Xunzi*, 22 *Rectification of Terms*, lines 57–58, 60–62)

It is the heart/mind that controls the emotions and desires and regulates behavior.

In discussing the mind, Xunzi recognized its role both in perception and in making free decisions. As for the emotions, it would appear that they are not attributed to the mind:

> The likes, dislikes, joy, anger, grief and happiness of human nature are what are meant by 'emotions.' The emotions being thus and the mind choosing among them is what is meant by 'reflection.' (Ibid., line 3)

For Xunzi the mind had both intellect and will.

Buddhism

In the pre-Qin and Han periods the mind was never considered the origin of the world. After the entry of Buddhism such a form of "idealism" became widespread. Zong Bing (375–443)* wrote a work titled *Discourse on Understanding the Buddha* in which he advocated "the mind as that which produces all things" and held that "all dharmas were empty" (*SBBY: Collected Great Brightness* 2, *Discourse on Understanding the Buddha*, p. 1a). Su Yan, Emperor Wu of the Liang dynasty, held that the mind was the original substance of the world:

> The mind is the root of functions. The root is one but the functions many. The many functions naturally flourish and decay but the one root remains unchanged.... Thus one knows that life and destruction, changes and movements depend on previous causes and the mixing and mutual inclination of good and evil are generated from actual circumstances and the mind is their root but it does not alter. By using its root without ceasing one can make the principle of becoming Buddha resplendent. By following the movement and mutual inclination of circumstances one can fully understand life and death. (*SBBY: Collected Great Brightness* 9, *Notes on Establishing Spiritual Brightness to Realise the Significance of the Buddha*, pp. 2a–b)

This is clearly an exposition of Buddhist doctrine.

Fan Zhen wrote of the mind/heart as being the physical human heart, one of the five organs. To it he ascribed the functions of thinking. This doctrine is to be found in his essay *Treatise on the Destruction of the Spirit*:

> Form is the stuff of spirit and spirit is the function of the form. (*Complete Liang Literature* 45, *Treatise on the Destruction of the Spirit*, p. 6b, p. 3209b)

Spirit is the knowledge of pain and itching and the ability to reflect on right and wrong. The latter is expounded in detail:

---

*Zong Bing *Zi:* Shao Wen, from Nieyang, Nanyang Commandery (northeast of the modern town of Dengxian, Henan Province). Pupil of Hui Yuan.

QUESTION: "The ability to reflect on right and wrong does not depend on the hands and feet. What does it depend on then?"

ANSWER: "Ability to reflect* on right and wrong is governed by the heart."

QUESTION: "Is the heart the heart which is one of the five organs or not?"

ANSWER: "It is."

QUESTION: "What distinctions do the five organs have while the heart alone has the ability to distinguish right and wrong?"

ANSWER: "Do not the seven apertures also display differences? And their roles and functions are unequal."

QUESTION: "Reflecting and thinking are without limit. How does one know† that they are governed by this heart?"

ANSWER: "The five organs each have their role and none of them are able to reflect. This is how one knows that the heart is the root of reflection." (*Liang History* 48, *Biography of Fan Zhen*, p. 668; also in *Complete Liang Literature* 45, *Treatise on the Destruction of Spirit*, p. 7b, p. 3210a)

The *Mencius* and the *Xunzi* did not specify the relationship between the faculties of thinking and the physical heart. Fan Zhen stressed too close an identification of the two.

The Early Song Dynasty

Zhang Zai proposed two themes in connection with the mind. The first is that it unites cognitive faculties with human nature:

> What unites human nature with knowing and awareness is what
> is called the 'mind.' (*SKQS* 697, *Correcting the Unenlightened*
> 1, *Ultimate Harmony*, p. 99a)

The second is that it governs both human nature and the emotions:

---

*The *Complete Liang Literature* edition reads "the significance of right and wrong."
† The *Liang History* edition reads, "How is it that there is ..."

> The mind governs human nature and the emotions. (*SKQS* 697, *Complete Books of Master Zhang* 14, *Remaining Surviving Notes on Nature and Principle*, p. 311b)

Not only do these two subjects go together but they complement each other.

> For thinking to fully use the mind one must know from whence the mind arises and then one can do so. (*SKQS* 697, *Correcting the Unenlightened* 7, *Great Mind*, p. 117a)

The origin of the mind lies in the unity of human nature and awareness:

> The oneness of being and beingless and the union of internal and external is the place from whence the human mind arises. (Ibid. 17, *Qian Cheng*, p. 143b)

From the context it is clear that the oneness of being and beingless is human nature and the union of internal and external refers to consciousness. Hence together they mean human nature and consciousness. There is no clear explanation, however, of the relation that exists between human nature and consciousness or between human nature and the emotions.

Cheng Yi distinguished between the substance and function of the mind, without, however, giving a clear account of what is intended by each term. The intercalated notes below are Cheng's own:

> The mind is one. It is said of the substance (this is calm and unmoving). It is also said of the function (this is affective and responds to the stimuli of the world). One should only look at how it appears to know which. (*SBBY: Collected Literary Works of Mr. Yin Chuan* 5, *Letter to Lu Dalin on the Mean*, p. 266b)

Zhu Xi

A more detailed explanation based on the writings of Zhang Zai and Cheng Yi is to be found in Zhu Xi's writings. Zhu Xi spoke in favor of the idea that the mind unites human nature and the emotions and added,

Human nature is the root; the emotions are the function. Human nature and the emotions both arise from the mind, hence the mind is able to lead them. This leading is like leading troops and refers to their being directed. Now, benevolence, justice, the rites and wisdom are human nature. Mencius says, "Benevolence, justice, the rites and wisdom are rooted in the heart/mind." Compassion, shame, yielding and the distinguishing of right and wrong have their root in the emotions. Mencius says, "the heart/mind of compassion, the heart/mind of shame, the heart/mind of yielding, the heart/mind of distinguishing between right and wrong." From this saying it can be seen that the mind is able to lead human nature and the emotions. (*Conversations* 98, p. 2513)

From this it can be seen that Zhang Zai and Zhu Xi derived their theory from the *Mencius*. Zhang and Zhu held that benevolence, justice, the rites, and wisdom belonged to human nature whereas compassion, shame, yielding, and the ability to distinguish between right and wrong belonged to the emotions. Hence the inclusion of both sets under the mind proved that the mind was capable of uniting and leading human nature and the emotions.

The mind is not, however, the physical human heart:

Spacious spirituality is the original nature of the mind. It is not that I am able to make it spacious. Regarding the seeing and hearing of the ears and eyes, what enables them to see and hear is the mind. Could it really have a form and shape? If the ears and eyes see and hear it, then it would have form and shape. But as for the spacious spirituality of the mind, could it really be a physical thing? (*Conversations* 5, p. 87)

The mind is what enables the senses to work and not something that the sense organs can perceive.

As for the heart, which is one of the five organs like the lungs and liver, it is indeed a thing. Nowadays when scholars talk about the mind which grasps, rejects, stores and dies, then this is naturally unfathomable intellectual clarity. Thus if the heart of the five organs is sick then one can use medicine to heal it.

But this mind cannot be healed by *acorus calamus, typha lat-ifolia*, devil's eye* or liquidambar fungus. (Ibid.)

Zhu Xi also wrote about the mysteriousness of the spiritual powers of the mind:

> This mind is very spiritual. It is so minute it can penetrate within a hair, a point, a thread or a mustard seed and know and be aware of it. At the same time there is nowhere in the vast expanse of the six directions that it is not able to be present. Or again while from the earliest times past to now there are thousands and ten thousands of years yet once thought of them appears then it goes there. Moving on into the future there are unknown thousands and ten thousands of years yet once the thought of them appears the mind can also go there. This unfathomable spiritual brightness is most spacious and most spiritual. It is indeed without pair! (*Conversations* 18, p. 404)

Whereas Zhang Zai spoke of "whence the mind arises," Zhu Xi gave a more detailed exposition of the subject:

> Consciousness is the principle of the mind. The ability to be conscious depends on the spiritual force of *qi*. (*Conversations*)
>
> First there was the principle of knowing and of con-sciousness. Before the principle knew or was conscious *qi* had gathered and formed shapes. Principle united with *qi* and then there can be knowing and consciousness. (*Conversations* 5, p. 85)

In other words, the mind is the product of the union of principle and *qi*. First there is principle. Within principle is the principle of knowing and of consciousness. If there is principle then there is *qi*. Once *qi* gathers then it produces forms. Principle and *qi* unite and then there can be knowing and consciousness. This is the spiritual force of *qi*.

---

*Herbert A. Giles defines this term as follows:"A herbaceous plant with round and downy leaves and red seeds, known as *gui mu*, devil's eye" Giles, *A Chinese-English Dictionary* (London: Bernard Quaritch; Shanghai: Kelly and Walsh, 1892), p. 375, no. 3675.

Zhu Xi also brought out the ruling role of mind:

> Human nature is the raison d'être of the mind. The mind rules over the body. (*Conversations* 5, p. 91)
>
> The mind is said of what rules over. It rules over both movement and stillness. It is not the case that when there is stillness it has no function and when there is movement that it then comes to rule. (*Conversations* 5, p. 94)
>
> This mind is what enables persons to have mastery over their bodies. It is one and not two. It is the master and not the object. It commands things and is not commanded by things. (*SBBY: Collected Writings of Zhu Wengong* 67.30, *Theory of Observing the Mind*, pp. 18b–19a)

The mind is the master of the body, or, in modern speech, it is the subjectivity of the person.

Zhu Xi held that the mind embraces nature, emotions, intentionality, and will:

> The mind takes nature as its substance.... What enables this mind to be present as such is principle. This is because it has human nature....
>
> The mind is the master of one body. Intentions are what are issued by the mind. Emotions are the motion of the mind. The will is the tendency of the mind. (*Conversations* 5, p. 89)

Intentions and will are expounded in more detail:

> The will is the tendency of the mind. It goes straight to its destination. The intentions are the means by which the will acts. They are the feet of the will. Any carrying out of an action, planning, moving is a matter of intention. Therefore Heng Qu [Zhang Zai] says, "When the will is focused on the public interest then the intentions are on the public interest."... The will and intentions both belong to the emotions. The term 'emotions' is broader in meaning. (*Conversations* 5, p. 96)

The will governs the general direction of conduct, whereas the intentions are involved in inspiring individual actions.

Zhu Xi's theory is more detailed than what preceded but it still has many points of obscurity about it.

Lu Jiuyuan and Wang Shouren

Whereas Zhu Xi separated the mind and human nature, Lu Jiuyuan deemed there to be no such separation. Lu's pupil Li Bomin recorded a conversation with his teacher on the subject:

> Bo Min asked, "How does one fully realize one's mind? How does one distinguish human nature, talent, mind and emotions?" The teacher said, "As for this question of my friend it is like the branches and leaves. Even though the formulation of the question is not my friend's mistake yet it is an error in the world today. The scholars now read books but only understand the characters and do not look for the blood and veins. As for emotions, human nature, the mind and talent they are all one and it is only the terms which are different.... If one really wants to use the different terms then one says that what is of heaven is nature and what is of human beings is mind. This is in conformity with what my friend said but in fact it is unnecessary to do so." (SKQS 1156, *Selected Sayings of Mr. Xiang-shan* 3, p. 580b)

Lu Jiuyuan held that the mind was principle:

> People all have this mind. Minds all have this principle. The mind is principle. (*SBBY: Complete Collected Works of Xiang Shan* 11, *With Li Zai*, p. 69b)

Moral awareness is a priori; the mind is consciousness of this a priori morality.

Wang Shouren expanded on Lu's theme that the mind is principle:

> The mind is not a lump of blood and flesh. Any aspects of knowing and consciousness are the mind. Such as the ears and eyes knowing how to see and hear, the hands and feet knowing how to feel and itch. This knowing and consciousness is the

mind. (*SBBY: Complete Books of Yang Ming* 3, *Instructions for Practical Living* C, p. 24a; WTC #323)

The same work records the following conversation with Wang:

> The teacher said, "See, what in this heaven and earth is the mind of heaven and earth?" He replied: "I once heard it said that human beings are the mind of heaven and earth."* He said: "What is it in the human person that is called the heart/mind?" He replied, "It is but a spiritual awareness." He said: "It is possible to know then that what fills up heaven and earth is this spiritual awareness." (Ibid., p. 26a; WTC #337)

To hold that the mind is spiritual awareness is to hold the same position as Zhu Xi. Yet Wang went on to differ from his predecessor:

> Wei Qian† asked, "How is knowledge the original substance of this mind?" The teacher said, "Knowledge is the principle made intelligent. It is in as much as it governs that it is called the mind and in as much as it is received from birth that it is called human nature." (*SBBY: Complete Books of Yang Ming* 1, *Instructions for Practical Living* A, p. 25b; WTC #118)

Zhu Xi believed that knowledge and consciousness were the result of the spiritual force of *qi* and not of principle, as Wang here maintained.

Wang Shouren justified his view that the mind is principle:

> All gentlemen want to know how I established this idea and main theme. Now how is it that I say that the mind is principle? It is only for the worldly folk that one separates mind and principle as two things and from this arise many maladies. As when the five earls drove out the barbarians and honored the house of Zhou. All came from a selfish mind and was not in accord with principle. Some people say that what they did was in accord with principle and only their minds were not pure

---

* *Record of Rites* 9, *Evolution of Rites*, p. 127.
† Ji Yuanheng (d. 1521). *Zi:* Wei Qian, pupil of Wang Shouren, died after release from prison, where he was held on false charges of conspiracy to revolt.

and so continue to admire their conduct. In fact they should say that externally they looked fine but that this was quite un-related to the mind. To separate the mind and principle into two results, unbeknownst to oneself, is the falsity of the way of the earls. Hence I say that the mind is principle and one should promote awareness of the fact that the mind and principle are one and then exert oneself with the mind and not merely ac-cumulate individual acts of justice externally. This is the truth of the Way of kingship. This is what I establish and mean. (*SBBY: Complete Books of Yang Ming* 3, *Instructions for Prac-tical Living C*, p. 24b; WTC #322)

This is to say that people should exert themselves to free the mind of all self-seeking and so make it evident that the mind is principle. This moral discipline is the basis for Lu Jiuyuan's and Wang Shouren's theory that the mind is principle.

Wang Fuzhi

In discussing the mind, Wang Fuzhi underlined the relation between the mind and the senses.

In the body of the human person the heart/mind occupies an important place. The spiritual awareness of the mind is sepa-rately dependent on the five organs and waits for the reactions of the five senses. The liver, spleen, lungs, kidneys, spiritual and material souls are the organs of the will and intentions. If one organ should fall from principle then the spirituality of the mind is impaired. Without the eyes the mind cannot distin-guish colors. Without the ears the mind cannot recognize sounds. Without the hands and feet the mind is not able to point or move. Should one organ lose its function then the spirituality of the mind is already harmed. Is it really possi-ble that one could have the mind alone and connect to the many functions and make its spiritual power effective? (*Elabo-ration on the Meanings of the* Book of History 6.3, *Bi Ming*, p. 176)

The spiritual awareness (cognitive power) of the mind rests on the foundation provided by the feelings and perceptions of the senses.

> The wind and thunder have no form but have shapes. The mind is without shape yet has awareness. Thus merely to think of something and then even if it be 1,000 *li* away it will be present in a flash. It is quicker than the wind or thunder. Although the emotions and talents of the mind are without form or shape and need to rely on what has been seen or heard to have substance, concerning what has not been experienced as seen or heard the mind cannot imagine its shape. (*Notes on Master Zhang's* Correcting the Unenlightened 3b, *Enlightenment Resulting from Sincerity*, p. 134)

The mind has the ability to imagine. It can imagine things far away, but this imagination must be based on what has been seen or heard. One cannot imagine what has never been seen or heard of. In commenting on Zhang Zai's phrase about what the human mind comes from, Wang Fuzhi has this to say:

> The inner mind unites to external things so as to result in awareness. The mind is generated from this. . . . Hence from what has not been seen or heard human beings cannot produce their mind. (*Notes on Master Zhang's* Correcting the Unenlightened 9a, *Qian Cheng*, p. 276)

The mind comes from the union of inner and outer. It does not exist independent of things. Wang Fuzhi brought out the roots of the mind in the senses.

Dai Zhen

The tradition of the Chengs and of Zhu Xi held that principle was in the mind since the mind had human nature and human nature is principle. Lu Jiuyuan and Wang Shouren and their followers said that the mind was principle. They held that the mind was human nature and since human nature was principle so principle is in the mind. In the mid-Qing period Dai Zhen opposed the former theory and also the latter theory. Instead he proposed the theory that principle is amid states of affairs and the mind is able to distinguish principles:

> Mencius says, "People's mouths agree in having the same tastes; their ears agree in enjoying the same sounds; their eyes agree in recognizing the same beauty: shall their minds alone be without that of which they similarly approve?"* Understanding principle and respect delights the mind as tastes delight the mouth, sounds delight the ear and colors delight the eye, this being human nature. Tastes, sounds, colors are related to things but enter into contact with my blood and *qi*. Principle and respect have to do with affairs and enter into contact with my mind and faculty of knowledge. Blood, *qi*, mind and the faculty of knowledge have their own abilities. The ability of the mouth is to distinguish tastes. The ability of the ears is to distinguish sounds. The ability of the eyes is to distinguish colors. The ability of the mind is to distinguish principle and respect. Tastes, sounds and colors are in things and not in me but they come into contact with my blood and *qi* and then I am able to distinguish them and take pleasure in them. The most pleasurable is necessarily the best of them. Principle and respect are analyzed from out of the conditions governing affairs and situations and come into contact with my mind and cognitive faculty. Then I am able to distinguish them and take pleasure in them. What is most pleasurable about them is what is most accomplished. (*An Evidential Study of the Meaning of Terms in the* Book of Mencius *A*, p. 269)

Colors, sounds, and tastes are all in things and not in the self. They are objective and the object of the attention of the senses. Principle and respect are in affairs. They are also objective and are the objects discerned by the mind and cognitive faculty. Dai Zhen explained in more detail how principle is in things using the metaphor of light:

> Speaking then of affairs and things, it is not the case that outside of affairs and things there is a separate principle and re-

* *Mencius 6, Gaozi A #7*; Legge, *Chinese Classics*, 2:406.

spect. If there is a thing there must be a norm. The norm can be used to correct the thing. It is as simple as that. As for the human mind, it is not the case that there is a principle to give to it and put into the mind. The spiritual awareness of the mind with respect to affairs and things is quite enough to know the unchanging norm of that thing just as light is only able to illuminate and fulfill its rationale. Should its light increase its illumination does not err. (Ibid. #1, *Li*, p. 7)

Principle and respect are in affairs and things, that is, they are in the relations of one thing to another and not in the mind. The mind is able to know them. Just as light is able to illuminate things, so then things are the objects of that illumination. Dai Zhen believed that principles of reason and morality are objective and not within the mind. While on one hand stressing the objectivity of principles, Dai Zhen was also underlining the mind's ability to discriminate and recognize principles. This is a valuable new contribution. Dai believed, however, that not only can the mind distinguish principles, it can also take pleasure in the same. Pleasure is not simply one person's intellectual grasp. It involves the feelings. Dai Zhen did not explain how one's perception of moral principles differs from one's moral feelings.

Ancient Chinese philosophy never resolved the problem of the relation between awareness of moral principles and moral feelings. Mencius said,

The office of the mind is to think. (*Mencius* 6, *Gaozi A*, #15)

He also said,

What is it that the mind is in sympathy with? It is principle and it is respect. The sages only apprehended before me that of which my mind approves along with other people. Therefore the principles of our nature and the determinations of respect are agreeable to my mind, just as the flesh of grass and grain-fed animals is agreeable to my mouth. (Ibid. #7)

That the mind is able to deem principle and respect correctly is the fruit of thought. Principle and respect being pleasing to my mind is not only a matter of thought but one of moral feelings. What then is the relation between 'thinking' and 'taking pleasure in'? It would seem that Mencius joined the two together. This joining was explicitly stated by Wang Shou-ren in the course of remarks on the conscience:

> The conscience is but the mind that is able to distinguish right and wrong. Right and wrong are but liking and disliking. If one only likes and dislikes then one will have fully grasped right and wrong. (*SBBY: Instructions for Practical Living* C, p. 16a; WTC #288)

The mind that can distinguish right and wrong is the cognitive mind, whereas liking and disliking are emotions. What is the relation between cognition and emotions? Wang Shouren seemed to think that they are one and the same. In other words, one can say that, though without any ex-plicit claim to be doing so, from Mencius to Dai Zhen Chinese philosophy united moral knowledge with moral feeling.

53. Intention, Will

Yi, Yi-zhi
意, 意志

The term yi *in ancient Chinese philosophy may mean both 'idea' and 'intention,' that is, it can be cognitive or voluntative. In this section only the latter use is discussed.* Zhi *refers to the will. The combination* yi-zhi *is the modern term for 'will' and for 'intention.'*

Intention

The sense of 'intention' is present in the following texts:

> If one cultivates one's intentions, one can take greater pride in them than in wealth and honors. If the Way and what is right is given weight then one will scorn kings and dukes. Taken up by inner examination one will slight external things. (*Xunzi* 2, *On Self-Cultivation*, line 19)

The tendency of the heart/mind is what is known as the intentions. (*Luxuriant Gems of the Spring and Autumn Annals* 77, *Following the Way of Heaven*, p. 452)

The intentions are the direction taken by the mind and the impetus to action.

The *Great Learning* advocated making one's intentions sincere:

By making one's intentions sincere is meant not cheating oneself. Thus one hates hateful smells, likes pretty colors. This is called self-enjoyment. Hence the gentleman must examine himself carefully while he is alone. In private there is no evil that the mean person will not do but on seeing the gentleman he will try to disguise himself, concealing his evil and revealing what is good. The other sees him as if he saw his lungs and liver, so what use is the disguise? This shows that what is truly within will be shown outside. Therefore the gentleman must be careful with himself when alone. (*Great Learning* 6, pp. 366–367)

People all have a will that likes the good and dislikes what is wrong. This can be called a good conscience. In all places and at all times to follow this good conscience is what is meant by making one's intentions sincere. To watch over oneself when alone is demanded by the task of making one's intentions sincere.

Will

Confucius asserted the independence of the will:

The three armies* can lose their generals but a common person cannot lose his or her will. (*Analects* 9, *Zi Han* #25, p. 224)

A human being cannot be without a will. According to Confucius the human will should be "oriented to the Way" (*Analects* 4, *Li Ren* #9,

---

*Legge, *Chinese Classics* 1:198 n. 10.2. One army has 12,500 soldiers. The king has six armies and a great state has three.

p. 168; *Analects* 7, *Shu Er* #6, p. 196) or "attuned to the Way" (*Analects* 4, *Li Ren* #8, p. 168).

Mencius contrasted the will and *qi*:

> The will is the general of *qi*; *qi* is what fills the body. The will is first to arrive; *qi* follows. Thus it is said: "Maintain one's will and do no violence to one's *qi*." (*Mencius* 2, *Gongsun Chou A*, #2)

Mencius was claiming that the person needs to be governed by the will and not by *qi*. This should not be to the detriment of one's *qi*, however.

54. Conscience, Innate Moral Knowledge
Liang Xin, Liang Zhi
良心, 良知

Wang Shouren is the philosopher of the conscience in Chinese philosophy. As always, Professor Zhang gives the prehistory of the terms that were to form the term 'liang xin' (conscience) in Wang's thought. The chief source of the terminology is the Mencius.

History of the Terms

The question of a priori innate moral awareness is expressed by two similar terms in the *Mencius: liang zhi*, good knowing, and *liang xin*, good heart/mind. The former may be translated as 'innate knowledge' or 'intuitive knowledge.' The latter is normally translated as 'conscience.'

> The trees of Mount Niu were once beautiful. Being situated, however, in the borders of a large State, they were hewn down with axes and hatchets. How could they retain their beauty? . . . And so of what belongs to human beings: shall it be said that the mind of any human being was without benevolence and respect? The way in which a person loses his conscience is like the way in which trees are denuded by axes and hatchets. Hewn

down day after day can the mind retain its beauty? (*Mencius* 6, *Gaozi A* #8)

The context shows that the conscience is the awareness of benevolence and respect.

The term *liang zhi* is found in another passage of the *Mencius*:

> The ability possessed by people who have not acquired it by learning is intuitive ability [*liang neng*] and the knowledge acquired by them without the exercise of thought is their intuitive knowledge [*liang zhi*]. Children carried in the arms all know to love their parents, and when they are grown a little, they all know to love their elder siblings. Filial affection for parents is the working of benevolence. Respect for elders is the working of respect. There is no other reason for those feelings: they belong to all under heaven. (*Mencius* 7, *Exhausting the Mind A*, #15)

Intuitive knowledge is clearly awareness of moral principles and attitudes.

The meaning of the term '*liang*' in the expressions 'intuitive ability,' 'intuitive knowledge,' and 'conscience' was a matter of varying opinions among Han and Song Confucians. The *Explanation of Words and Characters* (5b, p. 111) defines *liang* as 'good.' Hence conscience means 'a good heart/mind.' Zhao Ji commented on the phrase 'intuitive ability':

> To not study and yet to be able to do *x* means that one depends on human nature's own ability. This is what is best [most *liang*]. It is the greatest ability human beings can have. (*Correct Meaning of the* Mencius 13, *Exhausting the Mind A* #15, p. 529)

In the Qing dynasty, Jiao Xun made his own remarks on the passage:

> Intuitive ability is said of the greatest type of ability. Intuitive knowing is said of the greatest type of knowing. The greatest type of knowing and the greatest type of ability are what one is most able to do and know; that is the peak of ability and of knowing. (Ibid.)

Zhu Xi commented on the phrase 'conscience' in the *Mencius*:

The conscience is the naturally good heart/mind, that is, the mind of benevolence and justice. (*Collected Notes on the* Mencius 11, *Gaozi A*, p. 88)

On the term *liang* as used in 'intuitive ability' and 'intuitive knowledge,' he notes,

'*Liang*' is what is naturally good. (Ibid. 13, *Exhausting the Mind A*, p. 103)

Thus from the glosses it seems that the reading of *liang* as 'good' is indeed correct. From the point of view of thought it is also correct to interpret the Mencian terms as meaning what is naturally good, whether of ability, mind, or knowledge. What is at stake is one's a priori moral awareness. This is given by heaven.

Cheng Hao, Cheng Yi, Zhu Xi, and Lu Jiuyuan all continued in the tradition established by the *Mencius* of an a priori moral awareness. Their common point of view is well expressed by Cheng Hao:

Innate ability and innate knowledge have no cause but they come from heaven and are not dependent on human beings. (*SKQS* 698, *Surviving Works of the Two Chengs* 2a, p. 23a)

Wang Shouren

In the Ming dynasty Wang Shouren advocated "the extension of the innate knowledge of the good."* This represented a development of the thought of Mencius. By "innate knowledge" Wang meant a priori moral awareness, intuitive ability to make moral judgments, and subjective self-awareness.

Wang held that the conscience is the ability to distinguish between right and wrong:

The conscience is simply the mind that is able to distinguish right and wrong. Right and wrong are simply liking and disliking. If one can but like and dislike then one will fully grasp

---

*Wing-Tsit Chan describes this as Wang's greatest contribution to Chinese philosophy. See Chan, *Source Book*, p. 656.

right and wrong. If one can but distinguish right and wrong then one can fully cope with the myriad affairs and the myriad changes. (*SBBY: Complete Books of Yang Ming* 3, *Instructions for Practical Living C*, p. 16a; WTC #288)

The mind that can distinguish right and wrong is one that knows what is good and what is evil and is able to choose between them. Wang formulated four axioms to sum up his teaching:*

Being without good or evil is the substance of the mind;
There being good and evil comes about with the movement
   of intentions;
Knowing good and knowing evil is the conscience;
Doing good and removing evil is the investigation of things.
(Ibid., p. 21a; WTC #315)

Wang Shouren emphasized that the conscience is the subject's own self-consciousness:

That small conscience of yours is the norm governing your own house and the place of your own thoughts and concepts. When other things are 'so' it recognizes them as 'so'; when other things are 'not-so' it recognizes them as 'not-so.' (Ibid., pp. 2b–3a; WTC #206)
    The conscience is originally complete and whole. When things are 'so' then it knows them as 'so'; when things are 'not-so' it knows them as 'not-so.' If we but rely on it with regard to what is 'so' and 'not-so,' everything will be correct. This conscience is, furthermore, your perspicacious teacher. (Ibid., p. 12a; WTC #265)

This conscience is an inner awareness possessed a priori by all human beings. Wang believes that the conscience is the principle of heaven:

The principle of heaven is in the human mind from of old until now without end or beginning. The principle of heaven is the conscience. (Ibid., p. 15b; WTC #284)

---

*For a discussion of the importance of these axioms in Wang's thought see ibid., pp. 688–689.

Conscience operates only in music, sex, wealth and profit. If one can extend one's innate consciousness of the good such that it is pure and clear, without any hinderance, then all one's dealings with music, sex, wealth and profit will be instances of the operations of the principle of heaven. (Ibid., p. 25a; WTC #327)

The conscience is also able to perceive the principle of heaven through the intercourse of sounds and colors.

In human beings the conscience goes along with you as you are. It is not possible to extinguish it. Even the thief knows that he should not be a thief. If one calls him a thief, he will still feel ashamed. (Ibid., p. 3a; WTC #207)

The conscience is the inner awareness of what is right. It suffices for one to be attentive to it for all evil thoughts to go away:

If a person knows the knack of the conscience then no matter how many evil thoughts and wrong desires abound once it [the conscience] is awakened all will naturally disappear. Truly it is a grain of spiritual cinnabar which can turn iron into gold. (Ibid., pp. 3a–b; WTC #209)

The term 'extension' in the expression "extension of the innate knowledge of the good" is derived by combining the phrase "conscience [innate knowledge]" from the *Mencius* with the notion of extension of knowledge found in the *Great Learning*. Wang combined the two expressions into one. In the *Great Learning* the expression 'extension of knowledge' means 'to attain to knowledge.'* Wang used the expression to mean extending one's knowledge to the utmost:

We extend our knowledge, that is, we go on reaching out to the limits imposed. Today the conscience sees something as such. If we keep to the limits of today's knowing we can go on to the utmost. Tomorrow the conscience will have new intuition and then one keeps to the limits of tomorrow's knowl-

---

* *Great Learning* 5, p. 365.

edge and presses on to fill up the limits to the utmost. (Ibid.,
p. 5b; WTC #225)

To extend one's conscience in this way is to increase one's inner moral awareness to the utmost.

The school of the Chengs and Zhu Xi considered benevolence, justice, the rites, and wisdom to be the principle of heaven; that is, they made the basic Confucian moral norms into the guiding lines of heaven and earth. Wang Shouren considered that the same four norms were the principle of heaven but he situated them in the conscience. He saw them as demands put on the inner mind. The former school raised principle up to heaven; the latter placed it in the human mind. Both schools protected the Confucian moral concepts. Although Wang Shouren's notion of extending innate knowledge of the good can be described as maintaining the Confucian values, it is more than that. He showed a spirit of independence that is not bound to tradition.

> What is valuable about learning is gained in the mind. If I examine something in the mind and find it untrue, even if it be the words of Confucius, I would not dare to consider it true. How much less from people inferior to Confucius? If I examine something in the mind and find it to be true, even though the words be from ordinary folk, I would not dare to hold them false. How much less those of Confucius!" (Ibid. 2, *Instructions for Practical Living B, Letter in Reply to Vice-Minister Luo Zheng'an,** p. 27a; WTC #173)

The authority of the mind is superior to that of Confucius. The right and wrong discerned by the mind are superior to those stated by Confucius.

> With respect to details and circumstances the conscience is like the carpenter's square and compass to areas and lengths. The changes of details and circumstances cannot be predicted just as areas and lengths are infinite and cannot be all measured. . . . If one does not realize that in an instant of thought in one's mind and conscience a minute mistake in the beginning can

---

*Luo Qinshun (1465–1547). *Zi:* Yun Sheng; *Hao:* Zheng An, from present-day Jiangxi Province. This letter dates from 1520.

lead to an infinite error in the end, then what is the point of study? . . . Shun did not tell his father before he married. Is it really that he first examined previous cases of those who did not tell their fathers before they married and used this as a norm? Then from what book could Shun get such a norm or what persons could he ask in order to do this? Is it not rather that he looked for it as a concept of conscience in his mind, weighed up the pros and cons and could do no other? Wu did not first bury his father before leading the army to battle. Is it really the case that there were cases of people who did not bury their fathers before leading troops to battle who could serve as a norm? Then from what book could Wu get such a norm or what persons could he ask in order to do this? Is it not rather that he looked for it as a concept of conscience in his mind, weighed up the pros and cons and could do no other? If Shun's mind was not sincere about having no posterity and Wu's mind was not sincere about saving the people, then the former not telling his father before marrying and the latter not burying his father before leading the army to battle, would be the greatest cases of being unfilial and unloyal. And later people do not fully employ their consciences so as to carefully examine what corresponded to what was right and what was principled in their mind. Rather they wanted to indulge in empty discussions about changeable things and maintain that this is the root of affairs and hope to not be at a loss when things come to pass. They are far off the point. (Ibid., *Letter in Reply to Gu Dongqiao,** pp. 8a–9a; WTC #139)

Whatsoever one encounters, it is not necessary to find precedents in books or ask advice of others. One should look in one's mind. One's notion of the conscience or weighing the matter should resolve the problem. This is clearly an attack on sticking too literally to what one is taught and a recipe for the development of the independence of the individual. This also emphasizes the individual's own self-consciousness. In the course of history

*Gu Lin (1476–1545), a poet and official.

Wang Shouren's theory has had a role in destroying outmoded and corrupt traditions.

Innate knowledge and innate moral awareness of the conscience are to be upheld. Mencius' praise of ability attained without learning and knowledge achieved without thought was unrealistic, however. Human moral awareness is rooted in social history. It is over a long period of history that people recognize what they ought to do and what they ought not to do. This sociohistorical moral awareness becomes the person's own moral awareness. It is having this awareness that is termed 'innate knowledge' or 'conscience.' The duty of cultural education is to develop and nurture this moral awareness.

Part Three
Epistemology

I. Theory of Knowledge

Chinese philosophers were not concerned with how knowledge was acquired but rather with what knowledge should be acquired and what ought to be the object of knowledge and research.

55. Knowledge, Wisdom
Zhi¹, Zhi⁴
知, 智

The Mohist logicians attempted an analysis of different types of knowing; Xunzi distinguished 'knowing' (zhi, first tone) from 'wisdom' (zhi, fourth tone). Later philosophy raised such questions as the nature of moral knowledge and the relationship of the knower to the object known.

In the pre-Qin period epistemology was more highly developed among the Mohists and in the *Xunzi*. Although the subject arose in Song and Ming philosophy it was treated in a more sporadic manner. One problem that has always been treated along with knowledge in Chinese philosophy is that of action.

Pre-Qin: The Value of Knowledge

Confucius treated knowledge, benevolence, and courage as on a par:

> The one who knows does not go astray; the one who is benevolent does not worry and the one who is courageous does not fear. (*Analects* 9, *Zi Han* #28, p. 225)
>
> The way of the gentleman is threefold but I am not able to practice it: the one who is benevolent does not worry; the one who knows does not go astray and the one who is courageous does not fear. (*Analects* 14, *Xian Asked* #30, p. 286)

Confucius himself claimed that

> At forty, I did not go astray. (*Analects* 2, *On Administration* #4, p. 146)

This implies that he had then attained the level of the one who knows. Confucius was opposed to people claiming that they know when in fact they do not. He told Zi Lu (known as You):

> You, shall I teach what knowing is? When you know something to admit that you know it and when you do not know something to admit that you do not know it: this is knowing. (*Analects* 2, *On Administration* #17, p. 151)

Confucius was opposed to taking lack of knowledge as knowledge:

> There are those who do not know and yet act. I do not do that. Hearing much and choosing what is good and following it; seeing much and remembering it is the second kind of knowing. (*Analects* 7, *Shu Er* #27, pp. 203–204)

Thus, though proclaiming the virtues of knowledge, Confucius gives no analysis of knowledge as such.

Mencius said that the mind that can discriminate 'so' and 'not-so' is the starting point of knowledge. (*Mencius* 2, *Gongsun Chao A*, #6). 'So' and 'not-so' refer mainly to right and wrong, though they would also include 'true and false.' In talking of knowledge, however, Mencius did not limit himself to ethics:

> "To raise something high one must begin from the top of a mound; to dig deep down one must begin in a stream or marsh." Should one who practices administration and does not follow the way of the former kings be said to have knowledge? (*Mencius* 4, *Li Lou A*, #1)
>
> What I dislike about your knowledgeable ones is the effort they put into their argumentation. If those knowledgeable persons would only do as Yu did to the water then there would be nothing to dislike in their knowledge. In dealing with the water Yu found it the easiest passage. If the knowledgeable persons would find the path of greatest simplicity their knowledge would also be great. Heaven is so high and the stars so distant that if we investigate their phenomena one can know

the solstice of a thousand years ago just by sitting and ex-trapolating. (*Mencius* 4, *Li Lou B*, #26)

Here knowledge includes astronomical lore but again Mencius did not explain what knowledge itself is.

Pre-Qin Analysis of Knowledge

The Mohists gave the most detailed analysis of knowledge in the pre-Qin period:

> The '*zhi*' (intelligence/consciousness) is the capability.
> The 'intelligence': it being the means by which one knows, one necessarily does know. (Like the eyesight.) (*Mohist Canons* A3, p. 267)

The term *zhi* (to know) here refers to the subjective power by which one knows, the intelligence.

> '*Zhi*' (knowing) is the connecting.
> 'Thinking': by means of one's intelligence one seeks something, but does not necessarily find it. (Like peering.) (*Mohist Canons* A5, p. 267)

Here 'knowing' refers to being able to know external things.

> '*Zhi*' (understanding/wisdom) is the illumination.
> 'Understanding': by means of one's intelligence, in dis-course about the thing one's knowledge of it is apparent. (Like clearness of sight.) (*Mohist Canons* A6, p. 267)

In this definition knowledge is an intellectual grasp of facts that are ar-ranged by discourse or sorting and classifying.

In these three definitions the Mohists included three levels of human knowing. There is recognition and there is knowing. Recognition is more superficial than knowing. To know someone's name is a case of recogni-tion. To understand why a person does something is a case of knowing. Thus in ancient Chinese 'knowing' includes both 'awareness of' and 'un-derstanding of.'

The *Canons* give a further analysis:

> '*Zhi*' (know). By hearsay, by explanation, by personal experi-
> ence. The name, the object, how to relate, how to act.
>
> Having received it at second hand is knowing by 'hear-
> say.' Knowing that something square will not rotate is 'by ex-
> planation.' Having been a witness oneself is knowing 'by per-
> sonal experience.' What something is called by is its 'name.'
> What is so called is the 'object.' The mating of name and ob-
> ject is 'relating.' To intend and to perform are to 'act.' (*Mohist
> Canons* A80, p. 327)

Thus there are three types of ways of acquiring knowledge. The first is by
listening to what someone else says, the second by rational deduction, and
the third by one's own direct experience. Any form of knowing must encompass the name of the object known. The name of the object should
match the reality of the object. The reality includes the actual use of the
object and thus comprises both purpose and action. For the Mohists action
was a form of knowing; knowing cannot be divorced from reality.

There is a definition similar to those included under Canons 3–6
above in the *Zhuangzi*:

> Knowing is the connecting, knowledge is the representa-
> tion, what knowledge does not know is as though peered at.
> (*Zhuangzi* 23, *Geng Sang Chu*, line 71; *Mohist Canons*, p. 268)

By 'knowing is the connecting' is to be understood knowledge acquired
through the senses connecting to objects. By 'knowledge is the represen-
tation' is to be understood knowledge acquired through rational reflection. The highlighting of what is not known is a feature of Daoist thought.

In the *Guanzi* a distinction was made between what is known and
the means by which one knows:

> People all desire to know but no one looks for the means by
> which to know. What is known is 'that.' The means by which to
> know is 'this.' If one does not cultivate the 'this,' how can one
> ever know 'that'? (*Guanzi* 36, *Technique of the Heart A*, 2:6)*

'This' is the subjective element, 'that' the object known.

---

*The text is amended by Wang Niansun. Allyn W. Rickett follows this amendment;
see *Kuan-Tzu: A Repository of Early Chinese Thought*, Hong Kong: Hong Kong University
Press, 1965, p. 174, n. 109.

The *Xunzi* distinguished knowledge and wisdom:

> That in a person by which they know is called knowledge. That knowledge which matches reality is called wisdom. (*Xunzi* 22, *On the Rectification of Terms*, line 5)

The first of these definitions corresponds to what the *Mohist Canons* described as the 'capability.' The second refers to what the *Canons* called 'illumination,' that is, understanding by means of intelligence. The *Xunzi* also says how human beings can know:

> To be able to know is the nature of human beings; what can be known are the principles of things. (*Xunzi* 21, *The Removal of Prejudices*, lines 78–79)

Human beings are able to know and the principles of things can be known. The *Xunzi* gives a longer account of the process of knowing:

> The organs of members of the same kind with the same emotions perceive things in the same way.... The mind collects the knowledge of the senses. It is because the mind collects knowledge that it is possible to know sound through the ear and form through the eye. But the collection of knowledge must also depend on the natural organs first registering it according to its classification. If the five organs register it without knowing what it is, and the mind collects it without understanding it, then everyone says there is no knowledge. (*Xunzi* 22, *On the Rectification of Terms*, lines 16, 19–20)

The collection of knowledge is not merely a passive activity but an active summoning through the senses.* It underlines the work of the mind. The 'registering' undertaken by the sense organs corresponds to the Mohist 'connecting.' According to the *Xunzi* the mind can not only know sounds and forms but can also know the Way:

> The key to administration is to know the Way. How can a person know the Way? By the mind. How does the mind know? By being spacious, united and still. The mind never ceases to store [things] yet there is still what is called 'spaciousness.' The

---

*See Chan, Wing-tsit, A *Source Book in Chinese Philosophy* (Princeton: Princeton University Press, 1963), p. 125, n. 33.

mind never ceases to have plurality yet it still has what is called 'unity.' The mind never ceases to move, yet it still has what is called 'stillness.' When persons are born they have knowledge. If there is knowledge there are ideas. Ideas are stored. Yet there is still what is called 'spaciousness.' This spaciousness means that what is already stored does not interfere with what is about to be received. When the mind is born it has knowledge. Knowledge contains differences. These differences consist of perceiving more than one thing at the same time. To perceive more than one thing at a time is 'plurality.' Yet the mind has what is called 'unity.' The unity of the mind means that 'this one' does not interfere with 'that one.' When the mind sleeps it dreams. When it rests it goes off on its own accord. When it is employed it reflects. Thus the mind is never not moving. Yet it has what is called 'stillness.' Stillness means that dreams and fantasies do not confuse one's knowledge. (*Xunzi* 21, *The Removal of Prejudices*, lines 34–39)

By practicing methods that lead to the spaciousness, unity, and stillness of the mind one can know the Way. By 'spaciousness' is to be understood that one's mind is empty and free of prejudice. By 'unity' is to be understood concentration on the task at hand, and by 'stillness' is meant that dreams and fantasies do not interfere in the course of knowing.

The Confucians of the Han and Tang periods did not produce any new theories of knowledge. The Buddhist Consciousness-Only School gave a detailed analysis of knowing. Its main tenets came from India and so will not be discussed here.*

The Song Dynasty

Zhang Zai referred to knowledge as that which unites inner and outer:

People say that they have knowledge and that they receive through the ears and eyes. In receiving they unite what is from inner and outer. If one knows how to unite inner and outer

---

*Interested readers may consult Chan, *Source Book*, pp. 370–95. Chan notes that this school produced texts that were the most difficult to read and translate of all the Buddhist schools.

without the ears and eyes then one's knowledge goes far beyond that of other people. (*SKQS* 697, *Correcting the Unenlightened* 7, *Great Mind*, p. 116b)

Knowledge is largely dependent on what comes from the outside. The outside world bestirs the subject, who then knows:

> How is it that people know? It is because things have similarities and differences in form and because there are constant changes occurring so the unity of inner and outer by the ears and eyes calls for natural talent and then one can be said to know already as if automatically. (Ibid., p. 117a)

Zhang Zai distinguished two kinds of knowledge. What can be known by the union of inner and outer accomplished by means of the senses is knowing by seeing and hearing, whereas the knowing that lies without the ears and eyes is what intellectual nature knows:

> The knowing of seeing and hearing is gained when things interact with one and so one knows. It is not something that intellectual nature can know. What intellectual nature knows does not appear in the seeing and hearing. (Ibid., pp. 116a–b)

Intellectual nature knows the wondrous changes of heaven and earth:

> The *Changes* speak of going to the utmost of the wondrous and knowing transformation. This is not something that the force of knowledge can achieve but rather it occurs when virtue is full and benevolence at its peak. . . .
>
> Going to the utmost of the wondrous and knowing transformation is not something that can be gained by forcing the process of thought but rather comes from cultivating oneself fully and to the limit. Thus by merely honoring virtue externally a gentleman can never come to the highest knowledge. (*SKQS* 697, *Correcting the Unenlightened* 4, *Wondrous Transformation*, pp. 109b, 110a)

Intellectual knowledge has moral cultivation as its basis. Although Zhang Zai had his reasons for thus establishing knowledge on the basis of morality, in claiming that this kind of knowledge is not the result of the exercise of thought and reflection he fell into error. Knowledge of heaven and earth and their wondrous transformations should still be considered to be due to the force of knowledge.

Cheng Yi did not distinguish clearly between the ability to know and what one knows:

> Knowledge is something I naturally have yet if one cannot bring it to perfection then one is not able to acquire anything. The perfection of knowing must entail having the Way. Thus it is said that the perfection of knowledge consists in the investigation of things. . . .
>
> The perfection of knowledge consists in the investigation of things. It is not a matter of exercising oneself from the outside. I already have this ability. It is because of things that I am led astray and then the principle of heaven is extinguished. Thus the sage wants to investigate them. (*SKQS* 698, *Surviving Works of the Two Chengs* 25, pp. 254a–b)

It is not clear what Cheng Yi meant by 'knowing.' It would seem to be a case of perception but it could also be what is perceived. Thus he says that he naturally has it and also that if one cannot bring it to perfection then one cannot acquire it.

The phrase "the perfection of knowledge consists in the investigation of things" comes from the *Great Learning*. Zhu Xi's exposition of knowledge, like that of Cheng Yi, also contains two aspects and is found in his commentary on the same phrase.

> The phrase "the perfection of knowledge consists in the investigation of things" means that if I want to perfect my knowledge I must look to things and fully understand their principles. The moral nature of the human mind means that it is never without knowing while all things under heaven are never without principles. When the principle is not fully understood it is only because one's knowledge does not go far enough. Therefore the Great Learning begins teaching and one must lead the students to go from what they already know about the principles of things to go on to fully know them and one must ask the students to go on to the end. Simply by long

use of force one day one will suddenly penetrate the principles and then all the outside and inside, fine and rough of every thing will be comprehended and in the entire substance and great function of my mind there will be nothing that is not clear. This is what is meant by investigating things and this is what is called the perfection of knowledge. (*Chapter and Verse Commentary on the* Great Learning, pp. 6a–b)

In this passage the knowing of the mind is contrasted with the principles of things known. 'Knowing' is here to be taken as the ability to know. In the clause "one's knowledge does not go far enough" 'knowledge' refers to the ability to know and also the content of what is known, with the stress falling largely on the latter aspect.

The Ming-Qing Era

Wang Shouren discussed knowledge solely as moral awareness:

> To know is the original substance of the mind. The mind can naturally know. When one sees one's father one naturally knows to show filial affection. When one sees an older sibling one naturally knows how to respect him as an older sibling. When one sees an infant about to fall into a well, one naturally knows to be compassionate. This is all the work of the conscience; one need not look for anything outside. (*SBBY: Instructions for Practical Living A*, p. 5a; WTC #8)

Here knowledge is portrayed as a knowledge of filial piety, respect for elder siblings, and compassion. All these are moral issues.

Both Zhu Xi and Wang Shouren advocated a priori views. Zhu Xi held that principle is in the mind, whereas Wang Shouren said that without mind there is no principle. Wang Tingxiang was opposed to these a priori forms of knowledge:

> The infant in the womb is only able to drink and eat. When it comes out of the womb it is able to see and hear. This is the knowing which is part of heaven-given nature. Wondrous transformation can never influence it. As for what is known by

practice, understanding, experience and questioning this is all knowledge that belongs to the human sphere. The affection of father, mother, older and younger siblings is the result of accumulated practice and close intimacy. Why is it so? Suppose that after the birth of the child the parents gave it to others to foster and it grew up knowing only its foster parents. Now were it to suddenly meet its real parents on the road, it would look on them as ordinary people. It might possibly insult or mock them. Can this really be called the knowing of heaven-sent nature? Thus from the example of the affection between parents and child it can be seen that the knowledge of any thing or affair whatsoever that is acquired through practice, understanding, experience or questioning is from human beings and is not given by heaven. (*Elegant Descriptions A*, p. 836)

This example proves quite clearly that the affection of the family is born of accumulated experience of living together and is not innate. He earlier said,

If one does not see nor hear the principles of things, even though one be a sage or philosopher one could not just, by thinking of them, know them. Take the case of an infant which when born is shut up in a dark room and is not able to touch things. When it grows up and comes out then it will not even be able to distinguish ordinary things. How much less would it know how far away and how high heaven and earth are, how deep and dark spirits and ghosts are, the changes of events under heaven from of old until now? By examining to the utmost limits could it attain and know them? (Ibid.)

Although he had not actually carried out the experiment himself, nonetheless what he says conforms to reality. Wang Tingxiang's critique of innate a priori knowledge is both thorough and convincing.

One problem that has always been treated along with knowledge in Chinese philosophy is that of action, or practice. Here we cite just one example from Wang Tingxiang:

One earnestly practices and carries out so as to keep to the heart of what is right and principled. (*Prudent Words* 1, *Qian*, p. 778)

'Practice' here refers to ethical conduct.

Wang Fuzhi discussed the origin of knowledge and awareness:

When forms, spirit and things all come together then there is
knowing and awareness. (*Notes on Master Zhang's* Correcting
the Unenlightened 1a, p. 33)

'Forms' in this context means the sense organs; 'spirit' is the mind itself
and 'things' are external objects. It is when all three come together that
there is knowing and consciousness.

Wang gave a detailed analysis of the ability to know and that which
one knows:

If one circumscribes something and then makes it the object of
a function then it is called 'that which.' To add a function to
the circumscribed area such that it [the function] has an effect
is called 'ability.' ... Thus if the function is to be taken as the
'that which' then there must be a reality which is its substance.
To take the function as the function and to be able to add an
effect is what is called 'ability.' But there must be a reality for
this function. There is a substance and a function then one
goes along with the ability and so the function is able to be
used for the substance and so one is able to assist its 'that
whichness.' When substance and function are united in relying on the reality and do not turn their back on its cause
then names and realities each call forth the other. (*Elaboration
on the Meaning of the* Book of History 5.5, *Shao Gu Wu Yi*,
p. 1483)

That which is known is the external area faced by the subject. To be able
to know is for the subject to add its function to the external area. What is
known must have its substance, whereas the ability to know must have a
function. The function of the subject is called forth by that which is known
and must correspond to it. The ability to know and that which is known
are distinct and should not be confused nor spoken of in the same breath.

The one who is accorded filial piety is the father. It is not appropriate to say that filial piety is the father. The one who is
cherished is the child. It is not appropriate to say that cherish-

ing is the child. That which is climbed is a mountain. It is not appropriate to say that climbing is the mountain. That which is forded is a stream. It is not appropriate to say that the fording is a stream. (Ibid., p. 1485)

The object known and the ability to know are two and not one. Wang Fuzhi concludes,

> With regard to whatsoever falls in the realm of the principles of things and of human relationships, the ability [to know] comes from the function of the ears, eyes and thoughts of the mind; 'that which' [is known] is not within, thus the mind is like utmost space. It is only when it is affected that it responds. Ability does not lie outside; thus to act benevolently depends on oneself. If one returns to oneself then one will certainly be sincere. (Ibid., p. 1486)

The ability to know and that which is known are distinguished as inner to outer. On one hand one must affirm the ability of the subject to move and on the other one must recognize the reality of the object. Wang Fuzhi's remarks on the ability and object of knowledge were largely directed against subjective idealists who would restrict the object yet still hope to attain to the ability.

56. Thought

Si, Lü

思, 慮

Thinking is not purely the normal activity of the mind, although the Mohists analyzed such matters, but rather the grasping of moral or ultimate principles. Early uses also included meditation.

The Spring and Autumn Period

The concept *si* has a very early origin. In the *Great Plan* chapter of the *Book of History*, it is listed as the fifth of five affairs:

Second: the five affairs: The first is called 'appearance'; the second 'speech'; the third 'seeing'; the fourth 'hearing'; the fifth 'thinking.' The [virtue of] appearance is called 'respect,' of speech 'logic,' of seeing 'clarity,' of hearing 'distinctness,' of thinking 'perspicacity.' Respect becomes manifest in seriousness, logic in orderliness, clarity in wisdom, distinctness in deliberation and perspicacity in sageliness. (*The Book of History* 5.4, *The Great Plan* #6, pp. 225–226 [Legge, pp. 326–327])

Ma Rong notes that

Perspicacity is comprehension. (*Yuhan Shanfang* vol. 1: *Commentary of Mr. Ma on the* Book of History 3, p. 389a)

The *Explanation of Words and Characters* says,

Sageliness is comprehension. (*Explanation of Words and Characters* 12a, p. 250a)

The standard of thinking is comprehension, that is, understanding the principles of affairs. The *Great Plan* lists thinking after seeing and hearing, thus implying that perception by the senses precedes thinking.

Confucius mentioned thinking in connection with study:

Studying without thinking is useless; thinking without studying is dangerous. (*Analects 2, On Administration* #15, p. 150)

This dictum is indeed apposite and still as valid today as when it was first uttered. To study is to receive the learning of previous generations; to think is to reflect oneself on what happens and establish conclusions independently. Study and thought are both required; neither can be neglected. Confucius believed that of the two study is the foundation:

I have spent the whole day without eating and the whole night without sleeping so as to think. It was of no use. Far better to study. (*Analects 15, Duke Ling of Wei* #30, pp. 302–303)

Merely to study, though, would be of no use:

The master said, "Ci, do you think I am one who studies a lot and remembers it all?" He [Zi Gong] replied, "Is it not so?"

> He [Confucius] said, "No. I take the One to thread it all
> through." (*Analects* 15, *Duke Ling of Wei* #2, p. 295)*

Study involves the tasks of learning and committing to memory, whereas
thought enables one to thread everything together into one whole. Simply
by study one cannot produce a synthesis of everything. The term translated 'thread' is explained in the *Guang Ya* as follows:

> 'Guan' [to thread] is to pierce through. (*Guang Ya* 5, *Ex-
> plaining Words*, p. 58)

In other words, all that one has studied is to be knit together with one
basic principle that can penetrate every part of knowledge.

The Warring States Period

Mencius placed special emphasis on thinking. Thinking is the function of
the mind, in contrast to the various functions of the five sense organs.

> The sense of the ears and eyes do not think and are obscured
> by things. Things connect with things and then lead them
> away. The organ of the mind is thinking. By thinking it gains
> the [right view of affairs]. If one does not think then one does
> not acquire [the right view]. These are what heaven has given
> to human beings. Let one first stand in what is most important
> and then the lesser things cannot take away from one. (*Mencius*
> 6, *Gaozi A*, #15)

What is it that the mind thinks about? Mencius says that it is principle and
respect:

> With respect to tastes mouths have the same likings; with re-
> spect to sounds ears have the same pleasures; with respect to
> beauty eyes have the same standards; as for minds why do they
> alone not have something to agree on? Indeed, they do, namely

---

* Duan-mu Ci. *Zi*: Zi Gong, from Wei, 31 years younger than Confucius. He served in
government in Lu and Wei. See J. Legge, *The Chinese Classics* (Oxford: Clarendon, 1893;
reprint, Taibei: Southern Materials Centre, 1985), 1:115–116.

principle and respect. The sages simply grasped what my mind,
in common with all others, likes before I did. (Ibid., #7)

In other words, thinking attains to principles and respect, that is, to moral
norms.

In a meditation text similar to a passage discovered at Mawangdui,
Changsha, *16 Canons* 15,* the *Inner Training* chapter of the *Guanzi*
stresses the importance of thinking:

> Concentrate your '*qi*' until you become Spirit-like, and the
> myriad things are complete [within]. Can you concentrate? Can
> you adhere to the One? Can you know good fortune from bad
> without resorting to divination? Can you halt [at the right
> place]? Can you stop [when you ought to stop]? Can you forgo
> seeking from others but rather obtain fulfillment in yourself?
> Think about it! Think about it! And again think about it! If
> you think about it and it still is not comprehended, [you may
> believe] the spirits will make it comprehensible. Yet [it is com-
> prehended] not through the power of the spirits, but through
> the utmost development of your own essence and *qi*. When
> the four parts of the body have become correct and the blood
> and breath have become quiescent, you may make your in-
> tellect adhere to the One and concentrate your heart. Your
> ears and eyes will not go astray. And even though [the Way]
> be distant, it will seem as if near. Thought and inquiry pro-
> duce knowledge. (*Guanzi* 49, *Inner Training*, 2:129; Rickett,
> pp. 164–165)

A very similar text is to be found in the chapter titled *Technique of the
Heart B*:

> Can you concentrate? Can you adhere to the One? Can you
> know good fortune from bad without resorting to divination?
> Can you halt [at the right place]? Can you stop [when you
> ought to stop]? Can you refrain from asking of others but
> rather obtain fulfillment in yourself? Therefore it is said: Think

---

* See R. D. S. Yates, *Five Lost Classics* (New York: Ballantine, 1997), p. 153.

> about it! If you think about it and its meaning is still not ap-
> prehended, [you may believe] the spirits will teach it. Yet [its
> meaning is apprehended] not through the power of the spirits,
> but through the utmost development of your own essence
> and *qi*. (*Guanzi* 37, *Technique of the Heart B*, 2:16; Rickett,
> p. 169)

Although it is hard to be certain which of these pieces is the older, it would appear from the remark "therefore it is said" in the latter that it must be posterior. These passages clearly underline the importance of thinking and seem to attribute a role of assistance to ghosts and spirits. In reality it is one's essence and *qi* that help.

Some Daoist works underline immediate consciousness without the need for thinking. The opening line of a chapter by an otherwise unknown hermit and anarchist in the *Zhuangzi* reads as follows:

> Menders of their nature by vulgar study, trying to recover what
> they originally were; muddlers of the desires by vulgar think-
> ing, trying to perfect their enlightenment—we may call them
> the blinkered and benighted people. (*Zhuangzi* 16, *Menders of
> Nature*, line 1; Graham, *Chuang-tzu*, p. 171)

According to this view it is impossible to attain enlightenment through thinking. An even more explicit rejection of thought is given in chapter 22:

> If one neither thinks nor reflects, one can know the Way.
> (*Zhuangzi* 22, *Knowledge Roams North*, line 5)

This passage makes the attainment of the highest form of consciousness dependent on not thinking or reflecting.

When Confucius and Mencius spoke of thinking they used the term *si*; when the Mohists mentioned the same idea they used the term *lü*. The *Mohist Canons* described thinking as a matter of seeking on the analogy of peering at something without necessarily managing to see it:

> 'Lü' (thinking/forethought) is the seeking.
>> 'Thinking': by means of one's intelligence one seeks
>> something, but does not necessarily find it. (Like peering.)
> (*Mohist Canons* A4, p. 266)

The *Xunzi* also used the term *lü*:

The liking, disliking, joy, anger, grief and happiness of human nature are called emotions. When the mind selects from among these emotions this is called thinking (*lu*). When the mind thinks and can act accordingly, this is called acquired training. (*Xunzi* 22, *On the Rectification of Terms*, lines 3–4)

Lü is also expressed by the phrase *si-lü*:

The sages gathered their thoughts (*si-lu*) and became familiar with habitual behavior and its causes and thence produced the rites and justice and instituted legal systems. (*Xunzi* 23, *The Nature of Man Is Evil*, line 24)

Si-lü refers to the selective activity of the mind.

The Medieval Period

Writing in the late fifth century A.D., Fan Zhen also used the term *lu* to talk about thought:

QUESTION: If the body is the same as the soul, are the hands also the soul?

REPLY: All are part of the soul.

QUESTION: If all are part of the soul and the soul can think, the hands must also be able to think?

REPLY: The hands have sensitive powers but do not have intellectual powers.

QUESTION: Are they two or one?

REPLY: Sensation is also reasoning: sensation is superficial and reasoning is profound.

QUESTION: If thus, there must be two reasonings. If there are two reasonings, are there two souls?

REPLY: Human beings are but one entity; how can they have two distinctive souls?

QUESTION: If there are not two, how does it come about that there are sensitive powers as well as intellectual powers?

REPLY: As hands and feet differ though there is but one person. Reasoning and sensation also differ yet belong to one soul.

QUESTION: If intellectual powers are not concerned with hands and feet, what is concerned with them?

REPLY: The mind is the source of all intellectual operations. (*Complete Liang Literature* 45, *Treatise on the Destruction of the Spirit*, p. 3210a)

Thinking is related to the discernment of right and wrong, true and false and is not related to sensations of pain and itching.

Zhou Dunyi drew together both Confucian and Daoist viewpoints and thus affirmed the value of thought as well as nonthought:

It is said in the Great Plan that "thought should be penetrating and profound. . . . Such thinking leads to sageliness." Having no thought is the foundation and thinking penetratively is its function. With subtle incipient activation becoming active on the one hand, and with sincerity becoming active in response, on the other—having no thought and yet penetrating all—thus is one a sage. One cannot penetrate subtlety without thought, and cannot penetrate all without profound thought. Thus the ability to penetrate all comes from the ability to penetrate subtlety, and the ability to penetrate subtlety comes from thinking. Therefore, thinking is the foundation of the sage's effort and is also the subtle, incipient activation of good fortune and misfortune. (*SKQS* 697, *Comprehending the* Book of Changes 9, *Thought*, pp. 34a–b)

From thought one penetrates subtlety and from subtlety one can penetrate everything. Without thought one cannot understand anything. Such is the sage. Thus although Zhou put lack of thought on the highest plane he still recognized the importance of thought.

The Modern Period

Among the later Confucian thinkers only Wang Fuzhi's comments deserve notice. Wang built on the Mencian theory that thinking is the proper activity of the mind:

Mencius' talk of this 'mind' is a treasure that has no equal in all time.... Only the mind thinks and then benevolence and justice are obtained from it and what is obtained can only be benevolence and justice. Consider a person who is hungry who thinks of eating, or one who is thirsty who thinks of drinking, or who is young who thinks of sex, or who is strong and thinks of fighting or who is old and thinks of getting. None of these cases can truly be said to be cases of 'thinking.' Even if one thinks of the object one might not get it and if one does not think of it one might still obtain it. What the thinker can acquire or not acquire is only benevolence and justice.... Only thinking of justice and principle is indeed thinking and is indeed the office of the mind. Thinking of eating and of sex and the like is not the office of the mind and cannot properly be called 'thinking.' Mencius' talking about thinking is a treasure that has no equal in all time and it is said that thinking sincerely is the way for human beings and this especially to complete and clarify what Zi Si says about the reality of integrity. Thinking is the way for human beings . . . and that in which human beings differ from birds and beasts is this alone. (*Great and Full Explanation on Reading the Four Books* 10.1, *Mencius: Gaozi A* #26, pp. 699, 700, 705)

According to Wang, only thinking about justice and principle merits the designation 'thinking.' This is what distinguishes human beings as human. Thinking about principle and justice means being able to engage in rational and moral debate. Wang in fact put the stress on the moral debate.

57. Technique of the Mind

Xin Shu

心術

The mind, xin, *needs to be managed by an art or technique,* shu, *to preserve it from prejudice.*

The *Guanzi*

The expression 'technique of the mind' is found in the *Guanzi* and in the *Xunzi*. Two chapters of the *Guanzi* bear the phrase in their titles.* Yet, as Rickett points out, only the content of the first of these two chapters bears any relation to the title.† The main theme of this technique is the necessity of inner cultivation.

> In the body the mind holds the place of the prince. The duties of the nine apertures represent the separate offices. If the mind is fixed on the Way, the nine apertures [will function] correctly. If it becomes filled with desire and lust, the eyes will not see colors and the ears will not hear sounds. (*Guanzi* 36, *Technique of the Heart* A, 2:1; Rickett, *Guanzi*, p. 172)
>
> The ears and eyes are the sense organs for seeing and hearing. If the mind does not interfere in the activities of seeing and hearing, the sense organs will be able to maintain their separate functions. Now if one's mind has desires, one's eyes will not see when things pass by nor will one's ears hear when there are sounds. Therefore it is said, "If those on high depart from the Way those below will neglect their work." Therefore the technique of the mind consists in controlling the apertures through non-activity. (Ibid., 2:5; Rickett, *Guanzi*, p. 172)

This states the major principles that the mind should observe.

In the *Seven Standards* chapter of the *Guanzi* the expression is also found, but here it refers to six patterns of mental behavior found among the people.

> Being factual, sincere, liberal, generous, temperate or altruistic are called "techniques of the mind." (*Guanzi* 6, *Seven Laws*, 1:71; Rickett, *Guanzi*, p. 129)
>
> Issuing orders that must be observed while not know-

---

*Author's note: These two chapters are the work of philosophers of the Warring States period in Qi who admired the thought of Guan Zhong. The names of the authors are not known with any certainty. Recent claims that they were Song Xing and Yin Wen are without any sure foundation.

†Rickett, *Kuan-tzu*, pp. 154–155.

ing the techniques of the mind is not possible. (Ibid.; Rickett, *Guanzi*, p. 130)

The *Xunzi*

The *Removal of Prejudices* chapter in the *Xunzi* calls for the removal of one-sided ways of looking at things so that one might be able to achieve an all-around vision. Being prejudiced toward one point of view is described as the public disaster of the technique of the mind.

> Everything that people suffer from comes from being prejudiced towards one twisted thing and so shut out from the great principles.... Desire is a prejudice, evil a prejudice, beginning a prejudice, ending a prejudice, distant a prejudice, near a prejudice, expansive a prejudice, shallow a prejudice, ancient a prejudice, present a prejudice. Any of the myriad things that is different can be a prejudice. This is the great disaster of the technique of the mind.... The sages know the disaster of the technique of the mind and see the calamity of prejudice and blindness, thus they are without desire and without hate, without beginning or ending, without near or distant, without expansiveness or shallowness, without antiquity or the present. They can equally well get rid of all the myriad things and maintain the balance level. Therefore, all the differences are not able to prejudice them nor confuse their norms. (*Xunzi* 21, *The Removal of Prejudices*, lines 1, 6–7, 28–29)

The *Xunzi* does not actually say what the technique of the mind is, but from the context it would seem to mean the way of thinking and the kind of thought patterns. The disaster to which it is subject is to be inclined toward one point of view.

The *Record of Rites*

The third text that discusses the phrase is the *Record of Music* in the *Record of Rites*:

> The people have the nature of blood, *qi*, a mind and knowl-
> edge and do not have constancy in grief, joy, happiness and
> anger. These respond to things and are then moved and from
> this the technique of the mind takes shape. Therefore, at a
> trembling and quavering sound the people are anxious and
> fearful. At a sound that is expansive, slow, easy, rich, cultivated
> and clear the people are full of joy. At a rough, bold and con-
> tinuously martial sound the people are strong and courageous.
> At a ceremonious, solemn and reverent sound the people are
> respectful. At a soothing, harmonious and gentle sound the
> people are tender and loving. At a licentious, passionate and
> violent sound the people are depraved and disordered. (*Record
> of Rites* 19, *Record of Music*, p. 211)

Zheng Xuan commented on the expression 'technique of the mind' by
saying,

> Technique is that from which something comes. (*SKQS* 116,
> *Record of Rites* 38, *Record of Music*, p. 114b)

This means the way in which the mind expresses itself.
Kong Yingda said,

> Technique is said of the path by which something comes.
> 'Form' means that it is seen. This is because it is moved by
> things it encounters and then the path from which the tech-
> nique of the mind comes is formed and visible. (*SKQS* 116, *Com-
> mentary on the* Record of Rites 38, *Record of Music*, p. 115a)

'Form' refers to the attitudes produced by the music: anxious and fearful,
full of joy, strong and courageous, respectful, tender and loving, and de-
praved and disordered. This is what the text means by the technique of the
mind.

Thus in all these three texts the meaning of the phrase under discussion is the same. It can be summarized as referring to the attitude of
the inner mind or the method of thinking.*

---

*Author's note: The expression is still current in modern Chinese, as when one says
that the technique of the mind of a person is not correct. This refers to the goals of the person
or the ways used to achieve those goals.

58. Innate Moral Knowledge

Dexing suo Zhi

德性所知

'That which is known by virtuous nature' (De xing suo zhi) and the 'mind that has the Way' (Dao xin, for the latter see concept 59) are phrases that refer to innate moral knowledge. The mind is ultimately geared to moral realities and needs to keep itself focused on them.

The expression 'moral nature' is found in the *Mean and Harmony*, but it reached its development as a philosophical concept in the Song and post-Song periods. It is very similar to Kant's practical reason. No Chinese thinker, however, has analyzed it to the same degree that Kant has. The fullest expression of it in China is to be found in Wang Fuzhi's definition of it as loving good and hating evil. Nonetheless, no Chinese philosophers give an adequate exposition of the topic.

Moral Nature

The original context of the phrase is as follows:

> How great is the way of the sage! Like overflowing water, it sends forth and nourishes all things, and rises up to the height of heaven. All-complete is its greatness! It embraces the three hundred rules of ceremony, and the three thousand rules of conduct. It waits for the proper person and then it is trodden. Hence it is said, "Only by perfect virtue can the perfect path, in all its courses, be made real." Therefore the gentleman honors his moral nature and maintains constant inquiry and study, seeking to carry it out to its breadth and greatness, so as to omit none of the more exquisite and minute points which it embraces and to raise it to its greatest height and brilliancy, so as to pursue the course of the Mean. He cherishes his old knowledge and is continually acquiring new. He exerts an

honest, generous earnestness, in the esteem and practice of all propriety. (*Mean and Harmony* 27, p. 13 [Legge, pp. 422–423])

Zheng Xuan commented on this text, as follows:

Moral nature is nature at its most sincere. 'The Way' is like 'coming from.' If you ask about study. Study is sincerity. (*SKQS* 116, *Record of Rites* 53, *Mean and Harmony*, p. 373a)

This comment is in line with an earlier passage from the same work that reads,

Intelligence resulting from sincerity is called 'human nature' and sincerity resulting from intelligence is called 'teaching.' (*Mean and Harmony* 21, p. 11 [Legge, pp. 414–415])

Zheng Xuan related moral nature to the nature of the sage. Zhu Xi notes,

Moral nature is what I receive from the correct principle of heaven. (*Chapter and Verse Commentary on the* Mean and Harmony #27, p. 13)

Moral nature is the a priori nature of all persons, which has principle for its content. Although the theories of Zheng and Zhu differed, both held moral nature to be the root nature of morality, that is, the human nature, which from birth is naturally inclined to good.

Moral Nature and Knowledge

Zhang Zai discussed what moral nature knows.

The knowing of seeing and hearing is gained when things interact with one and so one knows. It is not something that moral nature can know. What moral nature knows does not appear in the seeing and hearing. (*SKQS* 697, *Correcting the Unenlightened* 7, *Great Mind*, pp. 116a–b)

Knowledge acquired by seeing and hearing is knowledge gained through the senses. What moral nature knows transcends sensory perception. What moral nature knows is wondrous transformation.

The *Changes* speak of going to the utmost of the wondrous and knowing transformation. This is not something that the force of knowledge can achieve but rather it occurs when virtue is full and benevolence at its peak. . . .

Going to the utmost of the wondrous and knowing transformation is not something that can be gained by forcing the process of thought but rather comes from cultivating oneself fully and to the limit. Thus by merely honoring virtue externally a gentleman can never come to the highest knowledge. (*SKQS* 697, *Correcting the Unenlightened* 4, *Wondrous Transformation*, pp. 109b, 110a)

By exerting oneself in morality one can reach the highest plane of knowledge, fathom the wondrous, and know transformations. Zhang Zai believed that knowledge is the union of inner and outer:

People say that they have knowledge and that they receive through the ears and eyes. In receiving they unite what is from inner and outer. If one knows how to unite inner and outer without the ears and eyes then one's knowledge goes far beyond that of other people. (*SKQS* 697, *Correcting the Unenlightened* 7, *Great Mind*, p. 116b)

The way to unite the inner and outer is what moral nature knows.

The knowing of seeing and hearing is gained when things interact with one and so one knows. It is not something that moral nature can know. What moral nature knows does not appear in the seeing and hearing. (Ibid., pp. 116a–b)

The uniting of inner and outer is what moral nature knows.

Cheng Yi did not talk of *what* moral nature knows but of the knowledge possessed by moral nature. The formulation differs only slightly from that of Zhang Zai but the meaning is quite different. Cheng Yi was talking about self-consciousness.

The knowledge [possessed by] seeing and hearing is not that possessed by moral nature. Things interact with things and so one knows them. This is not an internal matter. This is what is now called an extensive thing and a person of many abilities.

The knowledge of moral nature is not attached to seeing and hearing. (*SKQS* 698, *Surviving Works of the Two Chengs* 25, p. 255a)

Wang Fuzhi explains moral nature as follows:

Moral nature is not the nature of ears, eyes, mouth and body but what is possessed by the root of the mind, namely benevolence, justice, rites and wisdom. It is always present in the mind and though still cannot be forgotten, though moving cannot get lost. It does not incline to anything seen, heard, spoken or discussed but its virtue is all complete. (*Notes on Master Zhang's* Correcting the Unenlightened 2a, *The Heavenly Way*, p. 72)

Moral nature is liking good and disliking evil:

To like good and hate evil is moral nature. (Ibid. 3b, *Sincerity Resulting in Enlightenment*, p. 136)
　　The knowledge of moral nature is to follow principle and return to the source, dealing directly with the principle of the great beginning of the myriad things of heaven and earth. Thus it is what I get from heaven and what is said directly to me. (Ibid. 4a, *Great Mind*, pp, 144–145)

This is to say that the knowledge possessed by moral nature is knowledge of the principles and origins of the myriad things of heaven and earth.

Dai Zhen

Dai Zhen also held that man has moral nature:

Let us now approach this problem by comparing the human physical form with moral nature. The human physical form begins by being immature and small, but in the end it becomes mature and large; moral nature begins in ignorance, but ends in wisdom. As one grows in size and maturity, one's physical form depends on what one eats and drinks. It grows daily and is not a case of returning to its beginning. Moral nature depends upon learning, through which it progresses until one is wise, and this too is, quite obviously, not a case of returning to its beginning. (*An Evidential Study of the Meaning of Terms in the* Book of Mencius *A*, #14, p. 281)*

Xunzi stressed learning because he believed that virtues do not come from within but must be acquired from without. Mencius stressed learning because he believed that virtues are something we have within us but must be supported from without. The reason why food and drink can nourish the body's blood-and-*qi* is because the *qi* utilized does not come from a source different from that of the *qi* originally received from heaven and earth. Thus, although the nourishment comes from without, it can be transformed into blood-and-*qi* to fortify whatever is within. It is not possible that the inside does not have any originally endowed *qi*, but having acquired *qi* from outside, it is fortified. The same is true of the relation of inquiry and learning to human nature. When someone through inquiry and study joins his individual nature to the moral nature of the ancient sages and worthies, he is making use of what these sages and worthies said about moral nature to strengthen one's own moral nature. (Ibid. *B*, #26, p. 300)

All people have their own moral nature, which begins in ignorance and must go through inquiry and learning in order to develop. The content of moral nature is spelled out thus:

Desires are the natural tendencies of one's blood-and-*qi*; loving admirable virtue is the natural tendency of one's knowing mind. This was how Mencius explained the goodness of human nature. According to the natural tendency of our knowing mind, there is none who is not pleased with principle and justice; it is just that most of us have not fully grasped principle or that our actions are not in complete accord with justice. (Ibid. *A*, #15, p. 285)

---

*This translation and subsequent ones are largely based on Ann-ping Chin and M. Freeman, *Tai Chen on Mencius: Explorations in Words and Meaning* (New Haven: Yale University Press, 1990). The translators note that this passage contains an attack on Zhu Xi, who described learning as a return to the beginning.

Mencius had previously quoted a verse from the *Book of Songs*:

> Heaven engenders the mass of peoples;
> For any given thing there is a rule;
> The people have this normal nature;
> They tend to this admirable virtue.
> (*Book of Songs: Zheng Min*, p. 71 [Ode 260, #1])

Dai Zhen said that loving this admirable virtue is the natural tendency of the knowing mind. This is moral nature. Moral nature is to love the good.

In the Song dynasty Zhu Xi and Lu Jiuyuan had had a dispute about the role of study.

> Zhu Yuanhui [Zhu Xi] once wrote to one of his students say-ing, "Lu Zijing [Lu Jiuyuan] taught people only the doctrine of 'honoring the moral nature.' Therefore those who have studied under him are mostly scholars who put their beliefs into practice. But he neglected to follow the path of study and inquiry. In my teaching is it not true that I have put somewhat more emphasis on 'following the path of study and inquiry'? As a consequence, my pupils often do not approach his in putting beliefs into practice." From this it is clear that Yuanhui wanted to avoid two defects [failure to honor the moral nature and failure to practice] and combine the two merits [following the path of study and inquiry and practicing one's beliefs]. I do not believe this to be possible. If one does not know how to honor one's moral nature, how can one talk about following the path of study and inquiry? (*SKQS* 1156, *Complete Works of Xiang Shan: Selected Sayings* 1, p. 544b) [Chan, So, *Source Book*, p. 582 tr.]

Lu Jiuyuan believed that honoring the moral nature is what is most im-portant. Dai Zhen, in contrast, emphasized study:

> As for the Song period Lu [Jiuyuan] and the Ming period Chen [Liang] and Wang [Shouren], their learning is all a matter of empty talk and discussion. They pretended to honor moral nature so as to magnify their fame and dismissed the way of

inquiry and study. But then how can it be said to be honoring moral nature? (*Collected Literary Works* 9.3, *Letter to Shi
Zhongming on Study*, p. 184)

Dai Zhen believed that one must take the way of study and inquiry before
one can come to honor moral nature.

59. The Mind That Has the Way

Dao Xin

道心

A concept that is very close to moral nature is 'the mind that has the Way.'
The earliest reliable source for this phrase is the *Xunzi*:

> Previously, when Shun ruled over all under heaven, he did not
> need to issue proclamations and yet the myriad things were
> done.... Therefore the *Classic of the Way* says, "The human
> mind is anxious; the mind of the Way is subtle." If one be-
> comes as intelligent as a gentleman, one can then know the
> sources of anxiety and subtlety. (*Xunzi* 21, *The Removal of
> Prejudices*, lines 53, 54–55)

Whether the *Classic of the Way* is actually the name of a book is not clear.
The quotation given here also appears in the apocryphal and unreliable
"old text" version of the *Book of History*, which reads,

> The human mind is anxious; the mind which has the Way is
> subtle. Be discriminating, be undivided, that you may sincerely
> hold fast the Mean. (*Book of History* 2.2.2 #16, *Counsels of the
> Great Yu*, pp. 61–62)

It may be that the first part of this quotation was drawn from the *Xunzi*.

The two Chengs built on the old glosses on the phrase 'the human
mind is anxious; the mind which has the Way is subtle.' Zhu Xi produced a
more comprehensive analysis of 'human mind' and 'mind which has the
Way':

The spacious spirituality and knowing awareness of the mind is but one alone yet some reckon that it has the distinction of the human mind and mind which has the Way. If this were so then the one would be born of the selfishness of form and *qi* while the latter would draw its origin from the rectitude of nature and destiny and then that by which one knew or was conscious would not be the same. Therefore the one would be perilous and unstable while the latter would be subtle and hard to see. Now no person does not have this bodily form, hence even though one has the highest wisdom one could not be without a human mind and also none do not have this nature so even though one were the most stupid yet one could not be without the mind which has the Way. The two come together within the same square inch of space.... It is necessary that the mind which has the Way should always be the master of a person and the human mind should ever listen to its commands; then what is perilous will be stabilized and what is subtle will appear and movement and stillness will act together and there will be no going to excess or falling short. (*Preface to the Chapter and Verse Commentary on the* Mean and Harmony, p. 1)

The human mind and the mind that has the Way are two aspects of the one mind. The human mind is constituted by the selfishness of form and *qi*, whereas the mind that has the Way is the rectitude of nature and destiny. Zhu Xi further defined it as follows:

There is but this one mind. Knowing and awareness rise from the desires of the ears and eyes, and this is the human mind. When knowing and awareness arise from justice and principle then this is the mind which has the Way....

The mind which has the Way is when knowing and awareness acquire the Way and principle. The human mind is when knowing and awareness acquire sounds, colors, smells and tastes.... A person has only one mind but knowing and awareness acquiring the Way and principle is the mind which has the Way and knowing and awareness acquiring sounds, colors, smells and tastes is the human mind. (*Conversations* 78, pp. 2009, 2010)

The mind that has the Way is the recognition of the Way and principles, whereas the human mind is the recognition of ordinary things. Zhu Xi gives an example.

> When hungry one thinks of eating and when thirsty of drinking; this is the human mind. Whether or not one then eats or drinks is [a decision made by] the mind which has the Way.... When hungry one wants to eat and when thirsty one wants to drink; this is the human mind. To attain to the rectitude of eating and drinking is the mind which has the Way.... The human mind is that mind which when hungry thinks of eating and when cold thinks of wearing clothes. To be hungry and to think of the consequences of eating, to weigh up whether it is right to eat or not; to be cold and think of the consequences of wearing clothes, to weigh up whether it is right to wear clothes or not is the mind which has the Way.

Thus to be concerned about material things is a matter for the human mind but to be concerned with spiritual and intellectual things is a matter for the mind that has the Way.

In other words, the mind that has the Way is pure moral consciousness.

Conclusion

Moral nature is nature; the mind that has the Way is mind. In Zhu Xi's philosophy nature and mind are strictly separated. Moral nature consists of the principles of morality, whereas the mind that has the Way is awareness of morality. In fact, though, both are consciousness of morality.

60. Research

Ge Wu; Zhi Zhi

格物致知

The phrase 'the perfection of knowledge lies in the investigation of things' provoked great philosophical debate from the Song dynasty onward. The de-

bate focuses on the direction in which research should be conducted. Is it to be turned toward the rational principles that govern the way we see the world, or is it a matter of empirical investigation into the norms governing the physical world? Modern science depends on both aspects, on logically coherent paradigms, and on empirically derived norms.

The Great Learning

In a passage memorized by all Chinese students for the past thousand years, the *Great Learning* expounds a program for bringing peace to the world by first cultivating oneself, one's family, and one's state:

> The Way of great learning is to make bright virtue shine, to love the people and to stop only in the highest good. When one knows where to stop then one is settled; when settled then one can be quiet. When quiet then one can be secure. When secure then one can reflect. When reflective then one can obtain [the goal]. Things have roots and branches; affairs have endings and beginnings. To know what is first, what last is to come close to the Way. Of old those who wanted to make their bright virtue shine under heaven first regulated their States. Those who wanted to regulate their States first managed their households. Those who wanted to manage their households first cultivated themselves. Those who wanted to cultivate themselves first rectified their hearts. Those who wanted to rectify their hearts first integrated their thoughts. Those who wanted to integrate their thoughts first perfected their knowledge. The perfection of knowledge consists in the investigation of things. Once things are investigated then one attains to the perfection of knowledge. Once knowledge is perfected then one's thoughts are integrated.... From the Son of Heaven to the common people it is all one and the same, all must consider the cultivation of themselves as the root. It has never been the case that if the root is disordered the branches can be managed. It has never been such that what is of greatest impor-

tance received the least attention and what is of least importance received the most attention. (*The Great Learning*, p. 1)

The commentary on the text "the perfecting of knowledge" says,

> This is called knowing the root. This is called the perfecting of
> knowledge. (*The Great Learning: Commentary* #5, p. 3)

This comment is very brief, whereas commentary on the other items
mentioned is much more expansive. From the Han onward, however,
there were many thinkers who expressed opinions of all kinds on what the
investigation of things and the perfection of knowledge were. Here only a
few will be selected.

Zheng Xuan translated the verb *ge* not as 'to investigate' but as 'to
come':

> '*Ge*' is to come and 'things' are affairs. If one's knowledge of
> the good is deep then good things will come. If one's knowl-
> edge of evil is deep then evil things will come. This says that
> affairs and circumstances come according to people's moral
> tendencies. (*SKQS* 116, *Zheng Xuan's Notes on the* Record of
> Rites 60 *Great Learning*, p. 475b)

This explanation is very superficial and does not fit the original context of
the phrase.

Song Interpretations

Cheng Hao and Cheng Yi laid special emphasis on the *Great Learning* and
developed a new theory of the investigation of things. Cheng Yi explained
ge as 'to arrive at' and *ge wu* as 'fully comprehending principles':

> The perfection of knowledge lies in arriving at things. '*Ge*' is
> 'arriving at' as when one says that the ancestors 'arrive' [at the
> sacrificial offerings]. Over and above every thing is a principle.
> One must fully comprehend and arrive at their principles.
> There are many starting points to reach to a full comprehen-
> sion of principles. Some may read books and discourse clearly
> on justice and principle. Some may discuss people and things
> of past and present and discriminate what is right and wrong

about them. Some respond to affairs and come into contact with things and stick with what ought to be done. These are all cases of fully comprehending principles.... One must arrive at one thing today and another thing tomorrow, accumulate one's experience and gather it all and then one can synthesize it all. (*SKQS* 698, *Surviving Works of the Two Chengs* 18, p. 151a)

Zhu Xi based his reflections on the work of Cheng Yi. Zhu believed the text of the *Great Learning* to be defective, so he wrote a chapter of commentary on the investigation of things to supply the "missing" section:

"This is called knowing the root. This is called the perfecting of knowledge. The fifth chapter of the commentary." This should explain the meaning of "the investigation of things lies in the perfection of knowledge" but the text has been lost. I have dared to take the views of Master Cheng to supply it as follows: The meaning of the expression, "The perfection of knowledge lies in the investigation of things" is this: If we wish to carry our knowledge to the utmost, we must investigate the principles of all things we come into contact with, for the intelligent mind of human beings is certainly formed to know, and there is not a single thing in which its principles do not inhere. But so long as all principles are not investigated, human knowledge is incomplete. On this account the *Great Learning*, at the outset of its lessons, instructs the learner, in regard to all things in the world, to proceed from what knowledge one has of their principles, and pursue one's investigation of them until one reaches the extreme point. After exerting oneself in this way for a long time, one will suddenly find oneself possessed of a wide and far-reaching penetration. Then, the qualities of all things, whether external or internal, the subtle or the coarse, will all be apprehended, and the mind, in its entire substance and its relations to things, will be perfectly intelligent. This is called the investigation of things. This is called the perfection of knowledge. (*Chapter and Verse Commentary on the* Great Learning: *Commentary* #5, p. 3 [Legge, pp. 365–366])

Whether the text of the *Great Learning* was actually missing a piece is hard to say. Zhu Xi's insertion is made contrary to the norms of exegesis. The call to "investigate the principles of all things we come into contact with," however, is a very important point.

Wang Shouren's Reading

Wang Shouren disagreed with Zhu Xi's view that the text of the *Great Learning* was defective and also rejected Zhu's interpretation of the phrase under discussion. Wang Shouren explained *ge* as 'rectify.'

> The term '*ge*' in '*ge wu*' is the same as the '*ge*' in Mencius' saying that "A great person rectified [*ge*] the ruler's mind."* It means to take what is not right out of the mind so as to maintain complete the rectitude of one's original nature. (*SBBY: Instructions for Practical Living A*, p. 5a; WTC #7)

In other words, *ge wu* is explained as rectifying one's mind. As for 'thing,' Wang believed that it is simply the presence of an idea:

> What emanates from the mind is the will. The original substance of the will is knowledge, and wherever the will is directed is a thing. For example, when the will is directed toward serving one's parents, then serving one's parents is a 'thing.' When the will is directed toward serving one's ruler then serving one's ruler is a 'thing.' When the will is directed toward being benevolent to all people and feeling love toward things, then being benevolent to all people and feeling love toward things are 'things,' and when the will is directed toward seeing, hearing, speaking and acting then each of these is a 'thing.' Therefore I say that there are neither principles nor things outside the mind. (Ibid., p. 4b; WTC #6)

Wang Shouren denied the existence of things outside the mind; hence the investigation of things is a matter of interior cultivation. He criticized Zhu Xi's wanting to investigate the principles of all things:

* *Mencius* 4, *Li Lou A* #20.

What Zhu Xi meant by the investigation of things is "to investigate the principles of all things we come into contact
with." To investigate the principles in things to the utmost as
we come into contact with them means to look in each individual thing for its so-called definite principles. This means to
apply one's mind to each individual thing and look for principle in it. This is to divide the mind and principle into two. To
seek for the principle in each individual thing is like looking for
the principle of filial piety in parents. If the principle of filial
piety is to be sought in parents, then is it actually in my own
mind or is it in the person of my parents? If it is actually in the
person of my parents, is it true that as soon as the parents pass
away the mind will lack the principle of filial piety?... What is
true here is true of all things and events. From this we know
the mistake of dividing the mind and principle into two....
What I mean by the investigation of things and the extension
of knowledge is to extend* the innate knowledge of my mind
to each and every thing. The innate knowledge of my mind
is the same as the principle of heaven. When the principle of
heaven in the innate knowledge of my mind is extended to all
things, all things will attain their principle. To extend the innate knowledge of my mind is the matter of the extension of
knowledge, and for all things to attain their principle is the
matter of the investigation of things. In these the mind and
principle are combined into one. (Ibid. B, *Letter to Gu Dongqiao*, pp. 4b–5a; WTC #135)

From our present point of view we would describe this text as idealist.
Outside the mind there are no principles or things. Wang wrongly characterized his opponents as looking for the principles of filial piety in the
parents whereas what they are actually doing is looking for principles,
which all things have. It may be that Zhu Xi's explanation is not in accord
with the original text of the *Great Learning*, but it is still of immense
value. Wang's theory is totally at variance with the original meaning of the
Great Learning.

---

*Wang reads *zhi* as 'extend' rather than 'perfect.'

Wang Fuzhi's Reading

Wang Fuzhi treated the investigation of things and the perfection of knowledge as two separate things. Although the two are related they are nonetheless distinct.

> There are two kinds of knowing things. The two complement each other and yet each has its own role. The investigation of things is to gather widely from numerous phenomena and seek eveidence from ancient times to the present so as to fully understand the principles. To perfect one's knowledge is to vacate one's mind so as to give rise to clarity and to think so as to fully comprehend what is hidden. If one does not perfect one's knowledge then things have nowhere to be attached to and the diversity of things leads one's attention astray. If one does not investigate things then one does not know their use and one permits one's knowledge to fall into evil. (*Elaboration on the Meanings of the* Book of History 3.8, *Talking of Fate* B2, p. 76)

To investigate things is to examine things and phenomena so as to obtain their principles. To perfect one's knowledge is to vacate the mind and think profoundly so as to fully attain the minute and hidden aspects of principles. Investigation involves both examining and synthesizing. Perfecting one's knowledge comprises analyzing concepts.

Wang Fuzhi further says,

> Overall the work of investigating things is a matter for the functioning of the mind and the ears and eyes. Study and inquiry are paramount and thinking and discriminating help them. What is thought and discriminated about are the objects provided by study and inquiry. The work of perfecting knowledge is only a matter for the mind. Thinking and discriminating are paramount and study and inquiry help them. What is studied is with a view to resolving doubts raised by thinking and discriminating. (*Great and Full Study After Reading the Four Books* 1.2, *Great Learning: Sagely Scripture*, p. 12 [1975 ed.])

Wang Fuzhi considered study and inquiry paramount in the investigation of things and thinking and discriminating paramount in the perfection of knowledge. The *Mean and Harmony* says,

> Study it extensively. Inquire about it thoroughly. Think about it carefully. Discriminate on it clearly. Practice it earnestly. (*Mean and Harmony* #20, p. 11)

It is from this passage that Wang Fuzhi drew his program of study, inquiry, thinking, and discrimination. Wang stressed that rather than working from principles to things one should try "going into affairs so as to fully comprehend their principles" (*Extensive Discourse to Supplement Zuo's Commentary on the Spring and Autumn Annals* B, p. 2b, *Duke Zhao Year 7, Shi Wenbo Discusses a Solar Eclipse* [Guangxu year 25, Huaiji shuzhuang shiyin]) but also recognized that the perfection of knowledge, involving the mind alone, which thinks so as to reach to the hidden depths of principles, is also needed.

Yan Yuan's Reading

Yan Yuan brought a new interpretation to the phrase 'the investigation of things':

> Those who talk about the perfection of knowledge today mean no more than reading books and talking about inquiry, study, thinking and discriminating, without realizing that the perfection of knowledge does not lie in these at all. Take, for example, one who wants to understand the rules of propriety. Even if one reads a book on the rules of propriety hundreds of times, inquires and asks scores of times, thinks and discriminates scores of times, one cannot be considered to know them at all. One simply has to kneel down, bow, and otherwise move, hold up the jade wine-cup with both hands, hold the present of silk, and go through all these oneself before one really knows what the rules of propriety really are. Those who know propriety in this way know them perfectly. Or take, for example, one who desires to know music. Even if one reads a music score hun-

dreds of times, and inquires, studies, thinks and discriminates scores of times, one cannot know music at all. One simply has to strike and blow musical instruments, sing with one's own voice, dance with one's own body, and go through all these oneself before one knows what music really is. Those who know music this way know it perfectly. This is what is meant by "When things are investigated knowledge is perfected." Thus I conclude that 'thing' is to be understood as 'thing' in the "three things"* and '*ge*' is to be understood as 'kill' [*ge*] in "killing wild beasts with one's hands." It is the '*ge*' of "killing [*ge*] with one's hands." ... Thus faced with a *fu* turnip, a very wise gardner might not know that it can be eaten even if from its appearance and color and looks it seems to be edible and also he does not know how bitter its taste is. So one must grasp it, take it and put it in one's mouth before one knows its bitter taste. Hence I say that the hand must seize [*ge*] the thing before one knows it perfectly. (*Collected Works of Yan Yuan, Corrections of Wrong Interpretations of the Four Books* 1, *Great Learning*, p. 159)[†]

Yan Yuan interpreted *ge* as "to physically lay hold of." In order to gain full knowledge of something one must oneself lay one's hands on the object in question. This puts the emphasis on actual experience.

Conclusion

Thus Zheng Xuan read *ge* as 'to come,' Cheng and Zhu as 'to investigate,' Wang Shouren as 'to rectify,' and Yan Yuan as to 'lay hold of.' Each reading has evidence in its favor. The *Er Ya* reads as follows:

'*Ge*' is to come. (*Er Ya* 2, *Explaining Words* 10, p. 5b)

---

*According to the *Rites of Zhou* the three things are (1) the six virtues: wisdom, benevolence, sageliness, justice, fidelity, harmony, (2) the six forms of conduct: filial piety, friendship, concord, marriage, employment, and compassion and (3) the six arts: ritual, music, archery, charioteering, calligraphy, and math (*Rites of Zhou* 2.1, p. 21, lines 3–4), *Diguan Situ*.

[†] This translation is heavily indebted to Chan, *Source Book*, p. 708.

The same work also states,

> '*Ge*' is to investigate. (*Er Ya* 1a, *Explaining Glosses* 5, p. 1a)

With respect to the occurrence of the term in the *Mencius* Zhao noted,*

> '*Ge*' is to rectify. (*Correct Meaning of the* Mencius 7, *Li Lou A*, p. 309)

With respect to a passage of the *Xunzi* Yang Liang noted,

> '*Ge*' is said of the one who seizes what is at some distance. (*Zhuzi Jicheng: Xunzi* 15, *Debate on the Principles of Warfare*, p. 184)

But none of these glosses would seem to fit the context of the *Great Learning*. Here it would seem that the meaning of the phrase *zhi zhi* (perfecting knowledge) is a matter of knowing the root and what comes first and what last. Thus *ge wu* is a matter of being able to discriminate between the root and the branches, between what is first and what last. The oldest character index defines *ge* as a measure:

> '*Ge*' is to measure. (*SKQS* 1051, *Cang Jie Pian* 2, p. 40)

Thus it could mean to measure and weigh the long and short of things. This meaning includes the sense of comparing the root and branches, the first and last. This is the gloss that fits the context of the *Great Learning*.

That may be the original meaning of the phrase in the *Great Learning*, but after the Cheng brothers and Zhu Xi promoted the *Great Learning* as a canonical text the phrase *ge wu* became an empty category subject to whatever interpretation the reader cared to give it. Each of the philosophers examined gave it his own reading in the light of his own epistemology and methodology. Thus the investigation of things and the perfection of knowledge became a hot topic in Song, Yuan, Ming, and Qing philosophy, a concept in its own right. The debates about it have added an important chapter to Chinese philosophy.

---

* *Correct Meaning of the* Mencius 7, *Li Lou A* #20, p. 309.

II. Philosophy of Language

61. Naming, Rectification of Names

Ming, Zheng Ming

名, 正名

Although Chinese philosophers did not entirely neglect the question of the different nature of names and how naming worked, they—especially those in the Confucian tradition—often were driven by the question of how an official's actual performance measured up to the name or title he held. Meanwhile, the Daoists could see beyond names to the nameless Way.

Rectification of Names

The subject of the rectification of names was raised by Confucius in response to Zi Lu's question about how to govern the state of Wei.

> Zi Lu asked, "If the prince of Wei entrusted you with the administration of [Wei] what would you do first?" The Master said, "I must first rectify names!" Zi Lu said, "You would do that! Are you so far from practical matters? Why would you rectify names?" The Master said, "How uncultured you are, You [Zi Lu]! With regard to what he does not know about the gentleman should be careful. If names are not rectified then speech does not match. If speech does not match then affairs are not completed. If affairs are not completed then rites and music do not flourish. If rites and music do not flourish then punishments and penalties will be off the mark. If punishments and penalties are off the mark then the people will have nowhere to put hand or foot. Therefore the gentleman's names must be such that they can be spoken and his speech must be such that it can be practiced. With regard to his speech the gentleman simply requires that there be nothing incorrect about it." (*Analects* 13, *Zi Lu* #3, pp. 263–264)

The context indicates clearly that the rectification of names is a political issue. At the same time the connection between the rectification of names and speech is brought out, and this is a matter for epistemology.

It is not now possible to determine precisely what the political objectives of Confucius' program for Wei were. According to Sima Qian, the context is given by the relationship of father to son in 492–489 B.C. in Wei.* The prince of Wei was Lord Zhe of Wei. Lord Zhe fought with his father Kuai Kui for the rulership of the state. Kuai Kui was the eldest son of Duke Ling of Wei (d. 493 B.C.). He offended his father and was forced into exile. When Duke Ling died the people chose Zhe to be their ruler but Kuai Kui procured the help of the state of Jin. The *Spring and Autumn Annals* records that

> In the summer, Zhao Yang of Jin led troops and set up the heir apparent of the Duke of Wei, Kuai Kui, in Qi. (*Spring and Autumn Annals* 12, *Duke Ai* 2, p. 796)

There is no clear indication either in the *Analects* or in the *Spring and Autumn Annals* as to what Confucius' attitude toward this situation was. The Qing Confucian scholar Quan Zuwang† had this to say:

> Confucius calls Kuai Kui the heir apparent; thus there is no doubt that he was the one appointed by Duke Ling to succeed him. *Zuo's Commentary* names him the 'eldest son' and thus states the same thing clearly. Not only this but it is also certain that after he became a fugitive, even though Duke Ling was angry, he was not deprived of his position. From *Zuo's Commentary* one can see that Duke Ling wanted to appoint the son of one of his concubines, Ying, as heir but Ying refused. This shows that Duke Ling wanted to deprive [Kuai Kui] but failed to do so. This is also stated clearly. Hence Kuai Kui had not been rejected by Duke Ling. He had offended his father and fled into exile but on hearing of [his father's] death had rushed

---

*On this incident see J. Makeham, *Name and Actuality in Early Chinese Thought* (Albany: SUNY Press, 1994), pp. 35–44.

† Quan Zuwang (1705–1755). *Zi:* Shao Yi, *Hao:* Xie Shan, known as Mr. Xie Shan, from Yinxian, Zhejiang (near Ningbo). He was a scholar and editor who edited and added to Huang Zongxi's *Scholarly Records of Song and Yuan Confucian Scholars.*

back. The people of Wei could not refuse him. Kuai Kui's return is what has a name while the rejection by the people of
Wei is without a name.... Therefore Confucius' rectification of
names is simply a matter of rectifying his name as 'heir apparent.' Since he is the heir apparent the people of Wei cannot
refuse him. (*SBCK* [Taiwan Shangwu vol. 86], *Outer Collected
Works of the Jieqi Pavillion* 36.7, *Discussion of the Rectification
of Names*, pp. 886b–887a)

A century or so later, Liu Baonan wrote,

> What is the rectification of names? It is to rectify the name of
> the heir apparent. The *Spring and Autumn Annals: Duke Ai*
> year two reads: "In the summer, Zhao Yang of Jin led troops
> and set up the heir apparent of the Duke of Wei, Kuai Kui, in
> Qi." Kong [Yingda], in his Commentary, notes, "The name
> heir apparent is used when the father is alive. When Kuai Kui's
> father died he was called the heir apparent and the people of
> Jin took him. By declaring him heir apparent they rectified the
> name of heir apparent to name him ruler. The *Spring and Au-
> tumn Annals* take his original name of heir apparent before
> he had yet got the State of Wei. There was nothing that could
> be criticized in him; thus it writes 'heir apparent.'" According
> to this the name of heir apparent is not kept as a mere empty
> name by the *Spring and Autumn Annals*. Hence it is evident
> that this rectification of names is to rectify the name of the heir
> apparent. (*The Correct Meaning of the* Analects 16, *Zi Lu*,
> p. 281)

The opinions of Quan and Liu deserve notice.

The *Collected Exegesis of the* Analects quotes Ma Rong explaining the
rectification of names thus:

> It is to correct the names of the hundred affairs. (*The Correct
> Meaning of the* Analects: *Collected Exegesis of the* Analects 16,
> *Zi Lu*, p. 280)

This is an old theory of Han Confucians. The scope of the hundred affairs
is much greater than political matters alone. In the dialogues of Confucius

and his disciples there are many instances in which the discussion concerns
the analysis of the meaning of names.

> Zi Gong said, "Suppose the case of someone who widely ben-
> efited the people and was able to help the masses. What would
> you say of such a person? Could he be called benevolent?" The
> Master said, "Why speak only of benevolence, such a one must
> be a sage. Even Yao and Shun were still concerned about this."
> (*Analects* 6, *Yong Ye* #28, p. 194)

This is to distinguish the names 'benevolence' and 'sage.'

> Zi Zhang asked, "How can an official be said to be outstand-
> ing?" The Master said, "What do you mean by outstanding?"
> Zi Zhang replied, "He should be renowned in the State and at
> home." Confucius said, "That is renown. It is not being out-
> standing. One who is outstanding is straight of character and
> dedicated to justice. He examines what is said and observes
> people's faces and is concerned about humbling himself before
> others. Such a one is outstanding in the State and in the family.
> The one who is renowned seems to adopt benevolence but acts
> contrary to it and remains thus with no self-doubt. He will be
> renowned in the State and at home." (*Analects* 12, *Yan Yuan*
> #20, pp. 259–260)

This is to distinguish the name 'renown' from 'distinction.'

> Master Ran left the court [of the Ji family]. The Master said,
> "Why are you so late?" He replied, "There was government
> business." The Master said, "As for this business, if it were
> really government affairs, though I am not now in office, I
> should have been consulted." (*Analects* 13, *Zi Lu* #14, p. 268)

Confucius did not see how the Ji family could have been engaged in government business, which was proper only to the prince and not to a family,
who in fact aimed at usurping power. This is to distinguish between
'business' and 'government.' These can all be taken as examples of Confucius' rectification of names. I believe that Confucius' rectification of
names was aimed at settling the meaning of terms and determining the

correct name for all things. Ma Rong's "rectification of the hundred affairs" is correct. Zheng Xuan explained the rectification of names as follows:*

> It means the rectification of written words. (*Yuhan Shanfangji Yishu*, vol. 3 [Taiwan: Wenhai], *Notes of Mr. Zheng on the* Analects, p. 1648a)

This is to fall into a very narrow and biased interpretation. Nowadays most people explain the rectification of names on the basis of another passage of the *Analects* that reads,

> Let the ruler be a ruler and the minister a minister. (*Analects* 12, *Yan Yuan* #11, p. 256)

Or it is claimed that to rectify names is to rectify the real object according to the name. Neither interpretation is correct. Confucius clearly said that it is names he wants to rectify and not things. True, Confucius did demand a change in the custom of the time and hoped that "by his Way he can change all under heaven,"† but that is another question. The rectification of names is the determination of the meaning of terms.

Confucius discussed the rectification of names but did not explain what he meant by 'names.'

Daoism

The *Laozi* refers to the name that cannot be named:

> The Way which can be spoken of is not the everlasting Way. The name which can be named is not the everlasting name. (*Laozi* 1/MWD 45)

With respect to this text Wang Bi notes:

> The Way which can be spoken of and the name which can be named are visible things and have shape and form and do not

---

* Makeham (*Name and Actuality*, p. 43) gives a longer quotation from Zheng Xuan and analyzes its importance in the history of thought.
† Said by Mencius of the Mohists (*Mencius* 1, *Duke Wen of Teng A* #5).

refer to perennity. Thus what cannot be spoken of cannot be named. (*Explanation of Wang Bi's Notes on the* Laozi 1, p. 1)

The Way that can be spoken of is not the everlasting Way, and the name that can be named is not the everlasting name. This indicates the relative nature of the name. Although the *Laozi* suggests this deep meaning it does not prove its existence in detail.

Using the form of a fable the *Zhuangzi* talks about the problem of names and real objects:

> Yao abdicated the empire to Xu You.... Xu You said, "If you administer the empire then the empire is administered so why should I take your place? Would it be just for the name? The name belongs to the real object. Would it be for the real object?" (*Zhuangzi* 1, *Going Rambling Without a Destination,* line 25)

Here the name and the real object are contrasted. The name belongs to the real object and must be determined by the real object. In the later corpus of the *Zhuangzi* the subject also appears:

> The name remained in the real object; the duty was suited to the moment. (*Zhuangzi* 18, *Utmost Happiness,* line 39)

The *Guanzi* contrasts names and real objects:

> Things have definite forms. Forms have definite names. One who makes names conform [to real objects] is called a sage.... "Things have definite forms; forms have definite names"; this says that names should not exceed real objects and real objects should not fall behind names.... One examines speech to rectify names; thus one is called a sage....
>
> Names are what the sage uses to make a record of the myriad things. (*Guanzi* 36, *Technique of the Heart A,* 2:9)

Names are used to record the myriad things. They are the symbols of the myriad things. Names and reality must be in agreement.

Logical Approaches

The sixth chapter of Gongsun Long's work is titled *Discussion of Names and Real Objects*. Most of the chapter is quoted here:*

> Heaven and earth and what is produced from them are things. A thing is a thing by virtue of what makes it that thing and nothing more: this is reality. Real objects are real objects by virtue of what makes them these real objects and are not empty: this is position. Taking something from its position makes it lose its position. Placing it in its position makes it rectified.... Its rectification is to rectify what makes it a real object. To rectify what makes it a real object implies the rectification of its name.
>
> Once its name is rectified, then follows, that 'that' is 'this.' In calling it 'that,' while 'that' does not affirm it, 'that' then is 'that' and does not react to it. In calling it 'this' and 'this' does not affirm it, 'this' is then 'this' and does not react to it. By taking 'it' as being in agreement, it is in disagreement. If it is then in disagreement, it will cause confusion. Therefore 'that' agrees with 'that,' and 'that' affirming it, means it will respond to 'that.' 'This' agrees with 'this,' and 'this' affirming it, means it will respond to 'this.' Taking anything as being in agreement makes it agree with it. That it agrees with the agreement is the rectification of this agreement. Therefore 'that' and 'that' stops at 'that' and 'this' and 'this' stops at 'this'—which is possible. 'That' and 'this' is but 'that.' Moreover, 'this' and 'this' is 'that.' In that case, 'this' becomes 'that,' which is impossible.
>
> A name must be identified by its real object. Knowing that 'this' is not 'this,' and knowing that 'this' is not in 'this,' then it cannot be called ['this']. Knowing that 'that' is not 'that,' and knowing that 'that' is not in 'that,' then it cannot be called ['that']. (*Gongsun Long* 6, *Discussion of Names and Real Objects*, pp. 39, 40–41)

---

*Graham says that this chapter is a forgery dating from sometime between 300 and 600. He describes it as "a mixture of banality and nonsense" (A. C. Graham, *Disputers of the Tao* [La Salle: Open Court, 1989], p. 82).

What makes a thing a thing is the real object that determines the nature of any thing. What makes a real object is the position, that is, the spatio-temporal siting of the thing. Each thing has its own position among the mass of things. This is called 'being rectified.' Names are the appellations of things. Confirming the relations between names and real objects is what the rectification of names is about. To rectify names is to see if name '*x*' is fitted to object *x*, name '*y*' to object *y* so that '*x*' applies only to *x* and '*y*' only to *y*. If '*x*' applies to both *x* and *y* then it is not rectified. Gongsun Long's writing is far from easy to follow but the general meaning is clear: each name applies strictly to only one kind of object.

The Mohists gave the most detailed analysis of names.

> One uses names to refer to real objects. (*Later Mohist Logic*, p. 482 [NO11])
>
> '*Ju*' (to refer to, pick out by name from others) is to present the analogue for the real object.... (A31 C)
>
> [Example: 'tiger' explained by a picture?] ... To inform about this name is to refer to the other real object. (*Later Mohist Logic*, p. 285 [A32 E])
>
> What something is called by is its 'name.' What is so called is the 'real object.' (*Later Mohist Logic*, p. 327 [A80 E])

These examples all show that names are used to identify real objects. The Mohists claimed that there is a relationship between names and real objects.

The Mohists also distinguished different categories of names.

> '*Ming*' (name). Unrestricted: classifying: private.
>
> 'Thing' is 'unrestricted'; any real object necessarily requires this name. Naming something 'horse' is 'classifying'; for 'like the real object' we necessarily use this name. Naming someone 'Jack' is 'private'; this name stays confined in this real object. The sounds which issue from the mouth all have the name. (For example, surname and style name). (*Later Mohist Logic*, p. 325 [A78])

There are three kinds of names: unrestricted, classifying, and private. Unrestricted names such as 'thing' are those that apply to general things. Any object can be called a 'thing.' Classifying names are those that apply to a category of objects as 'horse' applies to the class of horses. Private names apply to only one individual as 'Jack' refers to one person only.

The Mohists also mentioned the principles of the rectification of names.

> You cannot use 'that' for this without using both 'that' for this and 'this' for that. Explained by: their being different. (B68 C)
>
> It is admissible for the person who uses names rightly to use 'that' for this and 'this' for that. As long as one's use of 'that' for that stays confined to that, and one's use of 'this' for this stays confined to this, it is admissible to use 'that' for this. When 'this' is about to be used for that, it is likewise admissible to use 'that' for this. If 'that' and 'this' stay confined to that and this, and accepting this condition you use 'that' for this, then 'this' is likewise about to be used for that. (*Later Mohist Logic*, p. 440 [B68 E])

This text uses 'this' and 'that' to speak of the rectification of names. It is very similar to the work of Gongsun Long. It is hard to say which of the two texts came first. In the *Mohist* passage one is presented with three different situations with regard to what is possible. 'X' may be used for x and 'y' for y. For 'x' to be used for both x and y and 'y' to be used for both y and x is not admissible. If the two names 'x' and 'y' are used for the two real objects x and y, this is also admissible. In discussing the rectification of names the Mohists chiefly focused on the relation of names to real objects.

The *Xunzi* discusses three topics: the reason for having names, the causes for the similarities and differences in names, and the fundamental principles on which names are instituted. On the first topic the reasoning is as follows:*

> Different peoples have different forms and different minds and yet understand each other. Different things have names and real objects which can be linked together. When the distinc-

---

*This translation is indebted to the notes of Yang Liuqiao, *Xunzi Gushi* (Xinzhu: Yangzhe, 1987), p. 618 ff.

tion between the noble and the humble is not clear and similarities and differences are not discriminated, under such circumstances, there is bound to be danger that ideas will be misunderstood and work will encounter difficulty or be neglected. Therefore men of wisdom sought to establish distinctions and instituted names to indicate real objects, on the one hand to clearly distinguish the noble and the humble and, on the other, to discriminate between similarities and differences. When the distinctions between the noble and the humble are clear and similarities and differences are discriminated, there will be no danger of ideas being misunderstood and work encountering difficulties or being neglected. This is the reason for having names. (*Xunzi* 22, *On the Rectification of Names*, lines 13–15)

This passage gives the reasons for instituting names. People have different physical bodies and different minds but they are able to understand each other and can have a common view of different kinds of things. If names and real objects are confused then distinctions will also be confused. The purpose of names is to clarify the distinction between humble and noble and to discriminate between similarities and differences.

On the causes for the similarities and differences in names the *Xunzi* says,

What are the causes for the similarities and differences in names? I say: It is because of the natural organs. The organs of members of the same species with the same feelings perceive things in the same way. Therefore things are compared and those that are seemingly alike are generalized. In this way they share their conventional name as a common meeting ground. Forms, bodies, colors, and patterns are distinctions made by the eye. Clear and unclear sounds, tunes, leading melodies, and unusual sounds are distinctions made by the ear. Sweet, bitter, salty and insipid, peppery and sour, and unusual tastes are distinctions made by the mouth. Fragrant and putrid smells, fresh and spoiled smells, smells of rotten meat, rancid and sour smells, and unusual smells are distinctions made by the nose. Pain and itching, cold and heat, smooth and rough, light and heavy are distinctions made by the body. Speaking and acting* and the feelings of pleasure, anger, sorrow, joy, liking and disliking and desire are distinctions made by the mind. The mind collects the knowledge of the senses. It is because the mind collects knowledge that it is possible to know sound through the ear and form through the eye. But the collection of knowledge must also depend on the natural organs first registering it according to its classification.... These are the causes for the similarities and differences in names. (Ibid., lines 15–20, 21)

This is to say that the similarities and differences in names depend on what is registered by the sensory organs and on how the mind knows and understands.

On the fundamental principles on which names are instituted, the *Xunzi* says,

Then, accordingly, names are given to things. Similar things are given the same name and different things are given different names.... Knowing that different real objects should have different names, one should let different real objects always have different names. There should not be any confusion in this respect. And similar real objects should always have similar names.... There are things which have the same appearance but are in different places, and there are things which have different appearances but are in the same place. These can be distinguished. When two things have the same appearance but are in two different places, although they may be grouped together, they are to be called two real objects. When the appearance changes but the real object is not different, it is called transformation. When there is transformation but no difference in reality, this is called one real object. This is the way real objects are examined and their number determined. This is the fundamental principle on which names are instituted. (Ibid., lines 21, 22–23, 27–29)

* See ibid., p. 621 n. 8.

Thus the fundamental principle on which names are instituted is that like objects have the same name and unlike objects different names so that names and real objects correspond to each other.

The *Xunzi* also distinguishes between common names and generic names but does not give the same depth of analysis found among the Mohists.

> For although the myriad things are innumerable, sometimes we want to speak of them as a whole and so we call them 'things.' 'Things' is a great common name. We carry the process further and generalize. In generalizing, we find more things to generalize. We go on and will not stop until there is nothing more general. Sometimes we want to speak of one section of things, and so we call them 'birds' and 'beasts.' 'Birds' and 'beasts' are great particular names. We carry the process further and particularize. In particularizing, we find more things to particularize. We go on and will not stop until there is nothing more particular. (Ibid., lines 23–25)

The great common names are what the Mohists called 'unrestricted names,' whereas the great particular names are what the Mohists called 'classifying names.'

With the *Xunzi* the Confucian theory of the rectification of names reached its maturity.

Later Writers

In the chapter titled *The Profound Examination of Names and Appellations*, Dong Zhongshu gave a clear definition of names:

> Names are the first chapter of the great principle. One records the meaning of the first chapter in order to spy into its affairs and then 'so' and 'not-so' can be known, going contrary to and going along with make themselves evident. Their standard penetrates to heaven and earth.... The sages of old uttered words and symbolized heaven and earth and called them 'appellations'; they cried out and sent forth their commands and called them 'names.' As words names were a cry and an order. As words appellations were an utterance and a symbolizing.

Uttering and symbolizing heaven and earth are appellations. Crying out and ordering are names. Although names and appellations have different sounds yet their roots are common: both are cries and appellations which fully express the intentions of heaven.... Names, then, are what the sages use to express the intentions of heaven and they cannot not be examined. The ruler who receives the decree [of heaven] is one who is given it by the intention of heaven. Thus the one who has the appellation of the Son of Heaven looks on heaven as his father and serves heaven by the way of filial piety.... Names outnumber appellations. Appellations are for the great whole. Names name distinctions, separations, divisions and what is apart. Appellations are broad and general; names are detailed and specific.... Therefore, affairs all go along with names and names all go along with heaven. (*Luxuriant Gems of the Spring and Autumn Annals* 35, *The Profound Examination of Names and Appellations*, pp. 285–288)

Dong called titles such as Son of Heaven, king, prince, lord and prime minister 'appellations' and the names of the myriad things 'names.' He believed that names and appellations are determined by heaven's intentions. When compared with the theory of the *Xunzi* this may only be described as retrogression.*

Xu Gan is best known for his work on names. He says:

Names are what are used to name real objects. When a real object is established its name follows it. It is not the case that the name is first established and then the object follows it. Thus when a long form is established then it is named 'long'; when a short form is established it is named 'short.' It is not the case that there are first the names 'long' and 'short' and that long and short objects follow them.... People only know that names [titles] are good but they do not know that false goodness is no goodness at all. This is a great mistake. (*SKQS* 696, *Discourses That Hit the Mark* 11, *Examining Falsity*, p. 487a)†

---

* For Makeham's analysis of Dong Zhongshu see *Name and Actuality*, pp. 88–93.
† See ibid., p. 7.

The main drift of this passage is to attack false titles. Titles should correspond to real objects. On the question of the relation between names and real objects Xu Gan was heir to the correct view of pre-Qin thinkers.

The Tang writer Han Yu advocated definite names and empty positions.

> Extensive love is called benevolence. Acting and being in the right is called justice. To proceed according to these is called the Way. To have enough in oneself and not to depend on anything outside is called virtue. Benevolence and justice are definite names. The Way and virtue are empty positions. Thus the Way comprises both the gentleman and the mean man and virtue encapsulates both misfortune and good fortune. (*SBBY: Collected Works of Mr. Chang Li* 11.1, *An Inquiry on the Way*, p. 129a)

Benevolence and justice have a definite content; thus they are called definite names. The way and virtue are like empty boxes that may be occupied by differing contents; thus they are called empty places. The way is the way of the gentleman and the way of the mean person. Both are called ways. Virtue has unlucky virtue and lucky virtue and both are called virtue. Han Yu's distinction of definite names and empty places is indeed worthy of notice.

These are the major points in the development of ancient Chinese theories of naming.

61A. Concept
Gai-nian
概念

Although brief, this section deserves a mention since Professor Zhang's work is titled a study of concepts and categories. The term used for 'concept' is a modern one, used to translate an imported word but, as ever, Professor Zhang is aware of its ancient roots.

Having discussed names, we cannot avoid the topic of concepts (*gai-nian*). The term 'concept' is a borrowed word. In ancient Chinese the word used was 'name.' There was also the term *nian*. In the *Explanation of the Characters* this term is defined as follows:

'Nian' is to be constantly thinking of. (*Explanation of the Characters*, p. 217a)

In the *Er Ya, nian* is glossed as follows:

'Nian,' to think. (*Er Ya* 1b, *Explanation of Glosses B* 22, p. 3a)

The term *nian* refers to what is thought of. In *Zuo's Commentary* Zang Wuzhong of Lu is reported as telling the chief minister of the state that he should consider carefully before giving rewards to bad men:

Think [*nian*] whether you should give this to this person. (*Zuo's Commentary* 9, *Xiang* 21, p. 487)

The term *nian* is now incorporated into the Chinese binome for 'concept,' *gai-nian*. It refers to the content of the thought, whereas 'name' refers to the way in which something is thought. One concept may be expressed by a number of names and one name can be used to express different concepts. Languages differ, so the names they use differ, but the concept they express may be the same. 'Concept' has a more profound meaning than does 'name.'

62. Idea

Yan-yi

言意

We have already seen in concept 53 the use of *yi* to mean 'intention.' Another use of the same term is 'idea.'

Concerning a passage in the *Record of Rites* Zheng Xuan notes:

'*Yi*' is 'an idea.' (*SKQS* 115, *Record of Rites* 13, *Royal Institutions C*, p. 288b)

The text being commented on says:

Ideas set out the order of importance. (*Record of Rites* 5, *Royal Institutions*, p. 79)

Meanings are greater than the words that try to express them:

The Master said, "Written characters do not fully express speech and speech is not the full expression of ideas." "Is it impossible, then, to know the meaning of the sages?" The Master said, "The sages made the symbols so as to fully express their ideas." (*Great Commentary* 1.12, p. 302)

Language does not suffice to fully express meaning; symbols can compensate and provide a full expression.

The world values the Way when it is written in a book. A book is no more than speech. Speech has value. What is valuable in it is thought. Thought is about something. What thought is about cannot be transmitted by words. (*Zhuangzi* 13, *The Way of Heaven*, lines 64–65)

The *raison d'être* of the bait is to get the fish. Once the fish is caught one can forget the bait. The *raison d'être* of the trap is to catch the rabbit. Once the rabbit is caught one can forget the trap. The raison d'être of words is to express ideas. Once the ideas are grasped one can forget the words. Where can I find someone who forgets words and can speak with him or her? (*Zhuangzi* 26, *External Objects*, lines 48–49)

The authors of these passages held that meaning is a mystery too great to be expressed by language.

The Mohists, on the other hand, believed that language could express meaning:

To attend to what you hear so that you grasp the idea is discernment by the mind. . . .

To make a case for what you say so that the idea can be seen is the subtlety of the mind. (*Mohist Names and Objects* 9, p. 478)

One uses names to refer to objects, uses propositions to dredge out ideas. (Ibid., p. 482)

Language is the expression of meaning.

The *Xunzi* confirms the Mohist position:

> Propositions combine the names of different real objects so as to expound one idea. (*Xunzi* 22, *On the Rectification of Terms,* line 39)

Thus there are three different points of view regarding the expression of ideas in language. The *Great Commentary* held that language cannot fully express ideas but that symbols can, the Daoists held that language can never express ideas fully, and the Mohists and Xunzi believed that language can express ideas.

In the Wei-Jin period there was a dispute about the question of language and ideas. Wang Bi used the example of the bait and the trap from the *Zhuangzi* quoted above to argue that symbols express ideas, but once one has grasped the idea one can forget the symbol:

> Symbols produce ideas. Language clarifies symbols. For fully expressing ideas nothing can rival symbols and for fully expressing symbols nothing can rival language.... Ideas are expressed fully by symbols and symbols are expressed fully by language. Thus language is able to clarify symbols. Once the symbol is grasped then the language can be forgotten. Thus symbols are able to contain ideas. Once the idea is grasped then the symbols can be forgotten. It is just as the *raison d'être* of the trap is to catch rabbits and once the rabbit is caught one can forget the trap or the *raison d'être* of the bait is to catch the fish and once the fish is caught one can forget the bait.... Therefore the one who keeps hold of the language is not the one who grasps the symbol. The one who keeps hold of the symbol is not the one who grasps the idea.... Thus one establishes the symbol so as to fully express the idea and then the symbol can be forgotten. (*Collected Works of Wang Bi: Summary Norms on the* Book of Changes 4, *Clarifying Symbols,* p. 609)

Wang Bi was writing in opposition to the scholars who attached great importance to the hexagrams and wording of the *Book of Changes.* His stress on the philosophical meaning of the text as opposed to its use in divination was to have lasting impact. By claiming that one could forget the language and symbols, however, he was paving the road to an overly mystical interpretation.

Ouyang Jian* wrote in opposition to Wang Bi's theory and argued that language adequately expresses ideas. There is no necessary relation between language and objects. Objects exist even if the names or the language used to describe them are wrong. Ouyang then asks, "Why bother rectifying terms?" The answer is that without language objects cannot be spoken of:

> If principle is to be acquired in the mind, unless there is language it cannot be explained. When x is determined to be a given sort of thing unless there is language it cannot be discerned.... Names go along with things and change; language accompanies principles and alters. This is like a sound being issued and the echo replying, a form existing and its shadow following on. It is not possible to split them into two. Since they are not two it [language] cannot but fully express [ideas]. (*Complete Jin Literature, juan* 109, p. 2084)

Language expresses the principles that are present in the mind and so is determined by the same principles. Hence it can express the content of those principles.

---

*Ouyang Jian (c. 270–300). *Zi*: Jian Shi, from Nan Pi, Bohai (now Hebei Province). He was killed after involvement in court politics. His only surviving philosophical work is the *Thesis That Language Adequately Expresses Ideas*. A biography may be found in *Jin History* 33, *Biography of Shi Bao*, pp. 1009–1010.

III. Theory of Truth

63. Authenticity

Zhen, Cheng

真, 誠

The term *zhen*, 'authentic,' is first found in the *Laozi*. In all three occur-rences of the term it is an adjective but no explanation of it is given:

Within it [the Way] is essence; its essence is most authentic.
(*Laozi* 21/MWD 65)
Substance is authentic like change. (*Laozi* 41/MWD 3)
Cultivate it in yourself and your virtue will then be au-thentic. (*Laozi* 54/MWD 17)

In the *Zhuangzi* 'authentic' is contrasted with 'inauthentic,' and 'authentic knowing' is recommended.

How is it that the Way is so hidden that there is authenticity and inauthenticity? How is that speech so hidden that there is 'so' and 'not-so'? (*Zhuangzi* 2, *The Sorting Which Evens Things Out*, line 25)
If you try to grasp its nature and never do so, that neither adds to nor takes from its authenticity. (Ibid., line 18)

The authentic is the real, what is really so. Concerning authentic knowing the *Zhuangzi* says,

Knowing depends on some object to which it must corre-spond. Yet what it depends on is never fixed. How do I know that the doer I call 'heaven' [that is, nature] is not a person? How do I know that the doer I call a 'person' is not heaven? Moreover, there can only be authentic knowing if there is an authentic person. (*Zhuangzi* 2, *The Teacher Who Is the Ulti-mate Ancestor*, lines 3–4)

Authentic knowing sees things as they really are.*
Authenticity means that inner and outer correspond to each other:

---

* Author's note: In modern Chinese the binome *zhen-li*, 'authentic-principle,' is used for the term 'truth.' It is like Zhuangzi's authentic knowing, to truly recognize reality.

The authentic is the most essential, the most sincere. What is not essential and not sincere cannot move people. Thus forced weeping, however sorrowful, will not make one grieve. Forced anger, however solemn, carries no sway. Forced affection, however much one smiles, is not returned. Authentic sorrow, even though it be silent, leads to grief. Authentic anger, even though not yet expressed, wins respect. Authentic affection, even without a smile, wins a response. For one who is authentic inside, the spirit moves to the outside and this is why one should value authenticity. (*Zhuangzi* 31 *The Old Fisherman*, lines 32–34)

In the same way the Daoists used 'authentic' the Confucians spoke of integrity [*cheng*].*

The Master said, "The gentleman advances in virtue and attends to his business. He is loyal and trustworthy and thereby advances in virtue. He pays attention to his words and establishes his integrity and thereby attends to his business." (*Book of Changes* 1, *Qian Hexagram: Literary Commentary*, p. 7)

'Integrity' is associated with 'words'; that is, 'integrity' is the standard by which to measure speech. To have integrity is to be genuine. In the passage of the *Zhuangzi* quoted above the essential and sincere are used to explain authenticity. The word translated 'sincere' is the same as that translated by 'integrity' in the *Book of Changes*.

64. Three Tests, Evidence and Verification
San Biao, Xiao Yan
三表, 效驗

Under this heading are grouped four theories of verification drawn up by the Mohists (three tests), Xunzi (discrimination and verification), Han Fei (verification), and Wang Chong (experiential evidence).†

---

* Author's note: Thus it can be seen that 'authenticity' and 'integrity/sincerity' mean the same thing. Yet the Confucian term 'integrity' has a deeper meaning. It refers to the objective norm and also to the highest sphere of morality.

† On this section see Graham, *Disputers of the Tao*, pp. 36–39.

Xunzi, Han Fei, and Wang Chong all have theories of verification that correspond to the three tests of the Mohists. All three are close in meaning, but here they are discussed separately.

The Mohist 'Three Tests'

The Mohists wrote about speech having three tests:

> Speech must have three tests. What are the three tests? Master Mozi said, "There is the root of it [speech], its origin [evidence in favor of,] and its use. Where is its root? Its root lies far back in the activities of the sage kings of old. Where is its origin? Its origin lies below in investigating the realities perceived by the ears and eyes of the hundred clans. Where is its use? One applies it in punishments and administration and observes whether it matches what is of benefit to the State, hundred clans and people. This is what is meant by saying that speech has three tests." (*Mozi* 35, *Rejection of Destiny A*, lines 7–10)

The tests are three ways of judging the truth of what is said. The first is to appeal to ancient authority. The second is to look at the experience of ordinary people. The second test is pragmatic: Is what is said of benefit to the people? The first test appeals to historical authority, the second to empirical observation, and the third to practical implementation. In combining authoritative, empirical, and pragmatic forms of truth the Mohist theory is rich and profound. It is the finest example of a theory of truth in ancient Chinese philosophy.

The *Xunzi*: Discrimination and Verification

The *Xunzi* uses the term *fu yan*, 'discrimination and verification':

> One who speaks well of the past will certainly support [his arguments] with evidence from the present. One who speaks well of heaven [nature] will certainly support [his arguments] with verification from the human sphere. In any discussion the important things are discrimination and verification [*fu yan*].

Thus one can sit down and talk about things; get up and put them into practice and they will be effective. (*Xunzi* 23, *The Nature of Man Is Evil*, lines 44–45)

On the term *fu* as used in *fu yan*, the *Explanation of the Characters* says,

'*Fu*' is to be trustworthy. In the Han system it was a section of bamboo six inches long which was broken in half so that the two pieces matched. (*Explanation of the Characters* 5a, p. 96a)

Thus verification is like the testing of the two parts of the bamboo tally to see that they match. The verification is shown in the use and effectiveness of what is said. Thus the *Xunzi*'s theory implies that speech and actions go together.

Han Fei

Han Fei assessed the doctrines of the Confucianists and the Mohists as follows:

Confucius and Mozi both followed the ways of Yao and Shun, and though their behavior differed, yet each claimed to be following the authentic Yao and Shun. But since one cannot call Yao and Shun back to life how is one to decide whether it is the Confucianists or the Mohists who are telling the truth? Now over seven hundred years have passed since Yin and early Zhou times, and over two thousand years since Yu and early Xia times. If we cannot even decide which of the present versions of Confucian and Mohist doctrine are the authentic ones, how can we hope to scrutinize the ways of Yao and Shun, who lived three thousand years ago? Obviously we can be sure of nothing! One who claims to be sure of something for which there is no evidence is a fool, and one who acts on the basis of what cannot be proved is an imposter. Hence it is clear that those who claim to follow the ancient kings and to be able to describe with certainty the ways of Yao and Shun if they are not fools are imposters. (*Hanfeizi* 50, *Eminence in Learning*, #1)

By 'evidence' the text means investigating in all fields and verifying. In the *Eight Canons* the *Hanfeizi* says,

> Regarding speech one gathers together evidence from all angles: one must consider from the point of view of the earth, reflect from the point of view of heaven, test from the point of view of things and consider with respect to human beings. When all four concur then one will have a proper view of the matter. (*Hanfeizi* 48, *Eight Canons*, #4)

Verification involves examining from all angles.

Han Fei advocated a pragmatic assessment of speech and action.

> Speech and action need to be judged according to their utility and effectiveness. In sharpening an arrow-head with a stone one must not be careless or the point will be unable to pierce even an autumn hair. Moreover one cannot call a person who does so a good archer since he has no constant model. To hit a standing target from a distance of ten paces is not because one is a brilliant archer like Yi or Peng Meng but because there is a constant model.... So now in listening to speech and observing conduct if one does not judge according to utility and effectiveness then no matter how well-examined the speech or how firm the conduct it will be a theory of no use. (*Hanfeizi* 41, *Asking About Discrimination*, #1)
>
> The intelligent lord in listening to speech must weigh up its utility and in observing conduct must ask that it be effective. In that way he will not talk of empty and out-dated studies nor adopt cunning and deceptive conduct. (*Hanfeizi* 46, *Six Contraries*, #6)

What Han Fei considered useful and effective was what enriched the state and strengthened the army. Thus he rejected all literary learning and hence displayed a very narrow pragmatism. In fact, literary studies are not without their use for the people.

In saying that one who claims to be sure of something for which there is no evidence is a fool and that one who acts on the basis of what cannot be proved is an imposter, Han Fei was quite right, but his pragmatism is too narrow and thus erroneous.

Wang Chong

Wang Chong spoke of experience as determining the truth and falsity of what is said and discussed.

> In affairs there is nothing more intelligent than effectiveness and in discussions there is nothing more certain than proof. (*Balanced Inquiries* 67, *Simple Funerals*, p. 225)
>
> Anyone who discusses affairs and speaks contrary to fact or not in conformity with experiential evidence even though the theory sounds wonderful and be rich in ideas yet it would be wholly untrustworthy. (*Balanced Inquiries* 79, *Knowing Reality*, p. 257)

Wang criticized the Daoists as follows:

> The Daoists speak of spontaneity but do not know how to substantiate their claims by evidence; thus their theory of spontaneity has not yet proved trustworthy. (*Balanced Inquiries* 54, *On Spontaneity*, p. 179)

Claims must be substantiated by evidence gained from experience because this is the only means to prove their correctness. Experiential evidence is how things truly appear. Following the gloss of *xiao* in the *Guang Ya*, we can see that 'experiential evidence' is proof of what is real.*

Wang Chong gave a further analysis of experiential evidence and noted that sometimes one must distinguish between that which is real and that which is specious. The Mohists talked about ghosts and produced many instances of experiential evidence, but they are all specious.

> This argument has no sense and no meaning; thus they look to external evidence to establish the truth or falsehood of the facts. Trusting to what is heard and seen outside does not depend wholly on what is inside but is discourse based on what is supplied by ears and eyes and is not modeled on the meaning of the mind. What is discussed from the point of view of ears and eyes takes specious appearances as its basis and specious

---

* *Guangya*, p. 65, *xiao* (effectiveness) is *yan* (tested experience). I am here translating the combination *xiao yan* by 'experiential evidence.'

appearances as evidence and so denies what is real. Therefore truth and falsehood do not depend on ears and eyes but must rely on the meaning of the mind. The Mohist model does not use the mind to found things but relies on hearing and seeing and so no matter how brilliant and clear its experiential evidence is, it falls away from reality. (*Balanced Inquiries* 67, *Simple Funerals*, p. 225)

The distinction between truth based on "the meaning of the mind" and truth based on empirical evidence is perhaps to be compared to the distinction between coherence and correspondence theories of truth. Coherence theories demand that an argument be logically coherent, able to be judged by the mind independent of experience, whereas correspondence theories stress the role of the evidence gleaned by the senses. In the above passage Wang Chong would seem to be advocating a coherence theory of truth. Since we have seen him also arguing for an empirically based correspondence theory, it would be helpful if we knew how he envisaged the two working together. On this point he is silent.

'Experiential evidence' is a term that is in common use today. It applies to normal and correct empirical evidence. Modern scholars also recognize the evidence of the senses, illusion, and false impressions.

Chronology

Ruler	Dates
Eastern Zhou Dynasty	770–222 B.C.
Laozi	571–480
Confucius	551–479
King Goujian of Yue	496–465
Zi Si	493–406
Mozi	480–397
Sunzi	440–381
Shizi	390–330
Shang Yang	385–338
Song Xing	382–300
Sun Bin	380–320
Mencius	372–289
Hui Shi	370–300
Zhuangzi	360–280
Yin Wen	360–280
Shen Dao	350–275
Gongsun Long	330–242
Xunzi	330–227
Lu Buwei	290–235
Han Fei	280–233
Han Dynasty	206 B.C.–220 A.D.
Gongsun Hong	200–121
Dong Zhongshu	190–105
Liu An	179–122
Sima Tan	?–110
Sima Qian	145–86
Liu Xiang	79–8 B.C.
Yang Xiong	53 B.C.–18 A.D.
Liu Xin	46 B.C.–23 A.D.

Huan Tan	43 B.C.–28 A.D.
Wang Chong	27–107 A.D.
Ban Gu	32–92 A.D.
Xu Shen	55–149
Liu Yi	58–125
Ma Rong	79–166
Wang Fu	85–162
Zheng Xuan	127–200
Xun Yue	148–209
Zhao Qi	?–201
Xu Gan	171–218
Cao Zhi	192–232
He Yan	193–249
Ruan Ji	210–263

Three Kingdoms 222–265

Du Yu	222–284
Xi Kang	223–262
Liu Shao	fl. Three Kingdoms period, 222–265
Wang Bi	226–249

Jin Dynasty 265–420

Ouyang Jian	270–300
Sima Biao	240–306
Guo Xiang	252–312
Pei Gu	267–300
Ge Hong	284–364
Zhang Zhan	4th century
Dao An	312–385
Han Kangbo	?–385
Hui Yuan	334–416
Zheng Xianzhi	364–427

Zong Bing	375–443
Bhiksu Zhao	384–414

Northern-Southern Dynasties 420–589

Fan Zhen	448–515
Su Yan (Emperor Wu of Liang)	r. 502–549
Liu Jun	462–521
Huang Kan	488–545
Xiao Tong	501–531
Lu Deming	556–627
Kong Yingda	574–648

Sui Dynasty 589–618

Tang Dynasty 618–907

Cheng Xuanying	fl. 630–660
Li Shan	?–689
Hui Neng	638–713
Fa Zang	643–712
Emp. Tang Gaozong	r. 650–683
Empress Wu Zetian	r. 684–704
Li Dingzuo	8th century
Li Mi	722–789
Han Yu	768–824
Liu Yuxi	772–842
Liu Zongyuan	773–819
Li Ao	778–841

Five Dynasties 907–960

Xing Bing	932–1010

Northern Song Dynasty   960–1127

Hu Yuan	993–1059
Ouyang Xiu	1007–1072
Shao Yong	1011–1077
Zhou Dunyi	1017–1073
Sima Guang	1019–1086
Zhang Zai	1020–1077
Wang Anshi	1021–1086
Shen Kuo	1031–1095
Cheng Hao	1032–1085
Cheng Yi	1033–1107
Su Dongpo	1036–1101
Xie Liangzuo	1050–1103

Southern Song Dynasty   1127–1279

Zhu Xi	1130–1200
Chen Zhi	late 12th–early 13th c.
Lu Jiuyuan	1139–1192
Chen Liang	1143–1194
Ye Shi	1150–1223

Ming Dynasty   1368–1644

Lu Rong	1436–1494
Luo Qinshun	1465–1547
Wang Shouren	1472–1528
Ji Yuanheng	?–1510
He Tang	1474–1543
Wang Tingxiang	1474–1544
Gu Lin	1476–1545
Han Bangqi	1479–1555
Wang Gen	1483–1540
Zhou Heng	fl. 1510–1530

Liu Zongzhou	1578–1646
Adam Schall	1591–1666
Huang Zongxi	1610–1695
Fang Yizhi	1611–1671
Wang Fuzhi	1619–1692
Mao Qiling	1623–1716
Yan Yuan	1635–1704

Qing Dynasty	1644–1911
Li Gong	1659–1733
Hui Dong	1697–1758
Quan Zuwang	1705–1755
Dai Zhen	1723–1777
Cui Shu	1740–1816
Wang Niansun	1744–1832
Jiao Xun	1763–1820
Liu Baonan	1791–1855
Liu Gongmian	1824–1883
Guo Qingfan	1844–1896

The works used in compiling this chronology are listed below. In cases where dating is disputed, I have used the traditional dating followed by Zhang Dainian and mainland scholars. In many cases, especially for the pre-Qin era, dates are not exact. Hence this chronology should be viewed as a general guide and no more.

Fung Yu-Lan. *A History of Chinese Philosophy*, trans. Derk Bodde (Princeton: Princeton University Press, 1952–53).

Loewe, Michael, ed. *Early Chinese Texts: A Bibliographical Guide* (Society for the Study of Early China and Berkeley: Institute of East Asian Studies, University of California, 1993).

Qian Mu. *Xianqin zhuzi xinian kaobian* (Shanghai: Shanghai shudian, 1992).

Twitchett, Denis, ed. *The Cambridge History of China*, vol. 3 (Cambridge: Cambridge University Press, 1979).

Zhang Dainian. *Zhang Dainian wenji* (Beijing: Qinghua daxue, 1990).

Zhexue dacidian: Zhongguo zhexueshi juan (Shanghai: Shanghai cishu chubanshe, 1985).

Zhongguo lishi dacidian: Sixiangshi juan (Shanghai: Shanghai cishu chubanshe, 1989).

Sources of Quotations

This list provides the reader with a way of finding the sources of works quoted in the text. Sources are listed alphabetically in the lefthand column, and the numbers of the concepts in which a source is quoted are given in the right-hand column. For instance, in concept 16 in the text, a work titled Pheasant Cap Master *is quoted; hence in this list the reader will find, under the title* Pheasant Cap Master, *the chapter quoted and, in the righthand column, the concept number (16). The Chinese sources of many of the quotations are also provided here following the words "Edition used," and "See also" signals secondary sources consulted by the translator.*

By and large, the translations of the Chinese quotations are my own. In cases where the translation in the text is taken directly from another trans-lator, it is noted in this list. For example, all translations of the Mohist Logic are from A. C. Graham's work. In cases where the translation was used in a modified form, this has also been noted. James Legge's translations of the classics have often been drawn upon, but his antiquated style has been altered and in some cases the translations changed for other reasons. In cases where the translation is mine but I have been helped to understand a passage by studying what others have done, I have tried to note each of these instances. Finally, in some cases, such as the translations from Laozi, *I have consulted many different translations and then did my own and in the process may also have been influenced by these translators.*

Abbreviations

MWD	Mawangdui
SBBY	*Sibu Beiyao*
SBCK	*Sibu Congkan*
SKQS	*Siku Quanshu*
WTC	Wing-Tsit Chan

Analects

1	*Xue Er*	32, 37
2	*On Administration*	38, 39, 55, 56
3	*Ba Yi*	32
4	*Li Ren*	13
5	*Gong Zhi*	2
6	*Yong Ye*	6
7	*Shu Er*	2, 6, 22, 44, 55
8	*Tai Bo*	1, 20, 39
9	*Zi Han*	1, 33, 39, 47, 53, 55
11	*Xian Jin*	15, 48, 50
12	*Yan Yuan*	6, 15, 39, 41
13	*Zi Lu*	37, 43, 48, 50, 62
14	*Xian Wen*	17, 55
15	*Duke Ling of Wei*	13, 39, 56
16	*Ji Shi*	39
17	*Yang Huo*	15, 39
18	*Weizi*	41
20	*Yao Says*	17, 39, 43

Edition used:

J. Legge, *The Chinese Classics*, vol. 1, *Confucian Analects*, The Great Learning *and* The Doctrine of the Mean (Oxford: Clarendon, 1893; reprint, Taibei: Southern Materials Centre, 1985).

Ancient Text Book of History 2.2, The Counsels of the Great Yu   59

Edition used:

J. Legge, *The Chinese Classics*, vol. 3, *The Shoo King or The Book of Historical Documents* (Oxford: Clarendon, 1893; reprint, Taibei: Southern Materials Centre, 1985).

Apocryphal Book of Changes   23

Edition used:

Siku Quanshu Zhou Yi Qian Zao Du.   53

Apocryphal Classic of Piety   6

Apocryphal Spring and Autumn Annals: Preface to Destiny and the Calendar   5

In *Selections of Refined Literature* 1b, *Poem on the Eastern Capital*.

Edition used:
Wen Xuan (Shanghai: Shanghai Shudian, 1988).
See also D. R. Knechtges, *Wen Xuan, or Selections of Refined Literature* (Princeton: Princeton University Press, 1982).

Ban Gu, *Quoting the Classics*   23

Editions used:
Complete Later Han Literature; Yan Kejun, ed., *Quan shanggu Sandai, Qin-Han, San-Guo, Liu Chao Wen* (Beijing: Zhonghua Shuju, 1959).

————, *Understandings of the White Tiger Studio*   17

Edition used:
Wu Zeyu, ed., *Baihutong shuzheng* (Beijing: Zhonghua Shuju, 1994).

Bhiksu Zhao

On the Unreal Void	20
The Immutability of Things	25

Edition used:
Fancheng Hsu, *Three Theses of Seng-Zhao* (Beijing: Chinese Social Sciences, 1985).
See also Wing-Tsit Chan, *A Source Book in Chinese Philosophy* (Princeton: Princeton University Press, 1963), pp. 343–356.

The Book of Changes

Text	6, 20, 28, 43, 63
Great Appendix	2, 3, 11, 15, 22, 23, 24, 25, 26, 27, 29, 33, 34, 39, 62
Treatise of Remarks on the Trigrams	3, 11, 24, 39, 44
Orderly Sequence of the Hexagrams	7
Literary Commentary	9, 11, 28
Commentary on the Decision	37, 41, 43n
Symbolism Commentary	43n

Edition used:

Z. D. Sung, *The Text of Yi King* (Taibei: Wenhua Tushu, 1988).

The Book of History

Edition used:

J. Legge, *The Chinese Classics*, vol. 5, *The Shoo King or The Book of Historical Documents* (Oxford: Clarendon, 1893; reprint, Taibei: Southern Materials Centre, 1985).

The Book of Lord Shang

Editions used:

The Chinese University of Hong Kong Institute of Chinese Studies, *A Concordance to the Shangjunshu* (Taibei: Commercial Press, 1992); J. J. L. Duyvendak, *The Book of Lord Shang* (London: Arthur Probsthain, 1936).

The Book of Songs

Editions used:

J. Legge, *The Chinese Classics*, vol. 4, *The She King or The Book of Poetry* (Oxford: Clarendon, 1893; reprint, Taibei: Southern Materials Centre, 1991). Chinese only: *Maoshi Yinde* (Shanghai: Shanghai Guji, 1986).

Cang Jie Pian   60

Edition used (Chinese only):

Congshu jicheng chubian, vol. 1051 (Shanghai: Shangwu, 1936).

Edition used:

Cheng Yi, *Yi Cheng Zhuan* (Taibei: Shijie Shuju, 1988).

—————, *Pure Words of the Two Chengs*   18, 33

Edition used:

Siku Quanshu 698.

—————, *Reply to Master Heng Qu's Letter on
Calming Human Nature*   40

In *Mr. Mingdao's Collection of Literary Works.*

Edition used:

Sibu Beiyao: Collected Literary Works of Mr. Yin Chuan.

—————, *Surviving Works of the Two Chengs*   1, 2, 3, 5, 11, 15,
                                                                         16, 17, 24, 25, 29,
                                                                         30, 33, 35, 38, 39,
                                                                         40, 49, 50, 54, 55,
                                                                         58, 60

Edition used:

Siku Quanshu 698.

Classic of Piety 9, Sheng Zhi   46

Edition used (Chinese only):

Xiaojing Yinde (Shanghai: Shanghai Guji, 1986).

Cui Jing, *Penetrating the Mystery of the Book of Changes*   32

In Li Dingzuo, *Collected Exegesis of the Zhou Yi.*

Edition used:

Siku Quanshu 7, *Collected Exegesis of the Zhou Yi.*

Dai Zhen (1742–1777), *An Evidential Study of the Meaning of Terms in the* Book of Mencius   2, 3, 5, 29, 32, 39,
                                                                         49, 50, 52, 58

Edition used (Chinese only):

Mengzi ziyi shuzheng (Beijing: Zhonghua Shuju, 1982).

See also Ann-ping Chin and M. Freeman, *Tai Chen on Mencius: Explorations in Words and Meanings* (New Haven: Yale University Press, 1990).

————, *Inquiry into Goodness*   2, 58

Edition used:

Cheng Chung-ying, *Tai Chen's* Inquiry into Goodness: *A Translation of the Yuan Shan* (Honolulu: East-West Center Press, 1971).

————, *Letter to Shi Zhongming on Study*   58

In *Collected Literary Works* 9.3.

Edition used:
Daizhen Wenji (Shanghai: Shanghai Guji, 1980).

Dong Zhongshu, *Luxuriant Gems of the Spring and Autumn Annals*

3	*Bamboo Forest*	38
4	*Jade Courage*	14
6	*Kingly Way*	5, 14
13	*Emphasizing Administration*	5, 14
29	*Models of* Ren *and* Yi	39
30	Ren *and Wisdom*	39
35	*Profound Examination of Names and Appellations*	6, 36, 39, 49, 50
38	*The Response to the Five Agents*	12
42	*The Meaning of the Five Agents*	12
43	Yang *Is Noble;* Yin *Is Humble*	11
47	*The Place of* Yin *and* Yang	11
48	*The Ending and Beginning of* Yin-Yang	11
49	*The Significance of* Yin-Yang	11
50	Yin-Yang *Emerging and Entering Above and Below*	11
58	*The Mutual Generation of the Five Agents*	12
65	*Suburban Talks*	1
77	*Following the Way of Heaven*	53
81	*Heaven, Earth*, Yin *and* Yang	5

Edition used:

Su Yu, *Chunqiu Fanlu Yizheng*, ed. Zhong Zhe (Beijing: Zhonghua Shuju, 1992).

Gao Heng, *Laozi Zhenggu*   8

Edition used:
Laozi Zhenggu, 3d ed. (Taibei: Taiwan Kaiming, 1973).

Ge Hong, *The Master Who Grasps the Simple 1, Expounding the Abstruse*   9

Editions used:
Sibu Beiyao; E. Feifel, "Pao-P'u Tzu: Nei Pien, Ch. 1–3," *Monumenta Serica* 6 (1941): 113–211; J. R. Ware, *Alchemy, Medicine, and Religion in the China of* AD *320: The Nei P'ien of Ko Hong* (Cambridge: MIT Press, 1966).

Gong Yang Commentary 2, Duke Huan, Year 11   47

Edition used:
J. Legge, *The Chinese Classics*, vol. 5, *The* Ch'un Ts'ew, *with the* Tso Chuen (Oxford: Clarendon, 1893; reprint, Taibei: Southern Materials Centre, 1985).

Gongsun Long 6, Names and Reality   7, 61

Edition used:
Sibu Beiyao: Gongsun Long
See also M. Perleberg, *The Works of Kung-sun Lung-Tzu* (Hong Kong: Local Printing Press, 1952).

The Great Learning   39, 41, 53, 60

Edition used:
J. Legge, *The Chinese Classics*, vol. 1, *Confucian Analects*, The Great Learning *and* The Doctrine of the Mean (Oxford: Clarendon, 1893; reprint, Taibei: Southern Materials Centre, 1985).

Guang Ya

Shi Gu 2	15
Shi Gu 3	10, 44, 45
Shi Yan	46, 64

Edition used (Chinese only):

Congshu Jicheng 1160 (Shanghai: Shangwu Yinshuguan, 1936).

Guanzi

Editions used:

Zhao Shouzheng, ed., *Guanzi Tongjie* (Beijing: Beijing Jingji Xueyuan, 1989); for reference in #35 see *Ershierzi: Guanzi* (Shanghai: Shanghai Guji, 1986).

See also W. Allyn Rickett, *Kuan-tzu: A Repository of Early Chinese Thought* (Hong Kong: Hong Kong University Press, 1965), for chs. 36, 37, and 49; W. Allyn Rickett, *Guanzi: Political, Economic and Philosophical Essays from Early China*, vol. 1 (Princeton: Princeton University Press, 1985), for chs. 1, 2, 6, 11, and 30.

Guo Xiang, *Notes on Zhuangzi*

Edition used:
Siku Quanshu 1056.

Han Bangqi, *Following Record of Testing, Seeing, and Hearing*   23n

Edition used:
Siku Quanshu 1269, *Collected Works of Yuanluo.*

Han History
21 *Gazette of the Calendar A*   3, 23
30 *Gazette of Arts and Literature: Summary of the Philosophers*   16, 39
58 *Biography of Gong-sun Hong*   37

Edition used:
Han Shu (Beijing: Zhonghua Shuju, 1962).

Han Kangbo, *Notes on the Great Commentary*   23, 32, 24, 25

Edition used:
Yan Lingfeng, ed., *Collected Editions of the Yi Jing* (Taibei: Chengwen, n.d., 1976), vol. 3.

Han Yu, *Original Nature*   49, 50

Edition used:
Sibu Beiyao: Collected Works of Mr. Chang Li.
See also Wing-Tsit Chan, *A Source Book in Chinese Philosophy* (Princeton: Princeton University Press, 1963).

———, *The Original Way*   39, 61

Edition used:
Sibu Beiyao: Collected Works of Mr. Chang Li.
See also Wing-Tsit Chan, *A Source Book in Chinese Philosophy* (Princeton: Princeton University Press, 1963), 454–456.

Hanfeizi
15 *Portents of Ruin*   47

Editions used:

Hanfeizi Suoyin (Beijing: Zhonghua Shuju, 1982); W. K. Liao, *The Complete Works of Han Fei-tzu*, 2 vols. (London: Arthur Probsthain, 1939, 1959).

He Shao, *Gazette of the Three Kingdoms* 28.8, *Biography of Zhong Hui*   50

He Tang, *Yin-Yang Guan Jian*   11

Edition used:
Bai Ling Xue Shan, Shanghai, fascicule 3.8.

He Tu kua Di Xiang   23

Edition used:
Congshu jichen chubian: Zhexue lei: Guweishu, juan 32, pp. 608–616, edited by Sun Ke, Beijing: Zhonghua Shuju, 1985.

He Xiu, *Notes on the Gongyang Commentary* 1, *Duke Yin* Year 1   5

Edition used:
Sibu Beiyao.

He Yan, *Collected Exegesis of the* Analects   47

Quoted in *Correct Meaning of the Analects*.

Edition used (Chinese only):

Sibu Beiyao: Lunyu Zhengyi.

———, *Discourse on the Way*   20

Quoted in Zhang Zhan, *Commentary on Liezi* 6, *Endeavour and Fate.*

Editions used:

Zhuzi Jicheng 3, *Liezi*; Wing-Tsit Chan, *A Source Book in Chinese Philosophy* (Princeton: Princeton University Press, 1963).

Huainanzi

3	*The Pattern of Heaven*	5, 10, 13, 37
8	*Ben Jing*	48
11	*Leveling Customs*	19
13	*Fanlun*	30
14	*Shuan Yan*	13
21	*Yao Lue*	30

Editions used:

Chinese University of Hong Kong Institute of Chinese Studies, *A Concordance to the Huainanzi* (Taibei: Commercial Press, 1992); Liu Wendian, Feng Yi, and Qiao Hua, *Huainan Honglie Jijie* (Beijing: Zhonghua Shuju, 1989) (p. 222 of this edition is used for the note of Gao You); J. S. Major, *Heaven and Earth in Early Han Thought: Chapters Three, Four and Five of the "Huainanzi"* (Albany: SUNY Press, 1993).

Huan Tan, *New Discourses*   9

Edition used:

Sibu Beiyao: New Discourses

Huang Kan. See Wang Bi, *Exegesis of the Analects*   47

Huang Zongxi, *Scholarly Records of Ming Confucians*

32	*Taizhou Scholarly Record* (Wang Gen)	17
47	*Scholarly Record of All Confucians*	49
62	*Scholarly Record of Ji Shan* (Liu Zongzhou)	49

Edition used:

Sibu Beiyao: Scholarly Records of Ming Confucians

———, *Tuxue Bianhuo*   8n

In *Song and Yuan Schools of Learning* 12, *School of Learning of Jianxi*.

Edition used:
Sibu Beiyao: Song and Yuan Schools of Learning

Hui Neng, *Platform Sutra*   32

Editions used:
Taishō Shinshū Daizōkyō 48 (no. 2008), *The Sixth Patriarch's Dharma Jewel Platform Scripture* (Taibei, 1990); Buddhist Text Translation Society, *The Sixth Patriarch's Sutra*, 2d ed. (San Francisco: Sino-American Buddhist Association, 1977).

Hui Yuan: *On the Sramana Baring His Right Shoulder*   32

Edition used:
Sibu Beiyao 55, *Hong Ming Ji* 5. For a translation into Japanese, see Kimura Eiichi, ed., *Eon Kenkyuu (Studies on Hui Yuan)* (Kyoto: Soobunsha, 1960).

Imperial Reader from the Taiping [983 A.D.] *Period*   5

Edition used:
Taiping Yulan (Beijing: Zhonghua Shuju, 1960).

The Inner Classic of the Yellow Emperor 66, *Great Treatise on Heaven, the Origin and the Thread*   10

Edition used:
Ershierzi (Shanghai: Shanghai Guji, 1986).

Jiao Xun (1763–1820), *The Correct Meaning of the Mencius*   54

Edition used (Chinese only):
Zhuzi Jicheng 1.

Jin History

Edition used:
Jin Shu (Beijing: Zhonghua Shuju)

Kong Yingda, *The Correct Meaning of the* Analects

Edition used: *Zhuzi Jicheng* 1.

———, *The Correct Meaning of the* Book of
Changes

Edition used:
The Correct Meaning of the Book of Changes,
Taibei: Zhonghua Shuju, 1986 *Siku Quanshu* 7.

———, *The Correct Meaning of the* Record of Rites

Edition used:
Siku Quanshu 115.

———, *Preface to the Correct Meaning of the* Book
of Songs

Edition used:
Siku Quanshu 69.

Laozi

19	39
20	7
21	2, 27, 44, 63
22	13
25	2, 7, 13, 16, 21
28 (Mawangdui)	8
35	27
37	2
38	44
39	13
40	16, 20
41	27, 44, 63
42	2, 11, 13, 16, 49
50	38
51	21, 31, 44, 46
52	20
54	63
55	15, 38
56	46, 49
58	16
59	15
63	44
64	21
65	16
73	38
75	15
78	16
79	44

Li Ao, *Book of the Recovery of Human Nature* 18, 50

Edition used:

Siku Quanshu 1078, *Collected Works of Li Wengong*.

See also Carsun Chang, *The Development of Neo-Confucian Thought* (New York: Bookman Associates, 1957); Wing-Tsit Chan, *A Source Book in Chinese Philosophy* (Princeton: Princeton University Press, 1963), pp. 456–459.

Li Dingzuo, *Collected Exegesis of the Zhou Yi* 23

Edition used:
Siku Quanshu 7.

Li Gong (1659–1733), *Commentary and*
  Notes on the Zhou Yi   23

Edition used:
Yan-Li Congshu (1923 ed.).

Li Shan in *Wen Xuan*   12

In *Selections of Refined Literature* 6, *Wei Capital Rhapsody* and 59 *Memorial Engraving for King Zhao of Qi at An Lu.*

Editions used:
Wen Xuan (Taibei: Wunan Tushei, 1991); D. R. Knechtges, *Wen Xuan or Selections of Refined Literature* (Princeton: Princeton University Press, 1982).

Liang History **48,** *Biography of* **Fan Zhen**   52

Edition used:
Liang Shu (Beijing: Zhonghua Shuju).

Liezi
  4 *Confucius*   25
  6 *Endeavour and Fate*   17

Editions used:
Zhuzi Jicheng 3; A. C. Graham, *The Book of Lieh-tzu* (London: John Murray, 1960). I have used Graham's translation of ch. 6; see concept 17.

Liu Jun, *Discourse on Distinguishing Fate*   17

Editions used:
Complete Liang Literature; Yan Kejun, ed., *Quan shanggu Sandai, Qin-Han, San-Guo, Liu Chao Wen* (Beijing: Zhonghua Shuju, 1959).

Liu Shao, *Gazette of Human Nature*

1 *Nine Points of Physiology* 43
4 *Material and Principle* 3

Edition used:
Siku Quanshu 848.

Liu Xi, *Shi Ming, Shi Yan Yu* 46

Edition used:
Siku Quanshu 221.

Liu Xiaoji, *Notes on* The World Speaks a New Language 4, *Literary Study* 51

Edition used:
Zhuzi Jicheng 8.

Liu Yi, *Song and Yuan Scholarly Records* 1, *Secure and Established Record* 32

Edition used:
Sibu Beiyao: Song and Yuan Scholarly Records

Liu Yuxi, *Discourse on Heaven* 1, 20, 46

Edition used:
Sibu Congkan (1929 ed.), *Collected works of Liu Mengde.*
See also H. G. Lamont, "An Early Ninth Century Debate on Heaven," *Asia Major* 18.2 (1973): 181–208; 19.1 (1974): 37–85.

Liu Zongyuan, *Discourse on Feudalism* 31

Edition used:
Sibu Beiyao: Collected Works of Liu Hedong.

———.

Replies on Heaven 5
Speaking of Heaven 1, 5

Edition used:
Siku Quanshu 1076, *Collected Works of Liu Hedong.*

See also H. G. Lamont, "An Early Ninth Century Debate on Heaven," *Asia Major* 18.2 (1973): 181–208; 19.1 (1974): 37–85.

Liu Zongzhou, quoted in Huang Zongxi.

Lu Jiuyuan, *Selected Sayings of Mr. Xiang Shan*   49, 50, 52, 58

Edition used:
Siku Quanshu 1156.

————, *With Li Zai*   52

Edition used:
Sibu Beiyao: Complete Collected Works of Mr. Xiang Shan.

Luo Qinshun, *Notes on Knowledge Painfully Acquired*   3

Editions used:
Yan Tao, *Kunzhiji* (Beijing: Zhonghua Shuju, 1990); I. T. Bloom, Notes on Knowledge Painfully Acquired: *A Translation and Analysis of the K'un-chih chi by Lo Ch'in-shun (1465–1547)*. Ph.D. diss., Columbia University, 1976.

Master Sun's Military Methods
  5 *Strategic Power*   31
  6 *Emptiness and Fullness*   12

Editions used:
Chinese University of Hong Kong Institute of Chinese Studies, *A Concordance to the Militarists* (Taibei: Commercial Press, 1992); Ralph D. Sawyer, *The Seven Military Classics of Ancient China* (Boulder, Colo.: Westview Press, 1993).

The Mean and Harmony   1, 7, 18, 33, 39, 41, 43, 44, 58

Edition used:
J. Legge, *The Chinese Classics*, vol. 1, *Confucian Analects,* The Great Learning *and* The Doctrine of the Mean (Oxford: Clarendon, 1893; reprint, Taibei: Southern Materials Centre, 1985).

Mencius

Edition used:

J. Legge, *The Chinese Classics*, vol. 2, *The Works of Mencius* (Oxford: Clarendon, 1893; reprint, Taibei: Southern Materials Centre, 1985).

Mozi

Editions used:

Mozi yinde; also Chan, Wing-Tsit, *A Source Book in Chinese Philosophy* (Princeton, N.J.: Princeton University Press, 1963). All the texts from chs. 40–45 are quoted directly from A. C. Graham, *Later Mohist Logic, Ethics, and Science* (Hong Kong: Chinese University of Hong Kong, 1978).

Mr. Lu's Spring and Autumn Annals

Edition used:

Chen Qiyou, *Lushi Chunqiu Jiaoshi* (Shanghai: Xuelin, 1984).

Ouyang Jian, *Thesis That Language Adequately Expresses Ideas*   62

Editions used:

Complete Jin Literature; Yan Kejun, ed., *Quan shanggu Sandai, Qin-Han, San-Guo, Liu Chao Wen* (Beijing: Zhonghua Shuju, 1959). This work is also found in Chen Menglei, ed., *Gujin tushu jicheng* 59, *Xuexing dian A* 79 *Yanyu bu Yiwen* 1, #8 (1894 ed., reproduced 1934).

Pei Gu, *Discourse Honoring Being*   20

In *Jin History* 35.2, *Biography of Pei Xiu*.

Edition used:

Jin Shu (Beijing: Zhonghua Shuju)

Pheasant Cap Master (Heguanzi)

5 *Flowing Round*   16

11 *Tailu*   5

Editions used:

Wu Shigong, ed., *Heguanzi Wu zhu* (Jiu He Tang Congshu, 1929); Carine Defoort, *The Pheasant Cap Master: A Rhetorical Reading* (Albany: SUNY Press, 1997).

Record of Rites

Edition used (Chinese only):

Chen Hao, ed., *Li Ji Jishuo* (Shanghai: Shanghai Guji, 1987).

Rites of Zhou 2.1, Officials of the Earth

Edition used (Chinese only):

Chinese University of Hong Kong Institute of Chinese Studies, *A Concordance to the Zhou Li* (Hong Kong: Commercial Press, 1993).

Ruan Ji, *Discourse on Fathoming Zhuangzi*

Editions used:

Complete Three Kingdoms Literature; Yan Kejun, ed., *Quan Shanggu Sandai, Qin-Han, San-Guo, Liu Chao Wen* (Beijing: Zhonghua Shuju, 1959).

Sayings of the States (Guo Yu)

Edition used (Chinese only):

Shanghai Shifan Daxue Guji Zhenglisuo Yanjiusuo, *Guo Yu* (Shanghai: Shanghai Guji, 1988).

Shao Yong: *The Book of the Supreme Principles Ordering the World*

Edition used:

Siku Quanshu 803.

See also K. Smith Jr., P. K. Bol, J. A. Adler, and D. J. Wyatt, *Sung Dynasty Uses of the* I Ching (Princeton: Princeton University Press, 1990).

Shen Dao 31, 38, 40, 47

Edition used:

P. M. Thompson, *The "Shen-Tzu" Fragments* (Oxford: Oxford University Press, 1979). All reading of the Chinese texts of this work are as in Thompson.

Shen Kuo, *Xu Bi Tan* 3

In *Meng Xi Bi Tan.*

Edition used:

Hu Daojing, ed., *Mengxi Bitan Jiaozheng* (Shanghai: Gudian Wenxue, 1957).

Shizi 19

In Lu Deming (556–627), *Explanations of the Writings of Zhuangzi*, in Guo Qingfan, ed., *Collected Exegesis of the* Zhuangzi.

Edition used (Chinese only):
Zhuzi Jicheng 3.

Sima Qian, *Records of the Historian*

47	*The Family of Confucius*	39n, 43n
74	*Biographies of Mencius and Xun Qing*	11, 12
130	*Summarised Discussion of the Six Schools*	32

Edition used (Chinese only):
Shi Ji, 2d ed. (Beijing: Zhonghua Shuju, 1982).

Spring and Autumn Annals 12, *Duke Ai* Year 2 48

Edition used:

J. Legge, *The Chinese Classics*, vol. 5, *The* Ch'un Ts'ew, *with the* Tso Chuen (Oxford: Clarendon, 1893; reprint, Taibei: Southern Materials Centre, 1985).

Su Yan (Emperor Wu of Liang), *Record of Establishing Spiritual Brightness as the Meaning of Buddhism*   32, 52

Editions used:

Complete Liang Literature; Yan Kejun, ed., *Quan shanggu Sandai, Qin-Han, San-Guo, Liu Chao Wen* (Beijing: Zhonghua Shuju, 1959); *Sibu Beiyao: Hong Ming Ji.*

Sun Bin's Military Methods 9, *Possession of Strategic Power*   31

Editions used:

Zhang Zhenze, *Sunbin Bingfa Jiaoli* (Beijing: Zhonghua Shuju, 1984); Ralph D. Sawyer, *Sun Pin: Military Methods* (Boulder, Colo.: Westview Press, 1995).

Tan Qiao: *The Book of Transformations, Discourse on the Way* 1   10

Edition used:
Siku Quanshu 849.

Wang Anshi, *Commentary on the Great Plan* 12

Edition used:
Siku Quanshu 1105, *Collected Writings of Lin Chuan.*

———, *Discussion of Justice* 6.6, *Human Nature and Emotions*   50

Edition used:
Siku Quanshu 1105, *Collected Writings of Lin Chuan.*

Wang Bi (226–249), *Commentary on the Book of Changes*   3, 25, 38, 45

———, *Commentary on the* Laozi   20, 21, 32

———, *Exegesis of the* Analects   20, 30

Edition used:

Lou Yulie, ed., *Laozi-Zhou Yi: Wang Bi zhu jiaoshi* (Taibei: Huacheng Shuju, 1983).

———, *Summary Norms on the* Book of Changes   3, 62

Wang Chong, *Balanced Inquiries*

Editions used:

Zhuzi Jicheng 7. Parts of chs. 13, 54, and 62 are in Wing-tsit Chan, *A Source Book in Chinese Philosophy* (Princeton: Princeton University, 1963); Alfred Forke, *Lunheng*, pt. 1, *Philosophical Essays of Wang Ch'ung*; pt. 2, *Miscellaneous Essays of Wang Ch'ung* (Shanghai: Kelly and Walsh; London: Luzac; Leipzig: Harrassowitz, 1907 and 1911).

Wang Fuzhi (1619–1692), *Discussion After Reading the* Mirror of Universal History 17

Edition used:

Sibu Beiyao:

See also A. H. Black, *Man and Nature in the Philosophical Thought of Wang Fu-Chih* (Seattle: University of Washington Press, 1989); I. McMorran, *The Passionate Realist: An Introduction to the Life and Political Thought of Wang Fuzhi (1619–1692)* (Hong Kong: Sunshine Book Co., 1992).

———, *Elaboration on the Meanings of the* Book of History

Edition used:

Shangshu yinyi (Beijing: Zhonghua Shuju, 1976).

See also A. H. Black, *Man and Nature in the Philosophical Thought of Wang Fu-Chih* (Seattle: University of Washington Press, 1989); I. McMorran, *The Passionate Realist: An Introduction to the Life and Political Thought of Wang Fuzhi (1619–1692)* (Hong Kong: Sunshine Book Co., 1992).

———, *Extensive Discourse to Supplement Zuo's Commentary on the Spring and Autumn Annals*   60

Edition used:

Huaiji Shuzhuang Shiyin (1900).

See also A. H. Black, *Man and Nature in the Philosophical Thought of Wang Fu-Chih* (Seattle: University of Washington Press, 1989); I. McMorran, *The Passionate Realist: An Introduction to the Life and Political Thought of Wang Fuzhi (1619–1692)* (Hong Kong: Sunshine Book Co., 1992).

———, *Great and Full Explanation on Reading the Four Books*

1	*Great Learning* (1975 ed.)	60
2	*Mean and Harmony*	43
3	*Mean and Harmony*	18
6	*Analects*	43
7	*Analects*	43
9	*Mencius*	3, 18
10	*Mencius*	3

See A. H. Black, *Man and Nature in the Philosophical Thought of Wang Fu-Chih* (Seattle: University of Washington Press, 1989); I. McMorran, *The Passionate Realist: An Introduction to the Life and Political Thought of Wang Fuzhi (1619–1692)* (Hong Kong: Sunshine Book Co., 1992).

———, *Notes on Master Zhang's* Correcting the Unenlightened

1	2, 10, 20, 27, 32, 33, 37, 55
2	32, 58
3	3, 18, 49, 52, 58
4	58
9	18, 27, 52

Edition used:

Zhangzi Zhengmeng zhu (Taibei: Heluo Tushu, 1975).

See also A. H. Black, *Man and Nature in the Philosophical Thought of Wang Fu-Chih* (Seattle: University of Washington Press, 1989); I. McMorran, *The Passionate Realist: An Introduction to the Life and Political Thought of Wang Fuzhi (1619–1692)* (Hong Kong: Sunshine Book Co., 1992).

———, *Outer Commentary on the* Book of Changes   15, 29, 32

Edition used:

Zhouyi Waizhuan (Beijing: Zhonghua Shuju, 1977).

See also A. H. Black, *Man and Nature in the Philosophical Thought of Wang Fu-Chih* (Seattle: University of Washington Press, 1989); I. McMorran, *The Passionate Realist: An Introduction to the Life and Political Thought of Wang Fuzhi (1619–1692)* (Hong Kong: Sunshine Book Co., 1992).

———, *Record of Thoughts and Questionings*

Inner Chapter	20, 25, 33
Outer Chapter	6, 16, 25

Edition used:

Wang Fuzhi, *Siwen lu* (Beijing: Guji Chubanshe, 1956).

See also A. H. Black, *Man and Nature in the Philosophical Thought of Wang Fu-Chih* (Seattle: University of Washington Press, 1989); I. McMorran, *The Passionate Realist: An Introduction to the Life and Political Thought of Wang Fuzhi (1619–1692)* (Hong Kong: Sunshine Book Co., 1992).

Wang Shouren (1472–1529), *Reply to Ji Mingde*   1

Instructions for Practical Living	1, 32, 36, 52, 54, 55, 60

Editions used:

Sibu Biyao, Complete Books of Yang Ming 2, *Instructions for Practical Living* 2; Wing-Tsit Chan, ed. and trans., *Instructions for Practical Living and Other Neo-Confucian Writings by Wang Yang-Ming* (New York: Columbia University Press, 1963).

Letter in Reply to Gu Dongqiao	7, 54, 60

Editions used:

For the quotation in concept 7 see *Siku Quanshu* 1265, *Collected Works of Wang Wencheng* 2, *Recorded Conversations: Instructions for Practical Living*; Wing-Tsit Chan, ed. and trans., *Instructions for Practical Living and Other Neo-Confucian Writings by Wang Yang-ming* (New York: Columbia University Press, 1963), #137; for the quotations in concepts 54 and 60 see *Sibu Beiyao, Complete Books of Yang Ming* 2, *Instructions for Practical Living* 2; Chan, *Instructions for Practical Living*, #135 and #139.

See also Julia Ching, trans., *The Philosophical Letters of Wang Yang-ming* (Canberra: Australian National University Press, 1972).

Editions used:

Sibu Beiyao, Complete Books of Yang Ming 2, *Instructions for Practical Living B*; Wing-Tsit Chan, ed. and trans., *Instructions for Practical Living and Other Neo-Confucian Writings by Wang Yang-ming* (New York: Columbia University Press, 1963).

See also Julia Ching, trans., *The Philosophical Letters of Wang Yang-ming* (Canberra: Australian National University Press, 1972).

Editions used:

Sibu Beiyao, Complete Books of Yang Ming 2, *Instructions for Practical Living* 2; Wing-Tsit Chan, ed. and trans., *Instructions for Practical Living and Other Neo-Confucian Writings by Wang Yang-ming* (New York: Columbia University Press, 1963); Julia Ching, trans., *The Philosophical Letters of Wang Yang-ming* (Canberra: Australian National University Press, 1972).

In *Complete Collected Works of Wang Yangming*.

Edition used:

Wang Yangming Quanji (Shanghai: Shanghai Guji, 1992).

See also Julia Ching, trans. and annot., *The Philosophical Letters of Wang Yang-ming* (Canberra: Australian National University Press, 1972).

Wang Tingxiang

Prudent Words   3, 5, 10, 11, 32, 55
Reply to He Bozhai's Theory of Creation   11

Editions used:

Wang Xiaoyu, ed., *Wang Tingxiang ji* (Beijing: Zhonghua Shuju, 1989). For *Debate on the Supreme Ultimate: Collected Works Stored in Mr. Zhang's House* 33.1; for *Reply to He Bozhai's Theory of Creation: Collected Inner Terrace* 4.

Xi Kang, *Discourse on Explaining Selfishness*   21

Edition used:

Complete Three Kingdoms Literature; Yan Kejun, ed., *Quan shanggu Sandai, Qin-Han, San-Guo, Liu Chao Wen* (Beijing: Zhonghua Shuju, 1959).

Xie Liangzuo, *Recorded Conversations of Shang Cai*   39

Edition used:

Siku Quanshu 698.

Xing Bing, *Commentary on the* Analects   39

Edition used:

Shisan jing zhushu.

Xu Gan, *Discourses That Hit the Mark*   39, 61

Edition used:

Siku Quanshu 696.

See also J. Makeham, *Name and Actuality in Early Chinese Thought* (Albany: SUNY Press, 1994).

Xun Yue (148–209), *Extended Reflections* 5.7, *Various Sayings B*   50

Editions used:

Sibu Beiyao; Ch'en Ch'i-yun, *Hsun Yueh and the Mind of Late Han China: A Translation of the* Shen-chien *with Introduction and Annotations* (Princeton: Princeton University Press, 1980).

Xunzi

Editions used:

Xunzi Yinde (Shanghai: Shanghai Guji, 1986); *Zhuzi Jicheng*, vol. 2, with commentary by Yang Liang and notes by Wang Niansun; Yang Liuqiao, *Xunzi Guyi* (Hsinchu: Yangcheh, 1987); Homer Dubs, *The Works of Hsuntze* (London, 1928; reprint, Taibei: Confucius Publishing, 1972) (I have consulted Dubs for chs. 21–23); John Knoblock, *Xunzi: A Translation and Study of the Complete Works*, vols. 1 and 2 (Stanford: Stanford University Press, 1988, 1990).

Yan Yuan *Preservation of Learning*

Editions used:

Yan-Li Congshu (1923 ed.); Mansfield Freeman, "Yan Yuan: Preservation of Learning," Monumenta Serica (1972); Wing-Tsit Chan, *A Source Book in Chinese Philosophy* (Princeton: Princeton University, 1963), pp. 704–706.

Questions on an Annotated Commentary on the
Analects 30

Edition used:
Siku Quanshu 47.

Yang Bojun, *Chunqiu Zuozhuan Zhu* 28

Edition used:
Chunqiu Zuozhuan Zhu (Beijing: Zhonghua Shuju, 1981).

Yang Xiong, *Call to the Soul* 5

Quoted in *Taiping Yulan* (Beijing: Zhonghua Shuju, 1960).

———, *Dispelling Ridicule (Jie Chao)* 5, 9

See *Complete Han Literature in Quan Shanggu Sandai, Qin-Han, San-Guo, Liu Chao Wen* (Beijing: Zhonghua Shuju, 1959), also *Taiping Yulan* (Beijing: Zhonghua Shuju, 1960).

———, *Ultimate Abstruseness* 9, 16

Editions used:
Zheng Wangeng, *Tai Xuan Jiaoshi* (Beijing: Beijing Shifan Daxue, 1989); M. Nylan, *Yang Hsiung: The Canon of Supreme Mystery* (Albany: SUNY Press, 1993).

Ye Shi (1150–1222), *Mean and Harmony* 33, 43

In *Other Collected Works of Mr. Shuixin.*

Edition used:
Ye Shi Ji (Beijing: Zhonghua Shuju, 1961).

Yuan Zhun, *Discussion of Material and*
Nature 32

Edition used:
Complete Jin Literature; Yan Kejun (ed.), *Quan Shanggu Sandai, Qin-Han, San-Guo, Liu Chao Wen* (Beijing: Zhonghua Shuju, 1959).

Zhang Zai, *Correcting the Unenlightened*

  1 *Great Harmony*   1, 2, 3, 5, 10, 11, 20, 24, 29, 32, 33, 37, 52

Edition used:

Siku Quanshu 697.

See also J. E. Kasoff, *The Thought of Chang Tsai (1020–1077)* (Cambridge: Cambridge University Press, 1984).

————, *Hengqu's Explanation of the* Book of Changes   25

Edition used:

Zhang Dainian, ed., *Zhang Zai Ji* (Beijing: Zhonghua Shuju, 1978).

See also J. E. Kasoff, *The Thought of Chang Tsai (1020–1077)* (Cambridge: Cambridge University Press, 1984).

————, *Recorded Sayings*   3, 7

Edition used:

Zhang Dainian, ed., *Zhang Zai Ji* (Beijing: Zhonghua Shuju, 1978).

See also J. E. Kasoff, *The Thought of Chang Tsai (1020–1077)* (Cambridge: Cambridge University Press, 1984).

Zhang Zhan, *Commentary on Liezi* 1, *Heaven's Gifts*   30

Edition used:

Zhuzi Jicheng 3

Zhao Qi, *Notes on the* Mencius   54

In *Correct Meaning of the* Mencius.

Edition used:
Zhuzi Jicheng 1.

Zheng Xianzhi, *Treatise on the Indestructibility of Spirit* 32

Edition used:
Sibu Beiyao 55, *Hong Ming Ji* 5.

Zheng Xuan, *Zheng Xuan's Notes on the* Book of Changes 23

Edition used:
Siku Quanshu 7 (Hui Dong, ed.): *Additions to Mr. Zheng's Zhou Yi.*

Notes of Mr. Zheng on the Analects   61

Edition used:
Yuhan Shanfangji yishu, vol. 3 (Taibei: Wenhai, 1974).

————, *Zheng Xuan's Notes on the* Record of Rites

21 *Evolution of Rites*	48
47 *Meaning of Sacrifices*	5
52 *Mean and Harmony*	33
53 *Mean and Harmony*	18
60 *Great Learning*	60

Editions used:
Siku Quanshu 115–116; Ruan Yuan (1764–1849), *Thirteen Classics annotated* (Taibei: Dahua shuju, 1977).

————, *Zheng Xuan's Notes on the* Rites of
Zhou   7

Edition used:
Siku Quanshu 90

Zhou Dunyi, *The Book of Comprehending*

1 *Integrity A*	18
2 *Integrity B*	18
3 *Integrity Is the Incipient Virtue*	26, 39
4 *Sagehood*	26
9 *Thought*	56
11 *Concordance and Transformation*	24

Zhuangzi

Editions used:

Zhuangzi Yinde (Shanghai: Shanghai Guji, n.d.) (Chinese only); Victor H. Mair, trans., *Wandering on the Way: Early Taoist Tales and Parables of Chuang Tzu* (New York: Bantam, 1994); A. C. Graham, *Chuang-tzu: The Inner Chapters* (London: Unwin, 1981). In concept 48 I have used Graham's translation of ch. 17.

Zhu Xi, *Appendix to Master Zhou's* Book of Comprehending   23

See Wing-tsit Chan, *Chu Hsi: New Studies* (Honolulu: University of Hawai'i Press, 1989); Wing-tsit Chan, trans., *Reflections on Things at Hand: The Neo-Confucian Anthology Compiled by Chu Hsi and Lu Tsu-ch'ien* (New York: Columbia University Press, 1967).

———, *Chapter and Verse Commentary on the*
Great Learning   55, 60

Edition used:

Sishu Wujing, vol. 1 (Beijing: Zhongguo Shudian, 1985).

See also Wing-tsit Chan, *Chu Hsi: New Studies* (Honolulu: University of Hawai'i Press, 1989); Wing-tsit Chan, trans., *Reflections on Things at Hand: The Neo-Confucian Anthology Compiled by Chu Hsi and Lu Tsu-ch'ien* (New York: Columbia University Press, 1967).

———, *Chapter and Verse Commentary on the*
Mean and Harmony   2, 18, 43, 55, 58

Edition used:

Sishu Wujing, vol. 1 (Beijing: Zhongguo Shudian, 1985).

See also Wing-tsit Chan, *Chu Hsi: New Studies* (Honolulu: University of Hawai'i Press, 1989); Wing-tsit Chan, trans., *Reflections on Things at Hand: The Neo-Confucian Anthology Compiled by Chu Hsi and Lu Tsu-ch'ien* (New York: Columbia University Press, 1967).

————, *Collected Notes on the* Analects   33

Edition used:

Sishu Wujing, vol. 1 (Beijing: Zhongguo Shudian, 1985).

See also Wing-tsit Chan, *Chu Hsi: New Studies* (Honolulu: University of Hawai'i Press, 1989); Wing-tsit Chan, trans., *Reflections on Things at Hand: The Neo-Confucian Anthology Compiled by Chu Hsi and Lu Tsu-ch'ien* (New York: Columbia University Press, 1967).

————, *Collected Notes on the* Mencius   49, 50, 54

Edition used:

Sishu Wujing, vol. 1 (Beijing: Zhongguo Shudian, 1985).

See also Wing-tsit Chan, *Chu Hsi: New Studies* (Honolulu: University of Hawai'i Press, 1989); Wing-tsit Chan, trans., *Reflections on Things at Hand: The Neo-Confucian Anthology Compiled by Chu Hsi and Lu Tsu-ch'ien* (New York: Columbia University Press, 1967).

————, *Conversations of Master Zhu Arranged Topically*

94 *The Books of Master Zhou*	12, 23, 24
95 *The Books of Master Cheng* 1	30, 32, 39, 49
98 *The Books of Master Zhang* 1	52

Editions used:

D. K. Gardner, *Learning to Be a Sage: Selections from the* Conversations of Master Chu, Arranged Topically (Berkeley: University of California Press, 1990); Wang Xingxian, ed., *Zhuzi Yulei* (Beijing: Zhongghua Shuju, 1994). Partial and scattered translations are found in J. P. Bruce, *The Philosophy of Human Nature by Chu Hsi* (London: Probsthain, 1922).

See also Wing-tsit Chan, *Chu Hsi: New Studies* (Honolulu: University of Hawai'i Press, 1989); Wing-tsit Chan, trans., *Reflections on Things at Hand: The Neo-Confucian Anthology Compiled by Chu Hsi and Lu Tsu-ch'ien* (New York: Columbia University Press, 1967).

———, *Exegesis of the Explanation of the Diagram of the Supreme Ultimate*   8, 23

Edition used:

Siku Quanshu 1101, *Collected Works of Zhou Yuangong*.

See also Wing-tsit Chan, *Chu Hsi: New Studies* (Honolulu: University of Hawai'i Press, 1989); Wing-tsit Chan, trans., *Reflections on Things at Hand: The Neo-Confucian Anthology Compiled by Chu Hsi and Lu Tsu-ch'ien* (New York: Columbia University Press, 1967).

———, *Explanation of the* Book of Comprehending 18

Edition used:

Siku Quanshu 1101, *Collected Works of Zhou Yuangong*.

See also Wing-tsit Chan, *Chu Hsi: New Studies* (Honolulu: University of Hawai'i Press, 1989); Wing-tsit Chan, trans., *Reflections on Things at Hand: The Neo-Confucian Anthology Compiled by Chu Hsi and Lu Tsu-ch'ien* (New York: Columbia University Press, 1967).

———, *The Original Meaning of the* Book of Changes   2, 23, 25, 28, 29

Editions used:

Yi Cheng Chuan; Yi Benyi (Taibei: Shijie Shuju, 1988).

See also Wing-tsit Chan, *Chu Hsi: New Studies* (Honolulu: University of Hawai'i Press, 1989); Wing-tsit Chan, trans., *Reflections on Things at*

Hand: The Neo-Confucian Anthology Compiled by Chu Hsi and Lu Tsu-ch'ien (New York: Columbia University Press, 1967).

——, *Reply to a Certain Person*   38, 45

In *Collected Writings of Zhu Wengong.*

Edition used:

Sibu Beiyao 56, *Collected Writings* 64, #33.7.

See also Wing-tsit Chan, *Chu Hsi: New Studies* (Honolulu: University of Hawai'i Press, 1989); Wing-tsit Chan, trans., *Reflections on Things at Hand: The Neo-Confucian Anthology Compiled by Chu Hsi and Lu Tsu-ch'ien* (New York: Columbia University Press, 1967).

——, *Reply to Huang Daofu*   5

In *Collected Writings of Zhu Wengong.*

Edition used:

Sibu Congkan.

See also Wing-tsit Chan, *Chu Hsi: New Studies* (Honolulu: University of Hawai'i Press, 1989); Wing-tsit Chan, trans., *Reflections on Things at Hand: The Neo-Confucian Anthology Compiled by Chu Hsi and Lu Tsu-ch'ien* (New York: Columbia University Press, 1967).

——, *Some Questions on the* Great Learning   3, 38, 45

Edition used:

Siku Quanshu 197.

See also Wing-tsit Chan, *Chu Hsi: New Studies* (Honolulu: University of Hawai'i Press, 1989); Wing-tsit Chan, trans., *Reflections on Things at Hand: The Neo-Confucian Anthology Compiled by Chu Hsi and Lu Tsu-ch'ien* (New York: Columbia University Press, 1967).

——, *Theory of Observing the Mind*   52

In *Collected Writings of Zhu Wengong.*

Edition used:

Sibu Beiyao: Collected Writings of Zhu Wengong 67.30.

See also Wing-tsit Chan, *Chu Hsi: New Studies* (Honolulu: University of Hawai'i Press, 1989); Wing-tsit Chan, trans., *Reflections on Things at Hand: The Neo-Confucian Anthology Compiled by Chu Hsi and Lu Tsu-ch'ien* (New York: Columbia University Press, 1967).

———, *A Treatise on Benevolence*   39

In *Collected Writings of Zhu Wengong.*

Edition used:

Sibu Beiyao, Collected Writings of Zhu Wengong 67.31.

See also Wing-tsit Chan, *Chu Hsi: New Studies* (Honolulu: University of Hawai'i Press, 1989); Wing-tsit Chan, trans., *Reflections on Things at Hand: The Neo-Confucian Anthology Compiled by Chu Hsi and Lu Tsu-ch'ien* (New York: Columbia University Press, 1967).

Zong Bing, *Discourse on Understanding the Buddha*   52

Edition used:

Sibu Beiyao: Hong Ming Ji.

Zuo's Commentary

1	Duke Yin	Year 4	44
2	Duke Huan	Year 6	22, 27
3	Duke Zhuang	Year 8	44
		Year 32	22
4	Duke Min	Year 2	44
5	Duke Xi	Year 4	44
		Year 5	44
		Year 15	27
		Year 16	11
		Year 24	44
		Year 27	39
		Year 33	39
6	Duke Wen	Year 5	12
		Year 7	44
7	Duke Xuan	Year 15	16, 39
8	Duke Cheng	Year 2	44
		Year 3	45
		Year 6	12
9	Duke Xiang	Year 3	12
		Year 9	28
		Year 21	48

	Year 24	44
	Year 27	12
10 Duke Zhao	Year 1	5, 11
	Year 12	39
	Year 17	2, 30
	Year 18	2
	Year 20	37
	Year 25	12
	Year 32	12, 33
11 Duke Ding	Year 4	39

Edition used:

J. Legge, *The Chinese Classics*, vol. 5, *The* Ch'un Ts'ew, *with the* Tso Chuen (Oxford: Clarendon, 1893; reprint, Taibei: Southern Materials Centre, 1985).

Texts Used for Translating Terms

Bodde, Derk. "On Translating Chinese Philosophic Terms," *Far Eastern Quarterly* 14 (1955): 235–237.

Smith, K, Jr., P. K. Bol, J. A. Adler, and D. J. Wyatt, *Sung Dynasty Uses of the* I Ching (Princeton: Princeton University Press, 1990).

Tang Yijie, "Questions Concerning the Categorical System of Traditional Chinese Philosophy," *Social Sciences in China* (winter 1982): 190–211.

Zhang Dainian, "On Levels of Values," *Social Sciences in China* (winter 1990): 22–30.

Also available in The Culture & Civilization of China series

Three Thousand Years of Chinese Painting
Richard M. Barnhart, Yang Xin, James Cahill, Nie Chongzheng,
Wu Hung, and Lang Shaojun

Chinese Architecture
Fu Xinian, Guo Daiheng, Liu Xujie, Pan Guxi, Qiao Yun,
and Sun Dazhang
English text edited and expanded by Nancy S. Steinhardt

Balanced Discourses
A Bilingual Edition
Xu Gan
English translation by John Makeham
Introductions by Dang Shengyuan and John Makeham